MORAL CHOICES

in contemporary
society

MORAL CHOICES

in contemporary society

A COURSES BY NEWSPAPER READER

EDITED BY PHILIP RIEFF AND
ISAAC FINKLE

COURSES BY NEWSPAPER IS A PROJECT OF
UNIVERSITY EXTENSION,
UNIVERSITY OF CALIFORNIA, SAN DIEGO

FUNDED BY
THE NATIONAL ENDOWMENT FOR THE HUMANITIES

PUBLISHER'S INC.  DEL MAR, CA

Copyright © 1977 by the Regents of the University of California. All rights reserved.
Printed in the United States of America.

Library of Congress Cataloging in Publication Data
Main entry under title:

Moral choices in contemporary society.

"A Courses by newspaper reader."
1. Social ethics. 2. United States—Moral con-
ditions. I. Rieff, Philip, 1922–   II. Finkle,
Isaac, 1952–
HM216.M65   301.41'7973   76-51460
ISBN 0-89163-023-6
ISBN 0-89163-022-8 pbk.

iv

ACKNOWLEDGMENTS

Cover art: R.K. Evans.

Chapter 1 4: Reprinted by permission from *The Christian Science Monitor.* © 1976 The Christian Science Publishing Society. All rights reserved; 7: Reprinted with permission of Macmillan Publishing Co., Inc. from *Ethics* by A.C. Ewing. Copyright 1953 by A.C. Ewing; 9: Reprinted with permission of Macmillan Publishing Co., Inc. from *Preface to Morals* by Walter Lippmann. Copyright 1929 by Walter Lippmann, renewed 1957 by Walter Lippmann; 11: From *Situation Ethics* by Joseph Fletcher. Copyright © MCMLXVI, W.L. Jenkins. Used by permission of the Westminster Press; 14: Used by permission from *The Reformed Review*, March 1967; 16: Used by permission from *The Washington Post*, May 5, 1976; 17: Used by permission of the author from *The Listener*, August 1, 1974; 18: Reprinted by permission of Wallace, Aitken & Sheil, Inc. Copyright © 1976 Harper's Magazine, Inc.; 20: Abridged from pp. 196–7, 201, 202, 203, 204–5, 211–2, and 216 in *The Moral Rules* by Bernard Gert. Copyright © 1966, 1967, 1970 by Bernard Gert. By permission of Harper & Row, Publishers, Inc.; 23: From *The Origin and Development of Moral Ideas* by Edward Westermarck, Macmillan, 1906; 24: From *Folkways* by William Graham Sumner, Copyright 1906 by William Graham Sumner; copyright 1940 by Ginn and Company. Used with permission.

Chapter 2 32: From *The Collected Papers of Sigmund Freud*, edited by Philip Rieff, Basic Books, 1963; 33: Copyright 1929 by Alfred A. Knopf, Inc. Reprinted from *Assorted Articles* by D.H. Lawrence, by permission of Alfred A. Knopf, Inc.; 35: From "The Fourth Revolution" by Jessie Bernard. Reprinted with permission from *The Journal of Social Issues*, April 1966; 41: This article first appeared in *The Humanist*, January/February 1976 and is reprinted by permission; 44: Reprinted by permission of *Psychology Today* magazine. Copyright © 1975 Ziff-Davis Publishing Company; 46: From *The New Sexuality*, edited by Herbert A. Otto. Copyright © 1971 Science and Behavior Books; 48: Reprinted by permission of William Morrow & Co., Inc. from *Playing Around: Women and Extramarital Sex* by Linda Wolfe. Copyright © 1975 by Linda Wolfe; 50: Used with permission of the author from *Life*, November 6, 1970.

Chapter 3 56: Used by permission of the author from *The New York Review of Books*, November 13 and November 27, 1975; 57: From *Marriage and Society* by E.O. James. By permission of John de Graff, Inc.; 58: Copyright 1976 by Harper's Magazine. All rights reserved. Reprinted from the April 1976 issue by special permission; 62: From *The Death of the Family* by David Cooper. Copyright © 1970 by David Cooper. Reprinted by permission of Pantheon Books; 64: From the February 1930 issue of *American Mercury* by permission of the publisher, Box 1306, Torrance, CA 90505; 66: Reprinted by permission from *Journal of Comparative Family Studies*, Spring 1971; 70: Copyright Ms. Magazine, 1973. Reprinted with permission; 72: From *The Future of Marriage* by Jessie Bernard. Copyright © 1973. Used by permission of the author; 74: From *Love in the Western World* by Denis De Rougemont. Copyright © 1956. Reprinted by permission of Pantheon Books.

Chapter 4 80: Reprinted with permission of Macmillan Publishing Co., Inc. from *Abortion: Law, Choice and Morality* by Daniel Callahan. Copyright © 1970 by Daniel Callahan; 83: Reprinted with permission of *America*, 1967. All rights reserved. © 1967 by America Press, 106 W. 56 St., New York, NY 10019; 84: From *Ethical Issues in Medicine*, edited by E. Fuller Torrey, Little, Brown and Co., 1968, by permission of the publisher; 86: Reprinted by permission from *The New England Journal of Medicine*, November 28, 1974, pp. 1189–1190; 88: Excerpted by permission of the author and publishers from *The Morality of Abortion: Legal and Historical Perspectives*, John T. Noonan Jr., ed. Copyright © 1970 by the President and Fellows of Harvard College; 90: From Judith Jarvis Thomson, "A Defense of Abortion," *Philosophy & Public Affairs*, Fall 1971. Copyright © 1971 by Princeton University Press. Reprinted by permission; 93 and 95: From *Ethical Issues in Human Genetics*, edited by Bruce Hilton, *et al.*, Plenum Publishing Corp., 1973; 96: From "Abortion—Or Compulsory Pregnancy?" *Journal of Marriage and the Family*, May 1968. Copyright 1968 by National Council on Family Relations. Reprinted by permission; 98: From *Hastings Center Studies*, January 1974. Copyright © 1974 by Institute of Society, Ethics and the Life Sciences.

Chapter 5 104: Reprinted by permission of the publisher from *Soundings: An Interdisciplinary Journal*, Vol. LVII (Spring 1974), No. 1; 106: From pp. 6–11 in *Why Survive? Being Old in America* by Robert N. Butler. Copyright © 1975 by Robert N. Butler, M.D. By permission of Harper & Row, Publishers, Inc.; 109: From *Aging in America* by Bert Kruger Smith. Copyright © 1973 by Bert Kruger Smith. Reprinted by permission of Beacon Press; 110: Originally published in *Harper's*, July 1953. Copright 1953 by Elmer Davis; 111: From *Folkways* by William Graham Sumner. Copyright 1906 by William Graham Sumner; Copyright 1940 by Ginn and Company. Used with permission; 113: From *Youth in Old Age* by Alexander Leaf and John Launois. Copyright © 1975 by Alexander Leaf and John Launois. Used with permission of McGraw-Hill Book Company; 115: From *The Future of the Family*, edited by Louise Capp Howe, Simon & Schuster, 1972. Used with permission of Arlie Hochschild; 118: From *Old Age: The Last Segregation* by Claire Townsend. Copyright © 1970, 1971 by The Center for Study of Responsive Law. Reprinted by permission of Grossman Publishers; 121: From *The Coming of Age* by Simone de Beauvoir, Putnam, 1972. Copyright © 1972 Simone de Beauvoir; 122: From *Hastings Center Report*, April 1975. Copyright © 1975 by Institute of Society, Ethics and the Life Sciences.

Chapter 6 128: From *The Philosophical Review*, LXVII (1958), by permission; 129: Reprinted from *Commentary* by permission. Copyright © 1972 by the American Jewish Committee; 131: Reprinted with permission from *Dissent*, Fall 1973; 134: Reprinted with permission of *The Wall Street Journal*, © Dow Jones & Company, Inc. 1976. All rights reserved; 136: From *The Shame of Our Cities* by Lincoln Steffens, McClure Philips & Co., 1904; 138: © 1974 by The New York Times Company. Reprinted by permission; 140: Reprinted with permission from *National Review*, December 1970; 142: From *The Good Society* by Walter Lippmann. Copyright© 1936, 1937, 1943 by Walter Lippmann. By permission of Little, Brown and Co. in association with Atlantic Monthly Press.

Chapter 7 148: Reprinted from *Commentary* by permission. Copyright © 1975 by the American Jewish Committee; 150: Reprinted with permission from *New Republic*, January 17, 1976; 151: Reprinted by permission from *Partisan Review*, 42:4 (1975). Copyright © 1975 by P. R., Inc.; 153: Reprinted from the *Los Angeles Times*, October 19, 1976; 154: From *The Collected Papers of Sigmund Freud*, Edited by Philip Rieff, Basic Books, 1963; 156: From Bronislaw Malinowski, "An Anthropological Analysis of War," *American Journal of Sociology*, January 1946. Copyright 1946 by the University of Chicago Press; 159: From *Force, Order, and Justice* by Robert E. Osgood and Robert W. Tucker, The Johns Hopkins University Press. Copyright © 1967; 162: Reprinted by permission of Charles Scribner's Sons from *Moral Man and Immoral Society* by Reinhold Niebuhr. Copyright 1932 Charles Scribner's Sons.

Chapter 8 168: From Lon Fuller, *The Morality of Law*, Yale University Press, 1969; 168 and 171: From *Is Law Dead?* edited by Eugene V. Rostow, Simon & Schuster, 1971. By permission of the authors; 174: From *The Trial of the Catonsville Nine* by Daniel

CONTENTS

PREFACE

This is the sixth in a series of books developed for Courses by Newspaper. A national program oriented and administered by University Extension, University of California, San Diego, and funded by the National Endowment for the Humanities, Courses by Newspaper develops materials for college-level courses that are presented to the general public through the nationwide cooperation of newspapers and participating colleges and universities.

The program offers three levels of participation: interested readers can follow a series of newspaper articles that constitute the course "lectures"; they can pursue the subjects in supplementary books—a reader and a study guide—and with audio cassettes; and they can enroll for credit at one of the 200 participating colleges or universities or through the Division of Independent Study at the University of California, Berkeley. In addition, many community organizations offer local forums and discussion groups based on the Courses by Newspaper series.

This volume supplements the sixteen newspaper articles written especially for the sixth Course by Newspaper, MORAL CHOICES IN CONTEMPORARY SOCIETY, by prominent scholars from around the country. The newspaper articles will appear weekly in newspapers throughout the nation in the winter and spring of 1977.

The efforts of many people and organizations have contributed to the success of Courses by Newspaper, and we should like to acknowledge them here. Hundreds of newspaper editors and publishers have contributed valuable newspaper space to bring the series to their readers; and the faculties and administrations of the many colleges and universities participating in the program have cooperated to make credit available on a nationwide basis.

Deserving special mention at the University of California are Paul D. Saltman, vice-chancellor for academic affairs and professor of biology, who has chaired the faculty committee and guided the project since its inception, in addition to serving as the first academic coordinator in 1973; and Caleb A. Lewis of University Extension, who originated the idea of Courses by Newspaper. The faculty committee contributed many valuable ideas to the conception of this volume, as did Professors Harry N. Scheiber of the History Department and Kristin Luker of the Sociology Department. The members of the Courses by Newspaper staff—Cecilia Solis, Yvonne Hancher, Stephanie Giel, and Susan Rago—were vital to the success of this year's program. In addition, Linda Rill and Nancy Sjoberg assisted with photo research and permissions.

We also wish to thank the authors of the newspaper articles—Jean Lipman-Blumen, Christopher Lasch, Daniel Callahan, Robert Tucker, Lon Fuller, Ernest van den Haag, John P. Sisk, Hans Jonas, Martin Marty, and Kenneth B. Clark—for their suggestions for this book.

Finally, we wish to express our gratitude to our funding agency, the National Endowment for the Humanities. The Endowment, a federal agency created in 1965 to support education, research, and public activity in the humanities, has generously supported this nationwide program from its beginning. We wish particularly to thank James Kraft, program officer in the Office of Planning and Analysis, for his support and advice.

Although Courses by Newspaper is a project of the University of California, San Diego, and is supported by the National Endowment for the Humanities, the views expressed in course materials are those of the authors only and do not necessarily reflect those of the Endowment or the University of California.

J. L. S.

INTRODUCTION

In each of the sixteen sections of *Moral Choices in Contemporary Society,* the choices examined are subject, especially nowadays, to intense argument and considerable perplexity. In many instances, the more perplexed argue with each other all the more intensely, so that even declarations of certitude about what is right and wrong, good and evil, breathe in the American air of uncertainty. Morals matters may be in different condition elsewhere, but the editors of this volume doubt that the American condition is unique. Of extreme contentiousness on matters of morals and their manners of social, political, and scientific expression, America appears endlessly well supplied.

The contentions divided into sixteen chapters here, the editors believe, cut across differences in social class, level of education, and ethnic origin and are crucial to the future shape and direction of all peoples' lives. None of these arguments appears reducible to the social class, level of education, ethnic origin, or other attributes of the authors. Moral choices seem to have a way of asserting their own existence, however dependent they are made, by clever arguers, on determinants other than moral.

"Institutions" are defined sociologically as interrelated moral regulations that determine the regular conduct of groups of individuals. In every society such institutions as marriage and the family, as well as less obvious political and economic regularities of conduct, are primarily moral edifices. Continuing to use the institution of the family as an example, in every society there appear rules of conduct by which individuals of opposite sex and successive generations are organized, which specify the right and wrong ways of living together as a family.

Moralities are complex; they admit of, even teach, innumerable exceptions to their rules. Moralities may often involve several moral principles in conflict, which must be reconciled and yet may never quite achieve that happy condition. Upon examination, even the most fundamental principles are not simply applicable to every situation—for example, great thought has been devoted to the times when the rule "thou shalt not kill" is lifted, as in times of war. This complexity is inevitable because moral rules aspire to do justice to the countless exceptions in, and the variegated spheres of, life.

Living with—sometimes even facing directly—such perplexities of moral choice, all humans develop a certain capacity, to a greater or lesser degree, as experts on the subject of morality; it is practically everybody's special subject, granted the individuality of his or her existence. Ranging from great decisions to the most insignificant-looking fidelities and betrayals of our rights and wrongs, dos and don'ts, all of us employ this capacity, shaping it to our own concerns and being shaped by it as we make our decisions; or we find them being made for us. A certain degree of moral craft is inseparable from the experience of life itself. As that great modern moralist and critic of our traditional moralities, Friedrich Nietzsche, remarked: "All experience is moral experience." Within the infinite possibilities of life, moralities show their directing hand; what we do is, in a vast variety of ways, somehow decided to be done. As we expert moralists grow older, our lives become ever more faithful reflections of the moral decisions which we have made—or think not to have made—or are glad to have had made for us.

The opening chapter lays the groundwork for the rest of the book. This chapter aims to define the contours of our present moral condition: a condition in which traditional moral standards, "handed down" over the course of generations, are being questioned and not infrequently rejected as "outdated." Nevertheless, however they escape an old morality for something apparently new, humans cannot escape the necessity of moral choice; in rejecting or merely forgetting one set of moral standards, they must be explicitly or implicitly employing another.

Under "traditional" moral standards, significant choices in life appeared so self-evident that an individual gratefully nourished himself off the cultural bread and wine of custom. The lure of these choices was always pungently real in his life. Traditional man did not have to ponder, in deliberate search of a choice not readily at hand. Instead, he felt himself led, indeed chosen, to perform an act, and it was almost as unthinkable not to enact a custom as it is impossible never to eat. When, as on occasion, "fasting" was constrained, this was for him the exception that confirmed certain rules in his ordinary, everyday, eating life—like "feasting."

Nowadays, there are rapidly changing customs, fads, in both fasting and feasting. Matters of "good taste" and bad are constantly at issue—or left to change as if "change" itself were the best taste. Our fundamental notions about how humans ought to live have lost their past quality of self-evidence; everything, including whether to live or not, appears to be a matter of personal choice—and often not only choice, but of choice after choice. For example, should one get married? If so, to a member of the opposite sex or of the same sex or of both sexes? Communally? Moreover, under the current divorce rate the traditional monogamous marriage loses much of its meaning; now one has serial monogamy or again, choice after choice. It is this "openness" of moral choice, where none is binding, that distinguishes the contemporary moral situation most sharply from past ones.

After discussing these matters, the first chapter goes on to introduce some basic terms and relations of moral discourse and presents, in opposing pairs, varieties of modern moral argument appearing in everyday life as well as in the philosophical field of ethics. Finally, Chapter 1 examines how morality is organized within society.

Chapter 2 considers the morality (and immorality) of sexual relations. Because society has recognized that the power of the sexual urge is capable of subverting the ideals of any institution by upsetting the most intimately biological arrangements between its individuals, sexual activity has always been an object of social control and moral regulation. Along with articles on how changes in sex mores are and have been tied to larger moral and political changes, the second chapter is an arrangement of excerpts that reflect the contemporary conflict over when sex is right and what is its ideal—that is, most moral—form.

In the third chapter, the contentions are over marriage and the family, with more emphasis on the latter—and for the following reason: throughout the history of Christian culture, the family has been regarded as the garden where the seed of morality is implanted and receives nourishment enough to be transplanted to every other ground of societal existence. Some changes in the history of the family are discussed here from several perspectives; these historical perspectives are often at odds with one another. Looking ahead, the prospects of the family are variously assessed by some of our authors. The reader will find the family institution, as a regularity of human action, both defended and attacked for its utility to its individual members and for its contributions to the larger society. New forms of marriage are also considered, as is divorce.

Chapter 4 is taken up with the most intensely argued of all the moral issues facing Americans nowadays: abortion. The contributing authors—doctors, theologians, and numerous philosophers and religious scholars—argue here, often in total opposition, while considering and explaining the moral complexities of the issue.

In contrast to abortion, the question of how we should treat our aged, the issue of Chapter 5, seems to be rather ignored. This relatively neglected subject, like its object, takes on its special significance because the old represent, naturally, through the passage of raw time made meaningful, our cultural traditions; what is "passed over" to the rest of us must have arisen in the past and can become part of our lives only by being taken in through the generations in more or less formal teachings. But suppose the aged have "nothing" to teach? Then, to ignore the aged often means rejecting parts of our cultural heritage as merely obsolete. In addition to reflections on the aged as condemned to obsolescence, there are discussions of how aging affects the personality, sociological dissections of some stereotypes surrounding the aged, and anthropological studies of how other societies honor or despise their old people.

The next two chapters focus on the uses of power in domestic and international politics— that focus narrowing on the seeming perennial opposition between politics and morality. Can politics ever be moral? Can the struggle for power over others ever proceed by moral means or pursue moral ends? Does not power, however disguised or displayed, inevitably sacrifice the superiority of its ideals, whatever they might have been, to the superiority of force, however decent the individuals may be managing that force (for which "violence" is the final synonym)? These chapters analyze and debate the ends toward which present-day domestic and international politics appear directed. The editors have included defenses and rejections of familiar old political ends along with the advocacy of some relatively new ones.

Chapters 8, 9, and 10 consider issues that involve law and morals. Chapter 8 delineates the general relations of law to morality: the moral standard of justice that lies at the cornerstone of the law, the "internal morality" of the law to which it must adhere if it is to be just, and the balancing conflict of law and conscience as law acts as an outward check on the vagaries and rationalizing capacities of individual conscience. There is included a heated debate over the extent to which the law should be used to support the moral standards of the community, particularly those concerning sexual conduct.

Crime and punishment is the subject of the succeeding chapter. The morality of capital punishment is debated first and is followed by opposing suggestions for reform of our criminal justice system. Further, several articles analyze the moral justifications of punishment that serve as the foundation of our criminal justice system

and find them variously barbaric, contradictory, and necessary.

We hardly doubt the wrong suffered by the victims of rapes or assaults; we consider next whether, the old childhood maxim notwithstanding, words and images may strip us of our dignity and thus wrong us, as these violent crimes do, by trespassing upon that protected realm of personal integrity upon which all civilized intercourse rests. Chapter 10 discusses, in several styles of dignity, the question of the moral character of pornography and obscenity. It attempts, first, to define precisely the qualities of the obscene and the pornographic. Are they merely expressions of unconventional tastes in a sphere where each is entitled to his own; do they possess special literary merit in speaking about subjects shrouded in silence and anxiety; or do they cheapen intimacy and pervert human emotion? Individual pieces in this chapter make each of these claims. Additional excerpts trace the relation of obscenity and pornography to other cultural forces and assay their political consequences.

The pressing moral questions that developments in modern science pose to us are the topics of the next two chapters. Chapter 11 reflects on the history and meaning of the technological revolution, and then dwells upon the question of the contemporary control of technology. Chapter 12 is concerned specifically with ethical issues in medicine and biology; for instance, what limitations ought to be placed on scientific experiments that use humans as "guinea pigs"? With the free accessibility of abortion, the growing movement for a "death with dignity," and the ability to control the genetic endowment of individuals within easy reach, medicine is faced with novel moral questions, for the handling of which its traditional dedication to health and saving of lives is entirely inadequate. The issue of consent, central in this chapter, is common to all of these areas.

Few people consider their own deaths a matter of routine. However, without minimizing the importance of those unique and extraordinary occurrences that are turning points of our lives, one may claim that our routines, too, are charged with moral significance. After all, it is in the performance of our mundane activities—for example, our work, our play, our sport, and our business—that we spend most of our lives.

The next two chapters explore the different moral aims that have directed these daily activities in the past and those that continue to do so. The former considers how play and work differ, under what conditions they are richest with meaning and how we may best engage in them. The latter, the fourteenth chapter, presents the Marxist indictment of capitalism and liberalism's defense, and the comparative standing of honesty and corruption in the history of American business.

The next chapter analyzes the great moral issue that has always been prominent in American history: racism. The excerpts in this chapter describe the inner dynamics of racism—how it develops and operates both in the individual psyche and the wider culture—and then present some widespread, but often unnoticed, examples of it. Some also gingerly assess the ways in which racism might be overcome.

Moral education is the final subject. Here, too, there is much contention, for the form of moral education will vary according to what morality one wishes to teach. These excerpts propose both the substance of what must be taught to make individuals moral and the manner in which that should be done. In particular, they concentrate on what the schools, from grammar to university level, may do to inculcate and develop character.

From this brief overview of the book's contents, it should be clear that the editors' aim in *Moral Choices in Contemporary Society* is to highlight the clash of viewpoints within the extended spectrum of contemporary moral argument. The book consists of many brief excerpts, edited and placed in opposition to each other in order to accent the contentions between them.

The editors assume full responsibility for their editing and use of the articles within the context of this book; they may or may not be used as their authors intended. As edited, the excerpts from books and articles do not necessarily duplicate their authors' purpose; rather,

the materials have been selected and their focus sometimes sharpened to fulfill the editors' purposes of representing the great variety of moral argument in contemporary society or of providing background knowledge upon which informed moral judgments may be based.

In brief, the design of the book may be likened to a mosaic in which each small piece seems fitted to its place within the panoramic whole. That whole is the order of contention to be found within the present condition of moral argument.

There is one final principle of selection that the editors have established. As the title indicates, this book focuses on moral choices facing us today; therefore, only contemporary or near contemporary pieces have been chosen, even though older works that are classics may have provided more profound insights. If those classical pieces are not being re-presented in contemporary moral argument, then they are not presently living "choices." As a result, all the authors—with but very few exceptions—have lived in the twentieth century.

The editors acknowledge with gratitude the assistance of Mrs. Jane L. Scheiber, editorial director of Courses by Newspaper, who has checked and sometimes changed their decisions, making fine improvements of her own. Finally, we wish to thank Mrs. Martha Rosso for her rare combination of patience and speed in compiling many of the biographical notes about the individual authors.

P. R.
I. F.

Philadelphia
October 1976

1

THE
NATURE
OF
MORALITY

In this section, as in all the following sections, there is a wide spectrum of points of view on morality. These have been selected for the purpose of indicating the great diversity, even conflict, of analyses and positions on moral issues that presently exists.

This introductory chapter provides the background for the subsequent examination of specific controversial subjects. To open the chapter, Charlotte Saikowski surveys the present moral condition of America as the nation seeks to come to grips with economic, social, and political problems of the last quarter of the twentieth century. She notes that a "deep moral ambivalence" characterizes American society: ". . . on the one hand an absorption in material pleasure and breakdown of Judaeo-Christian morality and, on the other, a yearning and quest for a rejuvenation of moral and spiritual values."

Such issues cannot be fully comprehended, however, without a further understanding of how we arrive at moral judgments. Throughout the remainder of this chapter, therefore, two separate questions are addressed: "What is moral?" and "What is morality?" The first question is a directly practical one. It asks for moral argument that justifies or criticizes a given act or way of conduct. The answers to this question are all evaluations—good, bad, useful, or harmful.

The second question is more theoretical. It asks for some extramoral explanation—for example, religious, psychological, or anthropological—of how morality is to be understood. Moral judgments cannot be isolated from the rest of our thought: They need to be anchored with facts or by judgments drawn from our experience. Our knowledge, intuitions, and experience provide the foundation upon which the edifices of our moral judgments rest.

This exploration begins with an introduction to the study of ethics, a discipline that today, more often than not, ignores the second question above and concerns itself with the task of constructing and refining moral argument. A. C. Ewing describes the essential terms—good, duty, means, ends—of moral argument and then indicates how ethics alone provides an insufficient basis on which to make moral judgments.

Nor is simple adherence to outmoded rules sufficient for making moral judgments in a time of rapid change, argues Walter Lippmann in the following selection. Lippmann then describes that extra element—a certain quality of vision—that is needed in order to formulate a new morality.

One recent approach to formulating such a new morality is that provided by "situation ethics," presented in the next article by one of its leading proponents, Joseph Fletcher. Fletcher argues that love is the source of all moral action and is more important than any given prohibition. In "situation ethics," no moral principles are regarded as absolute, but are valid or not depending on how they make manifest the subject's love in any particular situation. There is a "healthy and primary awareness that 'circumstances alter cases.'"

In direct opposition to Fletcher, Elton M. Eenigenburg argues that love alone is not sufficient as a norm to guide our actions. Setting forth traditional Christian morality, he asserts that God's will, as revealed through His law, must be obeyed; God's revealed will is primary, and love, secondary.

Also opposed to situation ethics and the "new morality" is William Raspberry, who suggests that much of morality is not intellectual and does not require a process of reflection. For him, most moral action is not founded on a rational assessment of the consequences, but on "knee-jerk habits" and on an "a-logical feeling that there are things one simply does not do."

However, Donald Cupitt, in an amusing article, says that people today are unwilling to make snap moral judgments. In the absence of religious authority, they have turned to a presumed scientific impartiality that substitutes the word "social" for "moral" in moral judgments. "The moral norm becomes the majority opinion," and "social convention . . . become[s] in effect the only criterion of right and wrong."

There follows an example of such dependence on majority opinion for establishing moral norms: an ethical aptitude test, presented by Leonard C. Lewin. Such tests are used by personnel officers screening applicants for professional schools, businesses, and so on. The "correct" answers in such a test are those given by a majority of a representative sample of adult Americans. "The governing principle here is that whatever is is right."

In the next selection Bernard Gert considers the general question, Why ought people be moral at all? He provides several strands of argument, each one of which may be persuasive to different people, but remarks, with respect to these as with all such "important decisions about whether to act morally," reason is no guide.

This thread is then picked up by Edward Westermarck; he says that the nonrational guide to moral decision is "authority," which in turn emanates from a great leader. In the final selection, a position is stated opposing the theory that authority originates in the leadership of a great man. William Graham Sumner argues that all morality develops anonymously, out of custom. "The standards of good and right are in the mores," or folkways, according to Sumner, and changes in our mores are difficult to bring about.

NOTES ABOUT THE AUTHORS

Charlotte Saikowski, a journalist, is chief editorial writer of *The Christian Science Monitor.* She also coedited *Current Soviet Policies IV: The Documentary Record of the 22nd Congress of the Communist Party of the Soviet Union.* She wrote "American Morality: Hanging in the Balance" in 1976 after talking with more than fifty social critics across the United States, including theologians, social scientists, psychiatrists, educators, and business leaders.

Alfred Cyril Ewing was born in 1899 and has taught in British universities. His book *Ethics* was published in 1953.

Walter Lippmann was born in 1889. A journalist, editor, and author, he was a founder and associate editor of *The New Republic*. He later became editor of *The New York World*. His column "Today and Tomorrow" was syndicated in 250 newspapers and won Pulitzer prizes in 1958 and 1962. Widely regarded as one of the nation's foremost analysts of foreign affairs as well as political, social, and ethical problems, he wrote many books, including *Public Opinion, The Good Society,* and *A Preface to Morals,* which was published in 1929. He died in 1974.

Joseph Fletcher is an ordained minister of the Episcopal church. A former Dean of St. Paul's Cathedral in Cincinnati, he has also taught at St. Mary's College and at the Episcopal Theological School in Cambridge, Massachusetts, where he was Robert Treat Paine Professor of Social Ethics. Among his books are *The Church and Society* (1930) and *Morals and Medicine* (1954), which openly discussed such formerly taboo subjects as abortion and the right to die. *Situation Ethics,* published in 1966, became the focus of great controversy—denounced as "a deterioration in morals" and praised as "a watershed in the history of moral theology"—and it made an important contribution to the democratization of theological argument.

Elton M. Eenigenburg is dean of Western Theological Seminary in Holland, Michigan, where he joined the faculty in 1952. An ordained minister of the Reformed Church in America, he held several pastorates after receiving his doctorate from Union Theological Seminary at Columbia. He is the author of *The Life and Work of the Reformed Church in America.* The article reprinted here, one of many written by theologians in response to Fletcher's *Situation Ethics,* first appeared in *The Reformed Review* in 1967.

William Raspberry was born in Okolona, Mississippi, in 1935. He was educated at Indiana Central College and worked as a journalist on several newspapers before taking the post of instructor in journalism at Howard University. He is a commentator on Washington, D.C. television and also lectures on race relations.

Don Cupitt, born in 1934, is an Anglican clergyman and university lecturer. He is currently dean of Emmanuel College, Cambridge University, where he is also university lecturer in divinity. His major publications include *Christ and the Hiddenness of God, Crisis of Moral Authority, The Leap of Reason,* and *The Worlds of Science and Religion.* The article reprinted here, "Are Your Morals Socially Acceptable?" was originally delivered as a radio talk over BBC in 1974.

Leonard C. Lewin, born in 1916, has written numerous articles of satire, parody, and criticism. He is the author of *A Treasury of American Political Humor, Report from Iron Mountain,* and *Triage.* The article, "Ethical Aptitude Test," originally appeared in *Harper's* Magazine in October 1976.

Bernard Gert was born in 1934 and is professor of philosophy at Dartmouth College, where he joined the faculty in 1959. A contributor to numerous professional journals, he is editor of Hobbes' *Man and Citizen* as well as author of *The Moral Rules.*

Edward Westermarck was born in 1862 in Finland. A philosopher, sociologist, and anthropologist, he taught at the University of London from 1890 to 1930. His writings include *The History of Human Marriage* (1891), a three-volume work that went through five editions. *The Origin and Development of Moral Ideas,* excerpted in this chapter, was first published in 1906. He died in 1939.

William Graham Sumner, born in 1840, was a professor of sociology and economics at Yale University from 1872 to 1909. *Folkways* (1897) is his best-known work. Sumner died in 1910, and a collection of his notes became the basis of the posthumously published four-volume *The Science of Society* (1927–1929).

CHARLOTTE SAIKOWSKI

America's morality: Hanging in the balance

Walking down Fifth Avenue in New York recently, I passed a young man distributing handbills. The small blue bill, splashed with a picture of a naked woman, read: "Beautiful Girls of All Nationalities. Complete satisfaction, $10. The Conference Rooms, 15 W. 45th St."

Only a few blocks later another handbill, a larger one, was thrust in my hand. "Brethren," it proclaimed, "let us pray for God's people, and raise our voices to Him that He send a mighty Elijah witness, who will demonstrate the Spirit and power of God, and will preach the true Christ."

In these two commonplace incidents seemed to be embodied the deep moral ambivalence which today characterizes American society: on the one hand an absorption in material pleasure and breakdown of Judeo-Christian morality and, on the other, a yearning and quest for a rejuvenation of moral and spiritual values.

It is an ambivalence that afflicts many nations of the world which, in common with the United States, wrestle with profound economic and social problems and are groping for moral moorings to solve them.

What is happening to America? Is it indeed following the example of the Roman Empire and dissipating into a moral wasteland of hedonistic self-indulgence, criminal violence, institutional disorder, and loss of world influence? Or will the warning signals be heeded in time to check the rush toward moral chaos and awaken a new national effort toward self-regeneration and renewal?

One observation can be made with certainty. Speaking with more than 50 thoughtful American social critics across the nation—theologians, sociologists, political scientists, educators, business leaders, psychiatrists, politicians—one finds a widespread and growing concern about the moral condition of American society and a desire to do something about it.

"We are a society without a moral center, like a doughnut," says Max Stackhouse of the Andover Newton Theological School. "There are good things around the edges but there is no guideline."

Comments Lutheran sociologist Peter Berger of Rutgers University: "An enormous demoralization is going on, and that is the gist of our crisis. It is not just a crisis in the political arena but reaches down to private life. It goes from the bedroom to the White House. We are uncertain about our values and the meaning of life. Religion used to give us our values, but we now live in an age of secularization."

"Our standards have shriveled to a point where phoniness is now accepted," says historian Barbara Tuchman. "From TV to magazines, advertising has created a culture in which nobody expects either to say or to listen to or to hear the truth."

Upheavals of 1960s recalled

A host of other social analysts convey America's malaise in such words as "fatalism," "a debunking spirit," "a sense of helplessness," "a norm crisis," "moral drift," a "trough of national consciousness." Such book titles as *The Dying of the Light* and *Twilight of Authority* also reflect the current mood.

The evidence to back up such a pessimistic outlook is abundant. The social and political upheavals of the 1960s, including the tidal wave of permissiveness, have left moral confusion in their wake, even though the nation witnessed unprecedented economic and social progress in that period. Permissiveness, a don't-make-rules philosophy, is now institutionalized. Sex, violence, and the "new morality" are touted with unrestrained zeal. What one sociologist calls "the age of sensation" has invaded the media, the arts, music, with spiritually destructive consequences.

"Our high culture has become largely decadent and without a virtue of creative criticism," comments sociologist Richard Neuhaus. "We

4

practice the celebration of meaninglessness and collapse. It is called 'liberation' but it is anything but that. Far from freeing the individual it casts him adrift.''

With the move away from moral rules and the greater freedom of individual choice, crime in cities and suburbs—from robbery and murder to cheating on exams—has reached alarming proportions. Nor is the public always resistant to the glorification of brutality, as witness the enjoyment of violence in hockey, football, and other body-contact sports and the opposition of many to gun-control laws. The drug and alcohol culture has filtered down to schoolchildren, and, as Harvard ethicist Preston Williams notes, such questions as marijuana use are raised in "descriptive not moral ways."

Brown's interview in Playboy

It is symptomatic of the times that Gov. Edmund G. Brown Jr. of California should give an interview to *Playboy* magazine, which in its sales pitch can now quote the popular Democrat as saying: "I have 150 requests for interviews. But from now on, I'm going to refer them all to this one."

Thirteen states now have gambling lotteries. There is also a growing clamor for public toleration of homosexuality.

The institution of marriage is under severe strain, with divorces now topping a million a year. Only one out of two or three marriages is given a chance of surviving.

Other institutions, too, are under attack or floundering for a moral bearing. Opinion polls show widespread public cynicism about government, politicians, corporations. The churches, confronted with the scientific revolution and competing with what one theologian calls the "religion of the long weekend," are in trouble.

Many social critics note America's hedonism in the permissive use of energy and other world resources. The rush to buy big cars again seems to reflect, in the words of Harvard sociologist David Riesman, the nation's "exalted expectation" of endless consumption and unwillingness to believe in an energy problem.

"Permissiveness took hold because of the view that everything is to be enjoyed and taken," says philosopher Jacques Barzun.

One disturbing trend of recent years is the growing tolerance practiced in our increasingly pluralistic society. Not tolerance in the positive constitutional sense but in the sense of not wishing to impose standards of any kind on others and letting the other fellow "do his own thing." Many young people even flinch at the word "moral," preferring to use the term "values." "I don't want to judge another's values" is a sentiment heard frequently on campuses these days.

Accompanying such tolerance appears to be a decline in personal responsibility and loss of faith in oneself, a mood that leads people into such empty pursuits as astrology, gambling, and game shows. The Protestant work ethic and a sense of calling have often been replaced by the pursuit of security and money.

"We have a Huck Finn spirit now," comments Dr. Riesman, "a spirit of 'don't be a sucker, don't give as much as possible.'"

On a national scale, there has been an enormous "erosion of will" on social problems, as Harvard theologian Harvey Cox puts it, and a growing doubt that the present political and economic system can deal with them. The Great Society with its emphasis on racial justice and help for the disadvantaged has given way to lack of public concern and a feeling of apathy. This can be seen in the fact that the gap between the earnings of whites and blacks is again widening (after a narrowing during the 1960s) yet the problem is not addressed in the top reaches of government anywhere else. Kenneth Keniston of Massachusetts Institute of Technology points out the deplorable record of the United States in the care of its children, one quarter of whom do not have adequate health care.

Abroad, the United States now is viewed by many as a declining power. The National Science Foundation reports that America's international predominance in science and technology has suffered erosion in the last 15 years and other nations are increasing labor productivity faster. Concern is also spreading in Europe about the country's willingness and ability to conduct a strong, coherent foreign policy as leader of the West.

"We don't compete in the world anymore," laments Dr. Riesman.

One could go on. Yet, both in a historical and a current sense, the total picture is not filled solely with negatives. Indeed, in the opinion of many, the self-flagellation which Americans now are engaging in has gone to excess and perspective is called for. The moral crisis is seen to be caused not by Watergate, say, or other ills of society but by how these are viewed.

Michael Novak, popular social critic, believes that not only is there no moral decline in the nation but that Americans' "itch to be moral" has gotten out of control and made them unrealistic in their appraisal of themselves. The media, with their catalog of negatives, have added to the moral disillusionment.

"We are seeing the triumph of moralism over the whole public domain," he commented in his rambling home in Bayville, Long Island. "Our moral achievements are extraordinary. Corporate practice is no worse than it was 50 years ago. Government is in better shape because there are more centers of power."

Urban anthropologist Constance Perin also questions whether there is a moral disintegration. "There are more laws in society today and lots of them are being obeyed," she says. "Our structure is so legal now that it looks like a breakdown."

Certainly there is a rising surge of moral concern spawned by the Watergate scandals and the Vietnam war which, in the words of one scholar, "has given ethics respect again." The investigations of the CIA and other government agencies as well as of corporate business have led to clamor for new laws and reforms, federal and state. Many social groups—from doctors to lawyers to accountants—are re-examining themselves.

Groping for solutions

New stress is being laid on authority, self-discipline, and constraint. Some schools and universities, groping for solutions, are institut-ing moral-education courses and scrutinizing standards. For the second year now the National War College is giving a course in ethics. Penologists and judges are calling for tougher deterrence against criminals and delinquents.

The sexual promiscuity that seemed so rampant appears to be subsiding, perhaps in part because women are finding greater self-worth and independence. While permissiveness has had its tragic results, it has also resulted in less false prudishness and less hypocrisy. Marriage, although visibly in trouble, is still recognized by the vast majority of people as the only viable social and moral mechanism for the stability of society. Outstanding high-school students polled this year indicated they are less tolerant of drug use, more puritannical sexually, and more traditional in their view of marriage.

For all the woes of the churches, there is strong evidence of a reviving interest in religion and a search for "root meanings," especially in the fundamentalist Christian churches, the black churches, and the evangelical segments of the Roman Catholic and other mainline churches. In fact the strongest association of Americans in Bicentennial 1976 still remains a religious one, a fact not reflected in media coverage.

On balance, as one looks back at the 30-odd years since World War II, the gains of American society are astonishing. Blacks have made enormous progress, when one considers that not so long ago lunchrooms and buses were segregated in the South. In the 1940s and 1950s few people were concerned about disadvantaged children, or the environment, or the aged, or the rights of women, or world hunger. There is rising activism among people over 65.

There is also a whole new population in the schools, and it stays there longer. And, while the standards have dropped in the traditional three "R's," academic performance at the high-quality colleges, according to Harold Howe II of the Ford Foundation, is "better than ever."

Despite the tensions of recession, a better relationship now exists between labor and management, and the worker has improved his life. Trade unions are doing a better job of policing racketeering and are beginning to focus on the needs of women and the minorities. Union violence has declined.

Most importantly, if the traumas of Watergate and the Vietnam war demonstrated anything, it is the strength not the weakness of America's institutions.

"We may look bad against that American dream," remarks Mr. Howe. "But if we compare ourselves to the rest of the world, we look pretty good. We should not be deterred from being self-critical, but not in the context of 'going down the drain.'"

Transition and flux

In perspective, the United States is in a period of transition and flux. As a result of the rapid development of science and technology and the pluralization of its culture due to the influx of immigrants, the United States is moving into what sociologist Daniel Bell calls "the post-industrial society" and political scientist Zbigniew Brzezinski describes as the "technetronic era." Swept by a torrent of changing standards, it is now stunned by the more extreme modes of a licentious society and is beginning to contemplate the necessity of moral foundations and direction.

That America must recover its balance is imperative, for not only its freedom at home but its standing in the world is at stake. Ahead lie moral questions of unprecedented magnitude—not just the issue of whether two people should sleep together before marriage but, as scientific and medical technology advances, whether a new breed of mankind should be created in the test tube; whether triage—lifeboat ethics that would let the "unfit" and poorest of the poor starve—should be practiced to hold down the world's population; and who shall make the decisions as to whether a person (or a fetus) lives or dies. The moral choices appear to be growing harder because of the increasing complexity of the issues.

If Americans are to cope with these challenges they will have to sort out their values, reaffirm their fundamental moral order, and reach some consensus again on what they stand for.

A.C. EWING

Ethics

Ethics is concerned with two main kinds of question, first, with deciding the general principles on which ethical terms, i.e. good, bad, duty, etc., are to be applied to anything, and secondly with deciding precisely what these terms mean. Now there seems to be no possibility of validly deducing ethical propositions by some sort of logical argument from the nature of reality without first assuming some ethical propositions to be true; or at least if there is, the way to do so has not yet been discovered by anybody. This may be a disappointing conclusion, but it is borne out by the whole trend of philosophical thought on the subject. Consequently the only way in which we can develop a systematic theory of Ethics is by starting with the ethical judgements which we find ourselves in our practical thinking constrained to make. . . .

Again, we could not intelligently make any ethical judgements of any sort if we had not some understanding of the meaning of terms like good, duty, etc., yet it is a vital part of the business of Ethics to define their meaning as far as this is possible. So Ethics must in this respect also be regarded as completing a task which we have already begun before studying it at all. We have some idea of what "good," etc., mean before opening a single book on Ethics, yet Ethics helps us to understand their meaning better than we did before we studied it.

The two main ethical concepts are expressed respectively by the words "good" and "ought" (or "duty"). But these terms, especially the former, are very far from unambiguous, being in fact used in a variety of different senses, and it is necessary to distinguish one or two of these before starting. Particularly important is the distinction between good as a means and good as an end. If you are suffering from an illness it may be good for you to have an operation, but this certainly does not mean that it is in any way desirable as an end in itself, it only signifies that it is good in the sense of being a means to produce something else which is good. In this case the end is health. It may however be doubted whether even health is good in itself. We should not care whether our teeth were decayed or our appendix inflamed or not if we could be sure that the decay and inflammation would neither hurt us nor make us less efficient in engaging in any activity. This suggests that health is good only as a means to happiness and to any other ends we may seek to pursue in our activities. But there are some things, e.g. happiness and virtue, which seem to be good in their own right and not merely because they produce something else which is good. Practically everybody would value at least happiness even if it never produced any advantages beyond itself, provided only it did not do harm, and very many at least would take the same view about virtue. These things are called good-in-themselves, good as ends, or intrinsically good. Obviously this kind of goodness is more fundamental than the other. Something which is merely good as a means can be rationally valued only because it is liable to produce something else which is intrinsically good (or diminish something intrinsically evil as e.g. medicines diminish pain). On the other hand something that is good as a means may also be good as an end, and it is all the better if this is so. Thus kindness may be commended both because it is good in itself and because it produces happiness. The distinction between ends and means must therefore not be taken too rigidly. The very qualities which make virtue good as an end make it good as a means also. Further, we may easily come to love and prize for its own sake something that we originally valued only for its effects and still admit would have no value if it were not for these effects. The miser takes this attitude to his wealth, and we almost all take it in some degree to some particularly useful material objects. On this ground the distinction between end and means has been sharply attacked, e.g. by the American philosopher, John Dewey. But the question is not what we actually prize, it is what are the ultimate grounds why it is reasonable to prize it, and these can only be found in what is an end in itself, not what is merely a means.

People are liable to ask about everything— What is the use of it?—meaning—To what future end is it a good means? But unless some things were good-in-themselves and not only as means, nothing would be of any use at all. To value everything only as a means would be to do everything for the sake of a future benefit which never came. . . .

In order to decide what action we ought to take or it is right to take in a given situation, one at least of the questions we ought to ask is what the consequences of any proposed action will be. It is a disputed question among writers on Ethics whether the rightness of an action depends solely on its consequences or not, but certainly it depends at least partly on them. It is always an objection to performing a certain act that it will produce bad effects, whether it is always a completely conclusive objection or sometimes may be outweighed by other considerations. So in order to decide whether we ought to do something or not we either always or at least usually need to have a knowledge of what the consequences of the action are likely to be. This is knowledge of the type obtained by natural science, as is the knowledge which enables us to decide whether something is a good means to a given end. To obtain it what we need to know is what are the relevant causal laws. It is in itself not specifically ethical knowledge at all. But this knowledge is not sufficient: we need also to know whether the consequences anticipated are to be regarded as good or bad in themselves. Thus the decision as to what we ought to do depends partly on factual knowledge and partly on knowledge of what things are good or bad in themselves, which unlike the former is knowledge of a specifically ethical kind. Thus in order to know what is the right treatment for a particular invalid, we must know both what is likely to be the best medicine for curing him and that he ought to be cured. In this case it is the scientific kind of knowledge which presents the difficulty and not the specifically ethical, but this is by no means always so. We may be hard put to it to decide not only what are the most efficient types of atom bomb, but also when, if ever, we ought to use atom bombs.

This explains how it is that Ethics as a study is

not able to give us more help than it does in deciding how we ought to act. To decide this we require not only ethical knowledge but also an empirical knowledge of facts and causal laws, and this is supplied by the sciences or by the common-sense knowledge we all possess of people and physical things. Further, even the specifically ethical element in our knowledge is not capable of complete proof by reasoning but requires an intuitive grasp and valuation of the situation, at which a student of Ethics need not be more competent than another person. The result is that Ethics cannot serve practice in more than an advisory capacity. It cannot decide the issue by itself but can only suggest arguments and considerations that will help us in deciding it. But even this is an important role. Because Ethics cannot by itself decide all questions as to what we ought to do, we need not regard it as of no practical value. A person who has studied Ethics should, given goodwill, at least be more likely to look at all relevant sides of an ethical problem, ask the right questions, and avoid elementary confusions. If Ethics could really decide by itself what we ought to do, it would be not only a practical science but the only practical science, and it certainly is not that. It is a great service if it can even only *help* us substantially in deciding what we ought to do. We should add that this must be distinguished from persuading us to do what we know we ought. That is the function of the preacher and orator rather than of the student of Ethics or philosopher. . . .

It might be thought that we could not advance in Ethics at all if we had not first found out the definitions of the fundamental terms we employ. But this is not the case. For, even if we cannot give a definition of them, we have some idea as to what they mean, otherwise we could not employ them even fairly intelligently, as we do in our ordinary ethical thought, and we have some idea as to when they can be correctly applied. It is the business of Ethics to start with the imperfect apprehension of the meaning and application of "good," "duty," etc., which we have in daily life and develop it into something better, but it can only do this by studying the ethical judgements we ordinarily make, examining their nature and trying to fit them into that coherent system which, as I have said, is the aim of the thinker. To say that a fundamental ethical term cannot be defined is not to say that we cannot know what it means. It may be indeed that we shall never be able to define it and yet that we may know or come to know very well what it means. And this in two ways and senses of meaning; we may know what the quality, e.g. of goodness is itself by direct experience of it without being able to analyse it, and we may know to what things we may consistently apply the term, and our knowledge in both ways may be capable of improvement without our ever being able to give a precise definition at all. As a matter of fact it can be easily proved that there must be some terms which are indefinable in the sense of not being analysable, reducible to anything else. For if you define A by analysing it in terms of B and C, you must, for the definition to be intelligible, know what B and C are, and though you may analyse B and C also in terms of something else, you cannot go on in this way *ad infinitum*. If you are to analyse your concepts, sooner or later you must come to concepts which are just unanalysable. If so, it will not be a mark of human failure but an inevitable result of the logic of the concepts that we cannot define them. And to say this will be only to say that we cannot reduce them to anything else, not that we cannot know very much about them. Now, if there are any indefinable concepts, concepts as fundamental as good or ought are among those which are most likely to be indefinable. We may be able to say a great deal about them, but that is not to say that we can reduce them without residuum to something else, something not specifically ethical.

WALTER LIPPMANN

A preface to morals

The trouble with the moralists is in the moralists themselves: they have failed to understand their times. They think they are dealing with a generation that refuses to believe in ancient authority.

They are, in fact, dealing with a generation that cannot believe in it. They think they are confronted with men who have an irrational preference for immorality, whereas the men and women about them are ridden by doubts because they do not know what they prefer, nor why. The moralists fancy that they are standing upon the rock of eternal truth, surveying the chaos about them. They are greatly mistaken. Nothing in the modern world is more chaotic—not its politics, its business, or its sexual relations—than the minds of orthodox moralists who suppose that the problem of morals is somehow to find a way of reinforcing the sanctions which are dissolving. How can we, they say in effect, find formulas and rhetoric potent enough to make men behave? How can we revive in them that love and fear of God, that sense of the creature's dependence upon his creator, that obedience to the commands of a heavenly king, which once gave force and effect to the moral code?

They have misconceived the moral problem, and therefore they misconceive the function of the moralist. An authoritative code of morals has force and effect when it expresses the settled customs of a stable society: the pharisee can impose upon the minority only such conventions as the majority find appropriate and necessary. But when customs are unsettled, as they are in the modern world, by continual change in the circumstances of life, the pharisee is helpless. He cannot command with authority because his commands no longer imply the usages of the community: they express the prejudices of the moralist rather than the practices of men. When that happens, it is presumptuous to issue moral commandments, for in fact nobody has authority to command. It is useless to command when nobody has the disposition to obey. It is futile when nobody really knows exactly what to command. In such societies, wherever they have appeared among civilized men, the moralist has ceased to be an administrator of usages and has had to become an interpreter of human needs. For ages when custom is unsettled are necessarily ages of prophecy. The moralist cannot teach what is revealed; he must reveal what can be taught. He has to seek insight rather than to preach.

The disesteem into which moralists have fallen is due at bottom to their failure to see that in an age like this one the function of the moralist is not to exhort men to be good but to elucidate what the good is. The problem of sanctions is secondary. For sanctions cannot be artificially constructed: they are a product of agreement and usage. Where no agreement exists, where no usages are established, where ideals are not clarified and where conventions are not followed comfortably by the mass of men, there are not, and cannot be, sanctions. It is possible to command where most men are already obedient. But even the greatest general cannot discipline a whole army at once. It is only when the greater part of his army is with him that he can quell the mutiny of a faction.

The acids of modernity are dissolving the usages and the sanctions to which men once habitually conformed. It is therefore impossible for the moralist to command. He can only persuade. To persuade he must show that the course of conduct he advocates is not an arbitrary pattern to which vitality must submit, but that which vitality itself would choose if it were clearly understood. He must be able to show that goodness is victorious vitality and badness defeated vitality; that sin is the denial and virtue the fulfilment of the promise inherent in the purposes of men. The good, said the Greek moralist, is "that which all things aim at"; we may perhaps take this to mean that the good is that which men would wish to do if they knew what they were doing.

If the morality of the naive hedonist who blindly seeks the gratification of his instincts is irrational in that he trusts immature desire, disregards intelligence and damns the consequences, the morality of the pharisee is no less irrational. It reduces itself to the wholly arbitrary proposition that the best life for man would be some other kind of life than that which satisfies his nature. The true function of the moralist in an age when usage is unsettled is what Aristotle who lived in such an age described it to be: to promote good conduct by discovering and explaining the mark at which things aim. The moralist is irrelevant, if not meddlesome and dangerous, unless in his teaching he strives to give a true account, imaginatively conceived, of that which experience would show is desirable among the choices that are possible and necessary. If he is to be listened to, and if he is to deserve a hearing among his fellows, he must set himself this task which is so much humbler than to command and so much more difficult than to exhort: he must seek to anticipate and to supplement the insight of his fellow men into the problems of their adjustment to reality. He must find ways to make clear and ordered and expressive those concerns which are latent but overlaid and confused by their preoccupations and misunderstandings.

Could he do that with perfect lucidity he would not need to summon the police nor evoke the fear of hell: hell would be what it really is, and what in all inspired moralities it has always been understood to be, the very quality of evil itself. Nor would he find himself in the absurd predicament of seeming to argue that virtue is highly desirable but intensely unpleasant. It would not be necessary to praise goodness, for it would be that which men most ardently desired. Were the nature of good and evil really made plain by moralists, their teachings would appear to the modern listener not like exhortations from without, but as Keats said of poetry: "a wording of his own highest thoughts and . . . almost a remembrance."

JOSEPH FLETCHER

Situation ethics: The new morality

There are at bottom only three alternative routes or approaches to follow in making moral decisions. They are: (1) the legalistic; (2) the antinomian, the opposite extreme—i.e., a lawless or unprincipled approach; and (3) the situational. All three have played their part in the history of Western morals, legalism being by far the most common and persistent. . . .

There is an old joke which serves our purposes. A rich man asked a lovely young woman if she would sleep the night with him. She said, "No." He then asked if she would do it for $100,000? She said, "Yes!" He then asked, "$10,000?" She replied, "Well, yes, I would." His next question was, "How about $500?" Her indignant "What do you think I am?" was met by the answer, "We have already established *that*. Now we are haggling over the price." Does any girl who has "relations" (what a funny way to use the word) outside marriage automatically become a prostitute? Is it always, regardless of what she accomplishes for herself or others—is it *always* wrong? Is extramarital sex inherently evil, or can it be a good thing in some situations? Does everybody have his price, and if so, does that mean we are immoral and ethically weak? Let's see if we can find some help in answering these questions.

Approaches to decision-making

Legalism. With this approach one enters into every decision-making situation encumbered with a whole apparatus of prefabricated rules and regulations. Not just the spirit but the letter of the law reigns. Its principles, codified in rules, are not merely guidelines or maxims to illuminate the situation; they are *directives* to be followed. Solutions are preset, and you can "look them up" in a book—a Bible or a confessor's manual.

Judaism, Catholicism, Protestantism—all major Western religious traditions have been legalistic. In morals as in doctrine they have kept to a spelled-out, "systematic" orthodoxy. . . .

Statutory and code law inevitably piles up, ruling upon ruling, because the complications of life and the claims of mercy and compassion combine—even with code legalists—to accumulate an elaborate system of exceptions and compromise, in the form of rules for breaking the rules! . . .

Any web thus woven sooner or later chokes its weavers. . . .

What can be worse, no casuistry at all may reveal a punishing and sadistic use of law to hurt people instead of helping them. How else explain burning at the stake in the Middle Ages for homosexuals (death, in the Old Testament)? . . . But even if the legalist is truly *sorry* that the law requires unloving or disastrous decisions, he still cries, *"Fiat justitia, ruat caelum!"* (Do the "right" even if the sky falls down). He is the man Mark Twain called "a good man in the worst sense of the word." . . .

Antinomianism. Over against legalism, as a sort of polar opposite, we can put antinomianism. This is the approach with which one enters into the decision-making situation armed with no principles or maxims whatsoever, to say nothing of *rules*. In every "existential moment" or "unique" situation, it declares, one must rely upon the situation of itself, *there and then,* to provide its ethical solution.

The term "antinomianism" [means], literally, "against law." . . .

One form [of antinomianism] was libertinism—the belief that by grace, by the new life in Christ and salvation by faith, law or rules no longer applied to Christians. Their ultimate happy fate was now assured, and it mattered no more *what* they did. . . . The other form, less pretentious and more enduring, was a Gnostic claim to special knowledge, so that neither principles nor rules were needed any longer even as guidelines and direction pointers. They would just *know* what was right when they needed to know. They had, they claimed, a superconscience. . . .

While legalists are preoccupied with law and its stipulations, the Gnostics are so flatly opposed to law—even in principle—that their moral decisions are random, unpredictable, erratic, quite anomalous. Making moral decisions is a matter of spontaneity; it is literally unprincipled, purely *ad hoc* and casual. They follow no forecastable course from one situation to another. They are, exactly, anarchic—i.e., without a rule. They are not only "unbound by the chains of law" but actually sheer extemporizers, impromptu and intellectually irresponsible. They not only cast the old Torah aside; they even cease to think seriously and *care-fully* about the demands of love as it has been shown in Christ, the love norm itself. The baby goes out with the bath water! . . .

Situationism. A third approach, in between legalism and antinomian unprincipledness, is situation ethics. (To jump from one polarity to the other would be only to go from the frying pan to the fire.) The situationist enters into every decision-making situation fully armed with the ethical maxims of his community and its heritage, and he treats them with respect as illuminators of his problems. Just the same he is prepared in any situation to compromise them or set them aside *in the situation* if love seems better served by doing so.

Situation ethics goes part of the way with natural law, by accepting reason as the instrument of moral judgment, while rejecting the notion that the good is "given" in the nature of things, objectively. It goes part of the way with Scriptural law by accepting revelation as the source of the norm while rejecting all "revealed" norms or laws but the one command—to love God in the neighbor. The situationist follows a moral law or violates it according to love's need. For example, "Almsgiving is a good thing *if* . . ." The situationist never says, "Almsgiving is a good thing. Period!" His decisions are hypothetical, not categorical. Only the commandment to love is categorically good. "Owe no one anything, except to love one another." (Rom. 13:8.) If help to an indigent only pauperizes and degrades him, the situationist refuses a handout and finds some other way. He makes no law out of Jesus' "Give to every one who begs from you." . . .

There are various names for this approach: situationism, contextualism, occasionalism, circumstantialism, even actualism. These labels indicate, of course, that the core of the ethic they describe is a healthy and primary awareness that "circumstances alter cases"—i.e., that in actual problems of conscience the situational variables are to be weighed as heavily as the normative or "general" constants.

The situational factors are so primary that we may even say "circumstances alter rules and principles." . . .

Christian situation ethics has only one norm or principle or law (call it what you will) that is binding and unexceptionable, always good and right regardless of the circumstances. That is "love"—the *agapē* of the summary commandment to love God and the neighbor. Everything else without exception, all laws and rules and principles and ideals and norms, are only *contingent,* only valid *if they happen* to serve love in any situation. Christian situation ethics is not a system or program of living according to a code, but an effort to relate love to a world of relativities through a casuistry obedient to love. It is the strategy of love. This strategy denies that there are, as Sophocles thought, any unwritten immutable laws of heaven. . . .

In non-Christian situation ethics some other highest good or *summum bonum* will, of course, take love's place as the one and only standard—such as self-realization in the ethics of Aristotle. But the *Christian* is neighbor-centered first and last. Love is for people, not for principles; i.e., it is personal—and therefore when the impersonal universal conflicts with the personal particular, the latter prevails in situation ethics. . . .

Principles, yes, but not rules

It is necessary to insist that situation ethics is willing to make full and respectful use of principles, to be treated as maxims but not as laws or precepts. We might call it "principled relativism." To repeat the term used above, principles or maxims or general rules are *illuminators.* But they are not *directors.* The classic rule of moral theology has been to follow laws but do it *as much as possible* according to love and according to reason *(secundum caritatem et secundum rationem).* Situation ethics, on the other hand, calls upon us to keep law in a subservient place, so that *only* love and reason really count when the chips are down! . . .

Love only is always good

The rock-bottom issue in all ethics is "value." Where is it, what is its locus? Is the worthiness or worthness of a thing inherent *in* it? Or is it contingent, *relative* to other things than itself? Is the good or evil of a thing, and the right or wrong of an action, intrinsic or extrinsic? . . .

In Christian situation ethics nothing is worth anything in and of itself. It gains or acquires its value only because it happens to help persons (thus being good) or to hurt persons (thus being bad). The person who is "finding" the value may be either divine (God willing the good) or human (a man valuing something). Persons—God, self, neighbor—are both the subjects and the objects of value; *they* determine it to be value, and they determine it to be value for some person's sake. It is a value because somebody decided it was worth something. Oscar Wilde was clever but not deep when he said, "A cynic is a man who knows the price of everything, and the value of nothing." There is no other way to set value but by price, even though *money* is not always the truest measure. Good and evil are extrinsic to the thing or the action. It all depends on the situation. What is right in one case, e.g., lending cash to a father who needs it for his hungry family, may be wrong in another case, e.g., lending cash to a father with hungry children when he is known to be a compulsive gambler or alcoholic. . . .

Love is a predicate

Apart from the helping or hurting of people, ethical judgments or evaluations are meaningless. Having as its supreme norm the neighbor love commanded of Christians, Christian situation ethics asserts firmly and definitely: *Value, worth, ethical quality, goodness or badness, right or wrong—these things are only predicates, they are not properties.* They are not "given" or objectively "real" or self-existent. There is only one thing that is always good and right, intrinsically good regardless of the context, and that one thing is love. . . .

It is the *only* principle that always obliges us in conscience. Unlike all other principles you might mention, love alone when well served is always good and right in every situation. Love is the only universal. But love is not something we *have* or *are,* it is something we *do.* Our task is to act so that more good (i.e., loving-kindness) will occur than any possible alternatives; we are to be "optimific," to seek an optimum of loving-kindness. It is an attitude, a disposition, a leaning, a preference, a purpose.

When we say that love is always good, what we mean is that whatever is loving in any *particular* situation is good! Love is a way of relating to persons, and of using things. . . . It is not a virtue at all; it is the one and only *regulative principle* of Christian ethics.

ELTON M. EENIGENBURG

How new is the new morality?

The new moralists are united in opposing any ethics which puts a code of laws, rules, principles, or explicit regulations *prior* to, and *external* to, individuals in situations requiring ethical decision. To do so is to derive "right" and "wrong" at second hand. . . .

Their frequent condemnation of laws and rules, because these have a built-in content, ready to be applied, has seemed to say that any and all content is to be scorned. . . .

The *content* the new morality is opposed to is that which is in existence prior to the particular ethical problem. The love which is called into play arises *after* the ethical predicament has become apparent. The content of the first is legalistic, abstract, applicable to many cases of the same general kind. The content of the second is particular, concrete, and uniquely fitted to the special instance to which it is applied as a healing medicine. The first is deductive in its approach, starting with general principles, ready to be applied. The second is inductive, starting with persons. The first regards some things as being always inherently evil; other things as always inherently good. The second sees nothing as being inherently good or evil, except love (translated as "personal concern"), and indifference or actual malice. . . .

We shall now pose a more complicated problem in the sphere of interpersonal relationship. Bob and Betty have been dating one another for about a year. . . . Tonight they had attended a church dance and were now ostensibly on the way home.

But the night was yet young, and Bob's heart being full of love for Betty, he decided to park at the lake shore. Betty found herself in immediate agreement with the idea, and as this ageless story goes, one thing led to another until Bob found himself demanding from Betty, in the name of an eternal love that knows no dying, and with the incoherence such situations invariably call forth, the ultimate gift she was able to give him.

The new morality has been charged by its critics with being obsessed with such situations—and more than that, with encouraging a bland permissiveness in the area of sexual relationships. . . .

Some of the new moralists have been insistent that their approach, if followed through faithfully, will actually reduce sexual license. The logic of that claim is clear. If love's careful estimate of the need and welfare of the other person is always made, if, as Fletcher says, we are "who-askers" (that is, who will be helped or hurt) rather than "what-askers" (that is, what does the law prescribe), the vast amount of sexual practice in and out of marriage which simply "uses" the other person will be eliminated. . . .

What follows on the lake shore between Bob and Betty is closed to our sight. As far as general outcomes are concerned, they either did or they didn't. But as far as preliminary factors are concerned, the possibilities are many. If both had studied their textbooks in the new morality well, and had accepted the conclusions both rationally and emotionally, the conclusion of the matter is uncertain. They might have, or they might not have—depending upon love's directive, one in which the comprehensive need and welfare of Bob and Betty are properly calculated. . . . And calculations must take into account the far reaches of time, not just the span of an evening at the lake shore, with, perhaps, tomorrow's regrets.

That's the one extreme. The other is a rigid legal apparatus in which Bob and Betty, admonished a thousand times by parents, Bible, church, and the personal tragedies of others, that certain things, like the thing proposed now by Bob, were *dead wrong,* and that acquiescence to them could bring only terrors in this life and in the world to come, heroically flee the lake shore before it is too late. Between the extremes lie the sad mixtures and confusions thrust upon young people by the sophisticated relativisms of the times. These are the broken norms of the present. . . .

The same basic procedure might be followed through with problems from any ethical area whatsoever. While sexual practice in all of its ramifications provides the most dramatic focus for illustration, the implications of the new morality in every sphere of moral activity must be acknowledged and studied. There has been a method in our madness in providing this extensive discussion of new morality methodology before raising our principal question, How new is it? That question cannot be dealt with properly until one has seen something of the stark contrast between traditional approaches to moral problems, Catholic and Protestant, and what is now being proffered as "new," and yet as very old.

The new moralists are not to be held responsible for the invention of the title of their ethical method. It came in the first instance from one of the method's chief enemies, Pope Pius XII, who, in an allocution on April 18, 1952, denounced what he called "existential" or "situational" ethics. The pope protested that such a method might be used to justify a Catholic leaving the Roman Catholic Church if he felt it might bring him closer to God. Birth control might be defended on the claim that thereby personality was enhanced. On February 2, 1956, the Supreme Sacred Congregation of the Holy Office gave the title, "the New Morality," to it, and banned it from all Catholic academies and seminaries. Professor Fletcher and others would like very much to drop the ambiguous title and call the method "situation ethics." . . .

It becomes necessary at this point to raise the critical question whether the new moralists have not made the fundamental error of making a part to be the whole.

There can be no doubt that the methodology of New Testament ethics is that of love. God's own primary mode of securing his ends was by love! He requires the same of his people. But love is not *everything!* It is the divinely appointed way of serving God in trustful obedience; it is at the same time a dynamic force of great power. It is, however, the will of God that must be done; or better, God must be served in faithful obedience. His revealed will concerning that which delights him is his law. And so the law must be obeyed. That law is fulfilled when it is obeyed through love's instrumentality. Jesus himself said that he did not come to destroy the law, but to fulfill it. He did so with a love unsurpassable in its depth and embrace. Love as instrument is secondary, and functional to that primary thing, God's revealed will. In a great many instances it stands prior to man's obedience—or his disobedience. . . .

The content for a Christian situationalism is the will of God that must be done in love. Paul does not let his fellow Christians think that love can be understood without the specific detail which the life of Christian love demands. His letters have many references to the kind of morality required of God's people in this world, and much of this is in the form of specific commands, exhortations, ethical directives. Of course he did not spell out Christian ethics in the form of codes or tables of rules. But ordinary Christians, which most of us appear to be, want the details. We want to know how love works itself out in specific ways in Christ's church and in the community of the world. The Bible does not fail us here. . . .

An illustration of Paul's exhortations and demands in the area of the sex life can be found in I Cor. 6:9 to 7:40. Certainly there is not found here a code of rules standing by itself, or "over against" the Christian community with the police power of civil law behind it. Nevertheless, obedience to Christ in this area demands loving adherence to certain rules and principles which promote the spiritual and moral health of both the Christian person and the Christian community. . . .

Our conclusion is that the new morality is, after all, quite new. There are significant enough differences between it and the New Testament to make us refuse to accept its deliverances as a faithful rendering of the same. A factor we have not had space to discuss, but a very important one, is the very great difference between the communicative power of New Testament ethics and that of the new morality. The latter can speak meaningfully only to a very few—those who are able to master its dialectic. It is a specialists' ethic, a precious thing for an intellectual elite. One must go to a class to learn its technique. The common people heard Jesus gladly, and while they frequently gave little attention to his moral directives for life in the Kingdom, they were able, at least, to understand what they were. So with the writers of the New Testament. They have been understood by millions down through the centuries. Too often their ethical directives have been converted into hard legalisms. That was mostly a corruption of the method, not of the content.

Jesus and the apostles spoke to men where they were, on the level of their appreciations. God's demands were made as his will was revealed. The grace of God was promised and given—so that those who wished to obey might have at their disposal the means by which to obey. Forever there was a falling short of the goal—and always the exhortation to keep trying. The new morality is incredibly naïve. It takes a fellow and a girl at the lake shore—and demands of them a miracle of objective evaluation of a deeply passional situation, and with that, decision-making at a rational level the UN would be proud of. People aren't made like that, and so God had to make a lot of things pretty clear beforehand.

WILLIAM RASPBERRY

Honesty — without even thinking about it

I wish they wouldn't deal so much with the pragmatics of the thing: the amount of the reward the rich lady gave the honest cabbie, and the offer of a chauffeur's job at twice what he now earns.

But maybe that's what we've come to, now that even such formerly self-evident virtues as education and decent behavior are sold on the basis that they enhance employability and can therefore be translated into money.

Well, I don't think William E. Taylor, the cab driver who found all that money and jewelry in his taxicab last week, ever stopped to think about the reward he might get for trying to find its owner.

He says he never really examined the contents of the purse and was astonished when the police (to whom he had taken it) told him it contained some $42,000 worth of cash, travelers checks and jewelry.

Mrs. Edward N. Cole, whose husband is the retired president of General Motors, rewarded Taylor with $400 and an offer of an $18,000-a-year chauffeur's job.

Naturally, some people have been counting the reward money, weighing it against what Taylor might have netted if he had kept the most negotiable part of the cache for himself, weighing all that against the possibility of getting caught and losing everything—and then trying to figure out whether Taylor did the right thing.

Taylor, one hardly need add, is not one of those doing this moral arithmetic. Taylor, a 51-year-old grandfather and hacker of some 30 years' experience, is what you might call knee-jerk honest. He behaves honestly without even thinking about it.

The not thinking about it is, in fact, the best part of it. Some things are too central to a person's character to risk the contamination of logic.

Without getting too philosophical about it, I am convinced that the absence of certain knee-jerk habits of morality and decency is one of the major problems of our times. Some people who think about these things blame it on a turn away from religion.

If they are right, I suspect it is not because of waning faith in the Almighty but because it was in church and Sunday school that a lot of us developed our knee-jerk decency. We may have behaved ourselves initially out of fear that God would strike us dead with a bolt of lightning, but later on we were guided by simple yet powerful ideas of right and wrong, of conscience.

But what happens when parents don't go to church, or don't send their children to Sunday school? Who instills the knee-jerk attitudes? In many cases, including homes headed by very decent, very honest parents, the answer is: Nobody.

And as a result, there is often nothing to counterbalance the moral pragmatism children learn by watching their parents.

This isn't the whole explanation of what is happening to us, of course. Part of it is that all of us are more questioning these days: of politicians, of government officials, of teachers, of parents, of authorities of every sort. That, probably, is a good thing. In any case, there's nothing to be done about it.

But if a non-religious person is permitted to say so, that relentless questioning can lead to difficulty if there has not already been inculcated a set of internalized, bench-mark, knee-jerk beliefs, somewhere to stand while you're asking the questions.

Nor is it simply a matter of morality. Nearly all social relationships are easier when certain nonlogical conventions are observed.

Those conventions, those bench-mark feelings, tend to be established very early or not at all. After that, you've got to *think* about everything.

And so you get teen-age boys asking their teachers to explain why it is all right for girls to wear hats in the classroom, but not boys. Or why one should behave deferentially to adults. Or not cheat merchants. Or any of a number of other things that another generation had taken as beyond question.

And when you are reduced to answering these things on the basis of logic, you're dead.

The point could be made, I suppose, that the inability to come up with a logical answer to questions of convention may mean that the convention isn't worth preserving.

But the truth is, much of the basis of civilized behavior is convention, a sense not of the *logic* of things but of the *fitness* of things, the a-logical feeling that there are things one simply does not do.

Keeping a purse that doesn't belong to you, for instance. . . .

I was pleased to learn that Taylor has three children in college and another about to graduate from high school. They could use the proceeds of the reward.

They could also use a healthy dose of the knee-jerk attitude that produced the reward. I hope he remembered to give it to them.

DON CUPITT

Are your morals socially acceptable?

Have you noticed how often nowadays people use the word "social" as a euphemism for "moral"? If a new medical technique is said to have "serious social implications," what is meant is that its use might be morally wrong. An industrial concern may be urged to pursue more "socially responsible" policies. Wrongdoing, or crime, or both, are often spoken of as "anti-social behaviour." If we listen to the language used by people trained in the medical and social sciences, we often hear idioms of this kind, in which a straightforward moral word has been replaced by an awkward periphrasis.

Perhaps the reason is that people have an obscure feeling that plain moral words like "good" and "evil," "right" and "wrong," are unscientific, and possibly controversial. So the moral terms are replaced by seemingly less controversial terms such as "immature," "deviant," "disturbed" or "socially irresponsible." By using these terms, we seem to suppose that we can report that somebody is departing from the statistical norm without actually quite committing the unforgivable sin of passing moral judgment upon him.

People who talk like this are not, I think, setting out to make covert moral judgments. It is rather that they have been persuaded that they ought not to make moral judgments at all (forgetting that the judgment that one ought not to moralise is itself a moral judgment) and they sincerely believe that by predicating "anti-social behaviour" of someone they are avoiding moralising about him.

This desire to avoid making moral judgments can be taken to absurd lengths. The other day, I noticed the *Guardian*'s leader-writer clearly wishing to write "x is wrong"; but feeling constrained instead to say, "most people would find x quite unacceptable": which sounds like an innocuous generalisation about public opinion.

Why do people do this? Surely because the whole business of making moral judgments causes us acute embarrassment. It is only 20 years ago that Mrs. Margaret Knight caused a storm by arguing publicly that morality is logically independent of religious belief. But, in these two short decades, the dissociation has become complete. In the modern idiom, it is now "socially" quite "unacceptable" to defend a thesis about abortion from religious premises. But, in dispensing with religious authority as a basis for moral argument, we have unfortunately been unable to agree upon anything else. We have no settled criteria for rational moral argument about fundamental questions. So we resort to empirical statements about what most people do or do not approve. If only science is rational, then moral judgments must be rephrased as sociological generalisations. The moral norm becomes the majority opinion. Moral questions are decided by polling. Since public opinion is constantly changing, what is "socially unacceptable" today may hope, with the help of good publicity, to become "socially acceptable" in the future. Taking public opinion

as a moral guide in this way is what religious moralists call "worldliness" and regard as a sin, but nowadays there is no better way of reviling the opinion of a group than by calling them "a small minority." If the majority must be right, the minority must be in the wrong.

People fancied that by shaking off the yoke of religious authority they were liberating themselves. But, in fact, they have fallen under a far worse tyranny, that of fashion and public opinion. The final absurdity is that those who have allowed social convention to become in effect the only criterion of right and wrong are the very same people who denounce what they call conventional morality! After 25 centuries of grounding morality on God and the individual conscience, we may relapse into the tyranny of a tribal morality.

LEONARD C. LEWIN

Ethical aptitude test

This short test is one of a series prepared by the Institute of Situational Ethics of Washington, D.C., as part of a program to determine the ethical quotients of persons applying for admission to professional schools and of those seeking positions of responsibility in business, in government, and in other occupations involving policy decisions. The ISE is funded by the American Free Enterprise Foundation, a nonprofit, nonpartisan organization chartered to "support and advance the principles of clear thinking in American life."

Along with others in the series (Political Pragmatism, Business Practice, Professional Ethics, Personal Relations, et cetera) this quiz was administered to a representative sampling of 435 adult Americans. A summary of their responses is included. Readers who wish to determine their own EQs will find the scoring procedure and the correct answers, as computed by the senior fellows of the Institute, on page 20.

E.A.T. Series I: The value of life

The National Kidney Foundation has reported that many persons have offered to sell kidneys for transplantation.

1. Would this be improper?
2. Would it differ in principle from the common practice of selling blood?
3. If it is not improper, how should the price of a kidney be determined—by direct negotiation, by medical administrators, by governmental regulation, or in some other manner?

As with other goods and services, the medical care available to the rich is superior to that available to the poor. The difference is most conspicuous in the application of new and expensive lifesaving techniques.

4. Is ability to pay an acceptable basis for allocating such services? If not, how should they be apportioned?

Symptoms of life can now be sustained long after consciousness has expired, by means of artificial respirators and other devices.

5. In such cases, when available medical opinion confirms that the condition is irreversible, by what criterion should the decision to "pull the plug" be made, if at all?
6. Who should make the decision?

Many drugs of great potential life-saving value can be tested effectively only on human beings, but often with such risk to the subjects tested that only those who felt they had nothing to lose would willingly participate if they knew the dangers involved.

7. Under what circumstances, if any, would it be right to conduct such tests without ensuring that the persons tested had a clear and complete understanding of the risks they would be taking?

Before the establishment of the national fifty-five-mile-per-hour speed limit, automobile-related deaths were running at the rate of fifty to sixty thousand per year. (Current figures are somewhat lower.) Some studies indicate that a twenty-mile-per-hour speed limit would reduce this figure to 10,000 or less. Assume this estimate is correct; assume further that for each ten miles per hour the speed limit is set above twenty miles per hour the death toll rises by 10,000; take into account whatever other factors seem relevant.

8. What is a reasonable national speed limit?

Increasing concern is being expressed, notably on the grounds of safety and cost efficiency, about the wisdom of expanding the use of nuclear reactors as a source of energy in this country over the next twenty-odd years. Assume here—for the sake of argument—that substantial economic benefits could be proved.

9. What is the maximum acceptable twenty-year level of risk for such a program? (Express the answer in terms of statistically probable fatalities from nuclear accidents—for example, a 10 percent chance of 10,000 deaths, a 1 percent chance of 100,000 deaths, a .1 percent chance of 1 million deaths, et cetera.)
10. Given, as in these examples, the same risk *ratio*, which is preferable:
    (a) A greater chance of fewer deaths?
    (b) A smaller chance of more deaths?
    (c) Immaterial?

In many remote parts of the world, vast numbers of people die from famine, disease, and other generally predictable disasters.

11. How much should the average American be willing to spend annually to reduce the number of these deaths?

Three years ago, when the oil embargo was put into effect by the Arab states, and the escalation of oil prices was begun, some people proposed American military seizure of one or more of the principal oil-producing countries. Assume, again for the sake of argument, that such an action would result in a net gain for the American economy of $2 billion per year for ten years.

12. What is the maximum number of American deaths that such an action would warrant?
13. Of foreign deaths?
14. What are the principal criteria for establishing the relative value of human lives?
15. How much, in dollars, is the average human life worth?

19

Summary of responses

Where 80 percent or more of the respondents were in unqualified agreement, no comment is included. Numerical answers are weighted averages, to the nearest significant round figure.

1. No.
2. No.
3. By direct negotiation. (Nearly half, however, thought that medical administrators should regulate the *terms* of such sales.)
4. Yes. (Respondents who suggested that other factors should be considered—most often mentioned were productivity, achievement, and life expectancy—agreed that ability to pay afforded the only workable standard as well as a rough measure of productivity and achievement.)
5. The most generally cited criterion was unwillingness of the persons or institutions bearing the cost of the life-support systems to maintain them.
6. The same persons or institutions.
7. A consensus approved testing without informed consent on persons judged to be "unproductive" or "undesirable," the two words most commonly used. Definitions, where offered, varied widely.
8. Seventy-three miles per hour.
9. Seventy-eight percent of the respondents picked one of the three examples offered, all of which carry the same risk ratio.
10. (c).
11. $22.
12. 84,000.
13. 240,000.
14. The principal criterion cited by almost all respondents, in varying language, was potential economic productivity. Also mentioned by 10 percent or more were life expectancy, achievement, and character.
15. $28,000.

Scoring procedure: Questions 1, 2, 3, 5, 6, 7, 10, and 13 count one point each, questions 4, 9, 12, and 14 two points, questions 8, 11, and 15 three points, for a total of 25. Where numerical answers were called for, a deviation of up to 10 percent is considered correct, and up to 20 percent receives half credit. Adjustment: If you feel you may have been unduly influenced by the responses of others, *add* two points; if you are sure you were not influenced by the answers you read, *deduct* two. A score of 15 is par. The correct answers are those that appeared in the summary, since the governing principle here is that whatever is is right.

BERNARD GERT

Why should one be moral?

Many philosophers have held that the question "Why should one be moral?" is a senseless or pointless question. I believe that this is due to their misunderstanding of the question. They interpret the question as "Why would a rational man publicly advocate that one be moral?" Taken in this way, the question is pointless, for the answer is obvious. All rational men must publicly advocate that everyone act morally. But the question is not a request for a moral judgment. Rather, it is a request for a nonmoral practical judgment. Understood in this way the question becomes "Why would a rational man concerned for me advocate that I be moral?" This is not a senseless question. It may very well be that some rational men concerned for me will advocate that I not be moral. However, some rational men concerned with me will advocate that I be moral. Why they would advocate this provides the answer to the question "Why should one be moral?"

This question must be asked by someone who thinks you are concerned for him. To really appreciate its force, consider that you have been asked it by one of your children or a younger sister or brother. What would you answer? There are many things you could say. You could point out that it was generally in one's self-interest to be moral, that people who were moral were generally happier than those who were not. When talking to those whose character is not yet formed, this point takes on even more significance. If you were religious, you could add that God wants one to be moral, and that he will reward those who are. But you could say more than this. You could talk of your ideal of a man—one with all the virtues, moral and personal—and say that you wanted him to be such a man. To want him to become your ideal of a man certainly shows your interest in him. You could talk of integrity and dignity, pointing out that since he must publicly advocate obedience to the moral rules, it would be hypocritical not to be moral himself.

Finally you could point out to him that though you were concerned for him, you were also concerned for others, and that in large measure, you advocate his being moral, not so much out of your concern for him as out of your concern for everyone. There is nothing wrong, morally or otherwise, with advocating a course of action to someone for whom you are concerned, which is not advocated out of concern for him. As long as you would advocate this course of action to anyone for whom you are concerned, you need not advocate it out of your concern for him. If you have instilled in him a concern for others, then this final answer will have the most force. If you have not, then there is a good chance that none of your answers will seem persuasive. . . .

The question "Why should I be moral?" is most likely to be asked by those concerned with morality. . . . Providing an answer to this question is one good way of distinguishing bogus from genuine or justifiable morality. If we cannot give an answer to it, then we should begin to question the justification of that morality. But we do have a justification of some moral rules. With regard to these rules we should be able to give a satisfactory answer; though, of course, not one in terms of self-interest.

The moral rules prohibit causing evil. This provides us with a ready-made answer to our question. One should be moral because he will cause someone else to suffer evil if he is not. Note that this is a moral reason or answer to the question "Why should one be moral?" As such it should apply in all cases rather than merely generally. We can now distinguish between be-

ing moral and the reasons for being moral. Included among these reasons is what I shall call the moral reason, to avoid causing evil. Note that this is a perfectly acceptable answer to the question. It is one that might serve to convince someone who had actually asked the question. Pointing out to him that others will suffer because of his immoral action may be sufficient to make him give up that course of action. For he may not have thought of this, or have given it sufficient weight. . . .

I am not concerned now with the question "Why in general shouldn't I deceive, break my word, cheat, disobey the law, or neglect my duty?" The answer to these questions is . . . "You will cause someone to suffer evil consequences." Thus it might seem as if the answer to the question "Why in this particular case shouldn't I deceive, cheat, etc." is "It is likely or probable that your act will cause someone to suffer evil consequences." But in some cases this is not true. It is not likely or probable that your act will cause someone to suffer evil consequences. From the fact that disobeying these rules generally results in someone suffering evil consequences, it follows that many individual acts of this sort are likely to have these consequences. But it does not follow that some particular act is likely to have them. It is the offering of this reason in the cases where it does not fit that renders it suspect. It is a good reason not to violate a moral rule on a particular occasion that it is likely or probable that your act will cause someone to suffer evil consequences. But it is not a good reason when this is not likely or probable. . . .

The answer to the question "Why should I be moral?" when it is not likely that my action will have evil consequences for anyone is connected to the moral answer by means of the virtues. . . . Virtues and vices are built on habit and by precedent. Following the moral rule generally builds the virtue, and contrary action generally builds the vice. The reason for following the moral rule in the peculiar situation when no one would be harmed by an unjustified violation sounds like a prudential one, i.e., it builds your character. This may sound more like a Platonic reason of self-interest than a moral reason. But it is not, for a virtuous man is much less likely to cause evil consequences to others. Building one's virtue makes one less likely to unjustifiably break moral rules when it is likely that this will cause someone to suffer evil consequences. . . .

But the virtues need not figure solely as an aid to the moral answer to the question. There is what could be called the virtuous answer to the question "Why should I be moral?" This answer makes use of the fact that some men aspire to a good character. The most plausible view of a good character is that it contains all of the virtues, both moral and personal. If one aspires to a character of this sort, then he must act morally. For clearly one cannot have the moral virtues unless he acts morally. One who acts morally because he aspires to a good character need not even be concerned with others. Rather he need only be concerned with attaining a goal that he has set himself. It is certainly a worthy goal, one that all rational men would publicly advocate that all men aim toward. I do not think, however, that the virtuous answer will have much appeal to anyone for whom the moral answer has no force. Although one needs no reason for aspiring to a character which includes the moral virtues, it is very unlikely that one will aspire to it unless he does have a reason. The most persuasive reason for wanting such a character is the moral reason. But the virtuous answer, like the moral answer, is one that has an intrinsic connection to morality. Further, it always provides a direct answer for being moral.

There is a third answer that has an intrinsic connection to morality. This answer makes use of the fact that, as a rational man trying to reach agreement with all other rational men, one must publicly advocate the moral attitude toward the moral rules. One may be persuaded to act morally because reason, including his own, publicly requires acting in this way. I call this answer the rational answer to the question "Why should I be moral?" If one aspires to act in the way that reason publicly requires, then he must act morally. The rational answer is quite similar to the virtuous one: neither one requires concern for anyone else. Yet both can always provide a di-

rect answer for being moral. However, neither of them by itself seems to me to be very persuasive. Of course, one needs no reason for wanting to act as reason publicly requires. But unless one accepts the moral reason as persuasive, I do not see why he would want to act in this way. . . .

In the important decisions about whether to act morally, reason does not provide the guide. When morality and self-interest conflict, even when morality and the interests of friends or family conflict, reason takes no sides. Disappointing as this conclusion seems at first, we should see that any other conclusion would be worse. Were reason ever to prohibit acting morally, we would be forced, in the case of conflict, to advocate either irrational or immoral behavior. If reason was always to require acting morally, we would be forced to regard all immoral action as irrational, including that which was clearly in the self-interest of the agent. Contrasted with either of these alternatives, the conclusion seems far less disappointing than before. . . .

Those who think it difficult to give an affirmative answer to the question "Should I be moral?" should realize that it is also difficult to give an affirmative answer to the question "Should I be immoral?" And the difficulty of providing persuasive answers to the question "Why should I be moral?" is no greater than the difficulties of providing persuasive answers to the question "Why should I be immoral?" Unfortunately, in some societies, and in some parts of all societies, the answers to "Why should I be immoral?" may be more persuasive than the answers to "Why should I be moral?" It is, I think, the most important measure of a society—which answers are most persuasive to most of its citizens.

EDWARD WESTERMARCK

The origin and development of moral ideas

Besides the relative uniformity of moral opinions, there is another circumstance which tempts us to objectivise moral judgments, namely, the authority which, rightly or wrongly, is ascribed to moral rules. From our earliest childhood we are taught that certain acts *are* right and that others *are* wrong. Owing to their exceptional importance for human welfare, the facts of the moral consciousness are emphasised in a much higher degree than any other subjective facts. We are allowed to have our private opinions about the beauty of things, but we are not so readily allowed to have our private opinions about right and wrong. The moral rules which are prevalent in the society to which we belong are supported by appeals not only to human, but to divine, authority, and to call in question their validity is to rebel against religion as well as against public opinion. Thus the belief in a moral order of the world has taken hardly less firm hold of the human mind, than the belief in a natural order of things. And the moral law has retained its authoritativeness even when the appeal to an external authority has been regarded as inadequate. . . . Adam Smith calls the moral faculties the "vicegerents of God within us," who "never fail to punish the violation of them by the torments of inward shame and self-condemnation; and, on the contrary, always reward obedience with tranquillity of mind, with contentment, and self-satisfaction." . . .

Authority is an ambiguous word. It may indicate knowledge of truth, and it may indicate a rightful power to command obedience. The authoritativeness attributed to the moral law has often reference to both kinds of authority. The moral lawgiver lays down his rules in order that they should be obeyed, and they are authoritative in so far as they have to be obeyed. But he is also believed to know what is right and wrong, and his commands are regarded as expressions of moral truths. However, this latter kind of authority involves a false assumption as to the nature of the moral predicates, and it cannot be justly inferred from the power to command. Again, if the notion of an external lawgiver be put aside, the moral law does not generally seem to possess supreme authority in either sense of the word. It does not command obedience in any exceptional degree; few laws are broken more frequently. Nor can the regard for it be called the mainspring of action; it is only one spring out of many, and variable like all others. In some instances it is the ruling power in a man's life, in others it is a voice calling in the desert; and the majority of people seem to be more afraid of the blame or ridicule of their fellowmen, or of the penalties with which the law threatens them, than of "the vicegerents of God" in their own hearts. That mankind prefer the possession of virtue to all other enjoyments, and look upon vice as worse than any other misery, is unfortunately an imagination of some moralists who confound men as they are with men as they ought to be.

It is said that the authority of the moral law asserts itself every time the law is broken, that virtue bears in itself its own reward, and vice its own punishment. But, to be sure, conscience is a very unjust retributer. The more a person habituates himself to virtue the more he sharpens its sting, the deeper he sinks in vice the more he blunts it. Whilst the best men have the most sensitive consciences, the worst have hardly any conscience at all. It is argued that the habitual sinner has rid himself of remorse at a great cost; but it may be fairly doubted whether the loss is an adequate penalty for his wickedness. We are reminded that men are rewarded for good and punished for bad acts by the moral feelings of their neighbours. But public opinion and law judge of detected acts only. Their judgment is seldom based upon an exhaustive examination of the case. They often apply a standard which is itself open to criticism. And the feelings with which men regard their fellow-creatures, and which are some of the main sources of human happiness and suffering, have often very little to do with morality. A person is respected or praised, blamed or despised, on other grounds than his character. Nay, the admiration which men feel for genius, courage, pluck, strength, or accidental success, is often superior in intensity to the admiration they feel for virtue.

In spite of all this, however, the supreme authority assigned to the moral law is not altogether an illusion. It really exists in the minds of the best, and is nominally acknowledged by the many. By this I do not refer to the universal admission that the moral law, whether obeyed or not, ought under all circumstances to be obeyed; for this is the same as to say that what ought to be ought to be. But it is recognised, in theory at least, that morality, either alone or in connection with religion, possesses a higher value than anything else; that rightness and goodness are preferable to all other kinds of mental superiority, as well as of physical excellence. If this theory is not more commonly acted upon, that is due to its being, in most people, much less the outcome of their own feelings than of instruction from the outside. It is ultimately traceable to some great teacher whose own mind was ruled by the ideal of moral perfection, and whose words became sacred on account of his supreme wisdom, like Confucius or Buddha, or on religious grounds, like Jesus. The authority of the moral law is thus only an expression of a strongly developed, overruling moral consciousness. It can hardly . . . be said to "depend upon" the conception of the objectivity of duty. On the contrary, it must be regarded as a cause of this conception—not only, as has already been pointed out, where it is traceable to some external authority, but where it results from the strength of the individual's own moral emotions. As clearness and distinctness of the conception of an object easily produces the belief in its truth, so the intensity of a moral emotion makes him who feels it disposed to objectivise the moral estimate to which it gives rise, in other words, to assign to it universal validity. The enthusiast is more likely than anybody else to regard his judgments as true, and so is the moral enthusiast with reference to his moral judgments. The intensity of his emotions makes him the victim of an illusion.

WILLIAM GRAHAM SUMNER

Folkways

Definition and mode of origin of the folkways

If we put together all that we have learned from anthropology and ethnography about primitive men and primitive society, we perceive that the first task of life is to live. Men begin with acts, not with thoughts. Every moment brings necessities which must be satisfied at once. Need was the first experience, and it was followed at once by a blundering effort to satisfy it. . . . Experiments with newborn animals show that in the absence of any experience of the relation of means to ends, efforts to satisfy needs are clumsy and blundering. The method is that of trial and failure, which produces repeated pain, loss, and disappointments. Nevertheless, it is a method of rude experiment and selection. The earliest efforts of men were of this kind. Need was the impelling force. Pleasure and pain, on the one side and the other, were the rude constraints which defined the line on which efforts must proceed. . . . Thus ways of doing things were selected, which were expedient. They answered the purpose better than other ways, or with less toil and pain. Along the course on which efforts were compelled to go, habit, routine, and skill were developed. The struggle to maintain existence was carried on, not individually, but in groups. Each profited by the other's experience; hence there was concurrence towards that which proved to be most expedient. All at last adopted the same way for the same purpose; hence the ways turned into customs and became mass phenomena. Instincts were developed in connection with them. In this way folkways arise. The young learn them by tradition, imitation, and authority. The folkways, at a time, provide for all the needs of life then and there. They are uniform, universal in the group, imperative, and invariable. As time goes on, the folkways become more and more arbitrary, positive, and imperative. If asked why they act in a certain way in certain cases, primitive people always answer that it is because they and their ancestors always have done so. . . .

The folkways are "right"

The folkways are the "right" ways to satisfy all interests, because they are traditional, and exist in fact. They extend over the whole of life. There is a right way to catch game, to win a wife, to make one's self appear, to cure disease, to honor ghosts, to treat comrades or strangers, to behave when a child is born, on the war-path, in council, and so on in all cases which can arise. The ways are defined on the negative side, that is, by taboos. The "right" way is the way which the ancestors used and which has been handed down. The tradition is its own warrant. It is not held subject to verification by experience. The notion of right is in the folkways. It is not outside of them, of independent origin, and brought to them to test them. In the folkways, whatever is, is right. This is because they are traditional, and therefore contain in themselves the authority of the ancestral ghosts. When we come to the folkways we are at the end of our analysis. . . .

What is goodness or badness of the mores

It is most important to notice that, for the people of a time and place, their own mores are always good, or rather that for them there can be no question of the goodness or badness of their mores. The reason is because the standards of good and right are in the mores. If the life conditions change, the traditional folkways may produce pain and loss, or fail to produce the same good as formerly. Then the loss of comfort and ease brings doubt into the judgment of welfare (causing doubt of the pleasure of the gods, or of war power, or of health), and thus disturbs the unconscious philosophy of the mores. Then a later time will pass judgment on the mores. Another society may also pass judgment on the mores. In our literary and historical study of the mores we want to get from them their educational value, which consists in the stimulus or warning as to what is, in its effects, societally good or bad. This may lead us to reject or ne-glect a phenomenon like infanticide, slavery, or witchcraft, as an old "abuse" and "evil," or to pass by the crusades as a folly which cannot recur. Such a course would be a great error. Everything in the mores of a time and place must be regarded as justified with regard to that time and place. "Good" mores are those which are well adapted to the situation. "Bad" mores are those which are not so adapted. The mores are not so stereotyped and changeless as might appear, because they are forever moving towards more complete adaptation to conditions and interests, and also towards more complete adjustment to each other. People in mass have never made or kept up a custom in order to hurt their own interests. . . .

The mores have the authority of facts

The mores come down to us from the past. Each individual is born into them as he is born into the atmosphere, and he does not reflect on them, or criticise them any more than a baby analyzes the atmosphere before he begins to breathe it. Each one is subjected to the influence of the mores, and formed by them, before he is capable of reasoning about them. It may be objected that nowadays, at least, we criticise all traditions, and accept none just because they are handed down to us. If we take up cases of things which are still entirely or almost entirely in the mores, we shall see that this is not so. There are sects of free-lovers amongst us who want to discuss pair marriage. They are not simply people of evil life. They invite us to discuss rationally our inherited customs and ideas as to marriage, which, they say, are by no means so excellent and elevated as we believe. They have never won any serious attention. Some others want to argue in favor of polygamy on grounds of expediency. They fail to obtain a hearing. Others want to discuss property. In spite of some literary activity on their part, no discussion of property, bequest, and inheritance has ever been opened. Property and marriage are in the mores. Nothing can ever change them but the unconscious and imperceptible movement of the mores. Religion was originally a matter of the mores. It became a societal institution and a function of the state. It has now to a great extent been put back into the mores. Since laws with penalties to enforce religious creeds or practices have gone out of use any one may think and act as he pleases about religion. Therefore it is not now "good form" to attack religion. Infidel publications are now tabooed by the mores, and are more effectually repressed than ever before. They produce no controversy. Democracy is in our American mores. It is a product of our physical and economic conditions. It is impossible to discuss or criticise it. It is rhetoric. No one treats it with complete candor and sincerity. No one dares to analyze it as he would aristocracy or autocracy. He would get no hearing and would only incur abuse. The thing to be noticed in all these cases is that the masses oppose a deaf ear to every argument against the mores. It is only in so far as things have been transferred from the mores into laws and positive institutions that there is discussion about them or rationalizing upon them. The mores contain the norm by which, if we should discuss the mores, we should have to judge the mores. We learn the mores as unconsciously as we learn to walk and eat and breathe. The masses never learn how we walk, and eat, and breathe, and they never know any reason why the mores are what they are. The justification of them is that when we wake to consciousness of life we find them facts which already hold us in the bonds of tradition, custom, and habit. The mores contain embodied in them notions, doctrines, and maxims, but they are facts. They are in the present tense. They have nothing to do with what ought to be, will be, may be, or once was, if it is not now. . . .

Revolution

In higher civilization crises produced by the persistency of old mores after conditions have changed are solved by revolution or reform. In revolutions the mores are broken up. Such was the case in the sixteenth century, in the French Revolution of 1789, and in minor revolutions. A period follows the outburst of a revolution in which there are no mores. The old are broken up; the new are not formed. The social ritual is interrupted. The old taboos are suspended. New taboos cannot be enacted or promulgated. They require time to become established and known. The masses in a revolution are uncertain what they ought to do. . . . In the best case every revolution must be attended by this temporary chaos of the mores. It was produced in the American colonies. Revolutionary leaders expect to carry the people over to new mores by the might of two or three dogmas of political or social philosophy. The history of every such attempt shows that dogmas do not make mores. Every revolution suffers a collapse at the point where reconstruction should begin. Then the old ruling classes resume control, and by the use of force set the society in its old grooves again. . . .

What changes are possible

All these cases go to show that changes which run with the mores are easily brought about, but that changes which are opposed to the mores require long and patient effort, if they are possible at all. The ruling clique can use force to warp the mores towards some result which they have selected, especially if they bring their effort to bear on the ritual, not on the dogmas, and if they are contented to go slowly. The church has won great results in this way, and by so doing has created a belief that religion, or ideas, or institutions, make mores. The leading classes, no matter by what standard they are selected, can lead by example, which always affects ritual. . . . If we admit that it is possible and right for some to undertake to mold the mores of others, of set purpose, we see that the limits within which any such effort can succeed are very narrow, and the methods by which it can operate are strictly defined. The favorite methods of our time are legislation and preaching. These methods fail because they do not affect ritual, and because they always aim at great results in a short time. Above all, we can judge of the amount of serious attention which is due to plans for "reorganizing society," to get rid of alleged errors and inconveniences in it. We might as well plan to reorganize our globe by redistributing the elements in it.

"*We learned all about sex today. Big deal!*"

2

THE
DILEMMAS
OF
SEX

Erotic attraction is a great force in social
relations. It exerts such force, first, because
it is so general: Everyone is one sex or
another and, by virtue of his or her sex, has
sexual desire. By itself, sexual desire or
revulsion may lead individuals to form new
social relationships or break old ones. It can
both disrupt the best established social
relationships in a culture and solidify and make
formidable those that had been fragile.

Because of such power to direct our actions,
the sexual impulses have always been a
force to be reckoned with by morality: At
some point or other, every morality must
order and regulate them in one way or
another.

The first two articles in this chapter are
by two of the spokesmen most responsible for
the changing sexual mores in twentieth-
century America: Sigmund Freud and
D. H. Lawrence. Freud argues that "our
civilization is, generally speaking, founded on
the suppression of instincts." Sexual restraint,
Freud states, is not only necessary for
civilization, but it also serves to strengthen the
development of culture. Nonetheless, when
he assesses our "civilized sexual morality," he
emphasizes the evils of sexual restraint over
the cultural gain deriving from it. Lawrence
has been a leading literary influence on
twentieth-century thinking about sex. He
despises Freud's clinical approach to sex,
although he, too, remonstrates against
our "civilized sexual morality." For him, sex
is a mystery and is "inseparable from beauty."
He claims that "to love living beauty, you
must have a reverence for sex."

Whereas both Freud and Lawrence wrote in
the first part of the twentieth century, the
next article, by sociologist Jessie Bernard,
discusses the current sexual revolution.
Brought about by the confluence of a
normative subrevolution—"the resexualization
of the female body"—and a technological
subrevolution—"the increasing feasibility of
conception control"—today's sexual
revolution demands new norms and a new sex
ethos, according to Bernard.

29

Although recognizing some of the factors that Bernard cites, the recent papal "Declaration on Certain Questions Concerning Sexual Ethics" continues to uphold the traditional Christian sexual morality on which our civilization for well over a millennium has been based. The pope writes that sexual intercourse is moral only when performed within marriage because only then is the "finality" of the act—that is to say, its sacredness—respected.

For a position opposing traditional Christian morality, the editors have chosen the new sexual code from *The Humanist,* a statement composed by sex educators and psychologists. The code states that "the boundaries of human sexuality need to be expanded" and that "repressive taboos should be replaced by a more balanced and objective view of sexuality."

We then turn to a consideration of a question raised by the humanists: With whom is it permissible to have sexual relations? Two kinds of relationships that have traditionally been subjected to taboos—homosexual and adulterous—are discussed. Mark Freedman argues that "homosexuals may be healthier than straights," debunking the popular myth that gay people are mentally or emotionally "sick." He asks whether society is not "mistaken when it condemns a person on account of some variant lifestyle."

O. Spurgeon English then considers the extramarital affair, a phenomenon that appears to be increasing, particularly for married women. He views it, in certain circumstances, as having positive values: providing "inspiration and personal fulfillment." Linda Wolfe, however, in the next article, cites a danger inherent in extramarital sex: the loss of the primary emotional bond with one's marriage partner.

In the final article in this chapter, Derek Wright looks at our newly permissive society and warns that we may be subjecting ourselves to a "new tyranny of sexual 'liberation.'" While opposing rigid moral values regarding sexual conduct, he urges that we not lose sight of the total human relationship in our compulsion to take advantage of new freedoms.

(Some forms of sexual relationships are forbidden by law. For a discussion of attempts to regulate sexual conduct through the law, see Chapter 9 on law and morals. Related materials are also found in Chapter 10 on pornography and obscenity.)

NOTES ABOUT THE AUTHORS

Sigmund Freud, the founder of psychoanalysis, was born in 1856 in Moravia, formerly a province of Austria-Hungary and now part of Czechoslovakia. His great work was *The Interpretation of Dreams* (1899), and his works most widely read by American students include *Civilization and Its Discontents* and *Moses and Monotheism.* He fled to London in 1938 to escape the Nazis and died there the following year. Freud believed that dreams represented repressed desires, especially sexual desires, and were therefore an important key to the subconscious mind. According to Freud, too much suppression of sexual desires, in accordance with "civilized" sexual morality, would lead to neuroses. "'Civilized' Sexual Morality and Modern Nervousness" was first published in 1908.

D. H. Lawrence, an English novelist, essayist, and short-story writer, was born in 1885. His major works include *Sons and Lovers* (1913), *Women in Love* (1916), and *Lady Chatterley's Lover* (1928). "Sex Versus Loveliness" was also first published in 1928 in *Assorted Articles.* Lawrence died in 1930.

Jessie Bernard is a research scholar, Honoris Causa, at Pennsylvania State University. A sociologist, she has written extensively on marriage and the roles of women. Her books include *American Family Behavior, Remarriage: A Study of Marriage, The Sex Game, Women and the Public Interest,* and *The Future of Marriage.* "The Fourth Revolution," reprinted below, originally appeared in *The Journal of Social Issues* in 1966. Since that time, the women's liberation movement has greatly increased the pressures for new norms that Bernard outlines in her article.

The Sacred Congregation for the Doctrine of the Faith is part of the Roman Curia within the Catholic church whose responsibility it is to safeguard doctrine on faith and morals. Its prefect is Franjo Cardinal Seper, and its central headquarters is in Rome. The "Declaration on Certain Questions Concerning Sexual Ethics" was issued in December 1975.

The Humanist, a journal cosponsored by the American Ethical Union and the American Humanist Association, is devoted to bridging the gap between theory and practice in ethical and philosophical concerns. The editors requested Lester Kirkendall, a sexologist and professor of family life at the University of Oregon, to draft a new bill of sexual rights and responsibilities to reflect the humanists' belief in moral responsibility. Rewritten in the form printed below, it was endorsed by many prominent sexologists and appeared in the January/February 1976 issue of the journal.

Mark Freedman is a staff psychologist at the Northeast Community Mental Health Center in San Francisco. He has taught in Japan, Thailand, and Australia as well as at Western Reserve University, where he earned his Ph.D. in clinical psychology. "Homosexuals May Be Healthier Than Straights" first appeared in *Psychology Today* in 1975. The themes presented in this article are further elaborated in Freedman's book, *Personal Definition and Psychological Function.*

O. Spurgeon English is professor of psychiatry at Temple University in Philadelphia. His books include *Emotional Problems of Living, Introduction to Psychiatry,* and *Direct Analysis and Schizophrenia.* His article, "Positive Values of the Affair," was written for a collection of essays titled *The New Sexuality,* edited by Herbert A. Otto (1971). It is representative of a growing interest among some psychologists and sociologists in the positive aspects of sexuality. Many believe with Otto that "the fuller exploration and development of the regenerative aspects of man's sexual functioning can add new dimensions to self-perception and bring greater wholeness to man."

Linda Wolfe has worked as a free-lance journalist and for Time, Inc. She is the author of *The Literary Gourmet* and *Cooking of the Caribbean Islands.* Her most recent book, *Playing Around: Women and Extramarital Sex* (1976), was based on extensive interviews and presents many case studies of women involved in extramarital affairs. It should not be implied from the extract reprinted here that all women she interviewed were unhappy as the result of their affairs; we have selected merely one of many viewpoints.

Derek Wright is a psychologist whose books include *Introducing Psychology: An Experimental Approach* and *The Psychology of Moral Behavior.* "The New Tyranny of Sexual 'Liberation'" originally appeared in *Life* in 1970.

SIGMUND FREUD

"Civilized" sexual morality and modern nervousness

Our civilization is, generally speaking, founded on the suppression of instincts. Each individual has contributed some renunciation—of his sense of dominating power, of the aggressive and vindictive tendencies of his personality. From these sources the common stock of the material and ideal wealth of civilization has been accumulated. Over and above the struggle for existence, it is chiefly family feeling, with its erotic roots, which has induced the individuals to make this renunciation. This renunciation has been a progressive one in the evolution of civilization; the single steps in it were sanctioned by religion. The modicum of instinctual satisfaction from which each one had abstained was offered to the divinity as a sacrifice; and the communal benefit thus won was declared "holy." The man who in consequence of his unyielding nature cannot comply with the required suppression of his instincts, becomes a criminal, an outlaw, unless his social position or striking abilities enable him to hold his own as a great man, a "hero."

The sexual instinct—or, more correctly, the sexual instincts, since analytic investigation teaches us that the sexual instinct consists of many single component impulses—is probably more strongly developed in man than in most of the higher animals; it is certainly more constant, since it has almost entirely overcome the periodicity belonging to it in animals. It places an extraordinary amount of energy at the disposal of "cultural" activities; and this because of a particularly marked characteristic that it possesses, namely, the ability to displace its aim without materially losing in intensity. This ability to exchange the originally sexual aim for another which is no longer sexual but is psychically related, is called the capacity for sublimation. In contrast with this ability for displacement in which lies its value for civilization, the sexual instinct may also show a particularly obstinate

tendency to fixation, which prevents it from being turned to account in this way, and occasionally leads to its degenerating into the so-called abnormalities. The original strength of the sexual instinct probably differs in each individual; certainly the capacity for sublimation is variable. We imagine that the original constitution pre-eminently decides how large a part of the sexual impulse of each individual can be sublimated and made use of. In addition to this, the forces of environment and of intellectual influence on the mental apparatus succeed in disposing of a further portion of it by sublimation. To extend this process of displacement illimitably is, however, certainly no more possible than with the transmutation of heat into mechanical power in the case of machines. A certain degree of direct sexual satisfaction appears to be absolutely necessary for by far the greater number of natures, and frustration of this variable individual need is avenged by manifestations which, on account of their injurious effect on functional activity and of their subjectively painful character, we must regard as illness.

Further aspects are opened up when we take into consideration the fact that the sexual instinct in man does not originally serve the purposes of procreation, but has as its aim the gain of particular kinds of pleasure. It manifests itself thus in infancy, when it attains its aim of pleasurable gratification not only in connection with the genitalia, but also in other parts of the body (erotogenic zones), and hence is in a position to disregard any other than these easily accessible objects. We call this stage that of auto-erotism, and assign to the child's training the task of circumscribing it, because its protracted continuance would render the sexual instinct later uncontrollable and unserviceable. In its development the sexual instinct passes on from auto-erotism to object-love, and from the autonomy of the erotogenic zones to the subordination of these under the primacy of the genitals, which come into the service of procreation. During this development a part of the self-obtained sexual excitation is checked, as being useless for the reproductive functions, and in favourable cases is diverted to sublimation. The energies available for "cultural" development are thus in great part won through suppression of the so-called perverse elements of sexual excitation.

It would be possible to distinguish three stages in cultural development corresponding with this development in the sexual instinct: first, the stage in which the sexual impulse may be freely exercised in regard to aims which do not lead to procreation; a second stage, in which the whole of the sexual impulse is suppressed except that portion which subserves procreation; and a third stage, in which only *legitimate* procreation is allowed as a sexual aim. This third stage represents our current "civilized" sexual morality. . . .

In what relation [do] the possible injurious effects of . . . abstention stand to the benefit accruing to culture? . . .

Even he who admits the injurious results [neuroses] thus attributable to civilized sexual morality may reply that the cultural gain derived from the sexual restraint so generally practised probably more than balances these evils, which after all, in their more striking manifestations, affect only a minority. I own myself unable to balance gain and loss precisely: nevertheless I could advance a good many considerations as regards the loss. Returning to the theme of abstinence, already touched on, I must insist that yet other injurious effects besides the neuroses result therefrom, and that the neuroses themselves are not usually appraised at their full significance.

The retardation of sexual development and sexual activity at which our education and culture aim is certainly not injurious to begin with; it is seen to be a necessity, when one reflects at what a late age young people of the educated classes attain independence and begin to earn a living. Incidentally, one is reminded here of the intimate relations existing between all our civilized institutions, and of the difficulty of altering any part of them irrespective of the whole. But the benefit, for a young man, of abstinence continued much beyond his twentieth year, cannot any longer be taken for granted; it may lead to other injuries even when it does not lead to neurosis. It is indeed said that the struggle with such powerful instincts and the consequent strengthening of all ethical and aesthetic tendencies "steels" the character; and this, for some specially constituted natures, is true. The view may also be accepted that the differentiation of individual character, now so much in evidence, only becomes possible with sexual restraint. But in the great majority of cases the fight against sexuality absorbs the available energy of the character, and this at the very time when the young man is in need of all his powers to gain his share of worldly goods and his position in the community. The relation between possible sublimation and indispensable sexual activity naturally varies very much in different persons, and indeed with the various kinds of occupation. An abstinent artist is scarcely conceivable: an abstinent young intellectual is by no means a rarity. The young intellectual can by abstinence enhance his powers of concentration, whereas the production of the artist is probably powerfully stimulated by his sexual experience. On the whole I have not gained the impression that sexual abstinence helps to shape energetic, self-reliant men of action, nor original thinkers, bold pioneers and reformers; for more often it produces "good" weaklings who later become lost in the crowd that tends to follow painfully the initiative of strong characters. . . .

D. H. LAWRENCE

Sex versus loveliness

It is a pity that *sex* is such an ugly little word. An ugly little word, and really almost incomprehensible. What *is* sex, after all? The more we think about it the less we know.

Science says it is an instinct; but what is an instinct? Apparently an instinct is an old, old habit that has become ingrained. But a habit, however old, has to have a beginning. And there is really no beginning to sex. Where life is, there it is. So sex is no "habit" that has been formed.

Again, they talk of sex as an appetite, like hunger. An appetite; but for what? An appetite for propagation? It is rather absurd. They say a peacock puts on all his fine feathers to dazzle the peahen into letting him satisfy his appetite for propagation. But why should the peahen not put on fine feathers, to dazzle the peacock, and satisfy *her* desire for propagation? She has surely quite as great a desire for eggs and chickens as he has. We cannot believe that her sex urge is so weak that she needs all that blue splendour of feathers to rouse her. Not at all.

As for me, I never even saw a peahen so much as look at her lord's bronze and blue glory. I don't believe she ever sees it. I don't believe for a moment that she knows the difference between bronze, blue, brown, or green. . . .

These theories of sex are amazing. A peacock puts on his glory for the sake of a wall-eyed peahen who never looks at him. Imagine a scientist being so naïve as to credit the peahen with a profound, dynamic appreciation of a peacock's colour and pattern. Oh, highly aesthetic peahen!

And a nightingale sings to attract his female. Which is mighty curious, seeing he sings his best when courtship and honeymoon are over and the female is no longer concerned with him at all, but with the young. Well, then, if he doesn't sing to attract her, he must sing to distract her and amuse her while she's sitting.

How delightful, how naïve theories are! But there is a hidden will behind them all. There is a hidden will behind all theories of sex, implacable. And that is the will to deny, to wipe out the mystery of beauty.

Because beauty is a mystery. You can neither eat it nor make flannel out of it. Well, then, says science, it is just a trick to catch the female and induce her to propagate. How naïve! As if the female needed inducing. She will propagate in the dark, even—so where, then, is the beauty trick?

Science has a mysterious hatred of beauty, because it doesn't fit in the cause-and-effect chain. And society has a mysterious hatred of sex, because it perpetually interferes with the nice money-making schemes of social man. So the two hatreds made a combine, and sex and beauty are mere propagation appetite.

Now sex and beauty are one thing, like flame and fire. If you hate sex you hate beauty. If you love *living* beauty, you have a reverence for sex. Of course you can love old, dead beauty and hate sex. But to love living beauty you must have a reverence for sex.

Sex and beauty are inseparable, like life and consciousness. And the intelligence which goes with sex and beauty, and arises out of sex and beauty, is intuition. The great disaster of our civilization is the morbid hatred of sex. What, for example, could show a more poisoned hatred of sex than Freudian psychoanalysis?—which carries with it a morbid fear of beauty, "alive" beauty, and which causes the atrophy of our intuitive faculty and our intuitive self.

The deep psychic disease of modern men and women is the diseased, atrophied condition of the intuitive faculties. There is a whole world of life that we might know and enjoy by intuition, and by intuition alone. This is denied us, because we deny sex and beauty, the source of the intuitive life and of the insouciance which is so lovely in free animals and in plants.

Sex is the root of which intuition is the foliage and beauty the flower. Why is a woman lovely, if ever, in her twenties? It is the time when sex rises softly to her face, as a rose to the top of a rose bush.

And the appeal is the appeal of beauty. We deny it wherever we can. We try to make the beauty as shallow and trashy as possible. But, first and foremost, sex appeal is the appeal of beauty.

Now beauty is a thing about which we are so uneducated we can hardly speak of it. We try to pretend it is a fixed arrangement: straight nose, large eyes, etc. We think a lovely woman must look like Lillian Gish, a handsome man must look like Rudolph Valentino. So we *think*.

In actual life we behave quite differently. We say "She's quite beautiful, but I don't care for her." Which shows we are using the word *beautiful* all wrong. We should say: "She has the stereotyped attributes of beauty, but she is not beautiful to me."

Beauty is an *experience,* nothing else. It is not a fixed pattern or an arrangement of features. It is something *felt,* a glow or a communicated sense of fineness. What ails us is that our sense of beauty is so bruised and blunted, we miss all the best.

But to stick to the films—there is a greater essential beauty in Charlie Chaplin's odd face than ever there was in Valentino's. There is a bit of true beauty in Chaplin's brows and eyes, a gleam of something pure.

But our sense of beauty is so bruised and clumsy, we don't see it, and don't know it when we do see it. We can only see the blatantly obvious, like the so-called beauty of Rudolph Valentino, which only pleases because it satisfies some ready-made notion of handsomeness.

But the plainest person can look beautiful, can *be* beautiful. It only needs the fire of sex to rise delicately to change an ugly face to a lovely one. That is really sex appeal: the communicating of a sense of beauty.

And in the reverse way, no one can be quite so repellent as a really pretty woman. That is, since beauty is a question of experience, not of concrete form, no one can be as acutely ugly as a really pretty woman. When the sex glow is missing, and she moves in ugly coldness, how hideous she seems, and all the worse for her externals of prettiness.

What sex is, we don't know, but it must be some sort of fire. For it always communicates a sense of warmth, of glow. And when the glow becomes a pure shine, then we feel the sense of beauty.

But the communicating of the warmth, the glow of sex, is true sex appeal. We all have the fire of sex slumbering or burning inside us. If we live to be ninety, it is still there. Or, if it dies, we become one of those ghastly living corpses which are unfortunately becoming more numerous in the world.

JESSIE BERNARD

The fourth revolution[1]

The great fundamental social issues in the area of sex today have to do with the normative control of nonprocreative heterosexuality. Not that nonprocreative sexuality is a new phenomenon, for it is older than man himself, as we shall presently note. But because now it is possible "for the first time [in our history] to separate our reproductivity and our sexuality," that is, procreative and nonprocreative heterosexuality.

Four fundamental changes in sexuality

Once bisexual reproduction had evolved, the first great "sexual revolution" or evolutionary change may be said to have come when sex relations became social as well as merely biological in nature. The pollenization of plants was bisexual, but it was not social. The fish who deposited her eggs to be fertilized by a male was not in a social relationship with him. One might cavil about calling the sex life of insects social; but the relations between the sexes among many birds and mammals are undeniably social.

A second major change in the relations between the sexes occurred when mating was no longer restricted to the female estrus. This was the first adumbration of the separation of reproduction and heterosexuality, or between procreative and nonprocreative heterosexuality. Among animals which have a clear-cut mating season, the female's body shows readable signs of her condition when ovulation has taken place, and she either sends out unequivocal signals to the male that she is receptive or takes the initiative in seeking him out, presumably to ensure

1. There are sexual revolutions in process all over the world. The discussion here refers primarily to the West and especially to the United States. This revolution may be viewed as fourth not only in time but also as fourth in the so-called triple revolution of automation, population, and race. Or fourth in the series of revolutions noted by Ira Reiss: urban-industrial, romantic-love, and feminist.

fertilization of the ready ovum. Ovulation, "the female sex act," is the important thing; the female is in control of sex relations. Coupling does not occur out of season.

Among the primates, however, where there is no such clear-cut mating season—unless one wishes to interpret the annual spring swarming of college youth on Florida or Bermuda beaches as symptomatic of a vestigial "mating season"— the relationships between the sexes becomes vastly complicated. Ovulation is no longer determinative of sex relations. The female is no longer in control. The male may aggress or the female present herself to him even when she is not in estrus, when procreation is not likely. Reproduction is not, of course, divorced from heterosexuality; but heterosexuality is divorced from reproduction. . . .

The third great revolution came with culture, which placed both procreative and nonprocreative sexuality under normative controls. These cultural constraints were by no means standardized throughout the world or over time; but, in some form or other, they were universal.

The fourth or current sexual revolution has to do with the confluence of two cultural subrevolutions, one normative and one technological. The normative deals with the resexualization of the female body; the technological, with the increasing feasibility of conception control, which further separates procreative and nonprocreative heterosexuality. Both revolutions began some time ago. The resexualization of the female body began at the turn of the century; it was furthered by a series of so-called marriage manuals in which sexual satisfaction for women was emphasized and the responsibility for producing it made a male concern. The technology of conception control has a long history. What is revolutionary about it in recent years is that it has now become feasible on a mass scale.

Either of the two revolutions alone would have had great impact on the relations of the sexes; in combination the impact was exponentially increased. That is, if the female body had been resexualized at a time when contraception was still uncertain or if feasible contracep-tion on a mass scale had come in Victorian times, the impact of either would have been moderated. Occurring as they did together, they produced revolutionary changes, not so much with respect to procreative as with respect to nonprocreative sexuality. . . .

Female sexuality

Procreative sexuality demands nothing of women except ovulation; they can conceive in their sleep. If heterosexual relations—procreative or nonprocreative—are to be pleasurable to women, the pleasure must be derived from the "male sex act." Here the impact of cultural constraints has been determinative. They have enormously influenced the responsiveness of the female body to "the male sex act."

Much of the normative structure for the control—often suppression—of sex has had to do with the behavior of women who were, in effect, assigned the task of supporting the existing norms. This was feasible because of the greater sexual plasticity of women. . . . There have, for example, been centuries when the female body was not expected to be sexually responsive to the male sex act. In Victorian times women bragged of their frigidity; they were processed for it from childhood. Contrariwise, there have been centuries when female enjoyment of the male sex act has been permitted, if not necessarily actually cultivated; the female body was even viewed as especially lustful.

The current sexual renaissance reflects an era which encourages—compels or coerces, some might say—women to equal if not out-do men in the enjoyment of the male sex act.

Normative control of procreative sexuality

With the alleged exception of the Trobriand Islanders, who chose to ignore the relationship between sexual intercourse and conception, there has until recently tended to be practically universal acceptance of reproductive sexuality. When large numbers of births were needed to replenish precarious populations, in the absence of specific knowledge of the processes of ovulation, reproductive sex played a large part in the normative thinking of the relations between the sexes. Because we relied so heavily on parents, or at least families, to take care of children, we did what we could, with varying degrees of success, to restrict even reproductive sex relations to men and women who promised to cleave to one another till death did them part and who would be responsible for the care of all the children resulting from their union. Before or without such commitment, whether it occurred at the betrothal, as in Scandinavia, or at the marriage, sex relations were forbidden. . . .

In general, the normative structure with respect to procreative sex outside of marriage remains intact. Since we still rely heavily on parents for the rearing and socialization of children, we will probably continue to frown on out-of-wedlock births, however much we may attempt to mitigate the penalties of their status. But the issue will not necessarily be, as hitherto, the sex relations which produced the children; it may well be the irresponsibility of the partners in not preventing the conception. We will blame them for carelessness or irresponsibility rather than, as in the past, for sinfulness. There will, that is, continue to be consensus with respect to the wrongness of out-of-wedlock births, but the moral basis for the consensus will be disapproval of carelessness and irresponsibility rather than of extra-marital sex relations per se. . . .

Nonprocreative sexuality

It was early recognized that there was more to sexuality than reproduction, that sexuality had many forms and widespread societal ramifications, that it served psychological and social functions quite unrelated to reproduction. . . .

But it is by no means easy to specify exactly the nature, let alone the function, of nonprocreative sexuality. It is certainly not simple, unidimensional, or standardized. It is not even easy to define nonprocreative sexuality. Reproductive sexuality is, of necessity and even by definition, genital. The sperm must be deposited in the vagina. But nonprocreative sexuality, though it includes genital sex at one extreme, includes vastly more. Clearly self or manual masturba-

tion, homosexuality, bestialism, fellatio, cunnilingus, biting, petting, kissing, fetishism are sexual but not procreational. How about the pleasure derived from the sight of a beautiful nude body, in the flesh or in marble? Or the reactions to other kinds of stimuli which Kinsey reported? He defined them as sexual; they are not procreational. The pleasure congenial men and women derive from talking to one another—is this sexual? One has only to ask what would a society be like if all forms of sexuality were forbidden (except heterosexual relations for the conception of children) to begin to sense the widely ramifying functions of nonprocreative sexuality and the confusing problems of normative control which it raises.

Some current issues

A variety of current issues exists in the area of sex per se (as distinguished from such *family-*related matters as divorce, abortion, illegitimacy, prostitution, and the like). What, for example, should be our attitudes, or what should be the law, with respect to homosexuality, sexual deviancy, perversions, pornography, obscenity? At least with respect to homosexuality, a consensus appears to be in process of emerging, even among those who consider it wrong, which accepts private homosexual behavior between two consenting adults while at the same time restricting public demonstrations and protecting young men and boys from seduction. There appears to be a growing consensus that any manifestation of sex between adults which is acceptable and pleasurable to them in the privacy of their bedroom should be permitted without guilt or opprobrium. The courts seem to move in the direction of legitimizing fewer and fewer limitations on the written word.

A few years ago, there was an issue with respect to making contraceptive information freely available to married women at public expense; today that is no longer an issue. Many communities have incorporated the policy of using public funds for this purpose. It was recently an issue whether or not to supply such information to unmarried women; Brown University and the

37

University of New Hampshire seem to have settled that one: college women may have such information at the discretion of the college physician. The issue will probably now take the form of whether to supply such information at the high school level and, if so, under what circumstances.

With respect to extra-marital relationships of married women, no revolution as yet appears to have occurred nor an issue to have been raised. There are reports from time to time of "wife-swapping clubs" or of "key clubs" and there is reported to be widespread tolerance of affairs for married women. But there does not appear to be any movement to establish normative sanctions for, or even reluctant consent to, such standards; and in the case of Negro women, there are still strong normative sanctions against them on the part, at least, of the white population.

The sex relations of mature unmarried women, especially if they are discreet, appear to be accepted in large cities although not, as yet, elsewhere. The private, personal life of mature adults appears less and less to be a matter of public concern.

Beginning in the 1920's, the premarital sex relations of young women was a major social issue. Since most young women are married by their early twenties, the issue had to do essentially with teen-agers. The consensus which broke down and hence gave rise to issues was that premarital sex relations were always and unequivocally wrong under any circumstances. Ira Reiss has traced in detail the dissolution of that consensus and the issues which resulted. He has reported four major standards—abstinence, double standard, permissiveness without affection, and permissiveness with affection—which have successively replaced it (Reiss, *Premarital Sexual Standards in America*, 1960).

At the other end of the age continuum has been an issue dealing with elderly widowed women who remarry. When it was discovered that some elderly recipients of social security benefits were "living in sin" rather than marrying and thus losing their benefits, provision was made to protect their social security payments even if they remarried. . . .

Who's in charge here? The issue of female autonomy

One of the tenets of the fourth revolution is sexual equality for women. It posits, implicitly if not always explicitly, identical sexuality in men and in women. The ideal would be one which eliminated the so-called double standard: "no more sexual exploitation."

The old exploitative pattern—requiring women to "submit" to their husbands—has certainly all but disappeared. Men today are not likely to take advantage of a resisting young woman. But this does not mean that exploitation does not still exist. It may take the form of a subtler kind of coercion than a physical kind.

Girls and young women, for example, sometimes complain that if they do not acquiesce in men's urgings they are bludgeoned with the epithet "frigid." When the norms forbade all extramarital sex relations, a girl or woman could easily refuse male requests. When the norms are permissive, she has nothing to hide behind. If she does not wish to engage in sex relations—and most teenage girls probably do not—she is left in an exploitable position. If in the past she had to say no to safeguard her self-respect, she must now say yes for the same reason—to avoid the dreaded epithet "frigid."

The old norms gave men the prerogative of initiating sex relations. This privilege, too, was part of the double standard which the fourth revolution opposes. The rationale for this aspect of the double standard, as Reiss has pointed out, has been, in part, that female sex drive and desire in the West was less powerful in women, so they had less need than men actively to seek genital sex relations. It may well be argued, however, that the double standard was a protection for men. It does appear to be true that women can tolerate abstinence better than men. But their orgasmic capacities—because of briefer refractory periods—are greater than men's. It is possible for them to make greater demands on men than men can fulfill. True, a woman cannot aggress against a man sexually; she must incite or excite or stimulate him so that he can "aggress" against her. If she fails, both lose. The reverse is not true. He can "aggress" against her in her sleep.

No final answers

The widespread possibility of nonprocreational heterosexuality by no means solves the problem of the relations of the sexes. It is certainly true, as Reiss says, that "for the first time in many millennia, Western society is evolving sexual standards which will tend to make men and women better able to understand and live with each other." But there is no final, absolute, and all-purpose pattern for the relations of the sexes equally well suited for all groups, all times, and all places, no solution to the problem of the "best" relations between them. There must, perhaps, always be the seeds of potential hostility between them, intrinsic to the relationship. We tend to hate those we are dependent on; for they have power over us; they can exploit our weaknesses. And no matter what we may say or do, the sexes are dependent on one another; they need one another. But they are different. Some normative patterns of relationships between the sexes favor men, some favor women. A pattern, for example, which puts the initiative in the hands of men means that women will sometimes be approached when they are not ready; a pattern which puts the initiative in the hands of women means that there will be times when men are denied or times when demands are made on them which they are not ready to meet. (Of the two, perhaps the first is the less costly to both sexes.)

It might be argued that different answers are required at different times. It might be argued, for example, that the Victorian consensus was a suitable one for an age that required a vast investment of human energy in the creation of capital. It gave men the prerogative of determining when and how often they would have sex relations; it put them in a dominant sexual position; it freed them from having to concern themselves about pleasing women. They could concentrate on the "really important" masculine things like work, making money, building factories, expanding markets, creating empires, and the like. . . .

The Victorian sexual ethos, however, does not suit the twentieth century. A sex ethos for the twentieth century has to take the resexualization of women into account. It has to be one which reconciles the demands made on men by their work and the demands made on them by women. It has to be one also which reconciles the differences between the sexes in their respective life calendars. It has to be one, finally, which takes into account the separation of heterosexual relations and reproduction. If the achievement of nonprocreative sexuality has solved some issues, it has raised many more. Nor can we anticipate what they will be. For as yet we really do not know what the sexual renaissance ushered in by the fourth revolution implies for the future relations between the sexes.

SACRED CONGREGATION FOR
THE DOCTRINE OF THE FAITH

Declaration on certain questions concerning sexual ethics

According to contemporary scientific research, the human person is so profoundly affected by sexuality that it must be considered as one of the factors which gives to each individual's life the principal traits that distinguish it. In fact it is from sex that the human person receives the characteristics which, on the biological, psychological and spiritual levels, make that person a man or a woman, and thereby largely condition his or her progress towards maturity and insertion into society. Hence sexual matters, as is obvious to everyone, today constitute a theme frequently and openly dealt with in books, reviews, magazines and other means of social communication.

In the present period, the corruption of morals has increased, and one of the most serious indications of this corruption is the unbridled exaltation of sex. Moreover, through the means of social communication and through public entertainment this corruption has reached the point of invading the field of education and of infecting the general mentality. . . .

The people of our time are more and more convinced that the human person's dignity and vocation demand that they should discover, by the light of their own intelligence, the values innate in their nature, that they should ceaselessly develop these values and realize them in their lives, in order to achieve an ever greater development.

In moral matters man cannot make value judgments according to his personal whim: "In the depths of his conscience, man detects a law which he does not impose on himself, but which holds him to obedience. . . . For man has in his heart a law written by God. To obey it is the very dignity of man; according to it he will be judged."

Moreover, through his revelation God has made known to us Christians his plan of salvation, and he has held up to us Christ, the Saviour and Sanctifier, in his teaching and example, as the supreme and immutable Law of life: "I am the light of the world; anyone who follows me will not be walking in the dark, he will have the light of life."

Therefore there can be no true promotion of man's dignity unless the essential order of his nature is respected. Of course, in the history of civilization many of the concrete conditions and needs of human life have changed and will continue to change. But all evolution of morals and every type of life must be kept within the limits imposed by the immutable principles based upon every human person's constitutive elements and essential relations—elements and relations which transcend historical contingency.

These fundamental principles, which can be grasped by reason, are contained in "the divine law—eternal, objective and universal—whereby God orders, directs and governs the entire universe and all the ways of the human community, by a plan conceived in wisdom and love. Man has been made by God to participate in this law, with the result that, under the gentle disposition of divine Providence, he can come to perceive ever increasingly the unchanging truth." This divine law is accessible to our minds.

Hence, those many people are in error who today assert that one can find neither in human nature nor in the revealed law any absolute and immutable norm to serve for particular actions other than the one which expresses itself in the general law of charity and respect for human dignity. As a proof of their assertion they put forward the view that so-called norms of the natural law or precepts of Sacred Scripture are to be regarded only as given expressions of a form of particular culture at a certain moment of history.

But in fact, divine Revelation and, in its own proper order, philosophical wisdom, emphasize the authentic exigencies of human nature. They thereby necessarily manifest the existence of immutable laws inscribed in the constitutive elements of human nature and which are revealed to be identical in all beings endowed with reason.

Furthermore, Christ instituted his Church as "the pillar and bulwark of truth." With the Holy Spirit's assistance, she ceaselessly preserves and transmits without error the truths of the moral order, and she authentically interprets not only the revealed positive law but "also . . . those principles of the moral order which have their origin in human nature itself" and which concern man's full development and sanctification. Now in fact the Church throughout her history has always considered a certain number of precepts of the natural law as having an absolute and immutable value, and in their transgression she has seen a contradiction of the teaching and spirit of the Gospel.

Since sexual ethics concern certain fundamental values of human and Christian life, this general teaching equally applies to sexual ethics. In this domain there exist principles and norms which the Church has always unhesitatingly transmitted as part of her teaching, however much the opinions and morals of the world may have been opposed to them. These principles and norms in no way owe their origin to a certain type of culture, but rather to knowledge of the divine law and of human nature. They therefore cannot be considered as having become out of date or doubtful under the pretext that a new cultural situation has arisen.

It is these principles which inspired the exhortations and directives given by the Second Vatican Council for an education and an organization of social life taking account of the equal dignity of man and woman while respecting their difference.

Speaking of "the sexual nature of man and the human faculty of procreation," the Council noted that they "wonderfully exceed the dispositions of lower forms of life." It then took particular care to expound the principles and criteria which concern human sexuality in marriage, and which are based upon the finality of the specific function of sexuality.

In this regard the Council declares that the moral goodness of the acts proper to conjugal life, acts which are ordered according to true human dignity, "does not depend solely on sincere intentions or on an evaluation of motives. It must be determined by objective standards. These, based on the nature of the human person and his acts, preserve the full sense of mutual self-giving and human procreation in the context of true love."

These final words briefly sum up the Council's teaching—more fully expounded in an earlier part of the same Constitution—on the finality of the sexual act and on the principal criterion of its morality: it is respect for its finality that ensures the moral goodness of this act.

This same principle, which the Church holds from divine Revelation and from her authentic interpretation of the natural law, is also the basis of her traditional doctrine, which states that the use of the sexual function has its true meaning and moral rectitude only in true marriage. . . .

Today there are many who vindicate the right to sexual union before marriage, at least in those cases where a firm intention to marry and an affection which is already in some way conjugal in the psychology of the subjects require this completion, which they judge to be connatural. This is especially the case when the celebration of the marriage is impeded by circumstances or when this intimate relationship seems necessary in order for love to be preserved.

This opinion is contrary to Christian doctrine, which states that every genital act must be within the framework of marriage. However firm the intention of those who practice such premature sexual relations may be, the fact remains that these relations cannot ensure, in sincerity and fidelity, the interpersonal relationship between a man and a woman, nor especially can they protect this relationship from whims and caprices. Now it is a stable union that Jesus willed, and he restored its original requirement, beginning with the sexual difference. "Have you not read that the creator from the beginning made them male and female and that he said: This is why a man must leave father and mother, and cling to his wife, and the two become one body? They are no longer two, therefore, but one body. So then, what God has united, man must not divide." Saint Paul will be even more explicit when he shows that if unmarried people or widows cannot live chastely they have no other alternative than the stable union of marriage: ". . . it is better to marry than to be aflame with passion." Through marriage, in fact, the love of married people is taken up into that love which Christ irrevocably has for the Church, while dissolute sexual union defiles the temple of the Holy Spirit which the Christian has become. Sexual union therefore is only legitimate if a definitive community of life has been established between the man and the woman.

THE HUMANIST

A new bill of sexual rights and responsibilities

Sexuality has for too long been denied its proper place among other human activities. Physical eroticism has been either shrouded in mystery and surrounded by taboos or heralded far beyond its capacity, by itself, to contribute to the fullness of life. Human sexuality grows increasingly satisfying as life itself becomes more meaningful. The time has come to enhance the quality of sexuality by emphasizing its contributions to a significant life.

For the first time in history there need be no fear of unwanted pregnancy or venereal disease, if proper precautions are taken. The limitation of sexual expression to conjugal unions or monogamous marriage was perhaps sensible so long as reproduction was still largely a matter of chance, and so long as women were subjugated to men. Although we consider marriage, where viable, a cherished human relationship, we believe that other sexual relationships also are significant. In any case, human beings should have the right to express their sexual desires and enter into relationships as they see fit, as long as they do not harm others or interfere with their rights to sexual expression. This new sense of freedom, however, should be accompanied by a sense of ethical responsibility.

Fortunately, there is now taking place a worldwide reexamination of the proper place of sexuality in human experience. We believe that the humanization of sexuality is far enough advanced to make useful a statement of rights and responsibilities of the individual to society and of society to the individual. Accordingly we wish to offer the following points for consideration.

1. *The boundaries of human sexuality need to be expanded.* Many cultures have tended to restrict sexuality to procreation. Any other purposes of sexuality were regarded as derivative, were looked at askance, or were sternly disapproved. But the need to limit population growth, the widespread use of effective contraceptives, and the developments in reproductive technology have made the procreative aspects of sex less significant today. Responsible sexuality should now be viewed as an expression of intimacy for women as well as for men, a source of enjoyment and enrichment, in addition to being a way of releasing tension, even where there is no likelihood of procreation.

This integration of sexuality with other aspects of experience will occur only as one achieves an essentially balanced life. When this happens, sexuality will take its place among other natural functions. . . .

2. *Repressive taboos should be replaced by a more balanced and objective view of sexuality based on a sensitive awareness of human behavior and needs.* Archaic taboos limit our thinking in many ways. The human person, especially the female, has been held in bondage by restrictions that prescribed when, where, with whom, and with what parts of the body the sex impulse could be satisfied. As these taboos are dispelled and an objective reappraisal ensues, numerous sexual expressions will be seen in a different light. Many that now seem unacceptable will very likely become valid in certain circumstances. Extramarital sexual relationships with the consent of one's partner are being accepted by some. Premarital sexual relationships, already accepted in some parts of the world, will become even more widely so. This will very likely also be true of homosexual and bisexual relationships. The use of genital associations to express feelings of genuine intimacy, rather than as connections for physical pleasure or procreation alone, may then transcend barriers of age, race, or gender.

Taboos have prevented adequate examination of certain topics, especially with respect to female sexuality, thus blocking the discovery of answers to important sexual questions. Abortion is a case in point. By focusing only on the destruction of the fetus, many have avoided facing the other issues that are fundamental. They do not, for example, openly discuss ways of providing a comprehensive sex education program for both children and adults. There has been a long struggle over the issue of providing adequate information about available contraceptive procedures for those who wish them. Likewise, taboos that cause people to feel that viewing the genitals is an obscenity or that any verbal or visual expression of the sex act is pornographic undermine objectivity and lead to demands for censorship. The oversacramentalization of sex also inhibits open discussion by not allowing people to treat sex as a natural experience. . . .

3. *Sexual morality should come from a sense of caring and respect for others; it cannot be legislated.* Laws can and do protect the young from exploitation and people of any age from abuse. Beyond that, forms of sexual expression should not be a mat-

ter of legal regulation. Mature individuals should be able to choose their partners and the kinds of sexual expression suited to them. Certain forms of sexual expression are limiting and confining, for example, prostitution, sado-masochism, or fetishism. However, any changes in such patterns, if they are made, should come through education and counseling, not by legal prohibition. Our overriding objective should be to help individuals live balanced and self-actualized lives. The punishing and ostracizing of those who voluntarily engage in socially disapproved forms of sexual conduct only exacerbate the problem. Sexual morality should be viewed as an inseparable part of general morality, not as a special set of rules. Sexual values and sex acts, like other human values and acts, should be evaluated by whether they frustrate or enhance human fulfillment.

4. Physical pleasure has worth as a moral value. Traditional religious and social views have often condemned pleasures of the body as "sinful" or "wicked." These attitudes are inhumane. They are destructive of human relationships. The findings of the behavioral sciences demonstrate that deprivation of physical pleasure, particularly during the formative periods of development, often results in family breakdown, child abuse, adolescent runaways, crime, violence, alcoholism, and other forms of dehumanizing behavior. We assert that physical pleasure within the context of meaningful human relationships is essential, both as a moral value and for its contribution to wholesome social relationships.

5. Individuals are able to respond positively and affirmatively to sexuality throughout life; this must be acknowledged and accepted. Childhood sexuality is expressed through genital awareness and exploration. This involves self-touching, caressing parts of the body, including the sexual organs. These are learning experiences that help the individual understand his or her body and incorporate sexuality as an integral part of his or her personality. Masturbation is a viable mode of satisfaction for many individuals, young and old, and should be fully accepted. Just as re-

pressive attitudes have prevented us from recognizing the value of childhood sexual response, so have they prevented us from seeing the value of sexuality in the middle and later years of life. We need to appreciate the fact that older persons also have sexual needs. The joy of touching, of giving and receiving affection, and the satisfaction of intimate body responsiveness is the right of everyone throughout life.

6. In all sexual encounters, commitment to humane and humanistic values should be present. No person's sexual behavior should hurt or disadvantage another. This principle applies to all sexual encounters—both to the brief and casual experience and to those that are deeper and more prolonged. In any sexual encounter or relationship, freely given consent is fundamental, even in the marital relationship, where consent is often denied or taken for granted.

Perplexing questions are raised by these concepts. Those directly engaged in the encounter may hold widely differing points of view toward sexual conduct. This possibility makes necessary open, candid, and honest communication about current and future expectations. Even then, decisions are subjects of judgment and projection, and their outcomes are only slowly revealed.

No relationship occurs in a vacuum. In addition to the persons directly involved in the sexual relationship there are important others. The interests of these other persons are usually complex and diverse; no course of action will satisfy everyone. Some might prefer that no sexual involvement whatever occur and are disturbed if they are aware of it; others might be quite accepting under most circumstances. For this reason each individual must have empathy for others. One might ask oneself: "How would I want others to conduct themselves sexually toward me and others I care about?" "Am I at least as concerned for the happiness and well-being of my partner, and others involved, as for my own?"

There is also a broader consideration, namely, that each person contribute to creating a social atmosphere in which a full acceptance of responsible sexual expression will exist.

MARK FREEDMAN

Homosexuals may be healthier than straights

Ten years ago the word "homosexual" conjured up images of sad, neurotic deviants. But the open spirit of the last decade has improved our knowledge, and a clear picture of homosexuals today would show a great many men and women who live by their own values and whose emotional expressions aren't limited by traditional sex roles. Far from being sick, gays often function *better* than nongays. . . .

Traditionally, psychiatrists have based their views of homosexuality either on armchair speculation or on the analysis of homosexuals who enter therapy—a highly unrepresentative sample. It wasn't until 1957, in fact, that psychologist Evelyn Hooker of UCLA published the first really sound research on the personal adjustment of gay men. Hooker compared homosexuals and heterosexuals who were *not* in therapy after dividing them up into pairs of comparable age, intelligence and schooling and then giving them a battery of personality tests. Experienced clinical psychologists then rated each person's test results without knowing the man's sexual orientation.

It turned out that the judges couldn't separate homosexuals from heterosexuals any better than if they had simply flipped a coin. The ratings of the homosexuals weren't significantly different from those of the heterosexuals, and about two-thirds of both groups seemed to have normal personalities.

Hooker drew several tentative conclusions from her study. First, the clinical entity or "disease" called homosexuality does not exist. The forms of homosexual experience are as varied as the forms of heterosexual experience. Second, homosexuality may well be a deviation that is within the normal range of human behavior. And third, particular forms of sexual desire and expression may play a less important role in

personality structure than many psychiatrists assume. Subsequent studies confirm Hooker's findings.

Unfortunately, most of these experiments used male subjects, so I decided in 1967 to do my doctoral research on female homosexuals. My results show that by several different measures of personality, lesbians are no more neurotic or disturbed than heterosexual women.

But there was something else in the test results, something provocative on the face of it: in certain ways, the lesbians actually functioned better than the controls. . . .

Creative opposition

Many gay people have responded to social pressures against homosexuality by "centering," by discovering and living according to their own values. An intense quest for identity, purpose and meaning often begins quite early, certainly by the time young homosexuals begin to appreciate the tremendous social pressures against them.

My research on lesbians found them scoring higher than a control group on autonomy, spontaneity, orientation toward the present (as opposed to being obsessed with the past or anticipating the future), and sensitivity to one's own needs and feelings. . . . In 1972 Marvin Siegelman compared a nonclinical sample of lesbian and heterosexual subjects on similar personality inventories, and the lesbians scored higher than the controls on both goal direction and self-acceptance.

I've met a good number of gay people, men and women, who have centered. They don't reject all social conventions and mores, but rather choose among them and develop new patterns of behavior to substitute for whatever they reject. . . .

Feelings of separateness, in other words, have led some gay people to oppose the values and institutions of the dominant society. The point to recognize here isn't merely the *fact* of alienation but the consciousness of it, a consciousness that can lead naturally to creative responses. The same process occurs among the members of other minority groups that must endure discrimination. Among homosexuals, I believe, creative opposition has produced not only new social concepts but an increased sensitivity to the value of the individual person in our society.

Besides centering, there are two other ways in which some gays function better than nongays: sex roles may be more egalitarian and sexuality more expressive. . . .

Recent research shows that even educated Americans disapprove of sex-role deviation, especially of males acting like sissies. Most people, when questioned about the attributes of a mentally healthy person, devalue "feminine" traits; they don't consider most so-called female characteristics, such as gentleness, either socially or psychologically valuable—for men *or* women.

The freedoms of deviance

These conventional views are too narrow to be healthy. In some cases, deviation from stereotyped sex roles is a very good thing. Research and my own experience have convinced me that many gays show a wider range of emotional expression because they are not confined by the standard roles. Lesbians, for instance, may show "masculine" attributes such as assertiveness and aggression. My research also indicates that lesbians *accept* their natural aggressive feelings better than their heterosexual counterparts, and tend to seek the kinds of satisfaction from their work that men do. As for gay men, they're more able to express "feminine" emotions such as tenderness and even frank weakness than most nongay men. . . .

The shared wisdom of the gay world is that two men or two women living together as mates quickly see the limitations of stereotyped sex roles. Breadwinner/homemaker and dominant/submissive dichotomies just aren't as important to gays as they are to most people. Obviously, there are a great many exceptions to this tendency, but the point I am trying to make is that homosexuality *in some cases* leads to better-than-average functioning and to a fuller realization of certain fundamental values.

As with sex roles, so with sexuality. The gay life can lead to certain types of experience that many human beings, whatever their sexual orientations, value highly. Honesty and variety are two of these. . . .

Whether interested in group sex or not, a homosexual couple in bed may do as well as, or even better than, a heterosexual couple. A gay man knows what feels good to his partner because he knows what makes his own body feel good. A woman may find, in the intimate company of another woman, precisely those qualities of nurturance, warmth and tenderness that many men are incapable of expressing. . . .

As for lesbians, Andrea Obérstone recently compared 25 heterosexual and 25 homosexual women between the ages of 20 and 45, and found that both groups were well-adjusted and that both played mutual sexual roles most of the time. . . . The lesbians also seemed more satisfied in their relationships—emotionally, sexually, in friendship and in common interest. It seems, then, that many gay people know how to focus on sex as an expression of warmth, tenderness and sensuality. And at least part of the gay world engages in the sexual variety that many psychologists consider extremely valuable. . . .

The healthy attributes I've mentioned—centering, transcendence of sex roles, freer sexuality and candor—are probably the result of personality development as well as social pressure. I am not saying that millions of gay people in this country always function better than heterosexuals. The true picture is more complicated than that and in many cases much less fortunate. Social pressures can narrow and cripple a person. I suspect, in fact, that many homosexuals end up trying to fit society's ugly image of "the homosexual" rather than pursuing any of the positive roles and patterns I've mentioned.

Playing society's game

The stereotypical homosexual is supposed to be an anomaly, a defective specimen of his or her sex. For women, this means being rough, insensitive, bossy. For men, it means being oversensitive and weak. And it's true that many members of the homosexual minority accept the majority's evaluation of them; they play the part society prescribes. The pushy Jew, the shuffling black, and the scatterbrained female are

45

examples of the same tragic psychological process. Before the advent of gay liberation and the emergence of positive roles for gays, homosexuals often developed a very negative identity. . . .

More common . . . , and no doubt more satisfying, is the life of sheer pragmatism. The pragmatic gay person acknowledges the social dangers of homosexuality but is willing and able to live effectively despite them. Most outsiders would assume that such people are heterosexuals. In some cases they may talk about their gayness, but in general they disguise it. They have gay friends and nongay friends, and the quality that characterizes them best is adaptability.

Gay pragmatists probably have as good a chance of self-actualization as anybody else. They seek satisfaction in their work and attend to the needs of sex, companionship and surroundings. Alan Bell, who conducted a large sociological survey in the San Francisco Bay area for the Kinsey Institute, characterizes this large segment of the gay community as follows:

"They may report that their homosexual, minority status has developed in themselves very useful and important capacities for social criticism, enhanced their creative abilities, or made them more sensitive to the needs of others. . . . Others report a kind of freedom which they feel is seldom found by heterosexuals. Still others may report that their educational and occupational pursuits have benefited from their experience of homosexuality. Many describe a way of life replete with positive reinforcements quite apart from whatever sexual satisfactions they enjoy."

A new vitality

Since the gay-liberation movement began in 1969, a new group of gay people has emerged that may turn out to be even more successful than the rather positive picture of gay pragmatism just quoted. I'm referring to those personally liberated people who refuse to hide their sexual orientation. They know they're not sick. They feel society is mistaken when it condemns a person on account of some variant lifestyle.

These people are centered, and they know, for the most part, what they want to do with their lives. . . .

Gay people are different from other people and it would be silly to deny it. Exactly how all the differences develop is not yet clear; complex patterns of social learning probably account for most of them. What I have tried to show here, though, is that these differences reveal some extremely positive aspects of homosexuality. Gay people constitute a large and varied group, and they are capable of providing new kinds of personal fulfillment and social vitality.

O. SPURGEON ENGLISH

Positive values of the affair

Centuries of effort have shown, without room for equivocation, the incapacity of one man and one woman to make marriage the congenial and mutually growth-promoting arrangement wherein they can grow simultaneously as personalities. They furthermore fail as they grow older to increase their love, good will, and enjoyment of each other, as well as to become of greater interest to each other. Directly in line with this, they fail to become more in the way of individuals functioning as a source of pleasure and interest to their children as well as to their friends and fellow workers.

So, in this widespread individual effort on the part of many married people of both sexes to bring some added vivacity, inspiration, and personal fulfillment to themselves and to the other, they have, in addition to taking up bridge, golf, and riding, become involved in this phenomenon called the affair. The affair, incidentally, has been greatly on the increase in young people before marriage and greatly increased among younger married women in proportion to the number of men. However, since the men already have had such a long head start on the wives in this matter, it will be some time yet before the women catch up to the men, either in

46

numbers or frequency of involvement in an affair.

At any rate, this attraction and the frequency with which so many people of both sexes seek out and either enjoy or suffer through an affair, in spite of its complexity and its risk of denouncement by one or more persons if discovered, must indicate that it offers a highly rewarding combination of delights and elevation of moods as well as a necessary and welcome enhancement to that which the partner in marriage can supply. This is not stated as criticism of the partner in marriage, even though all too many will insist on interpreting the statement that way. Either or both of two marital partners may in themselves be remarkable people, but still unable to fulfill the role placed upon them by the rules of the institution of marriage that are little less rigid than those of a concentration camp. Incidentally, community criticism can sting harder than any metal contraption yet invented, not to mention that it is charged with the current of envy, jealousy, prudery, and fear of the wish to copy those involved in an affair. The values of an affair are such as cannot be substituted by anything else. The late comedian, W.C. Fields, made a statement concerning sex, which is an acceptable and uncriticizable one yet truthful, when he said, "There may be some things better than sex, and some things may be worse. But, there is nothing exactly like it."

The sexual relation far from being a devastating, destructive, dangerous, humiliating, degrading one for those who engage in it, stands as man's (and woman's) greatest source of emotional and mental well-being. It is man's greatest single act, which symbolizes his total social and personal meaning and significance to another person and hence extends itself by way of a long-sustained emotional reverberation through his whole life awareness; it brings that sense of satisfaction, which accumulates as we grow older and always reminds us that life has had meaning. . . .

To speak to the phenomenon of love for a moment (which should never be divorced from sex or sex from it, because both these phenomena are always mutually complementary to a

varying degree), love demands that we enjoy the one we claim to love, and that we wish him well and direct our energies to help him in the way he needs, i.e. educationally, emotionally, economically, or assuage his discomfort if in need or distress. We defy anyone to say the factor of love in a sexual relationship is never there at all, be it ever so slight. And, in the best sexual relationships known to an individual and to any historical recounting of them by the most eloquent of writers, the amount of love present and generated in largest measure *by* the sexual aspect of the relationship has approached the sublime and carries with it the highest form of devotion and dedication and help to the very essence of the human being or personality history has on record. Hence, to brand sexual relationships outside of marriage as neurotic is to disavow the elements of courage, the defiance of tradition (a phenomenon often praised in other human activities), the rewarding and fulfilling enrichments to the participants, all of which have drawn forth the awe, admiration, praise, and as well furnished inspiration for millions of people, and is only a sign of mental retardation in embracing a valuable part of man's endowment. . . .

People often enter into affairs without thought of consequences, or whether each is capable of living and taking care of much more than one person emotionally, i.e. of intending to give them sufficient tokens of their personal meaning and value to insure a continuity of the relationship. These considerations should be weighed so that an individual can form some estimate as to whether he is capable of making an affair of value, rather than a guilty piece of behavior, hectic and reproachful because one participant cannot be available when the other is free. Each should be able to appreciate the values in meeting together and take the experience for what it contains for them, an addition in one of life's adventures or a fortunate interlude handed them by fate, and into which they bring a side of themselves poorly or not at all understood or fulfilled at home. If replaced by the affair each should make himself a better mate or spouse at home, and people so often enough to invite the public to view the affair with less prejudice.

47

It is highly probable that most people who enter into an affair would have a difficult time living together as man and wife, were it possible to make an easy and uncomplicated change. Why? The answer to that question is simple and has long since been given by the one who first noted that man is basically not a monogamous animal and of course woman is not either. . . .

What of morals, what of ideals, what of Biblical and other ethical injunctions? . . . It must be noted that we are moving rapidly away from a society in which religion alone controls man's behavior, or even influences it greatly. Yearly, for better or worse, he is taking responsibility for his behavior into his own hands and living by the results. These results, good or bad, are his own decision and it is high time he took over this responsibility. He has been shunning it long enough with his prayers and incantations, rather than face up to a more honest appraisal of his own abilities and a better use of the assets given him long since by nature and mind power, and by God also for the believer. . . .

Hence, an affair is a venture that threatens to reduce in some measure the control man (or woman) holds upon those he committed himself to once upon a time. But, it has been shown in how many ways man errs and hurts himself, as well as others, by attempting to arrogate to himself so much control of others, and what is more, uses harsh means to maintain this control. A greater freedom for all has slowly been coming in the affairs of men, and the affair in marriage is but one of the many evidences of it. Therefore, rather than complain at mention of an affair, as if mention of it really exacerbated its practice, the reader is appealed to to give the affair, and at least these few comments in connection with it, consideration. Ignoring it will not cause it to disappear, and to give it higher meaning, prestige, and a place of usefulness and high purpose rather than one execrable conduct should lead to better human understanding and compassion for what has been found to be good for many.

LINDA WOLFE

Playing around

With Lydia Marks, a modern dance teacher and performer, I found myself debating the unanswerable: what is best for women? Lydia had been married for fourteen years to her second husband, with whom she had had three children, and had separated from him a year ago, when she was thirty-seven. Few women I met were as appealing or exciting in their physical style as Lydia, a slim dark woman with long, straight brown hair, long graceful arms and legs, and what I came to think of as a long smile as well. Whenever she smiled, her face became so animated that even when she returned to deep serious thought, her eyes remained animated, sparkling, still smiling for long mysterious moments afterwards. Men must have found her as intriguing as I did, for she had, from what I could gather, no dearth of lovers in her current separated state. But despite popularity and self-confidence, Lydia fiercely regretted the end of her rebellious experimental marriage and her abortive attempts at pragmatism about sex.

"I had three affairs during my fourteen-year marriage," she said, "and each one of them was ridiculous. I always started out casually, thinking 'What's the harm in this?' but then somehow I'd screw myself up. I can't be trusted when it comes to sex. I'm apparently not yet ready to separate it from love. And I wonder who is. I wonder whether any woman is.

"Each time I had an affair I'd start to believe I was in love with the man, even though I always said it was sex, not love, I was after, or adventure, not love, I needed. You have to understand that marriage makes people grow together like fungus on a tree. Something happens because of this that kills the physical excitement. In the beginning I couldn't wait to touch my husband. There were all the corny things. We were magnetized like in the movies. I remember we once ran toward each other from opposite ends of an airport. But after a while, we lost that. It seemed to me that it was only when a man was really separate and outside myself that I could look at him and feel excited. My husband and I had grown so close that sex was like being physically attracted to oneself. We agreed, as a result, that occasional affairs would be permissible for either of us, provided we kept them slight."

Lydia wanted me to know that this had not been a unilateral decision. Both she and her husband were to have the same privileges. They had had the kind of marriage in which everything was discussed and shared—the children's inoculations, Lydia's work, her husband's job, their political attitudes—the trivial and the broad. "So I had the first affair," Lydia went on. "I was already interested in women's liberation, and I had very strong attitudes about affairs. For one thing, I always felt it was very divisive for single women to have affairs with married men. They shouldn't be taking men away from their sisters. So I also determined it would be wrong for me as a married woman to have an affair with a married man, and I chose only among the single or separated. And of course I thought I was choosing men I wouldn't love. I had three children and I wanted above all to protect their lives.

"My first affair was with an old boyfriend. We had kept in touch over the years, having lunch from time to time. Finally we went to bed. And that's when I began noticing how tricky this business of love and sex is. Here I was sleeping with a man I had previously rejected as a marriage partner, yet suddenly I found myself contemplating divorce and pursuing this old relationship again. I felt I was in love.

"It took enormous control for me to break it off but I did. I was able to do it only because I had now met someone else, someone I was absolutely convinced could give me what I wanted sexually but with whom I couldn't possibly fall in love. He was a hippy guy, a real kook. Forty years old and still bearded and barefoot. He couldn't afford to take me to dinner. Anyone could have seen he wasn't for me. And of course even I saw it, until I was into the thing. Then

it started all over again—the worrying and wondering and wanting to be with him all the time. I even considered getting him together with my kids. I was lucky that time because he broke it off.

"I decided no more affairs. Too risky. But about two years later I got into another one. This last guy was even less appropriate than the one before. He was a chilly establishment type, the kind of guy who owns no shirts but his white ones and who wouldn't dream of having a conversation through the door while one of you was in the bathroom. But even so, overnight I was dreaming of shaking up my life and hooking up with him. I was wondering how the kids would take it while I knew inside myself he was no one I even wanted to take to a party. No one I even wanted to introduce to my friends. But sure enough, it all began all over again, and this time I even went so far as actually to separate from my husband. It was very painful. I was weeping all the time. My kids were weeping all the time. 'When are we going to see Daddy? Daddy doesn't love us anymore or else we'd all be together,' that kind of thing. I wanted to go right back home.

"But it was too late. My husband felt betrayed by me. His affairs had indeed been casual but mine had become inflated. He felt my love for him had become wobbly or else this wouldn't have happened. We're separated now, and in marital therapy, and I want to get back together but he's growing very distant. He wants a divorce. And of course, I blame myself. I see now that all affairs—even affairs with the unmarried—are dangerous because they can so quickly get out of perspective. The first thing you know, someone—it doesn't matter whether it's a man or a woman—is ready to run off from their marriage." . . .

The fear of separation—not the loss of a mate's exclusive sexuality—is, I believe, what underlies most people's anxieties concerning extramarital sex. It is as insurance against our anxieties that we consent to ethical proscriptions limiting ourselves from extramarital sex. We do not fear sexual sharing itself, but fear it

49

only because it can lead to the possible loss of a partner's emotional bond.

In experimental marriages the practitioners assume that they can avoid such loss of bonds by defusing sex, long a primary way of forming and experiencing attachment. But they fail. Sex keeps its volatility, at least when attachment is at issue—and often the participants in a sexual affair cannot themselves recognize what is at issue until after the fact of attachment. Therefore, I cannot see experimental marriage as the wave of the future, as some sexual utopians have predicted. It might even be argued that it aids new bonding by making the process easier, or at least more convenient. If extramarital sex were always about sex, perhaps open adultery might become popular. All too often, however, extramarital sex is not about extra sex but about extra marriage, extra emotional intimacy, or the need for a new or different primary bond of attachment.

DEREK WRIGHT

The new tyranny of sexual "liberation"

The much-vaunted sexual freedom that the sex researchers and their disciples insist we share is turning out to be a new bondage. We have escaped from one trap to be ensnared by another; for freedom from ignorance and fear is being bought at the price of submission to the tyranny of social norms and the authority of the "experts."

On the face of it the new ideology looks innocent enough. Like fresh air, exercise and wholesome food, sex does you good, and within certain broad and tolerant limits the more you have the better. Since knowledge emancipates, we cannot know too much about such things as the physiological possibilities for pleasure our bodies offer, the cultural relativity of sexual mores and, of course, how everyone else behaves.

However, complacently aware of its benefits, we have failed to pay enough attention to the fact that this kind of knowledge generates not freedom but social pressures. We begin to grade our sexual partners, as they us, though we do not talk about it. And standards are rising. Too often for the sex experts, the merely possible is instantly the optimal, and tomorrow, for the rest of us, the normal. How we pity or scorn the impotent and frigid! While, absurdly, some people use sex to exorcise their insecurities, others who find it difficult, distasteful or merely dull conclude that they are odd, outcast and, most desolating of all, inadequate. It is so easy to build a prison around a man by convincing him he is a prisoner. . . .

If we are to be truly liberated, if we are to understand and explore the contribution sexual arousal can make to relationships, if we are to make it possible once again for this activity to kindle the imagination and intellect, and if we are to do justice to the fact that man has a single nervous system whose functions are integrated and interdependent, then we must evolve a way of thinking about sex which sees it as embedded in a personal context. This will take time, for it means devising ways of classifying human response which cut across functional distinctions (like the current idea that we give each other "creative experiences"). But certain preconditions of this new perspective are plain enough.

In the first place, we must rid our minds finally of the idea that there are any special moral rules for sexual behavior. Sexual pleasure is never wrong. It is the deceit, disregard for others, exploitation and the like which sometimes go with it that are wrong. Secondly, when we go into the bedroom we must learn to shut the sexologists and the neighbors out; and we must fully expose the rich absurdity of wanting a sex life as "good" as others, or one which would meet the approval of Dr. Masters and Mrs. Johnson. Thirdly, the researchers and their attendant popularizers must turn their attention to the way sexual arousal interrelates with other ecstasies, such as those of work, power, hate, encounter with others, and mysticism. Conceived as an isolated function, sex is a meaningless aside, a cul-de-sac. But we find its meaning, not in some limited purpose it is said to serve, such as procreation or mental health, but through becoming aware of that whole texture of connectedness within which the sexual is only one component. True sexual liberation occurs when the sexual is dissolved into the fully personal and when sexual ideologies are discarded for the tedious pedantries they are.

"I believe I may have found where you went wrong."

HOWARD STRINGER

3

THE
FAMILY
AND
MORALITY

The family is the most intimate of all social institutions. It is the primary institution in Western society for the development of children's personality and character. The patterns of relations established within the family are etched deeply in the personality of the child: Precisely because of its very personal significance, the family is that social institution most resistant to change. When it finally succumbs to change, however, the effects of that change ramify through the entire society. Today, various social forces have converged upon the family, placing increasing strain on it. The following selections analyze, from myriad perspectives, these pressures for change bearing down on the family from the larger social context. The consideration of these issues raises the question of whether the traditional monogamous family is the best institution for satisfying the needs of both the individual and society today.

In the first article in this chapter, Christopher Lasch traces the process by which the family traditionally "reproduces cultural patterns in the individual" and "colors all of a child's subsequent experience." Analyzing the changing family from a Marxist perspective, Lasch argues that capitalism and the family have combined to produce children who are oriented toward immediate gratification of desires rather than toward achievement or moral action.

A very different conception of the family is put forward by E. O. James. He sees the family as formed by a sacramental marriage. A sacramental marriage is a Christian marriage in which "the relationship typif[ies] the union of God with His people and Christ with His Church" and "each lives the life of the other."

Also upholding the institution of the family is Michael Novak, who deplores both our increasing reliance on the state to solve all social problems and the individual's ruthless pursuit of self-fulfillment and "liberation." For Novak, the family is a moral force, protective of the individual, and, most importantly, a reminder of our own finitude: "The point of marriage and family is to make us realistic. For it is one of the secrets of the human spirit that we long not to be of earth, not to be bound by death, routine, and the drag of our bodies.''

The family is not championed by everyone, however. David Cooper believes that the entire institution of whatever type should be overthrown. He makes the case that the family has consequences that are often "lethal" but always "humanly stultifying" to the personalities of its members.

In the next three articles, the present condition and probable future development of the "liberated" American family are defended. Edward Sapir applauds the loosening of affective bonds between family members, the undermining of the stereotyped roles of mother and father, and the weakening of paternal authority. Together, these grant the individual greater independence from his or her family. In support of these changes, Sapir writes: "It is not well for any human being to be identified with an institution."

Suzanne Keller discusses challenges to our traditional family structure, including those from changing sex roles. She suggests that time may reveal "our most cherished preconceptions such that monogamy is superior to other forms of marriage or that women naturally make the best mothers," to be "yet another illusion, another example of made-to-order truths." She foresees "greater, legitimate variety in sexual and marital experience, new forms of communal living arrangements" and "multi-marriages."

One recent development that might be a step in the direction that Keller envisions is the marriage contract in which the spouses "affirm their individuality in this relationship" and then specify their aims, rights, and responsibilities. If these are not met "for a sustained period of time" then grounds shall exist for "termination of this CONTRACT according to the divorce laws."

Such renewable marriage contracts would, of course, sacrifice the security of a long-term commitment for freedom. Yet it was just such security that traditionally made the family the ideal institution for rearing children. In the next article, Jessie Bernard considers the future of parenthood, concluding that, contrary to popular opinion, "childless marriages are more satisfactory than others." In today's increasingly crowded world, the decision not to have children, once anathema, might prove the best course of action for some couples.

The final selection is a piece on the end of marriage—divorce. Denis De Rougemont considers what is morally involved "in choosing a man or a woman *for the rest of one's life*" and argues that at any time marriage remains a risk. There is no way to foresee how events and circumstances will affect one's marriage. He concludes that "actually everything depends on a decision . . . whereby we commit ourselves during the rest of our lives 'for better, for worse.'"

Christopher Lasch, a historian, was born in Omaha, Nebraska in 1932 and was educated at Harvard and Columbia Universities. On the faculty of the University of Rochester since 1970, he formerly taught at the University of Iowa and Northwestern University. He is the author of *The New Radicalism in America* (1965) and *The World of Nations* (1973). He is working on a major study of the American family. "The Family and History" is excerpted from a series of three review articles that appeared in *The New York Review of Books* in the fall of 1975.

E[dwin] O[liver] James is professor emeritus of the history of religion at the University of London. Born in 1886, he was educated at Exeter College, Oxford, and at University College, London. He was editor of the *Journal of the British Folklore Society* for twenty-five years and in 1970 wrote *Creation and Cosmology. Marriage and Society* was published in 1955.

Michael Novak, born in 1933, has had a varied career as writer and lecturer, and as an editor of *Christianity and Crisis* and *Christian Century*. He is currently associate director for humanities of the Rockefeller Foundation, having previously taught at the Old Westbury campus of the State University of New York. His many books include *Belief and Unbelief, The Rise of the Unmeltable Ethnics,* and, most recently, *The Joy of Sports.*

David Graham Cooper is a psychotherapist associated with several London hospitals. He was born and educated in Cape Town, South Africa. He is coauthor with R. D. Laing of *Reason and Violence,* and among his other works are *Psychiatry and Anti-Psychiatry* and *The Death of the Family,* published in 1970.

Edward Sapir, born in 1884 in what is now Poland, came to the United States in 1889 and became one of the leading linguists and anthropologists of his time. He was known especially for his studies of the Indians of the Northwest, and he served as anthropologist with the Canadian National Museum and as professor at the University of Chicago and at Yale. His most popular book, *Language,* was published in 1921. "What Is the Family Still Good For?" was written in 1930, at a time when the nineteenth-century norms of marriage and the family were beginning to be questioned. During the decade of the 1920s, the percentage of married couples remaining childless had just about doubled (from about 13 percent to approximately 24 percent); and the percentage of married women who entered the labor force had approximately doubled since the turn of the century (from about 5.5 percent to almost 12 percent). While Sapir could not anticipate that more than 40 percent of married women would be working outside the home in the 1970s, his essay showed amazing foresight in analyzing some of the major trends of the contemporary family. Sapir died in 1939.

Suzanne Keller, a sociologist, was born in 1927 in Vienna. Educated at Columbia, she has taught at the Massachusetts Institute of Technology and is now on the faculty of Princeton University. She is the author of *Beyond the Ruling Class* (1963) and *The Urban Neighborhood* (1968). "Does the Family Have a Future?" originally appeared in *The Journal of Comparative Family Studies* in 1971.

Jessie Bernard. See above, p. 31.

Denis De Rougemont was born in Switzerland in 1906 and was educated in Switzerland and Vienna. He is the director of the European Cultural Center in Geneva and is also president of the Congrès pour la Liberté de la Culture, also based at Geneva. Among his better known works is *Love Declared: Essays on the Myths of Love* (1963). The revised edition of *Love in the Western World,* from which the excerpt reprinted here was taken, was published in 1956.

55

CHRISTOPHER LASCH

The family and history

As the chief agency of "socialization," the family reproduces cultural patterns in the individual. It not only imparts ethical norms, providing the child with his first instruction in the prevailing social rules, it profoundly shapes his character, in ways of which he is not even aware. The family instills modes of thought and action that become habitual. Because of its enormous emotional influence it colors all of a child's subsequent experience.

The union of love and discipline in the same persons, the mother and father, creates a highly charged environment in which the child learns lessons he will never get over—not necessarily the explicit lessons his parents wish him to master. He develops an unconscious predisposition to act in certain ways and to re-create in later life, in his relations with lovers and authorities, his earliest experiences. Parents first embody love and power, and each of their actions conveys to the child, quite independently of their overt intentions, the injunctions and constraints by means of which society attempts to organize experience. If reproducing culture were simply a matter of formal instruction and discipline, it could be left to the schools. But it also requires that culture be embedded in personality. Socialization makes the individual want to do what he has to do; and the family is the agency to which society entrusts this complex and delicate task.

Of all institutions, the family is the most resistant to change. Given its importance, however, changes in its size and structure, in its emotional organization, and in its relations with the outside world must have enormous impact on the development of personality. Changes in character structure, in turn, accompany or underlie changes in economic and political life. The development of capitalism and the rise of the state reverberate in the individual's inner being. . . .

If the [nineteenth-century] nuclear family served the needs of a market society based on competition, individualism, and Emersonian "self-reliance," it did so . . . not by providing sons with appropriate "role-models," but by cutting itself off from the extended kinship group and the world of work. The family's isolation gave the relations between parents and children a new intensity, which enabled the young to become more fully autonomous than before even as it increased the psychic costs of socialization. It was not so much the internal structure of the family that changed as its relations to the outside world. As an institution defined above all as a refuge, a private retreat, the family became the center of a new kind of emotional life, a new intimacy and inwardness. . . .

From the moment the conception of the family as a refuge made its historical appearance, the same forces that gave rise to the new privacy began to erode it. The nineteenth-century cult of the home, where the woman ministered to her exhausted husband, repaired the spiritual damage inflicted by the market, and sheltered her children from its corrupting influence, expressed the hope on which bourgeois society has always rested—that private satisfactions can compensate for deprivations suffered in the realm of work. But the machinery of organized domination, which had impoverished work and reduced civic life to a competitive free-for-all, soon organized "leisure" itself as an industry. The so-called privatization of experience went hand in hand with an unprecedented assault on privacy. The tension between the family and the economic and political order, which in the early stages of bourgeois society protected the members of the family from the full impact of the market, gradually abated.

Today the peer group introduces the child to the illusory delights of consumption at an early age, and the family, drained of the emotional intensity that formerly characterized domestic relations, socializes him into the easygoing, low-keyed relationships that predominate in the outside world as well. Capitalism in its advanced stages has reduced conflict between society and the family to a minimum. Whereas in earlier times the family passed on the dominant values but unavoidably provided the child with a glimpse of a world that transcended them, crystalized in the rich imagery of maternal love, capitalism has now eliminated or at least softened this contradiction. The family, assisted by the health industry, the mass media, the monolithic national culture, and its mirror-image the counterculture, produces a type of personality primed not for "achievement," . . . but for immediate instinctual gratification—the perfect consumer, in short.

If the emotional intensity of bourgeois family life encouraged the child's identification with his parents, the father's withdrawal into the world of work created conditions that weakened this identification in the long run. The significance of a father's training his children for work, in societies where the family still serves as a center of production, is that it tempers the child's fantasies with practical experience, softening the early impression of an omnipotent, wrathful, and punitive father. . . .

The decline of the father's participation in family life makes this identification difficult or impossible. The child no longer wishes to succeed the father; he wishes merely to enjoy life without his interference.

At the same time, his desire to get rid of authority, starting with the father, has grown stronger than ever, not only because authorities interfere with his pleasure (as always) but because he has probably formed an exaggerated idea of their power. The absence, remoteness, or inaccessibility of the father does not mean that the child forms no ideas about him, it only means that those ideas will seldom be tested against everyday experience. The child imagines a remote, vindictive father and comes to see the world as starkly divided between power and impotence. He reduces all questions of justice and morality to questions of strength.

E. O. JAMES

Marriage and society

Christianity, under the influence of Judaism, . . . introduce[d] a personal conception of conjugal love which gave a new significance to the conjugal relationship. . . .

Love being that moral principle which leads one moral being to desire and delight in another, it reaches its highest expression in a personal relationship in which each lives in the life of the other. Once it is recognized that "God is love" and man made in the divine image is the object of His love, human personality is seen in a new light. . . .

It was on this conception of divine love that Christ based His teaching concerning a right relationship between God and man, and the mystery of redemption, which . . . was interpreted by St. Paul as spiritual union with the Church as His mystical body, comparable to that which existed ideally between husband and wife. In making the bond indissoluble, the Apostle gave a fresh emphasis to marriage as a life-union rooted and grounded in a love that binds together two personalities in an enduring relationship. . . . Instead of being a legitimate but unromantic means of peopling the world and maintaining either the State, the nation, or the family, it became a sacramental and holy condition of life consecrated to the noblest ends in an intimate personal communion of heart and soul. . . .

The idea that the relationship typified the union of God with His people and Christ with His Church on the analogy of bridegroom and bride, was . . . deeply laid in Holy Writ. . . . Once it was recognized that God is love, and society as He has constituted it consists of persons created in His image, animated by His spirit and united by love, monogamous marriage as a divine ordinance falls into its natural place in this scheme as the sphere in which the highest expression of human love between man and woman is experienced in an indissoluble personal relationship, symbolizing nothing less than the mystical union between Christ and the Church on whose behalf He gave His life in perfect self-oblation. Herein is love revealed in its essential nature and expressed in sacrifice; love doing and bearing what apart from love would not be willingly done or borne. . . .

Against this theological background love as a personal relationship acquired a new and deeper significance. For man and wife to be united in a "one-flesh" union as "joint-heirs of the mystery of life," symbolizing the bond between the Church and its divine Founder and Sustainer, raised the institution of marriage to a sacramental status in which much more than the lawful procreation of legitimate children was involved. Propagation unquestionably was, as it always had been, the practical purpose of matrimony, but in coming together to found a Christian family they were united in a permanent contract by sanctifying grace and undivided conjugal affection. Therefore, "what God hath joined together let not man put asunder." Person is united to person indissolubly on the principle of a common personality consecrated and hallowed by love, for "to find oneself in another, so that both are apprehended as one, is love." As this is realized in human relationships most completely in the nuptial fellowship rightly understood and lived, love is the fulfilling of the law of Christian marriage.

MICHAEL NOVAK

The family out of favor

We live in lucky times. So many, so varied, and so aggressive are the antifamily sentiments in our society that brave souls may now have (for the first time in centuries) the pleasure of discovering for themselves the importance of the family. Choosing to have a family used to be uninteresting. It is, today, an act of intelligence and courage. To love family life, to see in family life the most potent moral, intellectual, and po-

litical cell in the body politic is to be marked today as a heretic.

Orthodoxy is usually enforced by an economic system. Our own system, postindustrial capitalism, plays an ambivalent role with respect to the family. On the one hand, capitalism demands hard work, competition, sacrifice, saving, and rational decision-making. On the other, it stresses liberty and encourages hedonism.

Now the great corporations (as well as the universities, the political professions, the foundations, the great newspapers and publishing empires, and the film industry) diminish the moral and economic importance of the family. They demand travel and frequent change of residence. Teasing the heart with glittering entertainment and gratifying the demands of ambition, they dissolve attachments and loyalties. Husbands and wives live in isolation from each other. Children of the upwardly mobile are almost as abandoned, emotionally, as the children of the ghetto. The lives of husbands, wives, and children do not mesh, are not engaged, seem merely thrown together. . . .

To insist, in the face of such forces, that marriage and family still express our highest moral ideals, is to awaken hostility and opposition. For many, marriage has been a bitter disappointment. They long to be free of it and also of the guilt they feel, a residual guilt which they have put to sleep and do not want awakened. They loathe marriage. They celebrate its demise. Each sign of weakness in the institution exonerates them of personal failure. . . .

Yet, clearly, the family is the seedbed of economic skills, money habits, attitudes toward work, and the arts of financial independence. The family is a stronger agency of educational success than the school. The family is a stronger teacher of the religious imagination than the church. Political and social planning in a wise social order begin with the axiom *What strengthens the family strengthens society*. Highly paid, mobile, and restless professionals may disdain the family (having been nurtured by its strengths), but those whom other agencies desert have only one institution in which to find essential nourishment.

The role of a father, a mother, and of children with respect to them, is the absolutely critical center of social force. Even when poverty and disorientation strike, as over the generations they so often do, it is family strength that most defends individuals against alienation, lassitude, or despair. The world around the family is fundamentally unjust. The state and its agents, and the economic system and its agencies, are never fully to be trusted. One could not trust them in Eastern Europe, in Sicily, or in Ireland—and one cannot trust them here. One unforgettable law has been learned painfully through all the oppressions, disasters, and injustices of the last thousand years: *if things go well with the family, life is worth living; when the family falters, life falls apart.*

Unfashionable families

These words, I know, go against the conventional grain. In America, we seem to look to the state for every form of social assistance. . . . [Yet] virtually all Americans, outside our professional classes, are family people.

There are, perhaps, radical psychological differences between people who center human life in atomic individuals—in "Do your thing," or "Live your own life," et cetera—and people who center human life in their families. There may be in this world two kinds of people: "individual people" and "family people." Our intellectual class, it seems, celebrates the former constantly, denigrates the latter.

Understandably, to have become a professional means, often enough, to have broken free from the family of one's birth. (How many wounds suffered there!) To have become successful, often enough, leads to the hubris of thinking one can live, now, in paradise, emotionally unfettered, free as the will to power is free. . . .

Aggressive sentiments against marriage are usually expressed today in the name of "freedom," "openness," "play," or "serious commitment to a career." Marriage is pictured as a form of imprisonment, oppression, boredom, and chafing hindrance. Not all these accusations are wrong; but the superstition surrounding

them is. Marriage *is* an assault upon the lonely atomic ego. Marriage *is* a threat to the solitary individual. Marriage does impose grueling, humbling, baffling, and frustrating responsibilities. Yet if one supposes that precisely such things are the preconditions for all true liberation, marriage is not the enemy of moral development in adults. Quite the opposite. . . .

The solitary self

Before one can speak intelligently of marriage, one must discuss the superstition that blocks our vision. We lack the courage nowadays to live by creeds, or to state our doctrines clearly (even to ourselves). Our highest moral principle is flexibility. Guided by sentiments we are embarrassed to put into words, we support them not by argument but by their trendiness.

The central idea of our foggy way of life, however, seems unambiguous enough. It is that life is solitary and brief, and that its aim is self-fulfillment. Next come beliefs in establishing the imperium of the self. Total mastery over one's surroundings, control over the disposition of one's time—these are necessary conditions for self-fulfillment. ("Stand not in my way.") Autonomy we understand to mean protection of our inner kingdom—protection around the self from intrusions of chance, irrationality, necessity, and other persons. ("My self, my castle.") In such a vision of the self, marriage is merely an alliance. It entails as minimal an abridgment of inner privacy as one partner or the other may allow. Children are not a welcome responsibility, for to have children is, plainly, to cease being a child oneself.

For the modern temper, great dreads here arise. Sanity, we think, consists in centering upon the only self one has. Surrender self-control, surrender happiness. And so we keep the other out. We then maintain our belief in our unselfishness by laboring for "humanity"—for women, the oppressed, the Third World, or some other needy group. The solitary self needs distant collectivities to witness to its altruism. It has a passionate need to love humankind. It cannot give itself to a spouse or children.

There is another secret to this aggressive sen-

59

timent, dominated as it is by the image of enlightenment. Ask, "Enlightenment from what?" and the family appears: carrier of tradition, habit, prejudice, confinement, darkness. In this view, the seeds of reaction and repression, implanted by the family of one's birth, are ready to sprout as soon as one sets up a family of one's own.

The great escape

Theories of liberation, of course, deserve to be studied in the light of flesh, absurdity, and tragedy. There is a pervasive tendency in Western thought, possibly the most profound cultural undercurrent in 3,000 years (compared to it, C. S. Lewis said, the Reformation was a ripple on the ocean), in which liberation is imagined as a breaking of the bonds of finiteness. Salvation comes as liberty of spirit. "Don't fence me in!" The Fall results from commitments that "tie one down," that are not subject to one's own controlling will. One tries to live as angels once were believed to live—soaring, free, unencumbered.

The jading of everyday, the routines of weekdays and weekends, the endless round of humble constraints, are, in this view, the enemies of human liberty.

In democratic and pragmatic societies, the dream of the solitary spirit often transfers itself into a moral assault upon institutions, traditions, loyalties, conventions. The truly moral person is a "free thinker" who treats every stage of life as a cocoon from which a lovely moth struggles to escape the habits of a caterpillar. This fuzzy sentiment names each successive breakaway "growth" and "development." It describes the cumulative process as "liberation."

There is, of course, a rival moral tradition. I do not mean the conventional variant, which holds that fidelity to institutions, laws, conventions, and loyalties is sufficient. The more compelling alternative—call it "realist"—differs from the romantic undercurrent by associating liberation with the concrete toils of involvement with family and/or familial communities. The romantic undercurrent takes as the unit of analysis the atomic individual. The

realist alternative takes as the unit of analysis the family. To put it mythologically, "individual people" seek happiness through concentration upon themselves, although perhaps for the sake of service to others. Most television cops, detectives, cowboys, and doctors are of this tribe. The "family people" define themselves through belonging to others: spouse, children, parents, siblings, nieces, cousins, and the rest. For the family people, to be human is to be, so to speak, molecular. I am not solely I. I am husband, father, son, brother, uncle, cousin; I am a family network. Not solitary. On television, both *All in the Family* and *Good Times* have as a premise the molecular identity of each character. The dramatic unit is the family.

There is, beyond the simplicities of half-hour television, a gritty realism in family life. . . .

So much of modern life may be conceived as an effort to make ourselves pure spirits. Our meals are as rationalized and unsensual as mind can make them. We write and speak about sexual activity as though its most crucial element were fantasy. We describe sex as though it were a stage performance, in which the rest of life is as little as possible involved. In the modern era, the abstract has grown in power. Flesh, humble and humbling, has come to be despised.

So it is no surprise that in our age many resistant sentiments should war against marriage and family. Marriage and family are tribute paid to earth, to the tides, cycles, and needs of the body and of bodily persons; to the angularity and difficulties of the individual psyche; to the dirty diapers, dirty dishes, and endless noise and confusion of the household. It is the entire symbolic function of marriage and family to remind us that we come from dust and will return to dust, that we are part of the net of earth and sky, inspirited animals at play for our brief moment on this planet, keeping alive our race. The point of marriage and family is to make us realistic. For it is one of the secrets of the human spirit that we long *not* to be of earth, not to be bound by death, routine, and the drag of our bodies. We long to be other than we are. . . .

Today the atomic individual is as free as a bird. The threat to human liberation today is

60

that the flesh, the embodied psyche, earthy roots, bodily loyalties, will be dismissed with contempt.

The consequence of this freedom is likely to be self-destruction. Whoever nourishes spirit alone must end by the ultimate denial of the flesh. . . .

A return to the true conditions of our own humanity will entail a return, on the part at least of a dedicated few, to the disciplines and terrors of marriage and family. . . .

People say of marriage that it is boring, when what they mean is that it terrifies them: too many and too deep are its searing revelations, its angers, its rages, its hates, and its loves. They say of marriage that it is deadening, when what they mean is that it drives us beyond adolescent fantasies and romantic dreams. They say of children that they are piranhas, eels, brats, snots, when what they mean is that the importance of parents with respect to the future of their children is now known with greater clarity and exactitude than ever before. . . .

My dignity as a human being depends perhaps more on what sort of husband and parent I am, than on any professional work I am called upon to do. My bonds to them hold me back (and my wife even more) from many sorts of opportunities. And yet these do not feel like bonds. They are, I know, my liberation. They force me to be a different sort of human being, in a way in which I want and need to be forced. . . .

Family politics

It would be a lie, however, to write only of the difficulties of marriage and family, and not of the beauty. The joys are known. The more a man and a woman are in love, the more they imitate the life of husband and wife; long, sweet affairs are the tribute romances pay to matrimony. Quiet pleasures and perceptions flow: the movement of new life within a woman's belly; the total dependence of life upon the generosity and wisdom of its parents; the sense that these poor muscles, nerves, and cells of one's own flesh have recreated a message to the future, carried in relays generation after generation, carried since the dim beginnings. There may not be

a "great chain of being." But parents do forge a link in the humble chain of human beings, encircling heirs to ancestors. To hold a new child in one's hands, only ounces heavy, and to feel its helplessness, is to know responsibilities sweet and awesome, to walk within a circle of magic as primitive as humans knew in caves.

But it is not the private pleasures of family life that most need emphasis today. Those who love family life do not begrudge the price paid for their adulthood. What needs elucidation is the political significance of the family. A people whose marriages and families are weak can have no solid institutions. . . .

It is difficult to believe that the state is a better instrument for satisfying . . . human needs than the family. If parents do not keep after the children to do their schoolwork, can the large, consolidated school educate? Some have great faith in state services: in orphanages, child-care centers, schools, job-training programs, and nursing homes. Some want the state to become one large centralized family. Such faith taxes credulity. Much of the popular resistance to federal child care arises from distrust of social workers and childhood engineers who would be agents of state power. Families need help in child care, but many distrust the state and the social-work establishment.

Almost everything about both "liberal" and "conservative" economic thought neglects, ignores, or injures family networks. It is not benign neglect. Millions of dollars are spent on the creation of a larger and larger state apparatus. Resources are systematically taken from the family. Is this an accident? One by one, all centers of resistance to the state are being crushed, including the strongest, family. The trend does not augur well for our liberties. . . .

The family nourishes "basic trust." From this spring creativity, psychic energy, social dynamism. If infants are injured here, not all the institutions of society can put them back together. Familial arts that took generations to acquire can be lost in a single generation, can disappear for centuries. If the quality of family life deteriorates, there is no "quality of life." Again, emphasis on family life is politically important because it can unite people of diverse religious, ethnic, regional, and racial traditions. Families differ in their structures, needs, and traditional inclinations; but they share many basic economic and political necessities. . . .

In a word, a politics aimed at strengthening families, white and black, would be a politics of unity rather than of division. It would also have higher prospect of success. The chief obstacle in its execution is the mysterious contempt liberals unthinkingly manifest toward their own greatest source of advantage.

As Jean-Paul Sartre has taught us, it is bad faith to plead "to each his own," to permit intellectual laissez-faire. Actions speak louder than shrugs of the shoulder. To marry, to have children, is to make a political statement hostile to what passes as "liberation" today. It is a statement of flesh, intelligence, and courage. It draws its strength from nature, from tradition, and from the future. Apart from millions of decisions by couples of realistic love, to bring forth children they will nourish, teach, and launch against the void, the human race has no future—no wisdom, no advance, no community, no grace.

Only the emptiness of solitary space, the dance of death.

It is the destiny of flesh and blood to be familial.

DAVID COOPER

The death of the family

Let us sum up on some of the factors that operate within the family, often with lethal but always with humanly stultifying consequences. Later we shall explore the possibilities of reversing them.

Firstly, there is the gluing together of people based on the sense of one's own incompleteness. To take one classical form of this, let us consider the mother who feels incomplete as a person (owing to a complex set of reasons that usually includes, with contrality, her relationship with her mother, and the general suppression of extrafamilial social effectiveness in women). So in the whole colloidal system of the family she glues, say, her son onto herself, to be that bit of her self that she feels to be missing (the bit her mother "taught" her was missing) and the bit that actually is missing (the factor of objective social suppression). The son, even if he "succeeds" in leaving home and getting married, may never become more personally complete than her, because he has experienced himself during the most critical years of his "formation" as an appendage to her body—(her penis)—and to her mind—her mind-penis, or socially prescribed effectiveness. In the most extreme form of this symbiosis, his only exit might be by a series of acts that lead him to be designated schizophrenic (about one percent of the population are hospitalized at some point in their lives with this label), and transferred to the replica family of the mental hospital. Probably the only way that people, glued to each other in the family and in the replica families of social institutions, can unglue themselves is by using the warmth of love. The irony here is that love gets warm enough to accomplish this ungluing only if it traverses a region usually experienced as arctic: the region of total respect for one's own autonomy and for that of each other person one knows.

Secondly, the family specializes in the formation of roles for its members rather than in the laying down of conditions for the free assumption of identity. I do not mean identity in the congealed, essentialist sense, but rather a freely changing, wondering but highly active sense of who one is. Characteristically, in a family a child is indoctrinated with the desired desire to become a certain sort of son or daughter (then husband, wife, father, mother), with a totally enjoined, minutely prescribed "freedom" to move within the narrow interstices of a rigid lattice of relationship. Instead of the feared possibility of acting from the chosen and self-invented center of oneself, being *self-centered* in a good sense, one is taught to submit, or else, to live in an eccentric way of being in the world.

62

Here, "eccentric" means being normal or located in the normal—way off the center of oneself. . . .

Being a well-brought-up, eccentric, normal person means that one lives all the time relatively to others, and this is how the falsely splitting system originates in family indoctrination, so that one functions all the time in social groups in later life as one side or other of a duality. . . . In the family there is the built-in antithesis of the bringer-up (parents) and the brought-up (children). All possibilities of children bringing up their parents are relegated. The socially imposed "duty" of parents suppresses, finally, any joy that might shatter the division of roles. This obligation structure is then transported into every other institutional system subsequently entered by the person brought up in the family (I include, of course, adoptive families and orphanages, which follow the same model). One of the saddest scenes I know is when a child of six or seven plays school with desks and lessons arranged, under the parents' view, in precisely the same form that exists in the primary school. How might we reverse this abdication, and stop stopping the child teaching her or his secret wisdom that we make them forget because we forget that we have forgotten it?

Thirdly, the family, in its function as primary socializer of the child, instills social controls in its children that are patently more than the child needs to navigate his way through the obstacle race laid down by the extrafamilial agents of the bourgeois state, whether these be police, university administrators, psychiatrists, social workers, or his "own" family that passively re-creates his parents' family model—although the television programs these days are a bit different, of course. The child, in fact, is taught primarily not how to survive in society but how to submit to it. Surface rituals like etiquette, organized games, mechanical learning operations at school replace deep experiences of spontaneous creativity, inventive play, freely developing fantasies and dreams. These forms of life have to be systematically suppressed and forgotten and replaced by the surface rituals. It may take therapy, in the best sense, to revalue one's experience highly enough to register one's dreams properly, and to sequentially develop one's dreams beyond the point of dream stagnation that most people reach before the age of ten. If this happens on a wide enough scale, therapy becomes dangerous to the bourgeois state and highly subversive because radically new forms of social life are indicated. Suffice it to say for the moment, however, that every child, before family indoctrination passes a certain point and primary school indoctrination begins, is, germinally at least, an artist, a visionary and a revolutionary. How do we recover this lost potential, how do we start stepping backward on the inexorable march from the truly *ludic,* joyful play that invents its autonomous discipline, to the *ludicrous*—that is, normal, games-playing social behavior, obedient to a narrow set of rules?

Fourthly, . . . there is an elaborate system of taboos that is instilled in each child by its family. This, like the teaching of social controls more generally, is achieved by the implantation of guilt—the sword of Damocles that will descend on the head of anyone who prefers his own choices and his own experiences to those enjoined on him by the family and the wider society. If one loses one's head enough to openly disobey these injunctive systems, one is, poetically enough, decapitated! . . .

The taboo system that the family teaches extends well beyond the obvious incest taboos. There is a restriction of the sensory modalities of communication between people to the audiovisual, with quite marked taboos against people in the family touching, smelling or tasting each other. Children may romp with their parents, but demarcation lines are very firmly drawn around the erotogenic zones on both sides. There has to be a very carefully measured obliquity and stiltedness in, say, the way that growing-up sons have to kiss their mothers. Transexual hugging and holding are rapidly precipitated, in the minds of family members, into a zone of "dangerous" sexuality. Above all, there is the taboo on tenderness. . . . Tenderness in families may be felt, certainly, but not expressed unless it is formalized almost out of existence. One is reminded of the young man . . . who, on seeing his father in his coffin, bent over him and kissed his brow, saying, "There, father, I never dared do that while you were alive!" Perhaps if we realized how dead "alive" people are we might be prepared, goaded by despair, to take more of a risk. . . .

Blood is thicker than water only in the sense of being the vitalizing stream of a certain social stupidity.

The family, for want of a capacity for producing holy Idiots, becomes moronic.

EDWARD SAPIR

What is the family still good for?

Four trends . . . will serve as a convenient formula to make intelligible what seems to be happening within the family. Putting ourselves into the traditional attitude, let us now see what seems to have been lost in the course of development of the modern family.

I should say, first of all, that the family is no longer a self-going concern, no longer a self-sufficient castle in a semi-hostile world. Furthermore, parental authority has perceptibly lessened. . . . In the third place, personal relations within the family, the attitude of brother to sister, of sister to sister, son to mother, daughter to father, have no longer quite that self-evident or pre-ordained quality which seemed to go with defined kinship status. Once one assumed, for instance, that brothers and sisters were friends, though one knew from sad experience that they were not necessarily so. Finally, we can no longer lightly assume that woman is the sacred guardian of the domestic hearth. She may or may not be that, but she is likely to be a great many other things as well.

Are these truly losses, or are they really gains in disguise? They are certainly not unmixed evils. That the family is no longer a self-going concern is part loss, but it is part gain as well.

The traditional family tended to be a little ingrown, rather selfish in its outlook upon life. Its happiness tended to be smug; its unhappiness bred all the poisons of secrecy. That the family is now more directly plunged into the general economic scene has at least this advantage, that the average man and woman of today develops a greater concern for the fundamental mechanisms of society. He loses something of his dignity as a personality because he is rarely a primary economic agent, yet the indirect and even fictitious part which he plays in life does bring him significantly nearer to his fellowmen. There is an altogether new willingness to see the family as but a unit in a larger whole.

Few are so held by the illusions of the past as to claim that the lessening of parental authority is nothing but evil. There was a time when to be a father was to know what was good for one's children. In those days the word mother connoted an all-wise affection that was as mysterious and as immutable as the law of gravitation. And, reciprocally, to have a father and a mother was construed as equivalent to doing what you were told and being thankful therefor ever after. We have traveled a certain distance from these dull mythologies. Thanks to Shaw, to psychoanalysis, and to liberated common sense, we now know that a devoted mother can be silly and pernicious; that an idolatrous affection for the son may and often does go with a corroding hatred of the husband.

It is well that we thus tend to take little for granted in the parental relation. It is well that fathers and mothers are beginning to discover that it is hard work making their children's acquaintance, and that before they have done so it will be just as well not to bank too heavily on the innate love and wisdom which the mere fact of parenthood is supposed to give them. There is no reason why parents and children may not be the best of friends, but it is getting to be believed that frankness is a better preface to such friendship than the mysticism of blood.

It is not merely that much of the mythology has been squeezed out of the parent-child relation, but that the greater independence of the individual within the family has brought with it the necessity of taking some effort to establish any and all of the truly valuable relations that are implicit in the family instead of taking them for granted as *a priori* necessities. Brothers and sisters have to earn each other's esteem. Temperamental differences disqualify the close of kin for long-enduring friendship just as they disqualify complete strangers in the world outside the family. That the younger brother fags for the older is no longer felt to be a law of nature, nor need one make it a point of honor to distribute one's deferences evenly between the maternal and the paternal kinfolk. Grandparents are no longer semi-divine. Kinship is a glorious opportunity for the meeting of minds and hearts, but in itself it constitutes neither an obligation nor a privilege.

Finally, who can regret that woman has become a real person—that she is no longer merely the imprisoned symbol of an institution? The fact that there are as many kinds of mothers and as many kinds of wives as there are kinds of women is a little disconcerting, but it should no longer shock us. It used to be possible to say to a woman, "You are not behaving like a *real* mother," or, "You are not behaving like a *real* wife." Nowadays it seems more appropriate to find other terms in which to couch the sentiment back of this antique terminology. It would be wiser to say, "I am afraid we don't agree about the bringing up of the children," or, "You have every blessed right in the world to behave as you do, but I want to tell you frankly that I don't like it a bit."

On the whole, the latter method is a technical improvement. Normal men and women will often do as individuals what they are not so keen on doing as fathers, mothers, husbands and wives. It is not well for any human being to be identified with an institution. The normal woman will want to discover wifehood and motherhood through the flesh and the symbolisms of the flesh, which lead to the deepest sentiments we know of, rather than to be reading the breviary of family duty.

Do these changes in the constitution of the family and in the psychology of family relationships mean a negation of everything that is sig-nificant in the family, or are they but a killing off of useless symbols and attitudes in order that the ground may be prepared for a new family? Is it too much to hope that this new family may prove to be all the more significant because little is expected of it officially? Isn't it possible that the weakness of the present-day family in America lies not so much in the visible destructive tendencies as in our persistent attempt to combine a verbal loyalty to the traditional family with a sneaking acceptance of its loss of integrity?

Perhaps the American family seems insecure, not because the father's authority is now little, but because we still secretly believe that it ought to be great but that he is too cowardly to act out his wistful tyranny; not because the love of husband and wife cannot in the nature of things be a sufficient basis for family life, but because our inherited sense of the sinfulness of sex has made us unwilling to believe that love is sufficient; not because a woman's career outside of the home is really inimical to its preservation, but because a sense of daring sin still lingers about her choice of independence. In brief, the inertia of social sentiment is stronger than the inertia of social form. Long after the family has changed its form men and women will continue to think and feel that its older implications of sentiment are still extant, or that if they are not, they ought to be. Indeed, I think one may contend, with no sense of paradox, that the family is likely to remain as important a psychological factor as it has ever been, that we are mistaking surgery for murder, that we have been thinking too much about the institutional and therefore secondary aspects of the family and too little about the biological and psychological foundations of the institution. . . .

To conclude, we are not confronted with the threatened dissolution of the family; we are simply promised a clearing away of institutional clogs of all sorts which do not correspond to modern mentality and of indulgence in sentiments which we are beginning to see are harmful. All this does not mean chaos, but rather the emergence of cleanly defined psychological patterns which have intimate relevance for the life of the individual at the expense of superimposed institutional patterns which take little or no account of individual psychology. We may say that the family is needed for the following primary purposes: first, to give the sex relation its greatest emotional value; second, to rear children in an atmosphere of intelligent affection; third, to prepare the individual for the give and take of society; and fourth, to prepare the child unconsciously for satisfactory mating in the future. . . .

The old family institution, walled about by a make-believe psychology of status, ignored the elementary truth that the individuals within it were essentially the same people as the self-same individuals outside. A belated recognition of this truth creates some dizziness, but when the gasps have subsided and the eye is opened again, the family will be seen to be still there, a little cleaner, a little more truthful, a little happier.

SUZANNE KELLER

Does the family have a future?

The malaise of our time reflects not simply a temporary disenchantment with an ancient institution but a profound convulsion of the social order. The family is indeed suffering a seachange.

The family means many things to many people but in its essence it refers to those socially patterned ideals and practices concerned with biological and cultural survival of the species. When we speak of the family we are using a kind of shorthand, a label for a social invention not very different, in essence, from other social interventions, let us say the Corporation or the University, and no more permanent than these. This label designates a particular set of social practices concerned with procreation and child rearing; with the heterosexual partnerships that make this possible and the parent–child relations that make it enduring. As is true of all collective habits, once established, such practices are exceedingly resistant to change, in part be-

cause they evoke strong sentiments and in part because no acceptable alternatives are offered. Since most individuals are unable to step outside of their cultures, they are unable to note the arbitrary and variable nature of their conventions. Accordingly, they ascribe to their folkways and creeds an antiquity, an inevitability, and a universality these do not possess.

The idea that the family is universal is highly misleading despite its popularity. All surviving societies have indeed found ways to stabilize the processes of reproduction and child care else they would not have survived to tell their tale. But since they differ greatly in how they arrange these matters . . . the generalization does not help us explain the phenomenon but more nearly explains it away.

In truth there are as many forms of the family as there are forms of society, some so different from ours that we consider them unnatural and incomprehensible. There are, for example, societies in which couples do not share a household and do not have sole responsibility for their offspring; others in which our domestic unit of husband and wife is divided into two separate units, a conjugal one of biological parents and a brother–sister unit for economic sustenance. There are societies in which children virtually rear each other and societies in which the wise father does not know his own child. All of these are clearly very different from our twentieth-century, industrial-urban conception of the family as a legally united couple, sharing bed and board, jointly responsible for bearing and rearing their children, and formally isolated from their next of kin in all but a sentimental sense. This product of a long and complicated evolutionary development from prehistoric times is no simple replica of the ancient productive and reproductive institutions from which it derives its name and some of its characteristic features. The contemporary family really has little in common with its historic Hebrew, Greek, and Roman ancestors.

The family of these great civilizations of the West was a household community of hundreds, and sometimes thousands, of members ("familia" is the Latin term for household). Only some

66

of the members were related by blood and by far the larger part were servants and slaves, artisans, friends, and distant relations. . . .

The fallacy of universality has done students of human behavior a great disservice. By leading us to seek and hence to find a single pattern, it has blinded us to historical precedents for multiple legitimate family arrangements. As a result we have been rather impoverished in our speculations and proposals about alternative future arrangements in the family sphere.

A second common fallacy asserts that the family is *the* basic institution of society, hereby revealing a misunderstanding of how a society works. For as a social institution, the family is by definition a specialized element which provides society with certain needed services and depends on it for others. This means that you cannot tamper with a society without expecting the family to be affected in some way and vice versa. In the contemporary jargon, we are in the presence of a feedback system. Whatever social changes we anticipate, therefore the family cannot be kept immune from them.

A final fallacy concerns the presumed naturalness of the family in proof of which a motley and ill assorted grab bag of anecdotal evidence from the animal kingdom is adduced. But careful perusal of ethological accounts suggests that animals vary as greatly as we do, their mating and parental groupings including such novelties as the love death, males who bear children, total and guilt-free "promiscuity," and other "abnormal" features. The range of variation is so wide, in fact, that virtually any human arrangement can be justified by recourse to the habits of some animal species. . . .

Today the family and its social and psychological underpinnings are being fundamentally challenged from at least three sources: (1) from accumulated failures and contradictions in marriage; (2) from pervasive occupational and educational trends including the changing relations between the sexes, the spread of birth control, and the changing nature of work; and (3) from novel developments in biology. Let me briefly examine each.

It is generally agreed that even in its ideal form, the industrial-urban family makes great, some would say excessive, demands on its members. For one thing it rests on the dyadic principle or pair relationship which . . . is inherently tragic and unstable. Whether in chess, tennis, or marriage, two are required to start and continue the game but only one can destroy it. In this instance, moreover, the two are expected to retain their separate identities as male and female and yet be one in flesh and spirit. . . . Nor do children, the symbols of their union, necessarily unify them. . . . And yet their upbringing and sustenance, the moral and emotional climate, as well as the accumulation of economic and educational resources needed for survival, all rest on this small, fragile, essential but very limited unit. . . .

To these potentials for stress and strain must be added the loss of many erstwhile functions to school, state, and society, and with it something of the glamour and challenge of family commitments. Few today expect the family to be employment agency, welfare state, old age insurance, or school for life. . . .

Like most social institutions in the throes of change, moreover, the modern family is also beset by numerous internal contradictions engendered by the conflict between traditional patterns of authority and a new egalitarianism between husbands and wives and parents and children. . . .

One [current] trend, demographic in nature but bound to have profound social implications, concerns the lengthened life expectancy and the shortened reproductive span for women. Earlier ages at marriage, fewer children per couple and closer spacing of children, means: the girl who marries at twenty will have all her children . . . out of the home by her early forties. This leaves some thirty to forty years to do with as personal pleasure or social need dictate. . . . Hence what may in the past have been an individual misfortune has turned into a social emergency of major proportions. . . . Destined to outlive her husband, stripped of major domestic responsibilities in her prime years, what is she to do with this windfall of extra hours and years? Surely we must expect and prepare for a

67

major cultural shift in the education and up-bringing of female children. If women cannot afford to make motherhood and domestic concerns the sole foci of their identities, they must be encouraged, early in life, to prepare themselves for some occupation or profession not as an adjunct or as a last resort in case of economic need but as an equally legitimate pursuit. . . .

All in all, it would appear that the social importance of the family relative to other significant social arenas will . . . decline. Even today when the family still exerts a strong emotional and sentimental hold its social weight is not what it once was. All of us ideally are still born in intact families but not all of us need to establish families to survive. Marriage and children continue to be extolled as supreme social and personal goals but they are no longer—especially for men—indispensable for a meaningful existence. As individual self-sufficiency, fed by economic affluence or economic self-restraint, increases, so does one's exemption from unwanted economic as well as kinship responsibilities. Today the important frontiers seem to lie elsewhere, in science, politics, and outerspace. This must affect the attractions of family life for both men and women. For men, because they will see less and less reason to assume full economic and social responsibilities for four to five human beings in addition to themselves as it becomes more difficult and less necessary to do so. This, together with the continued decline of patriarchal authority and male dominance—even in the illusory forms in which they have managed to hang on—will remove some of the psychic rewards which prompted many men to marry, while the disappearance of lineage as mainstays of the social and class order, will deprive paternity of its social justification. For women, the household may soon prove too small for the scope of their ambitions and power drives. Until recently these were directed first of all to their children, secondarily to their mates. But with the decline of parental control over children a major erstwhile source of challenge and creativity is removed from the family sphere. This must weaken the mother-wife complex, historically sustained by the necessity and exaltation of motherhood and the taboo on illegitimacy.

Above all, the move towards worldwide population and birth control must affect the salience of parenthood for men and women, as a shift of cultural emphasis and individual priorities deflates maternity as woman's chief social purpose and paternity as the prod to male exertions in the world of work. Very soon, I suspect, the cultural presses of the world will slant their messages against the bearing and rearing of children. Maternity, far from being a duty, not even a right, will then become a rare privilege to be granted to a select and qualified few. . . .

This along with changing attitudes towards sex, abortion, adoption, illegitimacy, the spread of the pill, better knowledge of human behavior, and a growing scepticism that the family is the only proper crucible for child-rearing, creates a powerful recipe for change. World-wide demands for greater and better opportunities for self-development and a growing awareness that these opportunities are inextricably enhanced or curtailed by the family as a prime determinant of life-chances, will play a major role in this change. . . .

The trends that I have sketched would affect marriage, male-female, and parent-child relations even if no other developments were on the horizon. But there are. As yet barely discernible and still far from being applicable to human beings, recent breakthroughs in biology—with their promise of a greatly extended life span, novel modes of reproduction, and dramatic possibilities for genetic intervention—cannot be ignored in a discussion devoted to the future of the family.* . . .

We will have to come to terms with changing sexual attitudes and mores ushered in by what has been called the sexual revolution. This liberalization, this rejection of old taboos, half truths, and hypocrisies, also means a crisis of identity as men and women, programmed for more traditional roles, search for the boundaries

---

*Ed. note: See Chapter 12 for a discussion of these developments.

of their sexual selves in an attempt to establish a territoriality of the soul. . . .

Returning now to our main question—does the family have a future—it should be apparent that I expect some basic and irreversible changes in the decades ahead and the emergence of some novel forms of human togetherness. . . .

Thus if we dare to speculate further about the future of the family we will be on safe ground with the following anticipations: (1) a trend towards greater, legitimate variety in sexual and marital experience; (2) a decrease in the negative emotions—exclusiveness, possessiveness, fear and jealousy—associated with these; (3) greater room for personal choice in the kind, extent, and duration of intimate relationships, which may greatly improve their quality as people will both give and demand more of them; (4) entirely new forms of communal living arrangements in which several couples will share the tasks of child rearing and economic support as well as the pleasures of relaxation; (5) multi-stage marriages geared to the changing life cycle and the presence or absence of dependent children. Of these proposals, some, such as Margaret Mead's, would have the young and the immature of any age test themselves and their capacities to relate to others in an individual form of marriage which would last only so long as it fulfilled both partners. In contrast to this, older, more experienced and more mature couples who were ready to take on the burdens of parenthood would make a deeper and longer lasting commitment. Other proposals would reverse this sequence and have couples assume parental commitments when young and, having discharged their debt to society, be then free to explore more personal, individualistic partnerships. . . .

For the immediate future, it appears that most Americans opt for and anticipate their participation in durable, intimate, heterosexual partnerships as anchors and pivots of their adult lives. They expect these to be freer and more flexible than was true in the past, however, and less bound to duty and involuntary personal restrictions. They cannot imagine and do not wish a life without them.

Speculating for the long range future, we can-not ignore the potential implications of the emerging cultural taboo on unrestricted reproduction and the shift in public concern away from the family as the central preoccupation of one's life. Hard as it may seem, perhaps some day we will cease to relate to families just as we no longer relate ourselves to clans, and instead be bound up with some new, as yet unnamed, principle of human association. If and when this happens, we may also see a world of Unisex, Multi-sex, or Nonsex. None of this can happen, however, if we refuse to shed some of our most cherished preconceptions such that monogamy is superior to other forms of marriage or that women naturally make the best mothers. Much as we may be convinced of these now, time may reveal them as yet another illusion, another example of made-to-order truths.

Ultimately all social change involves moral doubt and moral reassessment. If we refuse to consider change while there still is time, time will pass us by. Only by examining and taking stock of what is can we hope to affect what will be. This is our chance to invent and thus to humanize the future.

THIS CONTRACT is entered into this 24th day of November, 1972, by and between HARRIETT MARY CODY and HARVEY JOSEPH SADIS, as the parties enter into a marriage relationship authorized by a Marriage License and by an Official of the State of Washington, County of King.

RECITALS OF FACT

1. HARRIETT MARY CODY is a woman 27 years of age, born on August 23, 1945, in Norfolk, Virginia, and the child of Hiram S. Cody Jr. and Mary V. Cody.
2. HARVEY JOSEPH SADIS is a man 26 years of age, born on April 12, 1946, in Seattle, Washington, and the child of Jean Sadis and Joseph Sadis.
3. HARRIETT and HARVEY are presently residing together in Seattle, Washington.

RECITALS OF INTENTION

HARRIETT and HARVEY desire to enter into a marriage relationship, duly solemnized under the laws of the State of Washington, the rights and obligations of which relationship differ from the traditional rights and obligations of married persons in the State of Washington which would prevail in the absence of this CONTRACT. The parties have together drafted this MARRIAGE CONTRACT in order to define a marriage relationship sought by the parties which preserves and promotes their individual identities as a man and a woman contracting to live together for mutual benefit and growth.

HARRIETT and HARVEY are of sound mind and body, have a clear understanding of the terms of this CONTRACT and of the binding nature of the agreements contained herein; they freely and in good faith choose to enter into this MARRIAGE CONTRACT and fully intend it to be legally binding upon themselves.

NOW, THEREFORE, in consideration of their affection and esteem for each other, and in consideration of the mutual promises herein expressed, the sufficiency of which is hereby acknowledged, HARRIETT and HARVEY agree as follows:

NAMES

HARRIETT and HARVEY affirm their individuality and equality in this relationship. The parties reject the concept of ownership implied in the adoption by the woman of the man's name; and they refuse to define themselves as husband and wife because of the possessory nature of these titles.

THEREFORE, THE PARTIES AGREE to retain and use the given family names of each party: HARRIETT MARY CODY and HARVEY JOSEPH SADIS. The parties will employ the titles of address, MS. CODY and MR. SADIS, and will henceforth be known as PARTNERS in this relationship.

RELATIONSHIPS WITH OTHERS

HARRIETT and HARVEY believe that their partnership will be enriched by the extent to which their respective needs can be met by relationships with others, rather than by a total dependence on each other to fulfill their needs. The parties have strong individual identities, with their own families, friends, careers, histories, and interests, and do not view themselves as an inseparable couple who do not exist apart from each other.

THEREFORE, THE PARTIES AGREE to allow each other as much time with other friends individually as they spend with each other. The parties also agree that invitations extended to one of them will not be assumed to have automatically been extended to the other.

The parties freely acknowledge their insecurities about sexual relationships beyond the partnership.

THEREFORE, THE PARTIES AGREE to maintain sexual fidelity to each other.

RELIGION

HARVEY freely admits the break with Jewish tradition represented by this CONTRACT with HARRIETT. But he fully intends to maintain the cultural and religious traditions of his Sephardic community insofar as possible. HARRIETT chooses not to embrace the Jewish religion.

THEREFORE, THE PARTIES AGREE to respect their individual preferences with respect to religion and to make no demands on each other to change such preferences.

THE PARTIES AGREE to continue the traditions associated with their respective religious holidays (Christmas, Hanukkah, Passover, Easter, Rosh Hashanah, Yom Kippur, Thanksgiving) and to include each other in the celebrations thereof.

CHILDREN

The joy and the commitment of the parties' relationship are not dependent on raising a family. HARRIETT and HARVEY will not be unfulfilled as individuals or as partners if they choose not to have children. At this time, the parties do not share a commitment to have children.

THE PARTIES AGREE that any children will be the result of choice, not chance, and THEREFORE the decision to have children will be mutual and deliberate. FURTHER, THE PARTIES AGREE that the responsibility for birth control will be shared. In the event of a pregnancy unwanted by either party, THE PARTIES AGREE to obtain an abortion of such pregnancy. A decision by one party to be sterilized will be supported emotionally and financially by the other.

CAREERS; DOMICILE

HARRIETT and HARVEY value the importance and integrity of their respective careers and acknowledge the demands that their jobs place on them as individuals and on their partnership. Commitment to their careers will sometimes place stress on the relationship. It has been the experience of the parties that insofar as their careers contribute to individual self-fulfillment, the careers strengthen the partnership.

THE PARTIES AGREE that, should a career opportunity arise for one of the parties in another city at any future time, the decision to move shall be mutual and based upon the following factors:

(a) The overall advantage gained by one of the parties in pursuing the new career opportunity shall be weighed against the disadvantages, economic and otherwise, incurred by the other;

(b) The amount of income from the new job shall not be controlling;

(c) Short-term separations as a result of such moves may be necessary.

HARVEY HEREBY WAIVES whatever right he may have to solely determine the legal domicile of the parties.

CARE AND USE OF LIVING SPACE

HARRIETT and HARVEY recognize the need for autonomy and equality within the home in terms of the use of available space and allocation of household tasks. The parties reject the concept that the responsibility for housework rests with the woman in a marriage relationship while the duties of home maintenance and repair rest with the man.

THEREFORE, THE PARTIES AGREE to share equally in the performance of all household tasks, taking into consideration individual schedules and preferences. Periodic allocations of household tasks will be made, in which the time involved in the performance of each party's tasks is equal.

THE PARTIES AGREE that decisions about the use of living space in the home shall be mutually made, regardless of the parties' relative financial interests in the ownership or rental of the home. Each party shall have an individual area within the home in an equal amount, insofar as space is available. . . .

EVALUATION OF THE PARTNERSHIP

HARRIETT and HARVEY recognize the importance of change in their relationship and intend that this CONTRACT shall be a living document and a focus for periodic evaluations of the partnership.

THE PARTIES AGREE that either party can initiate a review of any article of the CONTRACT at any time for amendment to reflect changes in the relationship. THE PARTIES AGREE to honor such requests for review with negotiations and discussions at a mutually convenient time.

THE PARTIES AGREE that, in any event, there shall be an annual review of the provisions of the CONTRACT . . . on or about the anniversary date of the CONTRACT.

THE PARTIES AGREE that, in the case of unresolved conflicts between them over any provisions of the CONTRACT, they will seek mediation, professional or otherwise, by a third party.

TERMINATION OF THE CONTRACT

HARRIETT and HARVEY may by mutual consent terminate this CONTRACT and end the marriage relationship at any time.

FURTHERMORE, THE PARTIES AGREE that the breach of a material provision of this CONTRACT for a sustained period of time shall constitute "cruel treatment or personal indignities rendering life burdensome" and shall serve as a ground for termination of this CONTRACT, according to the divorce laws of the State of Washington, under RCW 26.08.020.

THE PARTIES AGREE that in the event of mutual consent to terminate this CONTRACT or breach thereof, neither party shall contest the application by the other party for a divorce decree or the entry of such decree in the county in which the parties are both residing at the time of such application.

In the event of termination of the CONTRACT and divorce of the parties, the provisions of this Article . . . shall serve as the FINAL PROPERTY SETTLEMENT AGREEMENT between the parties. In such event, this CONTRACT is intended to effect a complete settlement of any and all claims that either party may have against the other, and a complete settlement of their respective rights as to alimony, property rights, homestead rights, inheritance rights, and all other rights of property otherwise arising out of their partnership.

At such time as there may be a child born of this partnership or adopted by the parties, THE PARTIES AGREE to amend this CONTRACT to make provisions for their respective rights and obligations in regard to the child in the event of termination of the CONTRACT (including provisions for support and education of the child).

DECISION-MAKING

HARRIETT and HARVEY share a commitment to a process of negotiations and compromise which will strengthen their equality in the partnership. Decisions will be made with respect for individual needs. THE PARTIES HOPE to maintain such mutual decision-making so that the daily decisions affecting their lives will not become a struggle between the parties for power, authority, and dominance. THE PARTIES AGREE that such a process, while sometimes time-consuming and fatiguing, is a good investment in the future of their relationship and their continued esteem for each other.

The future of marriage

Having children has always been viewed as one of the major functions of marriage. For a married couple to remain deliberately childless was anathema. "To contract before that they will have no children makes it no marriage, but an adultery," preached John Donne in a sermon on May 30, 1621, and doubtless all decent people agreed with him.

Parenthood expands marriage into a family, and everything changes. And the changes are not all for the better, for although having children may do a great deal for the character of parents, schooling them in unselfishness and sacrifice, it does not always do much for their marriage.

The future of parenthood

In the future, more married couples will fall into "adultery" as defined by John Donne; that is, we may expect fewer marriages to involve children. . . . The evidence for this conclusion is as yet not statistically documentable, but rather implicit in the general tenor of the times and in the antimotherhood ambience generated by the concern about population. And even those who do plan to have children will have fewer of them. The effects on both the husbands' and the wives' marriages of both these trends will be profound, and all to the good. . . .

The benign effects on marriage of childlessness

In the past, the concern of reformers and researchers has been with the effect of parents on their children. Increasingly, there is concern also for the effect that children have on the marriage of their parents. What we have had on this subject has been mostly an array of folk clichés: children held a marriage together, a child would win back a disaffected spouse, children forged a stronger bond between the parents, and the like. And when people are asked directly about the effect of children on their own happiness and that of their spouses, they give the predictable replies: children had added greatly to both their own and their partners' happiness.

But, the researchers ask, "can what the couples say be taken as evidence of the happiness-producing effect of a child in the early years of marriage?" and they answer "no" to their own question, or "only with reservations." For, as Burgess and Wallin have pointed out,

our society, like most, if not all, societies, glorifies the experience of parenthood. Children, especially in the period of early childhood, are culturally idealized as "bundles of joy." Parents who fail to regard them as such run the risk in many groups of being judged at best as unconventional and at worst as immoral or abnormal.[1]

Reluctant, therefore, as parents are to state that children have decreased rather than increased their marital happiness, this is exactly what, overall, the researchers find. . . .

Contrary to all the clichés, childless marriages that do survive are happier than marriages with children. Mothers far more than childless wives find marriage restrictive; slightly fewer are very happy. Far more, expectably of course, report problems in the marriage; considerably fewer report satisfaction in the marital relationship; and more feel dissatisfied with themselves.

The benign effect of childlessness is even more marked in the husbands' marriages than in the wives'. Thus, although there was only a small difference between childless men and fathers in the proportion expressing marital satisfaction, an impressively larger proportion of childless men than of fathers were very happy. Conversely, more fathers felt marriage to be restrictive, and more reported problems. Twice as many fathers as childless men felt dissatisfied with themselves; three times as many, inadequate. (Who, male or female, facing at least their teen-age children today *can* feel adequate or satisfied with themselves?) . . .

Childless marriages are more satisfactory than others; parents, especially those currently rais-

ing children, were definitely less apt to be satisfied with their marriages. Whatever the general social ambience, then—encouraging or discouraging to motherhood—the presence of children in the marriage had an admittedly negative effect.

The major concern of society with marriage has always rested on its concern for children. Where there are no children, marriage becomes a totally different relationship, one that calls for little if any public surveillance. If it weren't for babies and children, the problems associated with marriage, though never easy, would be vastly simplified. Men and women would continue to love each other and cease to love each other; they would continue to attract and cease to attract each other—but in ways quite different from those that characterize relationships in which children are involved. Already there is unofficial recognition of marriages with and without children. If there are no children, divorce is easier to get. And if, in addition, there is little property involved, marriage does, indeed, become a very private affair. To the extent that childlessness becomes common in the future, marriage will be increasingly private and personal and, for many husbands and wives, also more satisfactory.

Is childlessness harmful for women?

Some people argue that having children satisfies a fundamental, even instinctive, drive, especially in women, that childlessness may therefore have an adverse effect on them by depriving them of this channel for self-expression by frustrating an intrinsic need. Conversely, others argue that some women do not want children, even reject them, that the desire for children is a culturally imposed need and that if such pressures on women are relaxed they will not feel the need to bear children.

An enormous literature on the maternal instinct is far from convincing as an explanation for the desire of women for children. Still, there is no denying that birth does have a powerful, even mystical, claim on our imaginations. It has overwhelming significance for peoples of all times and climes. No more can one deny

[1]E. W. Burgess and Paul Wallin, *Engagement and Marriage* (Philadelphia: Lippincott, 1953), pp. 707–708.

that a well-fed happy infant is a pleasurable sight or that small children can be entertaining as well as enjoyable. But enjoying children is not the same as parenthood with all the responsibilities that go with it. Parents undoubtedly do love their children, but parenthood is not for everyone a fully rewarding experience. And when, in addition, there is no special praise forthcoming for having children, there will be less socially-induced sense of frustration for not having them.

DENIS DE ROUGEMONT

Love in the western world

The institution of marriage was founded on three sets of values which subjected it to *compulsions*. . . . But today the compulsions have been either relaxed or abandoned.

There were, in the first place, sacred compulsions. Pagan races have invariably made marriage the subject of a ritual, vestiges of which long survived in our own customs. The ritual covered the purchase, abduction, and exorcism of the bride. . . . Nowhere now is a betrothal very often the occasion for a lawyer's presence at a full-dress reception. And few couples feel any "superstitious" need of having their union "blessed" by a priest.

There were, in the second place, social compulsions. But today considerations of rank, blood, family interests, and even money, are receding into the background so far as democratic countries are concerned, and hence the mutual choice of a marriage partner tends more and more to depend on individual circumstances. That is why divorce is steadily on the increase. . . . Nowadays the honeymoon, to the extent that it survives and retains any significance, must be held to indicate a wish for escape from habitual social surroundings and an insistence on the private nature of what is called wedded bliss.

There were, finally, religious compulsions. But the modern mind, in so far as it is still able to distinguish between Christianity and sacred and social compulsions, recoils from it with horror. For a religious vow is taken for "time and eternity," which means that it makes no allowance for temperamental vagaries, alterations of character, and changes in taste and external circumstances, such as every couple must expect to experience. And it is on there being no such ups and downs that modern couples make what they call their "happiness" depend. . . .

From such a general decay of institutional obstructions a slackening of tension was bound to ensue, so that it is no wonder that there is now a vast confusion. Adultery has become a topic either for delicate psychological analysis or else for facetious jokes. Fidelity in marriage has become slightly ridiculous: it is so conventional. Strictly speaking, the two hostile moral systems are no longer in *conflict* (and hence no myth is any longer possible), but are approaching a state of mutual neutralization, which will be reached when the old values—not transcended, but abased—have finally dissolved. . . .

Once we ask ourselves what is involved in choosing a man or a woman *for the rest of one's life,* we see that to choose is to wager. Both in the lower and the middle classes the wiseacres urge young men "to think it over" before taking the decisive step. They thus foster the delusion that the choice of a wife or husband may be governed by a certain number of accurately weighable pros and cons. This is a crude delusion on the part of common sense. You may try as hard as you like to put all the probabilities at the outset in your own favour—and I am assuming that life allows you the spare time for such nice calculations—but you will never be able to foresee how you are going to develop, still less how the wife or husband you choose is going to, and still less again how the two of you together are going to. The factors involved are too diverse. Suppose you could weigh them as they are now (assuming them to be finite in number) and you were so deeply versed in the conduct of human affairs as to know the values of every one of them and their order, you would still be unable to foresee how a union entered upon with all the *facts* duly weighed was going to shape. Nature is said to have required several hundreds of thou-

74

sands of years for the selection of those species which now seem to us adapted to their surroundings. And yet we have the presumption to suppose that all of a sudden in the course of a single life we may solve the problem of the adaptation to one another of two highly organized physical and moral beings! For this is what all unsatisfactorily married persons suppose whenever they grow convinced that a second or third trial is going to yield a closer approximation to "happiness," notwithstanding that everything goes to show that even a hundred thousand trials would not provide the first inchoate and altogether empirical data upon which to build a science of "happy marriage." It needs to be recognized frankly that the problem with which we are confronted by the practical necessity of marriage becomes the more hopelessly insoluble the more we strive "to solve" it in a rational way.

True, I have not stated the case quite fairly; for as a rule everything happens as if the happiness of a married pair actually did depend on a finite number of factors—character, beauty, fortune, social position, and so on. But as soon as individual demands are put forward, these external data lose importance, and it is imponderables that determine our decision. Thereupon it is common sense that turns out to have argued unfairly in recommending that our choice should result from a mature and reasonable submission of the data to impersonal criteria.

But after all the logical fallacy is negligible; what matters is the moral fallacy which the logical implies. When a young engaged couple are encouraged to calculate the probabilities in favour of their happiness, they are being distracted from the truly moral problem. The attempt to minimize or to conceal the fact that, when considered objectively, a choice of this kind is a wager fosters the belief that everything depends on wisdom or on a set of rules, when actually everything depends on a *decision*. And yet, inasmuch as no set of rules can be anything but imperfect and provisional, if we are to be guided by rules we also need some kind of guarantee. But the only possible guarantee would be one supplied by the strength of the decision whereby we commit ourselves during the rest of our lives "for better, for worse." And it is precisely to the extent that we persuade ourselves that the matter is above all one of calculation and of weighing up that the decision in itself is made to seem secondary or superfluous. I therefore feel that it would be more appropriate, both to the essential nature of marriage and to the facts for young people to be taught that their choice must always have an arbitrary element, of which they are undertaking to bear the consequences, whether the consequences turn out happy or unhappy. I do not seek to defend acting on "rash impulse"; to the extent that probabilities can be weighed, it would be stupid not to weigh them. But I insist that the guarantee of a union in appearance sensible never lies in this appearance. It must lie in that irrational event, a decision that we venture upon in spite of everything and that lays the foundation of a new life in being a consent to take new chances.

Let me forestall any misunderstanding. "Irrational" in no way means "sentimental." To choose a woman for wife is not to say to Miss So-and-So: "You are the ideal of my dreams, you more than gratify all my desires, you are the Iseult altogether lovely and desirable—and endowed with a suitable dowry—of whom I want to be the Tristan." For this would be deceit, and nothing enduring can be founded on deceit. Nobody in the world can gratify me; no sooner were I gratified than I would change! To choose a woman for a wife is to say to Miss So-and-So: "I want to live with you just as you are." For this really means: "It is you I choose *to share* my life with me, and that is the only *evidence* there can be that I love you." If anybody says, "Is that all?"—and this is no doubt what many young people will say, having been led by virtue of the myth to expect goodness knows what divine transports—he must have had little experience of solitariness and dread, little experience indeed of solitary dread.

Alone a decision of this kind, irrational but not sentimental, sober but in no way cynical, can serve as the basis for a real fidelity; and I do not say: "A fidelity that will prove a recipe for 'happiness'"; I only say: "A feasible fidelity, because it is not being wrecked at birth by some necessarily inaccurate calculation."

FREE
ABORTION
ON DEMAND
NO FORCED
STERILIZATION
WAYNE WOMEN'S
LIBERATION

THE STORK
IS A DIRTY
BIRD

FREE
ABORTION
ON DEMAND
NO FORCED
STERILIZATION
WAYNE WOMEN'S
LIBERATION

free our
sisters
free ourselves

FREE
ABORTION
AND
CED
TION
EN'S
N

SISTERHOOD
IS
POWERFUL

Never to Laugh or Love

ABORTION

ABORTION
IS KILLING

thisisb

The Pro and Con of Abortion. *Women demanding the right to "biological self-determination" march in Lansing, Michigan, in March, 1971. In New York, a child attends an anti-abortion stand in September, 1973.*

4

_____

ABORTION

The subject of abortion is used in this unit as an example of an activity that has been thrust forward as a pressing moral issue largely as a result of moral change. This change has itself been accelerated by changing social and technological conditions. Since the mid-nineteenth century, abortions have been severely censured in Europe and America. Of course, abortions were performed during this period but "on the sly" because of the prevailing moral opinion. In England and America, as well as in the Catholic countries of Europe, abortion had so few advocates that it was not an open subject of value conflict; it was not, therefore, an "issue."

More recently, a number of social and technological conditions have developed—some of which John Noonan discusses later in this chapter—that may well have had the effect of increasing support for abortion. These include, for example, the decline of infant mortality, the great growth of population, the development and spread of more effective means of birth control, and the lessened opposition to premarital sex. Each of these developments may be easily adopted as a basis of a moral argument favoring abortion. Of course, such an argument in favor of abortion does not require reference to these conditions or support from them; the argument may stand in its own right.

The lead article is by Daniel Callahan, who believes that women have the moral right to choose an abortion. He is concerned, however, that women may view their moral responsibility for such a decision far too lightly and, therefore, abuse that right.

Next, the Catholic church's opposition to abortion—an opposition that has historically been supported by Judaism as well—is forcefully defended by George Williams. Not himself a Catholic, Williams wishes to "enlist as many Christian allies as possible" on the side of the church. He argues that, after the issue of peace, abortion (along with euthanasia) constitutes "the major moral issue of our society."

Then follows an attack on the Catholic view

on abortion, put forward by Robert Hall. He indicates how isolated the church is in our society in its opposition to abortion and points out that legally the fetus is not a person.

Next in this chapter comes the prevailing law on abortion in the United States. The famous 1973 Supreme Court decision, *Roe v. Wade,* established that abortion in the first trimester of pregnancy is exclusively a private matter, to be decided by the patient and her attending physician.

The views of one attending physician are presented by Bernard Nathanson, an American doctor who had been, from 1969 to 1972, a leading advocate for the repeal of antiabortion laws. He is now having second, very painful thoughts over his involvement with abortions: He notes with increasing certainty that he had, "in fact, presided over 60,000 deaths."

The remaining pieces in this chapter are contemporary philosophic examinations of the morality of abortion. With great cogency, John Noonan argues that social changes, including "the trend to reject all codes of morality" and "the trend to control one's environment and life through rational planning," are behind the wide acceptance that abortion has won among "educated American opinion." In conclusion, he refers to the "stumbling block" that all supporters of abortion must face: "the right to life of another person." Vigorous arguments in support of abortion, he claims, must argue that the fetus is not a human being.

The next selection is by Judith Thomson who joins issue immediately and asserts precisely that. A fetus, she writes, is no more a person than an acorn is an oak tree. She then proceeds to argue that even were it conceded that a fetus is a person from conception, abortion would still be permissible. This argument rests on the claim that a woman has "unqualified rights" over her own body.

The excerpt by Thomson deals mainly with the case for abortion when the mother's life is endangered by the continuation of her pregnancy; another situation, in which it is known that the fetus is genetically defective, is considered in the next pair of articles. Leon Kass concludes that he cannot provide "a satisfactory intellectual and moral justification for the practice of genetic abortion." In contrast, Henry David Aiken argues that "where there exists no possibility of anything approaching a truly human life," the right to biological life loses its *raison d'être,* and the claims of other family members must take precedence.

In the following selection, Garrett Hardin suggests that the real question regarding abortion is not "How can we justify abortion?" but "How can we justify compulsory pregnancy?" His answer: "By no means whatever."

In the final article, an intermediate position—which appears to be in accord with the Supreme Court decision—is staked out by Sissela Bok. She believes that women have "unqualified rights" to choose to abort while early in their term of pregnancy; later in term, however, abortion becomes infanticide—to which, she argues, no one has the right.

(For other issues regarding genetics and the ethics of medicine and biological research, see Chapter 12.)

NOTES ABOUT THE AUTHORS

Daniel Callahan, born in 1930, is director of the Institute of Society, Ethics and the Life Sciences, which he founded in 1969. From 1961 to 1969 he was executive editor of *Commonweal* magazine. He has held several academic appointments, and he is a consultant on medical ethics to the Judicial Council of the American Medical Association. The recipient of the Thomas More Medal for *Abortion: Law, Choice and Morality* (1970), excerpted here, he has written and edited many other books and articles, including *The Tyranny of Survival* and *Ethics and Population Limitation.*

George Hunston Williams, an ordained minister in the Unitarian and Congregational churches, was born in Ohio in 1914. He has been on the faculty of the Harvard Divinity School since 1947 and Hollis Professor of Divinity there since 1963. He is past chairman of the Governor's Commission on Birth Control and past president of Christian Action: Americans United for Life. His works include *The Last Catholic Modernist.* "The No. 2 Moral Issue of Today" was written in 1967 and appeared originally in *America.*

Robert E. Hall, born in 1924, was associate professor of obstetrics and gynecology at the Columbia-Presbyterian Medical Center in New York until 1973, when he entered the field of psychiatry. President of the Association for the Study of Abortion since it was founded in 1964, he has written extensively on the subject in addition to editing the two-volume work, *Abortion in a Changing World.* "Abortion—A Non-Catholic View" was first published in 1968.

Roe **v.** *Wade* was a landmark case decided by the United States Supreme Court on January 22, 1973. The case concerned a Texas statute that restricted legal abortions to those considered necessary to save the woman's life. The Court ruled, seven to two, that the statute was a violation of the right to privacy. The majority opinion was written by Justice Harry A. Blackmun. In a related case, *Doe* v. *Bolton,* the Court similarly invalidated a Georgia statute that restricted abortions to those necessary for the woman's health, to prevent the birth of a deformed child, or to pregnancies resulting from rape.

Bernard N. Nathanson, born in 1926, received his M.D. from McGill University. He was a lobbyist for New York State's liberal abortion law, passed in 1970. "Deeper into Abortion" originally appeared in the *New England Journal of Medicine* in 1974.

John T. Noonan Jr., born in 1926, received his law degree from Harvard and has also studied at Cambridge University. After practicing law in Boston, he became professor of law at Notre Dame University, and since 1967 he has been on the faculty of the University of California at Berkeley. He was consultant for the Papal Commission on the Family (1965–1966) and is the author of *Contraception: A History of Its Treatment by the Catholic Theologians and Canonists* (1965) and *The Morality of Abortion: Legal and Historical Perspectives* (1970), excerpted in this volume.

Judith Jarvis Thomson teaches philosophy at the Massachusetts Institute of Technology. "A Defense of Abortion" originally appeared in *Philosophy and Public Affairs* in 1971.

Leon R. Kass, a biologist, is Henry R. Luce Professor in the College of the University of Chicago. He formerly served as the Joseph P. Kennedy, Sr. Research Professor in Bioethics at the Kennedy Institute of Georgetown University and as executive secretary of the Committee on the Life Sciences and Sociology Policy, National Research Council of the National Academy of Sciences. He is a founding fellow and member of the board of directors of the Institute of Society, Ethics and the Life Sciences and has published widely in the field of bioethics. "Implications of Prenatal Diagnosis for the Human Right to Life" appeared in *Ethical Issues in Human Genetics* (1973), edited by Bruce Hilton.

Henry David Aiken was born in 1912 and received his doctorate from Harvard. He is Charles Goldman Professor of Philosophy at Brandeis University. Among his best-known works are *The Age of Ideology* (1955), *Reason and Conduct* (1962), and *The Predicament of the University* (1971).

Garrett Hardin is professor of human ecology at the University of California, Santa Barbara. He attracted national attention in 1968 with his essay "The Tragedy of the Commons" in which he called attention to the dangers of unregulated population growth. He is also the author of *Nature and Man's Fate* and *Population and Birth Control.* "Abortion—or Compulsory Pregnancy" originally appeared in *Journal of Marriage and the Family* in 1968 and was reprinted in *Population, Evolution and Birth Control: A Collage of Controversial Ideas,* edited by Hardin. His book, *Mandatory Motherhood: The True Meaning of Right to Life,* expands on this discussion.

Sissela Bok is a fellow of the Institute of Society, Ethics and the Life Sciences and is also a lecturer at the Harvard Medical School. Her article "Ethical Problems of Abortion," excerpted here, originally appeared in the institute's *Hastings Center Studies* in 1974.

DANIEL CALLAHAN

Abortion: Law, choice and morality

The strength of pluralistic societies lies in the personal freedom they afford individuals. One is free to choose among religious, philosophical, ideological, and political creeds; or one can create one's own highly personal, idiosyncratic moral code and view of the universe. Increasingly, the individual is free to ignore the morals, manners and mores of society. The only limitations are upon those actions which seem to present clear and present dangers to the common good, and even there the range of prohibited actions is diminishing as more and more choices are left to personal and private decisions. I have contended that, apart from some regulatory laws, abortion decisions should be left, finally, up to the women themselves. Whatever one may think of the morality of abortion, it cannot be established that it poses a clear and present danger to the common good. Thus society does not have the right decisively to interpose itself between a woman and the abortion she wants. It can only intervene where it can be shown that some of its own interests are at stake *qua* society. Regulatory laws of a minimal kind therefore seem in order, since in a variety of ways . . . society will be affected by the number, kind and quality of legal abortions. In short, with a few important stipulations, what I have been urging is tantamount to saying that abortion decisions should be private decisions. It is to accept, in principle, the contention of those who believe that, in a free, pluralistic society, the woman should be allowed to make her own moral choice on abortion and be allowed to implement that choice.

But pluralistic societies also lay a few traps for the unwary. It is not a large psychological step from saying that individuals should be left free to make up their own minds on some crucial moral issues (of which abortion is one) to an adoption of the view that one personal decision is as good as another, that any decision is a good

one as long as it is honest or sincere, that a free decision equals a correct decision. However short the psychological step, the logical gap is very large. As absence of cant, hypocrisy and coercion may prepare the way for good personal decisions. But that is only to clean the room, and something must then be put in it. The hazard is that, once cleaned, it will be filled with capriciousness, sentimentality, a thinly disguised conformity to the reigning moral taste, or strongly felt but inadequately analyzed moral opinions. This is a particular danger in affluent pluralistic societies, heavily dominated by popular tastes, communication media and the absence of shared values. Philosophically, the view that all values are equally good and all private moral choices on a par is all but dead; but it still has a strong life at the popular level, where there is a tendency to act as if, once personal freedom is legally and socially achieved, moral questions cease to exist. . . .

It is possible to imagine a huge number of situations where a woman could, in good and sensitive conscience, choose abortion as a moral solution to her personal or social difficulties. But, at the very least, the bounds of morality are overstepped when, either through a systematic intellectual negligence or a willful choosing of that moral solution most personally convenient, personal choice is deliberately made easy and problem-free. Yet it seems to me that a pressure in that direction is a growing part of the ethos of technological societies; it is easily possible to find people to reassure us that we need have no scruples about the way we act, whether the issue is war, the suppression of rebellion and revolution, discrimination against minorities or the use of technological advances. Pluralism makes possible the achieving of freer, more subtle moral thinking; but it is a possibility constantly endangered by cultural pressures which would simplify or dissolve moral doubts and anguish.

The question of abortion "indications" returns at the level of personal choice. I have contended that the advent of permissive laws should not mean a cessation of efforts to explore the problem of "indications." When a woman asks herself, as she ought, whether her reasons for wanting an abortion are sound reasons—which presumes abortion is a serious enough moral issue to warrant the need to provide oneself with good reasons for choosing it—she will be asking herself about justifiable indications. . . . [I would argue] that, with the possible exception of exceedingly rare instances of a direct threat to the physical life of the mother, one cannot speak of general categories of abortion indications as *necessitating* an abortion. In a number of circumstances, abortion may be a wise and justifiable solution to a distressed pregnancy. But when the language of necessity is used, the implication is that no other conceivable alternative is available. It may be granted, willingly enough, that some set of practical circumstances in some (possibly very many) concrete cases may indicate that abortion is the only feasible option open. But these cases cannot readily be determined in advance, and, for that reason, it is necessary to say that no formal indication as such (e.g., a psychiatric indication) entails a necessary, predetermined choice in favor of abortion.

The word "indication" remains the best word, suggesting that a number of given circumstances will bring the possibility or desirability of abortion to the fore. But to escalate the concept of an indication into that of a required procedure is to go too far. Abortion is *one* way to solve the problem of an unwanted or hazardous pregnancy (physically, psychologically, economically or socially), but it is rarely the only way, at least in affluent societies (I would be considerably less certain about making the same statement about poor societies). Even in the most extreme cases—rape, incest, psychosis, for instance—alternatives will usually be available and different choices, open. It is not necessarily the end of every woman's chance for a happy, meaningful life to bear an illegitimate child. It is not necessarily the automatic destruction of a family to have a seriously defective child born into it. It is not necessarily the ruination of every family living in overcrowded housing to have still another child. It is not inevitable that every immature woman would become even more so if she bore a child or another child. It is not inevitable that a gravely handicapped child can hope for nothing from

life. It is not inevitable that every unwanted child is doomed to misery. It is not written in the essence of things, as a fixed law of human nature, that a woman cannot come to accept, love and be a good mother to a child who was initially unwanted. Nor is it a fixed law that she could not come to cherish a grossly deformed child. Naturally, these are only generalizations. The point is only that human beings are as a rule flexible, capable of doing more than they sometimes think they can, able to surmount serious dangers and challenges, able to grow and mature, able to transform inauspicious beginnings into satisfactory conclusions. Everything in life, even in procreative and family life, is not fixed in advance; the future is never wholly unalterable.

Yet the problem of personal question-asking must be pushed a step farther. The way the questions are answered will be very much determined by a woman's way of looking at herself and at life. A woman who has decided, as a personal moral policy, that nothing should be allowed to stand in the way of her own happiness, goals and self-interest will have no trouble solving the moral problem. For her, an unwanted pregnancy will, by definition, be a pregnancy to be terminated. But only by a Pickwickian use of words could this form of reasoning be called moral. It would preclude any need to consult the opinion of others, any need to examine the validity of one's own viewpoint, any need to, for instance, ask when human life begins, any need to interrogate oneself in any way, intellectually or morally; will and desire would be king.

Assuming, however, that most women would seek a broader ethical horizon than that of their exclusively personal self-interest, what might they think about when faced with an abortion decision? A respect for the sanctity of human life should, I believe, incline them toward a general and strong bias against abortion. Abortion is an act of killing, the violent, direct destruction of potential human life, already in the process of development. That fact should not be disguised, or glossed over by euphemism and circumlocution. It is not the destruction of a human person—for at no stage of its development does the conceptus fulfill the definition of a person, which implies a developed capacity for reasoning, willing, desiring and relating to others—but it is the destruction of an important and valuable form of human life. Its value and its potentiality are not dependent upon the attitude of the woman toward it; it grows by its own biological dynamism and has a genetic and morphological potential distinct from that of the woman. It has its own distinctive and individual future. If contraception and abortion are both seen as forms of birth limitation, they are distinctly different acts; the former precludes the possibility of a conceptus being formed, while the latter stops a conceptus already in existence from developing. The bias implied by the principle of the sanctity of human life is toward the protection of all forms of human life, especially, in ordinary circumstances, the protection of the right to life. That right should be accorded even to doubtful life; its existence should not be wholly dependent upon the personal self-interest of the woman.

Yet she has her own rights as well, and her own set of responsibilities to those around her; that is why she may have to choose abortion. In extreme situations of overpopulation, she may also have a responsibility for the survival of the species or of a people. In many circumstances, then, a decision in favor of abortion—one which overrides the right to life of that potential human being she carries within—can be a responsible moral decision, worthy neither of the condemnation of others nor of self-condemnation. But the bias of the principle of the sanctity of life is against a routine, unthinking employment of abortion; it bends over backwards not to take life and gives the benefit of the doubt to life. It does not seek to diminish the range of responsibility toward life—potential or actual—but to extend it. It does not seek the narrowest definition of life, but the widest and the richest. It is mindful of individual possibility, on the one hand, and of a destructive human tendency, on the other, to exclude from the category of "the human" or deny rights to those beings whose existence is or could prove burdensome to others. . . .

The goal of these remarks is to keep alive in the consciences of women who have an abortion choice a moral tension; and it is to hope that they will be willing to bear the pain and the uncertainty of having to make a moral choice. It is the automatic, unthinking and unimaginative personal solution of abortion questions which women themselves should be extremely wary of, either for or against an abortion. A woman can, with little trouble, find both people and books to reassure her that there is no problem about abortion at all; or people and books to convince her that she would be a moral monster if she chose abortion. A woman can choose in advance the views she will listen to and thus have her predispositions confirmed. Yet a willingness to keep alive a moral tension, and to be wary of precipitous solutions, presupposes two things. First, that the woman herself wants to do what is right, realizing that what is right may not always be that which is most convenient, most easy or most immediately apt to solve a pressing problem. It is simply not the case that what one wants to do, or would like to do, or is predisposed to do is necessarily the right thing to do. A willingness seriously to entertain that moral perception—which, of course, does not in itself imply a decision for or against an abortion—is one sign of moral seriousness.

Second, moral seriousness presupposes one is concerned with the protection and furthering of life. This means that, out of respect for human life, one bends over backwards not to eliminate human life, not to desensitize oneself to the meaning and value of potential life, not to seek definitions of the "human" which serve one's self-interest only. A desire to respect human life in all of its forms means, therefore, that one voluntarily imposes upon oneself a pressure against the taking of life; that one demands of oneself serious reasons for doing so, even in the case of a very early embryo; that one use not only the mind but also the imagination when a decision is being made; that one seeks not to evade the moral issues but to face them; that one searches out the alternatives and conscientiously entertains them before turning to abortion. A bias in favor of the sanctity of human life in all of its forms would include a bias against abortion on the part of women; it would be the last rather than the first choice when unwanted pregnancies occurred. It would be an act to be avoided if at all possible.

A bias of this kind, voluntarily imposed by a woman upon herself, would not trap her; for it is also part of a respect for the dignity of life to leave the way open for an abortion when other reasonable choices are not available. For she also has duties toward herself, her family and her society. There can be good reasons for taking the life even of a very late fetus; once that also is seen and seen as a counterpoise in particular cases to the general bias against the taking of potential life, the way is open to choose abortion. The bias of the moral policy implies the need for moral rules which seek to preserve life. But, as a policy which leaves room for choice—rather than entailing a fixed set of rules—it is open to flexible interpretation when the circumstances point to the wisdom of taking exception to the normal ordering of the rules in particular cases. Yet, in that case, one is not genuinely taking exception to the rules. More accurately, one would be deciding that, for the preservation or furtherance of other values or rights—species-rights, person-rights—a choice in favor of abortion would be serving the sanctity of life. That there would be, in that case, conflict between rights, with one set of rights set aside (reluctantly) to serve another set, goes without saying. A subversion of the principle occurs when it is made out that there is no conflict and thus nothing to decide.

GEORGE H. WILLIAMS

The no. 2 moral issue of today

I hold that the Catholic Church is engaged at the forefront in a battle for the good of all mankind in its resolute opposition to abortion. In this struggle to preserve—or in many sectors to assert—the rights of unborn children regardless of the stage of gestation, may the Catholic Church enlist as many Christian allies as possible. . . .

The Catholic Church is here defending the very frontier of what constitutes the mystery of our being. At the other end of this front line is the struggle against euthanasia (in the strict and deliberate sense). Unless these frontiers are vigilantly defended, the future is grim with all the prospects of man's cunning and contrived manipulation of himself and others. Next to the issue of peace in the world, I feel the opposition to abortion and euthanasia constitutes the second major moral issue of our society (racial integration and the preservation of the family being third and fourth in the American perspective of priorities). In the cause of defending the rights of the unborn, all Christians should be rallied.

The Catholic position on abortion should not be assailed as "sectarian" or deplored by some Protestants as "too harsh" in the present ecumenical climate. Historically, the position is in fact Judeo-Christian. In antiquity, Christians clearly set themselves apart from the Greco-Roman paganism about them in their responsible sexual behavior and in their condemnation of infanticide and abortion. . . .

Christians, who have lived by the parable of the tiny mustard seed (Matt. 13:31 ff.), should be the most alert and sensitive in recognizing the plenitude of meaning in a concerted effort to safeguard the rights of the smallest and weakest—the invisible, the fetal, person at the very inception of his pilgrimage among the children of men.

Because opposition to abortion at any stage is the common line behind which all *faithfully* Christian and Jewish forces could, or at least should, be arrayed at this moment in the evolution of American society, I regret that Pope Paul has not yet been able to ascertain a moral solution to the problem of birth control within the context of natural law and scriptural-credal theological ethics. I regret it, because we are confronted by the wholly unprecedented problem of a technologically based population explosion and *our* generation's disproportionate exploitation of the earth's reserves heedless of the rights of future generations to the use of the world as God created it for us and all other creatures.

Surely as scriptural as the divine injunction to

be fruitful and multiply (Gen. 1:28) is the divine assignment laid upon man to be the steward of God's creation, e.g., Adam in Gen. 2:19ff. and Noah in Gen. 7. The time has come when man collectively must take thought of other creatures, and of the world, and of the preservation of sheer space and the myriad bounties of creation amid which human life can be fulfilled in dignity and family solidarity. . . .

The Church extends her protective concern to the natural resources of the world and to all its variegated forms of life. . . . Unlike men who selfishly exploit the world's resources and do not think of the oncoming generations, Christians are aware of their accountability for their stewardship of creation, all the more urgently now as they take command of the earth, and the sky, and the seas about them. With the technological elevation of man to his new estate, increasingly master of himself and his environment, the whole of creation groans in travail with him, waiting for the revealing of the sons of God (cf. Rom. 7:19, 22).

As you see, I feel that there is a close Christian connection between conservation of the world's resources and the problem of population explosion. In the realm of *voluntary* population control and family planning, we are dealing with life that might be—and, at our best, we are thinking of the good of unborn generations. In contrast, in the realm of abortion we are dealing with human life already unfolding in the womb. Here we confront the inviolability of the right of a person *in parvo*.* Here there can be no invasion of the right of this invisible, inarticulate person unless another moral principle of comparable magnitude in terms of life and death contravenes.

Accordingly, except 1) where conception by demonstrable rape has violated the right and dignity of the woman as a person, 2) where by incest "a biological crime" has been committed, whether by mutual consent or victimization, and 3) where a woman has unwittingly contracted a fatal burden, every human being formed in the womb has the right of access to the world with all the protection a civilized society can afford.

Ed. note: In miniature.

84

For all other pregnancies, besides the three above specified, there is at least the consent of mutual passion; and therefore the mother must be required and, if socially necessary, aided to bear her child; and the child conceived, whether in or out of wedlock, whether in a rich or an impoverished home, must have the full protection of society's laws.

For those defective pregnancies for which society is sometimes indirectly responsible through miscalculations of its regulatory agencies in the realm of drugs and medicine, society at large . . . should bear some or all of the burden of its stringent upholding of a basically humane law: either by subvention of families afflicted by sadness at a birth or by full custodial care of defective offspring beyond the competence of a parent to sustain it.

This is the kind of burden society must assume in its defense of the equality of all persons before the law. That same society should, at the same time, be unhampered in its vigilant efforts to reduce the incidences of defective births by all means that do not violate the basic human rights of all concerned.

ROBERT E. HALL

Abortion: A non-Catholic view

Until 1803 in the Western world, abortion before quickening (in the fourth or fifth month of pregnancy) was proscribed by neither religion nor law. In the East, meanwhile, infanticide was widely practiced and condoned. Not until 1861 was early abortion forbidden in England, as an Offense against the Person; not until 1869 was early abortion equated with murder by the Roman Catholic Church; not until 1835 was the first anti-early-abortion law passed in the United States (by Missouri); and not until 1943 the last such state law (by North Dakota). . . .

The position of the Roman Catholic Church rests upon its modern-day assumption that the fetus is a human being and its destruction murder. (Bear in mind that, with the exception of a three-year period in the sixteenth century, the Church did not equate abortion and murder till 1869.) Scientifically, of course, the fetus is not a human being for the simple reason that it cannot survive, even with outside help. An infant can survive with the help of an adult, an adult can survive on its own, but the fetus is dependent upon its mother's womb.

Legally, of course, the fetus is not a human being either. It cannot inherit, it cannot sue; upon extrusion from the womb it is not entitled to a birth or death certificate; and the abortionist is not charged with murder or punished as a murderer. Semantically, of course, feticide, infanticide, homicide, and suicide are explicit terms with fundamentally different meanings. Theologically, abortion for the reasons proposed by the American Law Institute* is sanctioned by most major non-Catholic religious groups. These groups obviously do not regard the fetus as a human being.

If the Catholic Church chooses empirically to disagree with science, law, semantics, and the other religions, this is of course the Church's prerogative. But for the Church imperiously to impose its unique position upon the rest of society is to defy the fundamental separation of Church and State.

Those of us who seek reform do not intend to force abortions upon those who do not want them. Why, then, must the majority who want reform be thwarted by the minority who do not?

If you regard the fetus as a potential human being rather than an actual human being, and if you examine abortion logically and thoroughly in this light, you must, I contend, ultimately reach the conclusion that all voluntary abortion is permissible. When a pregnant woman decides that she wants an abortion, who is qualified to deny her this right? To allow her this right only if her health is jeopardized or her fetus endangered is to endow the medical profession with

omniscience it does not possess. Ultimately, then, abortion must be the right of every woman.

Roe v. Wade

To summarize and to repeat:

1. A state criminal abortion statute of the current Texas type, that excepts from criminality only a *life-saving* procedure on behalf of the mother, without regard to pregnancy stage and without recognition of the other interests involved, is violative of the Due Process Clause of the Fourteenth Amendment.

(a) For the stage prior to approximately the end of the first trimester, the abortion decision and its effectuation must be left to the medical judgment of the pregnant woman's attending physician.

(b) For the stage subsequent to approximately the end of the first trimester, the State, in promoting its interest in the health of the mother, may, if it chooses, regulate the abortion procedure in ways that are reasonably related to maternal health.

(c) For the stage subsequent to viability, the State in promoting its interest in the potentiality of human life may, if it chooses, regulate, and even proscribe, abortion except where it is necessary, in appropriate medical judgment, for the preservation of the life or health of the mother.

2. The State may define the term "physician," as it has been employed in the preceding paragraphs of this . . . opinion, to mean only a physician currently licensed by the State, and may proscribe any abortion by a person who is not a physician as so defined.

In *Doe v. Bolton, post,* procedural requirements contained in one of the modern abortion statutes are considered. That opinion and this one, of course, are to be read together.

This holding, we feel, is consistent with the relative weights of the respective interests in-

---

Ed. note: "A licensed physician believes that there is substantial risk that continuance of the pregnancy would gravely impair the physical or mental health of the mother or that the child would be born with grave physical or mental defect, or the pregnancy resulted from rape . . . or from incest."

volved, with the lessons and examples of medical and legal history, with the lenity of the common law, and with the demands of the profound problems of the present day. The decision leaves the State free to place increasing restrictions on abortion as the period of pregnancy lengthens, so long as those restrictions are tailored to the recognized state interests. The decision vindicates the right of the physician to administer medical treatment according to his professional judgment up to the points where important state interests provide compelling justifications for intervention. Up to those points, the abortion decision in all its aspects is inherently, and primarily, a medical decision, and basic responsibility for it must rest with the physician. If an individual practitioner abuses the privilege of exercising proper medical judgment, the usual remedies, judicial and intra-professional, are available.

BERNARD N. NATHANSON

Deeper into abortion

In early 1969 I and a group of equally concerned and indignant citizens who had been outspoken on the subject of legalized abortion organized a political action unit known as NARAL—then standing for National Association for Repeal of Abortion Laws, now known as the National Abortion Rights Action League. We were outspokenly militant on this matter and enlisted the women's movement and the Protestant clergy into our ranks. We used every device available to political-action groups such as pamphleteering, public demonstrations, exploitation of the media and lobbying in the appropriate legislative chambers. In late 1969 we mounted a demonstration outside one of the major university hospitals in New York City that had refused to perform even therapeutic abortions. My wife was on that picket line, and my three-year-old son proudly carried a placard urging legalized abortion for all. Largely as a result of the ef-

forts of this and a few similar groups, the monumental New York State Abortion Statute of 1970 was passed and signed into law by Governor Nelson Rockefeller. Our next goal was to assure ourselves that low cost, safe and humane abortions were available to all, and to that end we established the Center for Reproductive and Sexual Health, which was the first—and largest—abortion clinic in the Western world. . . .

Some time ago—after a tenure of a year and a half—I resigned as director of the Center for Reproductive and Sexual Health. The Center had performed 60,000 abortions with no maternal deaths—an outstanding record of which we are proud. However, I am deeply troubled by my own increasing certainty that I had in fact presided over 60,000 deaths.

There is no longer serious doubt in my mind that human life exists within the womb from the very onset of pregnancy, despite the fact that the nature of the intrauterine life has been the subject of considerable dispute in the past. Electrocardiographic evidence of heart function has been established in embryos as early as six weeks. Electroencephalographic recordings of human brain activity have been noted in embryos at eight weeks. Our capacity to measure signs of life is daily becoming more sophisticated, and as time goes by, we will doubtless be able to isolate life signs at earlier and earlier stages in fetal development.

The Harvard Criteria for the pronouncement of death assert that if the subject is unresponsive to external stimuli (e.g., pain), if the deep reflexes are absent, if there are no spontaneous movements or respiratory efforts, if the electroencephalogram reveals no activity of the brain, one may conclude that the patient is dead. If any or all of these criteria are absent—and the fetus does respond to pain, makes respiratory efforts, moves spontaneously, and has electroencephalographic activity—life must be present.

To those who cry that nothing can be human life that cannot exist independently, I ask if the patient totally dependent for his life on treatments by the artificial kidney twice weekly is alive? Is the person with chronic cardiac disease, solely dependent for his life on the tiny batteries on his pacemaker, alive? Would my life be safe in this city without my eyeglasses?

Life is an interdependent phenomenon for us all. It is a continuous spectrum that begins in utero and ends at death—the bands of the spectrum are designated by words such as fetus, infant, child, adolescent, and adult.

We must courageously face the fact—finally—that human life of a special order is being taken. And since the vast majority of pregnancies are carried successfully to term, abortion must be seen as the interruption of a process that would otherwise have produced a citizen of the world. Denial of this reality is the crassest kind of moral evasiveness.

The fierce militants of the Woman's Liberation evade this issue and assert that the woman's right to bear or not to bear children is her absolute right. On the other hand the ferocious Right-to-Life legions proclaim no rights for the woman and absolute rights for the fetus.

But these "rights" that are held to be so obvious and so undeniable are highly suspect. None of us have "rights" that go beyond the inter-related life that is our common heritage on this planet. Our "rights" exist only because others around us care enough about us to see to it that we have them. They have no other source. They result from no other cause.

Somewhere in the vast philosophic plateau between the two implacably opposed camps—past the slogans, past the pamphlets, past even the demonstrations and the legislative threats—lies the infinitely agonizing truth. We are taking life, and the deliberate taking of life, even of a special order and under special circumstances, is an inexpressibly serious matter.

Somehow, we must not deny the pervasive sense of loss that should accompany abortion and its most unfortunate interruption of life. We must not coarsen our sensitivities through common practice and brute denial.

I offer no panacea. Certainly, the medical profession itself cannot shoulder the burden of this matter. The phrase "between a woman and her physician" is an empty one since the physician is only the instrument of her decision, and has no special knowledge of the moral dilemma or the ethical agony involved in the decision. Furthermore, there are seldom any purely medical indications for abortion. The decision is the most serious responsibility a woman can experience in her lifetime, and at present it is hers alone.

Can there be no help for the pregnant woman bearing the incalculable weight of this moral tension? Perhaps we could make available to her—though it should by no means be mandatory—a consultative body of unique design. . . . To meet the new moral challenges of the abortion decision, we may very well need specialists, some of new kinds, to serve on such a body—a psychohistorian, a human ecologist, a medical philosopher, an urbanologist-clergyman. The counseling that such a body could offer a pregnant woman would be designed to bring the whole sweep of human experience to bear on the decision—not just the narrow partisanship of committed young women who have had abortions and who typically staff the counselor ranks of hospitals and clinics now.

My concern is increased by the fact that the sloganeers, with their righteous pontifications and their undisguised desires to assert power over others, have polarized American reactions into dimly understood but tenaciously held positions. The din that has arisen in our land has already created an atmosphere in which it is difficult, if not impossible, for the individual to see the issues clearly and to reach an understanding free from the taint of the last shibboleth that was screamed in her ear.

Our sense of values has always placed the greatest importance upon the value of life itself. With a completely permissive legal climate for abortion (and I believe that we must have such a climate—that abortion must be unregulated by law) there is a danger that society will lose a certain moral tension that has been a vital part of its fabric. In pursuing a course of unlimited and uncontrolled abortion over future years, we must not permit ourselves to sink to a debased level of utilitarian semiconsciousness.

I plead for an honest, clear-eyed consideration of the abortion dilemma—an end to blind polarity. We have had enough screaming placards and mindless marches. The issue is human life, and it deserves the reverent stillness and ineffably grave thought appropriate to it.

We must work together to create a moral climate rich enough to provide for abortion, but sensitive enough to life to accommodate a profound sense of loss.

JOHN T. NOONAN

The morality of abortion

Educated American opinion today accords an acceptance to abortion which even a decade ago it did not enjoy. Estimates of its actual practice in America vary enormously; the highest plausible projection is 1000 percent greater than the lowest; and the range of probable error is too extreme to permit confidence in the guesses made. But the shift in influential sentiment is palpable. Respectable, serious, committed persons have contended that the planned termination of pregnancy has a social utility and humane character not appreciated by earlier generations. Response to these contentions among groups likely to determine attitudes toward abortion has ranged from benevolent tolerance to passionate conviction. Abortion, once regarded as a secret and loathsome crime, a medical disaster, or a tragic manifestation of human weakness, has been justified by the draftsmen of the American Law Institute, defended by the American Medical Association, applauded by the American Public Health Association, championed by Planned Parenthood–World Population, and publicized by the *New York Times*. . . .

What gave the demand [for abortion] wings was the population problem. . . .

The view of the world as a whole, or parts of the world, or the American way of life, all being overwhelmed by an increase of human beings, generated enormous interest in ways to curb the danger. . . .

Until the 1960s, "birth control," promoted as a way of restricting population, was more accurately described as "conception control."

Official literature of the planned parenthood associations stressed contraception as a way of avoiding both birth and abortion. It became apparent, however, that known means of contraception—[coitus interruptus, diaphragms, and progesterone pills]—were unsatisfactory to achieve a reduction of population growth in many areas. . . . For poor, little-educated, slightly motivated persons, none of these methods was highly desirable or efficient. The one spectacular success in meeting a population problem was Japan's reduction of growth, and this success was achieved less by contraceptive means than by the massive spread of abortion. The most efficient mechanism for preventing reproduction was the intrauterine device or I.U.D.; and uncertainty continued to exist as to whether it prevented fertilization or implantation; its status as contraceptive or abortifacient was arguable. Technological developments and the limited effectiveness of unquestionably contraceptive means thus combined to make devotion to contraception alone appear as a kind of fetish, indefensible and inexplicable except by reference to the history of thought about abortion. In 1968, Planned Parenthood–World Population publicly changed its stand and endorsed abortion as a means of population control. The action marked formally a transition which had already occurred. Abortion was now put forward as a rational solution to the crises connected with population growth.

Without the appeal to a serious public larger than the membership of a single profession, and without the zeal of a dedicated organization, the efforts of physicians to obtain professional autonomy would have had no great impact. Together, the divergent interests of physicians and those concerned with population control brought disciplined power to bear upon the abortion statutes and effectively spread a message favorable to abortion through the American communications media of newspapers, magazines, and television. Yet educated opinion could not so swiftly have been swayed toward an acceptance of abortion by organizational tactics alone. This opinion responded because the appeal addressed to it touched two deep contemporary currents: the trend to reject all codes of morality as exterior, authoritarian, and absolute, above all, to reject sexual codes as the most odious; and the trend to control one's environment and life through rational planning.

The desire to be free of a code of morality fed on a distrust of any abstract formulation of an "absolute," a conviction that many such formulations in the past had actually harmed human beings, and a disbelief in the existence of any authority capable of promulgating universal rules. Translated into practical judgment, this viewpoint perceived every law restricting sexual behavior as an arbitrary imposition of another's will on the sacred sphere of personal liberty. Statutes regulating abortion fell within this global rejection. Such statutes meant that intercourse between the sexes could not be engaged in freely without preparation unless a woman was willing to risk being forced to bear a child. Justifications for such statutes could not interest those who saw in their necessary effect an affront to a liberty especially prized. . . . A rational purpose for the statutes was even difficult to imagine. Although ancient law made by male-dominated societies had maintained that the fetus was part of the woman, and modern tort law had just recognized the fetus' independence, the American statutes were often pictured as made by men and animated by a special misogyny, as though a conspiracy against womankind had designed the punishment of the risk of pregnancy as a condition for coitus. Unrestricted access to contraceptives was not enough to remove the curse of the law. . . . A sure means of "backstopping" omissions or errors was necessary. In a society where all other legal restrictions on adult heterosexual relations had been repealed or abandoned, the existence of laws exacting the possibility of uninterrupted pregnancy as the price of natural intercourse appeared as an unbelievable anachronism. Not accidentally de Sade had been the first Western champion of the right and pleasures of abortion. Abortion was necessary if sexual revolution was to succeed.

Paradoxically, the desire to be free from external control imposed by another's code did not conflict with the desire to control one's circumstances through planning. The desires were reconcilable if the planning was done by the individual himself. With every technological advance, with every step in the mastery of the environment, the wish not to be subject to irrational accident, the wish to determine one's future, became stronger. To have one's energy and resources dissipated, one's plans spoiled, by a pregnancy that it lay in one's power to end seemed senseless self-denial. Viewed as a technique available at the personal option of a woman, abortion maximized both freedom and planning. . . .

A child who was not planned was spoken of as "an accident." The comprehensive category of "unwanted children" was created. Abortion, then, appeared as the surgically certain way of eliminating accidents, the completely effective way of preventing unwanted children. Through abortion the individual's control of the consequences of his sexual freedom was affirmed.

The desire for professional autonomy and the desire for efficient means to control population had given focus to forces in the culture wider than the special aims of organized groups. Converging, the desire for sexual autonomy and the desire for rational planning of one's future combined to shape the American response. College students, journalists, lawyers, physicians, professors, and opinion-makers came to share the attitude that abortion was acceptable. . . .

The stumbling block for those who reject abortion is the limit which the most humane, most libertarian, most autonomous of ethics must set: the right to life of another person. Absolute abstractions may be impossible, misleading, or harmful to human welfare; but the life of another person is not an abstraction. Belief in a transcendent source of authority and sanctity may be required for reverence toward those regarded as the image of God; but simple coexistence with other humans demands that the lives of some not be open to sacrifice for the welfare and convenience of others. If man can be recognized at all in the multiple forms of humanity, the notion of man necessitates respect for the human person's right to live. One person's freedom to obtain an abortion is the denial of another person's right to live.

To answer that the fetus is not human is to join issue. Proponents of abortion, for the most part, have not cared to make this contact with their opponents. In the appeal to principle, they have seen an obscurantism originating in religious dogma. For them, in this context at any rate, the question, "What is a man?" need not be answered. They are content to bypass what strikes them as fruitless speculation of a metaphysical sort. The relativity of morals, the subjectivity of knowledge, the lack of agreement on ethical principle, all these cautionary epistemological axioms, are deployed to turn off discussion of abortion by those who pronounce with conviction on the morality of war, the rights of conscientious objectors, and the wrong of capital punishment. In not responding when the question of humanity is raised in relation to abortion, they make their own decision as to who is human. "How long can a man turn his head and pretend that he just doesn't see?"

JUDITH JARVIS THOMSON

A defense of abortion

Most opposition to abortion relies on the premise that the fetus is a human being, a person, from the moment of conception. The premise is argued for, but, as I think, not well. Take, for example, the most common argument. We are asked to notice that the development of a human being from conception through birth into childhood is continuous; then it is said that to draw a line, to choose a point in this development and say "before this point the thing is not a person, after this point it is a person" is to make an arbitrary choice, a choice for which in the nature of things no good reason can be given. It is concluded that the fetus is, or anyway that we had better say it is, a person from the moment of conception. But this conclusion does not follow. Similar things might be said about the develop-

ment of an acorn into an oak tree, and it does not follow that acorns are oak trees, or that we had better say they are. Arguments of this form are sometimes called "slippery slope arguments"— the phrase is perhaps self-explanatory—and it is dismaying that opponents of abortion rely on them so heavily and uncritically.

I am inclined to agree, however, that the prospects for "drawing a line" in the development of the fetus look dim. I am inclined to think also that we shall probably have to agree that the fetus has already become a human person well before birth. Indeed, it comes as a surprise when one first learns how early in its life it begins to acquire human characteristics. By the tenth week, for example, it already has a face, arms and legs, fingers and toes; it has internal organs, and brain activity is detectable. On the other hand, I think that the premise is false, that the fetus is not a person from the moment of conception. A newly fertilized ovum, a newly implanted clump of cells, is no more a person than an acorn is an oak tree. But I shall not discuss any of this. For it seems to me to be of great interest to ask what happens if, for the sake of argument, we allow the premise. How, precisely, are we supposed to get from there to the conclusion that abortion is morally impermissible? Opponents of abortion commonly spend most of their time establishing that the fetus is a person, and hardly any time explaining the step from there to the impermissibility of abortion. Perhaps they think the step too simple and obvious to require much comment. Or perhaps instead they are simply being economical in argument. Many of those who defend abortion rely on the premise that the fetus is not a person, but only a bit of tissue that will become a person at birth; and why pay out more arguments than you have to? Whatever the explanation, I suggest that the step they take is neither easy nor obvious, that it calls for closer examination than it is commonly given, and that when we do give it this closer examination we shall feel inclined to reject it.

I propose, then, that we grant that the fetus is a person from the moment of conception. How does the argument go from here? Something like this, I take it. Every person has a right to life. So the fetus has a right to life. No doubt the mother has a right to decide what shall happen in and to her body; everyone would grant that. But surely a person's right to life is stronger and more stringent than the mother's right to decide what happens in and to her body, and so outweighs it. So the fetus may not be killed; an abortion may not be performed.

It sounds plausible. But now let me ask you to imagine this. You wake up in the morning and find yourself back to back in bed with an unconscious violinist. A famous unconscious violinist. He has been found to have a fatal kidney ailment, and the Society of Music Lovers has canvassed all the available medical records and found that you alone have the right blood type to help. They have therefore kidnapped you, and last night the violinist's circulatory system was plugged into yours, so that your kidneys can be used to extract poisons from his blood as well as your own. The director of the hospital now tells you, "Look, we're sorry the Society of Music Lovers did this to you—we would never have permitted it if we had known. But still, they did it, and the violinist now is plugged into you. To unplug you would be to kill him. But never mind, it's only for nine months. By then he will have recovered from his ailment, and can safely be unplugged from you." Is it morally incumbent on you to accede to this situation? No doubt it would be very nice of you if you did, a great kindness. But do you *have* to accede to it? What if it were not nine months, but nine years? Or longer still? What if the director of the hospital says, "Tough luck, I agree, but you've now got to stay in bed, with the violinist plugged into you, for the rest of your life. Because remember this. All persons have a right to life, and violinists are persons. Granted you have a right to decide what happens in and to your body, but a person's right to life outweighs your right to decide what happens in and to your body. So you cannot ever be unplugged from him." I imagine you would regard this as outrageous, which suggests that something really is wrong with that plausible-sounding argument I mentioned a moment ago.

In this case, of course, you were kidnapped, you didn't volunteer for the operation that plugged the violinist into your kidneys. Can those who oppose abortion on the ground I mentioned make an exception for a pregnancy due to rape? Certainly. They can say that persons have a right to life only if they didn't come into existence because of rape; or they can say that all persons have a right to life, but that some have less of a right to life than others, in particular, that those who came into existence because of rape have less. But these statements have a rather unpleasant sound. Surely the question of whether you have a right to life at all, or how much of it you have, shouldn't turn on the question of whether or not you are the product of a rape. And in fact the people who oppose abortion on the ground I mentioned do not make this distinction, and hence do not make an exception in case of rape.

Nor do they make an exception for a case in which the mother has to spend the nine months of her pregnancy in bed. . . . I suspect, in fact, that they would not make an exception for a case in which, miraculously enough, the pregnancy went on for nine years, or even the rest of the mother's life.

Some won't even make an exception for a case in which continuation of the pregnancy is likely to shorten the mother's life; they regard abortion as impermissible even to save the mother's life. Such cases are nowadays very rare, and many opponents of abortion do not accept this extreme view. All the same, it is a good place to begin: a number of points of interest come out in respect to it.

Let us call the view that abortion is impermissible even to save the mother's life "the extreme view." I want to suggest first that it does not issue from the argument I mentioned earlier without the addition of some fairly powerful premises. Suppose a woman has become pregnant, and now learns that she has a cardiac condition such that she will die if she carries the baby to term. What may be done for her? The fetus, being a person, has a right to life, but as the mother is a person too, so has she a right to life. Presumably they have an equal right to life. How is it supposed to come out that an abortion may not be performed? If mother and child have an equal right to life, shouldn't we perhaps flip a coin? Or should we add to the mother's right to life her right to decide what happens in and to her body, which everybody seems to be ready to grant—the sum of her rights now outweighing the fetus' right to life?

The most familiar argument here is the following. We are told that performing the abortion would be directly killing the child, whereas doing nothing would not be killing the mother, but only letting her die. Moreover, in killing the child, one would be killing an innocent person, for the child has committed no crime, and is not aiming at his mother's death. And then there are a variety of ways in which this might be continued. (1) But as directly killing an innocent person is always and absolutely impermissible, an abortion may not be performed. Or, (2) as directly killing an innocent person is murder, and murder is always and absolutely impermissible, an abortion may not be performed. Or, (3) as one's duty to refrain from directly killing an innocent person is more stringent than one's duty to keep a person from dying, an abortion may not be performed. Or, (4) if one's only options are directly killing an innocent person or letting a person die, one must prefer letting the person die, and thus an abortion may not be performed.

Some people seem to have thought that these are not further premises which must be added if the conclusion is to be reached, but that they follow from the very fact that an innocent person has a right to life. But this seems to me to be a mistake, and perhaps the simplest way to show this is to bring out that while we must certainly grant that innocent persons have a right to life, the theses in (1) through (4) are all false. Take (2), for example. If directly killing an innocent person is murder, and thus is impermissible, then the mother's directly killing the innocent person inside her is murder, and thus is impermissible. But it cannot seriously be thought to be murder if the mother performs an abortion on herself to save her life. It cannot seriously be said that she *must* refrain, that she *must* sit passively by and wait for her death. Let us look again at the case of you and the violinist. There you are, in bed with the violinist, and the director of the hospital says to you, "It's all most distressing, and I deeply sympathize, but you see this is putting an additional strain on your kidneys, and you'll be dead within the month. But you *have* to stay where you are all the same. Because unplugging you would be directly killing an innocent violinist, and that's murder, and that's impermissible." If anything in the world is true, it is that you do not commit murder, you do not do what is impermissible, if you reach around to your back and unplug yourself from that violinist to save your life. . . .

Suppose you find yourself trapped in a tiny house with a growing child. I mean a very tiny house, and a rapidly growing child—you are already up against the wall of the house and in a few minutes you'll be crushed to death. The child on the other hand won't be crushed to death; if nothing is done to stop him from growing he'll be hurt, but in the end he'll simply burst open the house and walk out a free man. Now I could well understand it if a bystander were to say, "There's nothing we can do for you. We cannot choose between your life and his, we cannot be the ones to decide who is to live, we cannot intervene." But it cannot be concluded that you too can do nothing, that you cannot attack it to save your life. However innocent the child may be, you do not have to wait passively while it crushes you to death. Perhaps a pregnant woman is vaguely felt to have the status of house, to which we don't allow the right of self-defense. But if the woman houses the child, it should be remembered that she is a person who houses it.

I should perhaps stop to say explicitly that I am not claiming that people have a right to do anything whatever to save their lives. I think, rather, that there are drastic limits to the right of self-defense. If someone threatens you with death unless you torture someone else to death, I think you have not the right, even to save your life, to do so. But the case under consideration here is very different. In our case there are only two people involved, one whose life is threatened, and one who threatens it. Both are innocent: the one who is threatened is not threatened because of any fault, the one who threatens does not threaten because of any fault. For this reason we may feel that we bystanders cannot intervene. But the person threatened can.

In sum, a woman surely can defend her life against the threat to it posed by the unborn child, even if doing so involves its death. And this shows not merely that the theses in (1) through (4) are false; it shows also that the extreme view of abortion is false, and so we need not canvass any other possible ways of arriving at it from the argument I mentioned at the outset.

LEON R. KASS

Implications of prenatal diagnosis for the human right to life

According to what standards can and should we judge a fetus with genetic abnormalities unfit to live, i.e., abortable? It seems to me that there are at least three dominant standards to which we are likely to repair.

The first is societal good. The needs and interests of society are often invoked to justify the practices of prenatal diagnosis and abortion of the genetically abnormal. The argument, full blown, runs something like this. Society has an interest in the genetic fitness of its members. It is foolish for society to squander its precious resources ministering to and caring for the unfit, especially for those who will never become "productive," or who will never in any way "benefit" society. Therefore, the interests of society are best served by the elimination of the genetically defective prior to their birth.

The societal standard is all-too-often reduced to its lowest common denominator: money. Thus one physician . . . has written: "Cost-benefit analyses have been made for the total

prospective detection and monitoring of Tay-Sachs disease, cystic fibrosis (when prenatal detection becomes available for cystic fibrosis) and other disorders, and in most cases, the expenditures for hospitalization and medical care far exceed the cost of prenatal detection in properly selected risk populations, followed by selective abortion." . . .

There are many questions that can be raised about this approach. First, there are questions about the accuracy of the calculations. Not all the costs have been reckoned. The aborted defective child will be "replaced" by a "normal" child. In keeping the ledger, the "costs" to society of his care and maintenance cannot be ignored—costs of educating him, or removing his wastes and pollutions, not to mention the "costs" in non-replaceable natural resources that he consumes. Who is a greater drain on society's precious resources, the average inmate of a home for the retarded or the average graduate of Harvard College? I am not sure we know or can even find out. Then there are the costs of training the physician, and genetic counselors, equipping their laboratories, supporting their research, and sending them and us to conferences to worry about what they are doing. An accurate economic analysis seems to me to be impossible, even in principle. And even if it were possible, one could fall back on the words of that ordinary language philosopher, Andy Capp, who, when his wife said that she was getting really worried about the cost of living, replied: "Sweet'eart, name me one person who wants t'stop livin' on account of the cost."

A second defect of the economic analysis is that there are matters of social importance that are not reducible to financial costs, and others that may not be quantifiable at all. How does one quantitate the costs of real and potential social conflict, either between children and parents, or between the community and the "deviants" who refuse amniocentesis and continue to bear abnormal children? Can one measure the effect on racial tensions of attempting to screen for and prevent the birth of children homozygous (or heterozygous) for sickle cell anemia? What numbers does one attach to any decreased willingness or ability to take care of the less fortunate, or to cope with difficult problems? And what about the "costs" of rising expectations? Will we become increasingly dissatisfied with anything short of the "optimum baby"? . . .

Finally, we should take note of the ambiguities in the very notion of societal good. Some use the term "society" to mean their own particular political community, others to mean the whole human race, and still others speak as if they mean both simultaneously, following that all-too-human belief that what is good for me and mine is good for mankind. Who knows what is genetically best for mankind, even with respect to Down's syndrome? . . .

In sum, societal good as a standard for justifying genetic abortion seems to be unsatisfactory. It is hard to define in general, difficult to apply clearly to particular cases, susceptible to overreaching and abuse (hence, very dangerous), and not sufficient unto itself if considerations of the good community are held to be automatically implied. . . .

A second major alternative is the standard of parental or familial good.

Yet there are ambiguities and difficulties perhaps as great as with the standard of societal good. In the first place, it is not entirely clear what would be good for the other children. In a strong family, the experience with a suffering and dying child might help the healthy siblings learn to face and cope with adversity. . . . I suspect that one cannot generalize. In some children and in some families, experience with suffering may be strengthening, and in others, disabling. My point here is that the matter is uncertain, and that parents deciding on this basis are as likely as not to be mistaken.

The family or parental standard, like the societal standard, is unavoidably elastic because "suffering" does not come in discontinuous units, and because parental wishes and desires know no limits. Both are utterly subjective, relative, and notoriously subject to change. . . .

Indeed, the whole idea of parental rights with respect to children strikes me as problematic. It suggests that children are like property, that they exist for the parents. . . .

The justification according to the natural standard might run like this. As a result of our knowledge of genetic diseases, we know that persons afflicted with certain diseases will never be capable of living the full life of a human being. Just as a no-necked giraffe could never live a giraffe's life, or a needle-less porcupine would not attain true "porcupine-hood," so a child or fetus with Tay-Sachs disease or Down's syndrome, for example, will never be truly human. They will never be able to care for themselves, nor have they even the potential for developing the distinctively human capacities for thought or self-consciousness. Nature herself has aborted many similar cases, and has provided for the early death of many who happen to get born. There is no reason to keep them alive; instead, we should prevent their birth by contraception or sterilization if possible, and abortion if necessary.

The advantages of this approach are clear. The standards are objective and in the fetus itself, thus avoiding the relativity and ambiguity in societal and parental good. The standard can be easily generalized to cover all such cases and will be resistant to the shifting sands of public opinion.

This standard, I would suggest, is the one which most physicians and genetic counselors appeal to in their heart of hearts, no matter what they say or do about letting the parents choose. Why else would they have developed genetic counseling and amniocentesis? Indeed, the notions of disease, of abnormal, of defective, make no sense at all in the absence of a natural norm of health. This norm is the foundation of the art of the physician and of the inquiry of the health scientist. . . .

Although possibly acceptable in principle, the natural standard runs into problems in application when attempts are made to fix the boundary between potentially human and potentially not human. . . . Attempts to induce signposts by considering the phenotypes of the worst cases [are] . . . difficult. Which features would we take to be the most relevant in, say, Tay-Sachs disease, Lesch-Nyhan syndrome, Cri du chat, Down's syndrome? Certainly, severe mental retardation. But how "severe" is "severe"? . . . Mental retardation admits of degree. It too is relative. Moreover it is not clear that certain other defects and deformities might not equally foreclose the possibility of a truly or fully human life. What about blindness or deafness? Quadriplegia? Aphasia? Several of these in combination? Not only does each kind of defect admit of a continuous scale of severity, but it also merges with other defects on a continuous scale of defectiveness. Where on this scale is the line to be drawn? after mental retardation? blindness? muscular dystrophy? cystic fibrosis? hemophilia? diabetes? galactosemia? Turner's syndrome? XYY? club foot? Moreover, the identical two continuous scales—kind and severity—are found also among the living. In fact, it is the natural standard which may be the most dangerous one in that it leads most directly to the idea that there are second-class human beings and sub-human human beings.

But the story is not complete. The very idea of nature is ambiguous. According to one view, the one I have been using, nature points to or implies a peak, a perfection. According to this view, human rights depend upon attaining the status of humanness. The fetus is only potential; it has no rights, according to this view. But all kinds of people fall short of the norm: children, idiots, some adults. This understanding of nature has been used to justify not only abortion and infanticide, but also slavery.

There is another notion of nature, less splendid, more humane and, though less able to sustain a notion of health, more acceptable to the findings of modern science. Animal nature is characterized by impulses of self-preservation and by the capacity to feel pleasure and to suffer pain. Man and other animals are alike on this understanding of nature. And the right to life is ascribed to all such self-preserving and suffering creatures. Yet on this understanding of nature, the fetus—even a defective fetus—is not potential, but actual. The right to life belongs to him. But for this reason, this understanding of nature does not provide and may even deny what it is we are seeking, namely, a justification for genetic abortion, adequate unto itself, which

does not simultaneously justify infanticide, homicide and enslavement of the genetically abnormal.

There is a third understanding of nature, akin to the second, nature as sacrosanct, nature as created by a Creator. Indeed, to speak about this reminds us that there is a fourth possible standard for judgments about genetic abortion: the religious standard. I shall leave the discussion of this standard to those who are able to speak of it in better faith.

Now that I am at the end, the reader can better share my sense of frustration. I have failed to provide myself with a satisfactory intellectual and moral justification for the practice of genetic abortion. Perhaps others more able than I can supply one. Perhaps the pragmatists can persuade me that we should abandon the search for principled justification, that if we just trust people's situational decisions or their gut reactions, everything will turn out fine. Maybe they are right. But we should not forget the sage observation of Bertrand Russell: "Pragmatism is like a warm bath that heats up so imperceptibly that you don't know when to scream." I would add that before we submerge ourselves irrevocably in amniotic fluid, we take note of the connection to our own baths, into which we have started the hot water running.

HENRY DAVID AIKEN

Life and the right to life

I conclude first that claims regarding the right to biological survival are entirely contingent upon the ability of the individual in question to make, with the help of others, a human life for himself. This means that in circumstances where there exists no possibility of anything approaching a truly human life, the right to biological or physical survival loses its own *raison d'être* and, hence, that the merciful termination of life, in the bio-physical sense, is acceptable or perhaps even obligatory. Other things equal (which they rarely are), the rights of parents to accept the onus of caring for a radically defective child which has no capacity for enjoying a human life may be acknowledged. But then this is owing not to the child's right but to the human rights of its parents. And when the care of such a child seriously endangers the well-being of others, including in particular the members of its own family, parental rights (which are themselves, of course, always conditional) must give way to other, more exigent claims.

GARRETT HARDIN

Abortion — or compulsory pregnancy?

The abortion problem is, I think, a particularly neat example of a problem in which most of the difficulties are actually created by asking the wrong question. I submit further that once the right question is asked the whole untidy mess miraculously dissolves, leaving in its place a very simple public policy recommendation. . . .

Who wants compulsory pregnancy?

The question "How can we justify an abortion?" plainly leads to great difficulties. It is operationally unmanageable: it leads to inconsistencies in practice and inequities by any moral standard. All these can be completely avoided if we ask the right question, namely: *"How can we justify compulsory pregnancy?"*

By casting the problem in this form, we call attention to its relationship to the slavery issue. Somewhat more than a century ago men in the Western world asked the question: "How can we justify compulsory servitude?" and came up with the answer: *"By no means whatever."* Is the answer any different to the related question: "How can we justify compulsory pregnancy?" Certainly pregnancy is a form of servitude; if continued to term it results in parenthood, which is also a kind of servitude, to be endured

for the best years of a woman's life. It is difficult to see how it can be argued that this kind of servitude will be more productive of social good if it is compulsory rather than voluntary. A study made of Swedish children born when their mothers were refused the abortions they had requested showed that unwanted children, as compared with their controls, as they grew up were more often picked up for drunkenness, or antisocial or criminal behavior; they received less education; they received more psychiatric care; and they were more often exempted from military service by reason of defect. Moreover, the females in the group married earlier and had children earlier, thus no doubt tending to create a vicious circle of poorly tended children who in their turn would produce more poorly tended children. How then does society gain by increasing the number of unwanted children? No one has volunteered an answer to this question.

Of course if there were a shortage of children, then society might say that it needs all the children it can get—unwanted or not. But I am unaware of any recent rumors of a shortage of children.

Alternatives: True and false

The end result of an abortion—the elimination of an unwanted fetus—is surely good. But is the act itself somehow damaging? For several generations it was widely believed that abortion was intrinsically dangerous, either physically or psychologically. It is now very clear that the widespread belief is quite unjustified. . . .

In tackling questions of this sort, it is imperative that we identify correctly the alternatives facing us. (All moral and practical problems involve a comparison of alternative actions.) Many of the arguments of the prohibitionists implicitly assume that the alternatives facing the woman are these:

abortion——no abortion

This is false. A person can never do nothing. The pregnant woman is going to do something, whether she wishes to or not. (She cannot roll time backward and live her life over.)

People often ask: "Isn't contraception better

than abortion?" Implied by this question are these alternatives:

abortion———contraception

But these are not the alternatives that face the woman who asks to be aborted. She *is* pregnant. She cannot roll time backward and use contraception more successfully than she did before. Contraceptives are never foolproof anyway. . . . Abortion is not so much an alternative to contraception as it is a subsidiary method of birth control, to be used when the primary method fails—as it often does.

The woman *is* pregnant: this is the base level at which the moral decision begins. If she is pregnant against her will, does it matter to society whether or not she was careless or unskillful in her use of contraception? In any case, she is threatening society with an unwanted child, for which society will pay dearly. The real alternatives facing the woman (and society) are clearly these:

abortion———compulsory pregnancy

When we recognize that these are the real, operational alternatives, the false problems created by pseudo-alternatives vanish.

Is potential value valuable?

Only one weighty objection to abortion remains to be discussed, and this is the question of "loss." When a fetus is destroyed, has something valuable been destroyed? The fetus has the potentiality of becoming a human being. A human being is valuable. Therefore is not the fetus of equal value? This question must be answered.

It can be answered, but not briefly. What does the embryo receive from its parents that might be of value? There are only three possibilities: substance, energy, and information. As for the substance in the fertilized egg, it is not remarkable: merely the sort of thing one might find in any piece of meat, human or animal, and there is very little of it—only one and a half micrograms, which is about a half of a billionth of an ounce. The energy content of this tiny amount of material is likewise negligible. . . .

Clearly, the humanly significant thing that is contributed to the zygote by the parents is the information that "tells" the fertilized egg how to develop into a human being. This information is in the form of a chemical tape called "DNA," a double set of two chemical supermolecules each of which has about three billion "spots" that can be coded with any one of four different possibilities, symbolized by A, T, G, and C. . . . The DNA constitutes the information needed to produce a valuable human being. The question is: is this information precious? I have argued elsewhere that it is not:

> Consider the case of a man who is about to begin to build a $50,000 house. As he stands on the site looking at the blueprints a practical joker comes along and sets fire to the blueprints. The question is: can the owner go to the law and collect $50,000 for his lost blueprints? The answer is obvious: since another set of blueprints can be produced for the cost of only a few dollars, that is all they are worth. (A court might award a bit more for the loss of the owner's time, but that is a minor matter.) The moral: *a non-unique copy of information that specifies a valuable structure is itself almost valueless.*

> This principle is precisely applicable to the moral problem of abortion. The zygote, which contains the complete specification of a valuable human being, is not a human being, and is almost valueless. . . . The early stages of an individual fetus have had very little human effort invested in them; they are of very little worth. . . .

> A set of blueprints is not a house; the DNA of a zygote is not a human being. . . .

People who worry about the moral danger of abortion do so because they think of the fetus as a human being, hence equate feticide with murder. Whether the fetus is or is not a human being is a matter of definition, not fact; and we can define any way we wish. In terms of the human problem involved, it would be unwise to define the fetus as human (hence tactically unwise ever to refer to the fetus as an "unborn child"). Analysis based on the deepest insights of molecular biology indicates the wisdom of sharply distinguishing the information for a valuable structure from the completed structure itself. It is interesting, and gratifying, to note that this modern insight is completely congruent with common law governing the disposal of dead fetuses. Abortion-prohibitionists generally insist that abortion is murder, and that an embryo is a person; but no state or nation, so far as I know, requires the dead fetus to be treated like a dead person. Although all of the states in the United States severely limit what can be done with a dead human body, no cognizance is taken of dead fetuses up to about five months' prenatal life. The early fetus may, with impunity, be flushed down the toilet or thrown out with the garbage—which shows that we never have regarded it as a human being. Scientific analysis confirms what we have always known.

SISSELA BOK

Ethical problems of abortion

A failure to ask what the respect for life ought to protect lies at the root of the confusion about abortion and many other difficult decisions concerning life and death. I shall try, therefore, to list the most important reasons which underlie the elemental sense of the sacredness of life. Having done so, these reasons can be considered as they apply or do not apply to the embryo and the fetus.

1. Killing is viewed as the greatest of all dangers *for the victim.*
  • The knowledge that there is a threat to life causes intense anguish and apprehension.
  • The actual taking of life can cause great suffering.
  • The continued experience of life, once begun, is considered so valuable, so unique, so absorbing, that no one who has this experience should be unjustly deprived of it. And depriving someone of this experience means that all else of value to him will be lost.
2. Killing is brutalizing and criminalizing *for the killer.* It is a threat to others, and destructive to the person engaged therein.
3. Killing often causes *the family of the victim and others* to experience grief and loss. They may have been tied to the dead person by affection or economic dependence; they may have given of themselves in the relationship, so that its severance causes deep suffering.
4. *All of society,* as a result, has a stake in the protection of life. Permitting killing to take place sets patterns for victims, killers, and survivors that are threatening and ultimately harmful to all.

These are neutral principles governing the protection of life. They are shared by most human beings reflecting upon the possibility of dying at the hands of others. . . .

Turning now to abortions once more, how do these principles apply to the taking of the lives of embryos and fetuses?

Reasons to protect life in the prenatal period

Consider the very earliest cell formations soon after conception. Clearly, most of these *reasons* for protecting human life are absent here.

This group of cells cannot suffer in death, nor can it fear death. Its experiencing of life has not yet begun; it is not yet conscious of the loss of anything it has come to value in life and is not tied by bonds of affection to other human beings. If the abortion is desired by both parents, it will cause no grief such as that which accompanies the death of a child. Almost no human care and emotion and resources have been invested in it. Nor is a very early abortion brutalizing for the person voluntarily performing it, or a threat to other members of the human community. The only factor common to these few cells and, say, a soldier killed in war or a murdered robbery victim is that of the *potential* denied, the interruption of life, the deprivation of the possibility to grow and to experience, to have the joys and sorrows of existence.

For how much should this one factor count? It should count *at least* so much as to eliminate the occasionally voiced notion that pregnancy and its interruption involve only the mother in the privacy of her reproductive life, that to have an abortion is somehow analogous with cutting one's finger nails.

At the same time, I cannot agree that it should count enough so that one can simply equate killing an embryo with murder, even apart from legal considerations or the problems of enforcement. For it *is* important that most of the reasons why we protect lives are absent here. . . .

The reasons, then, for the protection of lives are minimal in very early abortions. At the same time, some of them are clearly present with respect to *infanticide,* most important among them the brutalization of those participating in the act and the resultant danger for all who are felt to be undesirable by their families or by others. . . .

Dividing lines

If, therefore, very early abortion does not violate these principles of protection for life, but infanticide does, we are confronted with a new kind of continuum in the place of that between less human and more human: that of the growth in strength, during the prenatal period, of these principles, these reasons for protecting life. In this second continuum, it would be as difficult as in the first to draw a line based upon objective factors. Since most abortions can be performed earlier or later during pregnancy, it would be preferable to encourage early abortions rather than late ones, and to draw a line before the second half of the pregnancy, permitting later abortions only on a clear showing of need. For this purpose, the two concepts of *quickening* and *viability*—so unsatisfactory in determining when humanity begins—can provide such limits.

Before quickening, the reasons to protect life are, as has been shown, negligible, perhaps absent altogether. During this period, therefore, abortion could be permitted upon request. Alternatively, the end of the first trimester could be employed as such a limit, as is the case in a number of countries.

Between quickening and viability, when the operation is a more difficult one medically and more traumatic for parents and medical personnel, it would not seem unreasonable to hold that special reasons justifying the abortion should be required in order to counterbalance this resistance; reasons not known earlier, such as the severe malformation of the fetus. After viability, finally, all abortions save the rare ones required to save the life of the mother, should be prohibited because the reasons to *protect* life may now be thought to be partially present; even though the viable fetus cannot fear death or suffer consciously therefrom, the effects on those participating in the event, and thus on society indirectly, could be serious. This is especially so because of the need, mentioned above, for a protection against infanticide. . . .

As technological progress pushes back the time when the fetus can be helped to survive independently of the mother, a question will arise as to whether the cutoff point marked by viability ought also be pushed back. Should abortion then be prohibited much earlier than is now the case, because the medical meaning of "viability" will have changed, or should we continue to rely on the conventional meaning of the word for the distinction between lawful and unlawful abortion?

In order to answer this question it is necessary to look once more at the reasons for which "viaability" was thought to be a good dividing-line in the first place. Is viability important because the baby can survive outside of the mother? Or because this chance of survival comes at a time in fetal development when the *reasons* to protect life have grown strong enough to prohibit abortion? At present, the two coincide, but in the future, they may come to diverge increasingly.

If the time comes when an embryo *could* be kept alive without its mother and thus be "viable" in one sense of the word, the reasons for protecting life from the point of view of victims, agents, relatives and society would still be absent; it seems right, therefore, to tie the obligatory protection of life to the present conventional definition of "viability" and to set a socially agreed upon time in pregnancy after which abortion should be prohibited.

To sum up, the justifications a mother has for not wishing to give birth can operate up to a certain point in pregnancy; after that point, the reasons society has for protecting life become sufficiently weighty so as to prohibit late abortions and infanticide.

Conflicting Images of Old Age. *Old man alone with his thoughts and poverty, and maestro Arthur Fiedler at the age of 80 with young members of the Boston Ballet Company.*

5

AGING
AND THE
AGED

The one conclusion that may be drawn from the articles in this chapter is that aging has extremely varied consequences. As Robert Butler writes later in this section, old people show a greater range of diversity—in their activity and their personality—than people at any other stage in life. The passage of time has permitted the vagaries of circumstance and the possibilities of character to draw their full weight.

No matter how varied their life in the present is, however, all old people face the same future. It is ineluctable that aging be closely identified with dying: The aged force us to confront the reality of death. It is only natural, too, that our treatment of the old is partly determined by the meaning that death holds for us.

As the aged represent the distant future that faces all of us, they equally represent the distant—or not so distant—past. They are the natural choice to transmit to the young the customs and the way of life that have developed in the past. These constitute the traditions of any people; the word "tradition" itself derives from a Latin root meaning "handing over." The old, then, are the natural "givers" of a people: They "hand over" the experience of a life formed by that people's culture.

The position of the aged in American culture is vulnerable because our culture is chiefly occupied with living in a present unencumbered by memories of the past. In this situation, a chief source of respect for the aged—as the repositories and teachers of tradition—is cut off. What is left, at that point, to determine the treatment of the aged is their nearness to death. In the opening piece of this chapter, Sidney Callahan and Drew Christiansen argue that the old are shabbily treated and indecently rejected because we have not learned to accept our "finitude and limitation." Our culture must be "re-oriented as a whole" in order to grant old people "dignity and autonomy."

The next selection dispels some of the stereotypes surrounding old age. Robert

Butler writes that the rates of physiological, psychological, and social aging differ greatly "within the person and from person to person." He then exposes the notions that the old are unproductive, inflexible, withdrawn from life, and serene to be nothing but "myths." Although it is mentioned only in passing in this particular excerpt, the notion that people over sixty-five lose their desire and capacity for sex is also a myth; Butler and others have found that old people are both capable and desirous of expressing their sexuality in a variety of ways.

Two contrasting personal views of what it means to be old are presented next. For Bert Kruger Smith, old age means the pain of loneliness, of being ignored, of being "a diminished me." In contrast, Elmer Davis finds that old age brings a certain freedom— "freedom that comes from the disappearance of ambition." No longer worried about the impact of their actions upon their careers, the old are uniquely free to act according to the dictates of their consciences.

These two views of the meaning of old age are followed by an account of two ways in which different societies treat their aged. William Graham Sumner illustrates how the mores of some primitive groups demand "conventional respect for the aged," who are valued "for their wisdom and counsel," while the mores of other groups regard the aged "as societal burdens" who "are forced to die, either by their own hands or those of their relatives."

The world's oldest people, in Abkhazia, Russia, in Hunza, Pakistan, and in Vilcabamba, Ecuador, are the subject of the next article by Alexander Leaf. Leaf attributes the extraordinary vitality of dozens of people well past the age of 100 in these communities at least in part to the active, central position they enjoy in their group. In contrast, many of the aged in the United States feel useless when they are forced to retire, and Leaf notes that "people who no longer have a necessary role to play in the social and economic life of their society generally deteriorate rapidly."

Recognizing that we cannot return to a pre-industrial society—and that the benefits of a traditional society for the aged are achieved only at a cost to the young—he urges a program of education and creative activities that would keep our old people integrated in their communities and give new meaning to their lives.

A different approach to coping with aging is suggested by Arlie Hochschild. On the basis of a sociological study of a low-income housing project for senior citizens, she concludes that not only do older people reject the idea of living with their children, but they also prefer to live in age-segregated communities. Such communities, she argues, permit old people to build "an order out of ambiguity" and develop sibling-type relationships that reduce their sense of isolation.

Many old people, however, are unable to care for themselves, and they spend their waning days in institutions. The decision to place an aged parent in a nursing home often arouses deep feelings of guilt in the children. In the next article, a letter written to Ralph Nader, who was investigating these institutions, suggests that it is the proprietors of nursing homes and not the children who are really acting immorally.

In the next selection, Simone de Beauvoir argues that it is not just our old-age policy that is scandalous, but our entire economic and social system, which treats people only as wage earners and not as whole human beings.

In the final excerpt, H. Tristram Engelhardt uses the insights of two philosophers, Georg Wilhelm Friedrich Hegel and Charles Hartshorne, to explore the meaning of human mortality. He concludes that man is a finite being and, therefore, must learn to accept the inevitability of death. Engelhardt contends that the search for the elixir of immortality is dangerous to the quality of human life and quotes Seneca, the Roman philosopher and tragedian, for support: "The wise man . . . lives as long as he should, not as long as he can." (The issue of the right to die is discussed in Chapter 12.)

102

Sidney Callahan is the author of many books and articles on sex, parenthood, and women, including *The Illusion of Eve, Beyond Birth Control, The Working Mother,* and *Parenting: Principles and Politics of Parenthood.* She has also contributed a regular column to the *National Catholic Reporter.* **Drew Christiansen** is a Jesuit priest and a special editor of *Theological Studies.* "Ideal Old Age" first appeared in 1974 in *Soundings.*

Robert N. Butler, born in 1927, is a psychiatrist who specializes in gerontological problems. He is a consultant at the Washington Psychoanalytic Institute and holds adjunct faculty appointments at the Washington School of Psychiatry as well as George Washington and Howard Universities. *Why Survive? Being Old in America* was published in 1975.

Bert Kruger Smith is an executive associate of the Hogg Foundation for Mental Health in Austin, Texas. In 1971 she attended the White House Conference on Aging. In addition to *Aging in America,* excerpted here, she has written *Your Non-learning Child.*

Elmer Holmes Davis, born in 1890, was a reporter for the *New York Times,* a news broadcaster and commentator on CBS and ABC radio, and, during World War II, director of the Office of War Information. He was also the author of several novels and short stories, including *Giant Killer, Morals for Moderns,* and *Love Among the Ruins.* One of the few public figures to speak out against the threat that Senator Joseph McCarthy posed to American freedoms, he wrote a series of essays entitled *But We Were Born Free.* Davis died in 1958.

William Graham Sumner. See above, p. 3.

Alexander Leaf is Jackson Professor of Clinical Medicine at Harvard Medical School and chief of Medical Services at Massachusetts General Hospital. Fascinated by tales of longevity among the people of the Caucasus in Russia, Vilcabamba in Ecuador, and Hunza in Pakistan, Leaf traveled to these remote regions to examine and study dozens of centenarians. *Youth in Old Age* (1975) is the report of his findings.

Arlie Hochschild is a sociologist at the University of California, Berkeley. She is the author of *The Unexpected Community: A Study of an Old Age Subculture.* "Communal Living in Old Age" was first published in 1972 in *The Future of the Family,* edited by Louise Kapp Howe.

Ralph Nader, born in 1934, has become internationally famous for his work as a consumer advocate. In his first book, *Unsafe at Any Speed* (1965), Nader indicted the United States automobile industry for being more concerned with profits than safety. Since then, he and his staff have studied numerous other industries, including meat and poultry, natural gas, coal, and color TV, pointing out hazards that he believed were endangering Americans' health. His report on nursing homes appeared in 1971.

Simone de Beauvoir, a French author, was born in 1908. In addition to teaching at the University of Paris, she is author of *The Second Sex, Force of Circumstance, The Prime of Life,* and *Coming of Age* (1972), excerpted here.

H. Tristram Engelhardt was born in 1912 and has been on the faculties of Tulane and Baylor Universities. He is at present clinical associate professor of physiology and medicine at the University of Texas Medical School. He is a frequent contributor to the *Hastings Center Report* and is editor, with Daniel Callahan, of *Science, Ethics and Medicine.*

SIDNEY CALLAHAN and DREW CHRISTIANSEN

Ideal old age

Old age is a painful subject in America. For one thing aging presents difficult and complex problems, and for another, most unforgivably, there's no future in it. Aging can only lead to death, another sore subject inspiring massive denial and avoidance. In an uncanny way the problems of old age expose the weakest points in our value system and social order. Obviously reforms of our health care, housing, and social security arrangements for old people are imperative; but perhaps more important, there is a need for cultural restitution. What viable ideals of old age do we possess? Few young persons can imagine their own old age without a shudder of fear. Sheer incredulity may blot out their thought processes. We are privately and publicly unprepared to be old. . . .

Avoidance

In youth-oriented, power-obsessed culture, the aging body and lack of productive status produce loathing. Not surprisingly, Americans have a minor tradition of avoiding old age by suicide. There exists a going-out-in-glory image in which a person at the height of power and beauty executes a narcissistic love-death solo, refusing decay and diminishment. As Norman Mailer has written in *Marilyn,* "The unspoken logic of suicide insists that an early death is better for the soul than slow extinction through a misery of deteriorating years." Leaving a beautiful corpse and avoiding old age are accomplished at a stroke, with the agent still in full control. Hemingway's death is a model of the suicidal response to the prospect of aging and impotence. The choice made is for death before diminishment.

The only acceptable ideal of old age we really possess in America is an old age without change, without limits, without loss. The old person need make no concessions, no changes in the face of age. Above all, the old person continues working and producing, controlling valued resources like money and sex. Power and position are not given up, nor is physical activity curtailed. With men, young wives are married and children are born well into the seventies; women take younger lovers. But most important, the admired old person continues to work: "He died with his boots on." "He died in harness." Unfortunately, in our complicated work world and economy, only a very few old people can maintain their careers after sixty-five and so live the dominant ideal. Unlike the old in the remote high altitudes of Vilcabamba, Abkhazia or Hunza, who regularly live into their hundreds, we cannot keep working in our fields within a simple agrarian society of scarcity.

With us, only the exceptional old person can keep participating in status-giving positions. It takes an unusual talent not to retire or to be able to control great political power like the aged Adenauer, Churchill, Golda Meir, or Chou En-lai. Great wealth may also give old persons power and status and keep them participating in the society without concessions. In addition, the exceptionally gifted artist can keep producing into old age, as in the case of Picasso, Casals, Segovia, Martha Graham, or Louise Nevelson. On a more trivial level a few older persons a la Dietrich or Cary Grant can even keep their youthful looks and sexual appeal. But how many aged can live without loss, without discontinuity? An ideal old age which can be lived only by the very rich, very talented, or very powerful is not viable. The exceptional person who can live untouched by age provides no cultural model or hope for a cultural restitution for the old.

Only a reappraisal of our conception of dignity, autonomy, and the human life cycle can cope with the inevitable changes of old age. Physical and social losses for most persons are as inevitable and inexorable as the passing of time. The question is what can be done under the given conditions in each individual life. In a way old age is a living parable of human freedom and necessity. . . .

Life cycle and time

Taking the life cycle approach to old age one sees the new life task of the last stage of life as a review of one's life, a final coming to terms with one's self, one's story, and one's world. The fact that the old live without an extended future creates a whole new situation and stance in regard to time. When you have more of a past than a future, then the present you have must be lived without a reliance on many of the external structures and necessities of other stages of life. Since our culture emphasizes the view that time is an ascending curve and we are perpetually oriented toward future goals and future achievements, the readjustments in old age can be difficult. We value the young, economically and in every other way, because they have future potential; to be divested of one's future promise can be painful, even panic-producing.

But the pattern of most human lives remains inevitable. After emerging from the family of origin into freedom, one marries and establishes the family of procreation with its defined tasks. When children grow up and leave, the elderly person again emerges from family tasks into "a second limbo," or time of becoming, without defined goals. Usually this freedom from necessary family tasks is increased and intensified by retirement and a lack of economically productive work. These enforced social disengagements at the end of life force old people to come to terms with freedom in the present dimension. How an individual meets this challenge of "role relinquishment" and freedom from tasks determines the success of old age. In the seventh age of man his enforced rest, leisure, and retirement can either be a Sabbath or a Sunday, Bloody Sunday. The so-called "Sunday neurosis" which attacks many in Western societies is a pale preview of the free-time problems of old age. . . .

Family

For an ideal old age with regard to family and kinship the same principles of dignity, autonomy, and interdependency apply. The older person who can choose his relationships with his family or intentional family, and maintain independence without isolation, can also maintain dignity. Almost every study of older persons, even in areas like East London in which the extended family is very much intact, discovers that most older persons wish to live near but not with their families. An independent base, a room of one's own, seems as necessary to the older person as to anyone else in maintaining integrity. If the older person can still be needed by his kin, or fictive kin, he can maintain that interdependency which aids in self-respect and social stimulation.

If independence can be maintained and family ties and mutual aid kept up, the older person can avoid the total age segregation and dependency of the old-age home. . . . No one at any stage in a life cycle can do without the stimulation and broadening influence of those in other stages and ages. Age segregation in America is a damaging aspect of the culture, affecting most severely the very young and the very old. In fact, with both the old and the very young we see the weaknesses and the price of our individualistic system.

Concluding remarks

If attention is to be paid, dignity and autonomy maintained, and an ideal of old age made possible in America we must indeed reorient our culture as a whole. Those latent aspects of life which we all share and which are manifest in old age must be emphasized and developed. Particularly important is the need to develop an un-American consciousness of finitude and limitations. As we become more aware that we live on a small planet with precious few resources, we become ecologically conscious. Saving, reusing, recycling, and a frugal use of energy become duties. This approach to reality is supremely appropriate to old age when human resources are declining and every scrap of power and ability must be cherished and used wisely. The old are experts in personal ecology. They have much to teach us about living with limitations and recognizing our finitude.

It is no accident, perhaps, that every culture which has given respect and dignity to the old has also been a culture which valued frugality and the wise use of every human resource. In such cultures, the body is seen as a subjective actor rather than as a luxurious object for display attractive only in its youth. Only a wasteful affluent culture can afford to throw away the experience of the old and dispense with the services of people no longer in their prime. Now that we are coming to understand finitude and our planetary problems of conservation we have a chance to reperceive old age. The wise old person making good use of limited time and depleted resources, with clearly established priorities, may be more of a cultural model than the young male slashing through the forests, fiercely intent on indiscriminate exploration, exploitation, consumption, and production. As the warrior male recedes in prominence—and dominance—old people will be more one with the rest of us. But society's reconciliation with old people, or with any powerless group, is a difficult task. We have suggested that a new ideal of old age may achieve this reintegration, because the ideal identifies a life task intrinsic to old age and because the ideal, as a public symbol of the place of old people in society, gives recognition, autonomy, and dignity to them. . . . The reason we have chosen an image in which old people personally appropriate the process of loss and limitation is that the core problem of aging is how to find dignity and autonomy in loss.

[One] . . . objection to our ideal of old age would maintain that old age can be of no interest in a culture of unparalleled social change. With the radical changes which technology brings about within the span of a single generation, there is no basis for interest in the lives of old people. They have nothing to teach a "prefigurative" generation. Their sapiential authority and integrity is as inadequate to the interpretation of life in the post-industrial age as it is to communicating the latest techniques of data processing.

Implicit in this objection is the notion that memory is the only form of knowledge old people possess. Indeed, the memories the old have of their own youth may be of little relevance to today's young people. But coming to final terms with the present is quite another thing. They are the old people in a technological society, and their problems are equally due to the impairments of age and to those brought on by advanced techniques which steal the very liberties we were promised they would bring. Old people have to face up to the basic deception in the technological myth: the belief that there can be growth without limit. Just as old people are pioneers in the use of leisure, they can be pioneers too in the creative use of limits.

ROBERT N. BUTLER

Why survive?
Being old in America

In addition to dealing with the difficulties of physical and economic survival, older people are affected by the multitude of myths and stereotypes surrounding old age:

An older person thinks and moves slowly. He does not think as he used to or as creatively. He is bound to himself and to his past and can no longer change or grow. He can learn neither well nor swiftly and, even if he could, he would not wish to. Tied to his personal traditions and growing conservatism, he dislikes innovations and is not disposed to new ideas. Not only can he not move forward, he often moves backward. He enters a second childhood, caught up in increasing egocentricity, and demanding more from his environment than he is willing to give to it. Sometimes he becomes an intensification of himself, a caricature of a lifelong personality. He becomes irritable and cantankerous, yet shallow and enfeebled. He lives in his past; he is behind the times. He is aimless and wandering of mind, reminiscing and garrulous. Indeed, he is a study in decline, the picture of mental and physical failure. He has lost and cannot replace friends, spouse, job, status, power, influence, income. He is often stricken by diseases which, in turn, restrict his movement, his enjoyment of food, the pleasures of well-being. He has lost his desire and capacity for sex. His body shrinks, and so too does the flow of blood to his brain. His mind does not utilize oxygen and sugar at the same rate as formerly. Feeble, uninteresting, he awaits his death, a burden to society, to his family and to himself.

In its essentials, this view I have sketched approximates the picture of old age held by many Americans. As in all clichés, stereotypes and myths there are bits of truth. But many of the current views of old age represent confusions, misunderstandings or simply a lack of knowledge about old age. Others may be completely inaccurate or biased, reflecting prejudice or outright hostility. Certain prevalent myths need closer examination.

The myth of "aging"

The idea of chronological aging (measuring one's age by the number of years one has lived) is a kind of myth. It is clear that there are great differences in the rates of physiological, chronological, psychological and social aging within the person and from person to person. In fact, physiological indicators show a greater range from the mean in old age than in any other age group, and this is true of personality as well. Older people actually become more diverse rather than more similar with advancing years. There are extraordinarily "young" 80-year-olds as well as "old" 80-year-olds. Chronological age, therefore, is a convenient but imprecise indicator of physical, mental and emotional status. For [our] purposes . . . old age may be considered to commence at the conventionally accepted point of 65.

We do know that organic brain damage can create such extensive intellectual impairment that people of all types and personalities may become dull-eyed, blank-faced and unresponsive. Massive destruction of the brain and body has a "leveling" effect which can produce increasing homogeneity among the elderly. But most older people do not suffer impairment of this magnitude during the greater part of their later life.

The myth of unproductivity

Many believe the old to be unproductive. But in the absence of diseases and social adversities, old

people tend to remain productive and actively involved in life. There are dazzling examples like octogenarians Georgia O'Keeffe continuing to paint and Pope John XXIII revitalizing his church, and septuagenarians Duke Ellington composing and working his hectic concert schedule and Golda Meir acting as her country's vigorous Prime Minister. Substantial numbers of people become unusually creative for the first time in old age, when exceptional and inborn talents may be discovered and expressed. What is most pertinent to our discussion here, however, is the fact that many old people continue to contribute usefully to their families and community in a variety of ways, including active employment. The 1971 Bureau of Labor Statistics figures show 1,780,000 people over 65 working full time and 1,257,000 part time. Since society and business practice do not encourage the continued employment of the elderly, it is obvious that many more would work if jobs were available. . . .

The myth of disengagement

This is related to the previous myth and holds that older people prefer to disengage from life, to withdraw into themselves, choosing to live alone or perhaps only with their peers. Ironically, some gerontologists themselves hold these views. One study, *Growing Old: The Process of Disengagement,* presents the theory that mutual separation of the aged person from his society is a natural part of the aging experience. There is no evidence to support this generalization. Disengagement is only one of many patterns of reaction to old age.

The myth of inflexibility

The ability to change and adapt has little to do with one's age and more to do with one's life-long character. But even this statement has to be qualified. One is not necessarily destined to maintain one's character in earlier life permanently. True, the endurance, the strength and the stability in human character structure are remarkable and protective. But most, if not all, people change and remain open to change throughout the course of life, right up to its termination. . . . The notion that older people become less responsive to innovation and change because of age is not supported by scientific studies of healthy older people living in the community or by everyday observations and clinical psychiatric experience.

A related cliché is that political conservatism increases with age. If one's options are constricted by job discrimination, reduced or fixed income and runaway inflation, as older people's are, one may become conservative out of economic necessity rather than out of qualities innate in the psyche. . . . Once again diversity rather than homogeneity is the norm.

The myth of "senility"

The notion that old people are senile, showing forgetfulness, confusional episodes and reduced attention, is widely accepted. "Senility" is a popularized layman's term used by doctors and the public alike to categorize the behavior of the old. Some of what is called senile is the result of brain damage. But anxiety and depression are also frequently lumped within the same category of senility, even though they are treatable and often reversible. Old people, like young people, experience a full range of emotions, including anxiety, grief, depression and paranoid states. It is all too easy to blame age and brain damage when accounting for the mental problems and emotional concerns of later life.

Drug tranquilization is another frequent, misdiagnosed and potentially reversible cause of so-called senility. Malnutrition and unrecognized physical illnesses, such as congestive heart failure, may produce "senile behavior" by reducing the supply of blood, oxygen and food to the brain. Alcoholism, often associated with bereavement, is another cause. Because it has been so convenient to dismiss all these manifestations by lumping them together under an improper and inaccurate diagnostic label, the elderly often do not receive the benefits of decent diagnosis and treatment.

Actual irreversible brain damage, of course, is not a myth, and two major conditions create mental disorders. One is cerebral arteriosclerosis (hardening of the arteries of the brain); the other, unfortunately referred to as senile brain disease, is due to a mysterious dissolution of brain cells. Such conditions account for some 50 percent of the cases of major mental disorders in old age, and the symptoms connected with these conditions are the ones that form the basis for what has come to be known as senility. But, as I wish to emphasize again, similar symptoms can be found in a number of other conditions which *are* reversible through proper treatment.

The myth of serenity

In contrast to the previous myths, which view the elderly in a negative light, the myth of serenity portrays old age as a kind of adult fairyland. Now at last comes a time of relative peace and serenity when people can relax and enjoy the fruits of their labors after the storms of active life are over. Advertising slogans, television and romantic fiction foster the myth. Visions of carefree, cookie-baking grandmothers and rocking-chair grandfathers are cherished by younger generations. But, in fact, older persons experience more stresses than any other age group, and these stresses are often devastating. The strength of the aged to endure crisis is remarkable, and tranquillity is an unlikely as well as inappropriate response under these circumstances. Depression, anxiety, psychosomatic illnesses, paranoia, garrulousness and irritability are some of the internal reactions to external stresses.

Depressive reactions are particularly widespread in late life. To the more blatant psychotic depressions and the depressions associated with organic brain diseases must be added the everyday depressions that stem from long physical illness or chronic discomfort, from grief, despair and loneliness, and from an inevitably lowered self-esteem that comes from diminished social and personal status.

Grief is a frequent companion of old age—grief for one's own losses and for the ultimate loss of one's self. Apathy and emptiness are a common sequel to the initial shock and sadness that come with the deaths of close friends and relatives. Physical disease and social isolation can follow bereavement. . . .

Ageism – the prejudice against the elderly

The stereotyping and myths surrounding old age can be explained in part by lack of knowledge and by insufficient contact with a wide variety of older people. But there is another powerful factor operating—a deep and profound prejudice against the elderly which is found to some degree in all of us. . . . Ageism makes it easier to ignore the frequently poor social and economic plight of older people. We can avoid dealing with the reality that our productivity-minded society has little use for nonproducers—in this case those who have reached an arbitrarily defined retirement age. We can also avoid, for a time at least, reminders of the personal reality of our own aging and death.

BERT KRUGER SMITH

An old woman speaks

What is it to be a human being? Am I but a reflection cast into the lives of other persons? The schizophrenic child often fears the mirror because he is not sure his likeness will be there. Perhaps the older person withdraws from the picture he knows he reflects in others.

Does a tree falling in the forest make a sound if there are no ears to hear it? Is a person human when he has shrunk into the basic core of self and others have moved away like loose-hanging folds of skin?

What is the sound I make when I am old? Shuffling for sustenance, napping for strength, dressing for no one, waiting for one certain visitor, I am a diminished me. No capital *I*. No self to fling free, a bird sailing skyward. There is only a small *i,* shriveled within the layers of the years.

The evening hours fall suddenly, shutting out the slanting light which livens the corners of my home. The evening hours are a door slammed shut against both friends and laughter.

Somewhere in the early sleepless morning, when daylight still brings flicker of promise, I lie young on my scarcely wrinkled bed and am warmed by the feel of husband-hands caressing me knowingly or of child-fingers on my face or of friend-touch on my hands. But those moments pass. Daytime brings no warmth, and at last I rise because I have always risen and go to prepare myself for a day which stays too shortly and a night which comes too soon.

I am an island, barren, surrounded by the waters of my life, my own shores drouth-pounded, desiccated. Only echoes skim the waters to my island-world—whispers and words, songs and laughter, carried by satellite of memory into my solitude.

Hands lie heavy on my lap—vein-ridged, spotted. Once they were like white birds in graceful flight over keys of a piano, stirring savory pots of food, gentling a crying child. Agile, useful, they were never still. Now they too are done with reaching out. They are folded inward. . . .

"I know; I know," they say. "There are problems with being old." But they do not know. Everyone has been a child. All can understand through muffled memory how childhood was. But none has been old except those who are that now.

Who can speak for the old? And who speaks to us? Once, when I was very ill, I lay unmoving on a bed. The doctor-voices, nurse-rustles all came to me, barely sounding through the layers of pain which separated us from one another. They talked about me then as if I were not a feeling, hearing human being. They talked above me and around me as they prepared needles and moved limbs. It was as if I had left my body there to be tended.

And now it is the same. No one looks at me—at me, into my eyes, into the core of me. It is "as if" I am like all who have lived too long, a being to be tolerated or bypassed or humored.

Can no one see that within my soul *I* exist? The person who loved and grieved and was? I too have hungered, been tormented by passion, known knife-thrust of pain. Stir the ashes of my being, blow tenderly to bring the flames to light.

ELMER DAVIS

Grandeurs and miseries of old age

I am almost sixty-four years old. That is not very old by modern standards, especially in a country whose benevolent government urges on me the advantages of being older still. When I am sixty-five, the Bureau of Internal Revenue assures me, I shall be able to deduct another $600 from my taxable income; and if I have the additional felicity to become blind, I can deduct some more.

I have no ambition to go blind at any age, despite this allurement; for that matter I am not anxious to be sixty-five, though I shall be unless I die pretty soon. My fan mail includes a good many gleeful predictions that I am going to be lynched; but barring that misfortune, I ought to be good for another ten or fifteen years if there is anything in the doctrine of hereditary longevity. But no matter how long I may last I am not persuaded that the best is yet to be, even by Catherine Drinker Bowen's eloquent disquisition in *Harper's* on the magnificence of age. I recognize and applaud her endeavor to reassure us that what is going to happen to all of us, whether we like it or not, is really something pretty good; but I cannot feel that the general public can draw much encouragement from the truly magnificent old age of the various worthies she mentions, notably Mr. Justice Oliver Wendell Holmes.

It is no doubt true, as she says, that "luck being equal, whether a man at eighty finds himself reaping the harvest or the whirlwind depends on how he has spent his forties and thirties and twenties." But luck is not equal; and it may be that to be an Oliver Wendell Holmes or a John Dewey at ninety you had to be a Holmes or a Dewey from the start, both in physical constitution and in potential mental capacity. . . .

There is, however, one offset to the inevitable infirmities, at least for us of the one per cent who have been lucky enough to be able to keep our noses above water; and that is freedom—freedom from the passions of youth. I don't mean what you mean; from that particular passion, I should imagine, few men or women are ever happy to be set free. We read in the pages of history that Sophocles the tragic poet, at the age of eighty-nine, was asked by some impertinent young squirt if he were still able to enjoy the pleasures of love. "My friend," said Sophocles solemnly, "I give thanks to the gods every day that I have been freed from that tyrannous desire." It is, however, the general opinion of men old enough to have an opinion that Sophocles was merely making the best of a bad job—whistling in the graveyard of his capacities.

The dominant passion of most young men—and middle-aged men, for that matter—is a lust for Success; they bend most of their efforts toward making a name, or a fortune, or both. But the time comes when they have either made it or not, and it is too late to do much more about it. Accordingly—always provided you have done well enough to keep afloat—ambition fades away; you no longer give a damn, or at any rate not much of a damn.

This too needs qualification, in both directions. A senator who in his eighties is defeated—as several senators have been—for re-election to a seat that he has held for thirty years probably feels even worse about it than he would have felt thirty years earlier; and those unfortunate novelists who under some obscure compulsion still push out a book a year, long after they have nothing left to say, probably hate unfavorable reviews just as much as they did in their youth.

Nor can you ever be quite sure when a man is through. Winston Churchill, at sixty-two, was a failure. He had been, at times, a considerable figure in each party, but now he was out of both parties. . . . Three years later he was called on to save his country, and he did it.

But not many of us are Churchills. . . . Nevertheless we of the one per cent can savor the sense of freedom that comes from the disappearance of ambition. When we were younger, getting and spending we laid waste our powers—and sometimes, in the headlong drive for success, some of us were in danger of laying waste something still more important, our conscience. A good many young men have sometimes been confronted with something that they know they ought to do; but if they did it, it might have an unfavorable if not disastrous effect on their future. They should have done it anyway, no doubt; but it is a good deal easier not to worry about the effect on your future when your future is behind you.

It is quite true that 'tis man's perdition to be safe when for the truth he ought to die—or, as the phrase is more likely to translate itself in these times, when for the truth he ought to lose his job, with small chance of getting another. But it is, emotionally if not ethically, a somewhat different matter to tell a young man with a wife and children whom he is barely able to support on his salary that for the truth, his wife and children ought to starve too. And that is a situation that increasingly comes up in the present drive, Congressional and local, against freedom of thought—particularly in the schools and colleges where above all freedom of thought must be preserved.

Professors and teachers in schools and colleges are tempted to pull in their horns, to say nothing at all; otherwise their students, or their students' parents, might report them to the American Legion—as has happened—and any deviation from the norm of reactionary thinking will be regarded as subversion. With the result also, as Mrs. Roosevelt reported after her nation-wide travels in the winter of 1953, that the young people who are just coming up and see what is happening begin to be afraid to think and afraid to act, for fear that something they may say or do now will be dug up and thrown at them twenty years later and ruin their careers. (Senator McCarthy has several times damned, or tried to damn, middle-aged men for what they did or said in college and have long since repudiated.) A despotism might be able to stand this loss of heart, though I doubt it; but a republic whose young people are in that state of mind is on its way downhill.

We have got to defeat this attack on the freedom of the mind; and I think we can defeat it if enough of us stand up against it—enough of all kinds of people, rich and poor, young and old. But it takes courage for a young man with a family to stand up to it; all the more obligation on those of us who have nothing left to lose. At any age it is better to be a dead lion than a living dog—though better still, of course, to be a living and victorious lion; but it is easier to run the risk of being killed (or fired) in action if before long you are going to be dead anyway. This freedom seems to me the chief consolation of old age.

WILLIAM GRAHAM SUMNER

Respect or contempt for the aged

Mores of respect or contempt for the aged

There are two sets of mores as to the aged: (*a*) in one set of mores the teaching and usages inculcate conventional respect for the aged, who are therefore arbitrarily preserved for their wisdom and counsel, perhaps also sometimes out of affection and sympathy; (*b*) in the other set of mores the aged are regarded as societal burdens, which waste the strength of the society, already inadequate for its tasks. Therefore they are forced to die, either by their own hands or those of their relatives. It is very far from being true that the first of these policies is practiced by people higher up in civilization than those who practice the second. The people in lower civilization profit more by the wisdom and counsel of the aged than those in higher civilization, and are educated by this experience to respect and value the aged. . . . In some cases we can see the two codes in strife. Amongst the ancient Teutons the father could expose or sell his children under age, and the adult son could kill his aged parents. There was no fixed duty of child to parent or of parent to child.

111

Ethnographical illustrations of respect to the aged

"The people of Madagascar pay high honor to age and to parents. The respect to age is even exaggerated." The Hovas always pay formal respect to greater age. If two slaves are carrying a load together, the younger of them will try to carry it all. In West Africa, "all the younger members of society are early trained to show the utmost deference to age. They must never come into the presence of aged persons or pass by their dwellings without taking off their hats and assuming a crouching gait. When seated in their presence it must always be at a 'respectful distance,'—a distance proportioned to the difference in their ages and position in society. If they come near enough to hand an aged man a lighted pipe or a glass of water, the bearer must always fall upon one knee." "Great among the Oromo is the veneration for the old. Failure in respect to age is considered an injury to the customs of the country. The aged always sit in the post of honor, have a voice in public councils, in discussions, and controversies which arise amongst citizens. The young and the women are taught to serve them on all occasions." The Hereros respect the old. Property belongs to an old man even after his son assumes the care of it. Milk pails and joints of meat are brought to him to be blessed. The old are well treated in Australia. Certain foods are reserved for them. Amongst the Lhoosai, on the Chittagong hills of southeastern India, "parents are reverenced and old age honored. When past work the father and mother are cared for by the children." The Indians on the northwest coast of North America "have great respect for the aged, whose advice in most matters has great weight." "Great is the respect for the aged" amongst the Chavantes, a Ges tribe of Brazil. . . . The Greenland Eskimo take care of their old parents. "The Ossetines [of the Caucasus] have the greatest love and respect for their parents, for old age in general, and for their ancestors. The authority of the head of the family, the grandfather, father, stepfather, uncle, or older brother is unconditionally recognized. The younger men will never sit down in the presence of elders, will not speak loudly, and will never contradict them." . . . The cases above cited are nearly all those of savages and barbarians. . . .

"The position of the Roman father assured him respect and obedience as long as he lived. His unlimited power of making a will kept his fate in his own hands." The power in his family which the law gave him was very great, but his sons never paid him affectionate respect. "It is remarkable that we do not hear so often of barbarous treatment of old women as of old men. Could love for mothers have been an effective sentiment? Under mother right the relation of child to parent was far stronger, and the relation to the maternal uncle was secondary and derivative with respect to that to the mother."

Killing the old

The custom of killing the old, especially one's parents, is very antipathetic to us. The cases will show that, for nomadic people, the custom is necessary. The old drop out by the way and die from exhaustion. To kill them is only equivalent, and perhaps kinder. If an enemy is pursuing, the necessity is more acute. All this enters into the life conditions so primarily that the custom is a part of the life policy; it is so understood and acquiesced in. The old sometimes request it from life weariness, or from devotion to the welfare of the group.

Killing the old in ethnography

The "Gallinomero sometimes have two or three cords of wood neatly stacked in ricks about the wigwam. Even then, with the heartless cruelty of the race, they will dispatch an old man to the distant forest with an ax, whence he returns with his white head painfully bowed under a backload of knaggy limbs, and his bare bronzed bowlegs moving on with that catlike softness and evenness of the Indian, but so slowly that he scarcely seems to get on at all." An old squaw, who had been abandoned by her children because she was blind, was found wandering in the mountains of California. "Filial piety cannot be said to be a distinguishing quality of the

Wailakki, or any Indians. No matter how high may be their station, the aged and decrepit are counted a burden. The old man, hero of a hundred battles, when his skill with the bow and arrow is gone, is ignominiously compelled to accompany his sons into the forest, and bear home on his shoulders the game they have killed." . . . An old Ponca chief was being deserted by the tribe with a little food and water, a trifling fire, and a few sticks. The tribe were driven on by hunger. The old chief said: "My children, our nation is poor, and it is necessary that you should all go to the country where you can get meat. My eyes are dimmed and my strength is no more. . . . I am a burden to my children. I cannot go. Keep your hearts stout and think not of me. I am no longer good for anything." This is the fullest statement we can quote, attributed to one of the abandoned old men, of the view of the proceeding which could make him acquiesce in it. The victims do not always take this view of the matter. This custom was common to all the tribes which roamed the prairies. Everyone who lived to decrepitude knew that he must expect it. A more recent authority says that Poncas and Omahas never left the aged and infirm on the prairie. They were left at home, with adequate supplies, until the hunting party returned. That shows that they had a settled home and their cornfields are mentioned in the context. The old watched the cornfields, so that they were of some use. By the law of the Incas the old, who were unfit for other work, drove birds from the fields, and they were kept at public cost, like the disabled. The Hudson's Bay Eskimo strangle the old who are dependent on others for their food, or leave them to perish when the camp is moved. They move in order to get rid of burdensome old people without executing them. The central Eskimo kill the old because all who die by violence go to the happy land; others have not such a happy future. . . . Many tribes in Brazil killed the old because they were a burden and because they could no longer enjoy war, hunting, and feasting. The Tupis sometimes killed a sick man and ate the corpse, if the shaman said that he could not get well.

ALEXANDER LEAF

Youth in old age

A striking feature common to all three cultures [Abkhazia, Hunza, and Vilcabamba] was the high social status of the aged. Each of the very elderly persons we saw lived with family and close relatives—often an extended household—and occupied a central and privileged position within this group. . . .

Even those well over 100 for the most part continued to perform duties which were essential and contributed to the economy of the community in which they lived. A few hours of weeding in the fields, feeding the poultry, tending flocks, picking tea, washing the laundry, cleaning house, or caring for grandchildren performed on a regular daily basis continued to provide a sense of usefulness for the elderly. The agrarian societies to which these old people belong lend themselves to this kind of participation. In addition, the old people are esteemed for the wisdom that is thought to derive from long experience and their word in the family group is generally the law.

In Hunza this last point was evident in the mechanism by which the state is governed. Thus, the Mir holds court daily at 10 A.M. with his council of elders. The latter is comprised of some twenty wise old men from each of the villages in the kingdom. They sit in a circle on carpets spread at the foot of the Mir's wooden throne and listen to all disputes among the citizens and other domestic affairs. . . .

We watched the strenuous, intricate performance of the folk dancers of Abkhasia in Sukhumi one evening with fascination. Interestingly, one dancer was dressed as a village elder and led and directed the dance group—symbolic recognition of the important role of the elderly in that society too. But their importance receives more than token recognition. Most continue with their work until the age of 100. There is no fixed or forced retirement age, and the elderly are not dismissed when they reach a certain age as occurs in our industrialized societies. Khfaf Lasuria of Kutol, age approximately 130, had applied for and received her old-age pension for only the past two years. Even when over 100 she was the recognized champion tea picker on her collective farm. When asked if he were helping in the construction of a new house springing up next to his, Selac Butba, age 121, responded, "Of course—they can't do without me." Temur Tarba, a vigorous, horse-riding member of the collective farm at Duripshi who had celebrated his hundredth birthday just three weeks before our visit, showed from his bearing and happy manner that he "had arrived." Only seven years earlier he had been designated as a Hero of Labor and was awarded this highest Soviet honor for his cultivation of corn. . . . Of the 15,000 elderly persons over the age of eighty whom Professor Pitzkhelauri* had studied, over seventy percent continue to be very active and more than sixty percent were still working on state or collective farms. They die quickly once a useful role in the community ceases.

People who no longer have a necessary role to play in the social and economic life of their society generally deteriorate rapidly. The pattern of increasingly early retirement in our own society takes a heavy toll of our older citizens. Industrialization caused a great migration from our farms to our cities in response to the needs for a labor force by factories and businesses. Mechanization of farming did much to maintain and increase productivity of farming so that fewer hands have been required. This too freed farm laborers of toil so that they moved to the cities, seeking jobs in our growing industries. But with automation of industry the need for laborers—except during times of rapid expansion, to keep our factories productive—has fallen off. The result has been a progressively earlier age of retirement and a shortening of the work week.

The retired person in our society all too often finds himself with no sustaining interests, with children who have no use for Dad or Mom, nor any room in their cramped urban apartments for parents. Even with economic independence the elderly find their children have moved away and made other friends and attachments. When visiting their children, they find their presence all too often tolerated rather than desired, especially if their visit becomes an extended one. They sense quickly that they have become a burden on their children, confirming in their own minds their uselessness. A search for friendship and companionship often drives them to centers where other retired elderly have congregated. The trailer parks in California, the hotels in Miami, and the housing and clubs for the elderly in every city are familiar examples of the retreat of the unneeded and often unwanted elderly from loneliness. All too often such groupings fail to satisfy the need. . . .

As continued technological advances accelerate the rate of change in our economy, the emphasis is on youth. In a traditional society like Hunza, which has changed little, wisdom comes with age because the old person has witnessed a wider range of the kinds of problems and the kinds of solutions which are effective in such a society. The greater adaptability possessed by the young affords them a distinct advantage over the conservatism and set ways of their elders in times of rapid change. . . . The heightened value of youth in these times of rapid change has provided the young with the economic independence to break ties with parents and elders who in a traditional agrarian society own the land, the sole source of livelihood. Furthermore, the wisdom of extensive experience, which in the static society of Hunza is justifiably highly prized in the elderly, loses its value in a rapidly changing society where the premium must be on adaptability rather than experience. . . .

If the only means by which the elderly can achieve status and deserve respect is a return to an unchanging traditional society—a most unlikely prospect, today—then we would have to weigh the gains for the elders against the possible loss to the young. In a traditional stable society the extended family structure clearly provides benefits for the old, but what are the costs to the young? Decision-making remains

*Ed. note: A leading Russian gerontologist.

the prerogative of the elderly, so there must be an associated limitation of choices for the young. But it is just the freedom to make their own decisions that motivates our youth to establish independent households. How restricted do the young (and even middle-aged) feel in traditional stable cultures? Do they rebel against a tyranny of their elders or do they accept this relation as in the nature of things, having known nothing different, and perhaps gain patience in the knowledge that in due time they will ascend to the status of their elders? There are clearly "cost benefits" to the individual and to society of social conditions which may favor respect for age versus freedom for youth. Can the one be had only at the expense of the other? Since there is little indication that society is likely spontaneously to return to stable traditional ways, it will take great ingenuity to develop conditions which will benefit both.

Retirement in our society is largely economically determined, and there seems to be no possibility of return to the agrarian existence of most of our forebears who lived in extended family groups. On the farm no one was too old to make some contribution to the social and economic life of the family. The chores might become less strenuous, but by performing them on a regular basis the elderly could always feel needed and useful.

It seems a corruption of the very purpose of our economy that, instead of freeing us from drudgery and need and allowing us all to enjoy a better life with the things it can produce, it holds us slaves to its dictates even though affluence is at hand. We can anticipate that continued automation of industry will bring earlier retirement and shorter working hours. The devastating effect of enforced leisure on the life span of the elderly and the happiness of all could be countered in part by educational programs. Such programs should have the purpose of arousing interest and demonstrating the possibility of hobbies or avocations to which people can turn with zest when their contribution to the industrial economy is no longer needed. The trend toward shorter working hours and earlier retirement makes the need for such education

urgent. Creative activities such as music and the arts, sports, and much-needed physical exercise, as well as crafts, gardening, and many other interests, need active cultivation. Involvement in services for less fortunate members of the community, in protecting the environment, and in other such socially constructive tasks can also be continued long after retirement. Self-fulfillment in such pursuits can provide the interest and joy of living that is so essential to a life-sustaining, wholesome mental state.

ARLIE HOCHSCHILD

Communal living in old age

Along with blacks, women and adolescents, the old have emerged as a "social problem"—a label usually given to people who lack power. There is not one social problem, but rather many. There is the problem of poverty, of poor health and of loneliness. Underlying all three is a condition that is hard to isolate as a "problem," a condition that cannot be changed without radically altering the entire society. Namely this: apart from a privileged elite for whom old age is a harvest of honor and riches, the old in America are not needed by society. . . .

As work becomes less important as a source of friendships for the old, neighborhoods tend to become more important, especially for the working and lower classes. The old in the United States today either live together with young people (in the same family or neighborhood) or separate from them (alone or with other old people). I will discuss why the first, more common and accepted setting often leads to isolation and why the second, newer and less approved, generally does not. I will also try to show how a new and increasingly common alternative to isolation is communities of old people. . . .

Integration

When one searches for an example of an old person living with his children, grandchildren and assorted relatives, the mind moves to other times and places. . . .

In the United States today only about 8 percent of people over sixty-five live with their children and grandchildren, and probably no more than this ever did in the past. About a fourth to a third of old people now live with an adult child (but not with a grandchild). A widowed grandmother may move in with her daughter and son-in-law, or a divorced man may live on with his mother and father. But it has been rare to see two generations of *intact* marriages living together, and since World War II it has become even more rare.

More often, old people live alone or with friends who are not related. This does not mean that the old are cut off from their children: 84 percent of American old people live less than an hour away from a child. But typically they do not live together.

And, more important, most old people do not *want* to live with their children. Many who do live with them do so because it saves money, not because it's a good social arrangement. Less than 10 percent of a recent national sample of old people said they wanted to live with a child or relative. Only 17 percent recommended it to other old people able to care for themselves. Even for ill or disabled old people, more (39 percent) recommended going to a nursing home or getting nursing care than recommended moving in with children (23 percent). . . .

Moreover, when the old live near young people outside the family, they usually do not make friends with them. In fact, the old person with young neighbors is often more isolated than his peer who lives near other old people. In a very important and excellent study of Cleveland residents, the sociologist Irving Rosow compared 1,200 old people living in three kinds of housing: one with a mix of ages ("normal"), one with quite a few old people ("age concentrated") and one with almost all old people ("age dense"). Those living with many other old people made the most friends. But even in the normal neighborhoods (with about 12 percent old people), most befriended not young people but others their own age. . . .

A mutual disinterest between young and old can, in varying degree, isolate the old. . . .

It has become a sad commonplace to associate being old with being alone. We call isolation a punishment for the prisoner, but perhaps a majority of American old people are in some degree isolated or soon will be. It has gradually come to seem "natural," and ironically age-integrated settings make it seem more so.

Separation

Old people live together in a number of places: private retirement villages for the well-to-do, public housing projects and rundown hotels for the poor. While most of the 9 percent of the U.S. population over sixty-five live in independent housing in age-integrated neighborhoods, they are only 3 percent of the population in some new suburbs and 30 percent in cities such as St. Petersburg, Florida. Since World War II, there has been a mushroom growth of old-age housing, drop-in centers and retirement settlements such as Ryderwood in Washington, Moosehaven in Florida, Sun City (which has over twelve thousand residents) in Arizona and the Rossmoor Leisure Worlds in California. . . .

Here the old person is not integrated with the young, but neither is he isolated. He may even find a new mate. One study found that almost a third of the married couples in a retirement community had met and married there.

Many outsiders feel ambivalent toward these new old-age subcultures, partly because they are based on leisure and partly because they separate old people from young people. But according to virtually all the reported research, the old people who live in them like the life and choose it freely.

A case in point

I recently worked and observed life in Merrill Court,[1] a California public housing project for poor people over sixty-two. Initially, I should confess, I felt that there was something sad about a group of old people living together, something artificial, maybe even depressing. But it soon

---

[1]This is not its real name.

became clear to me that they themselves were not depressed. They saw nothing sad about living together and felt a shade of pity for those who had to live alone. They felt they *had* problems, but they did not feel they *were* one.

The findings of this and other research suggest that the kind of communal life I found at Merrill Court was due more to the setting than to the particular characteristics of the people who happened to live there. Although the residents are not part of a random sample, their characteristics do not distinguish them so very much from this generation of American old people as a whole. Most of the residents were poor, rural-born Anglo-Saxon Protestant widowed females in their late sixties. . . .

The residents slept in separate apartments, but they did not live alone. Most waking hours were spent in each other's company, either over the telephone or over a cup of coffee. As a result, they kept an eye on each other and usually noted when someone was deviating from a routine. . . .

In addition to the private apartments, there was a large recreation room downstairs where [there] . . . was a hub of activity: there people were weaving rugs, knitting clothes, sewing aprons, cooking pies or practicing music—a five-piece band, including washtub bass, played in nursing homes for the "old folks" there. As people worked, they joked and gossiped and, if the mood was right, sang ballads. The activities changed from month to month, but the work, the gossip and the arranging did not. . . .

Liberation by separation

The similarity of the residents liberated them and liberated their topics of conversation. In a society that raises an eyebrow at those who do not "act their age," the old-age subculture of Merrill Court freed the old to dance a jig, to tell an off-color joke and to flirt without worrying about letting grandmotherly decorum slip. Among themselves, they developed a backstage talk about playing the role of old person. Just as one plays the role of woman to man and black person to white, so one plays the role of old person to young people. Thus, on occasions protected from the young, the old are able to drop the role. Outside such a community old people often try, with powder and wig, to "pass" as younger, but within such a community they don't need to.

To bring old people together is not to free them from all social constraint but to substitute old-age constraints for age-integrated ones. . . . On the other hand, there was much they could do and say together that they could not—or would not—with young people. . . .

Lifting the taboo on death

The residents talked with each other about other people's deaths and the prospect of their own quite freely, in straight-forward, noneuphemistic language. Death was a fact of life in the community: six residents died in the course of my three years of field work there. There was a collective concern with, as they put it, "being ready," facing up, and each death taught the residents something about it. They felt there was a "good" way and a "bad" way to die. One woman's death especially was the community's example of "the right way to die"—to face death rather than turn one's back on it, all the while living fully to the end. She was praised as much for remaining active as for having her will and burial arranged and being on good terms with her family.

They could not, in the same way, share these concerns with their young family and friends. In fact, it was from the young that they more often heard comments of denial such as "You don't look a day over fifty" or "You get younger every day." . . .

The age solidarity in Merrill Court tends to liberate the topic of death and the unembarrassed expression of grief. Only a small proportion of old people live in such old-age communities, but it is probably true that in general the old among the old feel less constrained to deny death or to observe the taboo on talk related to it. . . .

Conclusion

Deprived of function and power, old people have few clearly defined roles. The former roles that applied to a wife, a worker or a parent have faded with time. But the resulting ambiguity does not obtain in a community of old people such as this. If one is no longer a mother to a brood of small children, or a wife or a provider, one can be the club treasurer, a bowling partner, a volunteer worker in a nursing home or a neighbor's caretaker.

For friends lost through death there are replacements; at Merrill Court whenever an apartment is vacated, it is immediately filled by the first on a long list of applicants at the housing agency. If there is no longer work that "has to be done," something like it is there. With each new role come new customs and new notions of the right and wrong of it. The residents have built themselves an order out of ambiguity, a set of obligations to the outside world and to each other where few had existed before. Lacking responsibilities to the young, they take on responsibilities to each other, and if the outside world watches them less for being old, they watch each other more. They have renewed their social contract with life, on the basis of a new sibling solidarity.

Young people are not alone in their search for "relevant models." Since the parents of today's old people usually died earlier, in the social prime of middle age, an individual does not know what to expect of himself if he lives in pretty good health to a time when he is no longer needed and when he is isolated from others faced with the same dilemma. A community of peers in old life provides models for how to age, when, in this respect, the last generation of old people as well as the young are no help.

Communities of old people need not substitute for warm ties with young family and friends. But the decline of the extended family creates the need for a new social shelter, another pool of friendships, another bond with society apart from family. Old-fashioned values may fade, but the communal experiments of this generation of old people may forecast new social networks for the next.

Old age: The last segregation

July 10, 1970

Dear Mr. Nader:

One year ago, my parents, aged seventy-four and seventy-three, had a one-car accident in late afternoon on a rural country road in central Wisconsin. . . . My father hit the rearview mirror and was knocked unconscious on impact. My mother, however, was thrown against the dash and suffered a compression fracture of her spine, leaving her instantly paralyzed from the waist down, although completely conscious. . . .

The accident meant the end of my parents' life on the farm. . . .

On September 17, 1969, Dr. B. transferred my mother to * * * nursing home, under the care of Dr. M. He told my sister that under the circumstances it was impossible for my mother to live alone in the house; since my father was physically incapable of caring for her, the best solution at the moment was for her to be admitted directly to the nursing home where she would get continuing therapy and care. . . .

Our father continued to grow worse mentally, although he, like Mama, still had a body with the strength of an ox. . . . Ten days after his lung surgery he sat upright in the car and drove with my sister and her husband one hundred miles to the nursing home to be admitted as a patient with Mama, in a double room. He wanted desperately to be with her, and being with her seemed the only good thing we as a family could do for him at that point. . . .

I would like to skip over the next three months entirely, the memory is still so awful. I corresponded with my mother weekly; my father grew progressively worse, he hallucinated nights, got out of bed and crawled to my mother's bed and shook the rails, screaming out the nightmares he was living through. Nurses would rush in after Mama turned on her light, and with the help of a male aide would give my father a hypo and shove him back into bed. My mother, during this time, began to suffer increasing pain in her legs and lower back—nerve rejuvenation, the doctor called it— and did in fact regain slight movement in her right leg. Her nights were painful, and the little rest she was able to get was continually interrupted by my father. During the day they were left alone, and my mother had to watch my father constantly, ready to call for the nurses should he try to get out of bed or out of his chair and maneuver around. He was too weak to walk unaided. In short, for nine hundred dollars per month, plus medical care(!), my paralyzed mother was given the job of caring for my father twenty-four hours a day. Dr. M. never came to see either of them. . . .

In the meantime, both another sister in California and I had become terribly upset because Mama's letters indicated she was getting little if any rest at all during the nights. Both of us wrote to Dr. M. I wrote requesting that my father be moved across the hall into a separate room to insure that Mama would get some rest at night, and my sister wrote suggesting that Daddy might be better cared for at this point in the state mental hospital. We both wrote asking for advice, and asking that we get replies.

Neither of us received any acknowledgment of our letters. But on December 7, 1969, two nurses and a male aide rushed into my parents' room at the nursing home and forcibly removed my father into a waiting ambulance, in which he was transferred to the state hospital. My mother was frantic, and begged to know why. After a good while, Dr. M. came to see her and told her that Daddy had been transferred there at the request of two of her daughters. Since Daddy had grown uncontrollable and unsubduable, he judged it the best course of action. My mother telephoned my sister in Milwaukee to tell her the news. My sister was, understandably, terribly upset and extremely angry with both me and my sister in California. She phoned Dr. M. and he told her that we had both written to him and demanded that our father be put there.

I happen to be very careful about keeping copies of all my pertinent correspondence; I had only requested that Daddy be moved to a separate room, and had said, ". . . I want to make it clear that I am only one of eight children—certainly my decision alone shouldn't be the final one. . . ." I had asked for, and expected to receive, advice from the doctor.

Perhaps I need not even add that my father never had his medication checked or altered by Dr. M., nor were his dentures refitted. . . .

On January 20, 1970, my father died in the state hospital. He had starved himself into a living skeleton. . . . At Christmas he did not recognize my sister nor my brother when they came to see him. . . . In his dreams he was still whole and farming, and kept trying to get up and leave, saying that it was such a long, cold spring, and he had to get back to the farm to get the crops in. . . .

My father wanted to die, I know; I do not mean to make it sound as though he was neglected totally—he had willed himself to die. But his transfer from the nursing home to the state hospital was done cruelly and unnecessarily, with absolutely no thought for my mother, or for any of his children—let alone him.

And that left my mother. In January, I drove again to Wisconsin and saw her and talked at length with the therapist in charge of her, a very nice, personable young man. He told me that what Mama needed, now that Daddy was gone, was to get into * * * Rehabilitation Institute in Milwaukee. There was much she could learn to do for herself from a wheelchair, and she just was not learning to do it at the nursing home. "She's spoiled here," he said, "she's the only patient here who has a clear mind and the nurses all visit with her and do everything for her— they won't let her do anything for herself. . . ."

Can you get her there right away, I asked. I can't do it, he said apologetically. Dr. M. has to sign the order . . . I'm only the therapist. . . .

Mama had changed; her indomitable spirit, which shone through everything all that summer at the hospital, was gone. Everywhere nurses cluck-clucked over her; her catheter was well in evidence on her wheelchair, and she complained that her back brace (fitted on her directly after surgery) was never put on properly. She showed us the weals to prove it. I gave her a long Dutch-uncle talk about doing more for herself. . . . I told her, she must learn to be more self-sufficient in order to live anywhere else, and I told her she must plan on going to the rehabilitation institute. . . .

However, on Friday, April 17, my sister from California and I drove to see Dr. M. We asked him to admit Mama to the rehabilitation institute at once, and told him again of our hopes for her future. He stood in his office and laughed at us. He told us that our mother was an incurable invalid, that she could never expect to live outside an institution, and he hooted at me: "Why, do you realize it takes three nurses just to get her in and out of bed?" I asked him why, since she had come there from the hospital able to do it all by herself, and he changed the subject. He cited her back brace, her catheter, her constant night pain, all as irrefutable evidence that she would never be able to leave that nursing home.

And we looked at his flabby, vacuous face and saw that he looked at our mother and knew only a seventy-four-year-old farm woman who owned a 120-acre farm, thirty acres of good lake-shore property with cabin, and a value-increasing house in his town, not half a block away from his own house. He owned a nursing home filled with patients, and of all of them, our mother was the most secure financial liability he had, I know. He could keep her there until she died and own everything she had. . . .

Last winter my home-town newspaper did a series of articles on nursing homes. The tone of those articles was how awful it was the way families subject their elderly members to such places. That may be true in some cases but not always, and the villains who are so carefully never exposed are most of the time those grand, outstanding members of the medical profession at whose mercy the public is. . . .

After only five weeks at the Institute, my mother has proven what we in the family knew all along—that she is more than capable of taking care of herself, with only minimal supervision. The back brace was taken away at once; she had not needed it for six months, the doctor told me. She irrigates her own catheter,

controls her own bowel program, can wash and dress herself, and get in and out of bed without help. Her pain is due to muscle spasms; the medication prescribed by Dr. M. was diagnosed as a strong narcotic, which was discarded the first night at the Institute. In its place she has a muscle relaxant and a sleeping pill, and is sleeping soundly for the first time in nine months. She is using a sewing machine again, can work a rug loom, can roll over, turn herself, pull and drag herself anywhere on a mat or floor, and can do fifteen push-ups without getting even short of breath. She can work in a kitchen, do her own laundry and ironing and, in short, is as self-sufficient as any person can be without the full use of her legs.

She will be discharged from the Institute the first week in August and, I am happy to say, will then move in here with me. She is great, just great—I cannot tell you how much I am looking forward to having her here, nor how pleased my husband and kids are.

Far from the futile picture that charlatan owning the nursing home painted, she has a bright and full life ahead of her. . . .

But the best part of all is seeing Mama once again feeling useful and self-confident. If she had had to stay in that nursing home, she would have died. That is not just my opinion; the social worker told me the psychologist had confirmed it after all her tests at the Institute. The nursing home staff treated her as a total invalid and expected her to waste away and die. Far from caring about her future as a whole human being, that bastard of a doctor did his utmost to convince her children as well as her that her life was over. A caring family was the last thing he wanted for one of his patients.

I am convinced that my case is certainly not an exception. It is not only the nursing homes and the appalling care they give patients who need to be investigated, it is the doctors who own and live off them, and the cohorts who transfer patients to them.

The entire medical profession has one hell of a lot of answering to do for their treatment of elderly people. From the glib practitioners who recommend nursing homes as the only solution to distraught families to the money suckers who bleed the life's work of old people and call it "care." My mother . . . is lucky; her bills are in the thousands of dollars, but she has the money to pay them all and still live comfortably and well. What about all the old people who have only their homes when tragedy such as this strikes? I have learned a lot about such cases in the past year, believe me. I know about nursing homes that have their patients sign over all their property in return for "care" until they die. And I know about the homes themselves—the one my mother existed in for nine months, for example. She had a TV in her room, and every day all the nurses piled in to watch their favorite soap operas. She bought a paper every night, and during the night the nurses stole in and lifted it off her bed, thinking she was asleep; and she never got to finish reading it. . . . I could go on and on. . . . They took advantage of her clear mind and her money-paying ability, and treated her like a rotten vegetable ready to be discarded.

SIMONE DE BEAUVOIR

The coming of age

The vast majority of mankind look upon the coming of old age with sorrow or rebellion. It fills them with more aversion than death itself.

And indeed, it is old age, rather than death, that is to be contrasted with life. Old age is life's parody, whereas death transforms life into a destiny: in a way it preserves it by giving it the absolute dimension—"As into himself eternity changes him at last." Death does away with time. . . . But when [an old man] . . . was eighty, the present he was living through overlaid the past. This dominance of the present is saddening when it is a degradation or even a denial of what has been; and almost always this is so. Former happenings and acquired knowledge retain their place, but in a life whose fire

has died: they *have been*. When memory decays, they sink and vanish in a mocking darkness; life unravels stitch by stitch like a frayed piece of knitting, leaving nothing but meaningless strands of wool in the old person's hands. . . .

There is only one solution if old age is not to be an absurd parody of our former life, and that is to go on pursuing ends that give our existence a meaning—devotion to individuals, to groups or to causes, social, political, intellectual or creative work. . . . In old age we should wish still to have passions strong enough to prevent us turning in upon ourselves. One's life has value so long as one attributes value to the life of others, by means of love, friendship, indignation, compassion. When this is so, then there are still valid reasons for activity or speech.

But these possibilities are granted only to a handful of privileged people: it is in the last years of life that the gap between them and the vast majority of mankind becomes deepest and most obvious. When we set these two old ages side by side we can answer the question . . . : what are the inescapable factors in the individual's decline? And to what degree is society responsible for them?

The age at which this decline begins has always depended upon the class to which a man belongs. Today a miner is finished, done for, at the age of fifty, whereas many of the privileged carry their eighty years lightly. The worker's decline begins earlier; its course is also far more rapid. During his years of "survival" his shattered body is the victim of disease and infirmity; whereas an elderly man who has had the good fortune of being able to look after his health may keep it more or less undamaged until his death.

When they are old the exploited classes are condemned if not to utter destitution then at least to extreme poverty, to uncomfortable, inconvenient dwellings, and to loneliness, all of which results in a feeling of failure and a generalized anxiety. They sink into a torpid bewilderment that has physical repercussions: even the mental diseases from which they suffer are to a great extent the product of the system. Even if he keeps his health and his clarity of mind, the retired man is nevertheless the victim of that terrible curse, boredom. Deprived of his hold upon the world, he is incapable of finding another because apart from his work his free time was alienated, rendered sterile. The manual worker does not even manage to kill time. His gloomy idleness leads to an apathy that endangers what physical and intellectual balance he may still possess.

The injury he has suffered during the course of his life is still more radical. The reason that the retired man is rendered hopeless by the want of meaning in his present life is that the meaning of his existence has been stolen from him from the very beginning. A law, as merciless as Lassalle's "brazen law" of wages, allows him no more than the right to reproduce his life: it refuses him the possibility of discovering any justification for it. When he escapes from the fetters of his trade or calling, all he sees around him is an arid waste: he has not been granted the possibility of committing himself to projects that might have peopled the world with goals, values and reasons for existence.

That is the crime of our society. Its "old-age policy" is scandalous. But even more scandalous still is the treatment that it inflicts upon the majority of men during their youth and their maturity. It prefabricates the maimed and wretched state that is theirs when they are old. It is the fault of society that the decline of old age begins too early, that it is rapid, physically painful and, because they enter in upon it with empty hands, morally atrocious. Some exploited, alienated individuals inevitably become "throw-outs," "rejects," once their strength has failed them.

That is why all the remedies that have been put forward to lessen the distress of the aged are such a mockery: not one of them can possibly repair the systematic destruction that has been inflicted upon some men throughout their lives. Even if they are treated and taken care of, their health cannot be given back. Even if decent houses are built for them, they cannot be provided with the culture, the interests and the responsibilities that would give their life a meaning. I do not say that it would be entirely pointless to improve their condition here and now; but doing so would provide no solution

whatsoever to the real problem of old age. What should a society be, so that in his last years a man might still be a man?

The answer is simple: he would always have to have been treated as a man. By the fate it allots to its members who can no longer work, society gives itself away—it has always looked upon them as so much material. Society confesses that as far as it is concerned, profit is the only thing that counts, and that its "humanism" is mere window-dressing. . . .

Once we have understood what the state of the aged really is, we cannot satisfy ourselves with calling for a more generous "old-age policy," higher pensions, decent housing and organized leisure. It is the whole system that is at issue and our claim cannot be otherwise than radical—change life itself.

H. TRISTRAM ENGELHARDT

The counsels of finitude

[The philosophers] Hegel and Hartshorne are arguing for the obvious: that man is finite, though his expectations are not, that men must die though the values which man cherishes are as such enduring, living in the appreciation of whatever community of rational animals achieves them. Further, any one individual human achieves as *a* particular human only *a* particular grasp of such values. Thus societal progress depends on both new and energetic members embodying and achieving those enduring values in new ways. In so arguing, Hegel and Hartshorne presuppose two crucial premises: first that the amount of energy and resources is finite so that if one extended the human life span one would be forced to decrease the percentage which young persons constitute in the population; and second, that a certain fairly high percentage of young persons is necessary, if a society is to be dynamic. Hartshorne and Hegel presume in addition that old age itself is, in and of itself, encumbered by a certain monotony born out of the decrease in novel experiences. I have not explicitly examined those premises, but have rather displayed some of their consequences.

They are, though, not unlikely premises. The first, what may be called the finite resources premise, has some cogency when pushed all the way. If man achieves physical immortality and if resources are finite for the support of a population, then new members could not be added. The second premise, the youth-is-creative premise, is probably the more problematic— but probably only over the short run. That is, it might be the case that extending the human life span to one hundred and fifty or two hundred years might not have a profound effect on the tenor of society or prove a burden to those who live such long lives. But the premise is that somewhere there must be a limit and that surely within the present bounds of senility, that limit comes before any such extended longevity.

Thus, on the one hand, there are few, if any, practical, immediate consequences to this view. These reflections say nothing, for example, about what a reasonable human life span should be, about what a reasonable investment in prolonging the life of an elderly person would be, or about how one chooses between particular investments of societal resources in prolonging life. But, on the other hand, there are general implications which can in the end be drawn. Or at least, the foregoing suggests certain ways in which the relation of medicine to death can be viewed. In particular, it is plain that death is not the enemy of medicine.

In short, we are given a sense in which death is natural—namely, death is natural to men in that humans are contingent beings. Since each particular human being is not a necessary being, that person could possibly cease to exist and over the long run therefore surely will die. Further, an infinite life span for a finite being may be a difficult if not boring prospect, as Hartshorne suggests. Thus to the question why is man mortal, the answer is that he is a contingent, finite being and therefore dependent on an indefinite number of possible variables which could cause his death. But, though physical immortality is an absurdity, it does make sense to see a painful death or a premature death (less than the usual life span) as "unnatural" in the sense of violating a reasonable human hope—for a painless death and an average life span. Painful and premature deaths are properly the enemies of medicine, not death itself.

Thus, one can conclude with a fairly common-sense moral: if death is natural it follows that it is not medicine's enemy. At the most it is untimely death or painful death which stands out to be conquered by societal investment in medicine. Further, as a consequence, in establishing societal priorities for the control of the causes of death, the accent should fall on the control of those causes which result in painful or untimely death. The latter has been accomplished in great measure through the control of infectious diseases. But when, for example, considering a choice between investing resources in curtailing fatal diseases of old age groups versus those of younger age groups, the choice would favor the latter, and not on merely utilitarian grounds. Rather, the choice would reflect the fact that in the second case death occurred before the values open to those persons could have been achieved—values to which they could reasonably claim a right.

One should be careful here. The usual age at which death occurs in old age could change when and if the aging process could be slowed. Again, such slowing, if it were possible, would have to be done with serious thought concerning the values being balanced: the scope in time adequate to a rich, full life; the effect on the ability to add new members to the human community in which postponing death would result; the effect of the investment of resources in the prolongation of life, upon the resources available to support the general quality of life. The latter in particular must be an object of scrutiny, otherwise one will forget about achieving the purposes of life and society while frenetically attempting to prolong life. One will confuse ends with means, one will think that the goods which make the goodness of life are merely life, and forget that, as Seneca remarked, "The wise man . . . lives as long as he should, not as long as he can." Or, to put it another way, if one seeks primarily to save his life, he is likely to forget the purposes of life.

"Look, Nixon's no dope. If the people really <u>wanted</u> moral leadership,
he'd give them moral leadership."

6

POLITICS:
THE DOMESTIC
STRUGGLE
FOR POWER

In their complex relationship, politics and morals have never been on the best of terms. Plato and Aristotle wrote that the end of politics was the achievement of the best way of life, the life oriented to the Good, but in their own lifetimes both tried—and failed—to convince any politicians of this ideal. To this day, politics is often conducted according to the exact reverse of this classical Greek ideal in which the state is not subordinate to the good but superior to it. In this conception, the continued welfare and prosperity of the rulers *are* the highest moral ideals in that society. In such a state, justice, as Plato wrote in his immortal work, *The Republic,* "is the interest of the stronger"; what is *just* is whatever the rulers say it is. This is the deeper meaning of Lord Acton's famous epigram, "Power corrupts and absolute power corrupts absolutely." Graft and bribery are only the first steps in this process of moral corruption. The more advanced stages are marked by the denial that autonomous moral standards exist.

Despite all these dangers, however, morality cannot often shun political action. Some conditions may be so offensive, so threatening, or so evil that some form of political action is demanded in response. Then, even a lasting involvement in politics and desire for power with all its attendant temptations may be morally justified.

On the other side, even at its most immoral, politics must still sham a display of morality. It still must try to justify its acts by pointing to their moral ends. Even Stalin said that he was murdering Russians because, for instance, they "endangered the Revolution," or were "enemies of society," and not because he did not like them. The last is hardly seen as a moral ground for such an action while the first two may well be. In sum, at the core of the relation between politics and morals, there is an ever-present tension.

The first group of readings focuses on these moral ends of political action. John Rawls argues that justice is a "complex of three ideas: liberty, equality, and reward for services contributing to the common good." In his view, each person in a political system has an equal right to the greatest liberty compatible with a similar liberty for everyone. Inequalities can be justified only if they work to everyone's advantage and if positions leading to inequalities are open to all.

Irving Kristol and Michael Walzer come next, as antagonists in a debate over the relative benefits and disadvantages of equality. Kristol, taking issue with Rawls, rejects the goal of equality and claims that inequality of talents and achievements among men is "natural" and so, therefore, is inequality of reward. Furthermore, he believes that present urging of equality is specious: It is not really for equality at all, but is rather a symbol of disaffection with the spiritual emptiness of modern society. Walzer scoffs at Kristol's argument and argues the merits of the case for equality of income and power. In response to Kristol, Walzer writes that "there is no reason to think that 'human talents and abilities' in fact distribute themselves along a *single* curve, although income necessarily does. . . . There is no single talent or combination of talents which plausibly entitles a man to every available social good." Inequality, he claims, is arbitrary and, therefore, unjustifiable.

From the moral ends of political action, we turn to its immoral acts. The second group of articles focuses on the history of political corruption in America, and at the same time, raises the question of the relationship between means and ends in political action. In the lead piece, Jack Douglas defends Boss Tweed of Tammany Hall—whose name has become synonymous with corruption—as a masterful politician: Only Tweed had the insight, Douglas argues, to realize that motley New York, with its assorted ethnic fiefdoms, could be governed effectively only through corruption. What may be inferred from Douglas' article, Lincoln Steffens states clearly: In a classic piece of muckraking, Steffens indicts us private citizens for the corruption of our politics and politicians. Private greasing of the hand is not very different from public graft:

"The bribe we pay to the janitor to prefer our interests to the landlord's is the little brother of the bribe passed to the alderman to sell a city street, and the father of the air-brake stock assigned to the president of a railroad to have this life-saving invention adopted on his road."

The most recent episode of political corruption, Watergate, has stunned many analysts in desperate search for a motive. Archibald Cox, seeking "the long-range forces in the moral and political climate" that made Watergate possible, concludes that the failure to observe constraints upon means, no matter how worthy the ends, contributes "to some crumbling of the moral order." Thus, Cox argues that those who have opposed the government through physical confrontation or destruction of draft board records—although acting in the name of peace and justice—are partly responsible for the immoral condition of our society.

We turn next to a consideration of the morality of political action and the role of authority. Karl Marx, for whom the ends do justify the means, including violence, writes that all past political morality before the reign of the proletariat has been the result of domination of one class by another. In other words, all previous political morality has been no kind of morality at all but has been a tyranny based on the antimoral premise "might makes right."

Indeed, the role of might—or force—is one of the key issues in the on-going debate over what kind of political system is best. At present, liberalism, which is suspicious of restraints on the individual, is the most influential doctrine of political philosophy in America. James Burnham, however, pronounces liberalism to be "moribund." In addition, he criticizes it for weakening authority, which he holds to be necessary for any enduring and peaceful society. Placed by the editors in response is Walter Lippmann, who restates the classic case for liberalism and brings us back to the consideration of equality and liberty raised at the beginning of this chapter.

John Rawls, born in 1921, has been a professor of philosophy at Harvard since 1962. He earlier taught at Cornell and the Massachusetts Institute of Technology. His major work, *A Theory of Justice* (1971), was widely acclaimed as one of the most important modern works in political philosophy. He first set out the major thesis of this book in "Justice as Fairness," excerpted here, which appeared originally in *The Philosophical Review* in 1958.

Irving Kristol, born in 1920, is Henry Luce Professor of Urban Affairs at New York University and coeditor of the quarterly *The Public Interest.* He was formerly managing editor of *Commentary* magazine and cofounder of the English journal *Encounter.* Among his longer works are *The American Revolution as a Successful Revolution* and *On the Democratic Idea in America.* "About Equality," reprinted here, originally appeared in *Commentary* in 1972.

Michael Walzer was born in 1935 and educated at Brandeis and Harvard Universities. He has been on the faculty at Harvard since 1966. A member of the editorial board of *Dissent* since 1960, he is the author of *Obligations: Essays on Disobedience, War and Citizenship.*

Jack Douglas is professor of sociology at the University of California, San Diego, having also taught at Dartmouth, Wellesley, UCLA and Syracuse. He is the author of *The Social Meanings of Suicide.* His article on Boss Tweed, one of several works about the New York politician by various scholars to appear in the last few years, first was published in the *Wall Street Journal* in 1976.

Lincoln Steffens, journalist and social reformer, was born in 1866. In 1901 he became managing editor of *McClure's* magazine, in which he published a series of articles later collected in the volume *The Shame of the Cities* (1904). These exposés of corruption in business and politics earned him and his colleagues the title of "muckrakers." Steffens died in 1936.

Archibald Cox is Williston Professor of Law at Harvard Law School. He was special Watergate prosecutor from May 18, 1973 until October 21, when he was fired as the first step in what came to be known as the Saturday Night Massacre. He is author of *The Warren Court: Constitutional Decision as an Instrument of Reform.* "Ends" first appeared in the *New York Times Magazine* in 1974.

Karl Marx, born in 1818, is considered to be the founder of modern socialism and communism. His major works outlining his economic philosophy, written with Friedrich Engels, are *Das Kapital* and *The Communist Manifesto* (1847). Marx died in London in 1883. **Friedrich Engels,** born in 1820, was a German socialist who fled to England in 1850. In addition to collaborating with Marx, he wrote several other books and was engaged in manufacturing. He died in 1895.

James Burnham, born in 1905, was a professor of philosophy at New York University from 1929 to 1953. For the last twenty years he has been a member of the editorial board of the *National Review.* He is the author of several books on the subject of political power struggles. "Notes on Authority, Morality, Power" appeared in the *National Review* in 1970.

Walter Lippmann. See above, p. 3.

JOHN RAWLS

Justice as fairness

The conception of justice which I want to develop may be stated in the form of two principles as follows: first, each person participating in a practice,[1] or affected by it, has an equal right to the most extensive liberty compatible with a like liberty for all; and second, inequalities are arbitrary unless it is reasonable to expect that they will work out for everyone's advantage and provided the positions and offices to which they attach, or from which they may be gained, are open to all. These principles express justice as a complex of three ideas: liberty, equality, and reward for services contributing to the common good. . . .

The first principle holds, of course, only if other things are equal: that is, while there must always be a justification for departing from the initial position of equal liberty (which is defined by the pattern of rights and duties, powers and liabilities, established by a practice), and the burden of proof is placed on him who would depart from it, nevertheless, there can be, and often there is, a justification for doing so. . . .

It might be argued at this point that justice requires only an equal liberty. If, however, a greater liberty were possible for all without loss or conflict, then it would be irrational to settle on a lesser liberty. There is no reason for circumscribing rights unless their exercise would be incompatible, or would render the practice defining them less effective. . . .

The second principle defines what sorts of inequalities are permissible; it specifies how the presumption laid down by the first principle may be put aside. Now by inequalities it is best to understand not *any* differences between offices and positions, but differences in the benefits and burdens attached to them either directly or indirectly, such as prestige and wealth, or liability to taxation and compulsory services. Players in a game do not protest against there being different positions, such as batter, pitcher, catcher, and the like, nor to there being various privileges and powers as specified by the rules; nor do the citizens of a country object to there being the different offices of government such as president, senator, governor, judge, and so on, each with their special rights and duties. It is not differences of this kind that are normally thought of as inequalities, but differences in the resulting distribution established by a practice or made possible by it, of the things men strive to attain or avoid. Thus they may complain about the pattern of honors and rewards set up by a practice (e.g., the privileges and salaries of government officials) or they may object to the distribution of power and wealth which results from the various ways in which men avail themselves of the opportunities allowed by it (e.g., the concentration of wealth which may develop in a free price system allowing large entrepreneurial or speculative gains).

It should be noted that the second principle holds that an inequality is allowed only if there is reason to believe that the practice with the inequality, or resulting in it, will work for the advantage of *every* party engaging in it. Here it is important to stress that *every* party must gain from the inequality. Since the principle applies to practices, it implies that the representative man in every office or position defined by a practice, when he views it as a going concern, must find it reasonable to prefer his condition and prospects with the inequality to what they would be under the practice without it. The principle excludes, therefore, the justification of inequalities on the grounds that the disadvantages of those in one position are outweighed by the greater advantages of those in another position. . . .

Further, it is also necessary that the various offices to which special benefits or burdens attach are open to all. It may be, for example, to the common advantage, as just defined, to attach

---

[1] I use the word "practice" throughout as a sort of technical term meaning any form of activity specified by a system of rules which defines offices, roles, moves, penalties, defenses, and so on, and which gives the activity its structure. As examples one may think of games and rituals, trials and parliaments, markets and systems of property.

special benefits to certain offices. Perhaps by doing so the requisite talent can be attracted to them and encouraged to give its best efforts. But any offices having special benefits must be won in a fair competition in which contestants are judged on their merits. If some offices were not open, those excluded would normally be justified in feeling unjustly treated, even if they benefited from the greater efforts of those who were allowed to compete for them.

IRVING KRISTOL

About equality

There would appear to be little doubt that the matter of equality has become, in these past two decades, a major political and ideological issue. The late Hugh Gaitskell proclaimed flatly that "socialism is about equality," and though this bold redefinition of the purpose of socialism must have caused Karl Marx to spin in his grave—he thought egalitarianism a vulgar, philistine notion and had only contemptuous things to say about it—nevertheless most socialist politicians now echo Mr. Gaitskell in a quite routine way. And not only socialist politicians: in the United States today, one might fairly conclude from the political debates now going on that capitalism, too, is "about equality," and will stand or fall with its success in satisfying the egalitarian impulse. To cap it all, a distinguished Harvard professor, John Rawls, recently published a serious, massive, and widely-acclaimed work in political philosophy whose argument is that a social order is just and legitimate *only* to the degree that it is directed to the redress of inequality. To the best of my knowledge, no serious political philosopher ever offered such a proposition before. It is a proposition, after all, that peremptorily casts a pall of illegitimacy over the entire political history of the human race—that implicitly indicts Jerusalem and Athens and Rome and Elizabethan England, all of whom thought *in*equality

was necessary to achieve a particular ideal of human excellence, both individual and collective. Yet most of the controversy about Professor Rawls's extraordinary thesis has revolved around the question of whether he has demonstrated it with sufficient analytical meticulousness. The thesis itself is not considered controversial.

One would think, then, that with so much discussion "about equality," there would be little vagueness as to what equality itself is about—what one means by "equality." Yet this is not at all the case. . . .

It is clear that some Americans are profoundly and sincerely agitated by the existing distribution of income in this country, and these same Americans—they are mostly professors, of course—are constantly insisting that a more equal distribution of income is a matter of considerable urgency. . . .

Despite all the talk "about equality," [however,] no one seems willing to commit himself to a precise definition from which statesmen and social critics can take their bearings.

As with economists, so with sociologists. Here, instead of income distribution, the controversial issue is social stratification—i.e., the "proper" degree of intergenerational social mobility. The majority of American sociologists seem persuaded that the American democracy has an insufficient degree of such mobility, and it seemed reasonable to me that some of them—or at least one of them!—could specify what degree would be appropriate. . . .

I . . . regret to report that nowhere in our voluminous sociological literature will one find any such depiction of the ideally mobile society. Our liberal sociologists, like our liberal economists, are eloquent indeed in articulating their social discontents, but they are also bewilderingly modest in articulating their social goals.

Now, what is one to infer from this experience? . . .

I, for one, am persuaded that though those people talk most earnestly about equality, it is not really equality that interests them. Indeed, it does not seem to me that equality *per se* is much of an issue for anyone. Rather, it is a surrogate for all sorts of other issues—some of them of the highest importance; these involve nothing less than our conception of what constitutes a just and legitimate society, a temporal order of things that somehow "makes sense" and seems "right." . . .

The demand for greater equality has less to do with any specific inequities of bourgeois society than with the fact that bourgeois society is seen as itself inequitable because it is based on a deficient conception of the common good. The recent history of Sweden is living proof of this proposition. The more egalitarian Sweden becomes—and it is already about as egalitarian as it is ever likely to be—the more *enragés* are its intellectuals, the more guilt-ridden and uncertain are its upper-middle classes, the more "alienated" are its college-educated youth. Though Swedish politicians and journalists cannot bring themselves to believe it, it should be obvious by now that there are *no* reforms that are going to placate the egalitarian impulse in Swedish society. Each reform only invigorates this impulse the more—because the impulse is not, in the end, about equality at all but about the quality of life in bourgeois society. . . .

Somehow, bourgeois society seems incapable of explaining and justifying its inequalities—seems incapable of explaining and justifying how these inequalities contribute to or are consistent with the common good. This, I would suggest, derives from the growing bureaucratization of the economic order, a process which makes bourgeois society ever more efficient economically, but also ever more defenseless before its ideological critics.

For any citizen to make a claim to an unequal share of income, power, or status, his contribution has to be—and has to be seen to be—a human and personal thing. In no country are the huge salaries earned by film stars or popular singers or professional athletes a source of envy or discontent. More than that: in most countries—and especially in the United States—the individual entrepreneur who builds up his own business and becomes a millionaire is rarely attacked on egalitarian grounds. In contrast, the top executives of our large corporations, most of whom are far less wealthy than Frank Sinatra or

Bob Hope or Mick Jagger or Wilt Chamberlain, cannot drink a martini on the expense account without becoming the target of a "populist" politician. These faceless and nameless personages (who is the president of General Electric?) have no clear title to their privileges—and I should say the reason is precisely that they are nameless and faceless. One really has no way of knowing what they are doing "up there," and whether what they are doing is in the public interest or not.

It was not always so. In the 19th century, at the apogee of the bourgeois epoch, the perception of unequal contributions was quite vivid indeed. The success of a businessman was taken to be testimony to his personal talents and character—especially character, than which there is nothing more personal. This explains the popularity of biographies of successful entrepreneurs, full of anecdotes about the man and with surprisingly little information about his economic activities. In the 20th century, "entrepreneurial history," as written in our universities, becomes the history of the firm rather than the biography of a man. To a considerable extent, of course, this reflects the fact that most businessmen today are not "founding fathers" of a firm but temporary executives in a firm—the bureaucratization of modern society empties the category of the bourgeois of its human content. . . .

When the unequal contributions of individuals are perceived as nothing but the differential functions of social or economic or political roles, then only those inequalities absolutely needed to perform these functions can be publicly justified—and the burden of proof is heavy indeed, as each and every inequality must be scrutinized for its functional purport. True, that particular martini, drunk in that place, in that time, in that company, might contribute to the efficiency and growth of the firm and the economy. But would the contribution really have been less if the executive in question had been drinking water? . . .

The founding fathers of modern bourgeois society (John Locke, say, or Thomas Jefferson) all assumed that biological inequalities among men—inequalities in intelligence, talent, abilities of all kinds—were not extreme, and therefore did not justify a society of hereditary privilege (of "two races," as it were). This assumption we now know to be true, demonstrably true, as a matter of fact. Human talents and abilities, as measured, do distribute themselves along a bell-shaped curve, with most people clustered around the middle, and with much smaller percentages at the lower and higher ends. That men are "created equal" is not a myth or a mere ideology—unless, of course, one interprets that phrase literally, which would be patently absurd and was never the bourgeois intention. Moreover, it is a demonstrable fact that in all modern, bourgeois societies, the distribution of income is also along a bell-shaped curve, indicating that in such an "open" society the inequalities that do emerge are not inconsistent with the bourgeois notion of equality.

It is because of this "natural tyranny of the bell-shaped curve," in the conditions of a commercial society, that contemporary experiments in egalitarian community-building—the Israeli kibbutz, for instance—only work when they recruit a homogeneous slice of the citizenry, avoiding a cross-section of the entire population. It also explains why the aristocratic idea—of a "twin-peaked" distribution—is so incongruent with the modern world, so that modern versions of superior government by a tiny elite (which is what the Communist regimes are) are always fighting against the economic and social tendencies inherent in their own societies. Purely egalitarian communities are certainly feasible—but only if they are selective in their recruitment and are relatively indifferent to economic growth and change, which encourages differentiation. Aristocratic societies are feasible, too—most of human history consists of them—but only under conditions of relative economic lethargy, so that the distribution of power and wealth is insulated from change. But once you are committed to the vision of a predominantly commercial society, in which flux and change are "normal," in which men and resources are expected to move to take advantage of new economic opportunities—then you find yourself tending toward the limited inequalities of a bourgeois kind. . . .

But the real trouble is not sociological or economic at all. It is that the "middling" nature of a bourgeois society falls short of corresponding adequately to the full range of man's spiritual nature, which makes more than middling demands upon the universe, and demands more than middling answers. This weakness of bourgeois society has been highlighted by its intellectual critics from the very beginning. And it is this weakness that generates continual dissatisfaction, especially among those for whom material problems are no longer so urgent. They may speak about "equality"; they may even be obsessed with statistics and pseudostatistics about equality; but it is a religious vacuum—a lack of meaning in their own lives, and the absence of a sense of larger purpose in their society—that terrifies them and provokes them to "alienation" and unappeasable indignation. It is not too much to say that it is the death of God, not the emergence of any new social or economic trends, that haunts bourgeois society. And *this* problem is far beyond the competence of politics to cope with.

MICHAEL WALZER

In defense of equality

At the very center of conservative thought lies this idea: that the present division of wealth and power corresponds to some deeper reality of human life. Conservatives don't want to say merely that the present division is what it ought to be, for that would invite a search for some distributive principle—as if it were possible to *make* a distribution. They want to say that whatever the division of wealth and power is, it naturally is, and that all efforts to change it, temporarily successful in proportion to their bloodiness, must be futile in the end. We are then invited, as in Irving Kristol's recent . . . article, to reflect upon the perversity of those who would make the attempt. . . .

131

Kristol doesn't argue that we can't possibly have greater equality or greater inequality than we presently have. Both communist and aristocratic societies are possible, he writes, under conditions of political repression or economic underdevelopment and stagnation. But insofar as men are set free from the coerciveness of the state and from material necessity, they will distribute themselves in a more natural way, more or less as contemporary Americans have done. The American way is exemplary because it derives from or reflects the real inequalities of mankind. . . . "Human talents and abilities . . . distribute themselves along a bell-shaped curve, with most people clustered around the middle, and with much smaller percentages at the lower and higher ends." The marvels of social science!—this distribution is a demonstrable fact. And it is another "demonstrable fact that in all modern bourgeois societies, the distribution of income is also along a bell-shaped curve." The second bell echoes the first. Moreover, once this harmony is established, "the political structure—the distribution of political power—follows along the same way." . . .

The first bell is obviously the crucial one. The defense of inequality reduces to these two propositions: that talent is distributed unequally and that talent will out. Clearly, we all want men and women to develop and express their talents, but whenever they are able to do that, Kristol suggests, the bell-shaped curve will appear or reappear, first in the economy, then in the political system. It is a neat argument but also a peculiar one, for there is no reason to think that "human talents and abilities" in fact distribute themselves along a *single* curve, although income necessarily does. Consider the range and variety of human capacities: intelligence, physical strength, agility and grace, artistic creativity, mechanical skill, leadership, endurance, memory, psychological insight, the capacity for hard work—even, moral strength, sensitivity, the ability to express compassion. Let's assume that with respect to all these, most people (but different people in each case) cluster around the middle of whatever scale we can construct, with smaller numbers at the lower and higher ends. Which of these curves is

actually echoed by the income bell? Which, if any, ought to be?

There is another talent that we need to consider: the ability to make money, the green thumb of bourgeois society—a secondary talent, no doubt, combining many of the others in ways specified by the immediate environment, but probably also a talent which distributes, if we could graph it, along a bell-shaped curve. . . .

The difficulty here is that making money is only rarely a form of self-expression, and the money we make is rarely enjoyed for its intrinsic qualities (at least, economists frown upon that sort of enjoyment). In a capitalist world, money is the universal medium of exchange; it enables the men and women who possess it to purchase virtually every other sort of social good; we collect it for its exchange value. Political power, celebrity, admiration, leisure, works of art, baseball teams, legal advice, sexual pleasure, travel, education, medical care, rare books, sailboats—all these (and much more) are up for sale. The list is as endless as human desire and social invention. Now isn't it odd, and morally implausible and unsatisfying, that all these things should be distributed to people with a talent for making money? And even odder and more unsatisfying that they should be distributed (as they are) to people who have money, whether or not they made it, whether or not they possess any talent at all? . . .

It would not be any better if we gave men money in direct proportion to their intelligence, their strength, or their moral rectitude. The resulting distributions would each, no doubt, reflect what Kristol calls "the tyranny of the bell-shaped curve," though it is worth noticing again that the populations in the lower, middle, and upper regions of each graph would be radically different. But whether it was the smart, the strong, or the righteous who enjoyed all the things that money can buy, the oddity would remain: why them? Why anybody? In fact, there is no single talent or combination of talents which plausibly entitles a man to every available social good—and there is no single talent or combination of talents that necessarily must win the available goods of a free society. Kristol's bell-shaped curve is tyrannical only in a purely formal sense. Any particular distribution may indeed be bell-shaped, but there are a large number of possible distributions. Nor need there be a single distribution of all social goods, for different goods might well be distributed differently. Nor again need all these distributions follow this or that talent curve, for in the sharing of some social goods, talent does not seem a relevant consideration at all.

Consider the case of medical care: surely it should not be distributed to individuals because they are wealthy, intelligent, or righteous, but only because they are sick. . . . But in America today, the distribution of medical care actually follows closely the lines of the income graph. It's not how a man feels but how much money he has that determines how often he visits a doctor. Another demonstrable fact! Does it require envious intellectuals to see that something is wrong?

There are two possible ways of setting things right. We might distribute income in proportion to susceptibility-to-sickness, or we might make sure that medical care is not for sale at all, but is available to those who need it. The second of these is obviously the simpler. Indeed, it is a modest proposal and already has wide support, even among those ordinary men and women who are said to be indifferent to equality. And yet, the distribution of medical care solely for medical reasons would point the way toward an egalitarian society, for it would call the dominance of the income curve dramatically into question.

What egalitarianism requires is that many bells should ring. Different goods should be distributed to different people for different reasons. Equality is not a simple notion, and it cannot be satisfied by a single distributive scheme—not even, I hasten to add, by a scheme which emphasizes need. "From each according to his abilities, to each according to his needs" is a fine slogan with regard to medical care. Tax money collected from all of us in proportion to our resources (these will never correlate exactly with our abilities, but that problem I shall leave aside

for now) must pay the doctors who care for those of us who are sick. Other people who deliver similar sorts of social goods should probably be paid in the same way—teachers and lawyers, for example. But Marx's slogan doesn't help at all with regard to the distribution of political power, honor and fame, leisure time, rare books, and sailboats. None of these things can be distributed to individuals in proportion to their needs, for they are not things that anyone (strictly speaking) needs. They can't be distributed in equal amounts or given to whoever wants them, for some of them are necessarily scarce, and some of them can't be possessed unless other people agree on the proper name of the possessor. There is no criteria, I think, that will fit them all. In the past they have indeed been distributed on a single principle: men and women have possessed them or their historical equivalents because they were strong or well-born or wealthy. But this only suggests that a society in which any single distributive principle is dominant cannot be an egalitarian society. Equality requires a diversity of principles, which mirrors the diversity both of mankind and of social goods.

Whenever equality in this sense does not prevail, we have a kind of tyranny, for it is tyrannical of the well-born or the strong or the rich to gather to themselves social goods that have nothing to do with their personal qualities. . . .

For all our personal and collective resources, there are distributive reasons that are somehow *right,* that are naturally part of our ideas about the things themselves. So nature is reestablished as a critical standard, and we are invited to wonder at the strangeness of the existing order. . . .

The doctrine of right reasons suggests that we pay equal attention to the "different qualities," and to the "individuality" of every man and woman, that we find ways of sharing our resources that match the variety of their needs, interests, and capacities. The clues that we must follow lie in the conceptions we already have, in the things we already know about love and belief, and also about respect, obedience, education, medical care, legal aid, all the necessities of life—for this is no esoteric doctrine, whatever difficulties it involves. Nor is it a panacea for human misfortune . . . : it is only meant to suggest a humane form of social accommodation. There is little we can do, in the best of societies, for the man who isn't loved. But there may be ways to avoid the triumph of the man who doesn't love—who buys love or forces it—or at least of his parallels in the larger social and political world: the leaders, for example, who are obeyed because of their coercive might or their enormous wealth. Our goal should be an end to tyranny, a society in which no man is master outside his sphere. That is the only society of equals worth having. . . .

It is worth stressing that equality as I have described it does not stand alone, but is closely related to the idea of liberty. . . . Men are not free, not politically free at least, if *his* yes, because of his birth or place of fortune, counts seventeen times more heavily than *my* no. Here the case is exactly as socialists have always claimed it to be: liberty and equality are the two chief virtues of social institutions, and they stand best when they stand together.

JACK DOUGLAS

Boss Tweed's revenge

William Marcy Tweed has come down in popular American history as a grotesque figure of political corruption, a man of vile ambitions who created an all-powerful political ring to rob the treasury of New York City. This is the image that most of us learned from the funny caricatures of Tweed by Thomas Nast, originally published in *Harper's Weekly* as part of the reform campaign against Tweed and long a standard of American history texts. . . .

It was not until the 1960s that a few historians, especially John Pratt and Seymour Mandelbaum, began to show the underlying social and political forces which led Tweed to launch his program and which eventually destroyed that program

and him. This analysis, combined with a reading of Tweed's own statement after his fall, gives us a new picture of Tweed as a masterful politician who understood the city's problems as few others have and who tried to solve them in the only way he thought possible.

The New York City Tweed knew was roughly the same in its social composition and political structure as the city today. In 1860 the population was 813,669. Of this, 203,740 were born in Ireland; 119,984 in Germany; 27,082 in England, and so on. Less than half—383,345—were native-born whites. While the city lacked the large blocs of blacks, Puerto Ricans, Italians and Jews, the far greater proportion of foreign origin gave it at least as much heterogeneity and conflict as today. The municipal government was even more decentralized and feudal than now; the tug of war between state power and home rule just as intense; the quasi-class conflicts between business taxpayers and the demanders of public services almost exactly the same; and, consequently, politics every bit as Byzantine.

The "spoils system"

The only major difference between the politics of his day and those of today is that by our public standards, if not in comparison with our private actions, politics then were highly corrupt. It is this difference which led people so easily to accept the caricatures of Tweed and to fail to see the lessons of his downfall for our age. Tweed lived within, and wholeheartedly accepted, what we now stigmatize as the "spoils system." This was the legal way of doing things political. It consisted primarily of the granting of political positions for personal and party favors, but it also included the practice of "tax farming," which is the use of the powers of public office to generate payment for the official. . . .

These age-old practices gave the office holders a "cut" in the proceeds of the office and presumably gave them incentive to increase the proceeds by putting more pressure on the public. . . . Such measures were combined with vote buying, ballot-box stuffing and no clear distinction legally between campaign contributions, personal gifts and political bribes to produce a situation we today see as vastly corrupt.

In Tweed's day those out of power increasingly took the same view, but also used the same tactics to gain power. Most people, and certainly Tweed, accepted them as the reality of the day. As Tweed said of idealism in politics, "I don't think men are governed in these matters by ideas of what should be between man and man."

Though Tweed used all of these practices to gain personal power and wealth, he did so to further a basic social program, without which he would not have had his massive and devoted following. Boss Tweed . . . was a "reform politician." He was able to put together a powerful coalition of offices and interests in 1869 by overthrowing the "corrupt" machine of Fernando Wood. Tweed worked within Tammany Hall (which was Democratic) as his primary political base to produce this overthrow, but he then moved forcefully to create a power bloc of both Democrats and Republicans.

The basic program of what was to become known as the Tweed Ring, or Gang, was the usual amalgam of conflicting goals. To his closest friends, the Irish workers of Tammany Hall, he offered a broad program of social welfare and justice, including allowing them to form unions and strike. Since the Irish at that time were in the position of the blacks of the 1960s, this was vastly important to them and earned a devoted following. Along the same lines, but also appealing to some business and residential interests, he pushed forward with a public parks program, city construction, improving the docks and all the municipal programs that became so common in the 20th Century.

At the same time, and of vital importance to the businessmen in his coalition, he actually decreased the tax rate without raising tax assessments. As Seymour Mandelbaum summed it up, "His implicit motto was 'Something for everyone.' His tactical plan was 'Do it now.'"

As anyone except a modern Keynesian would anticipate, this vast increase in expenditures combined with a decrease in taxes produced an equally vast fiscal deficit. . . .

In July, 1871, a political enemy of Tweed got hold of a copy of the [municipal] books by accident and political chicanery. He turned them over to the *New York Times*. . . . It immediately began publishing the books to show that the Tweed Ring had committed fraud by paying phony bills and taking kickbacks on vastly inflated contracts. Bankers immediately refused to make further loans or buy any bonds.

The city faced default and bankruptcy unless it could pay $2.7 million interest on its bonds by Nov. 1. . . .

But a coalition of Tweed's enemies, informally orchestrated by his arch-Democratic rival, Samuel Tilden, formed a Committee of Seventy to solve the problems. This committee was controlled by bankers, was dedicated publicly to solving the fiscal crisis and was secretly aimed at increasing the power of the "minority"—the financial interests—at the expense of the populace who had voted for the payoff system that led to the crisis. Since there was no possibility of a state or federal bailout in those days, the officials gave in. A new acting comptroller was appointed, confidence was restored in the city's credit and an informal coaliton of bankers loaned the money needed to avoid default.

Tweed, of course, was scapegoated by everyone. Everyone, who could, squirmed clear by blaming Tweed, including those most closely involved in the kickback and book manipulation schemes. Tweed was the only one to go to prison. After a flamboyant escape to Spain, he was returned to prison and died there as a symbol of corruption.

The reason why

But why did he do it? Was it all personal greed as Nast and the other anti-Catholic forces insisted? If so, he must have been terribly inefficient at it, since he got very little out of it. He himself explained his reasons very clearly to an aldermanic committee appointed to investigate the whole thing. "The fact is New York politics were always dishonest—long before my time. There never was a time when you couldn't buy the

Board of Aldermen. A politician in coming forward takes things as they are. This population is too hopelessly split up into races and factions to govern it under universal suffrage, except by the bribery of patronage or corruption.''

Tweed had brilliantly analyzed the terrible conflictful electorate and weak government structure of New York City and used what Grover Cleveland later called ''the cohesive ties of public plunder'' to pull together a vastly complex coalition of groups to achieve both personal power and a public program. Either he didn't realize that such a massive payoff of the voters, especially when financed by technically illegal means, would eventually produce fiscal disaster, or else he counted on getting ''up and out'' before the fiscal chickens came home to roost.

He miscalculated but the history of the city, the state (and now the nation?) shows that his was a masterful understanding of the problems of getting rational coordination to deal with complex problems in a highly democratic society. He seems to have been striving to create a highly centralized city government, a less democratic one. His idea seems to have been to use massive payoffs in the short run to get the power that would allow a curtailment of the payoffs in the long run. But the very attempt to increase his power gravely threatened some parts of the coalition, especially his arch-rival among fellow Democrats, Samuel Tilden, so they secretly schemed with his open enemies to overthrow him.

Since Tweed, the city has been through many cycles of special interest ''corruption'' and reform politics. The normal pattern has been for the reformers to ride a tide of public outrage against special interest payoffs into power. They then destroy the central power built up by the ''corrupt'' interests because they believe that centralization of power corrupts. But without centralized power they themselves then become the victims of some special interest group, generally within their own coalition. They then become the corrupters or, more commonly, lose out to a new wave of reformers. . . .

It remains to be seen whether the fiscal take-over by the state will break this cycle or whether the state suffers so much from the same pluralistic conflicts that the problem will now be amplified by the greater size of the state. It is already clear, however, that Boss Tweed was one of the great social analysts in American history. History has given him his revenge.

LINCOLN STEFFENS

The shame of our cities

Do the people want good government? Tammany says they don't. Are the people honest? Are the people better than Tammany? Are they better than the merchant and the politician? Isn't our corrupt government, after all, representative?

President Roosevelt has been sneered at for going about the country preaching, as a cure for our American evils, good conduct in the individual, simple honesty, courage, and efficiency. ''Platitudes!'' the sophisticated say. Platitudes? If my observations have been true, the literal adoption of Mr. Roosevelt's reform scheme would result in a revolution, more radical and terrible to existing institutions, from the Congress to the Church, from the bank to the ward organization, than socialism or even than anarchy. Why, that would change all of us—not alone our neighbors, not alone the grafters, but you and me.

No, the contemned methods of our despised politics are the master methods of our braggart business, and the corruption that shocks us in public affairs we practice ourselves in our private concerns. There is no essential difference between the pull that gets your wife into society or for your book a favorable review, and that which gets a heeler into office, a thief out of jail, and a rich man's son on the board of directors of a corporation; none between the corruption of a labor union, a bank, and a political machine; none between a dummy director of a trust and the caucus-bound member of a legislature; none between a labor boss like Sam Parks, a boss of banks like John D. Rockefeller, a boss of railroads like J. P. Morgan, and a political boss like Matthew S. Quay. The boss is not a political, he is an American institution, the product of a freed people that have not the spirit to be free.

And it's all a moral weakness; a weakness right where we think we are strongest. Oh, we are good—on Sunday, and we are "fearfully patriotic" on the Fourth of July. But the bribe we pay to the janitor to prefer our interests to the landlord's is the little brother of the bribe passed to the alderman to sell a city street, and the father of the air-brake stock assigned to the president of a railroad to have this life-saving invention adopted on his road. And as for graft, railroad passes, saloon and bawdy-house blackmail, and watered stock, all these belong to the same family. We are pathetically proud of our democratic institutions and our republican form of government, of our grand Constitution and our just laws. We are a free and sovereign people, we govern ourselves and the government is ours. But that is the point. We are responsible, not our leaders, since we follow them. We *let* them divert our loyalty from the United States to some "party"; we *let* them boss the party and turn our municipal democracies into autocracies and our republican nation into a plutocracy. We cheat our government and we let our leaders loot it, and we let them wheedle and bribe our sovereignty from us. True, they pass for us strict laws, but we are content to let them pass also bad laws, giving away public property in exchange; and our good, and often impossible, laws we allow to be used for oppression and blackmail. And what can we say? We break our own laws and rob our own government, the lady at the customhouse, the lyncher with his rope, and the captain of industry with his bribe and his rebate. The spirit of graft and of lawlessness is the American spirit. . . .

The people are not innocent. That is the only "news" in all the journalism of these articles, and no doubt that was not new to many observers. It was to me. When I set out to describe the corrupt systems of certain typical cities, I meant to show simply how the people were deceived and betrayed. But in the very first study—St. Louis—the startling truth lay bare that corruption was not merely political; it was financial, commercial, social; the ramifications of boodle were so complex, various, and far-reaching, that one mind could hardly grasp them. . . . But when I went next to Minneapolis alone, . . . there were traces of the same phenomenon. The first St. Louis article was called "Tweed Days in St. Louis," and though the "better citizen" received attention the Tweeds were the center of interest. In "The Shame of Minneapolis," the truth was put into the title; it was the Shame of Minneapolis; not of the Ames administration, not of the Tweeds, but of the city and its citizens. And yet Minneapolis was not nearly so bad as St. Louis; police graft is never so universal as boodle. It is more shocking, but it is so filthy that it cannot involve so large a part of society. So I returned to St. Louis, and I went over the whole ground again, with the people in mind, not alone the caught and convicted boodlers. And this time the true meaning of "Tweed Days in St. Louis" was made plain. The article was called "The Shamelessness of St. Louis," and that was the burden of the story. In Pittsburgh also the people was the subject, and though the civic spirit there was better, the extent of the corruption throughout the social organization of the community was indicated. But it was not till I got to Philadelphia that the possibilities of popular corruption were worked out to the limit of humiliating confession. That was the place for such a study. There is nothing like it in the country, except possibly, in Cincinnati. Philadelphia certainly is not merely corrupt, but corrupted, and this was made clear. Philadelphia was charged up to—the American citizen.

ARCHIBALD COX

Ends

Why did the mistakes and misdeeds that we know as "Watergate" occur?

There was individual wrongdoing by any standard. The style and moral tone of any enterprise or organization is set by its leader. The published transcripts of Presidential conversations, whatever else they prove, amply demonstrate that the place of moral leadership was filled by shabby cynicism and sleazy scheming to hide responsibility. I wish to set these things aside to concentrate upon . . . the influence of long-range forces in the moral and political climate. . . .

[A discussion of one of the main] forces making for Watergate, the decline of morality and civility, is best pursued by the case method:

For the first case, choose one of the more aggressive tactics of confrontation pursued by student activists during the wave of unrest in 1968–71: the physical seizure of buildings, the bombing of the laboratory at the University of Wisconsin or of Harvard's Center for International Affairs Library, the burning of R.O.T.C. buildings, and the disruption of public meetings so that views distasteful to the activists were denied expression. Many participants in these activities were sincerely convinced of the righteousness of their objectives, such as forcing the university to abolish R.O.T.C. and alter its relations with portions of the surrounding community; they believed that they were morally right in engaging in disruption.

Case two is the Berrigans and the destruction of Selective Service records. The sincerity of their belief is generally acknowledged.

Daniel Ellsberg provides the third example. Dr. Ellsberg's motives appear to have been highly moral. He doubtless thought that he was performing a great service to both his country and to humanity by revealing the Pentagon Papers to increase the pressure to end the war in Indochina. Quite probably he committed no criminal offense. But if I understand the facts, Dr. Ellsberg violated a trust he had knowingly accepted when—in common but not legal parlance—he "stole" the Pentagon Papers.

The fourth case is that of Egil Krogh, the head of the "White House plumbers." Krogh has pleaded guilty to an indictment based upon his role in planning and directing the effort to obtain Dr. Fielding's files. Earlier, Krogh was indicted for perjury for falsely telling a grand jury that he had no knowledge of a trip to California by Howard Hunt in preparation for a possible burglary. Krogh, from everything I have learned, sincerely believes himself to be, and in that sense is, a highly moral man. At the time he approved the violation of Dr. Fielding's and Daniel Ellsberg's civil rights he sincerely viewed the action as a service to his country and humanity.

Does an important common thread run through these four cases? There is a wealth of distinctions ranging from trivialities to substantial differences in both conduct and justification, yet I doubt that the distinctions are critical. In each case, the conduct—the objective acts—was wrong because it violated standards that must be accepted if free men are to live together. In each case, the actor believed his wrong to be justified by the righteousness of his cause and the need for drastic means to achieve his objective.

Consider here the wisdom of Louis D. Brandeis, who was deeply convinced of the importance of "standards," and here he drew a distinction and made the point that dominates my thought: "One can never be sure of *ends*— political, social, economic. There must always be doubt and difference of opinion"; there is not the same margin of doubt as to *means*. Here "fundamentals do not change; centuries of thought have established standards. Lying and sneaking are *always* bad, no matter what the ends."

The Justice was speaking of the *Olmstead* wiretapping case, but his words fit the abstraction of copies of the Pentagon Papers and surely he would have included physical confrontation and barring the expression of another's distasteful opinions.

The point seems vital. If man is by nature a social being—if we are destined to live and work together—if our goal is the freedom of each to choose the best he can discern—if we seek to do what we can to move toward the realization of these beliefs, then surely some virtually absolute constraints upon the ways in which we pursue even the worthiest objectives (insofar as their worth can then be judged) furnish the best, perhaps the only, hope for man. What the constraints even upon means should be may be debatable around the periphery but surely the core includes refraining from physical aggression, lying and cheating, and includes respecting the rights of speech, privacy, dignity and other fundamental liberties of other men such as the Bill of Rights declares, by both government and private persons. I speak of these as "virtually absolute" because philosophers can pose examples calling for exceptions, chiefly in closed, authoritarian societies far removed from our conditions. Call the constraints "standards," as Brandeis did, the "rule of law," or "civility," or the "liberal tradition," as you will; they are constraints upon power and prerequisites of cooperation; and any serious erosion carries the greatest threat to the dream of freedom and justice. Disregard of the constraints by some breeds further disregard upon the part of others. Brute power becomes the determinant of what is falsely labeled "justice." Many of the greatest wrongs known to history were committed by men who were acting, according to the contemporary judgment of society as well as by their own lights, in the cause of truth and human welfare.

The willingness of one group to override constraints upon the means of pursuing social, political, moral or other human objectives generated willingness to override them on the part of others who had different goals but believed with equal conviction in their righteousness of purpose. In my view, each incident marked and contributed its share to some crumbling of the moral order.

Likening the role of Egil Krogh in the Ellsberg-Fielding break-in to Ellsberg's own breach of trust and to the radical tactics of physical con-

frontation has been criticized upon the ground that Krogh was a Government man while the others were outsiders, and that Krogh possessed while the others lacked a high degree of power. For many purposes these differences would be important. But I wish to insist a little that the argument gets the perspective wrong when we are attempting to appraise the weaknesses in our moral and political condition. It is the forgetting of the constraints upon methods of working our wills that counts because, despite short-run frustrations, such constraints furnish, as I have said, the best hope of combining liberty, change and progress. Constraints upon means cannot survive exceptions for those who think their power too small in proportion to the justice of their cause. Those who assert freedom to override the constraints in attacking the government cannot seriously suppose that government will observe the constraints if frightened; nor that they themselves will suddenly observe the constraints if, as they hope, they come to power.

KARL MARX AND FRIEDRICH ENGELS

Manifesto of the communist party

The history of all hitherto existing society is the history of class struggles.

Free man and slave, patrician and plebeian, lord and serf, guild master and journeyman, in a word, oppressor and oppressed, stood in constant opposition to one another, carried on an uninterrupted, now hidden, now open fight, a fight that each time ended either in a revolutionary reconstitution of society at large or in the common ruin of the contending classes. . . .

Does it require deep intuition to comprehend that man's ideas, views, and conceptions, in one word, man's consciousness, change with every change in the conditions of his material existence, in his social relations, and in his social life?

What else does the history of ideas prove than that intellectual production changes its character in proportion as material production is changed? The ruling ideas of each age have ever been the ideas of its ruling class. . . .

"Undoubtedly," it will be said, "religious, moral, philosophical, and juridical ideas have been modified in the course of historical development. But religion, morality, philosophy, political science, and law constantly survived this change.

"There are, besides, eternal truths, such as freedom, justice, etc., that are common to all states of society. But communism abolishes eternal truths, it abolishes all religion, and all morality, instead of constituting them on a new basis; it therefore acts in contradiction to all past historical experience."

What does this accusation reduce itself to? The history of all past society has consisted in the development of class antagonisms, antagonisms that assumed different forms at different epochs.

But whatever form they may have taken, one fact is common to all past ages, viz., the exploitation of one part of society by the other. . . .

The proletariat will use its political supremacy to wrest, by degrees, all capital from the bourgeoisie, to centralize all instruments of production in the hands of the state, i.e., of the proletariat organized as the ruling class, and to increase the total of productive forces as rapidly as possible.

Of course, in the beginning this cannot be effected except by means of despotic inroads on the rights of property and on the conditions of bourgeois production: by means of measures, therefore, which appear economically insufficient and untenable, but which, in the course of the movement, outstrip themselves, necessitate further inroads upon the old social order, and are unavoidable as a means of entirely revolutionizing the mode of production. . . .

When, in the course of development, class distinctions have disappeared and all production has been concentrated in the hands of a vast association of the whole nation, the public power will lose its political character. Political power, properly so called, is merely the organized power of one class for oppressing another. If the proletariat during its contest with the bourgeoisie is compelled, by the force of circumstances, to organize itself as a class, if, by means of a revolution, it makes itself the ruling class and, as such, sweeps away by force the old conditions of production, then it will, along with these conditions, have swept away the conditions for the existence of class antagonisms and of classes generally, and will thereby have abolished its own supremacy as a class.

In place of the old bourgeois society, with its classes and class antagonisms, we shall have an association in which the free development of each is the condition for the free development of all.

JAMES BURNHAM

Notes on authority, morality, power

Everybody knows that the sex/drug/pornography/incivility/obscenity/self-indulgence subculture is vile and rotten—not least those immersed in it, whose self-degradation and tendency to self-destruction is as obvious in real life as in those movies superficially seeming to glorify them. . . .

And everyone can see, merely by looking around, that the waves of the subculture lap widely over the general culture of our society: cf. the movies, plays, books, magazines, store fronts, drug-stocked pads, pornography shops, pot- and pill-soaked campus hangouts, routine public obscenities, flaunting of perversions, dirt-wallowing, etc. etc. . . .

Liberalism can do nothing to cleanse or halt this Augean wave; can only, in fact, smooth its advance. The secular relativism and permissiveness to which liberalism is committed provides no metaphysical foothold on which a stand might be taken. The logic of the liberal interpretation of free speech and the other civil rights not only cannot net the immoralist, but must on his demand successfully remove the checks and obstacles by which, over the millennia, society has restricted his field of operation. His civil rights are distilled into his right to do what he feels like, to the exclusion of the public's right to be protected from the signs and consequences of what he is doing. Two generations ago liberalism infiltrated the federal judiciary, and one generation ago took it over. Its successive decisions on pornography over this period, especially during the past two decades, draw out, step by step, the legal implications of liberal ideology. Let the logical order be put in the words of an accomplished liberal: "What the counter-culture embodies is an extension of the tendencies initiated sixty years ago by political liberalism and modernist culture. . . . It now seeks to take the preachments of personal freedom, extreme experience ('kicks' and 'the high') and sexual experimentation to a point in life-style that the liberal culture—which would approve of such ideas in art and imagination—is not prepared to go. Yet liberalism finds itself uneasy to say why. It approves a basic permissiveness, but cannot with any certainty define the bounds." (Professor Daniel Bell, *The Public Interest,* Autumn 1970.)

Whatever the past causal role of the immorality syndrome, it is a plausible guess that the early stages of a post-liberal American regime will include an anti-immorality campaign. The market may be way down now, but morality still has a promising future; some of the bears are likely to get caught short one of these days. . . .

American liberalism is moribund. (I use the adjective as my dictionary defines it: "in a dying state.") . . .

This is manifest in the writings of liberals. . . . Liberal writing has become a combination of stale formulas with wails. Oh woe is me! Our war, our cities, our crime, our housing, our TV, our youth, our aged, our poor, our air, our water, our drugs, our sewage, our blacks, reds, browns, and God knows our whites! Woe! Woe! . . . Schooling hasn't worked, so there must be more schooling. Welfare hasn't worked, so there must be more welfare. Public housing

by government regulation and antipoverty money haven't worked, so there must be more public housing, government regulation and antipoverty money. Spending billions hasn't worked, so we must spend trillions. . . .

Professor Bell may sum up: "In culture, as in politics, liberalism is now up against the wall." We all know what happens next when you are placed up against the wall. . . .

The innumerable reports on the causes of contemporary disorders—epidemic crime, arson, riots, confrontations, bombings and so on—invariably come up with the same sort of conclusions, which is not surprising since all the commissions, panels and conferences start from the same liberal premises. The "basic" causes are an environmental lack: poverty, inadequate education, malnutrition, discrimination, joblessness, bad housing. That is to say, "cause" is interpreted as meaning social or economic condition. The findings do not seem very plausible once we reflect that these conditions have existed in human society from its beginning, in orderly as in disorderly times and places. But even if they are correct, they do not answer the *political* question. Politics deals with power, with rule. From a political standpoint, the cause of increasing disorder is the decay in the *authority* of the ruler, the sovereign. The cure is the restoration of authority.

Authority rests on three primary factors: habit (custom), respect (reverence, awe) and fear. In our current disorders (Black Panthers, Weathermen, campus wreckers, military deserters, confronters of all sorts) the habit has been broken and the respect vanished (cf. the obscenities, rudeness, howling down of others). There remains only some of that proportion of the fear that is the reflection of force or the threat of force, and even this is much weakened by the knowledge that the use of force by the "authorities" is episodic and inept. (In designating the magistrates as "authorities" we recognize what in fact a functioning magistrate is: namely, one who has *authority*.)

Liberalism has always rejected the traditional ties of custom and respect as backwardness, prejudice and superstition. Now it confronts a generation of militants who take its lessons seriously. With custom and respect dissolved, only force remains. But liberalism has also—on principle, at least—rejected force, too, except as a last-minute recourse; and precisely because of that refusal to see force, in act or threat, as inevitably and continuously involved in human society, has never been able to understand force or use it wisely. Liberals always turn to force at the wrong moment in the wrong amount, and therefore bungle in using it.

The decay of authority is no sudden sickness, nor is it confined to political authority. The loss of authority by the political magistrates is, rather, an extension of its progressive withering throughout the structure of society. The weak voice of the magistrate in administering the state echoes the weakened voice of the father within the home, the teacher in school, the pastor in church, even of the commander within the traditional model of authority, the military. . . .

As guides in lieu of authority, liberalism recognizes only reason and individual conscience informed by reason. Authority based on custom, respect, force or any factor other than reason, is non-rational, hence invalid. Each man is a rational atom, seeking his own happiness, related only externally to other man-atoms. The claim of society can be asserted only quantitatively, through one or another variety of the utilitarian formula: Each individual, seeking his own happiness, will contribute to the greatest happiness of the greatest number. But when once I see through the utilitarian fraud and realize that there is no necessary coincidence between my individual search for happiness and the greatest happiness of the greatest number, existing society has no further moral claim on me, granted the metaphysical premises of liberalism. Thus, the Weathermen and the hippies, true descendants of their liberal ancestors. Even force has no claim beyond the physical fact, and thus the *authority* of the state's force vanishes if I am able to counter it or circumvent it. This violence-justifying conclusion from the liberal premises is drawn in the writings of many liberals today who are not aware of what the conclusion means in practice: for example, the

columnist Tom Wicker, and other journalists of his school, who equate the violence of those who are shooting police and blowing up buildings with "police violence" and the "violence" of the American Army in Vietnam. If the two forms of force are in truth equivalent, then authority is reduced simply to the question of which force prevails.

Liberalism cannot revive authority, and government cannot continue indefinitely without authority. We may therefore predict a regime that will be *authoritative* and thus not liberal. It will have to be authoritative. The question remains open whether that regime of the future becomes authoritative through a shift to Right or to Left, and whether it will end up not merely authoritative but authoritarian.

WALTER LIPPMANN

The good society

Of the development of liberty we have . . . seen only the beginnings: the emancipation even of Englishmen, let alone mankind, was not completed in 1859 when Mill wrote his *Essay on Liberty*. At best the foundation for the advancement of liberty had been laid in a few countries. But the advance itself has no visible end. Always there will remain to be liquidated subtler privileges and immunities; always there will remain to be checked the refinements of violence, fraud, intrigue, and conspiracy by which men bedevil themselves and their fellows. The ideal of a society in which all are equally free of all arbitrary coercion is a receding goal. From each new plateau in the ascent higher levels become visible.

If we scrutinize the progress of human emancipation, it appears to consist largely in a series of restraints upon the exercise of power by men over men. The organized liberty of mankind is established by laws and usages which seek to limit coercive authority, traditional prerogatives, vested rights, and all manner of predatory, violent, fraudulent dealing among men. . . .

Men have rebelled against arbitrary power because they collided with it in their work and in the enjoyment of their faculties. So while the constitutional means to liberty are in the main a series of negatives raised against the powerful, the pursuit of liberty is a great affirmation inspired by the positive energies of the human race. . . .

Thus we may think of the creative, the productive, and the adaptive energies of mankind as struggling to release themselves from the entanglements and perversions, the exploitation and the smothering, the parasitism and the obfuscation and the discouragement of aggressive, acquisitive, dogmatic, and arbitrary impulses. Men are moved to plant, but the seeds bear fruit with difficulty, so rank are the weeds which choke them. The cutting back of the weeds, the clearing of little spaces in which good things can grow, has been the task of human emancipation. Its method is to restrain arbitrariness. But its object is to disengage the human spirit in order that it may flourish. . . .

Though liberalism has often been identified with indifference, inaction, and nonresistance, it should now be evident that this is mere confusion. A doctrine which is opposed to all arbitrariness must mean the determination to resist arbitrariness, to check it, to cut it down, to crush it, wherever and whenever it appears. It cannot mean, for example, that in the seventeenth century the King was under God and the law, but that in the nineteenth century the owners of property were not, that in the twentieth century majorities, pluralities, mobs, or dictators are not, under God and the law. For liberalism all arbitrary power is evil. It matters not what are the titles or the pretensions or the promises of arbitrary power. It must be resisted and brought under control.

So liberalism is not quietism and weak government. That is the corruption of liberalism. In its vigorous periods liberalism has always meant rebellion against oppression and a determination to police aggression and acquisitiveness. Liberalism, therefore, is not the doctrine of laissez-faire, let her rip, and the devil take the hindmost. It does not envisage the demobilization of the police, the repeal of the laws, the disestablishment of legislatures and courts. On the contrary, the effective liberals have always been concerned with the development of the law, with the definition of rights and duties, with the organizing of constitutions, with the absorption of all power to coerce in the hands of duly constituted authorities, with the liquidation or regulation of all kinds of private and petty powers within the community. For the liberal, as distinguished from the anarchist, holds that mere unrestraint does not give the freedom of a voluntary society, that unrestraint merely inaugurates a competitive struggle in which the ruthless will exploit the rest. He insists that the promise of a voluntary life can be realized only as the law is strong enough to restrain aggressors at home and abroad. . . .

The ideal of equal rights for all and special privileges for none is inseparable from the pursuit of liberty. A free society is one in which inequalities in the condition of men, in their rewards, and in their social status do not arise out of extrinsic and artificial causes—out of the physical power to coerce, out of legal privilege, out of special prerogative, or out of fraud, sharp practice, necessitous bargaining.

This is no forcible leveling of men to a uniform condition of life. That is the tyrant's way. The libertarian does not demand that all the runners in the race must keep in step and finish together; he asks that they start from scratch and that none shall be permitted to elbow his rival off the track. Then the winner will be the best runner. The winner will not be the competitor who wangled a handicap from the judges, or obtained an advantage which had nothing to do with his ability to run the race. Manifestly, the liberal conception of equality does not promise to make all men equal in riches, influence, honor, and wisdom. On the contrary, its promise is that as the extrinsic inequalities imposed by prerogative and privilege are reduced, the intrinsic superiorities will assert themselves.

This, I believe, is the insight at the heart of the liberal conception of society.

Which Missile?

JOHN MALONEY IN THE LOS ANGELES HERALD-EXAMINER

7

POLITICS:
THE
INTERNATIONAL
STRUGGLE
FOR POWER

International politics differs in nuance from domestic politics but not in essentials. Some elements do not change: Tyrants, for instance, will be tyrants, whether in domestic or international politics. Two factors may be said to characterize the different qualities of international politics: There is greater self-sufficiency and insularity among nations, and their relations are less likely to be stably ordered. By self-sufficiency, we mean not only economic self-sufficiency and political self-government but also moral autonomy, while by insularity we mean to convey that nations look upon each other as strangers: strange in their looks, speech, customs, and ideas.

At first glance, this first factor would seem to increase the likelihood of international order because nations would have little need for and little interest in dealings with one another. Rarely, however, is a nation so self-sufficient that it could not become more self-sufficient, and, indeed, the trend in the world today is toward greater economic interdependence. Insularity is a more effective resistance against participation in international politics, but it has become almost impossible to maintain in the contemporary world. Now that international relations have penetrated the most remote kingdoms, the factors of self-sufficiency and insularity make nations at once proud, querulous, and circumspect. This accounts for the importance of formal protocol and the prominence of delicate negotiations in diplomacy.

In these circumstances, conflicts arise easily. Unlike domestic conflict, however, there is no really effective peace-keeping force, no army or police, no authoritative and independent court of appeal. Indeed, there is often little culture or custom which is held in common that may be relied upon to reduce tension. This lack of common culture makes it less likely that there will be commonly accepted legitimations of international power, that is, moral arguments that make the existing order of power appear right.

In the first piece of this chapter, Robert Tucker describes the emergence of a new chal-

145

lenge to the existing order, made by the poor and underdeveloped nations against the wealth and might of the powerful ones. This rising "egalitarianism" demands an inequality of treatment: "discrimination on behalf of the materially disadvantaged." Tucker indicates briefly, and in the following article Richard Barnet does so more emphatically, that this moral development rests upon changed political realities. The powerful must now give more help to the weak, so the challenge reads, because now the powerful are dependent upon the underdeveloped countries for vital raw materials. Barnet argues that "the issue is whether the security of Americans will be better served by trying to perpetuate the era of American hegemony after the conditions for it have passed or by taking the lead in building a more equitable international economic order and a less militarized international political order."

The next article addresses international politics in the near future in which it appears the "era of American hegemony" may already be a thing of the past. Hans Morgenthau sees America in both "moral and material decline." America's moral position vis-à-vis the Third World is precarious for two reasons: It sided with colonial powers after World War II, afraid that nationalist movements would turn Communist; and it is now unable "to stipulate moral principles with which to justify its positions and interests against its enemies and detractors." In the absence of any new order to take the place of the one previously maintained by the West, the threat of anarchy looms on the horizon. Morgenthau's article reveals the difficulty that has long plagued statesmen of formulating a foreign policy that is at once idealistic (based on moral principles) and realistic (based on actual conditions of power and self-interest).

In the next selection, Joseph Kraft questions whether morality has, indeed, any place in foreign policy at all. Noting the new wave of concern over this issue that surfaced during the 1976 presidential campaign, Kraft suggests that we should not commit ourselves to humanitarian programs if we are not able—

or willing—to fulfull our commitments. In this view, candid balance-of-power policy might ultimately be more moral than raising false hopes among the oppressed.

We turn next to the most significant element of international politics: the use of force. Political theorists generally think the use of force is inevitable because it is the most decisive tactic that can be employed in the struggle for power, and, as such, it is a natural part of politics. And yet, the most extreme use of force, war, is now so dangerous that it could be argued that in a third world war, there could be no winners—and perhaps no survivors. On political grounds, then, the case against war might be persuasive. The question then becomes: Are there grounds, other than political, that cause wars? In a letter to Albert Einstein, Sigmund Freud claims that a biological instinct of destruction exists in man that is the cause of that aggressive behavior that may erupt into war. Nonetheless, Freud betrays a cautious optimism that this destructive instinct may be controlled, either through the strengthening of emotional ties between men, or through the growth of culture that strengthens the intellect and checks the external action of aggressive impulses.

Bronislaw Malinowski rejects the theory put forward by Freud that there are biological determinants of war. From the perspective of an anthropologist, he writes, "war cannot be regarded as a fiat of human destiny in that it could be related to biological needs or immutable psychological drives. All types of fighting are complex cultural responses due not to any direct dictates of an impulse but to collective forms of sentiment and value."

It does not follow, however, that because fighting is not instinctual, it will soon be abandoned. However destructive force may be, it may also be a protector and guarantor of the peace. In the next selection, Robert E. Osgood and Robert W. Tucker argue that "since there is no other way for states to pursue what they regard as vital interests when other states are determined to oppose them, force must be as essential to international

146

politics in an anarchy as elections are to domestic politics in a democracy." Force is justified because only through force—or the threat of force—can states secure their ends and bring order out of chaos.

In the concluding piece, we get a notion of the volatile character of the relation of international politics and morality. Reinhold Niebuhr argues that nations are more selfish and more immoral than individuals and that the demands of patriotism preclude the critical self-reflection that moral thought and action require.

NOTES ABOUT THE AUTHORS

Robert W. Tucker, born in 1918, is professor of political science at Johns Hopkins University in Baltimore and holds a joint position with the School of Advanced International Studies in Washington, D.C. He is the author of *Nation or Empire? The Debate Over American Foreign Policy, The Radical Left and American Foreign Policy,* and *A New Isolationism.* He also coauthored *Force, Order and Justice.* "A New International Order" first appeared in *Commentary* in 1975.

Richard Barnet, who holds his law degree from Harvard, helped found the Institute for Policy Studies. He has served with several governmental agencies, including the Defense Department. Among his books on the subject of national defense are *Who Wants Disarmament?* (1961) and *Roots of War* (1972). "The Debate We Ought to Be Having" was first published in *The New Republic* in January 1976.

Hans Morgenthau, born in 1904, taught political science and law in his native Germany and in Switzerland and Spain before coming to the United States, where he became a naturalized citizen in 1943. He has held distinguished appointments at the University of Chicago and the City University of New York, and he is currently university professor at the New School for Social Research. Among his major works are *Politics in the Twentieth Century* and *A New Foreign Policy for the United States.* "The Decline of the West," excerpted here, first appeared in *Partisan Review* in 1975.

Joseph Kraft, born in 1924, is a syndicated columnist for the *Washington Post,* the *Chicago Daily News,* and other papers, having previously been on the staff of the *New York Times.* A member of the Council on Foreign Relations, he is the author of numerous journal articles and several books, including *The Grand Design, Profiles in Power,* and *The Chinese Difference.* "Has Morality a Place in Foreign Policy?" first appeared in the *Los Angeles Times* in October 1976.

Sigmund Freud. See above, p. 30.

Bronislaw Malinowski, born in 1884 in Poland, is widely recognized as the founder of social anthropology. He taught at the London School of Economics, the University of London, and Yale University. Among his many publications are *Sex and Repression in Savage Society* and several classic essays, including "A Scientific Theory of Culture" and "Magic, Science and Religion." His "Anthropological Analysis of War," excerpted in this volume, first appeared in the *American Journal of Sociology* in 1941. He died the following year.

Robert E. Osgood is dean of the Johns Hopkins School of Advanced International Studies and director of the Washington Center of Foreign Policy Research. Among his many books are *Alliances and American Foreign Policy, Ideals and Self-Interest in America's Foreign Relations, Limited War: The Challenge to American Strategy,* and *Force, Order and Justice* (1967), coauthored with Robert Tucker and excerpted here.

Reinhold Niebuhr, born in 1892, was a leading American theologian of the twentieth century. From 1928 to 1960 he was a professor at Union Theological Seminary in New York. Among his many published works are *Does Civilization Need Religion?, The Nature and Destiny of Man,* and *Moral Man and Immoral Society,* excerpted here and first published in 1932. Niebuhr died in 1971.

147

ROBERT W. TUCKER

A new international order?

What are the characteristics of the new egalitarianism that are expected to determine the future international system? In part, it is clear that the new egalitarianism resembles nothing so much as the old equality. If international society is on the threshold of a new era, it is not apparent in the commitment of the new states to an interdependence that precludes a freedom of action states have habitually claimed in the name of their sovereign equality. Westerners increasingly find a contradiction between the new egalitarianism, which is held to result largely from a growing interdependence, and the state's insistence upon its undiminished freedom of action, but the elites of the new states do not share this outlook. On the contrary, for the latter it is precisely the complete independence and sovereignty of the state that forms the most important—certainly the most emphasized—part of the new egalitarianism. It is the new states which with unwearying insistence have reiterated that the international order, based on the sovereign equality of states, must accord to every state the unrestricted right to determine its own course of political, economic, and social development. Thus the "full permanent sovereignty of every state over its natural resources and all economic activities," to use the words of the UN General Assembly's 1974 Declaration on the Establishment of a New International Economic Order, is an "inalienable right," the exercise of which is not to be subject to any external "economic, political, or other types of coercion." More generally, the principle of sovereign equality is interpreted to give every state the right to define its legitimate interests and, subject to limitations which remain uncertain, to take such measures as may be necessary for their defense. Save perhaps for the self-consciousness with which these claims to equality are made by the new states, there is little that is novel about them.

Nor is there any novelty in the insistent claim that the subjects of the new egalitarianism are

states and states alone. There is no warrant for seeing in the new egalitarianism the precursor of a growing equality *within* states. The growth of equality among states may prove quite compatible with a continuing, even a deepening, inequality among individuals within states. Whatever the meaning we may give to the equality of states, the assumption that the consequences of state equality need not be clearly distinguished from their consequences for individual equality can only lead to confusion and worse. The almost wholly abortive attempts since World War II to secure the effective internationalization of basic human rights afford a clear illustration of the point at issue. To the extent that the human-rights movement has made any progress—and such progress has been minuscule—it is not unfair to say that it has been made despite the insistent assertion by states of their rights—among which the right of equality has been paramount. The central thrust of the claim to equality in international politics and law not only remains a claim to the equality of states, it is a claim that serves today—as in the past—to reaffirm the view of the state as the exclusive guardian of the interests of, and sole dispenser of justice to, the human beings who comprise it. This claim shows few signs of receding today. Certainly, the new egalitarianism in no way challenges it. If anything, the new egalitarianism has given this claim renewed strength.

In some respects, therefore, the new egalitarianism is little more than a refurbished version of the old equality which was quite compatible with almost any and all forms of inequality. In other respects, though, the new egalitarianism is indeed new. The powerful are not to employ their power, certainly not their military power, against the weak on behalf of interests whose defense would have evoked the threat or use of force only a short time ago. Intended primarily to deny the legitimacy of armed intervention in response to action a government may take within its territorial jurisdiction, the prohibition has also been extended to cover so-called issues of "global management" (e.g., conflicting claims over the use and exploitation of the oceans and space). At the same time, the developed states are to acknowledge a duty to assist the underdeveloped states in the great task of reducing the material disparities among them. The prevention of nuclear war apart, this task forms the most important purpose of the new international order. Here again, the Declaration on the Establishment of a New International Economic Order may be cited as representative of the new egalitarianism. The principal purpose of the new order, the Declaration reads, is to alter a system wherein the developing countries "which constitute 70 per cent of the world population, account for only 30 per cent of the world's income." A substantial reduction of inequality in the global distribution of income forms the collective responsibility of the developed states. The framework within which this duty is to be implemented, however, must be one designed by the "whole international community," the collective decisions of the community reflecting the principle of political equality.

The logic of the new egalitarianism therefore requires discrimination on behalf of the materially disadvantaged. . . . Among unequals, the undeveloped nations have argued, equality of treatment leads to discrimination in favor of the stronger. Hence the conclusion that the discrimination shown in favor of the weaker, by virtue of the preferential standard, is equitable because it serves to reduce inequality.

Are the claims of the new egalitarianism, as articulated by Third World spokesmen, to be taken seriously? I see no reason why they should not. It is easy to show that they often combine two different standards: one for the developed states of the North, another for a largely undifferentiated South (comprising the very poor states, the emerging class, and the nouveaux riches). Thus the insistence that *every* state has exclusive control over its own resources cannot logically be reconciled with the insistence that *some* states have a duty to share their resources with others. Whereas the former claim risks nullifying the basis for an "international welfare order," the latter claim attempts to save such basis by proclaiming it the special duty of the favored few. It is for this reason that a detached, though not unsympathetic, Western observer of the new states' position can voice concern over the possibility that these states have "con- structed needless barriers to some of their central needs for the future—namely the acceptance by more affluent states of some level of duty to transfer resources to other states to meet the direst material needs of great sections of mankind." But logical consistency here could be maintained, and supposedly "needless barriers" removed, only by the concession in principle of a claim that responds to anxieties which are the result of a long history of domination and formal inequality. Rather than make such a concession, the new states find little difficulty in advancing logically inconsistent positions, or, more to the point, in insisting upon a double standard of conduct. Besides, this double standard can always be justified by invoking a past in which material disparities presumably arose because of what is seen as a double standard imposed on developing peoples.

If the claims of the new egalitarianism are not to be dismissed because they proclaim a double standard, they are also not to be dismissed because they gloss over divisions separating the countries of the South. The juxtaposition of Southern rhetoric with Southern realities has been undertaken many times. But what does the exercise prove apart from what we already know: that there are many conflicts of interest among the countries of the South and that, given normal expectations of state behavior, a number of these conflicts will persist and even deepen if for no other reason than as a result of markedly different rates of development? We did not need the oil crisis to demonstrate this, though it clearly has provided a very vivid demonstration. The devastating effects of current oil prices on many developing countries have been met with relative indifference by the major OPEC countries, thereby putting to rest the romantic notion that the new states would lead the way to humanity's moral regeneration. The most telling comment on this notion has come from a Senegalese official who is reported as having said about the world's response to the West African drought that while the United States "gives enough to allow itself an easy conscience," the infinitesimal assistance given by rich fellow Muslims in the Arab countries indicates the latter "have not reached the state of conscience."

149

RICHARD BARNET

The debate we ought to be having

The links of interdependence between the American economy and the world economy are so pervasive that isolationism is not a possibility for the United States. The choice is not whether the United States is to be integrally involved in the international system but the terms of the involvement. This is the crux of the debate we are not having. The self-perpetuating elite that has run our foreign policy for a generation have assumed that the United States cannot afford to share its power by accepting limits on its right to make crucial unilateral decisions—whether to use nuclear weapons, whether to invade other countries, whether to change the ground rules of the international monetary system. The strategy has been to perpetuate for as long as possible the preeminent military and economic position the United States enjoyed at the end of World War II. As the ruined economies of West Europe and Japan recovered and the Soviet Union became a formidable military rival, the tactics for achieving continued American preeminence have been modified. The issues concerning the management of the world economy and distribution of resources are crowding out the older issues of the cold war, many of which like Germany, Vietnam and Cuba have more or less been settled. But the resistance to sharing power remains. The hostile reaction of the Ford administration to the efforts of the poor countries to create a more equitable "new international economic order" reflects a deep-seated isolationism. We are in the unenviable position of defending privilege against the majority of people in an increasingly desperate world.

There is nothing exceptional about such a posture. Every great nation tries to hold on to what it has. But empires collapse because they lose touch with their own time and employ self-defeating strategies for maintaining their power. The issue is whether the security of Americans

will be better served by trying to perpetuate the era of American hegemony after the conditions for it have passed or by taking the lead in building a more equitable international economic order and a less militarized international political order. Candor, now in vogue as a political virtue, requires a painful assessment of the real conflicts between American comfort and the survival of a majority of mankind.

One of the most deceptive words in the foreign policy lexicon is "we." Discussion of the American national interest assumes that all Americans share the same interests, that what is a good U.S. policy for Anaconda in Chile or for Gulf Oil in Italy is necessarily a good policy for American wage earners and consumers. It has become clearer in recent months that CIA covert operations have to a significant degree been for the direct support of U.S.-based multinational corporations. That is one example—the Soviet wheat deal is another—of a foreign policy initiative from which the benefits flow to a small group of Americans and the costs are borne by a much larger segment of society. It is by no means clear that unemployed workers in Detroit, supermarket shoppers and small businessmen have the same foreign policy interests as the largest banks and corporations. Yet it is the representatives of these institutions who continue to make policy in the name of all Americans. There can be no serious consideration of alternative goals and policies without enlarging the circle of policy makers to include representatives of many domestic interests which are vitally affected by foreign policy decisions but which now have no voice in deciding what "we" do as a nation. Until foreign policy is seen for what it is—a reflection of present domestic policy and a context for evolving domestic policy—discussions will never rise above emotionalism and abstraction. A redefinition of America's role in the world will come, if it does, only as part of a process of redefining American society.

HANS MORGENTHAU

The decline of the West

Present concern with the decline of the West is caused by the obvious decline of American power. The defeat the United States has suffered in Indochina has not only been total but ignominious. Even if defeat had to be anticipated as inevitable, there was nothing inevitable about our inability to manipulate the modalities of defeat for the purpose of retreating from an untenable position with at least a modicum of poise. American power and influence used to be dominant in Turkey and Greece. The United States has succeeded in alienating both to the point where their effective membership in NATO is in question, and has failed in inducing them to compose their differences over Cyprus. We are reduced to watching passively the anarchy, threatening Communization, of our ally Portugal. We are unable to dissuade the Federal Republic of Germany, one of our closest allies, from selling a whole nuclear production cycle to Brazil, a transaction that, making the proliferation of nuclear weapons virtually inevitable, carries ominous implications for the survival of mankind.

The natural current concern with this decline of American power has obscured the relationship between that decline and the decline of the West in general. More particularly, it has obscured the fact that the United States owes its rise to predominance in the aftermath of the Second World War to the selfsame decline of the West, of which it now appears as the prime example. In other words, the decline of the West, the United States included, was preceded by the decline of the traditional nation-states of Western Europe, of which the United States was the main beneficiary. . . .

American simplistic anti-Communism was adequate to counter through containment the Soviet military threat. But, the counter-subversive programs America operated in the democratic countries of the West remained not only by and large ineffective but turned out to be counter-productive. What was difficult for the counter-subversive technicians of the American secret services to understand was that the hold which Communism has over large masses of the Western peoples is not primarily, let alone exclusively, the result of the machinations of Communist governments from abroad, but of indigenous conditions exploited but not created from abroad. Thus, the rigid ideological commitment to a dogmatic anti-Communism, reducing a complex reality to a simple juxtaposition between good and evil, has been demonstrated to be untenable on philosophical and historical grounds and proven to be a political and moral disaster. . . .

American moral and political commitment to anti-Communism succeeded only where the military and economic power of the United States could be effectively brought into play. It failed when its pure moral force was appealed to. Paradoxically, it failed not because the peoples whose freedom was at stake were not willing to listen to its message, but because America, the bearer of the message, did not know how to live up to it. The fear of Communism blocked the road to freedom. In the contest between the colonial powers of Europe and their colonies, the United States took the side of the former, not because it was in favor of colonialism, but because it was afraid that Communism might be the alternative to colonialism. The champion of freedom became the defender and restorer of the colonial status quo. Making common cause with the colonial powers, it shared with them the moral taint of colonialism. Thus America came to lose the peculiar moral aura which it thought had set it apart from all other nations.

Yet, while America's indiscriminate dogmatic opposition to Communism, or to what looked like Communism, compelled it to join the forces of the status quo, its libertarianism and anti-colonialist tradition evoked its sympathies with the aspirations of the Third World. That world had painted a picture of its condition flattering to itself and disparaging to their former colonial masters and the industrial nations at large. Their miseries and failures are presented as the responsibility of the developed nations, who have the moral obligation to right the

151

wrong they have done them. This moral dichotomy between the "good" members of the Third World and the "evil" colonial exploiters cut across the American dichotomy between "good" democratic capitalists and "evil" Communists. For many of the nations of the "free world" are sympathetic to one or the other brands of Communism, or at least to some brand of authoritarianism which bears the name of "Communism" or "Socialism."

Thus, what occurred on the moral plane was the opposite of what took place in the arena of power. In the latter, the United States benefited at the expense of its associates. On the former, it partook in the disrepute of its associates. Perhaps not surprisingly—considering the resentment that unchallengeable power evokes—the unprecedented power of the United States has not been matched by the reputation for the benevolent use of that power. That discrepancy produced the undoing of America's moral position. The Third World attacked the United States with the same arguments which America used to argue against colonialism, racism, and exploitation, perpetuated by its friends. Arguing within its traditional moral framework, the United States had no answer when its own arguments were turned against it. It had at least spoken as the champion of the downtrodden and the exploited in the name of equality and freedom, and now defended in its deeds the status quo of colonialism and exploitation in the name of anti-Communism. Foreign aid, parsimoniously and ineffectually dispersed, is a token tribute to the professed ideals of America. . . .

It is one of the great ironies of contemporary history that the moral and material decline of the West has in good measure been accomplished through the moral and material triumphs of the West. The Third World has shaken off the Western yoke by invoking the very moral principles of self-determination and social justice which the West has proclaimed and endeavored to put into practice. That, in the process, national self-determination was to become the ideology of new imperialisms and social justice the ideological disguise of servitudes new and old was to be expected. What points to the moral exhaustion of the West is its inability to stipulate moral principles with which to justify its positions and interests against its enemies and detractors. . . .

On the material plane the West has been made vulnerable to oil as a political weapon by its high technological development. The power which oil bestows upon oil-producing nations is the result of the technological development of modern industrial nations. Twenty or fifty years ago, oil did not bestow such power upon oil-producing nations because the use of oil as the lifeblood of modern industry was limited. The oil-consuming nations still operated in a buyer's market. If one source of oil was not available or was available only on conditions which were unacceptable to the consuming nation, that nation could go elsewhere and buy it there on more convenient terms. The contemporary situation is characterized by an imbalance between supply and demand to such an extent that the buyer's market has been transformed into a seller's market and nations which have large deposits of oil, cooperating as the oil-producing nations did during the fall of 1973, can apply a stranglehold to the consuming nations; or they can impose political conditions which the consuming nations can refuse to meet only at the risk of enormous political, economic, and social dislocations.

Thus, the vulnerability of highly developed industrial nations of the West to the supply of oil is a function of their industrial advancement. The shift of power from the oil-consuming to the oil-producing nations is a by-product of the former's industrial power. Industrial development has widened the gap between the advanced and backward nations in favor of the former, but it has supplied some of the latter with a new weapon: a quasi-monopoly of oil.

That weapon can be deadly, but it resembles nuclear power in that it is purely destructive. An oil-producing nation can bring an oil-consuming one to its knees, but it cannot govern it by virtue of its oil monopoly. Thus the potency of the oil weapon demonstrates dramatically the decline of Western power. Yet it indicates no substitute for that declining power—except the power of destruction.

The moral and material decline of the West is

an observable fact. What is not observable is the kind of order that could take the place of the fading one created and maintained by the power of the West. Instead of the outlines of a new order created and supported by a new center of power, what appears on the horizon of the civilized world is the specter of anarchy, with legal arrangements, institutions, and procedures being utterly out of tune with the objective technological conditions of the age.

JOSEPH KRAFT

Has morality a place in foreign policy?

Morality in foreign policy has been a constant theme in the presidential campaign. . . .

But now, in the name of morality, both Jimmy Carter and President Ford are making implicit commitments that they cannot keep in areas remote from American national interest. So there is a compelling need to ask what is morality in foreign policy.

The question has been driven front and center by the classic balance-of-power policy enunciated, and intermittently practiced, by Secretary of State Kissinger. He has tended to subordinate the smaller countries and to concentrate on relations with the powerful ones—notably Russia, China, Japan and Germany.

He has been indulgent toward the instruments of influence available to great powers—military force and the black art of secret intelligence. He has been less than absolutely scrupulous in squaring his policies with Congress and public opinion. He has been scornful of couching his deeds in the rhetoric of do-goodism.

The balance-of-power approach was acceptable as long as it worked. More specifically, while the Vietnam war lasted, particularly while chances of an indecisive or happy end seemed open, the Kissinger diplomacy commanded general approval. But the debacle in Vietnam showed that the United States has broken with its traditional policy of selflessly supporting the

good guys. It demonstrated that American policymakers had used all the dirty tricks in the game on behalf of the baddies.

Accordingly, some adjustment of approach was necessary. If public support for any foreign policy was to be developed, a greater emphasis on idealism and openness was required.

Kissinger himself, especially with the accession of Gerald Ford to the White House, began to consult more actively with Congress and the country, and to take up such humanitarian causes as hunger, nuclear proliferation and opposition to tyrannical government—particularly in southern Africa.

Jimmy Carter, in enunciating his foreign-policy stance, has gone way beyond the adjustment made by Kissinger. Carter has made morality and openness the center of his position on foreign policy. He has dumped on the use of military power and secret intelligence.

He has assumed a unilateral American responsibility for stopping the proliferation of nuclear weapons. He has implicitly acknowledged American responsibility to end tyranny in parts of the Communist world—notably Eastern Europe—and in Western Europe, Latin America, Africa and Asia.

President Ford has felt obliged to follow suit. He has recently taken his distances from Kissinger. He has pushed for an American role in southern Africa, where the United States has no vital interest and where matters are almost surely going to turn badly anyhow. Lastly, while making up for his goof in denying during the second debate that Russia dominated Eastern Europe, he has tended to accept the Carter proposition that there is an implicit American commitment to promote freedom in Eastern Europe.

Far from just making a necessary adjustment, in other words, the United States is now being pushed back to the old Wilsonian diplomacy. There is a renewed emphasis on America as a land chosen to play liberal missionary for the rest of the world.

Unfortunately, this development occurs when a variety of factors—including some public disposition to cut military forces—is working to reduce American influence in the world.

So we are witnessing an implicit expansion of

153

commitments coincident with a decrease in the capacity to make good on these commitments.

In these circumstances, what is moral in foreign policy becomes a hard question. To me anyway, there is nothing more immoral than raising false hopes in the breasts of people in Eastern Europe and southern Africa. They have been let down so many times that the least the United States can do is avoid a building of illusions bound to be disappointing.

Given a choice between Kissingerism and Wilsonianism, in other words, I would take the former, and primarily on deeply moral grounds.

SIGMUND FREUD

Why war?

VIENNA, *September, 1932.*

DEAR PROFESSOR EINSTEIN,

When I heard that you intended to invite me to an exchange of views on some subject that interested you and that seemed to deserve the interest of others besides yourself, I readily agreed. I expected you to choose a problem on the frontiers of what is knowable to-day, a problem to which each of us, a physicist and a psychologist, might have our own particular angle of approach and where we might come together from different directions upon the same ground. You have taken me by surprise, however, by posing the question of what can be done to protect mankind from the curse of war. . . .

You begin with the relation between Right and Might. There can be no doubt that that is the correct starting-point for our investigation. But may I replace the word "might" by the balder and harsher word "violence"? To-day right and violence appear to us as antitheses. It can easily be shown, however, that the one has developed out of the other; and if we go back to the earliest beginnings and see how that first came about, the problem is easily solved. . . .

It is a general principle, then, that conflicts of interest between men are settled by the use of violence. This is true of the whole animal kingdom, from which men have no business to exclude themselves. . . .

Such, then, was the original state of things: domination by whoever had the greater might—domination by brute violence or by violence supported by intellect. As we know, this régime was altered in the course of evolution. There was a path that led from violence to right or law. What was that path? It is my belief that there was only one: the path which led by way of the fact that the superior strength of a single individual could be rivalled by the union of several weak ones. *"L'union fait la force."** Violence could be broken by union, and the power of those who were united now represented law in contrast to the violence of the single individual. Thus we see that right is the might of a community. . . .

If we turn to our own times, we arrive at the same conclusion which you have reached by a shorter path. Wars will only be prevented with certainty if mankind unites in setting up a central authority to which the right of giving judgement upon all conflicts of interest shall be handed over. There are clearly two separate requirements involved in this: the creation of a supreme authority and its endowment with the necessary power. One without the other would be useless. . . .

I can now proceed to add a gloss to another of your remarks. You express astonishment at the fact that it is so easy to make men enthusiastic about a war and add your suspicion that there is something at work in them—an instinct for hatred and destruction—which goes halfway to meet the efforts of the warmongers. Once again, I can only express my entire agreement. . . .

According to our hypothesis human instincts are of only two kinds: those which seek to preserve and unite—which we call "erotic," exactly in the sense in which Plato uses the word "Eros" in his *Symposium,* or "sexual," with a deliberate extension of the popular conception of "sexuality"—and those which seek to de-

---

Ed. note: In union there is strength.

154

stroy and kill and which we class together as the aggressive or destructive instinct. As you see, this is in fact no more than a theoretical clarification of the universally familiar opposition between Love and Hate which may perhaps have some fundamental relation to the polarity of attraction and repulsion that plays a part in your own field of knowledge. We must not be too hasty in introducing ethical judgements of good and evil. Neither of these instincts is any less essential than the other; the phenomena of life arise from the operation of both together, whether acting in concert or in opposition. It seems as though an instinct of the one sort can scarcely ever operate in isolation; it is always accompanied—or, as we say, alloyed—with an element from the other side, which modifies its aim or is, in some cases, what enables it to achieve that aim. Thus, for instance, the instinct of self-preservation is certainly of an erotic kind, but it must nevertheless have aggressiveness at its disposal if it is to fulfil its purpose. So, too, the instinct of love, when it is directed towards an object, stands in need of some contribution from the instinct of mastery if it is in any way to possess that object. The difficulty of isolating the two classes of instinct in their actual manifestations is indeed what has so long prevented us from recognizing them.

If you will follow me a little further, you will see that human actions are subject to another complication of a different kind. It is very rarely that an action is the work of a *single* instinctual impulse (which must in itself be compounded of Eros and destructiveness). In order to make an action possible there must be as a rule a *combination* of such compounded motives. . . .

I should like to linger for a moment over our destructive instinct, whose popularity is by no means equal to its importance. As a result of a little speculation, we have come to suppose that this instinct is at work in every living being and is striving to bring it to ruin and to reduce life to its original condition of inanimate matter. Thus it quite seriously deserves to be called a death instinct, while the erotic instincts represent the effort to live. The death instinct turns into the destructive instinct if, with the help of special organs, it is directed outwards, on to objects. The living creature preserves its own life, so to say, by destroying an extraneous one. Some portion of the death instinct, however, remains operative *within* the living being, and we have sought to trace quite a number of normal and pathological phenomena to this internalization of the destructive instinct. We have even been guilty of the heresy of attributing the origin of conscience to this diversion inwards of aggressiveness. You will notice that it is by no means a trivial matter if this process is carried too far: it is positively unhealthy. On the other hand if these forces are turned to destruction in the external world, the living creature will be relieved and the effect must be beneficial. This would serve as a biological justification for all the ugly and dangerous impulses against which we are struggling. It must be admitted that they stand nearer to Nature than does our resistance to them, for which an explanation also needs to be found. . . .

For our immediate purpose then, this much follows from what has been said: there is no use in trying to get rid of men's aggressive inclinations. We are told that in certain happy regions of the earth, where nature provides in abundance everything that man requires, there are races whose life is passed in tranquillity and who know neither compulsion nor aggressiveness. I can scarcely believe it and I should be glad to hear more of these fortunate beings. The Russian Communists, too, hope to be able to cause human aggressiveness to disappear by guaranteeing the satisfaction of all material needs and by establishing equality in other respects among all the members of the community. That, in my opinion, is an illusion. They themselves are armed to-day with the most scrupulous care and not the least important of the methods by which they keep their supporters together is hatred of everyone beyond their frontiers. In any case, as you yourself have remarked, there is no question of getting rid entirely of human aggressive impulses: it is enough to try to divert them to such an extent that they need not find expression in war.

Our mythological theory of instincts makes it easy for us to find a formula for *indirect* methods of combating war. If willingness to engage

155

in war is an effect of the destructive instinct, the most obvious plan will be to bring Eros, its antagonist, into play against it. Anything that encourages the growth of emotional ties between men must operate against war. These ties may be of two kinds. In the first place they may be relations resembling those towards a loved object, though without having a sexual aim. There is no need for psychoanalysis to be ashamed to speak of love in this connection, for religion itself uses the same words: "Thou shalt love thy neighbour as thyself." This, however, is more easily said than done. The second kind of emotional tie is by means of identification. Whatever leads men to share important interests produces this community of feeling, these identifications. And the structure of human society is to a large extent based on them. . . .

I should like, however, to discuss one more question, which you do not mention in your letter but which specially interests me. Why do you and I and so many other people rebel so violently against war? Why do we not accept it as another of the many painful calamities of life? After all, it seems quite a natural thing, no doubt it has a good biological basis and in practice it is scarcely avoidable. . . . It is my opinion that the main reason why we rebel against war is that we cannot help doing so. We are pacifists because we are obliged to be for organic reasons. And we then find no difficulty in producing arguments to justify our attitude.

No doubt this requires some explanation. My belief is this. For incalculable ages mankind has been passing through a process of evolution of culture. (Some people, I know, prefer to use the term "civilization.") We owe to that process the best of what we have become, as well as a good part of what we suffer from. Though its causes and beginnings are obscure and its outcome uncertain, some of its characteristics are easy to perceive. . . . The psychical modifications that go along with the cultural process are striking and unambiguous. They consist in a progressive displacement of instinctual aims and a restriction of instinctual impulses. Sensations which were pleasurable to our ancestors have become indifferent or even intolerable to ourselves; there are organic grounds for the changes

in our ethical and aesthetic ideals. Of the psychological characteristics of culture two appear to be the most important: a strengthening of the intellect, which is beginning to govern instinctual life, and an internalization of the aggressive impulses, with all its consequent advantages and perils. Now war is in the crassest opposition to the psychical attitude imposed on us by the cultural process, and for that reason we are bound to rebel against it; we simply cannot any longer put up with it. This is not merely an intellectual and emotional repudiation; we pacifists have a constitutional intolerance of war, an idiosyncracy magnified, as it were, to the highest degree. It seems, indeed, as though the lowering of aesthetic standards in war plays a scarcely smaller part in our rebellion than do its cruelties.

And how long shall we have to wait before the rest of mankind become pacifists too? There is no telling. But it may not be Utopian to hope that these two factors, the cultural attitude and the justified dread of the consequences of a future war, may result within a measurable time in putting an end to the waging of war. By what paths or by what side-tracks this will come about we cannot guess. But one thing we *can* say: whatever fosters the growth of culture works at the same time against war.

I trust you will forgive me if what I have said has disappointed you, and I remain, with kindest regards,

Yours sincerely,
SIGM. FREUD

BRONISLAW MALINOWSKI

An anthropological analysis of war

I think that the task of evaluating war in terms of cultural analysis is today the main duty of the theory of civilization. In democratic countries public opinion must be freed from prejudice and enlightened as regards sound knowledge. The totalitarian states are spending as much energy, foresight, and constructive engineering on the task of indoctrinating the minds of their subjects as in the task of building armaments. Unless we scientifically and ethically rally to the counterpart task, we shall not be able to oppose them. At the same time the full cultural understanding of war in its relation to nationality and state, in its drives and effects, in the price paid and advantages gained, is necessary also for the problem of implementing any fundamental change.

The problem of what war is as a cultural phenomenon naturally falls into the constituent issues of the biological determinants of war, its political effects, and its cultural constructiveness. In the following discussion of pugnacity and aggression we shall see that even preorganized fighting is not a simple reaction of violence determined by the impulse of anger. The first distinction to emerge from this analysis will be between organized and collective fighting as against individual, sporadic, and spontaneous acts of violence—which are the antecedents of homicide, murder, and civic disorder, but not of war. We shall then show that organized fighting has to be fully discussed with reference to its political background. Fights within a community fulfil an entirely different function from intertribal feuds or battles. Even in these latter, however, we will have to distinguish between culturally effective warfare and military operations which do not leave any permanent mark either in terms of diffusion, of evolution, or of any lasting historical aftereffect. From all this will emerge the concept of "war as an armed contest between two independent political units, by means of organized military force, in the pursuit of a tribal or national policy." With this as a minimum definition of war, we shall be able to see how futile and confusing it is to regard primitive brawls, scrimmages, and feuds as genuine antecedents of our present world-catastrophe.

War and human nature

We have, then, first to face the issue of "aggressiveness as instinctual behavior"; in other words, of the determination of war by intrinsic-

ally biological motives. Such expressions as "war is older than man," "war is inherent in human nature," "war is biologically determined" have either no meaning or they signify that humanity has to conduct wars, even as all men have to breathe, sleep, breed, eat, walk, and evacuate, wherever they live and whatever their civilization. . . .

Can we regard pugnacity and aggressiveness and all the other reactions of hostility, hate, and violence as comparable to any vital sequence . . . ? The answer must be an emphatic negative. Not that the impulse of aggression, violence, or destruction be ever absent from any human group or from the life of any human being. If the activity of breathing be interrupted by accident or a deliberate act of another individual, the immediate reaction to it is a violent struggle to remove the obstacle or to overcome the human act of aggression. Kicking, biting, pushing, immediately start; a fight ensues, which has to end with the destruction of the suffocated organism or the removal of the obstacle. Take away the food from the hungry child or dog or monkey and you will provoke immediately strong hostile reactions. Any interference with the progressive course of sexual preliminaries—still more, any interruption of the physiological act—leads in man and animal to a violent fit of anger.

This last point, however, brings us directly to the recognition that the impulse of anger, the hostilities of jealousy, the violence of wounded honor and sexual and emotional possessiveness are as productive of hostility and of fighting, direct or relayed, as is the thwarting in the immediate satisfaction of a biological impulse.

We could sum up these results by saying that the impulse which controls aggression is not primary but derived. It is contingent upon circumstances in which a primary biologically defined impulse is being thwarted. It is also produced in a great variety of nonorganic ways, determined by such purely cultural factors as economic ownership, ambition, religious values, privileges of rank, and personal sentiments of attachment, dependence, and authority. Thus, to speak even of the *impulse* of pugnacity as biologically determined is incorrect. . . .

157

The contribution of anthropology to the problem of war

Glancing back over our previous arguments, we can see that we have arrived at certain theoretical conclusions, new to anthropological theory. It will still be necessary to show where our gains in clarity and definition are related to modern problems.

As regards the theoretical gains, we have shown that war cannot be regarded as a fiat of human destiny, in that it could be related to biological needs or immutable psychological drives. All types of fighting are complex cultural responses due not to any direct dictates of an impulse but to collective forms of sentiment and value. As a mechanism of organized force for the pursuit of national policies war is slow in evolving. Its incidence depends on the gradual development of military equipment and organization, of the scope for lucrative exploits, of the formation of independent political units.

Taking into account all such factors, we had to establish, within the genus of aggression and use of violence, the following distinctions: (1) Fighting, private and angry, within a group belongs to the type of breach of custom and law and is the prototype of criminal behavior. It is countered and curbed by the customary law within institutions and between institutions. (2) Fighting, collective and organized, is a juridical mechanism for the adjustment of differences between constituent groups of the same larger cultural unit. Among the lowest savages these two types are the only forms of armed contest to be found. (3) Armed raids, as a type of man-hunting sport, for purposes of head-hunting, cannibalism, human sacrifices, and the collection of other trophies. (4) Warfare as the political expression of early nationalism, that is, the tendency to make the tribe-nation and tribe-state coincide, and thus to form a primitive nation-state. (5) Military expeditions of organized pillage, slave-raiding, and collective robbery. (6) Wars between two culturally differentiated groups as an instrument of national policy. This type of fighting, with which war in the fullest sense of the word began, leads to conquest, and, through

this, to the creation of full-fledged military and political states, armed for internal control, for defense and aggression. This type of state presents, as a rule, and for the first time in evolution, clear forms of administrative, political, and legal organization. Conquest is also of first-rate importance in the processes of diffusion and evolution.

The types of armed contest, listed as (4) and (6) and these two only, are, in form, sociological foundations, and in the occurrence of constructive policy are comparable with historically defined wars. Every one of the six types here summed up presents an entirely different cultural phase in the development of organized fighting. The neglect to establish the differentiation here introduced has led to grave errors in the application of anthropological principles to general problems concerning the nature of war. The crude short-circuiting—by which our modern imperialisms, national hatreds, and worldwide lust of power have been connected with aggression and pugnacity—is largely the result of not establishing the above distinctions, of disregarding the cultural function of conflict, and of confusing war, as a highly specialized and mechanized phenomenon, with any form of aggression.

We can determine even more precisely the manner in which anthropological evidence, as the background of correct understanding and informed knowledge, can be made to bear on some of our current problems. In general, of course, it is clear that since our main concern is whether war will destroy our Western civilization or not, the anthropological approach, which insists on considering the cultural context of war, might be helpful.

Especially important in a theoretical discussion of whether war can be controlled and ultimately abolished, is the recognition that war is not biologically founded. The fact that its occurrence cannot be traced to the earliest beginnings of human culture is significant. Obviously, if war were necessary to human evolution; if it were something without which human groups have to decay and by which they advance; then war could not be absent from the earliest stages, in which the actual birth of cultural realities took place under the greatest strains and against the heaviest odds. A really vital ingredient could not, therefore, be lacking in the composition of primitive humanity, struggling to lay down the foundations of further progress.

ROBERT E. OSGOOD and ROBERT W. TUCKER

Force, order, and justice

Pugnacity and the emotional satisfactions of war may help to explain why states are sometimes bellicose, but they do not explain why states that would obviously prefer to secure their ends, whether offensive or defensive, without war habitually find it necessary to resort to war or the threat of war. They do not explain why war is endemic in international politics. The chief explanation for this phenomenon lies in the nature of the international system. More specifically, it lies in the conflicts among autonomous but interdependent political units that are organized for their own protection and advancement but that are not subordinate to a central political authority and police force. In this anarchical system, as in others where the sovereign authority and capacity to use force reside in independent political entities, armed coercion necessarily has a distinct utility that persuasion, negotiation, adjudication, and even nonviolent forms of coercion lack.

As in serious conflicts of interest within a community, force is the final argument after appeals to reason, sympathy, or tradition have failed, since it promises to gain an objective by direct means—by compelling one will to comply with another rather than by inducing one mind to consent to another. If men had an unlimited capacity to accommodate each other by appeals to reason and sympathy or custom, there would be no need for force. In fact, however, without organized force to prod reason, sympathy, and custom—or to compensate for

their absence—all but the most static and isolated societies would be in chaos.

Within a well-ordered political community the preponderant power of compulsion lies in the hands of a government commanding the consent of the governed. In such a government force provides the ultimate sanction for a system of orderly relations in which conflicts are normally resolved peacefully. In the relations of competing political groups independent of a central government, however, the power of compulsion must reside in each group. In this sense, therefore, wars occur between political groups simply because there is nothing to stop them. In international politics, moreover, the role of force, though not necessarily the propensity to war, is accentuated by the ability of popular states to mobilize mass loyalties, by the diversity of their interests and circumstances in a rapidly changing civilization, by their growing psychological, if not economic, interdependence, and by the great magnitude of the force they can marshal. Under these conditions the diffusion of force among a number of states in close communication with each other accentuates mutual suspicions and animosities and reinforces the need of every major state for its own armed force.

It is true that most wars are perpetrated by states who want something they do not have rather than by states that are content to defend what they already have. Hence the imprudence of defensive states neglecting their military power. On the other hand, even if all states were purely defense-minded—a utopian supposition—there would still be need for force. The very search for security in a system of politics without government compels reliance upon military self-help, which, in turn, fosters conflict and a competition for military power. The expansion of the meaning and conditions of national security to embrace tangible and intangible assets beyond the territorial boundaries of states makes this especially true. Only if all nations sought no more than the protection of their boundaries and, if at the same time, there were no conflicting requirements of such protection, could the competition for military power be avoided. But this prescription is a fantasy, if only because security has become so much broader a concept.

Increasingly, major powers feel compelled to protect their territory at places beyond their boundaries. Quite apart from the expanding range of their interests, they realize that the growing material and psychological interdependence of states—in conventional metaphor, the "shrinking" of the world—requires them to extend their defenses farther and farther into the surrounding international environment. To feel secure, they must guard against a variety of external developments that are far down the chain of threatening circumstances: developments affecting commercial and military lines of communication, the strength of friendly nations, the distribution of power, and the credibility of their will to use force.

Furthermore, the national entity that the governments of major powers are bound to secure transcends territory to include the protection of national rights and privileges, the maintenance of national prestige and honor, and even the vindication of political values in the world. The intangible quality of the ends encompassed in the concept of security is implicit in the identification of individual citizens with an abstract national personality. . . .

In its most general function force is an asset that is desirable in itself: desirable not from infatuation with power but from a purely utilitarian standpoint. For, like money, military power is an indispensable means for meeting future, unspecified, and largely unpredictable contingencies. . . .

For these reasons war and the threat of war are endemic in international relations. The fact that most states are at peace most of the time and some are at peace all of the time, the fact that many states with conflicts of interest do not arm against each other or raise the prospect of war, does not argue against the integral relationship of force to international politics. Since there is no other way for states to pursue what they regard as vital interests when other states are determined to oppose them, force must be as essential to international politics in an anar-

chy as elections are to domestic politics in an organized democracy. . . .

What is the alternative to a strategy of deterrence, with its potentially unlimited threat and its attendant risks, that does not at the same time abandon the ends of statecraft? Obviously, an "alternative" must abandon the means distinctive to statecraft in general and to a strategy of deterrence in particular. Is there such an alternative that can do so, however, without abandoning most of the ends of statecraft as well? The issue of means may be resolved simply by abandoning the *ultima ratio* of statecraft. To this extent, at least, pacifism has always formed an alternative, and continues to form an alternative today. In condemning war, for whatever reasons, pacifism abandons the means distinctive to statecraft. In refusing to threaten a potential aggressor with retributive measures, in refusing to confront an adversary with the prospect of returning like for like, pacifism abandons the constituent principle of statecraft. At the same time, it must abandon most of the ends of statecraft as well. For these reasons, pacifism cannot be regarded as an alternative political strategy. Nor has it been so regarded, whether by the few who have advocated it or by the many who have rejected it. In abandoning not only the means but most of the ends of statecraft as well, pacifism must be regarded as an alternative to statecraft per se. . . .

Nor is this all. It is clear that nonviolence, if it is to prove more than merely a prudential strategy the weak may in certain circumstances successfully employ against the strong, must assume not merely a change of sorts in men but something akin to their moral transformation. Men are not only expected to forego employing a means that has hitherto been central to social and political life, they are expected to forego the many ends this means has secured, and may still secure, for them. The latter point is critical though commonly neglected in discussions of nonviolence. The central issue nonviolence must raise is not so much whether it is compatible with the nature of man but whether it is compatible with the ends of man. We may well conclude that the evidence does not support the view that war is a biological necessity and that men are accordingly compelled by instinct to perpetuate this institution. It does not follow, however, that the disappearance of war is therefore primarily a matter of devising, by some "leap in our thinking," new methods or techniques of conflict resolution. Nor does it follow that the disappearance of war is primarily a matter of reversing the "learned link," if it be that, between violence and masculine courage. At the root of these and similar arguments is the common assumption that if man is not compelled by his nature to perpetuate the institution of war, he may resolve his conflicts by other and less destructive methods. If this assumption is unexceptionable, it is also rather beside the point in considering the prospects of a warless world. Of course, men may resolve their conflicts by methods other than war. But the decisive issue is whether they can always secure the ends they desire by methods other than war. For the past, at any rate, the evidence is overwhelming that war, the organized use of armed force, has been a means for securing a variety of desired ends, ends that could not be secured other than through war. . . .

It is only by denying, whether implicitly or explicitly, the ends men have sought through war, or by minimizing the significance of the ends that have often prompted men to war, that proponents of nonviolence can largely ignore the supreme difficulties in replacing war with nonviolent methods of conflict resolution.

These considerations indicate that if a commitment to nonviolence is nevertheless represented as an alternative to the predicament in which men presently find themselves, it is an alternative only in the sense that every vision of a "new beginning" in history is an alternative. We do not for this reason dismiss nonviolence. We simply do not find it very useful to speculate on such new beginnings.

If it does not seem useful to speculate on new beginnings that require the transformation of man, is it nevertheless useful to speculate on new beginnings that presumably require the transformation of the system rather than of man? Many would appear to think so. While

the serious advocacy of nonviolence remains confined to a very few, the goal of general disarmament has attracted a much larger and more impressive following. . . .

If general disarmament represents a possible alternative to the present system of self-help, in the sense that it is seen as leading to the transformation of this system, it does so only if attended by measures that go far beyond disarmament as such. For the abandonment of arms, even though accompanied by effective procedures of inspection and verification, would not thereby transform the present system. Without the development of supranational institutions for ensuring peace and security, and peaceful change, there would remain the possibility that states could at any time break the disarmament agreement and rearm. The threat of military force would therefore remain one of the instruments of diplomacy. Moreover, in the absence of effective collective procedures, war itself would remain the *ultima ratio* of diplomacy, though at one stage removed.

A distinction must be drawn, then, between proposals for disarmament that are limited to the disarmament process itself and proposals that place general disarmament within the broader framework of other and more comprehensive measures for the organization of peace and security. Whereas the former assume the continued reliance of states upon the traditional instruments of diplomacy, the latter assume that these instruments must be supplanted by new methods of resolving conflict and ensuring peace. Whereas the former assume the continuance by and large of the institution of self-help, in which each state remains at liberty to protect its interests as best it can with the means at its disposal, the latter assume that the scope of self-help will be severely restricted. Whereas the former necessarily assume that states may break the disarmament agreement and rearm, and that the threat of rearmament will therefore remain one of the instruments of diplomacy, the latter assume that effective peacekeeping institutions of a supranational character must ensure that states are not able to break the disarmament agreement and rearm. Whereas, finally, the former may accord only a modest role to law, the latter must give to law a central role. For the latter type of proposal is dependent upon the creation of a centralized security system within which states would be deprived of their traditional freedom not only to resort to armed force in the last resort but also to threaten seriously the security of their neighbors through other forms of coercion. Yet it is precisely because a centralized security system would have to be created for a society comprising very disparate and conflicting groups that these restraints on coercion would have to take a predominantly legal form and would have to be clearly defined. They would have to take a predominantly legal form because the forces other than law that normally operate within stable and cohesive domestic societies to restrain contending groups would remain—at least for a considerable time—weak and undeveloped. They would have to be very clearly defined because of the weakness of those forces other than law which in domestic societies serve both to restrain contending groups and to give meaning to the law itself. In the absence of those social forces other than law which largely give to the law its effectiveness while at the same time reducing the dependence upon law, "peace through law" can be attained only by giving to law a role of importance that it has rarely possessed in domestic society. And since the rule of law is still always the rule of men, this can only mean conferring an extraordinary power on those who are competent to apply and enforce the law. It is chiefly for these reasons that the recurrent demand of "peace through law" either appears impossible to satisfy or seems to hold out novel dangers if, by some miracle, it were suddenly to be satisfied.

REINHOLD NIEBUHR

The morality of nations

The selfishness of nations is proverbial. It was a dictum of George Washington that nations were not to be trusted beyond their own interest. "No state," declares a German author, "has ever entered a treaty for any other reason than self interest," and adds: "A statesman who has any other motive would deserve to be hung." "In every part of the world," said Professor Edward Dicey, "where British interests are at stake, I am in favor of advancing these interests even at the cost of war. The only qualification I admit is that the country we desire to annex or take under our protection should be calculated to confer a tangible advantage upon the British Empire." National ambitions are not always avowed as honestly as this, as we shall see later, but that is a fair statement of the actual facts, which need hardly to be elaborated for any student of history.

What is the basis and reason for the selfishness of nations? If we begin with what is least important or least distinctive of national attitudes, it must be noted that nations do not have direct contact with other national communities, with which they must form some kind of international community. They know the problems of other peoples only indirectly and at second hand. Since both sympathy and justice depend to a large degree upon the perception of need, which makes sympathy flow, and upon the understanding of competing interests, which must be resolved, it is obvious that human communities have greater difficulty than individuals in achieving ethical relationships. While rapid means of communication have increased the breadth of knowledge about world affairs among citizens of various nations, and the general advance of education has ostensibly promoted the capacity to think rationally and justly upon the inevitable conflicts of interest between nations, there is nevertheless little hope of arriving at a perceptible increase of international morality through the growth of intelligence and the perfection of means of communication. The development of international commerce, the increased economic interdependence among the nations, and the whole apparatus of a technological civilisation, increase the problems and issues between nations much more rapidly than the intelligence to solve them can be created. The silk trade between America and Japan did not give American citizens an appreciation of the real feelings of the Japanese toward the American Exclusion Act. Co-operation between America and the Allies during the war did not help American citizens to recognise, and deal sympathetically with, the issues of inter-allied debts and reparations; nor were the Allies able to do justice to either themselves or their fallen foe in settling the problem of reparations. Such is the social ignorance of peoples, that, far from doing justice to a foe or neighbor, they are as yet unable to conserve their own interests wisely. Since their ultimate interests are always protected best, by at least a measure of fairness toward their neighbors, the desire to gain an immediate selfish advantage always imperils their ultimate interests. If they recognise this fact, they usually recognise it too late. . . .

It is of course possible that the rational interest in international justice may become, on occasion, so widespread and influential that it will affect the diplomacy of states. But this is not usual. In other words the mind, which places a restraint upon impulses in individual life, exists only in a very inchoate form in the nation. It is, moreover, much more remote from the will of the nation than in private individuals; for the government expresses the national will, and that will is moved by the emotions of the populace and the prudential self-interest of dominant economic classes. . . .

In other words the nation is a corporate unity, held together much more by force and emotion, than by mind. Since there can be no ethical action without self-criticism, and no self-criticism without the rational capacity of self-transcendence, it is natural that national attitudes can hardly approximate the ethical. Even those tendencies toward self-criticism in a nation which do express themselves are usually thwarted by the governing classes and by a certain instinct for unity in society itself. For self-criticism is a kind of inner disunity, which the feeble mind of a nation finds difficulty in distinguishing from dangerous forms of inner conflict. So nations crucify their moral rebels with their criminals upon the same Golgotha, not being able to distinguish between the moral idealism which surpasses, and the anti-social conduct which falls below that moral mediocrity, on the level of which every society unifies its life. . . .

The social ignorance of the private citizen of the nation has thus far been assumed. It may be reasonable to hope that the general level of intelligence will greatly increase in the next decades and centuries and that growing social intelligence will modify national attitudes. It is doubtful whether it will ever increase sufficiently to eliminate all the moral hazards of international relations. There is an ethical paradox in patriotism which defies every but the most astute and sophisticated analysis. The paradox is that patriotism transmutes individual unselfishness into national egoism. Loyalty to the nation is a high form of altruism when compared with lesser loyalties and more parochial interests. It therefore becomes the vehicle of all the altruistic impulses and expresses itself, on occasion, with such fervor that the critical attitude of the individual toward the nation and its enterprises is almost completely destroyed. The unqualified character of this devotion is the very basis of the nation's power and of the freedom to use the power without moral restraint. Thus the unselfishness of individuals makes for the selfishness of nations. That is why the hope of solving the larger social problems of mankind, merely by extending the social sympathies of individuals, is so vain. Altruistic passion is sluiced into the reservoirs of nationalism with great ease, and is made to flow beyond them with great difficulty. What lies beyond the nation, the community of mankind, is too vague to inspire devotion.

The Laws of Moses and the Laws of Today

8

LAW
AND
MORALITY

There are strong and multifold strands uniting law and morals. There is, first, the general moral claim to obey the law. The law is held to be moral and he who wishes to disobey it—on moral grounds—bears the burden of proof to justify his act.

Even in cases of civil disobedience, however, the moral nature of the law is under-scored—because the legal punishment for disobedience is accepted. Indeed, civil disobedience is predicated upon a desire to make the law live up to its ideal of justice and become more moral. This ideal of justice is itself a tie between law and morals; as for the intimacy of this tie, it is enough to realize that the most effective critiques of our legal system are moral ones. A third strand binding law and morality is that many moral prohibitions, rights, and duties have also been made the subject of legal enforcement.

Nonetheless, there are differences between law and morals. The great majority of moral injunctions are rarely and only partially given legal sanction. There is no law against dishonoring one's parents, no law against laziness, none against slanderous gossip (only against libel), and none against dishonesty (only against fraud and perjury). Conversely, there are some laws whose only moral claim to our obedience is that they are the law. For instance, laws that Americans must drive on the right and pay taxes on April 15 are the result of arbitrary rule rather than of morality. These examples indicate that the relations between law and morals are various and complex; for the most part, the following selections address those areas in which the relations are in a state of conflict.

The opening piece, by Lon Fuller, intro-duces his conception of an "inner morality of law," which consists of procedural standards that the law must adhere to if it is to lay claim to legality. Fuller argues that only when a legal system fulfills these eight standards does there exist "a moral obligation to obey a legal rule." These standards, so to speak, are the infrastructure of the law's morality.

Assuming the law does meet these standards, what then is the extent of the citizen's obligation to obey the law? This is the subject of the next three selections, which consider the right of civil disobedience and the right of the minority to disobey the rules of the majority. In the first of these pieces, Eugene Rostow argues that "our society—as a society of consent—should not and indeed cannot acknowledge a right of civil disobedience." While recognizing that a citizen's obligations to other moral claims might conflict with his obligations to obey the law, the latter must take precedence, Rostow maintains, if a society is to remain free. In direct opposition to Rostow is Robert Wolff, who argues the case for philosophical anarchism. True "morality demands that each man freely and autonomously determine the guiding principles of his life," according to Wolff, and the authority of the state, even in a democracy, conflicts with this autonomy. Only if there were unanimous consent to all laws—a practical impossibility—would citizens be morally obligated to obey the law.

The third selection in this group is an excerpt from *The Trial of the Catonsville Nine* by Daniel Berrigan. The play is a dramatic account of the trial of nine men and women who, in obedience to their consciences and in a deliberate act of civil disobedience, set fire to Selective Service records at Catonsville, Maryland, to dramatize their opposition to a war that they believed to be immoral and illegal.

The next three excerpts debate another issue in which law and morals may conflict: Should society "legislate morals" and hold moral offenses such as homosexuality, drug abuse, or prostitution to be criminal offenses as well? In a celebrated exchange, Lord Devlin asserts that society has a right to preserve the moral system on which it is founded, for a weakening in the moral fiber of the citizenry will imperil the stability of any society. In response, H. L. A. Hart denies that "deviation from accepted sexual morality . . . threatens the existence of society. . . . As a proposition of fact it is entitled to no more respect than the Emperor Justinian's statement that homosexuality was the cause of earthquakes."

The next article in the design of this chapter is by Shirley Letwin, who believes that the entire argument over the legislation of morality is confused by a mistaken notion of a conflict between individualism and the law. In any discussion about the law, she maintains, the communal morality is at issue. For example, whether cohabitation is outlawed even though it is offensive may depend on other grounds—it might "entail surveillance incompatible with a civil association or . . . be impossible to enforce in any case." But consideration of the law was set in motion by moral concerns about the kind of civilization desired, and, therefore, whatever is decided, "the decision is a *moral* decision." In considering whether or not morality should be legislated, the reader might well ponder whether the criminal law is suited to prohibit moral deviancy, or whether laws prohibiting abortion, prostitution, homosexuality, and sodomy are often unenforceable and therefore breed cynicism and disrespect for the criminal law processes.

The final selection returns to a consideration from a different approach of the relative moral supremacy of conscience and the law when they come into conflict. John Silber uses a scene from the play *A Man for All Seasons* as an illustration "of the need to transcend the subjectivity of individual opinion about what is right, through an appeal to a society grounded in law." For Silber, the law is imperfect, but its imperfections prevent far greater moral evils from occurring.

Lon L. Fuller, born in 1902, is Carter Emeritus Professor of Jurisprudence at Harvard University. He previously taught at the universities of Illinois and Oregon and at Duke University. His many books include *The Morality of Law,* excerpted here and first published in 1964, and *Anatomy of the Law.*

Eugene V. Rostow, born in 1913, is Sterling Professor of Law at Yale, having joined the Law School there in 1938. From 1966 to 1969 he was undersecretary of state for political affairs, and he also served as president of the Atlantic Treaty Association. His books include *Planning for Freedom; Law, Power, and the Pursuit of Peace;* and *Peace in the Balance.* He also edited *Is Law Dead?* (1971), in which "The Rightful Limits of Freedom in a Liberal Democratic State" was first published.

Robert Paul Wolff, born in 1933, is a professor of philosophy at the University of Massachusetts, having previously taught at the University of Chicago and Columbia University. Among his many books are *A Critique of Pure Tolerance, Political Man and Social Man, In Defense of Anarchism,* and *About Philosophy.* The article reprinted here was published in *Is Law Dead?* (1971), edited by Eugene Rostow.

Daniel Berrigan, poet, author, and priest, was born in 1921. He now teaches theology at Woodstock College in New York. Active in the anti-Vietnam War movement, he was a founder of the Catholic Peace Fellowship. In May 1968, Daniel Berrigan, his brother Philip, and seven others set fire to Selective Service records from the local board in Catonsville, Maryland. *The Trial of the Catonsville Nine,* written in 1969, is Berrigan's dramatic account of the trial that followed and is based on actual court records. The defendants were found guilty and sentenced to jail. Among Berrigan's other works are *Night Flight to Hanoi, No Bars to Manhood, Prison Poems, America Is Hard to Find,* and *Lights On in the House of the Dead.*

Lord Patrick Devlin was born in 1905 and during his career in the law has held many distinguished posts, among them justice of the High Court, Queen's Bench Division. Since 1966 he has been High Steward of Cambridge University. He is author of *Trial by Jury* (1956) and *Woodrow Wilson's Neutrality* (1974). "The Enforcement of Morals," excerpted here, first appeared in 1959; in it he took issue with the report of the British Committee on Homosexual Offenses and Prostitution, generally known as the Wolfenden Report, which recommended that homosexual acts between consenting adults should no longer be a crime.

H(erbert) L. A. Hart, born in 1907, is a lawyer and philosopher and a leading authority on jurisprudence. A fellow of University College, Oxford, he is author of *The Concept of Law* (1961) and *Law, Liberty, Morality* (1963), excerpted here.

Shirley Robin Letwin, born in 1924, taught at Cornell University and the University of Chicago before becoming a fellow of the Radcliffe Institute for Independent Study. She is the author of many essays and monographs on social criticism. Her longer works are *Human Freedom* (1952) and *Pursuit of Certainty* (1965). She now lives in England. "Morality and Law" first appeared in *Encounter* in 1974.

John R. Silber, born in 1926, is president of Boston University. He previously taught philosophy and was dean of the College of Arts and Sciences at the University of Texas. He has published extensively in the field of legal philosophy and is associate editor of *Kant-Studien.* "The Thicket of Law and the Marsh of Conscience" was first published in *Harvard Magazine* in 1974.

LON FULLER

The morality of law

The attempt to create and maintain a system of legal rules may miscarry in at least eight ways; there are in this enterprise, if you will, eight distinct routes to disaster. The first and most obvious lies in a failure to achieve rules at all, so that every issue must be decided on an ad hoc basis. The other routes are: (2) a failure to publicize, or at least to make available to the affected party, the rules he is expected to observe; (3) the abuse of retroactive legislation, which not only cannot itself guide action, but undercuts the integrity of rules prospective in effect, since it puts them under the threat of retrospective change; (4) a failure to make rules understandable; (5) the enactment of contradictory rules or (6) rules that require conduct beyond the powers of the affected party; (7) introducing such frequent changes in the rules that the subject cannot orient his action by them; and, finally, (8) a failure of congruence between the rules as announced and their actual administration.

A total failure in any one of these eight directions does not simply result in a bad system of law; it results in something that is not properly called a legal system at all, except perhaps in the Pickwickian sense in which a void contract can still be said to be one kind of contract. Certainly there can be no rational ground for asserting that a man can have a moral obligation to obey a legal rule that does not exist, or is kept secret from him, or that came into existence only after he had acted, or was unintelligible, or was contradicted by another rule of the same system, or commanded the impossible, or changed every minute. It may not be impossible for a man to obey a rule that is disregarded by those charged with its administration, but at some point obedience becomes futile—as futile, in fact, as casting a vote that will never be counted. As the sociologist Simmel has observed, there is a kind of reciprocity between government and the citizen with respect to the observance of rules. Government says to the citizen in effect, "These are the rules we expect you to follow. If you follow them, you have our assurance that they are the rules that will be applied to your conduct." When this bond of reciprocity is finally and completely ruptured by government, nothing is left on which to ground the citizen's duty to observe the rules.

EUGENE V. ROSTOW

The rightful limits of freedom in a liberal democratic state: Of civil disobedience

All over the world—at least in societies which have or wish to achieve liberal governments—difficult problems have arisen in defining the boundary between individual freedom and public order.

In drawing that boundary, cultures like ours tend to resolve most doubts in favor of individual liberty. . . . Still, though our law goes to great lengths to protect the individual against the state, it has hardly abandoned its inherent right to protect the state against the individual, or the hostile group, and to insist on some deference to the prevailing code of social morality. . . .

In the United States, as in other countries, social protest is being expressed and dramatized in new and sometimes disturbing styles.

Wherever men look, they witness happenings which affront their sense of the right order of things—bombings, strange increases in the common crimes, turbulence at the universities, draft resistance, the rhetoric and sometimes the pantomime of revolution. In turn, these storms have stirred an intense preoccupation with the ancient philosophical problem of man's moral relation to the law. . . .

How should we evaluate the claims being put forward in the name of civil disobedience?

The case for civil disobedience

Is the highest form of moral liberty, as Rousseau contended, "obedience to self-imposed law," which alone makes man truly his own master?

Or is there an inalienable right of civil disobedience which citizens of conscience possess because they are moral beings—a right to disobey valid laws they do not approve, and to engage in organized programs of unlawful conduct (including some recourse to violence) by way of protest against such laws? . . .

An extensive literature asserts that there is a right of civil disobedience, and that the more disturbing features of the movements of protest to which society has been subjected—the turbulence, the violence, the shouting down of speakers, the campaigns to discredit authority and even due process of law—are all moral, legitimate, and indeed legal exercises of a kind of personal freedom which the law should now recognize as subsumed within the idea of liberty protected by the Constitution. Some proponents of civil disobedience contend that even if some of the occasions on which this "right" has been exercised have involved acts which in their view should be recognized as "excessive," and therefore "technically" illegal, society should be wise enough not to prosecute the men, women, and children of superior virtue who are responsible for them. They do no more, it is urged, than apply the tactics of the civil rights movement, and the philosophy of Martin Luther King, Jr., in other settings. If it was right, and legal, for black students to sit at the counter of a lunchroom in North Carolina twenty years ago, and ask for food despite a state law forbidding its sale to them, it is argued, then it must be also right, and legal, for Harvard students to sit in the dean's office and demand an end of R.O.T.C., the abolition of grades, or the employment of more blacks on Harvard construction projects.

Besides, it is said, even if some of the manifestations of civil disobedience go "too" far, one should put the blame not on those who have committed the "excessive" acts, but on the society whose callousness to injustice has driven morally superior persons to such extreme behavior. In any event, they contend, the "excessive"

protests are redeemed by their beneficent effects. They dramatize the views of the protesters for the media, and they jar our stolid and harassed institutions into reform. . . .

These are the main themes of the case for civil disobedience which have impressed and shaken public opinion without quite persuading it. Many of the writers, clergymen, professors, judges, and philosophers who support these views command wide respect. For our culture, there is deep resonance, calling up the memory of heroes and martyrs, in the comment of one of the leaders of draft resistance that what he did "may be a crime, but it is not a sin."

The obligation to obey valid law in a society of consent: The major premise

It is the thesis of this paper that our society—as a society of consent—should not and indeed cannot acknowledge a right of civil disobedience; that the moral and philosophical arguments advanced in support of such a right are in error; and that the analogies invoked in its behalf are inapplicable.

The major premise of my argument is the corollary of Jefferson's magisterial sentence . . . : The "just powers" of government derive from "the consent of the governed." It follows, I should contend, that in a society of consent the powers of government are just in Jefferson's sense: that is, they are legitimate, because authorized and renewed by procedures of voting all must respect. As a consequence, a citizen of such a society owes his fellow citizens, and the state they have established together, a moral duty to obey *valid* laws until they are repealed or fall into desuetude. I stress the word "valid" in the preceding sentence, to distinguish situations—of the utmost importance for our legal system—where the citizen is testing the constitutionality of a statute, an ordinance, or an official act. I cannot regard such tests as acts of disobedience to law. . . .

The individual owes other moral duties in his life—to his God, his family, his work, his conscience. Sometimes—often—there is conflict among the moral claims upon a man. But if man lives in a society of consent, and above all in a society of equality and of liberty, his relation to the valid laws of that society should be regarded as moral in character, and entitled to great weight in the hierarchy of moral claims he must face in the course of his life. If a man decides to commit an act of civil disobedience—for example, because he feels that what the law requires would breach his obligation to God—our culture would acknowledge at most his power, but not his right or privilege to do so. In such cases, the citizen faces a moral dilemma—he may resolve it in one way or another. But I can find no basis for saying that society has acknowledged, or must acknowledge, or should acknowledge his "right" to decide to violate the law. If the citizen should violate the law, then he should in turn acknowledge that he thereby breaches a covenant with moral dimensions, and is not committing a purely technical offense. To be sure, he would contend that he is breaking the law in order to avoid what he would regard as a greater sin. But the law too has a moral content; it represents the moral judgment of the majority, and its sense of justice. Under such circumstances, the individual should at least respect his duty to the law he has helped to make by accepting its penalties. . . .

The spacious tolerance of a free society is possible only if the laws are generally accepted and respected voluntarily, so that the role of force and coercion in the society can be kept to a minimum. The idea of a free society posits a much higher degree of civic responsibility on the part of each citizen than the concept of a tyranny or a system of paternalism. When a man elects to be a citizen of a society of consent, he necessarily undertakes a personal and far-reaching obligation to the laws, and his fellows do likewise. No such society could fulfill its aspirations, nor indeed remain free very long, unless this obligation were respected. . . .

The real problem in judging the ethical quality of social arrangements is not whether they achieve for the citizen the degree of moral autonomy which Robinson Crusoe possessed. Such a test would be chimerical, to say the least. Society must fulfill many functions and accommodate many jarring claims. In human societies, individual freedom and moral autonomy should not be viewed as absolutes, but as matters of more or less. Valid provisions made by the majority to provide for the common defense, for example, may well qualify individual freedom. It is not reasonable to judge the moral rightness of such accommodations by an absolute or Utopian standard.

Jefferson's standard—the standard of the American code of social justice—is drawn from two aspects of the idea of "consent." First, the individual has consented to the social compact: he has given his Platonic promise to obey the laws of the state where, as an adult, he has freely decided to stay. And, second, the society to whose code he has adhered is itself a society of consent. . . .

Conclusion

I started by recalling the view that law was the necessary condition and predicate of individual liberty. That is a proposition which unites "liberals" and "conservatives"—that is, those who prefer somewhat more to somewhat less individual freedom from official restraint. Personal freedom within organized society is made possible, this view holds, only by law—that is, by the influence of generally accepted rules and principles which satisfy the sense of justice of the community and assure the capacity of the citizen to live and seek fulfillment without being afraid of his fellows or of the state.

I examined the case for civil disobedience against the background of the strenuous and difficult processes of social change through which we are living, and in the perspective of Jefferson's thesis that the just powers of government derive from the consent of the governed. . . . On analysis the case for recognizing a right of civil disobedience can rest on only two grounds, apart from the argument of anarchism—first, Thoreau's claim that an elite within the society is exempted from the moral sanction of majority rule, and that its members should therefore be allowed to decide for themselves which laws to obey and which to disobey; and second, that citizens are justified in conducting demonstrations which violate valid positive law in order to dramatize their cause, and to precipitate change which might not otherwise come about, or come about so soon.

Thoreau's argument denies the moral premise of democracy—that of equality among citizens as citizens.

The second set of arguments, popular at the moment, amounts to no more than the claim that it is right to seek moral ends through the use of immoral means. In any event, there can be no showing that such tactics do more good than harm. And there is a great deal of evidence that progress has come in the United States only when the community as a whole accepts both the rightness of the ends sought and the rightness of the means used to achieve them. . . .

Every government and every society has an inherent right to insist on obedience to its laws, to restore order, and to assure its own survival.

Thus the idea of treating a right of civil disobedience as an aspect of personal liberty under the Constitution is at war with the moral principles on which this civilization, and any liberal civilization, rests; and it is equally at war with the possibility of social peace and of personal liberty.

Individual liberty can be respected and protected only in a society based on a shared understanding as to the broad aspirations of the law. Social concord in this sense requires a general acceptance of the citizen's moral obligation to obey valid law. Respect for the agreed limits of social conflict is essential if men are to live in liberty, and not, in Hobbes's phrase, as wolves.

The social compact of the United States is an unusual one. The power of the majority is checked and restrained in many ways, not least through the Supreme Court, enforcing a written Constitution. Our notion is that freedom is a corollary of agreed restraints on freedom; that man cannot be free, especially in a democratic society, unless the state, and the majority, are not free—unless they can be compelled to respect rights which are "subject to no vote," in Justice Jackson's vivid phrase—rights essential to the dignity of man in a free society and to the vitality of its public life.

These rules and customs, which are the glory of our Constitution and of our national life, could be destroyed, leaving not a rack behind, if we fail to insist that the citizen owes duties to the law equal to those the law owes to him. Without deference to valid law, individual liberty would always be in peril. Equality would find itself at war with freedom. And a revolt of the masses could lead, here as elsewhere, to majoritarian tyranny in one or another of its modern forms. By another path, the ideas of egalitarian anarchy could lead to the same result, by dissolving organized society into its individual atoms and inducing a war of all against all which could end only in the restoration of order by force.

In a society of consent, where democratic procedures of political action are open and functioning, the use of illegal means to achieve political ends cannot be justified, whether the ends sought be deemed major of minor, moral or political.

A prolongation of the tactics of riot, however, would have tragic consequences if fear comes to dominate the political atmosphere and if policy turns to a reliance on repression rather than on social progress as the primary method of order. Repudiating the principle of majority rule, as Jefferson said long ago, can lead only to military despotism. Violence and counterviolence, sooner or later, generate forces that demand social peace, even at the price of personal liberty.

It could happen here. We cannot expect to be immune from the experience of all mankind if we defy the principle of democratic consent, which thus far has been the essence of our destiny, and of our freedom.

ROBERT PAUL WOLFF

In defense of anarchism

Does a citizen have a moral obligation to obey the law? Are there any limits to the extent or force of his obligation? Are there circumstances in which he is relieved of any duty of obedience? What are those circumstances, and why?

These questions express, at one and the same time, the most fundamental issues of political philosophy and the most immediate personal choices facing young American men today. . . .

Throughout his paper, Professor Rostow takes it as beyond question that the citizens of a genuinely democratic state are morally obliged to abide by its laws. His principal aim is to show that, within the reasonable limits imposed by the imperfection of man and nature, the United States is such a democracy. . . .

All states claim legitimate authority, of course; and all *de facto* states succeed in imposing their claim on those who live within their borders. That, indeed, is all we mean when we accord *de facto* recognition to a regime. But the theory of democracy asserts that only one sort of state has a genuine moral *right* to claim legitimate authority. If we may borrow a term from the language of international law, we may express the theory of democracy in the proposition that only a state founded upon the consent of the governed has *de jure* legitimate authority. Or, to put the same point in the language of ethics, only the citizens of a democracy have an absolute moral obligation to obey the valid laws enacted by a genuinely representative legislature.

After long reflection, I have come to the conclusion that the theory of democracy is wrong. No one, not even a citizen of a true democracy, has an obligation to obey the law, save under conditions so special and difficult of fulfillment as hardly to constitute an exception at all. In short, I have come to believe that the doctrine known as philosophical anarchism is true. There are no circumstances, real or hypothetical, under which a state can validly demand the obedience of its subjects. Not even a state actually founded upon a real, historical social contract would have what I have called *de jure* legitimate authority.

This is a strong assertion, and I am well aware that I shall have difficulty persuading you of its truth. . . .

The theory of government by consent of the governed was advanced as the solution to a conflict which seems on first examination to be utterly irresoluble. On the one hand, morality demands that each man freely and autonomously determine the guiding principles of his life, and take full responsibility for the consequences of his own actions. . . .

Standing over against this principle of autonomy is the authority claimed by the state. If autonomy means anything at all, it means making one's own decisions, being no man's servant. But if authority means anything at all, it means the right to command, which is to say, the right to be obeyed. Authoritative commands are not mere threats, although they may be enforced by sanctions. Nor are they suggestions, even though the sovereign may choose to explain the reasons for his commands. When the state issues laws, it *claims* to have a right to expect obedience. That, indeed, is what distinguishes a state from a mere occupying army.

The problem faced by the early theorists of democracy was quite simply this: How can free and autonomous men submit to the authority of any state without truly losing their freedom? . . .

The solution lies in the nature of moral autonomy. To be free is not at all to be irresponsible, or licentious, or capricious. As Kant demonstrated, moral freedom consists in conforming one's behavior to principles which one lays down for oneself. The word "autonomous" literally means "giving laws to oneself," and so Kant argued that the truly moral man was simultaneously a lawgiver and a law obeyer. To obey the laws handed down by another is slavish servility—what Kant called heteronomy. To obey no law at all is irrational and irresponsible caprice. But to obey laws which one has legislated for oneself is the highest manifestation of human dignity. By the exercise of such autonomy, Kant said, men earned the right to be treated not as mere means or instruments, but as ends in themselves.

The extension of this doctrine to the political sphere is immediately obvious. When men submit to the commands of a ruler, they forfeit their freedom and become heteronomous slaves. When they submit to no laws at all, they sink into the caprice and chaos of anarchy. But when men submit to laws they have themselves made, then they are autonomous. Rule *of* the people is tyranny; rule *for* the people is at best benevolent tyranny. But rule *by* the people is *liberty,* which is to say, the union of individual autonomy with legitimate state authority.

This is a good argument. Indeed I think it can

fairly be described as the *only* good argument in the entire history of Western political theory. It faces squarely the conflict between conscience and state authority, and provides a coherent account of the way in which democracy is supposed to differ morally from all other forms of political society. What is more, it makes no spurious appeals to religious sanction, utilitarian consequences, or other irrelevant matters. Unfortunately, although it is the best justification that has ever been offered for the authority claims of any form of political society, it is nonetheless—in my opinion—wrong. Save under very special circumstances, rule *by* the people violates the moral autonomy of the individual, just as rule *of* and rule *for* the people do.

Consider the original argument. If freedom requires that each man submit only to laws which he himself has legislated, then obviously unanimous consent must be obtained before any law can be put in force. Under these stringent constraints, it would literally be true that each man would obey only himself and remain as free as before. Unanimous direct democracy—the system in which every citizen votes on all the laws and a single negative vote defeats any measure—is thus a theoretical solution to the conflict between individual autonomy and the state's claim to authority. . . .

How are we to handle those situations in which a unanimous consensus does not miraculously emerge from the debate? The answer springs unbidden to every mind: Take a vote, of course, and let the state be guided by the will of the majority! We are, all of us, so accustomed to majority rule that it is very difficult for us even to notice that it is one distinctive way among many for settling disputes, and not the inevitable, natural, unquestionably obvious way. . . . Nevertheless, I must ask your indulgence, for this familiar rule is in fact the Achilles' heel of the defense of democracy. The entire theory of government by consent of the governed rests upon the principle of majority rule, and that principle is utterly without justification. . . .

The question is whether majority rule can preserve the union of individual freedom and state authority which unanimous democracy achieves.

Needless to say, the problem is with those persons who are in the minority. When a vote is taken, the majority are clearly bound by the outcome because they have directly willed the law which has been enacted. To put the point rather simplemindedly, no senator who votes to go to war has any moral right to refuse induction, no matter what his conscience may tell him. But the minority have voted *against* the law, presumably because they believed it to be unwise, or immoral, or contrary to the interests of the nation. If the theory of democracy is to have any plausibility at all . . . then a proof must be found for the paradoxical proposition that in a majoritarian democracy, the minority have a moral obligation to obey the majority. What is more, we must show that a member of the minority, in submitting to the majority, is not merely forfeiting his freedom and bowing his knee to tyranny. . . .

Is there anything about majority rule which distinguishes it from all the various authoritarian or heteronomous forms of decision making, so that the moral liberty of the minority is preserved even though they, like the majority, have an absolute duty to obey validly enacted laws? . . .

The problem is always the same: Either the minority submit to the majority, thereby conforming to laws which they think are bad and against which they voted; or else the minority reserve to themselves the right to defy those laws which they consider too evil, in which case the fundamental authority of the state is negated. . . .

If a man has not signed his freedom away by a rash promise to obey the commands of the majority, whatever they may be; and if he has not directly voted for the laws which have been enacted; then he does not stand under any moral obligation to obey those laws *as such.* As a moral agent, he is of course responsible for the consequences of his actions, and he must therefore consider what will result *both* from his conformity to the law *and* from his defiance of it. But after he has weighed the goods and evils to the best of his ability, no one can say to him, "This is a democracy, and therefore irrespective of consequences you have a duty to obey the laws."

DANIEL BERRIGAN

The Trial of the Catonsville Nine

We were a group of concerned people
attempting to express to others
what we felt about the war
We began with a peace vigil
at one of the churches here
We prayed for peace
in response to the invitation
of religious leaders throughout the world
We followed this with a walk
demonstrating visually
our hope for peace
Things progressed   We had visits
with Maryland congressmen and senators
We wrote letters to them   and delivered
                                                        them
personally   in Washington
We met with silence
from all of them
We met
with hostility and apathy
One of the vigils in Washington
was at the home of McNamara
another was at the home of Rusk
Particularly Rusk indicated
his lack of concern
He said it was not his job
to deal with moral matters
He said
to the clergymen in the group
that it was their responsibility
to deal with the morality of the war
We did not need his homilies
We had been doing that for years
So we turned toward the military
We engaged in conversations
with the military hierarchy
They accepted no responsibility
for the direction of the war
The responsibility was not theirs
They were just taking orders

JUDGE
   You said "no response." You mean they did
not do what you asked them to do, is that it?

THOMAS LEWIS
   No response your honor . . .
   We were saying to the military
   This is wrong   This is immoral   This is
                                                                    illegal

And their response to this was
they were only obeying orders . . .
I then moved into civil disobedience
This is a legitimate form
of social protest   It is well documented
in Christianity
Civil disobedience was practiced
by the early Christians
The spirit of the New Testament deals
with a man's response to other men
and with a law that overrides
all laws   The one law
is the primary law of love and justice
toward other men
As a Christian
I am obligated
to the primary law of brotherhood
Men have responsibilities not only
to their immediate family
but to the world.

*   *   *

JUDGE
   At any rate, the defense has its test case. Now I
ask: Is the government ready to begin the final
argument?

PROSECUTION
   The government is ready, your honor.
   May it please the court and members of the
jury. It is now my responsibility to attempt,
in summary fashion, to review with you
the evidence that has been produced in this
courtroom.
   First of all, I want it clearly understood that
the government is not about to put itself in
the position—has not heretofore and is not
now—of conducting its policies at the end of
a string tied to the consciences of these nine
defendants. This trial does not include the issues of the Vietnam conflict. It does not include the issue of whether the United States
ought to be in the conflict or out of it.
   The government quite candidly admits that
the position these defendants took is reasonable—as to the fact that the war is illegal, that

it is immoral, that it is against religious principles, that any reasonable man could take that view. We do not even say that a person has to be insane to have the views that they have. No, we don't say that.

But this prosecution is the government's response, the law's response, the people's response, to what the defendants did. And what they did was to take government property and throw flammable material upon it and burn it beyond recognition. And that is what this case is about.

There are people, it hardly need be pointed out, who rely upon the files in Local Board No. 33 in Catonsville.

Suppose you were to acquit these people on the only basis possible, in view of everything they have conceded? Acquit them, that is, although they did those acts with the intention of hindering the Selective Service System and of burning the files and records. Suppose that because of their sincerity, their conscience, their religious convictions, they were entitled to be acquitted in this courtroom?

If these people were entitled to be acquitted by virtue of their sincerity and religion and conviction, then according to the same logic, should not the man who commits any other crime be also entitled to acquittal? . . .

It is your sworn duty to assert, by finding the defendants guilty, that our problems will not be solved, but will be increased beyond imagining, by people who deliberately violate the law under which we all live. . . .

DEFENSE

Ladies and gentlemen of the jury, this is an historic moment for all of us—for the judge, the jury, the counsel, the defendants. Undoubtedly, a great measure of personal reflection is required, even to begin to appreciate the meaning of this trial for us who participated in it.

As for those who did not, only the passage of time can tell whether the events of this courtroom will strike responsive chords both in our country and around the world. . . .

The court has agreed that this is a unique case. It shares the historic meaning of other great contests of law. The trial of Socrates was not merely a question of a man sowing confusion and distrust among the youth of Athens; the trial of Jesus could not be reduced to one of conspiracy against the Empire.

In a parallel way, there are overriding issues at stake in this case; I hope to bring them to your attention, within the limits the defense is allowed to touch on.

In the first place, we agree with the prosecutor as to the essential facts of the case. The defendants did participate in the burning of records.

You must have understood, because it was pointed out here, that the Selective Service System is an arm of the Federal government, for the procurement of young men for military service, as decided by the authorities of the United States. . . .

The defendants did not go to Catonsville to act as criminals, to frighten Mrs. Murphy,* or to annoy or hinder her. They were there to complete a symbolic act (first of all) which we claim is a free speech act. And secondly, they were there to impede and interfere with the operation of a system which they have concluded (and it is not an unreasonable belief, as the government has told you) is immoral, illegal, and is destroying innocent people around the world.

The defendants weren't burning files for the sake of burning files. If they were, I would not stand in this court to defend them. They burned the files at Catonsville for two reasons, both of which they admitted:

They wanted, in some small way, to throw a roadblock into a system which they considered murderous, which was grinding young men, many thousands of them, to death in Vietnam.

Also, they wanted, as they said, to reach the American public, to reach you. They were trying to make an outcry, an anguished outcry, to reach the American community before it was too late. It was a cry that could conceivably have been made in Germany in 1931 and 1932, if there were someone to listen and

---

Ed. note: Clerk at the Catonsville Selective Service Board.

act on it. It was a cry of despair and anguish and hope, all at the same time. And to make this outcry, they were willing to risk years of their lives.

The government has conceded that the defendants were sincere, it has conceded their truthfulness. The government has also conceded that it is reasonable to hold the views held by the defendants as to the illegality of this war.

So we come to the only issue left for you to decide: whether, in your opinion, they are guilty or innocent of crime. . . .

JUDGE

The jury may now begin their deliberations.

* * *

[All of the defendants were found guilty.]

PATRICK DEVLIN

The enforcement of morals

I think it is clear that the criminal law as we know it is based upon moral principle. In a number of crimes its function is simply to enforce a moral principle and nothing else. The law, both criminal and civil, claims to be able to speak about morality and immorality generally. Where does it get its authority to do this and how does it settle the moral principles which it enforces? Undoubtedly, as a matter of history, it derived both from Christian teaching. But I think that the strict logician is right when he says that the law can no longer rely on doctrines in which citizens are entitled to disbelieve. It is necessary therefore to look for some other source. . . .

In the belief that they cover the whole field, I have framed three interrogatories addressed to myself to answer:

1. Has society the right to pass judgement at all on matters of morals? Ought there, in other words, to be a public morality, or are morals always a matter for private judgement?

2. If society has the right to pass judgement, has it also the right to use the weapon of the law to enforce it?

3. If so, ought it to use that weapon in all cases or only in some; and if only in some, on what principles should it distinguish?

I shall begin with the first interrogatory and consider what is meant by the right of society to pass a moral judgement, that is, a judgement about what is good and what is evil. The fact that a majority of people may disapprove of a practice does not of itself make it a matter for society as a whole. Nine men out of ten may disapprove of what the tenth man is doing and still say that it is not their business. There is a case for a collective judgement (as distinct from a large number of individual opinions which sensible people may even refrain from pronouncing at all if it is upon somebody else's private affairs) only if society is affected. . . .

What makes a society of any sort is community of ideas, not only political ideas but also ideas about the way its members should behave and govern their lives; these latter ideas are its morals. Every society has a moral structure as well as a political one: or rather, since that might suggest two independent systems, I should say that the structure of every society is made up both of politics and morals. Take, for example, the institution of marriage. Whether a man should be allowed to take more than one wife is something about which every society has to make up its mind one way or the other. In England we believe in the Christian idea of marriage and therefore adopt monogamy as a moral principle. Consequently the Christian institution of marriage has become the basis of family life and so part of the structure of our society. It is there not because it is Christian. It has got there because it is Christian, but it remains there because it is built into the house in which we live and could not be removed without bringing it down. The great majority of those who live in this country accept it because it is the Christian idea of marriage and for them the only true one. But a non-Christian is bound by it, not because it is part of Christianity but because, rightly or

176

wrongly, it has been adopted by the society in which he lives. It would be useless for him to stage a debate designed to prove that polygamy was theologically more correct and socially preferable; if he wants to live in the house, he must accept it as built in the way in which it is.

We see this more clearly if we think of ideas or institutions that are purely political. Society cannot tolerate rebellion; it will not allow argument about the rightness of the cause. Historians a century later may say that the rebels were right and the Government was wrong and a percipient and conscientious subject of the State may think so at the time. But it is not a matter which can be left to individual judgement.

The institution of marriage is a good example for my purpose because it bridges the division, if there is one, between politics and morals. Marriage is part of the structure of our society and it is also the basis of a moral code which condemns fornication and adultery. The institution of marriage would be gravely threatened if individual judgements were permitted about the morality of adultery; on these points there must be a public morality. But public morality is not to be confined to those moral principles which support institutions such as marriage. People do not think of monogamy as something which has to be supported because our society has chosen to organize itself upon it; they think of it as something that is good in itself and offering a good way of life and that it is for that reason that our society has adopted it. I return to the statement that I have already made, that society means a community of ideas; without shared ideas on politics, morals, and ethics no society can exist. Each one of us has ideas about what is good and what is evil; they cannot be kept private from the society in which we live. If men and women try to create a society in which there is no fundamental agreement about good and evil they will fail; if having based it on common agreement, the agreement goes, the society will disintegrate. For society is not something that is kept together physically; it is held by the invisible bonds of common thought. If the bonds were too far relaxed the members would drift apart. A common morality is part of the bondage. The bondage is part of the price of society; and mankind, which needs society, must pay its price. . . .

The next question . . . to many minds may cause greater difficulty: to what extent should society use the law to enforce its moral judgements? But I believe that the answer to the first question determines the way in which the second should be approached and may indeed very nearly dictate the answer to the second question. If society has no right to make judgements on morals, the law must find some special justification for entering the field of morality: if homosexuality and prostitution are not in themselves wrong, then the onus is very clearly on the lawgiver who wants to frame a law against certain aspects of them to justify the exceptional treatment. But if society has the right to make a judgement and has it on the basis that a recognized morality is as necessary to society as, say, a recognized government, then society may use the law to preserve morality in the same way as it uses it to safeguard anything else that is essential to its existence. If therefore the first proposition is securely established with all its implications, prima facie society has the right to legislate against immorality as such. . . .

I think . . . that it is not possible to set theoretical limits to the power of the State to legislate against immorality. It is not possible to settle in advance exceptions to the general rule or to define inflexibly areas of morality into which the law is in no circumstances to be allowed to enter. Society is entitled by means of its laws to protect itself from dangers, whether from within or without. Here again I think that the political parallel is legitimate. The law of treason is directed against aiding the king's enemies and against sedition from within. The justification for this is that established government is necessary for the existence of society and therefore its safety against violent overthrow must be secured. But an established morality is as necessary as good government to the welfare of society. Societies disintegrate from within more frequently than they are broken up by external pressures. There is disintegration when no common morality is observed and history shows that the loosening of moral bonds is often the first stage of disintegration, so that society is justified in taking the same steps to preserve its moral code as it does to preserve its government and other essential institutions. The suppression of vice is as much the law's business as the suppression of subversive activities; it is no more possible to define a sphere of private morality than it is to define one of private subversive activity. . . .

In what circumstances the State should exercise its power is the third of the interrogatories I have framed. . . .

This then is how I believe my third interrogatory should be answered—not by the formulation of hard and fast rules, but by a judgement in each case. . . . The line that divides the criminal law from the moral is not determinable by the application of any clear-cut principle. It is like a line that divides land and sea, a coastline of irregularities and indentations. There are gaps and promontories, such as adultery and fornication, which the law has for centuries left substantially untouched. Adultery of the sort that breaks up marriage seems to me to be just as harmful to the social fabric as homosexuality or bigamy. The only ground for putting it outside the criminal law is that a law which made it a crime would be too difficult to enforce; it is too generally regarded as a human weakness not suitably punished by imprisonment. All that the law can do with fornication is to act against its worst manifestations; there is a general abhorrence of the commercialization of vice, and that sentiment gives strength to the law against brothels and immoral earnings. There is no logic to be found in this. The boundary between the criminal law and the moral law is fixed by balancing in the case of each particular crime the pros and cons of legal enforcement in accordance with the sort of considerations I have been outlining. The fact that adultery, fornication, and lesbianism are untouched by the criminal law does not prove that homosexuality ought not to be touched. The error of jurisprudence in the Wolfenden Report is caused by the search for some single principle to explain the division between crime and sin. The Report finds it in the principle that the criminal law exists for the protection of individuals; on this principle fornication in private between consenting adults is

outside the law and thus it becomes logically indefensible to bring homosexuality between consenting adults in private within it. But the true principle is that the law exists for the protection of society. It does not discharge its function by protecting the individual from injury, annoyance, corruption, and exploitation; the law must protect also the institutions and the community of ideas, political and moral, without which people cannot live together. Society cannot ignore the morality of the individual any more than it can his loyalty; it flourishes on both and without either it dies. . . .

H. L. A. HART

Law, liberty, morality

When we turn . . . to the positive grounds held to justify the legal enforcement of morality it is important to distinguish a moderate and an extreme thesis. . . . Lord Devlin seems to me to maintain, for most of his essay, the moderate thesis. . . .

According to the moderate thesis, a shared morality is the cement of society; without it there would be aggregates of individuals but no society. "A recognized morality" is, in Lord Devlin's words, "as necessary to society's existence as a recognized government," and though a particular act of immorality may not harm or endanger or corrupt others nor, when done in private, either shock or give offence to others, this does not conclude the matter. For we must not view conduct in isolation from its effect on the moral code: if we remember this, we can see that one who is "no menace to others" nonetheless may by his immoral conduct "threaten one of the great moral principles on which society is based." In this sense the breach of moral principle is an offence "against society as a whole," and society may use the law to preserve its morality as it uses it to safeguard anything else essential to its existence. This is why "the suppression of vice is as much the

178

law's business as the suppression of subversive activities."

By contrast, the extreme thesis does not look upon a shared morality as of merely instrumental value analogous to ordered government, and it does not justify the punishment of immorality as a step taken, like the punishment of treason, to preserve society from dissolution or collapse. Instead, the enforcement of morality is regarded as a thing of value, even if immoral acts harm no one directly, or indirectly by weakening the moral cement of society. I do not say that it is possible to allot to one or other of these two theses every argument used, but they do, I think, characterise the main critical positions at the root of most arguments, and they incidentally exhibit an ambiguity in the expression "enforcing morality as such." Perhaps the clearest way of distinguishing the two theses is to see that there are always two levels at which we may ask whether some breach of positive morality is harmful. We may ask first, Does this act harm anyone independently of its repercussion on the shared morality of society? And secondly we may ask, Does this act affect the shared morality and thereby weaken society? The moderate thesis requires, if the punishment of the act is to be justified, an affirmative answer at least at the second level. The extreme thesis does not require an affirmative answer at either level.

Lord Devlin appears to defend the moderate thesis. I say "appears" because, though he says that society has the right to enforce a morality as such on the ground that a shared morality is essential to society's existence, it is not at all clear that for him the statement that immorality jeopardizes or weakens society is a statement of empirical fact. It seems sometimes to be an *a priori* assumption, and sometimes a necessary truth and a very odd one. The most important indication that this is so is that, apart from one vague reference to "history" showing that "the loosening of moral bonds is often the first stage of disintegration," no evidence is produced to show that deviation from accepted sexual morality, even by adults in private, is something which, like treason, threatens the existence of society. No reputable historian has maintained this thesis, and there is indeed much evidence against it. As a proposition of fact it is entitled to no more respect than the Emperor Justinian's statement that homosexuality was the cause of earthquakes. Lord Devlin's belief in it, and his apparent indifference to the question of evidence, are at points traceable to an undiscussed assumption. This is that all morality—sexual morality together with the morality that forbids acts injurious to others such as killing, stealing, and dishonesty—forms a single seamless web, so that those who deviate from any part are likely or perhaps bound to deviate from the whole. It is of course clear (and one of the oldest insights of political theory) that society could not exist without a morality which mirrored and supplemented the law's proscription of conduct injurious to others. But there is again no evidence to support, and much to refute, the theory that those who deviate from conventional sexual morality are in other ways hostile to society.

There seems, however, to be central to Lord Devlin's thought something more interesting, though no more convincing, than the conception of social morality as a seamless web. For he appears to move from the acceptable proposition that *some* shared morality is essential to the existence of any society to the unacceptable proposition that a society is identical with its morality as that is at any given moment of its history, so that a change in its morality is tantamount to the destruction of a society. The former proposition might be even accepted as a necessary rather than an empirical truth depending on a quite plausible definition of society as a body of men who hold certain moral views in common. But the latter proposition is absurd. Taken strictly, it would prevent us saying that the morality of a given society had changed, and would compel us instead to say that one society had disappeared and another one taken its place. But it is only on this absurd criterion of what it is for the same society to continue to exist that it could be asserted without evidence that any deviation from a society's shared morality threatens its existence.

It is clear that only this tacit identification of a society with its shared morality supports Lord Devlin's denial that there could be such a thing

179

as private immorality and his comparison of sexual immorality, even when it takes place "in private," with treason. No doubt it is true that if deviations from conventional sexual morality are tolerated by the law and come to be known, the conventional morality might change in a permissive direction, though this does not seem to be the case with homosexuality in those European countries where it is not punishable by law. But even if the conventional morality did so change, the society in question would not have been destroyed or "subverted." We should compare such a development not to the violent overthrow of government but to a peaceful constitutional change in its form, consistent not only with the preservation of a society but with its advance.

SHIRLEY ROBIN LETWIN

Morality and law

To debate the relation between Law and Morality has recently become a fashionable preoccupation. What is supposed to be at issue is a conflict between liberty and legal restrictions on private conduct in order to protect "morality." But however the so-called conflict is formulated, it reflects a confusion about the character of law. The confusion rests on a failure to distinguish between two kinds of considerations that are intrinsic to law, both of which are "moral."

The bandying about of words such as "individualism" and "liberty" has served mainly to add acerbity to the confusion. Nevertheless the confusion is connected with the defence of what is commonly described as individualism. Though it is supposed to be a modern idea, the arguments in defence of individualism draw heavily on ancient sources. But the defenders of modern individualism have failed to see where it differs from its ancient models, and thus mistake its character and the questions that they are obliged to answer. As a result they have conjured up a conflict between individualism and communal morality which inspires the current debate on law and morality. . . .

The problem that individualists have to consider today may be illustrated by the following story.

A community that is Ostraban by descent has through a set of odd circumstances come to live apart from the parent country of Ostrabans. The New Ostrabans have lived for some 300 years in a different physical environment. They have in the course of this isolation developed quite a different style of life. Whereas the Old Ostrabans are very reserved and quiet, the New Ostrabans are ostentatious and bumptious. They consider it bad manners not to try to shout down everyone else in the room. Some curious developments in religious doctrine have led them to believe that the souls of children are taken over by the devil if children are disciplined before the age of fifteen. Their children are therefore permitted to kick their elders whenever and wherever the impulse takes them, to throw anything at hand, to break windows in houses, or commit any other violent act without reproof. There is a community fund for repairing such damages which are considered part of the normal routine of life. The New Ostrabans also consider it indecent to walk about with rubbish in their pockets or handbags and if they find any such bits of rubbish about them as they walk down the pavement, they just chuck it out. They have developed also a very special notion of the arts—all the Old Ostraban art is forbidden to the children as immoral. The art they favour obeys only one rule—it must be incoherent; it must preach the virtues of violating truth, honesty and chastity; and it must make an enormous noise. Indeed noise plays a fundamental part in this New Ostraban culture—silence or anything approaching silence is regarded as a sign of utmost wickedness or as a perversion.

Now this community of New Ostrabans decides for some reason to return to the homeland and claim their rights as Ostrabans. Racially they are much purer than those that remained at home because they have excluded anyone who married an outsider. The New Ostrabans are in fact warmly welcomed. They are hardworking and pay their rent. Employers easily take them on and landlords readily give them rooms. And so they settle in. But being tough pure Ostrabans, they are adamant about preserving their chosen manner of conducting themselves.

180

When they first arrive, they live together and it soon becomes evident that their part of Ostra, the capital, is unbearable for an Old Ostraban. Gradually the newcomers find their way to other parts of the homeland. It then appears that even one family of New Ostrabans can totally disrupt any community it enters. Where two or three New Ostraban families settle, it becomes impossible for the old residents to go on living anything like what they would consider a bearable life. Yet the New Ostrabans do not break any laws because there are no laws forbidding such behaviour. Behaviour such as theirs (in any but exceptional cases) had been unknown in Old Ostraban, which believed fervently in individual freedom and disdained to regulate anyone's behaviour. Nevertheless it is perfectly clear that the New Ostrabans will totally destroy what was once supposed to be civilisation in Ostraban. The Old Ostrabans gathered in great conclaves to consider the problem. But just how they could contain this disruption of their life without giving up their devotion to their fundamental moral belief in liberty, they could not discover.

A parallel story of a somewhat different sort points to the same moral. It is of another kind of invasion of Ostraban. As the doors are open to everyone, Ostraban suddenly finds itself with a large group of people who have nothing of their own that they wish to do, and adamantly refuse to run their own lives. They have all had a spell in the army and they loved it. They have decided that the worries and frustrations of making their own decisions and seeing them go wrong is more than they can bear. They want someone else to decide for them (just as in the army) what they are to do from the moment of rising to retiring, what they should wear and eat, where they should sleep and live and whom they should see. They want no responsibility whatsoever beyond executing orders, quite precise orders, leaving them in no doubt about what they should do here and now.

They are determined to have the government resolve for them permanently what the army had done temporarily. Moreover, as the sight of other men living differently and making their own lives for themselves disturbs their serenity, they want the government to decide everything for everyone. They are not given to violence; they are not revolutionaries. But whenever a public decision has to be made they exercise whatever influence or power they have to choose whatever alternative will further the sort of life they want. And again the Ostrabans find that they have no arguments against these foreigners.

The story in both cases is about a community that suddenly finds the life it values threatened by strangers. But whereas the ancient Greeks, who were very clear about their commitment to a certain view of civilisation, called such invaders "barbarians" and tried to drive them out, the Ostrabans are helpless. They had understood themselves to have no moral commitment because they were dedicated to leaving each man free to live as he chose. To restrict the invaders in any fashion seems to violate their deepest convictions. Yet if they do not make any such restriction, even deeper convictions (though hitherto never expressed) will also be violated.

The moral is that the commitment to liberty cannot be divorced from a commitment to some conception of what constitutes a civilised life. This is a moral conception, and will necessarily affect the laws. Moreover, the commitment to liberty is as much a moral commitment as a commitment to monogamy or to fidelity in marriage. About this the ancients had no doubt. But modern individualists, haunted as they are by imaginary perils of medieval obscurantism, parade their belief in liberty as an amoral idea, which obliges no one to believe anything. . . . Or else they try to secure liberty by denying . . . what makes it both valued and difficult to preserve—the uniqueness of every human being, which cannot be denied or destroyed without renouncing rationality.

The problem that modern individualism has now to face is not how to purify the law of morality, but how to distinguish between two different moral commitments intrinsic to the law. One is a commitment to the character of the association regulated by the law; the other, to one of the many patterns of civilisation compatible with this kind of association. . . . In other words, to say that the law is intrinsically moral is neither advocating certain laws, nor defending "the wisdom of the ages," nor foment-

181

ing revolution. It is saying only that when a number of men recognise the same authority, if they share a communal life, they will (whether or not they realise it) hold in common certain ideas about what is suitable, just, right, proper, seemly, decent. They want not only to be a community, and not only a community that is a civil association, but a civil association with a particular kind of civility. . . .

How differently moral considerations may enter into deliberations on law may be illustrated by considering possible responses to a question about marriage laws. It may be thought necessary to make or amend such laws because the cohabitation of a man and woman is believed to have a sacrosanct character and should neither take place nor be dissolved without due recognition of this character. This way of understanding marriage is very likely to be present in a theocracy. But it may also be part of the civility of a civil association. Or marriage may be thought of as a contract, much like any other contract, which the government will protect if certain conditions are observed, or allow to be broken if certain conditions are not met. Or the cohabitation of a man and a woman may be thought of as an act of friendship which may take place under an unlimited variety of conditions of no concern to any but the two persons involved. This might mean that children would be entirely the responsibility of the parents, however they may choose to understand that responsibility. If, however, it is thought desirable to set up public orphanages and other public institutions for bringing up such children, the civil association would be adulterating its character by turning itself into a nurse-maid as well as a rule-maker. To avoid doing so, it may be thought desirable to regulate the conditions of cohabitation, even though the relationship of lovers is understood as one of friendship. In this case, laws regulating the conditions of cohabitation will have been inspired by a concern for personal freedom, rather than by an attempt to impose any particular pattern of conduct.

But in all such discussions of proposed changes in the laws, the issue is never: Should the Law deal with Morality? but—What is our understanding of civility? Does it include the belief

that the conditions under which the members of the association become lovers, or choose to live together, are of *no concern* to anyone but themselves? Or does it include a conception of personal responsibility that excludes love-making or cohabitation at random? Even if the latter is chosen, nothing follows necessarily about what *laws* are desirable. There is no necessary connection between what is considered civil conduct and what is considered an appropriate subject to include in the public concern.

It is a gross confusion to suppose that a judgment to the effect that conduct is "indecent" carries an obligation to endorse legislation to that effect. It may be decided that although the reigning civility distinctly does not condone random cohabitation, any law designed to set up conditions of cohabitation or love-making might be too costly in financial terms, or would entail surveillance incompatible with a civil association, or would be impossible to enforce in any case. If it is concluded that no such law should be made or preserved for whatever reasons, it does not follow that Morality has been excluded from the domain of Law. The decision is a *moral* decision. Considerations other than moral may have entered into the deliberation, *e.g.* about the cost of enforcement (though considerations about the compatibility of enforcement with a civil association are certainly moral). But the deliberation was set in motion and concluded by moral ideas—ideas about the kind of association being governed by the law and about the civility that distinguishes that association. Apart from rules designating which side of the road shall be used by motorists, it is difficult to think of any subject entirely free of such considerations.

JOHN R. SILBER

The thicket of law and the marsh of conscience

The importance of the rule of law is brilliantly set forth in Robert Bolt's play *A Man for All Seasons,* in a passage dealing with Sir Thomas

More's impending confrontation with Henry VIII. More receives a visit from a devious and ambitious young man named Rich who appears to be spying on him in the guise of asking for a job. "Employ me," says Rich. "No," replies More. "Employ me!" says Rich desperately, and he turns to exit. Rich adds, "I would be steadfast!"

MORE: Richard, you couldn't answer for yourself even so far as tonight.

[Rich leaves and More takes counsel with his wife, Alice, his daughter, Margaret, and his prospective son-in-law, Roper.]

ROPER: Arrest him.

ALICE: Yes!

MORE: For what?

ALICE: He's dangerous!

ROPER: For libel; he's a spy.

ALICE: He is! Arrest him!

MARGARET: Father, that man's bad.

MORE: There is no law against that.

ROPER: There is! God's law!

MORE: Then God can arrest him.

ROPER: Sophistication upon sophistication!

MORE: No, sheer simplicity. The law, Roper, the law. I know what's legal, not what's right. And I'll stick to what's legal.

ROPER: Then you set Man's law above God's!

MORE: No, far below; but let me draw your attention to a fact—I'm *not* God. The currents and eddies of right and wrong, which you find such plain sailing, I can't navigate. I'm no voyager. But in the thickets of the law, oh, there I'm a forester . . .

ALICE: While you talk [Rich is] gone!

MORE: And go he should if he was the Devil himself, until he broke the law!

ROPER: So now you'd give the Devil benefit of law!

MORE: Yes. What would you do? Cut a great road through the law to get after the Devil?

ROPER: I'd cut down every law in England to do that!

MORE: Oh? And when the last law was down, and the Devil turned round on you—where would you hide, Roper, the laws all being flat? . . . If you cut them down—and you're just the man to do it—d'you really think you could stand upright in the winds that would blow them? Yes, I'd give the Devil benefit of law, for my own safety's sake.

Roper wants right to be done. He does not want to let the guilty go free or to accomplish less than the highest perfection demanded by the law of God. More is not insensitive to these higher demands, these loftier purposes. Like Roper, he prays, he reads the Bible, he understands theology, he is aware of the shortcomings of the law. But he would rather stand with the law of man and all its shortcomings than open wide the gates to the moral judgments of everyone, or anyone.

Without the constraint of law, not only Roper but anyone can decide what is right. He need not be deterred by what is legal. The imperative of conscience is a rationale open to any man, a guide to which every man can lay claim. Conscience is no better or wiser than the person to whom it speaks. Acutely aware of this, More recognizes that the voice of conscience is never backed by a Greek chorus authoritatively proclaiming, "That was the voice of God." He tries to convince his young colleague of the need to transcend the subjectivity of individual opinion about what is right, through an appeal to a society grounded in law. It is More's point that without the law only contingencies may differentiate the idealist Roper from the scoundrel Rich.

The view that Bolt here puts into More's mouth is strikingly reminiscent of Justice Brandeis's celebrated dissent in the Olmstead* case:

Decency, security, and liberty alike demand that government officials shall be subjected to the same rules of conduct that are commands to the citizen. In a government of laws, existence of the government will be imperiled if it fails to observe the law scrupulously. Our government is the potent, the omnipresent teacher. For good or ill, it teaches the whole people by its example. Crime is contagious. If the government becomes a lawbreaker, it breeds contempt for law; it invites every man to become a law unto himself; it invites anarchy. To declare that in the administration of the criminal law the end justifies the means—to declare that the government may commit crimes in order to secure the conviction of a private criminal—would bring terrible retribution.

---

*Ed. note: In Olmstead vs. United States (1928), the government's tapping of telephones to obtain evidence against a gang of bootleggers was held not to be an "unreasonable search" in violation of the Fourth Amendment. Justice Brandeis dissented.

"The way I see it, when you start tempering justice with mercy you've had it!"

9

CRIME
AND
PUNISHMENT

The concepts of crime and punishment presume the capacity of moral choice in the criminal. Guilt does not rest on the commission of a crime alone; it assumes that the actor was morally responsible for his action. For this reason, lunatics and children are usually exempted from the punishments meted out to normal adults. Neither the lunatic nor the child knows fully that what he is about to do is wrong and nonetheless chooses to do it.

In our society, punishment has three rationales: It is felt to be just to inflict pain on someone who has willfully inflicted it on someone else; it may impress on the criminal the wrongness of his deed, thereby serving to correct his character, such that in the future he will not perform acts he knows are wrong; it may increase the fear of punishment in others or strengthen their conviction that crime is wrong, thus deterring others from committing crime. The first two rationales obviously lose their force when the actors are not responsible for their acts; in such circumstances, any punishment may be thought to be unwarranted and unjust.

One argument against punishment maintains that crimes committed by ghetto residents fall under this category. It is claimed that the environment is the cause of crime and that the "criminals" have never had a choice open to them. In further defense of these crimes, they are said to be punishments of the larger society for its complicity in the dismal and degrading conditions of the ghetto. To punish these "criminals" then becomes so unjust as itself to approach a crime. In this argument, the familiar order is made topsy-turvy. Crimes become punishments and punishments crimes. It brings out, however, a fundamental condition of a just punishment: that those who condemn must be honored and blameless. Any attack on the moral legitimacy of the government or its legal system also becomes an attack on its right to punish.

The first three excerpts in this chapter deal with the most severe legal punishment in the United States—capital punishment. Ernest van den Haag argues that the death penalty is both

185

a just act and a deterrence. Faced with some uncertainty as to the extent of the deterrent, he measures the life of a convicted murderer against the lives of future victims—either of this criminal or of others who may be deterred by the death penalty—and finds that it is a risk worth taking. Then follows David Conway, who elaborates van den Haag's argument. Conway writes that this risk does not weigh the lives of potential victims against the lives of convicted criminals: What van den Haag advocates, he says, is taking the lives of convicted criminals and "risking that some further good will come of this." Given this restatement of van den Haag's description of capital punishment, Conway demands statistical proof that capital punishment deters future crime.

In the next excerpt, placed in opposition to van den Haag, Albert Camus makes the case against the imposition of the death penalty. Not only is its deterrent effect questionable, but it brutalizes those who must participate in its administration. The death penalty, Camus argues, is nothing better than revenge— premeditated murder that tortures its victim and treats a person like a thing. No group of men, he claims, has the moral right to exact it: The death penalty "can be legitimized only by a truth or a principle that is superior to man."

We leave the subject of capital punishment and consider an influential analysis of the social and psychological dynamics of crime and punishment. If, as Jerome Hall wrote, "the salient twentieth-century fact about criminal law is widespread skepticism of punishment," then the social science findings as represented by the following excerpt may well have contributed to it. Psychoanalysis and psychiatry have pointed out that law-abiding citizens need to punish criminals in order to purge themselves of their own desires to commit crimes. This perspective is outlined in our next selection by Karl Menninger, who states that "the vicarious use of the criminal for relieving the guilt feelings of 'innocent' individuals by displacement is no recent

theory, but it constantly eludes public acceptance." Clearly, this argument challenges the moral legitimacy of punishment: Menninger in fact titled his book, from which this excerpt is taken, *The Crime of Punishment.*

Sociologists have often written that crime is an inevitable part of any society. Indeed, the French sociologist Emile Durkheim has argued not only that crime is "normal" but also that it can make a positive contribution to our society by preparing the way for needed changes.

But for most people, crime must be punished, and it is to a consideration of our penal system that we now turn. Garry Wills makes a stinging indictment of our prison system, and he hopes for drastic reforms. It is, he claims, "our culture's neglected human sewer, charged and unworkable with human waste." He points out that with respect to its aims of revenge, deterrence, and rehabilitation, our present system is successful only at revenge. Prison sentences, he says, have only a minimal deterrent effect on others outside prison, and they are more likely to harden a criminal than to rehabilitate him.

James Wilson, agreeing that rehabilitation programs and sentences tailored to "fit the 'needs' of the individual offender" have not stopped the decade-old crime wave, nevertheless suggests that every person convicted of a serious offense be imprisoned for three years. This would cut the crime rate by as much as one-third, he claims, simply by incapacitating the criminals for that period of time.

Our concluding selection, in direct opposition to Wilson, is by David Bazelon, who asks us to consider the social costs and justice of "tough sentences." Even if they succeed in reducing crime, "will this approach make our society more just, or merely more repressive?" The trouble with the approaches championed by van den Haag and Wilson, Bazelon argues, is that they "fail to consider the social injustices that breed crime." In this view, it is not the criminal who should really be held responsible for crime but the society that tolerates unemployment, poverty, and racism.

Ernest van den Haag is a New York psychoanalyst and adjunct professor of social philosophy at New York University. Born in Holland in 1914, he has also taught at the New School for Social Research and at Vassar College. Author of many books, articles, and papers on the subject of delinquency, his latest work is *Punishing Criminals: Concerning a Very Old and Painful Question* (1975). "On Deterrence and the Death Penalty," excerpted here, appeared in *The Journal of Criminal Law, Criminology, and Police Science* in 1969; an earlier version appeared originally in *Ethics*.

David A. Conway is on the faculty of the department of philosophy at the University of Missouri. "Capital Punishment and Deterrence: Some Considerations in Dialogue Form" first appeared in 1974 in *Philosophy and Public Affairs*.

Albert Camus, a French novelist, journalist, essayist, and playwright, was born in 1913 in Algeria, which provides the setting for much of his fiction. He was deeply concerned with problems of individual freedom and responsibility and with the alienation of the individual from society. Among his best-known works are *The Stranger* (1942), *The Plague* (1947), and *The Fall* (1957). He won the Nobel Prize in literature in 1957, three years before his death. "Reflections on the Guillotine," as its name implies, was concerned primarily with capital punishment in France, but the objections Camus raises in this essay about the dehumanizing and brutal effects of capital punishment are not limited to any particular form of execution.

Karl Menninger, psychiatrist and author, was born in 1893. Cofounder, with his father, of the Menninger Clinic for psychiatric research and therapy in Topeka, Kansas, he was later joined by his brother and together they established the Menninger Foundation, of which he is chairman of the board. He taught psychiatry for many years at the University of Kansas. Among his multitude of published works are *Man Against Himself* (1938), *The Crime of Punishment* (1968), excerpted here, and *Whatever Became of Sin* (1974).

Garry Wills, born in 1934, is an adjunct professor of humanities at Johns Hopkins University, where he has taught since 1962. A syndicated newspaper columnist and lecturer, he is the author of *The Second Civil War, Man and Mask, Nixon Agonistes,* and *Bare Ruined Choirs.* "The Human Sewer" first appeared in *The New York Review of Books* in April 1975.

James Q. Wilson is Henry Lee Shattuck Professor of Government at Harvard University. A specialist in criminology as well as in urban affairs, he is former chairman of the National Advisory Council for Drug Abuse Prevention. His most recent book is *Thinking About Crime.*

David Bazelon, born in 1909, has been judge of the United States Circuit Court of Appeals for the District of Columbia since 1949. He is also a lecturer in psychiatry at the Johns Hopkins School of Medicine and he teaches sociolegal aspects of psychiatry at George Washington University. In 1975 he received the Distinguished Science Award of the American Psychiatric Association. "Tough Sentences Alone Won't Stop Crime" was first published in the *Los Angeles Times* in October 1976.

187

ERNEST VAN DEN HAAG

On deterrence and the death penalty

If rehabilitation and the protection of society from unrehabilitated offenders were the only purposes of legal punishment the death penalty could be abolished: it cannot attain the first end, and is not needed for the second. No case for the death penalty can be made unless "doing justice," or "deterring others," are among our penal aims. Each of these purposes can justify capital punishment by itself; opponents, therefore, must show that neither actually does, while proponents can rest their case on either.

Although the argument from justice is intellectually more interesting, and, in my view, decisive enough, utilitarian arguments have more appeal: the claim that capital punishment is useless because it does not deter others is most persuasive. I shall, therefore, focus on this claim. Lest the argument be thought to be unduly narrow, I shall show, nonetheless, that some claims of injustice rest on premises which the claimants reject when arguments for capital punishment are derived therefrom; while other claims of injustice have no independent standing: their weight depends on the weight given to deterrence.

Capital punishment is regarded as unjust because it may lead to the execution of innocents, or because the guilty poor (or disadvantaged) are more likely to be executed than the guilty rich.

Regardless of merit, these claims are relevant only if "doing justice" is one purpose of punishment. Unless one regards it as good, or, at least, better, that the guilty be punished rather than the innocent, and that the equally guilty be punished equally, unless, that is, one wants penalties to be just, one cannot object to them because they are not. However, if one does include justice among the purposes of punishment, it becomes possible to justify any one punishment—even death—on grounds of jus-

tice. Yet, those who object to the death penalty because of its alleged injustice, usually deny not only the merits, or the sufficiency, of specific arguments based on justice, but the propriety of justice as an argument: they exclude "doing justice" as a purpose of legal punishment. If justice is not a purpose of penalties, injustice cannot be an objection to the death penalty, or to any other; if it is, justice cannot be ruled out as an argument for any penalty.

Consider the claim of injustice on its merits now. A convicted man may be found to have been innocent; if he was executed, the penalty cannot be reversed. Except for fines, penalties never can be reversed. Time spent in prison cannot be returned. However, a prison sentence may be remitted once the prisoner serving it is found innocent; and he can be compensated for the time served (although compensation ordinarily cannot repair the harm). Thus, though (nearly) all penalties are irreversible, the death penalty, unlike others, is irrevocable as well.

Despite all precautions, errors will occur in judicial proceedings: the innocent may be found guilty; or the guilty rich may more easily escape conviction, or receive lesser penalties than the guilty poor. However, these injustices do not reside in the penalties inflicted but in their maldistribution. It is not the penalty—whether death or prison—which is unjust when inflicted on the innocent, but its imposition on the innocent. Inequity between poor and rich also involves distribution, not the penalty distributed. Thus injustice is not an objection to the death penalty but to the distributive process—the trial. Trials are more likely to be fair when life is at stake—the death penalty is probably less often unjustly inflicted than others. It requires special consideration not because it is more, or more often, unjust than other penalties, but because it is always irrevocable.

Can any amount of deterrence justify the possibility of irrevocable injustice? Surely injustice is unjustifiable in each actual individual case; it must be objected to whenever it occurs. But we are concerned here with the process that may produce injustice, and with the penalty that would make it irrevocable—not with the actual individual cases produced, but with the general rules which may produce them. To consider objections to a general rule (the provision of any penalties by law) we must compare the likely net result of alternative rules and select the rule (or penalty) likely to produce the least injustice. For however one defines justice, to support it cannot mean less than to favor the least injustice. If the death of innocents because of judicial error is unjust, so is the death of innocents by murder. If some murders could be avoided by a penalty conceivably more deterrent than others—such as the death penalty—then the question becomes: which penalty will minimize the number of innocents killed (by crime and by punishment)? It follows that the irrevocable injustice, sometimes inflicted by the death penalty would not significantly militate against it, if capital punishment deters enough murders to reduce the total number of innocents killed so that fewer are lost than would be lost without it.

In general, the possibility of injustice argues against penalization of any kind only if the expected usefulness of penalization is less important than the probable harm (particularly to innocents) and the probable inequities. The possibility of injustice argues against the death penalty only inasmuch as the added usefulness (deterrence) expected from irrevocability is thought less important than the added harm. (Were my argument specifically concerned with justice, I could compare the injustice inflicted by the courts with the injustice—outside the courts—avoided by the judicial process; *i.e.,* "important" here may be used to include everything to which importance is attached.)

We must briefly examine now the general use and effectiveness of deterrence to decide whether the death penalty could add enough deterrence to be warranted.

Does any punishment "deter others" at all? Doubts have been thrown on this effect because it is thought to depend on the incorrect rationalistic psychology of some of its 18th and 19th century proponents. Actually deterrence does not depend on rational calculation, on rationality or even on capacity for it; nor do arguments for it depend on rationalistic psychology. Deterrence depends on the likelihood and on the regularity—not on the rationality—of human responses to danger; and further on the possibility of reinforcing internal controls by vicarious external experiences.

Responsiveness to danger is generally found in human behavior; the danger can, but need not, come from the law or from society; nor need it be explicitly verbalized. Unless intent on suicide, people do not jump from high mountain cliffs, however tempted to fly through the air; and they take precautions against falling. The mere risk of injury often restrains us from doing what is otherwise attractive; we refrain even when we have no direct experience, and usually without explicit computation of probabilities, let alone conscious weighing of expected pleasure against possible pain. One abstains from dangerous acts because of vague, inchoate, habitual and, above all, preconscious fears. Risks and rewards are more often felt than calculated; one abstains without accounting to oneself, because "it isn't done," or because one literally does not conceive of the action one refrains from. Animals as well refrain from painful or injurious experiences presumably without calculation; and the threat of punishment can be used to regulate their conduct.

Unlike natural dangers, legal threats are constructed deliberately by legislators to restrain actions which may impair the social order. Thus legislation transforms social into individual dangers. Most people further transform external into internal danger: they acquire a sense of moral obligation, a conscience, which threatens them, should they do what is wrong. Arising originally from the external authority of rulers and rules, conscience is internalized and becomes independent of external forces. However, conscience is constantly reinforced in those whom it controls by the coercive imposition of external authority on recalcitrants and on those who have not acquired it. Most people refrain from offenses because they feel an obligation to behave lawfully. But this obligation would scarcely be felt if those who do not feel or follow it were not to suffer punishment.

Although the legislators may calculate their threats and the responses to be produced, the effectiveness of the threats neither requires nor depends on calculations by those responding. The predictor (or producer) of effects must calculate; those whose responses are predicted (or produced) need not. Hence, although legislation (and legislators) should be rational, subjects, to be deterred as intended, need not be: they need only be responsive.

Punishments deter those who have not violated the law for the same reasons—and in the same degrees (apart from internalization: moral obligation) as do natural dangers. Often natural dangers—all dangers not deliberately created by legislation (*e.g.,* injury of the criminal inflicted by the crime victim) are insufficient. Thus, the fear of injury (natural danger) does not suffice to control city traffic; it must be reinforced by the legal punishment meted out to those who violate the rules. These punishments keep most people observing the regulations. However, where (in the absence of natural danger) the threatened punishment is so light that the advantage of violating rules tends to exceed the disadvantage of being punished (divided by the risk), the rule is violated (*i.e.,* parking fines are too light). In this case the feeling of obligation tends to vanish as well. Elsewhere punishment deters.

To be sure, not everybody responds to threatened punishment. Non-responsive persons may be a) self-destructive or b) incapable of responding to threats, or even of grasping them. Increases in the size, or certainty, of penalties would not affect these two groups. A third group c) might respond to more certain or more severe penalties. If the punishment threatened for burglary, robbery, or rape were a $5 fine in North Carolina, and 5 years in prison in South Carolina, I have no doubt that the North Carolina treasury would become quite opulent until vigilante justice would provide the deterrence not provided by law. Whether to increase penalties (or improve enforcement), depends on the importance of the rule to society, the size and likely reaction of the group that did not respond before, and the acceptance of the added punishment and enforcement required to deter it.

Observation would have to locate the points—likely to differ in different times and places—at which diminishing, zero, and negative returns set in. There is no reason to believe that all present and future offenders belong to the *a priori* non-responsive groups, or that all penalties have reached the point of diminishing, let alone zero returns. . . .

The foregoing suggests the question posed by the death penalty: is the deterrence added (return) sufficiently above zero to warrant irrevocability (or other, less clear, disadvantages)? The question is not only whether the penalty deters, but whether it deters more than alternatives and whether the difference exceeds the cost of irrevocability. (I shall assume that the alternative is actual life imprisonment so as to exclude the complication produced by the release of the unrehabilitated.)

In some fairly infrequent but important circumstances the death penalty is the only possible deterrent. Thus, in case of acute *coups d'état,* or of acute substantial attempts to overthrow the government, prospective rebels would altogether discount the threat of any prison sentence. They would not be deterred because they believe the swift victory of the revolution will invalidate a prison sentence and turn it into an advantage. Execution would be the only deterrent because, unlike prison sentences, it cannot be revoked by victorious rebels. The same reasoning applies to deterring spies or traitors in wartime. Finally, men who, by virtue of past acts, are already serving, or are threatened by, a life sentence could be deterred from further offenses only by the threat of the death penalty.

What about criminals who do not fall into any of these (often ignored) classes? Prof. Thorsten Sellin has made a careful study of the available statistics: he concluded that they do not yield evidence for the deterring effect of the death penalty. Somewhat surprisingly, Prof. Sellin seems to think that this lack of evidence for deterrence is evidence for the lack of deterrence. It is not. It means that deterrence has not been demonstrated statistically—not that non-deterrence has been.

It is entirely possible, indeed likely (as Prof.

Sellin appears willing to concede), that the statistics used, though the best available, are nonetheless too slender a reed to rest conclusions on. They indicate that the homicide rate does not vary greatly between similar areas with or without the death penalty, and in the same area before and after abolition. However, the similar areas are not similar enough; the periods are not long enough; many social differences and changes, other than the abolition of the death penalty, may account for the variation (or lack of) in homicide rates with and without, before and after abolition; some of these social differences and changes are likely to have affected homicide rates. I am unaware of any statistical analysis which adjusts for such changes and differences. And logically, it is quite consistent with the postulated deterrent effect of capital punishment that there be less homicide after abolition: with retention there might have been still less. . . .

For all of these reasons, I doubt that the presence or absence of a deterrent effect of the death penalty is likely to be demonstrable by statistical means. The statistics presented by Prof. Sellin *et al.* show only that there is no statistical proof for the deterrent effect of the death penalty. But they do not show that there is no deterrent effect. Not to demonstrate presence of the effect is not the same as to demonstrate its absence; certainly not when there are plausible explanations for the non-demonstrability of the effect.

It is on our uncertainty that the case for deterrence must rest.

If we do not know whether the death penalty will deter others, we are confronted with two uncertainties. If we impose the death penalty, and achieve no deterrent effect thereby, the life of a convicted murderer has been expended in vain (from a deterrent viewpoint). There is a net loss. If we impose the death sentence and thereby deter some future murderers, we spared the lives of some future victims (the prospective murderers gain too; they are spared punishment because they were deterred). In this case, the death penalty has led to a net gain, unless the life of a convicted murderer is valued more highly than that of the unknown victim, or victims (and the non-imprisonment of the deterred non-murderer).

The calculation can be turned around, of course. The absence of the death penalty may harm no one and therefore produce a gain—the life of the convicted murderer. Or it may kill future victims of murderers who could have been deterred, and thus produce a loss—their life.

To be sure, we must risk something certain—the death (or life) of the convicted man, for something uncertain—the death (or life) of the victims of murderers who may be deterred. This is in the nature of uncertainty—when we invest, or gamble, we risk the money we have for an uncertain gain. Many human actions, most commitments—including marriage and crime—share this characteristic with the deterrent purpose of any penalization, and with its rehabilitative purpose (and even with the protective).

More proof is demanded for the deterrent effect of the death penalty than is demanded for the deterrent effect of other penalties. This is not justified by the absence of other utilitarian purposes such as protection and rehabilitation; they involve no less uncertainty than deterrence.[1]

Irrevocability may support a demand for some reason to expect more deterrence than revocable penalties might produce, but not a demand for more proof of deterrence, as has been pointed out above. The reason for expecting more deterrence lies in the greater severity, the terrifying effect inherent in finality. Since it seems more important to spare victims than to spare murderers, the burden of proving that the greater severity inherent in irrevocability adds nothing to deterrence lies on those who

---

1. Rehabilitation or protection are of minor importance in our actual penal system (though not in our theory). We confine many people who do not need rehabilitation and against whom we do not need protection (*e.g.,* the exasperated husband who killed his wife); we release many unrehabilitated offenders against whom protection is needed. Certainly rehabilitation and protection are not, and deterrence is, the main actual function of legal punishment, if we disregard non-utilitarian purposes.

oppose capital punishment. Proponents of the death penalty need show only that there is no more uncertainty about it than about greater severity in general.

The demand that the death penalty be proved more deterrent than alternatives cannot be satisfied any more than the demand that six years in prison be proved to be more deterrent than three. But the uncertainty which confronts us favors the death penalty as long as by imposing it we might save future victims of murder. This effect is as plausible as the general idea that penalties have deterrent effects which increase with their severity. Though we have no proof of the positive deterrence of the penalty, we also have no proof of zero, or negative effectiveness. I believe we have no right to risk additional future victims of murder for the sake of sparing convicted murderers; on the contrary, our moral obligation is to risk the possible ineffectiveness of executions. However rationalized, the opposite view appears to be motivated by the simple fact that executions are more subjected to social control than murder. However, this applies to all penalties and does not argue for the abolition of any.

DAVID A. CONWAY

Capital punishment and deterrence: Some considerations in dialogue form

P: I am happy to learn that our state legislature is trying to restore C.P.[1] Many of the legislators think they can pass a bill prescribing C.P. that the Supreme Court would not find unconstitutional.

O: Yes, that is true in many legislatures. But it is hardly something I am happy about. Not only do I think C.P. is wrong, but I see a

---

1. I shall use "C.P." for "capital punishment" throughout this paper.

192

great danger in the present situation. The prime question in the minds of too many legislators seems to be, How do we draft laws that the court would not object to? The more basic question, Is C.P. ethically justifiable? may be lost sight of altogether.

P: Perhaps, but if necessary, I think C.P. can be justified easily enough.

O: Are you some sort of retributivist?

P: Not at all. I hold that deterrence is the aim of punishment and that it is the central issue in the minds of legislators. They, as I am, are worried about the sheer lack of personal safety in our society.

O: I didn't know that you had any strong feelings on this subject.

P: I didn't until recently. Then I read an interview in a newspaper [*St. Louis Globe–Democrat*, January 6–7, 1973]. Ernest van den Haag, in response to questions from Philip Nobile, gives some arguments for C.P. that I find very convincing. And I would bet that legislators do too.

The preference argument

O: How can you think that C.P. is an effective deterrent? What about all of the statistical studies that have failed to show that this is true?

P: I admit that such studies are inconclusive. But I am not relying on them to show the deterrent value of C.P. A simpler fact will do the job. Consider this exchange in the van den Haag interview:

NOBILE: Is it true that capital punishment is a better deterrent than irrevocable life imprisonment?

VAN DEN HAAG: Yes, and that I can prove. I noticed a story in the paper the other day about a French heroin smuggler who pleaded guilty in a New York court because, as his lawyer admitted, he preferred irrevocable life imprisonment here to the guillotine in France.

In fact, all prisoners prefer life. For even if the sentence is irrevocable, as long as there's life, psychologically, there's hope.

O: . . . I do think this argument is worth taking seriously. For it is intuitively plausible, and it rests on an empirical premise which seems to me to be almost indisputably true. That is, almost all of us would, at least consciously, given the present choice between being subjected to life imprisonment and to C.P., choose the former. Still, the argument is not convincing.

P: Why not?

O: There are a couple of reasons. First, you are saying that if, given that I must choose between some punishment x and another punishment y, I would strongly prefer y, then it follows that knowing that x will be inflicted on me if I perform some action will more effectively deter me from performing that action than will knowing that y will be inflicted. But consider that, given the choice, I would strongly prefer one thousand years in hell to eternity there. Nonetheless, if one thousand years in hell were the penalty for some action, it would be quite sufficient to deter me from performing that action. The additional years would do nothing to discourage me further.

Similarly, the prospect of the death penalty, while worse, may not have any greater deterrent effect than does that of life imprisonment. In fact, I would imagine that either prospect would normally deter the rational man, while the man irrational enough not to be deterred by life imprisonment wouldn't be deterred by anything. So, the deterrent value of the two may be indistinguishable in practice even though one penalty may be definitely preferable to the other, if one is forced to choose between them.

P: I see. Still there could be potential killers who are deterred by one and not by the other.

O: Of course there *could be*. But have you forgotten what this discussion is about? You were supposed to have a proof that there are such people.

P: OK. What is your other argument?

O: Well, before, I argued that C.P. may not be an additional deterrent even if we assume that the criminal expects to be caught. But surely most do not expect to be caught or they hold no expectations at all, i.e. they are acting in "blind passion." In these cases, the punishment is irrelevant. If, however, we assume at least minimal rationality on the part of the criminal, he knows that there is some chance that he will be caught. Let us say that he believes that there is a one in ten chance that he will be, and also that the actuality of punishment x is sufficient to deter him from performing some actions from which punishment y would not deter him. It does not follow from this that a one in ten chance of x would deter him from performing any actions that a one in ten chance of y would not. . . . For instance, if it is important that I get to my destination quickly, I may be willing to (actually) be fined for speeding while I am not willing to (actually) smash up my car and possibly myself. The difference between the two "penalties," if actually inflicted, is very great, great enough that one deters and the other does not. If, however, I know that there is only a slight chance of either occurring, the deterrent effect of the threats may be virtually indistinguishable, and I may speed on my way.

There are, then, at least two reasons for not equating "what we fear the most" with "what will most effectively deter us." Both of these are overlooked by those of you who give the "preference argument."

The rational person–deterrent argument

O: What else did you find in the van den Haag interview?

P: Well, there is this.

NOBILE: Most capital crimes are crimes of passion in which family members or friends kill each other. You can't stop this sort of thing with the threat of execution.

VAN DEN HAAG: It's perfectly true that the irrational person won't be deterred by any penalty. But to the extent that murder is an act of passion, the death penalty has already deterred all rational persons.

O: And you agree with that?

P: I suppose not. It does seem to be a pretty clear case of *post hoc, ergo propter hoc* reasoning. Still, there is a smaller point to be made

193

here. Van den Haag says that C.P. has deterred rational persons. We do not know that it has. But, we also don't know that it hasn't. You opponents of C.P. are always saying something like, "Virtually all capital crimes are committed by persons in an irrational frame of mind. Therefore, C.P. (or any other punishment) cannot be regarded as a deterrent." So, you say, rational persons just do not (often) murder; I say, maybe they do not because of the threat of C.P. And so you cannot simply cite the fact that they do not as an argument against C.P.

o: I have to grant you that point. What you say has been often enough said before, and, yet, without attempting to answer the point, my fellow opponents of C.P. too often just go on saying "rational people seldom murder." We must seriously try to show that rational people seldom murder even in the absence of C.P., rather than just continuing to recite "rational people seldom murder."

The best-bet argument

o: Do you have any other arguments to trot out?

p: There is another in the van den Haag interview, and I have been saving the best for last.

o: Let's hear it.

p: All right.

NOBILE: You're pretty cavalier about executions, aren't you?

VAN DEN HAAG: If we have capital punishment, our risk is that it is unnecessary and no additional deterrence is achieved. But if we do not have it, our risk is that it might have deterred future murderers and spared future victims. Then it's a matter of which risk you prefer and I prefer to protect the victims.

NOBILE: But you're gambling with the lives of condemned men who might otherwise live.

VAN DEN HAAG: You're right. But we're both gambling. I'm gambling by executing and you're gambling by not executing.

We can see the force of this more clearly if we specify all of the possible outcomes. ("C.P. works" means "C.P. is a uniquely effective deterrent.") [See below.]

To make it more clear, suppose that we assign utility values in this way:

Each murderer saved (not executed)	$+5$
Each murderer executed	-5
Each innocent person saved (not murdered)	$+10$
Each innocent person murdered	-10

And assume also that, if C.P. works, each execution saves five innocents (a conservative estimate, surely). Potential gains and losses can be represented as:

$$
\begin{array}{ll}
\text{(a)} \quad \begin{array}{r} -5 \\ +50 \\ \hline +45 \end{array} & \text{(b)} \quad -5 \\[2em]
\text{(c)} \quad \begin{array}{r} +5 \\ -50 \\ \hline -45 \end{array} & \text{(d)} \quad +5
\end{array}
$$

Now we can clearly see that not only do we have less to lose by betting on C.P., but we also have more to gain. It would be quite irrational not to bet on it. . . .

o: But look, you have to admit that there is an unsavory air about the argument. Nobile is

	C.P. Works	C.P. Does Not Work
We bet C.P. works	(a) We win: Some murderers die, but innocents, who would otherwise die, are spared.	(b) We lose: Some murderers die for no purpose. The lives of others are unaffected.
We bet C.P. does not work	(c) We lose: Murderers live, but some innocents needlessly die.	(d) We win: Murderers live and the lives of others are unaffected.

right; the very notion of gambling with human lives seems morally repugnant.

P: Maybe. But the fact is, as van den Haag says, we are also gambling if we do not execute, so you would do so as much as I.

O: If so, then what your argument does is make very apparent the sort of point retributivists have always made. In Kantian terms, this sort of gambling with human lives is a particularly crude form of treating human beings as means rather than ends.

P: You are willing to take a retributivist position in order to avoid the force of the argument?

O: No. I will leave vengeance to the Lord, if he wants it. Anyway, I am not convinced there are not other reasons for rejecting your argument. I cannot get over the feeling that, in some sense, you are gambling with lives in a way that I am not.

P: Maybe that is a feeling that requires therapy to get over. Let me say it once more: If either of us loses our wager, human lives are needlessly lost. Granted, if you win yours, no life is lost at all, while if I win mine, the criminal loses his; but since he loses it and others gain theirs, that cannot be what is disturbing you. There is nothing disturbing about the prospect of saving many innocents.

O: Wait now. I think that I am beginning to see what is going on here. Look at your utility summary again. You rightly say that (a) which represents the situation *if* we bet on C.P. *and win* is the best possible outcome, while (c), the situation which results *if* we bet against it *and lose,* is the worst. Now if this were a case of pure uncertainty, if we had no idea at all whether C.P. deters, these outcomes might be the only thing to consider. But surely this is not such a case: We do have statistical studies; we do have some rudimentary knowledge of criminal psychology; at least, we have some common sense idea of how people behave and why. All of this may be very inconclusive, but still we cannot say we have total uncertainty.

P: No. I never imagined we did have that.

O: So when we are weighing the alternative outcomes, we cannot *just* consider which is most or least desirable; we must consider the probability of that outcome occurring, even though our probability estimates must be very subjective.

P: Of course. I had that in mind all along.

O: It seems to me that that might be at least obscured in van den Haag's statements and in your earlier ones. You sounded as if it were just a matter of both of us gambling and recommending that we decide which to take on the basis of the possible outcomes alone, without taking into account the probabilities of those outcomes occurring. Anyway, can we now, for the sake of argument if nothing else, find a probability we can agree on?

P: I really think that it is at least as likely that it deters as that it does not.

O: I can see no reason at all for such an evaluation.

P: All right. I was going to add that I will not insist on it. Grant me that there is at least a one in five chance that C.P. deters. That is asking little enough. And it is all I need for my argument. In fact, that such a low assessment of the probabilities is all that is needed is, essentially, the point of the argument.

O: Let's see how that works.

P: It's very simple. Even if there is only a .2 probability that C.P. works, the calculations come out this way: if we bet for C.P.,

(a) $(.2) \cdot (+45) = +9$. That is, there is a one in five chance of gaining 45 utility units. Similarly, there is a .8 chance that I would take a life needlessly.

(b) $(.8) \cdot (-5) = -4$

And, if we bet against C.P., then

(c) $(.2) \cdot (-45) = -9$

(d) $(.8) \cdot (+5) = +4$

So, even if it is improbable that C.P. deters, we should bet that it does.

O: But that calculation is all wrong.

P: Wrong? All I did was multiply possible outcomes by the probability of obtaining those outcomes. What can be wrong with that?

O: In (a), there is not a .2 chance of gaining 45 utility units. There is certainty of there being −5 utility units, a certainty of the criminal losing his life, and a .2 chance of a compensating +50 units, of C.P. being a deterrent. And in (b), there isn't a .8 chance of taking a life needlessly; there is a certainty of taking a life. That it is needless simply means there is no compensating gain. So the outcome for (a) is not +9, it is +5. Let me put the whole thing properly.

(a) $-5 + (.2) \cdot (+50) = +5$
(b) -5
(c) $+5 + (.2) \cdot (-50) = -5$
(d) $+5$

This looks very different than it did before. And once the betting situation is put in this way, the correct way, the source of the "worry" that the argument causes becomes clear, and we can seriously evaluate the argument.

P: I see how what you have said changes the advisability of the various wagers, but you seem to mean more than that.

O: I think I do. The argument was put badly from the start. It was put in a way which is reflected in your erroneous utility calculation. Van den Haag says, "It's a matter of which risk you prefer and I prefer to protect the victims." This immediately makes us think of the situation in a misleading way, for it seems to imply that while I would risk the lives of potential victims, he would risk the lives of convicted criminals. Or, minimally, it implies that there are risks of a like kind on both sides. But he isn't *risking* the lives of criminals; he is taking their lives and risking that some further good will come of this.

Put the same thing a slightly different way. It has been said in our discussion that on either bet, the result could be the needless loss of life. This makes the bets look more parallel than they are. If we bet your way, lives *have been lost,* and the risk is that this is needless. If we bet my way, it is *possible* that *lives may be lost,* needlessly. The differ-ence between *lives lost,* perhaps needlessly, and *perhaps lives lost,* strikes me as a very significant one.

Now it should be clear that there is a sense in which you are gambling and I am not. It is exactly the sense in which I would be gambling if I used my last ten dollars to buy a lottery ticket but would not be if I used the money for groceries. Opting for a certain good, rather than risking it on a chance of a greater future good, is exactly what we mean when we say we refuse to gamble. Not gambling is taking the sure thing.

On the plausible moral principle, gambling with human lives is wrong, I can, then, reject the "Best-bet Argument."

P: But if you understand "gambling" as not taking the sure thing, that moral principle is much too strong. Unless you have infallible knowledge that C.P. deters, on that principle it could never be justified, even under conditions in which you would want to adopt it. For even if it were ninety *percent* certain that it deters, you would still be gambling. And there are other circumstances in which we must gamble with lives in this way. Suppose you were almost, but not quite, certain a madman was about to set off all the bombs in the Western hemisphere. On that principle, you would not be justified in shooting him, even if it were the only possible way to stop him.

O: Yes, I suppose that I must grant you that. But perhaps my suppositions that gambling is taking the risk and that gambling with human lives is wrong, taken together, at least partially account for my intuitive revulsion with van den Haag's argument.

P: That may be. But so far, your intuitions have come to nothing in producing a genuine objection to the argument. I might add that I cannot even agree with your intuition that not gambling is taking the sure thing. Don't we sometimes disapprove of the person who refuses to take out life insurance or automobile liability insurance on the grounds that he is unwisely gambling that he will not die prematurely or be responsible for a highway accident? And he is taking the sure thing, keeping the premium money in his pocket. So, in common sense terms, failure to take a wise bet is sometimes "gambling."

O: You are right again. And I thank you.

P: For what?

O: For saying just what I needed to hear in order to get straight on this whole business. As I indicated before, once we properly set out the betting situation, it does not appear that you proponents *have* such a good bet. But in addition, I have (along with Nobile) been plagued by the feeling that there is something *in principle* wrong with the argument, that you would gamble with human lives while I would not. Now I understand that these two objections are actually only one objection.

P: How so?

O: Your insurance examples make the point. They show that what we intuitively think of as "gambling" is simply taking the more risky course of action, i.e. making a bad bet. So, my intuitive worry resulted simply from my conviction that your bet on C.P. is "gambling," i.e. that it is the riskier course of action; or, and this comes to the same thing, it is a *bad* bet.

P: So you admit that there is nothing in principle wrong with my argument. That it all depends on whether the bet on C.P. is a good bet.

O: I think I must. But that does not change my views about C.P. Once the bet is clarified, it should be clear that you are asking us to risk too much, to actually take a human life on far too small a chance of saving others. It is just a rotten bet.

P: But it is not. As I have said, the life of each murderer is clearly worth much less than the life of an innocent, and, besides, each criminal life lost may save many innocents.

O: This business about how much lives are "worth" seems pretty suspicious to me. According to some, human life qua human life is sacred and so all lives have the same value. According to others, the continued life of an innocent child is of much less im-

portance than that of a criminal, since it is the criminal, qua criminal, who needs a chance to cleanse his soul. Or we could consider the potential social usefulness of the individual. If we do this, it is by no means obvious that the average murderer has less potential than the average person (consider Chessman or Leopold).

P: How can you talk like that? Have you ever seen the battered, maimed body of an innocent child, raped and brutally murdered? Compare the value of that life against that of the beast who performed the deed, and then can you doubt that the child is worth 10,000 times the criminal?

O: That seems to me to be based on a desire for revenge against "the beast," rather than on any evaluation of the "value of different lives." I admit to sharing such feelings, in some moods, at least, but it is not at all clear how they are relevant. Anyway, let's drop this. I am willing to rely on my feelings and grant, for argument purposes, that the life of a murderer is worth somewhat less than that of an innocent.

The basic problem with your wager is simply that we have no reason to think C.P. does work, and in the absence of such reason, the probability that it does is virtually zero. In general, you proponents seem confused about evidence. First, you say C.P. deters. Then you are confronted with evidence such as: State A and State B have virtually identical capital crime rates but State A hasn't had C.P. for one hundred years. You reply, for instance, that this could be because State A has more Quakers, who are peace-loving folk and so help to keep the crime rate down. And, you say, with C.P. and all those Quakers, State A, perhaps, could have had an even lower crime rate. Since we do not know about all such variables, the evidence is "inconclusive." Here, "inconclusive" can only mean that while the evidence does not indicate that C.P. deters, it also does not demonstrate that it does not.

The next thing we see is you proponents saying that we just do not know whether

197

C.P. deters or not, since the evidence is "inconclusive." But for this to follow, "inconclusive" must mean something like "tends to point both ways." The only studies available, on your own account, fail to supply any evidence at all that it *does* deter. From this, we cannot get "inconclusive" in the latter sense; we can't say that "we just don't know" whether it deters; we can only conclude, "we have no reason to think it does." Its status as a deterrent is no different from, e.g. prolonged tickling of murderers' feet. It could deter, but why think it does?

P: That's an absurd comparison that only a professional philosopher could think of. Common sense tells us that C.P. is a likely deterrent and foot-tickling is not.

O: I don't see how we can rely very heavily on the common sense of a law-abiding man to tell us how murderers think and why they act. Common sense also tells us that pornography should inflame the passions and therefore increase sex crimes, but Denmark's recent experience indicates quite the opposite.

P: So you demand that we have definite, unequivocal evidence and very high probability that C.P. deters before it could be said to be justifiable.

O: No, I never said that. That is what most of my fellow opponents of C.P. seem to demand. In fact, even though this would probably horrify most opponents, I think the "Best-bet Argument" shows that that demand is too strong. Given the possible gains and losses, if there is even a strong possibility that it works, I do not think it would be irrational to give it another try. But we should do so in full cognizance of the betting situation. We would be taking lives on the chance that there will be more than compensating saving of lives. And, I also think that it is damned difficult to show that there is even a strong possibility that C.P. deters.

P: Not really. Consider the fact that, given a choice between life imprisonment and C.P., prisoners always prefer . . .

O: Good night.

ALBERT CAMUS

Reflections on the guillotine

"Nothing proves, indeed," say the conservatives, "that the death penalty is exemplary; as a matter of fact, it is certain that thousands of murderers have not been intimidated by it. But there is no way of knowing those it has intimidated; consequently, nothing proves that it is not exemplary." Thus, the greatest of punishments, the one that involves the last dishonor for the condemned and grants the supreme privilege to society, rests on nothing but an unverifiable possibility. . . .

What will be left of that power of example if it is proved that capital punishment has another power, and a very real one, which degrades men to the point of shame, madness, and murder?

It is already possible to follow the exemplary effects of such ceremonies on public opinion, the manifestations of sadism they arouse, the hideous vainglory they excite in certain criminals. No nobility in the vicinity of the gallows, but disgust, contempt, or the vilest indulgence of the senses. These effects are well known. Decency forced the guillotine to emigrate from Place de l'Hotel de Ville to the city gates, then into the prisons. We are less informed as to the feelings of those whose job it is to attend such spectacles. Just listen then to the warden of an English prison who confesses to "a keen sense of personal shame" and to the chaplain who speaks of "horror, shame, and humiliation." Just imagine the feelings of the man who kills under orders—I mean the executioner. What can we think of those officials who call the guillotine "the shunting engine," the condemned man "the client" or "the parcel"? The priest Bela Just, who accompanied more than thirty condemned men, writes: "The slang of the administrators of justice is quite as cynical and vulgar as that of the criminals." . . .

If, therefore, there is a desire to maintain the

death penalty, let us at least be spared the hypocrisy of a justification by example. Let us be frank about that penalty which can have no publicity, that intimidation which works only on respectable people, so long as they are respectable, which fascinates those who have ceased to be respectable and debases or deranges those who take part in it. It is a penalty, to be sure, a frightful torture, both physical and moral, but it provides no sure example except a demoralizing one. It punishes, but it forestalls nothing; indeed, it may even arouse the impulse to murder. . . . Let us call it by the name which, for lack of any other nobility, will at least give the nobility of truth, and let us recognize it for what it is essentially: a revenge.

A punishment that penalizes without forestalling is indeed called revenge. It is a quasi-arithmetical reply made by society to whoever breaks its primordial law. That reply is as old as man; it is called the law of retaliation. Whoever has done me harm must suffer harm; whoever has put out my eye must lose an eye; and whoever has killed must die. This is an emotion, and a particularly violent one, not a principle. Retaliation is related to nature and instinct, not to law. Law, by definition, cannot obey the same rules as nature. . . .

Let us leave aside the fact that the law of retaliation is inapplicable and that it would seem just as excessive to punish the incendiary by setting fire to his house as it would be insufficient to punish the thief by deducting from his bank account a sum equal to his theft. Let us admit that it is just and necessary to compensate for the murder of the victim by the death of the murderer. But . . . [capital punishment] is not simply death. It is just as different, in essence, from the privation of life as a concentration camp is from prison. It is a murder, to be sure, and one that arithmetically pays for the murder committed. But it adds to death a rule, a public premeditation known to the future victim, an organization, in short, which is in itself a source of moral sufferings more terrible than death. Hence there is no equivalence. Many laws consider a premeditated crime more serious than a crime of pure violence. But what then is capital punishment but the most premeditated of murders, to which no criminal's deed, however calculated it may be, can be compared? For there to be equivalence, the death penalty would have to punish a criminal who had warned his victim of the date at which he would inflict a horrible death on him and who, from that moment onward, had confined him at his mercy for months. Such a monster is not encountered in private life.

There, too, when our official jurists talk of putting to death without causing suffering, they don't know what they are talking about and, above all, they lack imagination. The devastating, degrading fear that is imposed on the condemned for months or years is a punishment more terrible than death, and one that was not imposed on the victim. . . . Long in advance the condemned man knows that he is going to be killed and that the only thing that can save him is a reprieve, rather similar, for him, to the decrees of heaven. In any case, he cannot intervene, make a plea himself, or convince. Everything goes on outside of him. He is no longer a man but a thing waiting to be handled by the executioners. He is kept as if he were inert matter, but he still has a consciousness which is his chief enemy.

When the officials whose job it is to kill that man call him a parcel, they know what they are saying. To be unable to do anything against the hand that moves you from one place to another, holds you or rejects you, is this not indeed being a parcel, or a thing, or, better, a hobbled animal? . . .

What man experiences at such times is beyond all morality. Not virtue, nor courage, nor intelligence, nor even innocence has anything to do with it. Society is suddenly reduced to a state of primitive terrors where nothing can be judged. All equity and all dignity have disappeared. . . . As a general rule, a man is undone by waiting for capital punishment well before he dies. Two deaths are inflicted on him, the first being worse than the second, whereas he killed but once. Compared to such torture, the penalty of retaliation seems like a civilized law. It never claimed that the man who gouged out one of his brother's eyes should be totally blinded. . . .

To cut short this question of the law of retaliation, we must note that even in its primitive form it can operate only between two individuals of whom one is absolutely innocent and the other absolutely guilty. The victim, to be sure, is innocent. But can the society that is supposed to represent the victim lay claim to innocence? Is it not responsible, at least in part, for the crime it punishes so severely? . . .

To simplify matters, let us say that our civilization has lost the only values that, in a certain way, can justify that penalty and, on the other hand, suffers from evils that necessitate its suppression. In other words, the abolition of the death penalty ought to be asked for by all thinking members of our society, for reasons both of logic and of realism.

Of logic, to begin with. Deciding that a man must have the definitive punishment imposed on him is tantamount to deciding that that man has no chance of making amends. This is the point, to repeat ourselves, where the arguments clash blindly and crystallize in a sterile opposition. But it so happens that none among us can settle the question, for we are all both judges and interested parties. Whence our uncertainty as to our right to kill and our inability to convince each other. Without absolute innocence, there is no supreme judge. Now, we have all done wrong in our lives even if that wrong, without falling within the jurisdiction of the laws, went as far as the unknown crime. There are no just people—merely hearts more or less lacking in justice. Living at least allows us to discover this and to add to the sum of our actions a little of the good that will make up in part for the evil we have added to the world. Such a right to live, which allows a chance to make amends, is the natural right of every man, even the worst man. The lowest of criminals and the most upright of judges meet side by side, equally wretched in their solidarity. Without that right, moral life is utterly impossible. None among us is authorized to despair of a single man, except after his death, which transforms his life into destiny and then permits a definitive judgment. But pronouncing the definitive judgment before his death, decreeing the closing of accounts when the creditor is still alive, is no man's right. On this limit, at least, whoever judges absolutely condemns himself absolutely. . . .

The age of enlightenment, as people say, wanted to suppress the death penalty on the pretext that man was naturally good. Of course he is not (he is worse or better). . . . But precisely because he is not absolutely good, no one among us can pose as an absolute judge and pronounce the definitive elimination of the worst among the guilty, because no one of us can lay claim to absolute innocence. Capital judgment upsets the only indisputable human solidarity—our solidarity against death—and it can be legitimized only by a truth or a principle that is superior to man.

In fact, the supreme punishment has always been, throughout the ages, a religious penalty. Inflicted in the name of the king, God's representative on earth, or by priests or in the name of society considered as a sacred body, it denies, not human solidarity, but the guilty man's membership in the divine community, the only thing that can give him life. Life on earth is taken from him, to be sure, but his chance of making amends is left him. The real judgment is not pronounced; it will be in the other world. Only religious values, and especially belief in eternal life, can therefore serve as a basis for the supreme punishment because, according to their own logic, they keep it from being definitive and irreparable. Consequently, it is justified only insofar as it is not supreme.

The Catholic Church, for example, has always accepted the necessity of the death penalty. It inflicted that penalty itself, and without stint, in other periods. Even today it justifies it and grants the State the right to apply it. The Church's position, however subtle, contains a very deep feeling that was expressed directly in 1937 by a Swiss National Councillor from Fribourg during a discussion in the National Council. According to M. Grand, the lowest of criminals when faced with execution withdraws into himself. "He repents and his preparation for death is thereby facilitated. The Church has saved one of its members and fulfilled its divine mission. This is why it has always accepted the death penalty, not only as a means of self-defense, but *as a powerful means of salvation. . . .* [My italics.]" . . .

But what is the value of such a justification in the society we live in, which in its institutions and its customs has lost all contact with the sacred? When an atheistic or skeptical or agnostic judge inflicts the death penalty on an unbelieving criminal, he is pronouncing a definitive punishment that cannot be reconsidered. He takes his place on the throne of God, without having the same powers and even without believing in God. He kills, in short, because his ancestors believed in eternal life. But the society that he claims to represent is in reality pronouncing a simple measure of elimination, doing violence to the human community united against death, and taking a stand as an absolute value because society is laying claim to absolute power. . . . Society proceeds sovereignly to eliminate the evil ones from her midst as if she were virtue itself. Like an honorable man killing his wayward son and remarking: "Really, I didn't know what to do with him." She assumes the right to select as if she were nature herself and to add great sufferings to the elimination as if she were a redeeming god.

KARL MENNINGER

The crime of punishment

Society secretly *wants* crime, *needs* crime, and gains definite satisfactions from the present mishandling of it! We condemn crime; we punish offenders for it; but we need it. The crime and punishment ritual is a part of our lives. We need crimes to wonder at, to enjoy vicariously, to discuss and speculate about, and to publicly deplore. We need criminals to identify ourselves with, to secretly envy, and to stoutly punish. Criminals represent our alter egos—our "bad" selves—rejected and projected. They do for us the forbidden, illegal things we *wish* to do and,

like scapegoats of old, they bear the burdens of our displaced guilt and punishment—"the iniquities of us all."

Them we can punish! At them we can all cry "stone her" or "crucify him." We can throw mud at the fellow in the stocks; he has been caught; he has been identified; he has been labeled, and he has been proven guilty of the dreadful thing. Now he is eligible for punishment and will be getting only what he deserves.

The vicarious use of the criminal for relieving the guilt feelings of "innocent" individuals by displacement is no recent theory, but it constantly eludes public acceptance. The internal economics of our own morality, our submerged hates and suppressed aggressions, our fantasied crimes, our feeling of need for punishment—all these can be managed in part by the scapegoat device. To do so requires this little maneuver of displacement, but displacement and projection are easier to manage than confusion or sublimination.

Hence, crowds of people will always join in the cry for punishment. Often their only interest in the particular victim is the fact that he is a labeled villain, and the extermination of villains is a "righteous act." The definition of villainy does not have to be a matter of common agreement or scientific investigation. It is enough that someone has been "fingered," accused, arraigned, sentenced. "He, not I, is the purveyor of evil, the agent of violence. Crucify him! Burn him! Hang him! Punish him!"

Crime in the news is often a kind of sermon; it is a warning, a reminder of the existence of evil and the necessity for good to conquer it. And are not the forces of good gradually overwhelming the forces of evil? We want to think so. It is the perennial hope of and for our civilization. Hence the wretched handling of the offender, from beginning to end, is part of a daily morality play—a publicly supported, moralistic ritual enactment, without benefit of clergy.

GARRY WILLS

The human sewer

We shudder our way past penitentiaries as by graveyards—with good reason. They are as nasty a little secret as sex and death have ever been—indeed, the three *infanda** run toward a common pool, our culture's neglected human sewer, clogged and unworkable with human waste. . . .

What on earth do we think we are accomplishing with our prison system? That question is hard to answer, because people who think as little as they can about prisons are bound to think confusedly. Analysis is abortive and disjointed. At least three conflicting views of the penal institutions are forced to live in uncomfortable league with each other—trying to find a justification for them in Revenge, or in Deterrence, or in Rehabilitation.

1) *Revenge:* The oldest of our culture's views on punishment is the *lex talionis,* an eye for an eye. Take a life, lose your life. It is a very basic cry—people must "pay" for their crimes, yield exact and measured recompense. No one should "get away with" any crime, like a shoplifter taking something unpaid for. The desire to make an offender suffer equivalent pain (if not compensatory *excess* of pain) is very deep in human nature, and rises quickly to the surface.

We are uneasy with the unabashed revenge motive for punishment, but we continue to talk of penalties as "payment." Payment to whom? In the original *lex talionis,* the commerce was explicit, and defensible as such. One "stole" an eye or a tooth from the God who was looking out for them, and had to pay back an eye or a tooth—or a treasure, or one's life. "Revenge is mine," said the Lord—but he used human instruments for exacting it. Our society is tactfully noncommittal about God now, so it can hardly claim to be collecting debts for him. Still, rather than give up the language of payment, we talk

of men "paying their debt to society." A man "owes" the society twenty years to life; pay now, no credit accepted. "Society" steps in to relieve the aggrieved party of those spiritual dangers associated with direct personal vengeance. If pain was inflicted, society exacts an answering quantum of pain from the offender. Prison is therefore geared to inflict pain—mental pain, if not physical; the suffering of various privations; loss of liberty, family, friends, conveniences, income. So prisons are *meant* to be awful—reformers hear a constant refrain that we should not make prison too soft on people (fat chance!) when they are there precisely in order to suffer. . . .

2) *Deterrence:* Yet this double-entry bookkeeping, the endless totting up of eyes lost and eyes "gained," is not very economical in the long run. Once society has "gained" a certain number of eyes, what is it going to do with them? What is left in its account that can be used? You just have to build further dumps for the decomposing retinas. When men pay society their quanta of pain, society has nothing spendable as a result. What makes the whole thing worth such tremendous effort and expenditure? One answer is to say that the man who "pays his debt" gives society something useful because he offers his body as an object lesson to others, who might commit the same crime if they did not see his grisly example set before them.

This was, of course, the reason for public execution and penance in the days before prisons were invented. People were locked in the stocks to be ridiculed. They were deprived of an ear or branded, to give all citizens a mnemonic lesson on the wages of crime. But our crooks are hidden away, not brandished in public. Certain parts of society are very aware of the prisons, but not in ways that scare them off—the ghettos commune with their prison-extensions, so as to make prison walls seem inevitable. Others are deterred—but mainly those who need no such harsh deterrence. The middle-class citizen is frightened of prison—just as he is scared to death of a ghetto. But his type also fears any loss of respectability—fines, bankruptcy, scandal, lost jobs and opportunities. All those things

---

**Ed. note:* Things not to be spoken of.

202

hedge his actions, deter him, even apart from jail—which is a comparatively distant threat.

We have just heard bright and prominent people telling us that mere loss of office was punishment enough for the "high" social types of Watergate. There is, in that argument, an admission that prisons are not maintained to deter the deterrable, but to sequester the undesirables, the nonrespectables (and therefore the nondeterrables). We talk of making society safe from the criminal; but most criminals are taken from parts of society that are not safe anyway. The prisons just add ghettos to ghettos, making them all worse in the process.

Deterrence is a simple principle of life, and it often works—as in the disciplining of young children. But even there it only works within a general frame of useful affection and mutual benefit—and only if a specific person is made aware of an immediate penalty: "If you go outside the yard, you will not get a lollypop." That gives a two-year-old pause. Yet even in this enclosed area of mutual awareness, it has a milder effect (if any) on the three-year-old who overhears the threat. The problem of a deterrence theory of prisons is that it aims its "lesson" at those outside prison. The convict is turned into a teaching instrument for the enlightenment of others—unspecified others who do not, for the most part, even advert to the man inside the walls. The lesson being taught is remote, diffuse, aimed at an undifferentiated "they" out in the crowd. This would blunt the lesson even for rational, informed, and adverting parts of the presumed audience—much more so for those beyond the reach of such indirect pedagogy, the compelled or impulsive or culturally hardened types on whom the treatment of third parties makes no impression at all.

So we have this situation: the deterrable are mainly deterred by other things short of prison, and the imprisonable are by and large undeterrable. That sounds crazy, but not nearly so crazy as what we find in the present circumstances. If deterrence worked, the more people we had in prison (thus the more teaching examples there were), the more would their lesson be conveyed across the walls. But today we have record numbers of men and women in prison, and a record crime rate—one growing, not decreasing. Even if you grant all the questionable contentions of the deterrence theorists, you still have to add one incontrovertible fact at the end of their demonstration. The education has not educated. The deterrents have not deterred.

3) *Rehabilitation:* Forced back and back, from one indefensible position to another, the advocate of the prison system has to try one last grisly excuse, though it is visibly the thinnest. Yet logic compels him. If the criminal's punishment does not deter others, out in the undifferentiated crowd, the system should at least try to deter the criminal it has caught from repeating his crime. This prompts the Rehabilitation approach to prisons, circling back to the Enlightenment-monastery rationale. But the statistics on recidivism are even more damning than evidence on the ineffectiveness of deterrence. Prisons teach crime, instill it, inure men to it, trap men in it as a way of life. How could they do otherwise? The criminal is sequestered with other criminals, in conditions exacerbating the lowest drives of lonely and stranded men, men deprived of loved ones, of dignifying work, of pacifying amenities. (Those in Attica lacked proper psychiatric care, religious exercises, and a drug program—and they were nagged at by petty indignities like having to get along on one roll of toilet paper per month.) Smuggling, bullying, theft, drug traffic, homosexual menace are ways of life. . . .

Are we serious about rehabilitation? Then the last place we should send a person is to one of our prisons. Do we want to deter others? The best way is not by hidden brutalization but by making society participate in the reclamation of people still present to the public's concern. (Of course, none of these socially useful goals should even be pretended to if all we want is revenge.)

Solitude, deprivation, the breaking up of families, the loss of meaningful work, the denial of heterosexual congress—all the staples of our prison system—do not "reform" human beings, but destroy them. We no longer have any excuse for not knowing that. The record is too clear. We have been far too successful at breaking down dignity and hope. The harder we work along these prior lines of effort, the more we must harm and cripple ourselves. . . .

The situation is hideous, and growing worse. And until we do something about it, we are all the prisoners of our own prisons.

JAMES Q. WILSON

Lock 'em up

As much as anything, our futile efforts to curb or even understand the dramatic and continuing rise in crime have been frustrated by our optimistic and unrealistic assumptions about human nature. Considering that our society is in the grip of a decade-old crime wave despite a decade-long period of prosperity, it is strange that we should persist in the view that we can find and alleviate the "causes" of crime, that serious criminals can be rehabilitated, that the police can somehow be made to catch more criminals faster, and that prosecutors and judges have the wisdom to tailor sentences to fit the "needs" of the individual offender.

I argue for a sober view of man and his institutions that would permit reasonable things to be accomplished, foolish things abandoned, and utopian things forgotten. A sober view of man requires a modest definition of progress. A 20-percent reduction in robbery would still leave us with the highest robbery rate of almost any Western nation but would prevent about 60,000 robberies a year. A small gain for society, a large one for the would-be victims. Yet a 20-percent reduction is unlikely if we concentrate our efforts on dealing with the causes of crime or even if we concentrate on improving police efficiency. But were we to devote those resources to a strategy that is well within our abilities—to incapacitating a larger fraction of the convicted serious robbers—then not only is a 20-percent reduction possible, even larger ones are conceivable.

Most serious crime is committed by repeat-ers. What we do with first offenders is probably far less important than what we do with habitual offenders. A genuine first offender (and not merely a habitual offender caught for the first time) is in all likelihood a young person who, in the majority of cases, will stop stealing when he gets older. This is not to say we should forgive first offenses, for that would be to license the offense and erode the moral judgments that must underlie any society's attitude toward crime. The gravity of the offense must be appropriately impressed on the first offender, but the effort to devise ways of re-educating or uplifting him in order to insure that he does not steal again is likely to be wasted—both because we do not know how to re-educate or uplift and because most young delinquents seem to re-educate themselves no matter what society does. . . .

Only a tiny fraction of all serious crimes leads immediately to an arrest, and only a slightly larger fraction is ultimately "cleared" by an arrest, but this does not mean that the police function is meaningless. Because most serious crime is committed by repeaters, most criminals eventually get arrested. . . . Studies suggest that the chances of a persistent burglar or robber living out his life, or even going a year, with no arrest are quite small. Yet a large proportion of repeat offenders suffers little or no loss of freedom. Whether or not one believes that such a penalty, if inflicted, would act as a deterrent, it is obvious that it could serve to incapacitate these offenders, and thus, for the period of the incapacitation, prevent them from committing additional crimes.

We have a limited (and declining) supply of detention facilities, and many of those that exist are decrepit, unsafe, and overcrowded. But as important as expanding the supply and improving the decency of the facilities is the need to think seriously about how we wish to allocate those spaces that exist. At present, that allocation is hit or miss. A 1966 survey of more than 15 juvenile correctional institutions disclosed that about 30 percent of the inmates were young persons who had been committed for conduct that would not have been judged criminal were it committed by adults. They were runaways, "stubborn children," or chronic truants—problem children, to be sure, but scarcely major threats to society. Using scarce detention space for them when in Los Angeles more than 90 percent of burglars with a major prior record receive no state prison sentence seems, to put it mildly, anomalous.

In a joint study, Prof. Reuel Shinnar of City College of New York and his son Shlomo have estimated the effect on crime rates in New York State of a judicial policy other than that followed during the last decade or so. Given the present level of police efficiency and making some assumptions about how many crimes each offender commits per year, they conclude that the rate of serious crime would be only *one-third* what it is today if every person convicted of a serious offense were imprisoned for three years. This reduction would be less if it turned out (as seems unlikely) that most serious crime is committed by first-time offenders, and it would be much greater if the proportion of crimes resulting in an arrest and conviction were increased (as also seems unlikely). The reduction, it should be noted, would be solely the result of incapacitation, making no allowance for such additional reductions as might result from enhanced deterrence or rehabilitation.

The Shinnar estimates are based on uncertain data and involve assumptions that can be challenged. But even assuming they are overly optimistic by a factor or two, a sizable reduction in crime would still ensue. . . .

Though intellectually rewarding, from a practical point of view it is a mistake to think about crime in terms of its "causes" and then to search for ways to alleviate those causes. We must think instead of what it is feasible for a government or a community to do, and then try to discover, by experimentation and observation, which of those things will produce, at acceptable costs, desirable changes in the level of criminal victimization. . . .

Some persons will shun crime even if we do nothing to deter them, while others will seek it out even if we do everything to reform them. Wicked people exist. Nothing avails except to set them apart from innocent people. And many people, neither wicked nor innocent, but watchful, dissembling and calculating of their opportunities, ponder our reaction to wickedness as a cue to what they might profitably do. We have trifled with the wicked, made sport of the innocent and encouraged the calculators. Justice suffers, and so do we all.

DAVID L. BAZELON

Tough sentences alone won't stop crime

A chorus of voices is telling us that one way to reduce crime is for judges to impose tougher sentences. Led by Harvard's James Wilson and New York University's Ernest van den Haag, this group argues that increasing the number of offenders sent to prison will decrease the crime rate either by removing the more prolific criminals from the streets or by deterring others from yielding to temptation. . . .

What can society really expect from these proposals? Of course, all these proposals are almost certain to increase the number of prisoners, even if sentences are shortened. Most state systems are already overcrowded; many are operating at 130% or more of capacity. In one state the department of corrections has stopped issuing a capacity figure "because we keep passing it." Based on population increases *alone,* this nation will have 455,000 adults behind bars in 1985— an increase of 120,000 from 1970.

Can society expect harsher sentences to deter crime? The white-collar offender may weigh the risks of punishment, but the street offender— the one who is the cause of our alarm—probably does not. With no job, no opportunity, no close family ties, he may well believe he has more to gain than he has to lose.

Also, even *if* it is true that we can reduce crime simply by locking up enough lawbreakers, we must ask—for how long and at what cost to them and ourselves? Even if it succeeds, will this approach make our society more just, or merely more repressive?

Most disturbing, all these proposals fail to consider the social injustices that breed crime. . . . Can it be true that this nation would rather build a new prison cell for every slum dweller who turns to crime than try to alleviate the causes of his lawlessness?

If the present debates over corrections are aimed at making prisons less brutal and sentencing more fair, then the effort is worthwhile. But if they are aimed at reducing crime, they are dangerously off-target. They are dangerous because they risk repression and greater suffering. They are off-target because they encourage society to expect magic cures rather than facing the real causes of crime.

One of the few clues that we *do* have about the sources of street crime is that a viable family structure is crucial for social integration. A child needs a family because that is where his roots and his education are.

But many poverty parents have less time and energy for their families. They are easily overwhelmed simply by the struggle for survival. A frantic and harassed mother is not a natural mother, and a father filled with failure and desperation is not a real father and he may not even stay around long enough to try. A parent who cannot put food on the table cannot convey to a child a sense of order, purpose or self-esteem.

I am not saying poverty equals crime. That would be silly. I am merely stating the obvious: that poverty—and the deprivation and discrimination that so often go with it—creates the conditions that make street crime more likely. . . .

One step we *can* take is to guarantee to every family an income sufficient to enable parents to provide the kind of home environment their children need. Of course, we cannot be sure that more given directly to the family will prevent delinquency, but there's no chance of preventing delinquency without it. Most important, it is right for its own sake.

We can also make sure that there are sufficient job opportunities to provide a real alternative to crime for youths and adults. Unemployment among black teenagers ages 16 to 19 is now at 34%. For the poverty areas of our cities, the figure is put at 57%. The boredom of free time, the desire for money in the pocket, resentment about having no access—even by hard work—to the things that most of society enjoys—these are the ingredients of crime by youths.

Crime is not surprising. What amazes me is that so many deprived Americans accept their lot without striking out. Surely violent crimes among these people would be much more prevalent but for their religion, their welfare checks, and their alcohol. I am stunned by those who point to the many docile poor and say, "Their poverty doesn't force them to break the law, so why should it force others to?" How can anyone find comfort or righteousness in social peace bought at the price of deadened souls?

Prison reform and tougher sentencing seem like hollow promises when we realize that it is *this* kind of crime with *these* causes that we are really talking about. At worst, the present attacks on crime are repressive. At best, they are mere nibbling.

The temptation to mind our own business runs strong. Justice Oliver Wendell Holmes once remarked that if the law "stood on the moral grounds proposed for it," it would have to take account of offenders' "abnormal instincts, want of education, lack of intelligence, and all the other defects which are most marked in the criminal classes."

In other words, we would have to consider whether society can really hold responsible a poverty-stricken and deprived black youth from the inner city who kills a Marine who taunts him with a racial slur; a thief who steals to feed his family; and a narcotic addict who buys drugs for his own use.

"I shall now quote the passages I consider obscene."

10

PORNOGRAPHY
AND
OBSCENITY

This chapter is designed upon the assumption that all arguments on the morality of pornography and obscenity presuppose that art and speech possess a double-edged character. With equal effect, art and speech may either edify us and teach us forms of respect, or they may debase us and teach us varied forms of disrespect. It seems reasonable to say that the power of art and speech to undermine morality—however great that may be—is as strong as their power to strengthen it.

This assumption is at odds with one frequently expressed position that simultaneously claims that sublime art develops and refines the moral sense and denies that art has the power to coarsen or blunt it. On these latter claims, the entire debate on pornography and obscenity becomes trivial because they cannot possibly have any baneful moral consequences. That position commits the logical fallacy of *petitio principii,* that is, of assuming precisely what must be proved. Needless to say, all the excerpts that follow in this chapter assume the existence of a debate and argue one side or the other on its merits.

To begin this chapter, John Sisk considers the spread of obscene sexual language in American culture. He believes that the fashion of using such language signifies something far more important than bad taste—that it bespeaks a burgeoning hatred for civilization and moral restraints as such.

Sisk's piece is followed by two articles concerned with the political implications of pornography and obscenity. Walter Berns restates the classical argument on the harmful political consequences of pornography. He maintains that pornography promotes shamelessness in the polity and a lack of self-discipline in general. As a result, the stability of self-government and democracy is threatened. The excerpt from an article by Marshall Cohen opposes Berns head-on. Cohen declares that the effect of pornography in America is more likely to be greater acceptance of "the system" and conformity to it than "the rape of republican institutions."

Joining Cohen in defense of pornography is

W. Cody Wilson, who summarizes the findings of the United States Commission on Obscenity and Pornography, of which he was chairman. Wilson claims that no serious moral objections against pornography can be sustained because the most reliable empirical studies on the problem provide evidence that exposure to pornography has no harmful consequences that can be proven, producing neither criminal behavior nor bad character.

In the next excerpt we turn to purely aesthetic considerations. In quite an amusing fashion, George Steiner makes a standard objection to pornography—that it is boring. He claims that pornography is inescapably monotonous because the imaginative possibilities of its subject matter—sexual gratification—have severely finite "natural" limits. But a more serious objection for Steiner is pornography's "onslaught on human privacy, on the delicate processes by which we seek to become our own singular selves, to hear the echo of our specific being." This publicity of sex, of what was once private, is dehumanizing and enslaving, according to Steiner.

Then Peter Michelson defends pornography, claiming that pornography is "a way of knowing" just like any literature. Further, he states that pornography is a "natural" product of the "contemporary moral and aesthetic imagination" in which the true is much more likely to be the ugly or the grotesque than the beautiful.

In contrast, Edward J. Mishan makes the case that pornography harms children, undermines respect for parents, and debases love. While recognizing some of the evils of which Mishan speaks, Arthur Lelyveld, in the final article in this chapter, argues that censorship is always and everywhere an evil. In his view, freedom cannot be limited without being destroyed.

John P. Sisk, born in 1914, is professor of English literature at Gonzaga University, where he began as a teaching fellow in 1938. He has contributed numerous critical essays and reviews to both learned and popular journals, and he is the author of *A Trial of Strength,* which won the Carl Foreman Award for the best short novel in 1961, and *Persons and Institutions.* "The Promise of Dirty Words" first appeared in *The American Scholar* in 1975.

Walter Berns, born in 1919, is professor of political science at the University of Toronto, having previously taught at Yale and Cornell. He is the author of *Freedom, Virtue and the First Amendment* (1957) and *Constitutional Cases in American Government* (1963). "Pornography vs. Democracy" was first published in *The Public Interest* in 1971.

Marshall Cohen is professor of philosophy at the City University of New York. He is editor of the journal *Philosophy and Public Affairs* and has edited *The Philosophy of John Stuart Mill* for the Modern Library.

W. Cody Wilson, born in 1926, was director of the Behavioral Sciences Advanced Research Project Agency in Washington, and he has taught at Harvard, UCLA, and the University of Texas. He has published widely in the field of adolescent personality development, and from 1968 to 1970 he chaired the United States Commission on Obscenity and Pornography. The article reprinted here appeared in *The Annals of the American Academy of Political and Social Science* in 1971.

George Steiner, born in 1929 in France, became a United States citizen in 1944. He has been a member of the Institute for Advanced Study at Princeton and is now a fellow of Churchill College, Cambridge, and professor of English and comparative literature at the University of Geneva. Recipient of many literary prizes, he delineated his interest in social change in his recent book, *In Bluebeard's Castle: Notes Toward the Redefinition of Culture.* "Night Words," excerpted here, first appeared in *Encounter* in 1965.

Peter Michelson teaches English at Northwestern University in Evanston, Illinois. *The Aesthetics of Pornography* was published in 1971.

E. J. Mishan divides his time between England, where he is professor of economics at the London School of Economics, and the United States, where he is visiting professor at the University of Maryland. He has also taught at American University in Washington, D.C. His books include *The Costs of Economic Growth* and *Technology and Growth: The Price We Pay.* "Making the World Safe for Pornography," excerpted here, first appeared in *Encounter* in 1972.

Arthur Lelyveld, rabbi of Fairmont Temple in Cleveland, Ohio, has served as president of the American Jewish Congress and vice-president of the American Jewish League for Israel. He has been deeply concerned with the causes of world peace and civil rights, and he was severely beaten by segregationists while serving in Mississippi with the Commission on Race and Religion of the National Council of Churches.

JOHN P. SISK

The promise of dirty words

When Barbara Lawrence's short essay, "Dirty Words *Can* Harm You," appeared . . . in *Redbook,* it was no more likely to endear her to tough-talking feminist extremists than to their male counterparts for whom *Portnoy's Complaint* is in the grand tradition of liberating obscenity. Professor Lawrence argued that much of our brutally frank and currently voguish sexual vocabulary is "implicitly sadistic or degrading to women" in its intent "to reduce the human organism (especially the female organism) and human functions (especially sexual and procreative) to their least organic, most mechanical dimension." . . .

Beneath the denigration of women . . . is another, and in its implication even more disturbing, motive which, consciously or unconsciously, uses the denigration of women as a means of expression. One of the best ways to see how this happens is to observe how one of our older contemporaries, Iago, behaves in Shakespeare's *Othello.*

Iago is not only a great denigrator of women, but he is also typical of the modern debunker. . . . His problem is how to maintain some kind of control in a universe that must be meaningless if he is to be safe, but in which he is continually threatened by mysterious, meaningful powers. He belongs with those characters in Shakespeare . . . who have temporarily or permanently lost faith and for whom the denigration of women is both symptom and symbol. Such persons dwell in their "critical" hell from which escape is made difficult or impossible by their fear of salvation. This hell, however spiritually sterile and even agonizing, lends itself to the illusion not only that it is all of reality but that it is quite controllable by those smart enough or tough enough to act on this information.

Iago demythologizes and denigrates in the interest of limiting and organizing his world. . . .

From Iago's point of view, of course, the impulse to degrade and desecrate is liberating, and few people can read or watch the play without sharing some of his liberated zest as he transgresses against, and transcends, the moral and social norms that restrict his adversaries. In the end, reality proves to be far too complicated for him. . . . The most favorable position one could take toward him would require pushing this liberational element as far as it would go. In that case it would become clear that we want to get rid of Iago for the same reason that we want to get rid of Sade: we can't stand that much freedom and that much reality. We prefer to be captives of value structures and self-transcending (therefore self-denying) causes, even at the cost of living derivative and hypocritical lives.

Considered in such extreme terms, it is easy to see the true hierarchy of Iago's hates and degradations. Before all else he hates civilization and culture for the intolerable burdens they are and the ego-diminishing service they command after one has lost faith in them as meaningful enterprises. . . . All . . . [Iago's] actions are directed to the survival of the isolated self; he acts like a man driven by the fear that if he ceases to raise hell he will cease to exist. Hence he is a compulsive degrader who anticipates the fate of the modern *isolato* whose ideal, at its most extreme, is total autonomy. For him, therefore, acts of degradation become not only substitutes for virtue but indispensable means of self-definition and survival. . . .

A certain amount of degrading activity—ranging from the merely tension-relieving, through the good-natured, comic, and farcical, to the ugly and vicious—is the inevitable by-product of any ongoing cultural process. The existing body of denigrating and desecrating obscenities in a society is a reflexive record of the extent to which it has been pressed by its pieties. . . .

The dirty words that Barbara Lawrence objects to always appear in contexts where they are the familiar cultural reactions to forces that threaten to overpower, overawe, or overabstract. There is a variety of reasons for them, some of which are bound up with the legitimate needs of literature (to say nothing of the exigencies of nightclub comics). Sociologically, they correspond to that "real language of men" with which Wordsworth believed he could re-identify only by smashing the icons of poetic diction. Hence, like many degrading gestures, they may function to keep the lines of communication clear, though their tendency to establish themselves as a new poetic diction is by now notorious. But the dirty words are also vehicles to carry the modern gnostic conviction that culture is basically evil—evil because it restricts free expression of impulse while it imposes ego-limiting commitments and roles, and imprisoning piety-fictions. . . .

Pornography, dependent as it is on images of youthfulness and on displays of sexual energy possible only to the young, is one of the extreme forms of youth cult. It is a kind of pastoral in which the sex-seeking male is liberated from the burdens of age and the burdens of community-making as they are experienced in loving relations between men and women. Male pornography degrades woman as a person in order to be free of her as a person, but ultimately to degrade culture; and the converse is of course true of female pornography. As the objective correlative of the masturbatory urge, it is the purest and most gnostic form of sex. This is what has made it so available in the past decade as an all-purpose liberation symbol, and why attempts have been made to see it as a serious art form. Insofar as it is believed to be genuine art, pornography can command respectful attention for doing what art is now widely respected for doing: for opposing culture in the interest of authentic "living."

WALTER BERNS

Pornography vs. democracy: The case for censorship

Pornography and the taste for it are not new phenomena. What is new is the fact that it can display itself openly in the marketplace, so to speak, whereas in the past it had been confined by the laws to the back alleys, or to the underworld where its sales were limited not by a weakness of the potential demand but rather by the comparative inaccessibility of the market. Prodded by the civil libertarians, the Supreme Court made pornography a growth industry by giving it a license to operate in the accessible and legitimate market, thereby bringing buyer and seller together. . . . So long as a work is not "*utterly* without redeeming social value" (and the emphasis is the Supreme Court's), it cannot be proscribed even if it is "patently offensive" and is found by a jury to appeal to a "prurient interest." All that is needed to save any work from the censor, or the police, is some college professor willing to testify as to its "social value" or "social importance," and there is no shortage of such professors with such testimony. . . .

Underlying this unfortunate development is the familiar liberal idea of progress. Rather than attempt to inhibit artists and scientists, the good polity will grant them complete freedom of expression and of inquiry, and will benefit collectively by so doing. What is good for the arts and sciences is good for the polity: this proposition has gone largely unquestioned among us for 200 years now. The case for censorship rests on its denial, and can be made only by separately examining its parts. What is good for the arts and sciences? What is good for the polity? The case for censorship arises initially out of a consideration of the second question.

The case for censorship is at least as old as the case against it, and, contrary to what is usually thought today, has been made under decent and even democratic auspices by intelligent men. To the extent to which it is known today, however, it is thought to be pernicious or, at best, irrelevant to the enlightened conditions of the 20th century. It begins from the premise that the laws cannot remain indifferent to the manner in which men amuse themselves, or to the kinds of amusement offered them. . . .

We turn to the arts—to literature, films, and the theatre, as well as to the graphic arts . . . for the pleasure to be derived from them, and pleasure has the capacity to form our tastes and

213

thereby to affect our lives. It helps determine the kind of men we become, and helps shape the lives of those with whom and among whom we live. So one can properly ask: Is it politically uninteresting whether men derive pleasure from performing their duties as citizens, fathers, and husbands or, on the other hand, from watching their laws and customs and institutions being ridiculed on the stage? Whether the passions are excited by, and the affections drawn to, what is noble or what is base? Whether the relations between men and women are depicted in terms of an eroticism wholly divorced from love and calculated to destroy the capacity for love and the institutions, such as the family, that depend on love? . . .

To speak in a manner that is . . . obviously political, there is a connection between self-restraint and shame, and therefore a connection between shame and self-government or democracy. There is, therefore, a political danger in promoting shamelessness and the fullest self-expression or indulgence. To live together requires rules and a governing of the passions, and those who are without shame will be unruly and unrulable; having lost the ability to restrain themselves by observing the rules they collectively give themselves, they will have to be ruled by others. Tyranny is the natural and inevitable mode of government for the shameless and self-indulgent who have carried liberty beyond any restraint, natural and conventional.

Such, indeed, was the argument made by political philosophers prior to the 20th century, when it was generally understood that democracy, more than any other form of government, required self-restraint, which it would inculcate through moral education and impose on itself through laws, including laws governing the manner of public amusements. . . .

Such an argument was not unknown among thoughtful men at the time modern democracies were being constituted. It is to be found in Jean-Jacques Rousseau's *Letter to M. d'Alembert on the Theatre.* Its principles were known by Washington and Jefferson, to say nothing of the antifederalists, and later on by Lincoln, all of whom insisted that democracy would not work

without citizens of good character. And, until recently, no justice of the Supreme Court and no man in public life doubted the necessity for the law to make at least a modest effort to promote that good character, if only by protecting the effort of other institutions, such as the church and the family, to nourish and maintain it. The case for censorship, at first glance, was made wholly with a view to the political good, and it had as its premise that what was good for the arts and sciences was *not* necessarily good for the polity.

There was no illusion among these thinkers that censorship laws would be easy to administer, and there was a recognition of the danger they represented. One obvious danger was that the lawmakers will demand too much, that the Anthony Comstocks* who are always with us will become the agents of the law and demand not merely decency but sanctity. Macaulay stated the problem in his essay on Restoration Comedy** (mild fare compared to that regularly exhibited in our day):

And if it be asked why that age encouraged immorality which no other age would have tolerated, we have no hesitation in answering that this great depravation of the national taste was the effect of the prevalence of Puritanism under the Commonwealth.

To punish public outrages on morals and religion is unquestionably within the competence of rulers. But when a government, not content with requiring decency, requires sanctity, it oversteps the bounds which mark its proper functions. And it may be laid down as a universal rule that a government which attempts more than it ought will perform less. . . . And so a government which, not content with repressing scandalous excesses, demands from its subjects fervent and austere piety, will soon discover that, while attempting to render an impossible service to the cause of virtue, it has in truth only promoted vice.

Ed. note: Anthony Comstock (1844–1915) was a zealous reformer and secretary of the Society for the Suppression of Vice in New York.

**Ed. note:* The Restoration was the reestablishment of monarchy in England under King Charles II (1660–1685). Thomas Macaulay (1800–1859) was a British writer and statesman.

The truth of this was amply demonstrated in the United States in the Prohibition era, when the attempt was made to enforce abstemiousness and not, labels to the contrary, temperance. In a word, the principle should be not to attempt to eradicate vice—the means by which that might conceivably be accomplished are incompatible with free government—but to make vice difficult, knowing that while it will continue to flourish covertly, it will not be openly exhibited. And that was thought to be important.

It ought to be clear that this old and largely forgotten case for censorship was made by men who were not insensitive to the beauty of the arts and the noble role they can play in the lives of men. Rousseau admitted that he never willingly missed a performance of any of Molière's plays, and did so in the very context of arguing that all theatrical productions should be banned in the decent and self-governing polity. Like Plato he would banish the poets, yet he was himself a poet—a musician, opera composer, and novelist—and demonstrated his love for and knowledge of poetry—or as we would say, the arts—in his works and in his life. But he was above all a thinker of the highest rank, and as such he knew that the basic premise of the later liberalism is false. A century later John Stuart Mill could no longer conceive of a conflict between the intrinsic and therefore legitimate demands of the sciences and the intrinsic and therefore legitimate demands of the polity. Rousseau had argued that the "restoration" of the arts and sciences did not tend to purify morals, but that, on the contrary, their restoration and popularization would be destructive of the possibility of a good civil society. His contemporaries were shocked and angered by this teaching and excluded Rousseau from their society, and taught by them and more directly by Mill and his followers—Justice Douglas, for example—we might tend to dismiss it as the teaching of a madman or fool. Are we, however, still prepared to stand with Mill and his predecessors against Rousseau, to argue that what is good for science is necessarily good for civil society? Or have certain terrible events and conditions prepared us to reconsider that

issue? If so, and especially in the light of certain literary and theatrical events, we might be prepared to reconsider the issue of whether what is good for the arts is necessarily good for civil society. . . .

Censorship, because it inhibits self-indulgence and supports the idea of propriety and impropriety, protects political democracy; paradoxically, when it faces the problem of the justified and unjustified use of obscenity, censorship also serves to maintain the distinction between art and trash and, therefore, to protect art and, thereby, to enhance the quality of this democracy. We forgot this. We began with a proper distrust of the capacities of juries and judges to make sound judgments in an area that lies outside their professional competence; but led by the Supreme Court we went on improperly to conclude that the judgments should not be made because they cannot be made, that there is nothing for anyone to judge. No doubt the law used to err on occasion; but democracy can live without "Mrs. Warren's Profession,"* if it must, as well as without *Fanny Hill***—or to speak more precisely, it can live with the error that consigns "Mrs. Warren's Professon" to under-the-counter custom along with *Fanny Hill*. It remains to be seen whether the true friend of democracy will want to live in the world without under-the-counter custom, the world that does not know the difference between "Mrs. Warren's Profession" and *Fanny Hill*.

Ed. note: Play by George Bernard Shaw, dealing with the causes of prostitution. First produced in 1902, it was immediately banned.

**Ed. note:* John Cleland's novel, properly entitled *Memoirs of a Woman of Pleasure,* was surreptitiously circulated from the mid-eighteenth century, when it was written, until 1963, when it was published in New York. It was the subject of a landmark Supreme Court decision, which held that, although it described explicit sex acts, it was of high literary merit and therefore entitled to the protection of the First Amendment.

MARSHALL COHEN

Pornography vs. democracy: Dissenting opinion

I confess that I find little merit in Berns' specific suggestions; indeed, they are among the most implausible known to me. For there is little reason to believe that pornographic literature rouses men to such transports of lust that they will fling themselves upon the body politic. (Is Denmark a case in point?) In general, I am impressed by the argument of Tocqueville and Mill that modern democracies are biddable and conformist, and am skeptical of the classical argument that democracies are by nature unruly and self-indulgent. Insofar as pornographic literature and sexual permissiveness have any effect, it seems as likely to be of the kind that Marcuse detects—an increased willingness to accept "the system"—as it is to be of the kind that Berns fears—the rape of republican institutions. The harms Berns has in mind are too remote and implausible to provide a reasonable ground for restraining speech, and it is worth remembering that Berns is interested in restraining not only obscenity but, like Marcuse, vicious speech quite generally. Neither of these extravagant men provides the kind of guidance we need in the delicate area of First Amendment freedoms.

If the argument from sexual permissiveness to political debauchery is unpersuasive, so is the far more plausible argument that finds some connection between pornographic representations and various other kinds of undesirable, and even criminal, behavior. It is not enough to say as some say, on principle, that we should content ourselves with punishing criminal acts and not try to reach the states, conditions, and actions that give rise to them. There is nothing in principle objectionable about a prohibition on drunken driving. But the analogy between drunken driving and randy reading is tenuous indeed. Self-abuse is not to be compared to death

on the highways and it is questionable whether the frequency of sex crimes is significantly increased by the availability of pornography (recent Danish experience suggests the opposite). . . .

It does not follow from what I have urged that no concessions can be made to the section of the public that finds pornographic representations disgusting and offensive, and here I think that Richard Kuh in *Foolish Figleaves?* makes some sensible suggestions. Indeed, two of his proposed statutes are, I think, substantially acceptable on liberal principles and to Court opinion as well. For it is one thing to say that the publication or sale of obscene materials ought to be free and another to say that these materials may be forced upon people. In *Redrup* v. *New York* the Court indicates that it will not protect "an assault on individual privacy by a publication in a manner so offensive as to make it impossible for unwilling individuals to avoid exposure to it." The Court rests the argument on the proper ground, the invasion of privacy, and the control of public nuisances, insofar as the notion of a public nuisance is understood to require such an invasion of privacy, is perfectly acceptable. Such an approach would permit the prevention of "offensive public displays" of the kind that Kuh seeks to control. Times Square can go. It is possible, too, that some proper constitutional ground can be found for prohibiting sales to minors. . . .

I would confine myself to prohibiting public nuisances by law and hope that other institutions could raise the level of literary taste. Surely a liberal society is capable of distinguishing between art and trash (and, I should think, of seeing that this is not the distinction between "Mrs. Warren's Profession" and *Fanny Hill*). The circulation of pornography, even of hard-core pornography, does not undermine this distinction or anything else that is fundamental to our social arrangements. The same cannot be said for the interpretation of the First Amendment that Berns has been circulating for some years now. If widely accepted, it would constitute a far greater threat to the Republic than all the pornography now in print, here and in Denmark.

W. CODY WILSON

Facts versus fears: Why should we worry about pornography?

Many of the data that exist at the present regarding pornography are either the direct or indirect products of the needs and interests of the U.S. Commission on Obscenity and Pornography which began its work in 1968 and made its report in 1970. The Commission, created by Congress, was assigned four specific tasks: (1) to analyze existing laws, (2) to ascertain the volume of traffic and patterns of distribution for obscene and pornographic materials, (3) to study the effects of these materials on the public, and (4) to recommend policy. A review of the existing empirical literature in 1968 concluded that "we still have precious little information from studies of humans on the questions of primary import to the law . . . the data 'stop short at the critical point.' Definitive answers on the determinants and effects of pornography are not yet available." The Commission spent two years and nearly one million dollars in research on these tasks. The result was not a "definitive answer"—but there are, now, a few facts with which to think about the issues.

Extent of exposure

In retrospect it may seem incredible that in 1968 there were no "facts" about people's experience with erotic materials. Alfred C. Kinsey and his associates had collected information on this topic, but it had never been adequately analyzed and reported. Any estimate was necessarily a projection of one's own personal experience or one's own private fears and fantasies. Each individual was a repository of information about such experiences, but this experience had never been collated to provide a description of the typical experience in our society.

In 1969 several investigators began to ask selected individuals about their experiences with pornography or explicit sexual materials. . . .

These several studies of selected samples are quite consistent in their results and suggest that experience with explicit sexual materials sometimes called pornography is rather widespread in our society.

This hypothesis was tested by conducting face-to-face interviews with approximately 2,500 adults selected in such a way that their responses could be generalized to the total adult population of the United States. This survey asked questions about seeing pictorial depictions and reading verbal depictions of the following five types: emphasizing the sex organs of a man or woman; mouth-sex organ contact between a man and woman; a man and woman having sexual intercourse; sexual activities between people of the same sex; and sex activities which included whips, belts, or spankings. Eighty-four percent of the men and 69 percent of the women in this representative national sample reported having been exposed to at least one of these kinds of depictions.

Experience in the United States is very similar to that in Denmark. In a survey of a representative sample of 398 men and women in Copenhagen, 87 percent of men and 73 percent of women reported that they had "consumed" at least one "pornographic" book, and similar percentages had "consumed" at least one "pornographic" magazine. . . .

Empirical studies of adult sex criminals

Although there has been for some time a considerable amount of concern about possible harmful and anti-social consequences of exposure to explicit sexual materials, almost no controlled empirical studies had been carried out until relatively recently.

In 1964, one study reported no significant differences between matched groups of delinquent and nondelinquent youth in the number of "sensational" books they had read. In 1965, a book from the Kinsey Institute reported no significant differences in exposure to sexual materials among white male sex offenders, males who were not sex offenders, and volunteer nonoffender males from the general population.

More recent research provides elaboration on these findings.

Long intensive clinical interviews regarding sexual history were conducted with sex offenders in a California state hospital for the criminally insane and with a group from the general population which was similar in age, ethnic group membership, and socio-economic status. Particular attention was paid to experience with explicit sexual materials during adolescence and pre-adolescence, with the aim of checking out the idea that early exposure to sexual materials produces sexual deviance and sexual criminals. The investigators did find a correlation between exposure to sexual materials in adolescence and pre-adolescence and the committing of sexual offenses—but it was in a direction opposite to that embodied in our cultural myths. Sex offenders (rapists and pedophiles) had had significantly *less* experience with explicit sexual materials in adolescence and pre-adolescence than had the normal control subjects from the general population!

Similar results were obtained independently by investigators in other geographical regions using other research methods. . . .

The California study also included groups of homosexuals, trans-sexuals, and customers of adult bookstores and movie theaters. These groups also reported less experience with explicit sexual materials in adolescence and pre-adolescence than did the control subjects.

These several investigators also inquired about more recent experience, as adults, with sexual materials. In general, the results indicate that the recent experience of sex offenders and other population subgroups with depictions of sex is very similar. When differences are observed they are usually in the direction of the sex offender having less experience. . . .

Other antisocial consequences

Two other "antisocial orientations" have been studied in terms of their relationship to exposure to explicit sexual material: "bad moral character" and "calloused sexual attitudes toward women."

Psychologists found a moderate correlation between exposure to explicit sexual materials and "bad moral character," but pointed out that the raw correlation tells nothing about the direction of causation. After a further complicated causal analysis they concluded that bad moral character "causes" exposure to explicit sexual materials—not that exposure to sexual materials leads to development of bad moral character!

An experimental investigation tested the hypothesis that "calloused" sexual attitudes in males would increase after exposure to explicit sexual stimuli. Results showed that exposure to two erotic films did not increase already established frequencies of exploitive sexual behavior; and "calloused" sexual attitudes toward women *decreased* immediately after viewing the erotic films, and continued to decrease slightly 24 hours and two weeks later!

Other consequences

A number of experimental studies have been conducted recently to investigate the effects of exposure to explicit sexual materials.

As a group these studies indicate: (1) exposure to explicit sexual stimuli produces sexual arousal in most people; (2) there is no general increase in sexual behavior following exposure to sexual stimuli; (3) there is no change in the type of sexual behavior one engages in as a result of exposure to sexual materials; (4) there is no change in attitudes regarding what is acceptable sexual behavior; (5) there is a marked increase in the likelihood of individuals talking about sex in the 24-hour period following exposure to explicit sexual materials—many subjects, especially married people, rate this a highly desirable consequence, since it often results in a breakdown of communication barriers that have retarded the solving of marital conflicts; and (6) attempts to censor by cutting out more explicit depictions tend to increase the arousal value of sex-related materials.

Finally, a representative sample of American adults reports that, on the basis of their own knowledge regarding the consequences of exposure to explicit sexual materials, these consequences tend to be positive or harmless rather than harmful. For example, approximately 40 percent report that such materials have provided information about sex to themselves or someone they know personally; roughly 35 percent report on the basis of their own knowledge that these materials excite people sexually, and a similar number say they provide entertainment; and approximately 25 percent report that these materials improve the sex relations of some married couples, and a similar number report that exposure to sex materials produces boredom with such materials. On the other hand, few people report first-hand knowledge of harmful consequences such as breakdown of morals, rape, or driving people sex crazy.

Conclusions

The facts that have been briefly summarized here would appear to be sufficient to begin to reassure and calm most reasonable and rational people regarding the threat and danger of pornography. . . . Indeed, the majority of the members of the Commission on Obscenity and Pornography concluded that explicit sexual materials could not be considered to play a significant role in the causation of delinquent or criminal behavior among youth or adults. Rather, they concluded that much of the "problem" regarding materials which depict explicit sexual activity stems from the inability or reluctance of people in our society to be open and direct in dealing with sexual matters.

The response of the Commission on Obscenity and Pornography was in many respects a conservative one. In the past half decade, five other nations have had official commissions study and make recommendations in this area: Denmark, Sweden, West Germany, Great Britain, and Israel. Each of these commissions had many fewer empirical facts to guide their considerations than did the United States Commission. Yet each of these commissions arrived at essentially similar conclusions and recommendations: there is no evidence that explicit sexual materials are harmful, and legal restrictions which inhibit freedom of the press and of speech should be repealed.

GEORGE STEINER

Night words: High pornography and human privacy

Is there any science-fiction pornography? I mean something *new,* an invention by the human imagination of new sexual experience? Science fiction alters at will the coordinates of space and time; it can set effect before cause; it works within a logic of total potentiality—"all that can be imagined can happen." But has it added a single item to the repertoire of the erotic? I understand that in a forthcoming novel the terrestrial hero and explorer indulges in mutual masturbation with a bizarre, interplanetary creature. But there is no real novelty in that. Presumably one can use anything from seaweed to accordions, from meteorites to lunar pumice. A galactic monster would make no essential difference to the act. It would not extend in any real sense the range of our sexual being.

The point is crucial. Despite all the lyric or obsessed cant about the boundless varieties and dynamics of sex, the actual sum of possible gestures, consummations, and imaginings is drastically limited. There are probably more foods, more undiscovered eventualities of gastronomic enjoyment or revulsion than there have been sexual inventions since the Empress Theodora resolved "to satisfy all amorous orifices of the human body to the full and at the same time." There just aren't that many orifices. . . . In short: given the physiological and nervous complexion of the human body, the number of ways in which orgasm can be achieved or arrested, the total modes of intercourse, are fundamentally finite. The mathematics of sex stop somewhere in the region of *soixante-neuf;* there are no transcendental series. . . .

The plain truth is that in literary erotica as well as in the great mass of "dirty books" the same stimuli, the same contortions and fantasies, occur over and over with unutterable monotony. In most erotic writing, as in man's wet dreams, the imagination turns, time and time again, inside the bounded circle of what the body can experience. The actions of the mind when we masturbate are not a dance; they are a treadmill. . . .

The sensibility of the writer is free where it is most humane, where it seeks to apprehend and re-enact the marvelous variety, complication, and resilience of life by means of words as scrupulous, as personal, as brimful of the mystery of human communication, as the language can yield. The very opposite of freedom is cliché, and nothing is less free, more inert with convention and hollow brutality, than a row of four-letter words. Literature is a living dialogue between writer and reader only if the writer shows a twofold respect: for the imaginative maturity of his reader, and, in a very complex but central way, for the wholeness, for the independence and core of life, in the personages he creates.

Respect for the reader signifies that the poet or novelist invites the consciousness of the reader to collaborate with his own in the act of presentment. He does not tell all because his work is not a primer for children or the retarded. He does not exhaust the possible responses of his reader's own imaginings, but delights in the fact that we will fill in from our own lives, from resources of memory and desire proper to ourselves, the contours he has drawn. . . .

The novels being produced under the new code of total statement shout at their personages: strip, fornicate, perform this or that act of sexual perversion. So did the S.S. guards at rows of living men and women. The total attitudes are not, I think, entirely distinct. There may be deeper affinities than we as yet understand between the "total freedom" of the uncensored erotic imagination and the total freedom of the sadist. That these two freedoms have emerged in close historical proximity may not be coincidence. Both are exercised at the expense of someone else's humanity, of someone else's most precious right—the right to a private life of feeling.

This is the most dangerous aspect of all. Future historians may come to characterize the present era in the West as one of a massive on-slaught on human privacy, on the delicate processes by which we seek to become our own singular selves, to hear the echo of our specific being. This onslaught is being pressed by the very conditions of an urban mass-technocracy, by the necessary uniformities of our economic and political choices, by the new electronic media of communication and persuasion, by the ever-increasing exposure of our thoughts and actions to sociological, psychological, and material intrusions and controls. Increasingly, we come to know real privacy, real space in which to experiment with our sensibility, only in extreme guises: nervous breakdown, addiction, economic failure. Hence the appalling monotony and *publicity* —in the full sense of the word—of so many outwardly prosperous lives. Hence also the need for nervous stimuli of an unprecedented brutality and technical authority.

Sexual relations are, or should be, one of the citadels of privacy, the nightplace where we must be allowed to gather the splintered, harried elements of our consciousness to some kind of inviolate order and repose. It is in sexual experience that a human being alone, and two human beings in that attempt at total communication which is also communion, can discover the unique bent of their identity. There we may find for ourselves, through imperfect striving and repeated failure, the words, the gestures, the mental images which set the blood to racing. In that dark and wonder ever renewed both the fumblings and the light must be our own.

The new pornographers subvert this last, vital privacy; they do our imagining for us. They take away the words that were of the night and shout them over the rooftops, making them hollow. The images of our love-making, the stammerings we resort to in intimacy, come pre-packaged. From the rituals of adolescent petting to the recent university experiment in which faculty wives agreed to practice onanism in front of the researchers' cameras, sexual life, particularly in America, is passing more and more into the public domain. This is a profoundly ugly and demeaning thing whose effects on our identity and resources of feeling we understand as little as we do the impact on our nerves of the perpet-

220

ual "sub-eroticism" and sexual suggestion of modern advertisement. Natural selection tells of limbs and functions which atrophy through lack of use; the power to feel, to experience and realize the precarious uniqueness of each other's being, can also wither in a society. And it is no mere accident (as Orwell knew) that the standardization of sexual life, either through controlled license or compelled puritanism, should accompany totalitarian politics.

Thus the present danger to the freedom of literature and to the inward freedom of our society is not censorship or verbal reticence. The danger lies in the facile contempt which the erotic novelist exhibits for his readers, for his personages, and for the language. Our dreams are marketed wholesale.

Because there were words it did not use, situations it did not represent graphically, because it demanded from the reader not obeisance but live echo, much of Western poetry and fiction has been a school to the imagination, an exercise in making one's awareness more exact, more humane. My true quarrel with the *Olympia Reader** and the *genre* it embodies is not that so much of the stuff is boring and abjectly written. It is that these books leave a man less free, less himself, than they found him; that they leave language poorer, less endowed with a capacity for fresh discrimination and excitement. It is not a new freedom that they bring, but a new servitude. In the name of human privacy, enough!

**Ed. note:* A collection of pornographic literature edited by Maurice Girodias (New York: Grove Press, 1965).

PETER MICHELSON

The aesthetics of pornography

To understand the contemporary working of pornography we must conceive the term in its widest context. Originally it signified writings about prostitutes. But as we have come to recognize that the fantasy archetype represented in the prostitute is not at all unique to her, and as amateur promiscuity has increasingly supplied erotic fantasy material, pornography has revealed a new and larger being, *homo sexualis.* This has two images, the erect phallus and the carnal woman. The phallic symbol has become not only a psychological and literary commonplace, but also a cultural joke, and we are long since accustomed to finding one in everything from a new Buick to the Empire State Building. But the female image of *homo sexualis*—the essential pornographic image—is never funny, even in parody. Al Capp's cartoon women, for example, parody this image, enormously breasted and buttocked. But even the parody rides the edge of lust, and these images are much more desirable than ridiculous. For the pornographic world is peopled with men of limitless potency and women of limitless libido. O, the protagonist in *Story of O,* is a good contemporary example. No concerns in the narrative are allowed to obscure the translation of her total existence into terms of sexuality. Sex becomes the metaphor for being. In sophisticated pornography *homo sexualis* metaphors the erotic dimension of imagination and is the basis of erotic fantasy. The fantasy in this case is archetypal, and is not dissipated even by ejaculation. In other words, in this expanded sense of the term, pornography creates an image of human sexuality which not only inspires erotic gratification but also suggests the anthropological dimensions of sexual libido.

This view of pornography, then, regards it in its broadest and best sense as the literature of sexuality. And it has therefore the same degree of dignity and complexity potential to it that

221

the libido itself demands as an aspect of human nature. . . . In whatever art form, pornography documents both man's neurotic and his archetypal concern with sexuality. The neurotic (not to be confused with the pathological) engagement with pornography is the private confrontation of the individual psyche with its sexual needs. The larger cultural engagement with pornography is the public confrontation with archetypal—and usually subliminal—sexual impulses. Pornography then, for better or worse, is the imaginative record of man's sexual will. . . .

On the one hand, hard core or commercial pornography is static. Its ends are served by the simplest of descriptive techniques and rhetorical gambits. But, on the other hand, there is another and higher form of pornography which might be called *literary*. Rather than being only an exploitation of orgasm stimuli, it is rather an exploration of human sexuality. This is real pornography . . . and it does exploit its subject. But it does more than exploit. We are, as Freud observed, *all* of us more or less neurotic. One aspect of human neurosis is the rhythm of expectation and frustration which marks our sexual lives. Pornography on its lowest level exploits this rhythm by providing easy fantasy gratifications. But on its highest level it *explores* this rhythm, its moral and psychic implications, and to the degree that it does this it is poetic in the highest sense. This kind, of course, is the pornography being absorbed into what we call Literature, and it is represented by such works as O. The fact of pornography's evolution out of its own genre and into the larger literature means that pornography must also be considered as a rhetorical device for that literature. Faulkner, for example, although no mere pornographer, is certainly one of the most pornographic of modern writers. He often uses pornographic scenes and situations (the cockpit copulation in *Pylon,* the romance of Mink Snopes in *The Hamlet,* etc.) to articulate his total scheme. It is perhaps in this latter rhetorical role that pornography will assume its best form and have its greatest significance.

What I have been arguing is that pornography, like any literature, is a way of knowing.

The irony of its subject, sex, is the irony of another social pariah, the whore. We either deny its existence or privately acknowledge our private intimacies with it; and we are correspondingly either astonished or embarrassed to meet it on the street. Critically, if we don't ignore pornography altogether, we condescend to it like reformed sugar-daddies. Legally we invoke "contemporary community standards" against it as if they were not a fantasy morality derived from vestigial Puritanism rather than human experience. And thus we insure our ignorance of what it can tell us about—the interaction of moral imagination and sexual being. Meanwhile science, having escaped community standards and academic condescension in the guise of a white coat, goes on documenting a reality we deny our imagination.

Further, we forget that contemporary pornography is a natural product of the contemporary moral and aesthetic imagination. Our sense of the beautiful has become too psychologically complex to permit its reduction to either moral idealism or artistic formalism. For Plato the True was necessarily the Beautiful. For us the true is much more likely to be the ugly or grotesque. . . . Our literature adopts an aesthetic that aims to reveal the ugly as the true, and it often uses the sexual libido, which our culture has turned into a species of the ugly, as part of its rhetoric.

For the eighteenth and nineteenth centuries ugliness was artistically tolerable only when used as a dialectical agent (e.g. satire) to enforce the idea of a beautiful and harmonious Nature. It was an aesthetic which conceived of Nature, and therefore Truth and Beauty, as an archetypal norm that dismissed all aberrations as irrelevant. Contemporary aesthetic practice uses this process but reverses the values. Like Satan, it says, "Evil, be thou my good," and plays the role of devil's advocate, using the ugly to penetrate a cosmos no longer thought to be either benevolent or harmonious. It is at best indifferent, at worst malign. The ugly, then, becomes an ironic figure of revelation, exposing an implacable universe unrelieved by moral or spiritual design. Sartre's concepts of *slime* and

222

nausea are eloquent statements of an aesthetic of the ugly. Pornography, the kind represented by the *Story of O,* is a manifestation of the ugly. It does not romanticize sexuality; sex . . . is not beautiful. It is simply there, at the center of man's life. And its meaning is that it *is there,* dominating love, aspiration, happiness, all human experience. Its extravagance is often fearful because it so ruthlessly reflects our own libido.

Perhaps, as Freud suggests, our sexual impulse cannot be gratified without our becoming cultural outlaws. Perhaps sexuality requires being worked out through cultural taboos. If so, this argues a fearful human necessity. A fact of life that may be true, but hardly what we can think of as beautiful. . . . Pornography is part of this contemporaneous urgency to pursue the true. It too explores the unknown and therefore fearful in us. Our glimpses into that world refute our private and public lies. We can keep going— into the psyche as into space—and risk the dislocations that new knowledge brings, or we can collapse at the naked sight of ourselves. Not to explore the impulse to pornography is a form of denying human sexuality. We are, willy-nilly, brought to the overriding question of the modern imagination: how much deceit can we afford?

EDWARD J. MISHAN

Making the world safe for pornography

Turning . . . to the substantive issue concerning the social consequences of the spread of the erotic and the pornographic, two opinions in favour are offered by "permitters." The strong opinion is that it is positively beneficial, and the more cautious opinion is that the growing availability of such stuff does no harm—or, more cautious still, that it does no more harm than a number of other things that are socially acceptable. Let us examine these beliefs in that order.

Supporting the first opinion is the *Report* of the Arts Council's Working Party: "The so-called permissive society may have its casualties: the repressive society almost certainly has a great deal more.[1] Repressed sexuality can be toxic both to the individual and society. Repression can deprave and corrupt." . . .

Let us . . . [consider] the emphatic assertions about the evils of "repression." I place the word in quotes because it is not properly indicative of psychological malaise. As understood by psychiatrists, repression is a mechanism for dealing with emotional phenomena—memories, desires, impulses, fantasies—a mechanism whose proper function is necessary to a person's mental health. It is *over*-repression—which is what people usually mean by the word repression—that entails emotional maladjustment. So also does *under*-repression.

However, under- and over-repression are not social but *individual* maladies. Over-repression of sexuality results in a reduced ability, or total inability, to enjoy physically the sexual act. Its causes lie deeply embedded in the psyche. Though it can sometimes be treated successfully by psychiatry, so far as I know, exposure to erotica, or pornography, is not reckoned by the profession to be an essential part of the treatment. On the contrary, although the over-repressed individual might well become a voyeur, such exposure can only aggravate his sexual frustration. No matter how "permissive"

---

[1]This is as good a place as any to remind the reader that the terms "permissiveness" and the "permissive society," even where they are restricted to sexual aspects, are misleading. The "permissiveness" being debated is that which, if extended, initially offers the public increased opportunities for excitation, not for gratification. For nobody in authority is challenging any person's right to engage in sexual activity with other persons in any way he wishes, as often as he wishes, with willing adult partners. Permission to indulge and enjoy is not the issue at all. The permissiveness that is at issue is whether complete license should be extended to writers, impresarios, actors, and film producers to depict sexual activity of any variety in public places, and permission for the public to pay and stare.

the cinema or theatre becomes, no matter how vividly copulation is depicted, sexual gratification eludes the victim of over-repression. While those well-enough adjusted to enjoy sexual activity are not unduly arrested by erotic images, these can have a pathological attraction for the sexually unfulfilled. Some of the starved inmates of Nazi concentration camps were so far obsessed with visions of food that, when rescued and offered food, they would not eat it. They either gazed at it rapturously or sought to hoard it. The parallel with orgasmic starvation may be thought forced, but not by all psychiatrists.

Yet hope springs eternal in the human breast, and if repeated failure depresses, it can also feed an inner fury that seeks somehow to force egress into the citadels of sensation. But drinking the salt water of pop porno—gazing fixedly at live shows—contemplating photos of swollen proportions, staring orifices, and bizarre postures—act on the victim's fevered imagination, generating exaggerated visions of sexual gratification quite unrelated to that which is naturally attainable—so adding further to his frustrations and tempting him into sado-masochistic practices, or into intemperate attacks on his image of a grudging "establishment," in the vain hope of release. . . .

To sum up on the alleged virtues of "permissiveness" in contrast to the so-called toxicity of "repression," if the stricter proprieties of the Victorians presented no real barrier to sexual adventures (though one was well advised to have decent regard to the establishment hypocrisies of society to get the best out of it), it is perhaps unnecessary to seek "liberation" by the defiant cultivation of sexual "permissiveness." What is more to the point, the causes of frigidity and sexual despair are manifold—over-repression being rather a loose way of referring to some of them. And there is no evidence whatsoever that their incidence has diminished along with the growth of erotica and pornography. Frigidity and other forms of sexual failure may yield to medical and psychiatric skills. They do not yield to public manifestations of increased "sexual permissiveness," though they are likely to be aggravated by them.

The sex lobby

Turning now to the more cautious proposition that the spread of sexual content in literature and public entertainment can do no harm. . . .

To insist that, say, a reading of literature in general can *never* do harm is to take up an indefensible position. For it is commonly believed by those who condemn censorship of art and literature that they can do a powerful lot of good. Taken at its face value such a position amounts to the belief that, *although art and literature can do a great deal of good, they can never do any harm*—reassuring, perhaps, but hardly convincing. They knew better than this in Antiquity. If Plato would ban poets from the ideal city it was because, aware of the power of art for good and evil in society, he did not wish to risk the stability of the social order in order to entertain the populace.

It would be more convincing, then, if those favouring the abolition of all censorship explicitly acknowledged the influence of art and literature, and also of the screen, theatre, and television, in moulding people's behaviour and character. They could reasonably add that, in any particular case, the resultant effect might not be clearly perceived; that one might not always be able to determine in advance whether the impact of certain works would be benign or otherwise. But they could hardly avoid the conclusion that continued exposure to some sorts of art and literature was better than, or worse than, others in their effect on the character of people and, therefore, on society as a whole. . . .

The pornographic society

It is time to bring some thought to bear on the harmful consequences society may suffer if current trends toward increasing pornography continue. . . .

In order to avoid tedious qualifications at every turn in the argument, let us project existing trends and think in terms of an emergent "Pornographic Society," one in which all existing restraints have vanished. There are no legal checks on any form of erotic experience, "natural" or "unnatural," and no limit with respect to place, time, scale, or medium, in the depiction of what today would be called the carnal and lascivious. Neither are there any limits placed on the facilities for autoeroticism, or for participating in any activity, heterosexual, homosexual, bestial, or incestuous, sado-masochistic, fetishistic, or just plain cruel. Provided actors, audience, and participants are willing, provided there is a market for the "product," no objection is entertained. . . .

Can pornography be part of the good life?

It is time to turn about in our minds some of the facets of the problem posed by the concept of the Pornographic Society; namely, whether such a society is compatible with the Good Life, *any* good life.

First, allowing that family life will continue in such a society, what are we to make of the effect on the child's psychology of his apprehension of a society obsessed with carnal indulgence? It has been alleged, occasionally, that children are immune to pornography; that, up to a certain age, it does not signify. Though this allegation cannot draw on any evidence since they are not in fact exposed, when young, to sexual circuses, we need not pursue this controversial question here because, presumably, there does come an age when they begin to understand the significance of what is happening about them. It is appropriate, then, to question the effect on the child's emotional life, in particular his regard and feelings for his parents.

Is it not just possible that the child needs not only to love his parents but to esteem them? In his first gropings for order and security in a world of threatening impulse, does he not need to look up to beings who provide assurance, who appear to him as "good" and wise and just? Will such emotional needs not be thwarted in a society of uninhibited sexual device? I do not pretend to know the answers to these questions, but no one will gainsay their importance. In view of the possibly very grave consequences on our children's children, would it not be an act of culpable negligence to allow current trends toward an increasingly promiscuous society to continue without being in sight of the answers?

Consider next the quality of love in such a society. Three closely related questions arise.

Treated simply as a physical exploit with another body, and divorced from the intrusion of sentiment, is sexual fulfilment possible? David Holbrook, for one, has doubts whether this is possible. Indeed, he concludes that the so-called sexual revolution is "placing limits on people's capacities to develop a rich enjoyment of sexual love by reducing it to sexuality." Nor has Irving Kristol any brief for the more visible manifestations of the sexual revolution:

There are human sentiments . . . involved in this animal activity. But when sex is public the viewer does not—cannot—see the sentiments. . . . He can only see the animal coupling. And that is why, when men and women make love, as we say, they prefer to be alone—because it is only when you are alone that you can make love, as distinct from merely copulating in an animal and casual way.

The second question that comes to mind in this connection is whether romantic love will become obsolete in a society of unfettered sexual recourse.

The "savage" in Aldous Huxley's brilliant satire, *Brave New World,* who commits suicide in despair, tried for romantic love but could obtain only instant sex. There might well continue to be sexual friendships, sexual rivalries, sexual jealousies. But the sublimation of sex, thought to be the well-spring of creative imagination and of romantic love, would be no more. One of the great sources of inspiration of poetry and song, of chivalry and dedication, throughout the ages would have dried up. . . .

The third related question is about the quality of love in general that can be expected to emerge along the road to such a society. One wonders if it would really be possible to love other people very much, or to care for them as persons very much in a world without opportunity for sublimation. Can such virtues as loyalty, honour, compassion, sacrifice, charity, or tenderness, flourish in an environment of uninhibited public exhibitionism and pornography?

Taking a wider perspective of the scene, one wonders whether it is possible to unite unchecked public sexual indulgence with the continued progress of any civilisation—thinking of civilisation in terms not merely of increasing scientific advance and technological innovation but in those, also, of a refinement of taste and sensibility. Let the reader ponder on the question at his leisure, bearing in mind the reflection that whereas the emergence in the past of a new civilisation, or of a new age within the matrix of an existing civilisation, has indeed always been associated with a rapid displacement of old conceptions, values, and purposes by new ones, it has never been associated with a mass movement toward unbridled sexual licentiousness. . . .

Thus, a first experiment of this kind just might be the last experiment ever. Goaded on by the predatory forces of commercial opportunism, expectations of carnal gratification—aroused by increasingly salacious spectacles, and increasing facilities for new sexual perversions—would soar beyond the physical limits of attainments. In the unrelenting search for the uttermost in orgiastic experience, cruel passions might be unleashed, impelling humanity into regions beyond barbarism. One has only to recall the fantastic sadistic barbarities of the Nazi era—and to recall also that in 1941 the Nazis were within an ace of winning the War—to accept this conjecture as neither far-fetched nor fanciful, and to recognise that civilisation is indeed but skin-deep.

ARTHUR LELYVELD

Censorship

I am against censorship.

This essay will argue that freedom to speak, to publish, or to communicate from stage, screen or any other public media should be subject to only two inhibitions. The first is that which flows naturally from public taste. The people can choose to reject what is offered, to ignore it, or even to condemn it. The second inhibition is that which may result from the provision for after-the-fact, due-process review under carefully drawn laws prohibiting demonstrable injury to human welfare or human rights.

Censorship is something quite different. It is always and everywhere an evil. Censorship means the screening of material by an authority invested with power to ban that which it disapproves. A censor is someone appointed to regulate public morals and judge public taste. And who is that paragon to whom we would be willing to entrust such authority? And who, if he be such a paragon, would be willing to accept the responsibility?

In 1644, John Milton published his *Areopagitica: A Speech for the Liberty of Unlicensed Printing* when printing was the major medium for the dissemination of ideas. Milton's essay should have been the last word on censorship for it limned the dangers with unmatched eloquence:

. . . there is not aught more likely to be prohibited than truth itself; whose first appearance to our eyes bleared and dimmed with prejudice and custom, is more unsightly and implausible than many errors. . . .
And though all the winds of doctrine were let loose to play upon the earth, so Truth be in the field, we do injuriously by licensing and prohibiting, to misdoubt her strength. Let her and Falsehood grapple.

What Milton held in defense of the absolute right to publish applies also to judgments about what is obscene and what is not obscene. One man's obscenity is another man's customary mode of expression. In art and in drama, as well as in literature, it is only the arrantly self-certain who would know where to cry halt.

But having enlisted on the side of freedom, we need not slough off the social problems which come in the wake of license. Those who would exploit prurience for profit have been quick to take advantage of the new freedom. American sex movies today are a billion-dollar-a-year business with low costs yielding astronomical profits. The marquees along New York's 42nd Street which advertise "Adult Movies" become more brazen day by day. But compared to the huge nudes on billboards abutting Piccadilly Circus which thrust oversized breasts into the London night, the 42nd Street display looks positively decorous. The four-letter word, long tabooed in polite society, is today a commonplace used even by distinguished professors of theology.

During this last decade, public acceptance of these trends has been deepening with amazing speed. *Portnoy's Complaint* and its genre make *Fanny Hill* and *Lady Chatterley's Lover* look like Sunday School primers. . . .

There is no denying that the new freedom affords a refreshing release from furtiveness and from clandestine "dirtiness." Why, then, are some aspects of this flood of uninhibited expression so offensive? The counter-reaction is being expressed not only by the descendants of *Watch and Ward* but also by impressive public personalities. Recently, a professor of pediatric psychiatry gave voice to his fear that the brutality and the cheapness of current sex displays may diminish the meaning, the loveliness— and hence the joy—of the future love life of mankind.

D. H. Lawrence, whose *Lady Chatterley's Lover* was a landmark case in the battle against censorship, professed that he himself would censor "real" pornography "rigorously," and for the same reasons as those given by the psychiatrist just referred to. Said Lawrence:

Pornography is the attempt to insult sex, to do dirt on it. Take the very lowest instance, the picture postcard sold underhand . . . What I have seen of them have been of an ugliness to make you cry . . . they make the sexual act trivial and cheap and nasty.

. . . But how to deal effectively with such social evils? If absolute freedom to show and tell brings abuses in its train, is censorship a warranted and effective remedy? John Milton said "no" with a trenchant and unforgettable analogy:

. . . evil manners are as perfectly learned without books a thousand other ways which cannot be stopped . . . And he who were pleasantly disposed, could not well avoid to liken it to the exploit of that gallant man, who thought to pound up the crows by shutting his park gate.

A helpful distinction is available in the Jewish view of this matter; it is a distinction founded largely on intent. When the ancient rabbis were teaching or expounding the traditional sources, they spoke and wrote with the utmost freedom and frankness, as did the Biblical material on which they based their discussion. But when the intent was to demean, "to do dirt" on sex, to insult sex or deprecate sex, then this was inadmissible coarseness. In Hebrew the phrase used was *nibbul peh:* literally, "disfigurement of the mouth." Says one Talmudic teacher:

Everyone knows why the bride is brought into the bridal-tent, but anyone who befouls that moment with his mouth, even if seventy years of good have been decreed for him, has it changed into seventy years of evil.

And this judgment applies with equal force to anyone who *listens* to foul and leering speech and who remains silent.

Note, however, that *the penalty for coarseness is not legal action but moral condemnation.* The text itself speaks with perfect freedom about sexual intercourse. Condemnation falls only on that which is intentionally degrading and lewd.

The Bible contains abundant references to the sex act, homosexual as well as heterosexual, to rape, to prostitution, and to fornication. The Bible refers without self-consciousness to natural functions, and the Bible preserves some of the world's most beautiful erotic poetry. It is noteworthy that the same authorities who were banning Rousseau's *Confessions* were putting into the hands of youngsters the story of David and Bathsheba, of Judah and Tamer, and of Lot and the men of Sodom. Had they been consistent they would have banned Chaucer's *Canterbury Tales,* the plays of Ben Jonson, and the works of Shakespeare.

Indeed, as most legal authorities agree, it is impossible to arrive at a reasonable, workable definition of obscenity for purposes of censorship. It is this difficulty that leads many jurists toward an absolutist interpretation of the First Amendment. In the words of Justice Hugo Black:

My view is, without deviation, without exception, without any ifs, buts, or whereases, that freedom of speech means that you shall not do something to people either for the views they have, or the views they express, or the words they speak or write.

Freedom of expression, if it is to be meaningful at all, must include freedom for "that which we loathe," for it is obvious that it is no great virtue and presents no great difficulty for one to accord freedom to what we approve or to that to which we are indifferent.

This is the heart of the dilemma. That which I hold to be true has no protection if I permit that which I hold to be false to be suppressed—for you may with equal logic turn about tomorrow and label my truth as falsehood.

The same test applies to what I consider lovely or unlovely, moral or immoral, edifying or unedifying. . . .

But, praised be the law, this same freedom makes possible our right to condemn, to decry and to attack, as effectively as we can, that which is in our view tawdry or salacious or nauseating. To affirm freedom is not to applaud that which is done under its sign. Thomas Jefferson showed vigor and indignation as he made this point:

I deplore . . . the putrid state into which our newspapers have passed, and the malignity, the vulgarity, and the mendacious spirit of those who write them. . . . These ordures are rapidly depraving the public taste.

It is, however, an evil for which there is no remedy: Our liberty depends on the freedom of the press and that cannot be limited without being lost.

. . . But I have a right to want the law to prevent you from *imposing* your "ordures" on me. The law cannot create morality and taste, but it can prevent you from rubbing my nose in what I consider to be execrable. This is what Oliver Wendell Holmes, Jr., meant when he said "my right to swing my arm ends at the point at which your nose begins." It should be added that our new devices for instantaneous and universal communication make "your arm" far longer than it used to be, and it may well be necessary for legal authorities to give careful consideration to whether or not an extension of the doctrine of "clear and present danger" is required. . . .

Ignored in the hullaballoo about the report of the Commission on Obscenity and Pornography is the fact that the Commission has recognized this dilemma, and has affirmed the propriety of legislative action to protect the individual's right to make his own choices as to what he wishes to see and to hear. Its majority report includes this declaration:

Certain explicit sexual materials are capable of causing considerable offense to numerous Americans when thrust upon them without their consent. The commission believes that these unwanted intrusions upon individual sensibilities warrant legislative regulation and it further believes that such intrusions can be regulated effectively without any significant interference with consensual communication of sexual material among adults.

If this is an acceptable limitation, then it is certainly *a fortiori* true, as the Commission recognizes, that "explicit sexual materials," particularly those that brutalize and insult sex, should not be thrust upon children. But here we are desperately confused. It is possible to be degradingly lewd while fully clothed. I would rather my own children saw *The Lovers* than have had them see the late Marilyn Monroe in *Some Like It Hot,* a movie in which adultery and transvestitism were leering jokes. Many motion pictures rated for general audiences seem to me far more harmful than many that are rated "Restricted."

And this is where we came in. Legislation will not lighten the complexity of these problems, and censorship will not solve them. We can but hope that more and more men will come to have respect for human life and for the potentialities of human relationship. And as for that which is depraved and disgusting in our own time, we can only wait for taste and good judgement to reassert themselves after the first wild release.

Fortunately, there is some evidence that pornography has its own cure built into it—after a relatively short time pornography produces ennui. . . .

Repression, on the other hand, as the Prohibition experiment showed us, creates an unwholesome, heightened desire for that which is forbidden. No one bothers to write a crudity on a wall or on a placard exposed to public view unless such a writing is considered banned and appropriate only to secret places, such as the cubicle of a men's room.

It isn't easy. But I have seen freedom and I have seen repression. Freedom is better.

"But, Galileo—why should you study moon craters when right here
at home most people don't have satisfactory bathrooms yet?"

11

SCIENCE AND MORALS: FREEDOM OF INQUIRY AND THE PUBLIC INTEREST

Essentially, science is the pursuit of truth: How then could it ever be held to be immoral? Clearly only if the truth itself or some truths were immoral—a charge that is rarely made nowadays.

It is not scientific truth in itself that is challenged ethically, but the uses to which it is put. Many argue that there is nothing inherent in the scientific discovery that insures it will be used for moral ends. The polio vaccine, for instance, may inoculate people against polio, but it may also be used to cause it.

Another moral problem of technology arises with the ignorance of scientists of all the consequences of a particular scientific application. It might turn out, for instance, that the successful vaccine had unintended harmful side effects, which had not been foreseen. In such a case, one might say that the doctors were morally negligent in not proceeding more carefully in the use of the vaccine.

These examples refer to the applications of science—to the technology of atomic energy, computers, and biological compounds—not to the scientific formulas that underlie them. How many of us know modern evolutionary theory, relativity theory, the Heisenberg Uncertainty Principle, or Godel's Proof? These are all the business of experts. But the possible uses to which theories may be put very likely have a momentous impact on our way of life. It is not surprising, therefore, that the moral debate that has surrounded science has most frequently concentrated on the way our technologies ought to be developed.

Modern science developed in close relation to technology: It is not too much to say that they were wedded to each other. The possibilities of technology for improving our lives were first clearly seen by Francis Bacon in the early seventeenth century. In the first selection in this chapter, Lewis Mumford recalls Bacon's vision and analyzes how much the practice of contemporary science has changed since Bacon's time. Mumford argues that the scientist in the twentieth century "has forfeited the qualities that were exalted, in the seventeenth century, as the very hallmark of the scientist—his detachment from worldly gains and his disinterested pursuit of truth." Science has become the servant of corporate organizations or of governments that use it for their own ends of power and riches that may not have humane consequences.

C. P. Snow, in the next article, displays more optimistic faith in the beneficent consequences of science. He remains convinced of the goodness promised by technology and of the high moral standards of scientists because he sees scientific inquiry as itself a moral activity. He seems to believe that the moral character present in the pursuit of a discovery will carry over and affect how that discovery is used. Snow writes that there is "a built-in moral component right in the core of the scientific activity itself. The desire to find the truth is itself a moral impulse, or at least contains a moral impulse." In a passage of the same essay, which is not excerpted, Snow exhorts his fellow scientists to take up the challenge of overcoming hunger around the world.

But is the pursuit of truth always moral, or does the very search for knowledge sometimes entail evil? If it does, what is the responsibility of the scientist toward society? These questions are addressed in the next three articles in this chapter.

Robert Sinsheimer discusses the dangers inherent in research into recombinant DNA. The DNA molecule, present in every cell, determines the hereditary properties of an organism. It has now become possible to "recombine" fragments of DNA from different species, thus creating new forms of life. At the present time such recombination is possible only in a bacteria that is currently found in man. Sinsheimer calls attention to the dangers of releasing a new hybrid organism that could cause new forms of widespread disease. This possibility has caused demonstrations of public concern near some of the major biomedical centers where such research is taking place, such as Harvard University and the University of California, San Diego.

Beyond this danger, however, are unknown dangers we may face as man enters a new phase of technology in creating life. Recombinant DNA research can teach us much about our genetic structure and might have beneficial practical consequences, such as a cure for cancer and the repair of genetic defects in humans; but in the face of our awesome new powers, Sinsheimer suggests that caution may become an essential scientific virtue.

The current controversy over DNA research is reminiscent of the controversy that surrounded nuclear physics in the mid-century. Then, too, scientists knew they were embarking on research that could have disastrous consequences for humanity. The next selection is from the Report of the General Advisory Committee to the United States Atomic Energy Commission in October 1949. The committee, which included scientists who had developed the atomic bomb, recommended on moral grounds that the government halt its work on the "Super" or hydrogen bomb and that it make the public aware of the issues involved. Despite these recommendations, President Truman decided, on January 31, 1950, to proceed with the bomb. In the following very brief excerpt, Edward Teller takes the position that such political decisions are not the responsibility of the scientist, whose sole job is to find out how the laws of nature operate.

In the following article, Jacob Bronowski takes issue both with the idea that scientific research can be halted and with the idea that scientists are not responsible for the applications of their research. He recognizes that some scientists may feel morally obligated to work for the government; these scientists should clearly do so. But Bronowski sees a basic incompatibility between the aims of nationalism and the moral pursuit of the truth that is the essence of science. Scientists, Bronowski maintains, must "set an incorruptible standard for public morality." It is time, he argues, for scientists to disestablish themselves from the government that currently finances most of their research and to set up their own priorities and allocation of resources.

232

In the concluding selection in this chapter, Barry Commoner makes clear what he believes those priorities should be. He takes the position that scientists have been too narrow in their concerns and failed to realize the complexity of the world today. New technology has been developed without a clear recognition of the delicate balance of our environment. He concludes that "university scientists have a clear obligation to the society that supports us. We have no right to retreat behind the walls of our laboratories; instead, we must use our knowledge to help improve the world."

NOTES ABOUT THE AUTHORS

Lewis Mumford, born in 1895, is generally considered the leading American critic of twentieth-century architecture. His books range from art and architecture to the impact of technology on human life. His books include *Technics and Civilization, The Highway and the City, The Culture of Cities,* and *The City in History,* for which he received the National Book Award in 1961. "Science as Technology" originally appeared in the *Proceedings of the American Philosophical Society* for 1961.

C. P. Snow is a British peer who is also a novelist, scientist, and government adviser. He immortalized England's professional class in his eleven-volume series of novels *Strangers and Brothers.* His work on the relation of science to morality and culture includes *The Two Cultures and the Scientific Revolution.* "The Moral Un-neutrality of Science" first appeared in 1961 in *Science.*

Robert L. Sinsheimer is professor of biophysics and chairman of the Division of Biology at the California Institute of Technology. He is also chairman of the editorial board of the Proceedings of the National Academy of Sciences and the author of many research reports on nucleic acids.

The General Advisory Committee of the Atomic Energy Commission was established in 1946 "to advise the Commission on scientific and technical matters relating to materials, production, and research and development." Composed of nine civilians, its membership in 1949 included such notable scientists as James B. Conant, J. Robert Oppenheimer, and Enrico Fermi, all of whom had been instrumental in developing the atomic bomb.

Edward Teller, born in Hungary in 1908, came to the United States after fleeing the Nazi regime. He was among the group of scientists that went to Los Alamos to work on the atomic bomb during World War II, and he was responsible for much of the theoretical groundwork for a hydrogen bomb. In 1953 he joined the faculty of the University of California. In contrast to much of the scientific community during the 1950s, he strongly favored the continued testing and development of nuclear weapons. The recipient of the Atomic Energy Commission's Fermi Award in 1962, he is the author of *Our Nuclear Future* and *The Legacy of Hiroshima.*

Jacob Bronowski was both a scientist and a humanist. A mathematician by training, he was research professor and fellow of the Salk Institute for Biological Studies in La Jolla, California and director of the Council for Biology in Human Affairs there. His books reflect his broad interests and include *Science and Human Values, The Identity of Man, Nature and Knowledge,* and *The Ascent of Man,* which was made into a television series by the British Broadcasting Corporation. "The Disestablishment of Science" first appeared in *Encounter* in 1971. Bronowski died in 1974.

Barry Commoner is professor of plant physiology at Washington University in St. Louis. He is also the director of the Center of the Biology of Natural Systems and cochairman of the Scientists' Institute for Public Information. His interests encompass both science and the humanities, and his books *Science and Survival* and *The Closing Circle* have had a major impact on the environmental protection movement. "The Dual Crisis in Science and Society" first appeared in *Today's Education* in 1968.

233

LEWIS MUMFORD

Science as technology

The title of this paper, Science as Technology, would not have surprised or shocked Francis Bacon, for perhaps his most original contribution to the enlargement of the province of science was his understanding of its great future role in transforming the physical conditions of life. But I am sure that the conclusions that I shall finally present—conclusions in the form of doubts, challenges, and questions—would have shocked him quite as much as it will, I fear, shock many of those who . . . [read this paper], for his faith in science as a source of technology, and in technology itself as the final justification of science must now, after four centuries, be submitted to an historic evaluation and the pragmatic test. When Bacon's assumptions are rigorously examined, they should, I submit, lead to a modification of Bacon's original hopes and even a radical change in our own attitude toward many Baconian beliefs we have, somewhat blindly, taken to be axiomatic. . . .

What is most fresh and original in Bacon [is] his conception of the role of science as the spiritual arm, so to speak, of technology. . . .

But Bacon went further: he saw that curiosity, to be fully effective, must enlist, not solitary and occasional minds, but a corps of well-organized workers, each exercising a specialized function and operating in a restricted area. By the technological organization of science as he portrayed it in the *New Atlantis,* he proposed to fabricate an engine capable of turning out useful knowledge in the same fashion that a well-organized factory would, shortly after Bacon's prediction, turn out textiles or shoes. . . .

Bacon's conception of the organization of science as a technology did not altogether overlook the part played by individual creative minds: he even had a name for such seminal investigators, for he called them "Lamps," and indicated that their function was to "direct new experiments of a Higher Light, more penetrating into nature." But his peculiar contribution was to sense that, if the illuminations and insights of creative minds were to have the widest kind of application, they would need abundant collective support: state aid, corporate organization, systematic conferences and publications, liberal rewards and honors, and finally, public exhibition and celebration in museums of science and industry. It was these features of collective organization and state regimentation, not perhaps entirely unknown in pre-Christian Alexandria, that Bacon so presciently recognized, advocated, and exalted. . . .

In looking back over the fulfillment of Bacon's anticipations, it is plain that there were two critical points. The first occurred in the first half of the nineteenth century, when for the first time purely theoretic researches in physics, by Volta, Ohm, Henry, and Faraday, resulted, almost within a generation, in the invention of the electric telegraph, the dynamo, the electric motor; and within two generations in the invention of the telephone, the electric lamp, the x-ray, and the wireless telegraph: all of these being inventions that were not merely impracticable but technically inconceivable until pure scientific research made them live possibilities. The methods that were so fruitful in mechanics and electronics were then applied, with growing success, in organic chemistry and biology; though significantly enough the parts of technology with the longest accumulation of purely empiric knowledge, like mining and metallurgy, remained almost impervious to the advances of science.

The second critical point came during the first half of the twentieth century, along with a change of scale and magnitude partly brought about, almost automatically, by the expansion of the facilities for communication and the exploitation of new sources of power. This change lifted hitherto inviolable limits on human activities: a shot could be heard around the world by means of radio more than eleven times faster than it could be heard by the unaided ear a mile away. At this point, science itself became the technology of technologies; and as the mass production of scientific knowledge went hand in hand with the mass production of inventions and products derived from science, the scientist came to have a new status in society, equivalent to that earlier occupied by the captains of industry. He, too, was engaged in mass production.

The old image of the self-directed scientist still remains popular, particularly among scientists; but as science expands as a mass technology, the scientist himself becomes a servant of corporate organizations intent on enlarging the bounds of empire—by no means always "humane empire!"—and endowing themselves by means of invention with power and riches and worldly prestige. By this transformation the scientist has forfeited the qualities that were exalted, in the seventeenth century, as the very hallmark of the scientist—his detachment from worldly gains and his disinterested pursuit of truth. To the extent that his capacity for pursuing truth depends upon costly apparatus, collective collaboration, and heavy financial contributions from government or industry, he has lost, as Sir Charles Snow [has] pointed out . . . , the capacity to stand alone and to say No—even on matters like the mal-exploitation of nuclear energy that threatens the future of the human race.

Not merely have the sciences, then, become technologies, but the scientist himself, caught in the corporate process, is fast becoming the model of a docile, standardized, organization man, imprisoned by his own obsolete premises, incapable of making his escape without altering those premises. I hope I need not underline the moral that Snow properly drew from this. But there is a corollary that I would stress. Since science as technology has already submitted, often with great eagerness, to political and economic pressures, for the sake of the immense scientific opportunities offered, it cannot escape facing the consequences of this submission, and actively helping to rectify them. The scientist now has the obligation of erecting intellectual and social safeguards against the frequently malign consequences of scientific discoveries, even if the creation of these internal checks and balances slow up, or occasionally bring to a halt, the process of scientific investigation or technological application. As an agent of technology, science no longer has the immunities or the irresponsibilities that it claimed for itself during its great quarrels with the Church. Today, the greatest danger to science comes not from the hostility of traditional institutions but from the patronage of contemporary ones.

Now if the fulfillment of Bacon's dream deserves our respectful recognition of his prophetic insights, it also imposes upon us a special duty—that of dissociating ourselves from the mythology he so largely helped to promote, so as to appraise, in the light of historic experience, his unexamined premises. These premises are now so thoroughly institutionalized that most of our contemporaries continue to act upon them without even a quiver of doubt. But observe: science as technology presents a series of problems that science, as the disinterested examination of nature in search of rational understanding, never confronted; for already it shows the same deep irrationalities and absurdities that mass production in other fields has brought about. The chief premise common to both technology and science is the notion that there are no desirable limits to the increase of knowledge, of material goods, of environmental control; that quantitative productivity is an end in itself, and that every means should be used to expand the facilities for quantitative expansion and production. . . .

We are now faced . . . with the situation Goethe foresaw in the fable of the Sorcerer's Apprentice: we have achieved the magic formula for automatically increasing the supply of scientific knowledge; but we have forgotten the Master Magician's formula for regulating or halting the flood, and so are on the point of drowning in it. Science as technology gets its main financial support, and therefore its overall direction, from the national government, or from great industrial corporations like those engaged in exploiting new pharmaceutical preparations, chemical pest controls, or atomic energy, and from quasi-public philanthropic foundations exerting almost equally large powers. Though the professed aim of these organizations is truth and human welfare, they are governed in perhaps an even greater degree by the Baconian goals of riches and power. On these premises they have no concern with ordering science in accordance with some human measure, toward the fulfillment of broader human goals: for this means altering the method of mass production and slowing down the whole process. Our schools and universities are helpless to restore an organic balance, because they themselves have accepted the same ideology and rely for a large part of their activities upon endowments that are scaled to the prospects of continued expansion and quick turnover: indeed the very possibilities for professional promotion depend more upon the number of scientific papers published than upon long-term results that may not be visible for a generation or more. . . .

The greatest contribution of science, the most desirable of all its many gifts, far surpassing its purely material benefits, has been its transformation of the human consciousness, through its widening illumination of the entire cosmic and historic process, and its transfer to man of the power to participate, with his whole being, in that process. Has the time not come, then—in technology as in every other aspect of the common life—to re-examine our accepted axioms and practical imperatives and to release science itself from the humanly impoverished and underdimensioned mythology of power that Francis Bacon helped to promote?

C.P. SNOW

The moral un-neutrality of science

Scientists are the most important occupational group in the world today. At this moment, what they do is of passionate concern to the whole of human society. At this moment, the scientists have little influence on the world effect of what they do. Yet, potentially, they can have great influence. The rest of the world is frightened both of what they do—that is, of the intellectual discoveries of science—and of its effect. The rest of the world, transferring its fears, is frightened of the scientists themselves and tends to think of them as radically different from other men.

As an ex-scientist, if I may call myself so, I know that is nonsense. I have even tried to express in fiction some kinds of scientific temperament and scientific experience. I know well enough that scientists are very much like other men. After all, we are all human, even if some of us don't give that appearance. I think I would be prepared to risk a generalization. The scientists I have known (and because of my official life I have known as many as anyone in the world) have been in certain respects at least as morally admirable as any other group of intelligent men. . . .

So scientists are not much different from other men. They are certainly no worse than other men. But they do differ from other men in one thing. That is the point I started with. Whether they like it or not, what they do is of critical importance for the human race. Intellectually, it has transformed the climate of our time. Socially, it will decide whether we live or die, and how we live or die. It holds decisive powers for good and evil. *That* is the situation in which the scientists find themselves. They may not have asked for it, or may only have asked for it in part, but they cannot escape it. They think, many of the more sensitive of them, that they don't deserve to have this weight of responsibility heaved upon them. All they want to do is to get on with their work. I sympathize. But the scientists can't escape the responsibility—any more than they, or the rest of us, can escape the gravity of the moment in which we stand.

There is of course one way to contract out. It has been a favourite way for intellectual persons caught in the midst of water too rough for them.

It consists of the invention of categories—or, if you like, of the division of moral labour. That is, the scientists who want to contract out say, *we* produce the tools. *We* stop there. It is for *you*—the rest of the world, the politicians—to say how the tools are used. The tools may be used for purposes which most of us would regard as bad. If so, we are sorry. But as scientists, that is no concern of ours.

This is the doctrine of the ethical neutrality of science. I can't accept it for an instant. I don't believe any scientist of serious feeling can accept it. It is hard, some think, to find the precise statements which will prove it wrong. Yet we nearly

236

all feel intuitively that the invention of comfortable categories is a moral trap. It is one of the easier methods of letting the conscience rust. . . . Are we going to let our consciences rust? Can we ignore that intimation we nearly all have, that scientists have a unique responsibility? Can we believe it, that science is morally neutral?

To me—it would be dishonest to pretend otherwise—there is only one answer to those questions. . . .

Let me begin with a remark which seems some way off the point. Anyone who has ever worked in any science knows how much aesthetic joy he has obtained. That is, in the actual *activity* of science, in the process of making a discovery, however humble it is, one can't help feeling an awareness of beauty. The subjective experience, the aesthetic satisfaction, seems exactly the same as the satisfaction one gets from writing a poem or a novel, or composing a piece of music. . . .

That is not the end of it. The *result* of the activity of science, the actual finished piece of scientific work, has an aesthetic value in itself. The judgments passed on it by other scientists will more often than not be expressed in aesthetic terms: "That's beautiful!" or "That really is very pretty!" (as the understating English tend to say). The aesthetics of scientific constructs, like the aesthetics of works of art, are variegated. We think some of the great syntheses, like Newton's, beautiful because of their classical simplicity, but we see a different kind of beauty in the relativistic extension of the wave equation of the interpretation of the structure of deoxyribonucleic acid, perhaps because of the touch of unexpectedness. Scientists know their kinds of beauty when they see them. They are suspicious, and scientific history shows they have always been right to have been so, when a subject is in an "ugly" state. For example, most physicists feel in their bones that the present bizarre assembly of nuclear particles, as grotesque as a stamp collection, can't possibly be, in the long run, the last word. . . .

There is no doubt, then, about the aesthetic content of science, both in the activity and the result. But aesthetics has no connection with morals, say the categorizers. I don't want to waste time on peripheral issues—but are you quite sure of that? Or is it possible that these categories are inventions to make us evade the human and social conditions in which we now exist? But let us move straight on to something else, which is right in the grain of the activity of science and which is at the same time quintessentially moral. I mean, the desire to find the truth.

By *truth,* I don't intend anything complicated, once again. I am using the word as a scientist uses it. We all know that the philosophical examination of the concept of empirical truth gets us into some curious complexities, but most scientists really don't care. They know that the truth, as they use the word and as the rest of us use it in the language of common speech, is what makes science work. That is good enough for them. On it rests the whole great edifice of modern science. . . .

Anyway, truth in their own straightforward sense is what the scientists are trying to find. They want to find what is *there*. Without that desire, there is no science. It is the driving force of the whole activity. It compels the scientist to have an overriding respect for truth, every stretch of the way. That is, if you're going to find what is *there,* you mustn't deceive yourself or anyone else. You mustn't lie to yourself. At the crudest level, you mustn't fake your experiments.

Curiously enough, scientists do try to behave like that. A short time ago, I wrote a novel in which the story hinged on a case of scientific fraud. But I made one of my characters, who was himself a very good scientist, say that, considering the opportunities and temptations, it is astonishing how few such cases there are. We have all heard of perhaps half a dozen open and notorious ones, which are on the record for anyone to read—ranging from the "discovery" of the L radiation to the singular episode of the Piltdown man. . . .

But the total number of all these men is vanishingly small by the side of the total number of scientists. . . .

The remarkable thing is not the handful of scientists who deviate from the search for truth but the overwhelming numbers who keep to it.

That is a demonstration, absolutely clear for anyone to see, of moral behaviour on a very large scale.

We take it for granted. Yet it is very important. It differentiates science in its widest sense (which includes scholarship) from all other intellectual activities. There is a built-in moral component right in the core of the scientific activity itself. The desire to find the truth is itself a moral impulse, or at least contains a moral impulse. The way in which a scientist tries to find the truth imposes on him a constant moral discipline . . . the constant moral exercise of seeking and telling the truth. To scientists, who are brought up in this climate, this seems as natural as breathing. Yet it is a wonderful thing. Even if the scientific activity contained only this one moral component, that alone would be enough to let us say that it was morally un-neutral.

ROBERT L. SINSHEIMER

Caution may be an essential scientific virtue

Troubled scientists and confused laymen may wish that the recombinant DNA issue would go away, but it will not. Mankind is about to extend its dominion by redirecting the course of biological evolution. Inevitably, this must change not only the world in which we live, but also the way in which science functions in it.

It is the success of science that has ended its pleasant isolation from the strident conflict of interests and the often passionate clash of values. The great discoveries in molecular and cellular biology—in particular the elucidation of the structure and functions of the nucleic acids—have provided us with a definitive understanding of the nature of life. Earlier in this century splendid discoveries in physics and chemistry provided us with a definitive understanding of the nature of matter. From that understanding has come the technology to reshape the inani-

mate world to human purpose—and many are less than pleased with the consequences. Now the description of life in molecular terms provides the beginnings of a technology to reshape the living world to human purpose—to reconstruct our fellow life forms, each, as are we, the product of three billion years of evolution—into projections of the human will. And many are profoundly troubled by the prospect.

With the advent of synthetic biology we leave the security of that web of evolutionary Nature that, blindly and strangely, bore us and all of our fellow creatures. With each step we will be increasingly on our own. The invention and introduction of new living forms may well be irreversible. How do we prevent grievous missteps, inherently unretraceable? Can we in truth foresee the consequences, near- and long-term, of our interventions?

Genes, composed of DNA, provide the basic molecular blueprints for the design of living organisms. The recombination of genes providing new arrangements of DNA has always been a mechanism for the generation of genetic diversity *within species* (and thus an essential factor in evolution). However, the new technology of "recombinant DNA" provides the capability to recombine genetic material from the *most diverse* species, i.e., to mix genes from animals and plants and microorganisms, and thereby to produce novel organisms not derived by the usual evolutionary processes.

I suggest that it is impossible to predict from present knowledge the properties of such organisms and therefore the consequences of their introduction into our biosphere. Most would probably be innocuous. Some could, by design and selection, become of very great value for human purpose. Others might possibly, inadvertently, become a considerable peril to present human, animal or plant life.

If these novel organisms could be fully contained while they were under study, there would be much less cause for concern. However, the recombinant DNA technology is currently feasible only in microorganisms and in particular in the organism, *Escherichia coli,* a microbe indigenous to man, animals, soil and plants. The continued total containment of microorganisms

238

has never been accomplished even under the most stringent conditions. The proposed use in this work of "crippled" bacterial strains with reduced likelihood of survival outside the laboratory is certainly a valuable precaution; however, pragmatically, I suggest that the likelihood of error, of accident, of culture contamination, etc. will inevitably frustrate the goal of total containment.

Because we are concerned here with self-reproducing organisms, this hazard has a novel and irreversible character. Once released, and finding an appropriate ecological niche, these organisms cannot be recalled nor their manufacture ceased. They will be with us potentially forever.

By our wits mankind has become the master of the extant living world. Will short-sighted ingenuity now spawn new competitors to bedevil us?

The apparent significance of the potential hazard of recombinant DNA depends markedly upon the perspective in which the issue is seen.

Viewed narrowly the potential hazard seems slight. Most of the novel microorganisms will likely be innocuous. A few, by careful design and selection, will be of value for human purposes. A few might inadvertently be perilous. The chance of release of these organisms is statistically small, although it can hardly be null. The chance of a series of events necessary to produce a plague seems slim in any one experiment.

Viewed broadly, however—over long years, in numerous environs, with countless experiments—a far larger penumbra of hazard appears.

We are ignorant of the probable consequences, near- and long-term, of crossing the well-developed barriers to genetic recombination between species. We, and all higher organisms, figuratively live immersed in a sea of microorganisms. Our intimate and inevitable interactions with these ubiquitous forms—some beneficial, some pathological—are, however, on the metabolic level, not at the genetic level. The introduction of genetic intercourse between microorganisms and higher organisms may provide opportunities for the subsequent evolution of new forms of pathogens and new modes of transmission of disease. If the diseases concerned have long latent periods (as do cancers or slow virus diseases) they might not become apparent until the causative organisms had become widely disseminated.

Because of these potential major hazards of likely low but, in truth, incalculable probability, I would advocate extreme caution in the development of research in this field. I suggest such research be restricted to a small number of laboratories providing the maximum possible containment, under supervision, to insure that all possible precautions are in fact employed.

I would also advocate the transition as rapidly as feasible of such research from the *Escherichia coli* organism to some other organism adapted by nature to survival in only a very restricted and extreme environment and far less intimately associated with man. It is only the reservoir of knowledge accumulated over the past 25 years concerning *Escherichia coli* that makes it the organism of choice. An extensive program of research could likely provide alternatives within a few years, if the delay is accepted and the effort is made.

We can have no assurance that science will not bring us into a more dangerous world. The search for knowledge has often been hazardous; many explorers have faced great perils. Now the hazards can encompass the planet. For our knowledge now gives us great power and we may not continue to rely upon the resilience of Nature to protect us from our follies.

New circumstances bring new perspectives. As scientists we have had the rare luxury to pursue truth, unconflicted by compassion. Caution has been an unfamiliar virtue, while boldness and curiosity have been hallowed.

As we cut free the strands of our inheritance, a different blend of virtues may be in order and other traditions may be helpful.

We should not underestimate these stakes, now and in time to come. We will need to establish in each time a sense of limits commensurate with our finite vision and shaped by our sense of the moral—limits within which we believe we can explore without fear and with decency and beyond which we ought tread most gingerly. These limits will change continually as knowledge grows. In their definition and redefinition we should involve all who can help and respect all of those affected.

As scientists who seek to understand Nature we should not unthinkingly and irreversibly perturb it. As human beings we have a responsibility always to be concerned for our fellows and our fellow creatures and the future generations.

Report of the General Advisory Committee to the United States Atomic Energy Commission, October 30, 1949

Although the members of the Advisory Committee are not unanimous in their proposals as to what should be done with regard to the super bomb, there are certain elements of unanimity among us. We all hope that by one means or another, the development of these weapons can be avoided. We are all reluctant to see the United States take the initiative in precipitating this development. We are all agreed that it would be wrong at the present moment to commit ourselves to an all-out effort toward its development.

We are somewhat divided as to the nature of the commitment not to develop the weapon. The majority feel that this should be an unqualified commitment. Others feel that it should be made conditional on the response of the Soviet government to a proposal to renounce such development. The Committee recommends that enough be declassified about the super bomb so that a public statement of policy can be made at this time. Such a statement might in our opinion point to the use of deuterium as the principal source of energy. It need not discuss initiating mechanisms nor the role which we believe tritium will play. It should explain that the weapon cannot be explored without developing it and proof-firing it. In one form or another, the statement should express our desire not to make this development. It should explain the scale and general nature of the destruction which its use

would entail. It should make clear that there are no known or foreseen nonmilitary applications of this development. The separate views of the members of the Committee are attached to this report for your use.

J. R. Oppenheimer

October 30, 1949

We have been asked by the Commission whether or not they should immediately initiate an "all-out" effort to develop a weapon whose energy release is 100 to 1000 times greater and whose destructive power in terms of area of damage is 20 to 100 times greater than those of the present atomic bomb. We recommend strongly against such action.

We base our recommendation on our belief that the extreme dangers to mankind inherent in the proposal wholly outweigh any military advantage that could come from this development. Let it be clearly recognized that this is a super weapon; it is in a totally different category from an atomic bomb. The reason for developing such super bombs would be to have the capacity to devastate a vast area with a single bomb. Its use would involve a decision to slaughter a vast number of civilians. We are alarmed as to the possible global effects of the radioactivity generated by the explosion of a few super bombs of conceivable magnitude. If super bombs will work at all, there is no inherent limit in the destructive power that may be attained with them. Therefore, a super bomb might become a weapon of genocide.

The existence of such a weapon in our armory would have far-reaching effects on world opinion: reasonable people the world over would realize that the existence of a weapon of this type whose power of destruction is essentially unlimited represents a threat to the future of the human race which is intolerable. Thus we believe that the psychological effect of the weapon in our hands would be adverse to our interest.

We believe a super bomb should never be produced. Mankind would be far better off not to have a demonstration of the feasibility of such a weapon until the present climate of world opinion changes.

It is by no means certain that the weapon can be developed at all and by no means certain that the Russians will produce one within a decade. To the argument that the Russians may succeed in developing this weapon, we would reply that our undertaking it will not prove a deterrent to them. Should they use the weapon against us, reprisals by our large stock of atomic bombs would be comparably effective to the use of a super.

In determining not to proceed to develop the super bomb, we see a unique opportunity of providing by example some limitations on the totality of war and thus of limiting the fear and arousing the hopes of mankind.

James B. Conant
Hartley Rowe
Cyril Stanley Smith
L. A. DuBridge
Oliver E. Buckley
J. R. Oppenheimer

October 30, 1949

AN OPINION ON THE DEVELOPMENT OF THE "SUPER"

A decision on the proposal that an all-out effort be undertaken for the development of the "Super" cannot in our opinion be separated from considerations of broad national policy. A weapon like the "Super" is only an advantage when its energy release is from 100–1000 times greater than that of ordinary atomic bombs. The area of destruction therefore would run from 150 to approximately 1000 square miles or more. . . .

It is clear that the use of such a weapon cannot be justified on any ethical ground which gives a human being a certain individuality and dignity even if he happens to be a resident of an enemy country. It is evident to us that this would be the view of peoples in other countries. Its use would put the United States in a bad moral position relative to the peoples of the world.

Any postwar situation resulting from such a weapon would leave unresolvable enmities for generations. A desirable peace cannot come from such an inhuman application of force. The postwar problems would dwarf the problems which confront us at present.

The application of this weapon with the consequent great release of radioactivity would have results unforeseeable at present, but would certainly render large areas unfit for habitation for long periods of time.

The fact that no limits exist to the destructiveness of this weapon makes its very existence and the knowledge of its construction a danger to humanity as a whole. It is necessarily an evil thing considered in any light.

For these reasons we believe it important for the President of the United States to tell the American public, and the world, that we think it wrong on fundamental ethical principles to initiate a program of development of such a weapon. At the same time it would be appropriate to invite the nations of the world to join us in a solemn pledge not to proceed in the development or construction of weapons of this category. If such a pledge were accepted even without control machinery, it appears highly probable that an advanced stage of development leading to a test by another power could be detected by available physical means. Furthermore, we have in our possession, in our stockpile of atomic bombs, the means for adequate "military" retaliation for the production or use of a "super."

E. Fermi
I. I. Rabi

EDWARD TELLER

Back to the laboratories

The scientist is not responsible for the laws of nature. It is his job to find out how these laws operate. It is the scientist's job to find the ways in which these laws can serve the human will. However, it is *not* the scientist's job to determine whether a hydrogen bomb should be constructed, whether it should be used, or how it should be used. This responsibility rests with the American people and with their chosen representatives.

241

JACOB BRONOWSKI

The disestablishment of science

On 2 February 1939 my late friend and colleague Leo Szilard sent a letter to Professor J. F. Joliot-Curie in France in which he proposed that atomic physicists should make a voluntary agreement not to publish any new findings on the fission of uranium. It was a crucial time in history. The date was shortly after Munich; Hitler was riding high, and was clearly determined to make war. And just at this threatening moment, results were published which left no doubt that the atom of uranium could be split and neutrons released in the process. Szilard concluded that a chain reaction could be produced and warned Joliot-Curie, "In certain circumstances this might then lead to the construction of bombs which would be extremely dangerous in general and particularly in the hands of certain governments."

Far-sighted as Leo Szilard was, it is hard to believe that the events he feared could have been stopped even if the scientists he canvassed had accepted his invitation to silence. The embargo on publication that he tried to improvise was too crude to be realistic, in a field in which discoveries were being made so fast and their implications were so clear and so grave. At best Szilard's scheme could have been a stop-gap with which he might hope to buy a little time.

Yet it is revealing and important that a scientist with the standing of Leo Szilard should have put into words the favourite daydream of the bewildered citizen: to call a Moratorium on Science. It reminds us that scientists also feel helpless in the rush of events, which unseen hands seem constantly to direct towards more and more massive and unpleasant forms of death. We all want to buy time: a time to reflect, without next year's weapons programme already grinning behind our backs.

A proposal to call a moratorium on science, in a strict and literal sense, would be as unrealistic today as it was thirty years ago. It does not matter whether it is conceived as a moratorium on research, on publication, or on development, in the present system of support for science it could be imposed only by government action. And no government would agree to that in the middle of an arms race, when it is hidebound in the concept of negotiating from strength— which means by threat and counter-threat. . . .

In fact no scientist, and I hope no one who cares for the growth of knowledge, would accept a moratorium even if it were practicable. The tradition of free inquiry and publication has been essential in setting the standard of absolute truth in science: it is already eroded by secrecy in government and industry, and we need to resist any extension of that. On this ground certainly any idea of a literal stand-still in science is wrong-headed, and I do not take it seriously. But it would be shallow to find in the popular dream of a moratorium nothing more than this literal idea. There is something there that goes deeper, and that is the idea of *a voluntary agreement among scientists themselves.* For the layman sees that he will never put an end to misuse by letting governments tell scientists what to do: that leads only to the exploitation of science by those who know how to manipulate power. He sighs for a moratorium because he wants science used for good and is convinced that this can come about only by the action of scientists themselves.

If science is to express a conscience, it must come spontaneously out of the community of scientists. But of course this hope poses the crucial questions on which in the end the whole argument hinges. Is science as a discipline capable of inspiring in those who practise it a sense of communal responsibility? Can scientists be moved, as a body, to accept the moral decisions which their key position in this civilisation has thrust upon them?

These questions cut deep, and I do not think that any scientist now can sleep in peace by pushing them to the back of his mind. However, there are two distinct kinds of questions here, which engage different parts of his activity and personality. Both are questions of moral conscience. But I will distinguish the first kind by calling them questions of *humanity* and the second by calling them questions of *integrity*.

The questions of *humanity* concern the stand that a man should take in the perpetual struggle of each nation to outwit the others, chiefly in the ability to make war. Although the scientist is more often drawn into this (as a technician) than his fellow citizens, his moral dilemma is just the same as theirs: he must weigh his patriotism against his sense of a universal humanity. If there is anything special about his being a scientist, it can only be that he is more conscious than others that he belongs to an international community.

The second kind of moral questions, those of *integrity,* derive from the conditions of work which science imposes on those who pursue it. Like every form of research and scholarship—indeed, like every intellectual commitment—science is an endless search for truth, and those who devote their lives to it must accept a stringent discipline. For example, they must not be a party to hiding the truth, for any end whatever. There is no distinction between means and ends for them. Science admits no other end than the truth, and therefore it rejects all those devices of expediency by which men who seek power excuse their use of bad means for what they call good ends.

I begin with the questions of humanity. Since so much scientific and technical talent goes into advice and research on war, it is natural that the moral problem that stands largest in our minds (as it did in Leo Szilard's) is still the disavowal of war. . . .

No man who is able to see himself as others do can approve making war on civilians, and (as a consequence) using broadcast weapons—atomic bombs, napalm, orbiting missiles, and the like. Yet he also knows that every government that ordered the development of these indiscriminate weapons, anywhere in the world, did so as a duty to its own nation. This is why the man in the street wants scientists to turn away from such enterprises, or at the least to keep these dreadful secrets to themselves when they discover them. He knows that the heads of

state have no choice: each of them has been elected to protect the interests of his nation, and to be deaf and stony-hearted to the interests of humanity at large. In a world in which diplomacy still consists of national bargaining, and jockeying for positions of power, no statesman has a mandate for humanity, and therefore the man in the street turns to scientists in the desperate hope that they will act as keepers of an international conscience.

Some scientists will answer that they have a national duty, too, which is to disclose what they know to the head of state who has been elected to put it to whatever use he judges best. At a time of world war, when the survival of a nation may be at stake, most scientists will act like this; and they will have a better conscience than Klaus Fuchs, who thought himself entitled to do as he chose with scientific secrets. Even in time of peace, there will be some who will put national loyalty first. I think this is a matter of private conscience, which no man can adjudicate for another. Therefore scientists who feel that their ultimate loyalty is to their nation must be allowed to follow their conscience; and they should do so by working *directly for their government.*

But what I think is no longer tenable, in the times as they are, is the stance that Dr. Robert Oppenheimer tried to maintain, namely to be a technical adviser on weapons on some days and an international conscience on others. The rivalry of nations has now become too bitter, and the choices that it poses for the scientist too appalling, to make it possible to be involved in weapons and war policy and still to claim the right of personal judgment. And that is not merely a matter of professional independence: it comes from a deeper conflict with the morality of nationalism, government, and diplomacy.

Nationalism has now distorted the use of science so that it outrages the aspirations of the user. All over the world, from Jordan to Viet Nam, and from Nigeria to South America, men carry in their hands the most precise and expensive products of technology: automatic rifles, radar, infra-red glasses, homing rockets, and all the refined machinery of combat and terrorism.

Yet the Viet Cong sniper and the Negro infantryman on whom these gifts are heaped has them only to kill. Nothing like this has been given him at home to live with: he has no toilet there and no bath, not a stick of decent furniture and no tools, no medicines and no schooling to speak of. It is bad enough that the world is full of people who live in such misery; and it is an affront to humanity and morality that there should then be pressed upon them as the blessings of technical civilisation the beautiful instruments of murder.

It seems plain, therefore, in my analysis that unless a scientist believes as a matter of conscience that he owes it to his nation to work directly on war research, he should not accept any indirect part in it. If he chooses war research, he should work in a government department or establishment. But if he abhors the consequences of national war, he should also reject any contract, grant or project that comes to him from a military department, in any country.

This is not an easy counsel in those countries (chiefly the United States and Russia) where most research in the physical sciences, and much outside them, is financed by service and other government departments. For it does not apply only to work on weapons and strategy, but by historical momentum extends over a large area of fundamental and theoretical research.[1]

The support of science from military and allied funds has come about in a haphazard way. In the main, it grew after 1945 out of the crash methods to finance research which had been improvised during the War. . . .

This pattern of quasi-military support still persists, both in general research grants and in specific project costs and contracts, in much of the work done in physics and chemistry, for example. There is a similar pattern in the research financed by the space programme in the United States; again the theoretical and fundamental scientist finds himself at the end of a long pipeline which is not strictly military, and yet whose command of funds derives from a belief by government that the department is a useful outpost of technology as an instrument of competitive nationalism.

Because of these arrangements, it is convenient for a worker in the physical sciences to draw the money for his research, whatever it is, from one of these quasi-military pipelines. And since his university usually cannot pay for his research, and often (in the United States, for example) cannot survive without grants, he is compelled to go for help where the money is. So it comes about that physical scientists in different countries, who would not willingly work in war research, nevertheless get their funds from government departments whose main business is related to war, or which are at least sensitive to the wishes and displeasures of war departments.

It seems timely to decide now that this is a bad practice, and that grants for non-military research should not come from quasi-military sources. A scientist who accepts money from such a source cannot be blind to the subtle conformity that it imposes on his own conduct and on those who work with him, including his students. . . .

I have already said that most physicists who take money from government departments have nowhere else to go; so that if they were to refuse these grants, they would have to give up their research. This would be a hardship, but it is unlikely that it could last long. For the technical society that we live in cannot afford to let research languish, and will be forced to create

---

[1]Although I begin with the physical sciences, my theme is the dependence of all science now on government support, and I ought to give the reader some measure of that. To avoid an excess of detail, I will confine myself to two statistics: Where is basic research done, and who pays the piper there? In Soviet Russia, of course, the monopoly by government is absolute. In the United States between 1965 and 1970, 62% of the annual cost of basic research (which rose from 2.9 to 3.5 billion dollars in these years) was paid by the Federal Government, and 58% of it was done in the Universities. When research done outside the Universities is stripped from the total cost, the balance sheet becomes: 75% of the basic research done in the Universities is paid by Federal grants and contracts, and only 25% by other funds. This is for *basic research in all sciences together*. The disparity is even greater for the physical sciences alone, and for non-basic and development work.

new channels for support if the old channels are stopped up by the receivers themselves.

But it would be foolhardy to pretend that the transition period will be easy while it lasts. A deeply entrenched and politically powerful practice can be overthrown in time, but not without sacrifices meanwhile (in careers and even in scientific success) by those who take the first step in trying to break the monopoly of government patronage. Meanwhile, the longer we wait, the more deeply rooted this patronage becomes, and the harder to break.

I shall return later to the problem of creating a new organisation of support for non-military research. For the problem applies to all sciences, far beyond physics, and before I discuss it I must establish a case for detaching them also from government departments. To do so, I must move on from the inhumanity of war to the moral standing of government influence in general: that is, to the issue of scientific and intellectual *integrity*.

The traditional issue of conscience for scientists has been the use of their work to make war more terrible. But the problem that confronts us now is more fundamental and is all-embracing. Scientists can no longer confine their qualms to the uses and abuses to which their discoveries are put—to the development of weapons, or even to the larger implications of an irresponsible technology which distorts our civilisation. Instead they are face to face with a choice of conscience between two moralities: the morality of science, and the morality of national and government power.

My view is that *these two moralities are not compatible.* In world affairs, science has always been an enterprise without frontiers, and scientists as a body make up the most successful international community in the world. . . .

In domestic affairs . . . , the morality of power was laid down centuries ago by Machiavelli for *The Prince,* and is incompatible with the integrity of science. This is a more subtle and recent issue, which has grown up with the extension of government patronage to cover all branches of science.

A pervasive moral distortion, a readiness to use any means for its own ends, warps the machinery of modern government. The scientist who joins a committee becomes a prisoner of the procedures by which governments everywhere are told only what they want to hear, and tell the public only what they want to have it believe. The machine is enveloped in secrecy, which is called "security" and is used as freely to hoodwink the nation as to protect it. A great apparatus of evasion is constructed, a sort of plastic language without content, in which a pack of deliberate half-truths (and less) goes by the euphemism of "the credibility gap."

The scientist who goes into this jungle of 20th-century government, anywhere in the world, puts himself at a double disadvantage. In the first place, he does not make policy; he does not even help to make it, and most of the time he has no idea what shifts of policy his advice is meant to serve. And in the second (and oddly, for him, the more serious) place, he has no control over the way in which what he says in council will be presented to the public. I call this more serious for him, because *public respect for science is built on its intellectual integrity,* and the second-hand statements and the garbled extracts that are attributed to him bring that into disrepute.

Government is an apparatus which exercises power and which is bent on retaining it; and in the 20th century, more than ever before, it spends its time in trying to perpetuate itself by justifying itself. This cast of mind and of method is flatly at odds with the integrity of science, on which its intellectual values and its practical success alike are founded, and which consists of two parts. One is the free and total dissemination of knowledge: but since knowledge leads to power, no government is happy with that. The other is that science makes no distinction between means and ends: but since all governments believe that power is good in itself, they will use any means to that end. . . .

We live in a civilisation in which science is no longer a profession like any other. For now the hidden spring of power is knowledge; and more than this, power over our environment grows from discovery. Therefore, those whose profession is knowledge and discovery hold a place which is crucial in our societies: crucial in importance and hence in responsibility. This is true for everyone who follows an intellectual profession; in the sense that I have just described it, ours is an intellectual civilisation, and the responsibility of the scientist is, I repeat, only a particular case of the moral responsibility which every intellectual must accept. Nevertheless, it is fair to pin the responsibility most squarely on scientists, because their pursuits have for some time had the largest practical influence on our lives, and as a result have made them favoured children in the register of social importance—some would say, spoilt children. So other intellectuals have a right to ask of them, as favoured children, that they accept the moral leadership which their singular status demands. This calls both for a sensitive humanity and a selfless integrity, and it is the second of these that I am now stressing.

. . . Scientists have to renounce the creeping patronage of governments if they want to preserve the integrity of knowledge as a means and an end which thoughtful citizens (including their own students) prize in them. In my view, *there is now a duty laid on scientists to set an incorruptible standard for public morality.* The public has begun to understand that the constant march from one discovery to the next is kept going not by luck and not even by cleverness, but by something in the method of science: an unrelenting independence in the search for truth that pays no attention to received opinion, or expediency, or political advantage. We have to foster that public understanding, because in time it will work an intellectual revolution even in affairs of state. And meanwhile we as scientists have to act as guardians and as models for the public hope that somewhere there is a moral authority in man which can overcome all obstacles.

These considerations apply as much to those sciences (for example, the biological sciences) whose support comes from branches of government which have no military connections. For the moral issues that face the whole body of scientists now are no longer to be measured by the simple scale of war or peace. We see the growing involvement year by year of government in science and science in government; and unless we cut that entanglement, we endanger the integrity of all science, and undermine the public trust in it by which I set such store. The silent pressure for conformity exists whenever grants and contracts for research are under the direct control of governments; and then . . . no science is immune to the infection of politics and the corruption of power. . . .

The time has come to consider how we might bring about a separation, as complete as possible, between Science and Government in all countries. I call this the *disestablishment of science,* in the same sense in which the churches have been disestablished and have become independent of the state. It may be that disestablishment can be brought about only by the example of some outstanding scientists—as the great Kapitza refused the directions of Stalin in Russia, and Max von Laue refused to work for Hitler in Germany. But the immediate need is more practical. It is to have all scientists consider the form that disestablishment should take, and for which they would be willing to make common cause.

Evidently *the choice of priorities in research should not be left in the hands of governments.* This is a view that government departments will not like, so that scientists who hold it will need to be single-minded if they are to make it heard. They may have to refuse to apply for grants and contracts that are allocated directly by departments. Again, this would be a hardship for many scientists, who now have nowhere else to go for money and who would be forced to suspend their research. But they must be willing to face the hardship for a time if they are serious and united in the will to put science into the hands of scientists.

In the long run, the aim should be to get a single and overall fund or grant for research, to be divided by all the scientists in a country. This would be an effective form of disestablishment, and no doubt governments would accept it rather than watch research become moribund. . . .

Once there is a single grant for all research together, its division becomes the business of scientists themselves. They have plenty of practice now in sitting on panels that grade the applicants for the money assigned to each small section of a scientific topic. But in the future they will have to undertake to weigh section against section, topic against topic, field against field, and (at the top of this pyramid) each branch of science against the rest. This is a communal responsibility, and must be shared with the community by a form of representation which will have to be devised for the purpose. What is clear is that the representation must be direct, and specific to the joint social and scientific need; it must not be under the influence of government departments, for whom scientific priorities are simply an instrument of policy.

The disestablishment of science will compel the body of scientists to assign its own priorities on behalf of the community and with it, and divide the overall grant at its disposal accordingly. . . . The method is practical, and can be developed from known procedures.

So far, I have proposed two steps in the disestablishment of science: first, refusal to accept grants or contracts or projects directly from government agencies, and second, demand for a single national grant which is then to be allocated by the scientific community itself. There remains a third step in the more distant future, and yet it is the crucial step: the allocation of research as a single *international* undertaking.

The public in every nation in the world is looking for an international conscience—that is the point from which I began this article, and on which it hinges. For it knows that nationalism is an anachronism, and a dying form of civilisation. So the public everywhere looks to scientists to find a practical way to express the sense of international duty and decency which is so plainly waiting over the horizon. The reason for this trust is precisely that science is recognised as an international fellowship: international in its principles, and international as a body of men. . . .

It would be nice to believe that the computation of priorities in this way requires nothing more than scientific competence aided by social passion. But alas, even the disestablishment of science cannot make life so simple. There is no judgment of the importance of a field or a line of research that can be confined to its scientific potential. Every judgment in life contains a silent estimate of human and social values too, and the representatives of science will not be able to shirk that. There is no guarantee that scientists will make a better job of fitting science to humanity than has been done so far; but it is time that they faced their moral obligations and tried.

BARRY COMMONER

The dual crisis in science and society

Our present achievements in science and technology appear to contrast vividly with our present lack of achievement in solving social problems. We can nourish a man in the supreme isolation of outer space—but we cannot adequately feed the children of Calcutta or Harlem. We hope to analyze life on other planets—but we have not yet learned to understand our own neighbors. We are attempting to live on the moon—but we cannot yet live peacefully on our own planet.

The usual explanation of this frightening paradox is that we are competent in the realm of science because no value judgments are demanded and that we are tragically incompetent in dealing with each other because this requires adjustment between personal values and the social good—a capacity that frequently eludes us.

I should like to propose another explanation—that the contrast between our technological competence and our ethical ineptitude is only apparent. We are tragically blind, I believe, not only about our fellow-men but also about important aspects of nature; we are dangerously incompetent in our relations to the natural world as well as in our relations to each other.

Our society is threatened not only by a growing social crisis but also by a technological crisis. In our eager search for the benefits of modern science and technology, we have blundered unwittingly into serious hazards:

We used to be told that nuclear testing was perfectly harmless. Only now, long after the damage has been done, do we know differently.

We produced power plants and automobiles that enveloped our cities in smog—before anyone understood its harmful effects on health.

We synthesized and disseminated new insecticides—before anyone learned that they also kill birds and might be harmful to people.

We produced detergents and put billions of pounds of them into our surface waters—before we realized that they would pollute our water supplies because they do not break down in our disposal systems. . . .

We are fully prepared to conduct a nuclear war—even though we do not know whether its vast effects on life, on soil, and on the weather will destroy our civilization.

Clearly, we have compiled a record of serious failures in recent encounters with the environment. This record shows that we have thus far failed to understand the environment well enough to make new large-scale intrusions on it with a reasonable expectation of accurately predicting the consequences.

This failure raises two important questions about the relation between science and technology and human values. What are the relative roles of science and human desires in the resolution of the important issues generated by our failures in the environment? What are the causes of these failures, and how do they illuminate the dual crisis in technology and human affairs? How can we resolve the grave public issues that have been generated by our new assaults on the integrity of the environment?

Sometimes it is suggested that since scientists and engineers have made the bombs, insecticides, and autos, they ought to be responsible for deciding how to deal with the resultant hazards.

More cogently, it is argued that scientists and technologists are uniquely competent to resolve these issues because they are in possession of the relevant technical facts that are essential to an understanding of the major public issues generated by new technology. . . .

In my view, this argument has a basic flaw—the resolution of every social issue imposed on us by modern scientific progress can be shown to require a decision based on *value judgments* rather than on objective scientific laws.

What scientific procedure can determine, for example, whether the benefits to the national interest of nuclear testing outweigh the hazards of fallout? How can scientific method determine whether the proponents of urban superhighways or those who complain about the resultant smog are in the right? What scientific principle can tell us how to make the choice—which may be forced upon us by the insecticide problem—between the shade of the elm tree and the song of the robin?

Certainly, science can validly describe the hard facts about these issues. But the choice of the balance point between benefit and hazard is a value judgment; it is based on ideals of social good or morality or religion—not on science. And if this choice is a social and moral judgment, it ought to be made, not by scientists and technologists alone, but by all citizens.

How can a citizen make such judgments? Deciding these issues requires a confrontation between human values and rather complex scientific data that most citizens are poorly prepared to understand.

The solution demands a new duty of scientists. As the custodians of the technical knowledge relevant to these public issues, scientists have an obligation to bring this information before their fellow citizens in understandable terms.

But first, scientists themselves must determine the causes of our recent failures in the environment and learn from such a determination about the relationship between science and technology and human values. If we are to succeed as inhabitants of a world increasingly transformed by technology, we need to undertake a searching reassessment of our attitudes toward the natural world and the technology that intrudes on it. . . .

It is not a coincidence, I believe, that the scientific and technological problems affecting the human condition involve inherently complex systems. Life, as we live it, is rarely encompassed by a single academic discipline. Real problems that touch our lives and impinge on what we value rarely fit into the neat categories of the college catalog: medieval history, nuclear physics, molecular biology.

For example, to encompass in our minds the terrifying deterioration of our cities we need to know not only the principles of economics, architecture, and social planning, but also the chemistry of air quality areas, the biology of water systems, and the ecology of the domestic rat and the cockroach. In a word, we need to understand science and technology that are relevant to the human condition.

However, we, in the university community, have been brought up in a different tradition. We have a justified pride in our intellectual independence and know—for we often have to battle to maintain it—how essential this independence is to the search for truth. But academic people may sometimes tend to translate intellectual independence into a kind of mandatory disinterest in all problems that do not arise in their own minds—an approach that may in some cases cut them off from their students and from the real and urgent needs of society.

I believe we university scientists have a clear obligation to the society that supports us. We have no right to retreat behind the walls of our laboratories; instead, we must use our knowledge to help improve the world.

If we accept this obligation, how can we make it jibe with the principle of academic freedom, which holds that every scholar should be free to pursue the studies that interest him and free to express whatever conclusions the evidence and the powers of his mind may generate?

There is no simple answer to this question, but Alexander Meiklejohn,* who contributed much to the making of the modern American university, gave us a useful guide. According to Meiklejohn, academic freedom is not a special immunity from social responsibility but, on the contrary, a basic part of the duty that the university and the scholar owe to society.

The university, he believed, is an institution established by society to fill its own need for knowledge about the nature of the world and man. The scholar's search for the truth is thus not merely an obligation to himself, to his profession, or to the university, but to society. And in this search, open and unconstrained discourse is essential, for no scholar's work is complete or faultless.

Our duty, then, is not to truth for its own sake, but to truth for society's sake. In Meiklejohn's words: "Our final responsibility as scholars and teachers is not to the truth. It is to the people who need the truth." Hence, the scholar's duty inevitably becomes coupled with social issues. The scholar will become concerned not only with social needs, but with social goals as well. And if society expects the scholar to honor a duty toward the development of socially significant knowledge, society must equally honor his freedom openly to express a concern with social goals. Those whom we serve should see in our zeal for this freedom not the selfish exercise of privilege, but a response to these solemn obligations.

---

*Ed. note: Meiklejohn (1872–1964) was president of Amherst College from 1912–1924 and director of the Experimental College at the University of Wisconsin from 1927 to 1932. His books include *The Liberal College* and *Education Between Two Worlds*.

Deciphering the Genetic Code. *Nobel Prize-winner Maurice H. F. Wilkins studies model of DNA molecular structure, responsible for hereditary traits, in 1962. It is now possible deliberately to manipulate genes and thus produce new forms of life.*

12

SCIENCE
AND MORALS:
THE ETHICS
OF BIOMEDICAL
RESEARCH

The purpose of this chapter is to examine specific moral issues that have arisen with respect to biological research and medical practice. In the first half of the twentieth century, the science with the most revolutionary discoveries was physics; in the second half it promises to be biology. The changing of one's sex, and the transplantation of organs and the implantation of artificial ones, are just the beginnings of this revolution: Biology now has within its view the creation of human life in a test tube, the cloning or reproduction of a genetic code that would make possible the creation of identical human beings, and the power of genetic engineering (discussed to some extent in the previous chapter), in which the genetic code of a fetus could be altered at will.

To ponder the implications of these developments, a new field has arisen, biomedical ethics, or bioethics, for short. Most of the work within bioethics, however, has been devoted less to extraordinary problems, such as whether life should be created, than to problems faced everyday in biological research and medical practice. Two such problems will be discussed in the following excerpts: Under what conditions can human beings be used as the subjects of experiments, as human "guinea pigs"? and who has the final authority to decide upon medical treatment—the doctor, the patient, or the state?

In the first question, the rights of the individual are opposed to the benefits that might accrue to society from scientific research. As Hans Jonas points out in the opening article, at some time or other, the biological experiment must be performed on the human being. Jonas argues that human experimentation is inherently degrading, making the subject "a passive thing . . . His being is reduced to that of a mere token or 'sample.'" The only element that would make valid this reduction of being is "such authentic identification with the cause that it is the subject's as well as the researcher's cause—whereby his role in its service is not just permitted by him, but willed." Jonas then criticizes the new medical definition of death because it is being used as a pretext for maintaining the patients' organs in optimal state for transplantation. He believes "that no less than the maximum definition of death will do—brain death plus heart death plus any other indication that may be pertinent."

The next two selections deal further with the issue of human experimentation. In the first of these, William Curran reports on the Tuskegee Syphilis Study in which, beginning in 1932, a group of black men in the South were given syphilis and left untreated so that doctors could study the later stages of the disease. Studies such as this raise difficult problems about the morality of withholding medicine from a "control" group if there is any chance that the medicine could benefit the patient. The difficulty of weighing possible risks to the patient against medical progress is apparent in the next selection, a questionnaire submitted to investigators and administrators in a representative sample of research centers around the country by Bernard Barber and a research group on human experimentation. The questionnaire describes a hypothetical experiment on human beings; respondents were asked to indicate under which conditions they would approve such an experiment. The results of the survey showed that 54 percent were against doing this experiment at all, but 14 percent would have approved it even if the chances were only one in ten that a significant medical discovery might result.

The mere rise of a biomedical ethics signifies that the traditional manner of practicing medicine is felt to be in some way inadequate to cope with situations that confront doctors daily. Now, for instance, the supreme value that medicine since Hippocrates has always placed on life has been challenged by notions such as "death with dignity" and "the right to die," as exemplified in the case of Karen Ann Quinlan. A second change has occurred in doctor-patient relations: Previously doctors were expected to take full responsibility for their treatment, whereas today patients demand a greater role in deciding their treatment. These issues are discussed in the next

252

two selections. In the Quinlan case, the patient was comatose and obviously unable to make a decision for herself. Under these circumstances, who has the right to decide whether life-sustaining apparatus should be withdrawn and the patient allowed to die? Thomas Oden supports the decision of the lower court, which ruled that the parents do not have this right against the announced desire of the doctors to maintain the patient's life. According to Oden, there is no recognized "right to die," and "the instinct of the court in this case is more profound morally than the majority formal opinion: wherever human life exists, even in defective forms, it is to receive the protection of the state on a nonselective basis." The ruling of the lower court was, however, overturned by the New Jersey Supreme Court. Excerpts from this decision, arguing that the "right to die" is inherent in the right to privacy, constitute the next selection.

There follows excerpts from the California Natural Death Act, the first such state statute passed in the United States, signed into law on September 30, 1976. This act explicitly recognizes the right of a patient to die with dignity and to direct that life-supporting measures be halted when the patient deems life no longer worth living. Other provisions of the act, not reprinted here, are designed as safeguards to the patient and to the doctors and attendants, who are relieved of criminal and civil culpability in executing such a directive.

Jack Provonsha discusses other questions of life and death raised by the new technology. He suggests that "what is missing, in short, is a guiding norm, or value ideal, in relation to which the terms like right and wrong are meaningful." He argues that "moral rules serve the purpose of keeping human life human." It therefore makes no sense, in his view, to waste resources on prolonging life when life is meaningless.

The issue of what makes human life human is also raised in a consideration of the control of our genetic future, the subject of the final two selections in this chapter. Hermann Muller, one of the early, leading spokesmen for positive eugenics, argues that parents should help determine the genetic makeup of their offspring by selecting sperm from outstanding individuals that would be stored in a sperm bank. Such a process of germinal choice would express a "higher form of morality than that now prevalent." Hans Jonas takes issue not only with Muller's proposal, but with other proposals such as cloning and genetic engineering in which new life would be created. He asks what can the goals of genetic engineering be. The only answer he sees is a "supposed utility value of the products for the collective business of the group." He believes this utilitarian conception shall destroy the significance of humanity; it will "leave no one recognized as an end in himself."

NOTES ABOUT THE AUTHORS

Hans Jonas is Alvin Johnson Professor of Philosophy at the New School for Social Research in New York, where he joined the graduate faculty in 1956. He was born and educated in Germany. His books include the *Gnostic Religion* and *The Phenomenon of Life: Toward a Philosophical Biology*. "Philosophical Reflections on Experimenting with Human Subjects" first appeared in *Daedalus* in 1969; "Biological Engineering—a Preview" was published in his *Philosophical Essays* in 1974.

William J. Curran, born in 1940, is Frances Glessner Lee Professor of Legal Medicine at Harvard. "The Tuskegee Syphilis Study," reprinted here, first appeared in the *New England Journal of Medicine* in 1973.

Bernard Barber has been a member of the faculty of the sociology department at Barnard College since 1952 and department chairman since 1968. He is the author of *Science and Social Order, Social Stratification,* and *Drugs and Society.* The questionnaire reproduced in this volume was part of a national survey of 300 research facilities to determine whether human experimentation was being conducted under adequate safeguards for the subjects.

Thomas C. Oden is professor of theology and ethics at the Theological School of Drew University. "Beyond an Ethic of Immediate Sympathy" was one of five commentaries on the Karen Ann Quinlan case to appear in the February 1976 issue of *The Hastings Center Report.* The case concerned a twenty-one-year-old woman who had been in a coma for months and had suffered irreversible brain damage. Her parents sought the court's permission to withdraw the respirator that they believed was keeping her alive. On November 10, 1975, Judge Robert Muir of the Morris County, New Jersey Superior Court denied the parents' request.

The New Jersey Supreme Court is the highest court in the state of New Jersey. It heard the Quinlan case on appeal and on March 31, 1976 handed down a fifty-nine-page opinion upholding the "right to die" as part of the right of privacy.

The California Natural Death Act was introduced into the California Assembly as Bill No. 3060 in February 1976. Seven months later, after amendment by the California Senate, it was signed into law by Governor Brown. The bill was the first in the country to provide a procedure whereby a patient could provide in advance for the withdrawal of medical care in the event of a terminal illness.

Jack W. Provonsha is both a practicing physician and professor of the philosophy of religion and Christian ethics at Loma Linda University. A Seventh Day Adventist, he has a special interest in morals in medicine. He is the author of *God Is with Us.* "Keeping Human Life Human," reprinted here, was first published in *Spectrum* in 1974.

Hermann J. Muller, born in 1890, was an American geneticist who taught at the University of Texas and the University of Indiana as well as at the U.S.S.R. Institute of Genetics and the University of Edinburgh. In 1946 he was awarded the Nobel Prize for medicine for his work on the artificial transmutation of genes by X-rays. For more than forty years he advocated improving the human gene pool through germinal choice. He died in 1967.

253

HANS JONAS

Philosophical reflections on experimenting with human subjects

Experimentation was originally sanctioned by natural science. There it is performed on inanimate objects, and this raises no moral problems. But as soon as animate, feeling beings become the subjects of experiment, as they do in the life sciences and especially in medical research, this innocence of the search for knowledge is last and questions of conscience arise. The depth to which moral and religious sensibilities can become aroused is shown by the vivisection issue. Human experimentation must sharpen the issue as it involves ultimate questions of personal dignity and sacrosanctity. One difference between the human experiments and the physical is this: The physical experiment employs small-scale, artificially devised substitutes for that about which knowledge is to be obtained, and the experimenter extrapolates from these models and simulated conditions to nature at large. Something deputizes for the "real thing"—balls rolling down an inclined plane for sun and planets, electric discharges from a condenser for real lightning, and so on. For the most part, no such substitution is possible in the biological sphere. We must operate on the original itself, the real thing in the fullest sense, and perhaps affect it irreversibly. No simulacrum can take its place. Especially in the human sphere, experimentation loses entirely the advantage of the clear division between vicarious model and true object. Up to a point, animals may fulfill the proxy role of the classical physical experiment. But in the end man himself must furnish knowledge about himself, and the comfortable separation of noncommittal experiment and definitive action vanishes. An experiment in education affects the lives of its subjects, perhaps a whole generation of schoolchildren. Human experimentation for whatever purpose is always

also a responsible, nonexperimental, definitive dealing with the subject himself. And not even the noblest purpose abrogates the obligations this involves. . . .

"Identification" as the principle of recruitment in general

What is wrong with making a person an experimental subject is not so much that we make him thereby a means (which happens in social contexts of all kinds), as that we make him a thing—a passive thing merely to be acted on, and passive not even for real action, but for token action whose token object he is. His being is reduced to that of a mere token or "sample." This is different from even the most exploitative situations of social life; there the business is real, not fictitious. The subject, however much abused, remains an agent and thus a "subject" in the other sense of the word. The soldier's case . . . is instructive: Subject to most unilateral discipline, forced to risk mutilation and death, conscripted without, perhaps against, his will—he is still conscripted with his capacities to act, to hold his own or fail in situations, to meet real challenges for real stakes. Though a mere "number" to the High Command, he is not a token and not a thing. (Imagine what he would say if it turned out that the war was a game staged to sample observations on his endurance, courage, or cowardice.)

These compensations of personhood are denied to the subject of experimentation, who is acted upon for an extraneous end without being engaged in a real relation where he would be the counterpoint to the other or to circumstance. Mere "consent" (mostly amounting to no more than permission) does not right this reification. The "wrong" of it can only be made "right" by such authentic identification with the cause that it is the subject's as well as the researcher's cause—whereby his role in its service is not just permitted by him, but *willed*. That sovereign will of his which embraces the end as his own restores his personhood to the otherwise depersonalizing context. To be valid it must be autonomous and informed. The latter condition can, outside the research community, only be fulfilled by degrees; but the higher the degree of the understanding regarding the purpose and the technique, the more valid becomes the endorsement of the will. A margin of mere trust inevitably remains. Ultimately, the appeal for volunteers should seek this free and generous endorsement, the appropriation of the research purpose into the person's own scheme of ends. Thus, the appeal is in truth addressed to the one, mysterious, and sacred source of any such generosity of the will—"devotion," whose forms and objects of commitment are various and may invest different motivations in different individuals. The following, for instance, may be responsive to the "call" we are discussing: compassion with human suffering, zeal for humanity, reverence for the Golden Rule, enthusiasm for progress, homage to the cause of knowledge, even longing for sacrificial justification (do not call that "masochism," please). On all these, I say, it is defensible and right to draw when the research objective is worthy enough; and it is a prime duty of the research community (especially in view of what we called the "margin of trust") to see that this sacred source is never abused for frivolous ends. For a less than adequate cause, not even the freest, unsolicited offer should be accepted.

The rule of the "descending order" and its counter-utility sense

We have laid down what must seem to be a forbidding rule. Having faith in the transcendent potential of man, I do not fear that the "source" will ever fail a society that does not destroy it—and only such a one is worthy of the blessings of progress. But "elitistic" the rule is (as is the enterprise of progress itself), and elites are by nature small. The combined attribute of motivation and information, plus the absence of external pressures, tends to be socially so circumscribed that strict adherence to the rule might numerically starve the research process. This is why I [speak] . . . of a descending order of permissibility, which is itself permissive, but where the realization that it is a *descending* order is not without pragmatic import. Departing from the august norm, the appeal must needs

shift from idealism to docility, from high-mindedness to compliance, from judgment to trust. Consent spreads over the whole spectrum. . . . I merely indicate the principle of the order of preference: The poorer in knowledge, motivation, and freedom of decision (and that, alas, means the more readily available in terms of numbers and possible manipulation), the more sparingly and indeed reluctantly should the reservoir be used, and the more compelling must therefore become the countervailing justification.

Let us note that this is the opposite of a social utility standard, the reverse of the order by "availability and expendability": The most valuable and scarcest, the least expendable elements of the social organism, are to be the first candidates for risk and sacrifice. It is the standard of *noblesse oblige;* and with all its counter-utility and seeming "wastefulness," we feel a rightness about it and perhaps even a higher "utility," for the soul of the community lives by this spirit. It is also the opposite of what the day-to-day interests of research clamor for, and for the scientific community to honor it will mean that it will have to fight a strong temptation to go by routine to the readiest sources of supply—the suggestible, the ignorant, the dependent, the "captive" in various senses. I do not believe that heightened resistance here must cripple research, which cannot be permitted; but it may slow it down by the smaller numbers fed into experimentation in consequence. This price— a possibly slower rate of progress—may have to be paid for the preservation of the most precious capital of higher communal life.

Experimentation on patients

So far we have been speaking on the tacit assumption that the subjects of experimentation are recruited from among the healthy. To the question "Who is conscriptable?" the spontaneous answer is: Least and last of all the sick—the most available source as they are under treatment and observation anyway. That the afflicted should not be called upon to bear additional burden and risk, that they are society's special trust and the physician's particular trust—these are elementary responses of our moral sense. Yet the very destination of medical research, the conquest of disease, requires at the crucial stage trial and verification on precisely the sufferers from the disease, and their total exemption would defeat the purpose itself. In acknowledging this inescapable necessity, we enter the most sensitive area of the whole complex, the one most keenly felt and most searchingly discussed by the practitioners themselves. This issue touches the heart of the doctor-patient relation, putting its most solemn obligations to the test. Some of the oldest verities of this area should be recalled.

The fundamental privilege of the sick

In the course of treatment, the physician is obligated to the patient and to no one else. He is not the agent of society, nor of the interests of medical science, the patient's family, the patient's co-sufferers, or future sufferers from the same disease. The patient alone counts when he is under the physician's care. . . .

Nondisclosure as a borderline case

Then there is the case where ignorance of the subject, sometimes even of the experimenter, is of the essence of the experiment (the "double blind"-control group-placebo syndrome). It is said to be a necessary element of the scientific process. Whatever may be said about its ethics in regard to normal subjects, especially volunteers, it is an outright betrayal of trust in regard to the patient who believes that he is receiving treatment. Only supreme importance of the objective can exonerate it, without making it less of a transgression. The patient is definitely wronged even when not harmed. . . .

On the redefinition of death

My other emphatic verdict concerns the question of the redefinition of death—acknowledging "irreversible coma as a new definition for death." I wish not to be misunderstood. As long as it is merely a question of when it is permitted to cease the artificial prolongation of certain functions (like heartbeat) traditionally regarded as signs of life, I do not see anything ominous

in the notion of "brain death." Indeed, a new definition of death is not even necessary to legitimize the same result if one adopts the position of the Roman Catholic Church, which here for once is eminently reasonable—namely that "when deep unconsciousness is judged to be permanent, extraordinary means to maintain life are not obligatory. They can be terminated and the patient allowed to die." Given a clearly defined negative condition of the brain, the physician is allowed to allow the patient to die his own death by *any* definition, which of itself will lead through the gamut of all possible definitions. But a disquietingly contradictory purpose is combined with this purpose in the quest for a new definition of death, in the will to *advance* the moment of declaring him dead: Permission not to turn off the respirator, but, on the contrary, to keep it on and thereby maintain the body in a state of what would have been "life" by the older definition (but is only a "simulacrum" of life by the new)—so as to get at his organs and tissues under the ideal conditions of what would previously have been "vivisection."

Now this, whether done for research or transplant purposes, seems to me to overstep what the definition can warrant. Surely it is one thing when to cease delaying death, but another when to start doing violence to the body; one thing when to desist from protracting the process of dying, but another when to regard that process as complete and thereby the body as a cadaver free for inflicting on it what would be torture and death to any living body. For the first purpose, we need not know the exact borderline with absolute certainty between life and death— we leave it to nature to cross it wherever it is, or to traverse the whole spectrum if there is not just one line. All we need to know is that coma is irreversible. For the second purpose we must know the borderline; and to use any definition short of the maximal for perpetrating on a *possibly* penultimate state what only the ultimate state can permit is to arrogate a knowledge which, I think, we cannot possibly have. *Since we do not know the exact borderline between life and death,* nothing less than the maximum definition of death will do—brain death plus heart death plus any other indication that may be pertinent—before final violence is allowed to be done.

It would follow then, for this layman at least, that the use of the definition should itself be defined, and this in a restrictive sense. When only permanent coma can be gained with the artificial sustaining of functions, by all means turn off the respirator, the stimulator, any sustaining artifice, and let the patient die; but let him die all the way. Do not, instead, arrest the process and start using him as a mine while, with your own help and cunning, he is still kept this side of what may in truth be the final line. Who is to say that a shock, a final trauma, is not administered to a sensitivity diffusely situated elsewhere than in the brain and still vulnerable to suffering? a sensitivity that we ourselves have been keeping alive? No fiat of definition can settle this question. But I wish to emphasize that the question of possible suffering (easily brushed aside by a sufficient show of reassuring expert consensus) is merely a subsidiary and not the real point of my argument; this, to reiterate, turns on the indeterminacy of the boundaries between *life and death,* not between sensitivity and insensitivity, and bids us to lean toward a maximal rather than a minimal determination of death in an area of basic uncertainty.

There is also this to consider: The patient must be absolutely sure that his doctor does not become his executioner, and that no definition authorizes him ever to become one. His right to this certainty is absolute, and so is his right to his own body with all its organs. Absolute respect for these rights violates no one else's rights, for no one has a right to another's body. Speaking in still another, religious vein: The expiring moments should be watched over with piety and be safe from exploitation. . . .

Let me only say in conclusion that if some of the practical implications of my reasonings are felt to work out toward a slower rate of progress, this should not cause too great dismay. Let us not forget that progress is an optional goal, not an unconditional commitment, and that its tempo in particular, compulsive as it may become, has nothing sacred about it. Let us also remember that a slower progress in the conquest of disease would not threaten society, grievous as it is to those who have to deplore that their particular disease be not yet conquered, but that society would indeed be threatened by the erosion of those moral values whose loss, possibly caused by too ruthless a pursuit of scientific progress, would make its most dazzling triumphs not worth having. Let us finally remember that it cannot be the aim of progress to abolish the lot of mortality. Of some ill or other, each of us will die. Our mortal condition is upon us with its harshness but also its wisdom—because without it there would not be the eternally renewed promise of the freshness, immediacy, and eagerness of youth; nor, without it, would there be for any of us the incentive to number our days and make them count. With all our striving to wrest from our mortality what we can, we should bear its burden with patience and dignity.

WILLIAM J. CURRAN

The Tuskegee syphilis study

A great deal of publicity was given in late 1971 and early 1972 to reports of unethical practices in a long-term study of so-called untreated syphilis in a group of black men in six southern states. It was alleged that a United States Public Health Service study, also perhaps supported by certain foundations, had withheld effective treatment from these men and that many had died as a result. A cover story on human experimentation in *Medical World News* referred to subjects in the study as "victims" of the Tuskegee affair.

In 1972 an ad hoc advisory panel was formed to investigate the matter and to make recommendations to the Assistant Secretary for Health at the Department of Health, Education, and Welfare. The panel, with representation from medicine, law, religion, labor, education, health administration, and public affairs, held a series of meetings during 1972 and early 1973 and recently issued a report.

The report, with the abstention of the chairman, strongly criticizes the project. It was the conclusion of the group that the study was ethically unjustified even at its start in 1932. The finding of improper ethical conduct was made primarily on the basis of the failure to inform the subjects of the risks in joining the study and to gain their free and voluntary consent to being involved. Also, it was found that the study lacked a written protocol, lacked validity and reliability assurances, had questionable database validity, and had an overall experimental design of questionable value for such a long-term study.

When it came to evaluating the consequences in withholding penicillin from the "untreated" group, the majority were again forceful in concluding that the withholding was unethical. It was found that the subjects were not given any "choice" about continuing in the study once penicillin had become readily available.

After making these findings, the report proceeds to a further part of its charge, that referring to whether the study should be discontinued, and, if so, how the rights and health needs of subjects could be protected. The ad hoc panel recommended that the study be terminated immediately. It was further suggested that a select specialists' group be formed to protect the subjects, to assess their current health status, and to arrange for their treatment and care, if the subjects so desired. In an addendum to this portion of the report, Dr. Jay Katz, of Yale Law School, asserted that an additional reason for termination should have been listed: that it was his belief that the panel had been informed that "no scientific knowledge of any consequence would be derived from its continuance." Dr. Katz raised the very cogent question of why, if there was no scientific merit in the study, it had not been terminated sooner, before the appointment of the panel.

BERNARD BARBER

The ethics of experimentation with human subjects

A researcher plans to study bone metabolism in children suffering from a serious bone disease. He intends to determine the degree of appropriation of calcium into the bone by using radioactive calcium. In order to make an adequate comparison, he intends to use some healthy children as controls, and he plans to obtain the consent of the parents of both groups of children after explaining to them the nature and purposes of the investigation and the short and long-term risks to their children. Evidence from animals and earlier studies in humans indicates that the size of the radioactive dose to be administered here would only very slightly (say, by 5–10 chances in a million) increase the probability of the subjects involved contracting leukemia or experiencing other problems in the long run. While there are no definitive data as yet on the incidence of leukemia in the children, a number of doctors and statistical sources indicate that the rate is about 250/million in persons under 18 years of age. Assume for the purpose of this question that the incidence of the bone disease being discussed is about the same as that for leukemia in children under 18 years of age. The investigation, if successful, would add greatly to medical knowledge regarding this particular bone disease, but the administration of the radioactive calcium would not be of immediate therapeutic benefit for either group of children. The results of the investigation may, however, eventually benefit the group of children suffering from the bone disease. Please assume for the purposes of this question that there is no other method that would produce the data the researcher desires. The researcher is known to be highly competent in this area.

A. Hypothetically assuming that you constitute an institutional review "committee of one," and that the proposed investigation has never been done before, please check the *lowest* probability that *you* would consider acceptable for *your* approval of the proposed investigation. (Check only *one*)

( ) 1. If the chances are 1 in 10 that the investigation will lead to an important medical discovery.

( ) 2. If the chances are 3 in 10 that the investigation will lead to an important medical discovery.

( ) 3. If the chances are 5 in 10 that the investigation will lead to an important medical discovery.

( ) 4. If the chances are 7 in 10 that the investigation will lead to an important medical discovery.

( ) 5. If the chances are 9 in 10 that the investigation will lead to an important medical discovery.

( ) 6. Place a check here if you feel that, as the proposal stands, the researcher should not attempt the investigation, no matter what the probability that an important medical discovery will result. (*IF YOU CHECKED HERE,* please explain): _____

_____

B. Which of the above responses comes closest to what you feel the *existing institutional review committee* in your institution would make? ____ (Please write in the number of the response.)

C. Which of the above responses comes closest to what you feel the *majority of the researchers* in your institution would make, acting in their role as researcher rather than as a "committee of one"? ____ (Please write in the number of the response.)

_____

THOMAS C. ODEN

The Quinlan decision: Beyond an ethic of immediate sympathy

Joseph Quinlan requested that the court grant him "the expressed power of authorizing the discontinuance of all extraordinary means of sustaining the vital processes of his daughter Karen Ann Quinlan." A myriad of problems confronted Judge Robert Muir's Superior Court in Morristown, New Jersey, in the attempt to respond mercifully to this distressed family. . . .

While the media focused on the immediate agony of the family, the court properly focused on the complex facts and the substantive questions of law in the case, and to its credit did not fall victim to the old maxim, "hard cases make bad law." . . . Among Judge Muir's key findings:

1. "The judicial power to act in the incompetent's best interest in this instance selects continued life and to do so is not violative of a constitutional right."
2. "There *is* a duty to continue the life assisting apparatus, if within the treating physician's opinion, it should be done."
3. "There is no constitutional right to die that can be asserted by a parent for his incompetent adult child."
4. "Continuation of medical treatment, in whatever form, where its goal is the sustenance of life is not something degrading, arbitrarily inflicted, unacceptable to contemporary society or unnecessary."
5. "The Court does not consider the 'extraordinary' versus 'ordinary' discussion viable legal distinctions."
6. "Humanitarian motives cannot justify the taking of a human life."
7. "The fact that the victim is on the threshold of death or in terminal condition is no defense to a homicide charge."
8. "A patient is placed, or places himself, in the care of a physician with the expectation that

he (the physician) will do everything in his power, everything that is known to modern medicine, to protect the patient's life. He will do all within his human power to favor life against death.''

9. "The precedential effect on future litigation" of granting the Quinlan's request "would be legally detrimental."

Muir's judgment, if upheld, delivers a stunning blow to most of the key contentions of "right to die" proponents: that there is a constitutionally grounded right to die; that the court can and should establish "quality of life" criteria that would sanction treatment termination intentionally leading to death; that equal protection of nonsapient life is not a compelling interest of the court; that euthanasia belongs to the right of self-determination.

The withholding of life-sustaining treatment in irreversible cases (sometimes called "judicious neglect") may be appropriate where death is imminent with terrible pain, and where patient consent is unequivocally established. None of these three conditions was present in the Quinlan case.

When a case is taken out of the sphere of confidentiality (which "judicious neglect" absolutely requires), and placed before a court of equity requesting an anticipatory sanction of a deliberate action leading to a person's death, what do we learn? We learn that the court may limit options that otherwise might have been considered under the conditions of trustful confidentiality.

With heavy laden precedential consequence, the court cannot afford to send a signal to society that would indicate any slackness in its determination to protect innocent life equally and nonselectively. Since all parties agreed that Karen Quinlan is alive by all accepted medical and legal definitions, the court could do no other than see to it that she is protected, unless it wished to go against a heavy tradition of case law on the constitutional right to equal protection of life under law.

Harsh as this may sound to those who are concerned more with immediate sympathetic relief for an anguished family than with the hazardous potential consequences of such a merciful action for thousands of defenseless incompetents in the future, the deeper instincts of the law were right in this case. For if legal guardians are allowed to judge the worth and viability of human life, then we should not be surprised to see many "mercy killings" of newborn defectives, retardates, genetically handicapped, senile and feeble-minded persons whose lives could end under liberalized involuntary euthanasia rulings.

There is no responsibility more essential to the state than the protection of life, equally and nonselectively. Preservation of life is an elementary reason for government, as the Preamble to the U.S. Constitution clearly states.

Who is to decide what quality of life warrants its discontinuance? Where is the line to be drawn? Some have suggested "capacity for social relations," or "useful life," or "meaningful existence" as possible criteria. We have good reason to distrust all such definitions, each of which would open the gate for countless living persons to whom the state owes equal protection to be potential candidates for involuntary euthanasia, persons who by someone's definition are said to have a relatively low quality of life.

Unfortunately, the majority opinion of American moral commentators hastily threw their weight on the side of granting the request. This was predictable, since American bioethical reflection has too long functioned with a constricted and normless situation ethic (which too often amounts to an ethic of sentimental immediacy coupled with outraged self-righteousness). What popular American moral judgment has not learned to do is to reflect carefully beyond an ethic of immediate sympathy to an ethic of consequences and obligation.

The instinct of the court in this case is more profound morally than the majority moral opinion: wherever human life exists, even in defective forms, and perhaps especially in its defective forms, it is to receive the protection of the state on a nonselective basis.

Is the "right to die" included under the "right to privacy"? This connection is made only by the most remote applications of precedents, such as the Griswold case (1965), which rested on the absence of a compelling state interest in the distribution of contraceptives. In the Quinlan and other terminal-illness cases involving incompetents, we have a compelling state interest, the preservation of life.

American courts have never agreed with the theories of a few commentators that a right to die can be derived from the Ninth Amendment. The right to life is explicitly stated in the Fifth and Fourteenth Amendments. So it is hardly surprising that there are no constitutional guarantees arguing for a right to die, either in the case of suicide or euthanasia. In fact, if the state had failed to defend a comatose patient from an action deliberately intending to cause death, relatives or advocates for a dead Karen Quinlan could have asked for redress from the state for its failure to supply equal protection to her under law.

Does a court of equity have jurisdiction in effect to render a death sentence without a jury? It is doubtful. If Muir's judgment is successfully reversed in appeals, it will be the first time in American legal history that a human being who is universally recognized to be alive by every accepted definition is given what amounts to a death verdict in a case where there is no alleged culpability under the device of substituted judgment. The doctrine of substituted judgment, by which the court can substitute its judgment for the judgment of an incompetent, is chiefly used in business law, not where a life-or-death judgment is at stake.

"The authorization sought, if granted, would result in Karen's death," wrote Judge Muir. "This is not protection. It is not something in her best interests. . . . The single most important temporal quality Karen Anne Quinlan has is life. This Court will not authorize that life to be taken from her. . . . Such an authorization would be a homicide."

Excerpts from the Quinlan decision

The central figure in this tragic case is Karen Ann Quinlan, a New Jersey resident. At the age of 22, she lies in a debilitated and allegedly moribund state at Saint Clare's Hospital in Denville.

Joseph Quinlan (her adopted father) wished to be appointed guardian of the person and property of his daughter. It was proposed by him that such letters of guardianship should contain an expressed power to him as guardian to authorize the discontinuance of all extraordinary medical procedures now allegedly sustaining Karen's vital processes and hence her life, since these measures . . . present no hope of her eventual recovery. . . .

The matter is of transcendent importance, involving questions related to the definition and existence of death, the prolongation of life through artificial means.

Essentially . . . Karen Quinlan's father sought judicial authority to withdraw the life-sustaining mechanism temporarily preserving his daughter's life and his appointment as guardian of her person to that end. His request was opposed by her doctors, the hospital, the Morris County Prosecutor, the State of New Jersey, and her guardian ad litem.

The experts believe that Karen cannot now survive without the assistance of the respirator; that exactly how long she would live without it is unknown; that the strong likelihood that death would follow soon after its removal, and that removal would also risk further brain damage and would curtail the assistance the respirator presently provides in warding off infection.

It seemed to be the consensus not only of the treating physicians but also of the several qualified experts who testified in the case that the removal from the respirator would not conform to medical practices, standards and traditions.

When plaintiff and his family, finally reconciled to the certainty of Karen's impending death, requested the withdrawal of life-support mechanisms [Dr. Robert J. Morse] demurred. His refusal was based upon his conception of medical standards, practice and ethics described in the medical testimony.

The character and general suitability of Joseph Quinlan as guardian for his daughter, in ordinary circumstances, should not be doubted. The record bespeaks the high degree of familial love which pervaded the home of Joseph Quinlan and reached out fully to embrace Karen, although she was living elsewhere at the time of her collapse.

A communicant of the Roman Catholic Church, as were other family members, [Mr. Quinlan] first sought solace in private prayer looking with confidence, as he says, to the Creator, first for the recovery of Karen and then, if that were not possible, for guidance with respect to the awesome decision confronting him.

To confirm the moral rightness of the decision he was about to make, he consulted with his parish priest and later with the Catholic chaplain of Saint Clare's Hospital. He would not, he testified, have sought termination if that act were to be morally wrong or in conflict with the tenets of the religion he so proudly respects. He was disabused of doubt, however, when the position of the Roman Catholic Church was made known to him as it is reflected in the record in this case.

We know the position of that church as illuminated by the record before us. We have no reason to believe that it will at all be discordant with the whole Judaeo-Christian tradition, considering its central respect and reverence for the sanctity of human life.

We think the contention as to interference with religious beliefs or rights may be considered and dealt with without extended discussion. . . . Simply stated, the right to religious beliefs is absolute but conduct in pursuance therefore is not wholly immune from government restraint.

The public interest is thus considered paramount, without the essential dissolution of respect for religious beliefs.

We have no doubt, in these unhappy circumstances, that if Karen were herself miraculously lucid for an interval and perceptive of her irreversible condition, she could effectively decide upon discontinuance of the life-support apparatus, even if it meant the prospect of natural death.

We have no hesitancy in deciding, in the instance diametrically opposite case, that no external compelling interest of the state could compel Karen to endure the unendurable, only to vegetate a few measurable months with no realistic possibility of returning to any semblance of cognitive life. We perceive no threat of logic distinguishing between such a choice on Karen's part and a similar choice which, under the evidence in this case, could be made by a competent patient terminally ill, riddled by cancer and suffering great pain; such a patient would not be kept alive against his will on a respirator.

Ultimately, there comes a point at which the individual's rights overcome the state interest. It is for that reason that we believe Karen's choice, if she were competent to make it, would be vindicated by the law.

The sad truth, however, is that she is grossly incompetent and we cannot discern her supposed choice based on the testimony of her previous conversations with friends, where such testimony is without sufficient probative weight. Nevertheless, we have concluded that Karen's right of privacy may be asserted on her behalf by her guardian under the peculiar circumstances here present.

If [his] conclusion is in the affirmative, this decision should be accepted by society the overwhelming majority of whose members would, we think, in similar circumstances, exercise such a choice in the same way for themselves or for those closest to them.

The existence and nature of the medical dilemma need hardly be discussed at length, portrayed as it is in the present case and complicated as it has recently come to be in view of the dramatic events of medical technology. The dilemma is there, it is real, it is [continually] resolved in accepted medical practice without attention in the courts. It pervades the issues in the very case we here examine.

But insofar as the court, having no inherent

medical expertise, is called upon to overrule a professional decision made according to the prevailing medical practice and standards, a different question is presented.

The medical obligation is related to standards and practice prevailing in the profession. The physicians in charge of the case, as noted above, declined to withdraw the respirator. That decision was consistent with the proofs below as to the existing medical standards and practices.

However, in relation to the relief sought by plaintiff as representative of Karen's interest, we are required to re-evaluate the applicability of the medical standards projected in the court below. The question is whether there is such internal consistency and rationality in the application of such standards as would warrant their constituting an ineluctable bar to the effectuation of substitive relief for plaintiff at the hands of the court. We have concluded not.

The agitation of the medical community in the face of modern life-prolongation technology and its search for definitive policy are demonstrated in the large volume of relevant professional commentary.

The wide debate contrasts with the relative paucity of legislative and judicial guides and standards in the same field. The medical profession has sought to devise guidelines such as the "brain death" concept.

We glean from the record here that physicians distinguish between curing the ill and comforting and easing the dying; that they refuse to treat the curable as if they were dying or ought to die, and that they have sometimes refused to treat the hopeless and dying as if they were curable.

We think these attitudes represent a balanced implementation of a profoundly realistic perspective on the meaning of life and death and that they respect the whole Judaeo-Christian tradition of regard for human life.

Having concluded that there is a right of privacy that might permit termination of treatment in the circumstance of this case, we turn to consider the relationship of the exercise of that right to the criminal law. We are aware that such termination of treatment would accelerate Karen's death. The county Prosecutor and the Attorney General stoutly maintained that there would be criminal liability for such acceleration. Under the statutes of this state, the unlawful killing of another human being is criminal homicide.

We conclude that there would be no criminal homicide in the circumstance of this case. We believe, first, that the ensuing death would not be homicide but rather expiration from existing natural causes. Secondly, even if it were to be regarded as homicide, it would not be unlawful.

These conclusions rest upon definitional and constitutional bases. The termination of treatment pursuant to the right of privacy is, within the limitation of this case, ipso facto lawful. Thus, a death resulting from such an act would not come within the scope of the homicide statutes proscribing only the unlawful killing of another.

There is a real and in this case determinative distinction between the unlawful taking of the life of another and the self-determination.

California's Natural Death Act enacted September 30, 1976

7185.   This act shall be known and may be cited as the Natural Death Act.

7186.   The Legislature finds that adult persons have the fundamental right to control the decisions relating to the rendering of their own medical care, including the decision to have life-sustaining procedures withheld or withdrawn in instances of a terminal condition.

The Legislature further finds that modern medical technology has made possible the artificial prolongation of human life beyond natural limits.

The Legislature further finds that such prolongation of life for persons with a terminal condition may cause loss of patient dignity, unnecessary pain and suffering, and an unreasonable emotional and financial hardship on the patient's family, while providing nothing medically necessary or beneficial to the patient.

The Legislature further finds that there exists considerable uncertainty in the medical and legal professions as to the legality of terminating the use or application of life-sustaining procedures where the patient has voluntarily and in sound mind evidenced a desire that such procedures be withheld or withdrawn.

In recognition of the dignity and privacy which patients have a right to expect, the Legislature hereby declares that the laws of the State of California shall recognize the right of an adult person to make a written directive instructing his physician to withhold or withdraw life-sustaining procedures in the event of a terminal condition. . . .

7188. . . . The directive shall be in the following form:

DIRECTIVE TO PHYSICIANS

Directive made this _____ day of (month, year).

I _____, being of sound mind, willfully, and voluntarily make known my desire that my life shall not be artificially prolonged under the circumstances set forth below, do hereby declare:

1. If at any time I should have an incurable injury, disease, or illness certified to be a terminal condition by two physicians, and where the application of life-sustaining procedures would serve only to artificially prolong the moment of my death and where my physician determines that my death is imminent whether or not life-sustaining procedures are utilized, I direct that such procedures be withheld or withdrawn, and that I be permitted to die naturally.

2. In the absence of my ability to give directions regarding the use of such life-sustaining procedures, it is my intention that this directive shall be honored by my family and physician(s) as the final expression of my legal right to refuse medical or surgical treatment and accept the consequences from such refusal.

3. If I have been diagnosed as pregnant and that diagnosis is known to my physician, this directive shall have no force or effect during the course of my pregnancy.

4. I have been diagnosed and notified at least 14 days ago as having a terminal condition by _____, M.D., whose address is _____, and whose telephone number is _____. I understand that if I have not filled in the physician's name and address, it shall be presumed that I did not have a terminal condition when I made out this directive.

5. This directive shall have no force or effect five years from the date filled in above.

6. I understand the full import of this directive and I am emotionally and mentally competent to make this directive.

Signed _____

City, County and State of Residence _____

The declarant has been personally known to me and I believe him or her to be of sound mind.

Witness _____

Witness _____

. . .

7189. (a) A directive may be revoked at any time by the declarant, without regard to his mental state or competency. . . .

7190. No physician or health facility which, acting in accordance with the requirements of this chapter, causes the withholding or withdrawal of life-sustaining procedures from a qualified patient, shall be subject to civil liability therefrom. . . .

7195. Nothing in this chapter shall be construed to condone, authorize, or approve mercy killing, or to permit any affirmative or deliberate act or omission to end life other than to permit the natural process of dying as provided in this chapter.

JACK W. PROVONSHA

Keeping human life human

A premature infant girl was delivered to Phyllis Obernauer in the back seat of the family car en route to the hospital. Once in the hospital, Mrs. Obernauer was perplexed because the hospital staff and even her obstetrician seemed to avoid her. Finally came the crushing news: the infant had mongolism, with a major cardiac abnormality and an intestinal obstruction. The obstruction required immediate surgical intervention if the little girl were to survive. When informed of the condition, the mother looked ahead to the kind of life that lay before this infant and made a decision she didn't think herself capable of making: "Let the baby die."

The hospital staff was horrified by the mother's attitude, and her wish was not carried out. The local bureau of children's services obtained a court order and forced the intestinal surgery. Two months later, Mrs. Obernauer was presented with a live, still imperfect child and a medical and surgical bill for $4,000. She took the infant home with great reluctance. Months later, after being tempted on several occasions to end the child's life, she was still staying, "If there were a place where I could take this child today and she would be put to sleep permanently, I would do it."

At Johns Hopkins University Hospital in Baltimore, an almost identical birth occurred. Again, the parents refused surgery. This time, however, no court order was obtained. For fifteen days the infant survived. Its bassinet, on which hung the sign "nothing by mouth," was placed in a darkened room. Dehydration finally killed the child during a period of agony for parents, doctors, and nurses.

Which solution was the correct one?

Dr. Frank R. Ruff describes a patient who was admitted to the hospital with an inoperable bowel malignancy that had metastasized widely through his body. Nothing short of a miracle could save him, but his doctors tried. "Over his tired protests, they gave him x-ray therapy, chemotherapy, and other costly treatments. After several weeks they sent him home mentally exhausted, financially depleted, and physically only slightly improved. He died within a week. By the time his funeral was paid for, his death had left his wife virtually penniless."

Tony Gallo's physical and mental symptoms were finally diagnosed as uremia from chronic kidney failure. His age and hypertension ruled out a kidney transplant. He was placed on an artificial kidney machine that kept him alive but severely restricted his activities. Side effects of the dialysis were severe generalized itching and (worse, from Tony's standpoint) impotence. The family savings were quickly dissipated, and the Gallos remortgaged the house. Finally it was all getting to Tony. "Why do I have to be around? Why do I have to live like this?" he would ask his wife daily. "I could see it if I were getting better." Tippy Gallo could only say, "We love having you around. We want you forever."

One day shortly after his wife's birthday Tony decided he had had enough. "He ripped the tubes from his arm and walked out of the treatment room, leaving behind a trail of blood and shocked nurses. His wife pleaded with him to go back on the machine, telling him it was a sin to give up. A parish priest begged him. His sons threatened to sit on his chest and legs while a nurse put him back on the machine. 'He just told me it wasn't worth it any more. He wanted to die,' his wife says. Tony stuck to his decision, and a week later he was dead." Should he have been forced back on the dialysis machine?

I received this letter from a tired old man: "What would you regard as a natural death? Or is there no such thing? . . . I am eighty-seven years old, and I have been fighting off death all my life. Two years ago I fought off death from four kinds of urinary complaints, compaction, hardening of the arteries, chronic heart disease so severe that one attack left a lesion on my heart; and now I am in a life struggle with cancer. I have been on the operating table nine times; and I have also had two minor operations. My folks are terribly opposed to my treatments. Hospitals and doctors have cost me $16,000. . . . Because I have very little money left, they have put me under guardianship as an incompetent. Now, if I had not taken those treatments (and they said I would die if I didn't), wouldn't that have been the same as committing suicide? And if I committed suicide, wouldn't I lose eternal life? I am so anxious to go home. Oh, Lord, won't you please let up on me a little?"

An elderly mother wrote: "Dear Sons—This letter is not a request; it is an order. I have tried to live with dignity, and I want to die the same way. If my fate is such that I should become ill and unable to make a rational decision, you are hereby instructed to give the attending physi-

265

cian orders that he must not attempt to prolong my life by using extraordinary measures. If I am stricken with an illness that is irreversible and am unable to speak, please speak for me. I want no surgery, no cobalt, no blood transfusions, and no intravenous feedings. Instead, please see to it that the physician gives me plenty of medication and sedatives. This letter of instruction will relieve you of the burden of making the decision. It is made. I have made it. My thanks and my love. Mother."

How would you have answered the tired old man? Send him the mother's letter to her sons perhaps?

It is one of the ironies of our times that a wondrous technology has thrust upon us all kinds of new questions, or raised old questions in a variety of new ways at a time of diminished capacity to answer them. For many, the old certainties have disappeared—certainties about the nature of right and wrong—along with the social institutions (the family and the church) by which they were preserved and passed along from generation to generation. Never has man been faced with such difficult questions, yet possessing so little expertise by which to wrestle with them.

I do not propose in this brief presentation to outline what all of these questions are, nor to suggest, in any detail, methods for dealing with them. I have chosen, rather, to concentrate on one issue that seems to be escaping most bio-ethicians who are struggling with such matters these days. . . .

What is missing, in short, is a guiding norm, or value ideal, in relation to which the terms like right and wrong are meaningful.

This is surprising—given the fact of our common cultural heritage. When pushed, men usually discover an underlying common system of values (at least in the Western world) that we all owe to our common Judeo-Christian background, and continue to owe even if not every one of us is willing to pay his debts.

In such a culture, if it is true to itself, the highest place (on a scale of earthly things we value) is given to personal human existence. Nothing in all of God's earth is more impor-

tant. In such a setting, all rules, customs, practices, statutes, or whatever, become valid and enduring precisely to the extent that they create, support, and enhance this highest value. *Moral rules, in short, serve the purpose of keeping human life human.* . . .

To say this is to say nothing very new or astonishing. And it is to say something regarding which there is an astonishing degree of unanimity—whether one conceives of the rules as divine revelations given to guide man toward fulfillment of the Creator's intention for him (as I do), or in terms of the atheistic evolutionist's observations concerning what behavior patterns foster the survival and development of genus *Homo.* That unanimity derives, I repeat, from our common value heritage.

When there is confusion, disagreement usually has to do with what the term *human* means in the expression "keeping human life human.". . .

In the new technology, the questions themselves arise from the premises of our common heritage. Therefore, the best possibility of dealing with them must be found within the context of these premises. Since these are essentially Judeo-Christian questions, they therefore require Judeo-Christian (which is to say biblically based) answers.

How does one define *human* as over against merely animal in such a context? . . .

Inanimate things can be acted upon. Sub-human plant and animal life can be acted upon, and can react. Man shares with inanimate nature the capacity to be acted upon, and with subhuman life the additional capacity to react. But man shares only with God the power to act, to create, to initiate actions he did not have to initiate. Only man has this freedom, and thus only man of all earthly creatures can be held accountable, that is, can be held responsible for his actions. It is this freedom that sets man apart from lesser animals and by definition renders him human. It is this capacity which in fact underlies the highest of all his abilities— that described by the love commandment. Such freedom involves a certain level of self-consciousness, a time sense, the ability to reason abstractly, and above all the ability to select between live options.

If through disease or accident this volitional capacity is lost, man has ceased to be functionally human—in which case life's value diminishes proportionately. This altered value greatly conditions the amount of effort man would put into life preservation, particularly if that effort should logically better be expended elsewhere. For example, in competition for existence—and all that it implies both qualitatively and quantitatively—it makes moral nonsense to allow what is subhuman to take priority over human existence, or to compete with humanity in such a manner as to deprive it. If it came to such a choice, it would not be morally right to drain off technical or financial resources from children with human potential so as to satisfy the needs of functionally subhuman children. Fortunately this choice does not often face us.

It is even possible to develop a system of relative values giving guidance to our priorities in a situation of competing claims. Such a system would range upward from "thing" values at the bottom of the scale to personal values at the top, the ladder rungs in between arranged in the order of their proximity to, or resemblance to, the highest value—human personal life.

In competition, what was higher on such a scale would take priority over the lower. A "living thing," or even a potential human, would take a place subordinate to the actual human—as in the case of a fetus in competition with its mother's "human" existence. (Notice, I said not just "existence," or "life," but human existence—in the sense of my earlier definition of human.) An abortion becomes justifiable in the presence of a real threat to a relative quality of the mother's life—not merely to life itself. In a choice between two actual persons competing for the same resources—for example, a dialysis machine—qualitative factors (such as "what kind of life?" "how high up on the scale?") must enter into the equation.

Making judgments involving the value of human life as over against subhuman existence may be facilitated in other ways. It makes moral nonsense, I repeat, to waste resources that are required elsewhere to prolong meaningless existence. If the human quality of existence has disappeared, heroics become inappropriate.

There comes a time when it is morally necessary and right to "pull the plug" on empty "tissue survival."

There remain questions, of course. Can a mere man (even one with an M.D. degree) always be sure that the term "meaningless" applies—and if so, precisely when? And of course there are times when this is in doubt. Ought man to play God? The fact is that there are times when he must (without developing illusions, it is to be hoped). At times one has to make such judgments whether he wishes to or not. And he must make use of all the newer technical aids (such as electroencephalography and others) when he makes judgments.

So far, we've probably said nothing novel or startling. But there is one element (missing in some discussions of this subject) that we might do well to consider. Let me illustrate from a recent newspaper headline: "TRIPLE TRANSPLANT DONOR—SLAYING DILEMMA." The case involved the transplant of the still beating heart of a victim of a shooting. The legal question concerned who actually killed the donor, the gunman or the transplant surgeons? In the latter case, of course, the gunman could not be charged with murder (and presumably the doctors could).

This was not the first time a donor's heart was taken while it was still pulsating (transplant people have coined a phrase "pulsatile cadaver"), and of course technically the practice has much logic going for it. If the brain is dead (as tests indicated in the case above), who cares over much that other organs are still functioning? (It is probable that the transplant surgeon cares that they *are* still functioning.)

Who cares? I'm going to suggest that perhaps it should be the concern of all of us. Cerebral death alone cannot constitute, at least at present, the sole criterion of death—especially if we define cerebral in functional terms. Such death, at least in human terms, could occur in intrauterine and presumably "genetic" life. Thus, transplant surgeons could as easily use the hearts of institutionalized mental defectives as those of victims of gunmen. Nuremberg clearly pointed out the dangers down that road.

Donor subjects must not only *be* functionally dead (as far as their brains are concerned)—they must *mean* dead in terms of what the larger community considers evidence of death. Grandma who has suffered her final stroke and lies in an irreversible coma still *means* Grandma to her community. And until the changes can be rung on that meaning—that is, until Grandma comes to mean *corpse*—she must be granted what is due her status. And she will *mean* dead only when what it takes to provide that meaning has occurred—that is, when conventional signs of life have ceased and usually have been declared so by responsible people. . . .

In terms of our present discussion, how one relates to what *means* human will condition in important ways one's attitudes and sensitivities toward what *is* in fact human. Those institutionalized mental defectives *mean* human—not merely animal—even if in fact functionally they are not! Therefore we cannot exploit them as living organ banks, without endangering a crucial quality of our civilization, indeed our very humanity. The same must be said for Grandma with her cardiovascular accident—and, I might add, for unborn fetuses. If we are to protect our human sensitivities, we must be prepared also to treat with respect those symbolic individuals who are associated with the concept of humanity, but within the limits of a system of values that keeps human life human.

On that ladder scale of values ranging from inanimate things up to human persons, "symbolic humans," I think, should be placed somewhere just below potential humans. But again, they should not be permitted to take priority over actual humans in competition for our limited resources. Mainly what symbolic humans have a right to expect from us is whatever is required to keep our human sensitivities intact. Usually that will not involve costly and elaborate heroics—rather, simple acts of care and compassion such as keep *us* human as well as provide for their ease.

The naturalist Edwin Way Teale makes an intriguing statement: "It is those who have compassion for all life who will best safeguard the life of man. Those who become aroused only when man is endangered become aroused too late."

It seems to me that this statement could also be made to read, "It is those who have compassion for what symbolizes human life who will best safeguard the actual life of man." For surely it is the case that if we lose such compassion, all of those fancy gadgets and devices (and the things they can do that have thrust the new questions upon us) will have become wasted effort. It will all simply cease to be worth the doing in the short as well as the long run.

HERMANN J. MULLER

Means and aims in human genetic betterment

For persons who would concede the desirability of human genetic betterment, or at least the need of merely preventing genetic deterioration, the possibility of conducting it by some kind of parental selection should not be overlooked. . . .

There has for some time been . . . [a] possible method of parental selection, which . . . I discussed in a public lecture given at the University of Chicago in 1925. . . .

Unlike what is true of other forms of parental selection that have been suggested for man, this method does not work by attempting to influence either the size of families that people have or their choice of marriage partners. Neither does it attempt to influence people's evaluations of themselves. Its proposed mode of procedure is to establish banks of stored germ cells (spermatozoa), eventually ample banks, derived from persons of very diverse types but including as far as possible those whose lives had given evidence of outstanding gifts of mind, merits of disposition and character, or physical fitness. From these germinal stores couples would have the privilege of selecting such material, for the engendering of children of their own families, as appeared to them to afford the greatest promise of endowing their children with the kind of hereditary constitution that came nearest to their own ideals.

As an aid in making these choices there would

268

be provided as full documentation as possible concerning the donors of the germinal material, the lives they had led, and their relatives. The couples concerned would also have advice available from geneticists, physicians, psychologists, experts in the fields of activity of the donors being considered, and other relevant specialists, as well as generalizers. In order to allow a better perspective to be obtained on the donors themselves and on their genetic potentialities, as well as to minimize personality fads and to avoid risks of personal entanglements, it would be preferable for the material used to have been derived from donors who were no longer living, and to have been stored for at least 20 years. The technique of preparing semen in a medium containing glycerine and keeping it at the temperature of liquid nitrogen . . . provides a reliable and relatively inexpensive means of maintaining such material for an unlimited period without deterioration. . . .

With the coming of a better understanding of genetics and evolution the individual's fixation on the attempted perpetuation of just his particular genes will be bound to fade. It will be superseded by a more rational view, supported by just as strong a feeling, according to which the individual finds fulfillment in passing on to the future the best that he can find to represent him, by gathering that best from wherever it can be found in most concentrated form. And he will condemn as a childish conceit the notion that there is any reason for his unessential peculiarities, idiosyncrasies, and foibles to be expressed generation after generation. In these ways, as well as through the love and careful upbringing that he bestows upon his child of choice, he will achieve a form of continuance as worthy of himself as possible, one expressing a higher form of morality than that now prevalent.

HANS JONAS

Biological engineering — a preview

The biological control of man, especially genetic control, raises ethical questions of a wholly new kind for which neither previous praxis nor previous thought has prepared us. Since no less than the very nature and image of man are at issue, prudence becomes itself our first ethical duty, and hypothetical reasoning our first responsibility. To consider the consequences before taking action is no more than common prudence. In this case, wisdom bids us to go further and to examine the use of powers even before they are quite ready for use. One conceivable outcome of such an examination could be the counsel not to let those powers get ready in the first place, i.e., to stop certain lines of inquiry leading to them, considering the extreme seducibility of man by whatever power he has. And more than mere counsel could be indicated [if] . . . the powers can be acquired only by their actual exercise on the true "material" itself. This exercise, moreover, must be on a trial-and-error basis: that is, only through necessarily faulty biological engineering could we perfect the theory for eventually faultless biological engineering—which alone might be enough to interdict the acquisition of the art even if its foreseen final performance were approved.

Interference with the freedom of research is a grave ethical matter by itself, yet it is like nothing against the gravity of the ethical issues posed by the eventual success of that research; and bringing up the possibility of a self-imposed halt in these preliminary remarks at all is just to suggest a measure of the perils which a biological engineering fully matured and enfranchised might visit upon man. . . .

The general nature of biological engineering

Up to the present, all technology has been concerned with lifeless materials (most typically metals), shaping them into nonhuman artifacts for human use. The division was clear: man was the subject, "nature" the object of technological mastery (which did not exclude that man became mediately the object of its application). The advent of biological engineering signals a radical departure from this clear division, indeed a break of metaphysical importance: Man becomes the direct object as well as the subject of the engineering art. . . . Conventional engineering can always correct its mistakes; and not only in the planning and testing stages: even the finished products, automobiles for example, can be recalled to the factory for correction of faults. Not so in biological engineering. Its deeds are irrevocable. When its results show, it is too late to do anything about it. What is done is done. You cannot recall persons nor scrap populations. . . .

By the Baconian formula, science and technology increase man's power over nature. . . . Now man's impending control over his own evolution is hailed as the final triumph of this power—"nature" now significantly including man himself, reclaiming him as it were from his splendid isolation. But of whom is this a power over what and whom? Plainly, of the living over posterity; more correctly, of present men over future men, who are the defenseless objects of antecedent choices by the planners of today. The obverse of *their* power is the later servitude of the living to the dead. . . . [This] raises the question, unknown to dead-matter engineering, of what *right* anyone has to so predetermine future men; and, hypothetically granting the right, what *wisdom* he has that entitles him to exercise it. . . .

This brings me to the last point in this survey of the differences between conventional and biological engineering—that of *goals*. . . . Unless men themselves are conceived as being for the use of men, to be designed accordingly, the utilitarian rationale of all other technology fails us in the case of man's engineering of himself. What then are *its* aims? Surely not to create man—he is already there. To create better men? But what is the standard of better? Better adapted men? But better adapted to what? Supermen? But how do we know what is "super"? We stumble into ultimate questions as soon as we propose to tamper with the making of man. They all converge into one: in what image?

We must now descend from generalities to particulars, and from the "what is it?" to the "how done?" i.e., to the different—available or anticipated—modes of execution, which also differ in their ends.

Presently available modes

The possible *goals* define the *kinds* of biological control that are being contemplated, and in this second section of my paper, as later in the third, I shall discuss the ethical aspects of certain kinds of control distinguished by their ends. It may well be the case that certain ends are first suggested by the mere becoming available of the means; even then, they can serve to categorize the adopted course of action. According to this criterion, which answers to the question *why* something is to be done and thereby determines *what* is to be done, we can distinguish between protective, melioristic, and creative biological control. . . .

Negative or preventive eugenics. First, then, about protective or preventive control, whose best-known form is negative eugenics, that is, a mating policy that prevents the transmission of pathogenic or otherwise deleterious genes by barring their carriers from procreation. The congenital diabetic, e.g., is to be barred or restrained from producing offspring. I am not here concerned with the means of restraint, which may go all the way from persuasion to sterilization, from voluntary to compulsory, and which raise their own problems. I confine my attention to the rationale, which is twofold: humanitarian and evolutionary. The humanitarian relates to the well-being of the potential offspring individually, and for their own sake as it were, trying to avoid future misery. No possible violation of the rights of such potential offspring is involved in desisting from producing it, since there is no right to existence for hypothetical individuals not yet conceived. But though not the right *of* the merely imagined offspring, the right *to* offspring of the hindered progenitor is involved. He or she is asked to forgo it, and he can counter the appeal to his humanitarian responsibility, i.e., to his pity, with the claim that he, a sufferer from the disease himself, is the best judge on whether such a life is still worth living, and that he is prepared to take the risk (it is usually no more than that) on behalf of his offspring. There is merit to this at least in a number of cases—definitely where only one parent is afflicted, and arguably even where both are and the risk amounts to near-certainty. But the humanitarian appeal is strengthened, independently of the individual risk factor, by the evolutionary one, which argues that the *species* or population must be protected against the danger of deterioration of its gene pool through a progressive increase of deleterious factors—an increase threatened by the very protection which civilization affords to those factors otherwise held in check by natural selection. The diabetic can be told that he owes his very candidacy for procreation to the medical art which (through the provision of insulin) has kept him from perishing before reaching the proper age: as a *quid pro quo* he can be asked to sacrifice this one right in the interest of the species. This is ethically in order at the individual level. At the population level, negative eugenics is ostensibly modest, aiming at preservation rather than innovation, not presuming to improve on nature but wishing merely to redress its balance, disturbed by human intervention in the first place. This too seems to be in order, *if* the specter of a sickly and debilitated species otherwise to be expected from civilized conditions is true (which I cannot judge). Negative eugenics thus looks more like an extension of preventive medicine than a beginning of biological engineering. . . .

Positive or melioristic eugenics. We now move on to positive or melioristic eugenics, the much more ambitious, bolder, therefore also more dangerous program—which, of course, comprises negative eugenics as an automatic byproduct of its larger schemes. Far from bent on preserving, it wants to improve the quality of the race and make it more perfect than nature has made it. . . .

A chief method of improving the race is seen in selective breeding, but this time with positive and not merely negative selection. Planned mating, based on genetic charts of the partners, family histories, etc., is to take the place of amateurish amatory choices. . . . This then leads to the institution of human studs, eugenically certified semen donors, eventually also ovum donors, with artificial insemination (and inovulation) replacing the sexual act—thus to a complete separation of love and sex from procreation, of marriage from parenthood, and so on. All this, mark you, not in order to avert a mortal danger to the race but to improve the race; not under the pressure of extreme emergency but from gratuitous choice. But *what* choice, concretely? Who is to judge the excellence of the specimens—of the semen and ovum donors, and by what standards? Let us remember that it is much easier to identify the undesirable than the desirable, the *malum* than the *bonum*. That diabetes, epilepsy, schizophrenia, hemophilia are undesirable, to afflicted and fellow men alike, is noncontroversial. But what is "better"—a cool head or a warm heart, high sensitivity or robustness, a placid or a rebellious temperament, and in what proportion of distribution rather than another: who is to determine that, and based on what knowledge? The pretense to such knowledge alone should be sufficient ground to disqualify the pretender. And whatever the standards of selection agreed or hit upon—is standardization as such desirable?

Discounting humanistic values, which are always debatable (and outside the scientists' domain), biologists are agreed on the plain biological value of the prolix manifoldness in the gene pool, with its vast reserve of presently "useless" traits the only safeguard of adaptability to novel conditions. . . . It sounds almost trivial to add the point . . . that genetic traits come in packages, in which even the decidedly undesirable may be linked with the desirable (e.g., sickle-cell anemia with protection against malaria)—then, of course, also vice versa: the decidedly desirable with the undesirable—and that we simply *cannot* know what linkages we are affecting, what in effect we are jettisoning in adopting, and what adopting in jettisoning, when we single out "separate" traits for either condemnation or promotion. And, apart from such technicalities, can there be any forecast of how the selection will work out in the continued combinations of reproduction? Except for the most unequivocal objects of *negative* eugenics, surely in the dreamland of positive genetic perfectibility, we are *not* buying greater certainty

271

with surrendering the unplanned for the planned. Why then exchange the blissful blindness of personal mating choices for the doctored ignorance of arrogant art? Its only certainty is the impoverishment of the genetic stock, apart from the destruction of basic, not to say sacred, interpersonal values.

Futuristic modes

Cloning. The two kinds of genetic control discussed so far, negative and positive eugenics, both based on selective breeding, suffer from the uncertainty injected by the lottery of bisexual reproduction with its unpredictable chances of crossing-over and recombination—which guarantee that no two individuals are the same. This frustrating interference of nature and chance the planners can circumvent by the device of *cloning*. It is at once the most unorthodox device in its method and the most slavish in its goal.

Cloning is a form of asexual reproduction, like that found in many plants side by side with the sexual mode and, unlike the latter, resulting in exact genetic replications of the parent organism. It rests on the ability of normal, diploid cells to germinate. . . . The method, which so far has succeeded with some amphibians (e.g., a frog), involves inserting the nucleus of the chosen body cell (intestinal in the known case) into an enucleated ovum of the kind, which then behaves as if fertilized. Actual adult individuals (also some monstrosities) have been thus generated. . . .

What is brought about by cloning? A genetic double of the donor, with the same degree of resemblance of phenotype as is known from identical twins. Clone and donor are indeed identical twins with a time lag. . . .

[The] *ethical* issue we wish to raise [is] . . . what to *be* a clone would mean for the subject concerned; and here the case of the distinguished donor merely serves to bring into sharper light what would apply to all cases, i.e., to the cloning proposition as such. . . .

The focal question of essence is that of unprejudiced selfhood, and it can be attacked from the situation of a twinhood that lacks contemporaneity. The situation of identical twins (or triplets, etc.) has its own problems, . . . [but]

one essential feature . . . sets it . . . apart from . . . cloning: the "multiplets" who have to face the reiteration of their genotype in one another are strictly contemporaneous, none has a head start, and none has to relive a previously completed life. It is irrelevant to what extent the genotype actually dominates individual history, and how far "identity" here goes in determining the final effect. What matters is that the sexually produced genotype is a novum in itself, unknown to all to begin with and still to reveal itself to owners and fellow men alike. Ignorance is here the precondition of freedom: the new throw of the dice has to discover itself in the guideless efforts of living its life for the first and only time, i.e., to *become* itself in meeting a world as unprepared for the newcomer as this is for himself. None of the siblings, though continually confronted with his likeness, suffers from the precedence of a firstcomer who has already demonstrated the potentials of his being (at least one set of them) and thereby preempted their authenticity for him. . . .

Contrary to the equality of twins, the replication of a genotype [by cloning] creates inherently unequal conditions for the phenotypes concerned—and an inequality deadly for the clone. Here it is where our argument substitutes a manifest right to ignorance for any hidden right (which we need neither deny nor affirm) to a unique genotype. . . .

The simple and unprecedented fact is that the clone knows (or believes to know) altogether too much about himself and is known (or is believed to be known) altogether too well to others. Both facts are paralyzing for the spontaneity of becoming himself, the second also for the genuineness of others' consorting with him. It is the known donor archetype that will dictate all expectations, predictions, hopes and fears, goal settings, comparisons, standards of success and failure, of fulfillment and disappointment, for all "in the know"—clone and witnesses alike; and this putative knowledge must stifle in the pre-charted subject all immediacy of the groping quest and eventual finding "himself" with which a toiling life surprises itself for good and for ill. . . . In brief, he is antecedently robbed of the *freedom* which only under the pro-

272

tection of ignorance can thrive; and to rob a human-to-be of that freedom deliberately is an inexpiable crime that must not be committed even once. . . .

The ethical command here entering the enlarged stage of our powers is: never to violate the right to that ignorance which is a condition for the possibility of authentic action; or: *to respect the right of each human life to find its own way and be a surprise to itself.* . . .

The engineering potential of molecular biology.

The advent of molecular biology (genetics) has opened up new and more ambitious prospects, speculative at present, but sound enough theoretically to warrant hypothetical discussion. It is the possibility of direct intervention in genotypes by what is called, in anticipation, "genetic surgery" and would amount to taking over also the second, "mutational" agency of evolution: first the substitution of single genes (desirable for undesirable, pathogenic ones) in the chromosomal nucleus of gametes or zygotes, i.e., in the starting points of future individuals—the intent being corrective rather than innovative; but then also the adding to and reshuffling of the given DNA pattern—the rewriting as it were of its script, which a complete "cracking" of the genetic code together with microtechniques still to be developed makes at least conceivable: ultimately, a kind of DNA architecture. This would result in the production of new *types* of creatures, in the deliberate generation of freaks and, mediately, future lines of freaks; and when practiced on a human take-off basis, would depose the image of man as an object of ultimate respect and renounce allegiance to its integrity. It would be a metaphysical breach with the essence of man as well as the most reckless gamble in view of the utter unpredictability of the consequences—the blundering of a blind and arrogant demiurge at the delicate heart of creation. . . .

By definition, none of the products of inventive, or "freakish," engineering will have been produced for its own sake; utility was the only rule of its conception. The expansion hence to the universal view that men are for the use of men, entirely appropriate to engineering products, will be irresistible and leave no one recognized as an end in himself. But if no member of the class, then why the class? The very being of mankind for its own sake looses its ontological ground. . . .

Concluding appeal. We have been moving for some stretch now at the very boundaries of things human and of possible discourse about them. A spectral sense of unreality must have communicated itself to the reader, which I share. Yet he would be wrong to regard the discourse therefore as otiose. The danger is that we may be gliding into fateful beginnings unawares, innocently as it were by the thin edge of the wedge, namely pure science. I have tried, in discussing these borderline cases, to suppress the metaphysical shudder I feel at the idea of man-made homunculus. To let it out now with an archaic word, the production of human freaks would be an abomination; let alone the unspeakable thought of human-animal hybrids which, quite consistently, has not failed to enter the list.

Steering clear of metaphysics and categories of the sacred, which this topic makes it not easy to do, I resort at the end, and with reference to the whole field of biological control, to the plainest of moral reflections: Deeds with no accountability are wrong when done to others. The moral dilemma in all human-biological manipulation, other than negative—and the greater, the more artificial the procedure and goal—is this: that the potential accusation of the offspring against his makers will find no respondent still answerable for the deed, and no possible redress. Here is a field for crimes with complete impunity to the perpetrator. This also should call forth the utmost scrupulousness and sensitivity in applying the rising powers of biological control on man. And though much more is involved, the simple ethics of the case are enough to rule out the direct tampering with human genotypes (which cannot be other than amateurish) from the very beginning of the road—that is, impalatable as it sounds to modern ears, at the fountainhead of experimental research.

"*Run for your life! It's boredom, spawned by technological advances and overabundance of leisure.*"

13

THE MORALITY OF WORK AND PLAY

Work, play, and sport take up most of our waking time and available energies. It is no wonder, then, that moral evaluations and significances get attached to them.

Regarding work, Luther, in his concept of the "vocation," thought that each job, no matter how lowly, served as an occasion to glorify God on earth; and the Puritans believed that achievement in one's work was a sign that one had been elected to salvation. Play, too, has had moral esteem accorded to it. The famed child psychologist, Jean Piaget, has demonstrated that children's games are an important means by which a child learns the meaning of moral rules. As for sport, the Greeks thought that sport developed divine qualities of grace and beauty, while the English relied on sport to develop qualities of character.

One often thinks of work, play, and sport as denoting separate activities. However, one can find frequent occasions where our ordinary usage of language combines them. We speak, for example, of a golfer "working" at his putting, Muhammed Ali "playing" with his opponent, and a scientist "toying" with his equations. Under what category does art fall? How, for instance, should one describe the activity of a budding pianist in an international piano competition—as work, play, or sport? Both the moral evaluations of work, play, and sport and their relations to one another are discussed in the following selections.

The highest moments we experience in work, or sport occur when we accomplish or perform something at the limit of our capacities that has a significance beyond the mere performance. The significance may be a reward that attends the accomplishment such as money, acclaim, or glory. The greatest significance, however, has always been attributed to experiences of insight or feeling that possess meaning. This "unity of power and meaning" defines those highest moments of ours that the theologian Paul Tillich referred to as "spiritual."

In the first selection by Richard Burke, we can see how work and play can be combined to achieve such "unity of power and meaning." Play enables man "to endow his life with form and meaning. What art, religion and philosophy are for the few, play is for the many: a free, intrinsically satisfying activity, governed by rules of man's own making and giving rise to a finite, meaningful world that man can call his own." Work, on the other hand, is not "a mere means to an end"; rather, it brings satisfaction "from having helped to bring a new 'whole' into existence." Burke carefully lists and analyzes various types of play and work and concludes that they need not be incompatible, for the same activity may be both work and play. Both are activities of a "free agent," and the combination of both elements in the same activities "accounts for their powerful and lasting fascination."

There follows a piece by Max Weber, who describes the passionate devotion and effort that he thinks a truly dedicated scholar or scientist must give to his work. While such dedication to work can be rewarding, a preoccupation with success in work can also exact a heavy price, as Nicholas Lemann points out in the next selection. Lemann notes that ambitious young people today go to where what they are doing "is done at its very best." But this "mobility ethic" means that one imposes a single external standard— that of success—on one's life. The result is "a less than ideal moral climate" in which "ambition, allowed to become the preeminent human motive, dissolves the nobler qualities of life."

For many people, however, the determining factor in work is not the drive for success but automation. In the next article, Daniel Bell discusses how automation will "give a new character to work, living and leisure." Not only will it increase the mental tension surrounding work, but it may also end "the measurement of work" and make the team, not the individual, the important work unit. Indeed, the organization of work that is then performed by machine may come to supplant the actual performance of the work. Bell believes that automation will increasingly eliminate the meaning and the moral significance that work has always had in Western civilization.

According to Friedrich Juenger, mechanization due to technology has progressed so far that it has infiltrated our play, making it "sterile." Games that have become dependent on elaborate tools and the "increasing mechanization of motion" Juenger terms "sports." Modern sports, he claims, "lack completely all spontaneous movement, all free improvisation," and are "essentially unartistic and unspiritual by nature." The Olympic games of the Greeks, he says, were "not sports but festivals of a religious character."

A further look at modern sports is presented in the next pair of articles by two football players. The first of these is an exposé of "the abuses and hypocrisy of college football" by Gary Shaw, who played for the University of Texas Longhorns. According to Shaw, the coaches treated the players as objects, regimented their lives, sacrificed their education, and subordinated all human values to pursuit of the goal of producing a winning football team. Shaw argues that the popularity of football in America goes "right to the core of the American psyche," with its ethos of competition and its "survival-of-the-fittest" code. While Shaw does not discuss the big-business aspects of sports and the buying and selling of players that has characterized many professional sports, he makes it clear that even at the college level, many athletes are treated like so much "meat on the hoof."

Taking a far more positive view of organized sports is Lance Rentzel, who portrays the close, supportive bond that develops among teammates who work and suffer together. Although he recognizes that he was, in many ways, different from the other members of the Dallas Cowboys, he nevertheless writes that he "would be nothing without being a part of the team. Football had been the opening door for everything that was worthwhile" in his life.

Organized sports are, of course, a kind of work for those participating in them. In the final selection, however, we leave the world of work and sport and turn to a consideration of leisure. Josef Pieper recognizes that we are so accustomed to defining our lives by work that the notion that "'we work in order to have leisure' . . . sounds immoral, as though directed at the very foundations of human society." For Pieper, leisure is not merely the absence of work, but it is "a receptive attitude of mind, a contemplative attitude, and it is not only the occasion but also the capacity for steeping oneself in the whole of creation." It is thus of a "higher order" than the active life, for only leisure allows us to grasp "the world as a whole" and to "reach out to superhuman, life-giving existential forces." For Pieper, that spiritual "unity of work and power" mentioned by Tillich would not be possible in work or sport, but only in leisure.

NOTES ABOUT THE AUTHORS

Richard Burke was born in 1930 and was educated at Columbia and the University of Wisconsin. A specialist in learning theory, he has taught experimental psychology at Temple University in Philadelphia. "'Work' and 'Play'" was first published in *Ethics* in 1971.

Max Weber, born in 1864, was a leading sociologist in Germany. He wrote a number of works on religions and their impact on other aspects of society, the most famous being *The Protestant Ethic and the Spirit of Capitalism.* He died in 1920.

Nicholas Lemann is an editor of *The Washington Monthly.* "Going Home," excerpted here, appeared in the November 1967 issue of the journal.

Daniel Bell has been professor of sociology at Harvard University since 1969, having previously taught at the University of Chicago and Columbia University. He is coeditor of *The Public Interest.* Among his best-known works are *The End of Ideology, The Radical Right,* and *The Coming of Post-Industrial Society. Work and Its Discontents,* excerpted here, was first published in 1956.

Friedrich Georg Juenger, born in 1898, is a poet, novelist, and essayist. Among his longer works is *Neitzsche. The Failure of Technology,* excerpted in this volume, was published in 1949.

Gary Shaw played football for the University of Texas Longhorns, having entered the university as a freshman in 1963. He quit the football team in his senior year. After a variety of odd jobs, he returned to the University of Texas graduate school in 1969. *Meat on the Hoof: The Hidden World of Texas Football* was written in 1972.

Lance Rentzel played professional football for the Minnesota Vikings, the Dallas Cowboys, and the Los Angeles Rams. *When All the Laughter Died in Sorrow,* excerpted here, is his autobiography, written in 1972. In it he tells not only of his tragic problem of exhibitionism, but also of the psychology of sport and of the American tendency to deify sports heroes. Rentzel now lives in Los Angeles.

Josef Pieper, born in 1904 in Germany, teaches philosophy and theology at the University of Munster (Germany). He is the author of *The End of Time: A Meditation on the Philosophy of History, In Tune with the World,* and *Leisure, the Basis of Culture,* first published in 1952 and excerpted here.

277

RICHARD BURKE

"Work" and "play"

"All work and no play makes Jack a dull boy." Most jingles rhyme better than this one, but no proverb is truer. The complement is also true. I venture to add, without argument, a new item to our store of conventional wisdom: "All play and no work makes Jack a big jerk." We don't so often realize, however, that simply alternating between work and play is not very satisfying either, if the work is drudgery and the play is merely recuperation to enable us to go back to work again. This has been the lot of most people throughout history, and it is not an enviable one. The lucky few are not the leisure class, if that means "all play and no work," but those whose activities combine elements of both. We all know someone whose job is so satisfying, so rewarding to him that he would rather "work" than do anything else, regardless of product or profit. And some people are so serious about their leisure activity, whether it be golf, bridge, or the piano, that it absorbs more of their energy and discipline than their work does. I wish to maintain in this essay that the most satisfying kind of work shares in the freedom and plasticity of play; that the most satisfying kind of play (in the long run) is purposeful and disciplined, like work; and that the good life for both individuals and societies must include plenty of both kinds of activities. As John Dewey put it, "Both [play and work] are equally free and intrinsically motivated, apart from false economic conditions which tend to make play into idle excitement for the well to do, and work into uncongenial labor for the poor."

The above thesis sounds plausible, I suppose; but any attempt to justify it runs into the notorious difficulty of defining both "play" and "work." . . .

"Play"

I submit that the following activities are all clearly examples of "play" and that a defini-tion which excludes any of them is therefore inadequate.

1. A one-year-old child rolling a toy across the floor or wearing his cereal on his head instead of eating it—or a kitten, puppy, or young chimpanzee doing the same things
2. A five-year-old boy engrossed in building a tower by himself or a girl making a dress for her doll
3. A pair of ten-year-old boys wrestling but laughing and taking care not to hurt one another—or two wolves doing the same thing
4. Two or more people of any age playing a game or sport, whether of skill or of chance, whether for money, for a prize, for the satisfaction of winning, or simply "for the fun of it"
5. A lone person playing a game or sport, etc.
6. Impersonation of someone or something else ("playing a role") without the intent to deceive
7. Variation for the sake of novelty, such as "doodling" while taking notes or decoration of a utilitarian object
8. Making a game out of a monotonous activity to avoid boredom, such as counting the red cars passed while driving home from the country
9. Putting on a performance for the amusement of an audience, whether for money, etc. (see no. 4)

This list is not intended to be exhaustive or exclusive: numbers 7 and 8 may be the same phenomenon, or numbers 6 and 9. It is simply a list of *examples* of play, chosen to be as uncontroversial as possible. There are interesting borderline cases, such as hiking or swimming, an evening of casual conversation, practicing a musical instrument, sexual "foreplay," the song of birds. For our purpose, however, the above list is long enough. Several observations follow directly from it:

a) Play cannot be a distinct type of observable behavior, since several of the paradigms (nos. 2, 6, 9) can involve almost any sort of behavior. A Martian would often fail to recognize play when he saw it, without some knowledge of the motives of the participants. This rules out a behaviorist approach.

b) Adults play as well as children, and not only when they are being childish (nos. 4–9); so we cannot define play as essentially a preparation for more mature activity.

c) Not all play is competitive, or social, or governed by rules (nos. 1, 2, 5, 7, 8); our definition must include free exploration of one's environment and experimentation with one's own faculties.

Let me try to formulate a defintion that will include all the paradigms on the list. A few common features emerge: freedom from compulsion, completeness of the activity itself apart from its result, and a certain artificial or "pretend" quality which is unobservable and hard to pin down but which is nevertheless present, I think, in the organized games and performances of adults, and even in the random exuberance of the child. I would define "play," therefore, as *activity which is free, complete in itself, and artificial or unrealistic.* I might add that play is often governed by rules, either explicit (as in a game) or implicit (there are rules of impersonation, for example); and that it often involves a test or contest. . . .

In itself, play is "not serious" in the sense that it contrasts with hard, everyday reality; with more earthy activities like eating, working, fighting, sex. It can be, however, and often is pursued with an attitude of rapt concentration and dogged persistence that surpasses these "more serious" activities. The difference is not in the degree of absorption involved, or in the value placed on the activity by the participant, but in its relationship to the life of man. Play is not just an attitude of mind: it is a type of *activity* in the world, normally associated with a certain attitude but not reducible to it. Play involves a representation or rehearsal of life, especially its agonistic aspects, according to tacit rules of simplification and projection. A child's play world is composed of elements drawn from his experience but rearranged so as to be more manageable and meaningful. The same is true

of many sports and games, whether of skill or chance: each generates a finite microcosm, where the things that can happen are strictly delimited. Not only do they take place in delimited areas—stadium, court, casino, board, etc.—and within fixed time limits, but according to rules which artificially equalize the conditions of competition between players and specify which few of their countless characteristics and actions will count as relevant to each game. The result is an artificially simplified world, in which each act has one and only one meaning. Each game is a system of symbolic acts, the meanings of which are drawn from real life but then refined and purified of connotations and ambiguities so that they can be combined in new and interesting ways. The best example is probably chess, drawn from military tactics in ancient India. Performances and impersonations likewise take place in microcosms, governed by the symbols and conventions of the theater. This description applies equally well, however, to the exploratory play of small children, except that the simplification is not for the sake of novelty and amusement but results from the child's inability to deal with more complex situations. Freud and Piaget are relevant here, but they adopt a patronizing attitude toward those who love this simpler world of symbols and conventions. . . .

Here lies the true significance of play in the life of man: in its more complex forms, it develops his creative, imaginative ability, enabling him to live not only in the "real" world but also in countless symbolic worlds of his own making. No doubt this makes him a more efficient solver of practical problems; but it also enables him to endow his life with form and meaning. What art, religion, and philosophy are for the few, play is for the many: a free, intrinsically satisfying activity governed by rules of man's own making and giving rise to a finite, meaningful world that man can call his own. . . .

"Work"

Perhaps "work" refers to an entirely different aspect of activity, different from play but not incompatible with it. In order to see whether this is true, let me begin again and assemble another list of paradigms, this time of work:

1. Physical toil, such as digging, hauling or lifting heavy objects, etc.
2. Physical toil performed by an ant or a mule
3. Physical toil performed by a machine
4. Any repetitive task, physical or mental, such as turning a screw on an assembly line or adding up columns of figures in an office
5. Assembling, arranging, or shaping materials into a product (and the product of such assembling or shaping)
6. Problem solving, practical or theoretical, such as untying a knot or designing a scientific experiment
7. Supervising the work of others
8. The proper functioning of any part of any machine
9. Providing a service for others, as does a butler or a babysitter
10. Any occupation for which one gets paid, either in money or in kind

This list tells us that work can be either physical or mental, either repetitive drudgery (nos. 1, 4) or creative activity (nos. 5, 6). It can apparently be performed by persons, animals, or machines (nos. 2–5, 8, even 6). Note that it need not be active in any overt way (nos. 6, 7, and some forms of nos. 9 and 10), so that a Martian would also fail to recognize these types of work when he saw them. The most striking thing about this list, however, is the way the various activities fall into clusters: paradigms 1–4 are of exhausting, or repetitive activity; 5–7 all involve arranging parts (materials, ideas, or people) so that they form a whole; and 8–10 refer to the functioning of a part in a whole. In paradigms 9 and 10, the "whole" is a social nexus in which one person takes the part (or part of the part) of another, or in which people participate in a common task and share in a common product (wealth). Is there a common idea underlying all three clusters? . . .

A single formula, then, seems to cover all types of work: *activity which is part of a larger whole or serves to unite parts into a whole.* This applies to intellectual as well as physical work and

to supervisory as well as menial functions. At the minimum, being paid for any activity proves that one is at least part of an economic whole to which others are willing to acknowledge one's contribution, even if the activity itself seems quite unproductive, like that of a business or government sinecure. An activity can be *for the sake of the whole,* then, regardless of whether this is the motive of the participant on any given occasion. . . .

Work has turned out *not* to be the simple opposite of play. Like play, work is the activity of a free agent. The discipline imposed on work by the whole of which it is a part, or which it is producing, is a freely accepted discipline; indeed, the concept of "discipline" applies only to a will that is free not to accept it. Play, too, may involve acceptance of the discipline of a whole—as a member of a team, or with an effort to perfect one's game—and to this extent it shares in the nature of work. The term "teamwork" is perfectly accurate and points to a whole range of activities which partake in both work and play.

Nor is work necessarily an activity incomplete and unsatisfying in itself, a mere means to an end. At the outset we noted that there is a kind of satisfaction from many kinds of work: Veblen called it "the instinct of workmanship." We can now see that this satisfaction must be derived from having helped to bring a new "whole" into existence. Whether this whole is a "work of art" or not, the feeling is an aesthetic one.

Finally, there is a kind of work which is not "realistic": in which the imagination soars to create ideal realms of truth, goodness, and beauty which give order and purpose to our mundane lives. In religion, art, science, and philosophy man creates symbols and values which transcend actual existence and are thus "artifice"; but there is no activity which better "serves to unite parts into a whole."

Conclusion

What, then, is the true relationship between work and play? We must conclude, I think, that each is a characteristic human activity associated with a characteristic attitude but that these are such as to be perfectly compatible with each other in the same activity at the same time. An athlete or a musician striving to perfect his technique, or to function smoothly in a team or an orchestra—regardless of whether he is a professional—can be said to be "working at playing." An architect experimenting with aesthetic effects, or a factory worker making a game out of his monotonous task, might equally well be said to be "playing at working" (except that in English, at least, this suggests that he is only pretending to work). . . .

There are some activities which are either "working at play" or "playing at work," and it is hard to tell which. The fine arts have all the characteristics of play, but people work so hard at them and *typically* take them so seriously—in our culture, anyway—that they seem to pass beyond the bounds of my definition. It is difficult to think of Michelangelo or Dostoevsky as "playing" when they created their somber masterpieces; but how about Paul Klee? Or John Cage? Twentieth-century art in general seems to be recapturing the spirit of play, together with discipline, that has characterized the arts among many peoples. Similarly, while the free play of imagination is essential to creativity in mathematics, philosophy, and the sciences, the element of discipline is so important that it seems impertinent to call them forms of play.

There are occupations which allow for autonomy, intrinsic satisfaction, and creativity, thus participating in the nature of play. My own occupation, that of a college professor, is one of these; and there are many others (but not enough) in business and the professions, in the arts and journalism, in certain crafts. There are also games which call for every ounce of intelligence, resourcefulness, and perseverance a man can muster. These continue to fascinate whole populations of mature adults; they are not just "recreation" but valuable activities in their own right.

I have tried to show that there are elements of both work and play in certain very satisfying activities and that it is the combination of these elements that accounts for their powerful and lasting fascination. In order to do this, I have had to define both terms and to show that there is no contradiction in applying both of them to the same activity at the same time. What matters is not to decide whether a free, satisfying, creative activity in which parts are disciplined by participation in a whole should be called basically "work" or "play" but to see to it that more people get to spend more of their time this way! My formula for utopia is simple: it is a community in which everyone plays at work and works at play. Anything less would fail to satisfy me for long.

MAX WEBER

Science as a vocation

I believe . . . you wish to hear [about] the *inward* calling for science. In our time, the internal situation, in contrast to the organization of science as a vocation, is first of all conditioned by the facts that science has entered a phase of specialization previously unknown and that this will forever remain the case. Not only externally, but inwardly, matters stand at a point where the individual can acquire the sure consciousness of achieving something truly perfect in the field of science only in case he is a strict specialist.

All work that overlaps neighboring fields, such as we occasionally undertake and which the sociologists must necessarily undertake again and again, is burdened with the resigned realization that at best one provides the specialist with useful questions upon which he would not so easily hit from his own specialized point of view. One's own work must inevitably remain highly imperfect. Only by strict specialization can the scientific worker become fully conscious, for once and perhaps never again in his lifetime, that he has achieved something that will endure. A really definitive and good accomplishment is today always a specialized accomplishment. And whoever lacks the capacity to put on blinders, so to speak, and to come up to the idea that the fate of his soul depends upon whether or not he makes the correct conjecture at this passage of this manuscript may as well stay away from science. He will never have what one may call the "personal experience" of science. Without this strange intoxication, ridiculed by every outsider; without this passion, this "thousands of years must pass before you enter into life and thousands more wait in silence"—according to whether or not you succeed in making this conjecture; without this, you have *no* calling for science and you should do something else. For nothing is worthy of man as man unless he can pursue it with passionate devotion.

NICHOLAS LEMANN

Going home

A curious fact: geographical mobility in America has been rising steadily since 1900. . . . In 1970 only a little more than half of the population had been living in the same house for five years. . . . In the big cities, of course, the figures are proportionally higher; in Washington, D.C., the most extreme example, less than half the city's population and less than a quarter of its white population was born there.

These figures don't go into the telling detail they might, but it's safe to say that mobility runs highest at the top end of the spectrum—the young, bright, and ambitious are the ones who are moving, and the old and poor the ones who are staying put. . . .

A simplified moral universe

A series of things . . . seems to go along with geographical mobility. When you go where what you're doing is done at its very best, you're essentially submitting yourself to judgment by external standards. It is this condition that underlies the mobility ethic; success and failure in the great metropolises and huge institutions take on an overriding importance. How good you are is determined according to well-established

rules, and in moving into the big cities and institutions you accept those rules and seek success as it is presently defined.

In other words, the tendency is to impose a single external standard on one's life—one didn't leave home, after all, for the sake of family or friends or familiar places and institutions, so those things recede in importance. Even friendship, if one's friends are the people with whom one works, hinges on success; it's not that your friends desert you if you switch jobs, it's just that the bonds of interest that once held you together have dissolved. In such a simplified moral universe, it's easy to see how contact with the most dizzying heights of success can bring on weak knees in even the most admirable people.

So it is that a great deal of the much-chronicled excitement of the Northeast is the sense of being near the most important events and best people of the day—that is, in the atmosphere of greatest possible success according to external standards. The unfortunate characteristics of this view of the world are manifold. It seems unsurprising, for instance, that although Washington is a fairly affluent metropolis, it lags behind others in things like United Way contributions per capita. When people are off to work practically at sunrise to beat the traffic in from the suburbs, when they have working breakfasts, working lunches, and working dinners, when they drag themselves home at night carrying full briefcases, the kind of extracurricular community activities and concerns they might have gotten involved in back home become, well, just out of the question.

The mobility ethic and its concomitant emphasis on success also create a less than ideal moral climate. With jobs and professional status so important, getting and keeping as many credentials as possible takes on an importance so great as to override things like the quality and consequence of one's work. Idealism, which ought to be at the very center of things, is instead purely a luxury to be cast aside when opportunity beckons or disapproval is threatened. Ambition, allowed to become the preeminent human motive, dissolves the nobler qualities.

Countervailing forces

This is not to say that all these sins aren't present in other places besides the Northeast; no doubt they are, and no doubt ambitious people behave ambitiously no matter where they are. But where people grow up there are certain countervailing forces at work on them, on which they base their identity—work, yes, and status and approval, but family and friends and community as well. They have a complex series of loyalties, and a wide circle of acquaintances outside their particular line of work, and a direct stake in the fate of their city or town. All this does more than perhaps enrich their lives in a way that the exciting big city cannot; it also makes it more likely that they will have more perspective on what they are doing. If one's sense of identity derives from family and long-time associations as well as work, it's easier to deal with failure, old age, and the rest of the unpleasant aspects of life. They do not absolutely destroy one's identity, as they might in a place away from all those old associations.

The web of countervailing loyalties in a small town also ties people together, so that they understand one another and their fates are intertwined. One of the worst consequences of bigness in general in America is that it fragments society to the point where people don't have to live with the consequences of what they do, indeed don't understand the effects of their actions. . . .

The balance needs to be better struck. . . . If it isn't, everybody and every place loses.

DANIEL BELL

Work and its discontents

Automation . . . will have enormous social effects. Just as factory work impressed its rhythms on society, so the rhythms of automation will give a new character to work, living, and leisure.

Automation will change the basic composition of the labor force, creating a new *salariat* instead of a *proletariat,* as automatic processes reduce the number of industrial workers required in production. In the chemical industry, for example, output rose, from 1947 to 1954, over 50 per cent, while the number of "blue-collar" workers increased only 1.3 per cent. At the same time, the number of non-production workers, that is, professional, supervisory, clerical, and sales personnel, increased by 50 per cent. In 1947, the ratio of production workers to non-production workers was 3:1. In 1954, in a seven-year period, the ratio had dropped to 2:1. . . .

For the individual worker, automation may bring a new concept of self. For in automation men finally lose the "feel" of work. Whatever the derogating effects, the men who use power-driven tools sense these instruments, almost as in driving an automobile, as an extension and enlargement of their own bodies, their machines responding, almost organically, to their commands and adding new dexterity and power to their own muscle skills. As a machine tender, a man now stands outside work, and whatever control once existed by "setting a bogey" (i.e., restricting output) is finally shattered. As one steelworker said, "You can't slow down the continuous annealer in order to get some respite." With the new dial-sets, too, muscular fatigue is replaced by mental tension, by the interminable watching, the endless concentration. (In the Puritan morality, the devil could always find work for "idle hands," and the factory kept a man's hands busy. But that morality ignored the existence of the fantasy life and its effects. Now, with machine-watching, there will be idle hands but no "idle minds." An advance in morality?)

Yet there is a gain for the worker in these new processes. Automation requires workers who can think of the plant as a whole. If there is less craft, less specialization, there is the need to know more than one job, to link boiler and turbine, to know the press and the borer and to relate their jobs to each other.

Most important, perhaps, there may be an end, too, to the measurement of work. Modern industry began not with the factory but with the measurement of work. When the worth of the

283

product was defined in production units, the worth of the worker was similarly gauged. Under the unit concept, the time-study engineers calculated that a worker would produce more units for more money. This was the assumption of the wage-incentive schemes (which actually are output-incentive schemes) and of the engineering morality of a "fair day's pay for a fair day's work."

But under automation, with continuous flow, a worker's worth can no longer be evaluated in production units. Hence output-incentive plans, with their involved measurement techniques, may vanish. In their place . . . may arise a new work morality. Worth will be defined not in terms of a "one best way," not by the slide rule and stop watch, not in terms of fractioned time or units of production, but on the basis of planning and organizing and the continuously smooth functioning of the operation. Here the team, not the individual worker, will assume a new importance; and the social engineer will come into his own. And work itself? . . .

In Western civilization, work, whether seen as curse or as blessing, has always stood at the center of moral consciousness. "In the sweat of thy brow," says Genesis, "shalt thou eat bread." The early Church fathers were intrigued about what Adam did before the Fall; in the variety of speculations, none assumed he was idle. He devoted himself to gardening, "the agreeable occupation of agriculture," said St. Augustine.

In the Protestant conception, all work was endowed with virtue. "A housemaid who does her work is no farther away from God than the priest in the pulpit," said Luther. Every man is "called," not just a few, and every place, not just a church, is invested with godliness. With Zwingli, even with dour Calvin, work was connected with the joy of creating and with exploring even the wonders of creation.

In the nineteenth century, beginning with Carlyle, man was conceived as *homo faber,** and human intelligence was defined as the capacity for inventing and using tools. If man in the Marxist sense was "alienated" from himself,

---

Ed. note: Man the artisan.

284

the self was understood as a man's potential for "making" things, rather than alienation as man being broken into a thing itself. (Man will be free when "nature is his work and his reality" and he "recognizes himself in a world he has himself made," said Marx in his early philosophical-economic manuscripts, adopting an image that A. E. Housman later turned into a lament.) In the same vein, John Dewey argued that a man "learned by doing," but the phrase, now a progressive-school charade, meant simply that men would grow not by accepting prefigured experiences but by seeking problems that called for new solutions. ("Unlike the handling of a tool," said Dewey, "the regulation of a machine does not challenge man or teach him anything; therefore he cannot grow through it.")

All these are normative conceptions. In Western history, however, work has had a deeper "moral unconscious." It was a way, along with religion, of confronting the absurdity of existence and the beyond. Religion, the most pervasive of human institutions, played a singular symbolic role in society because it faced for the individual the problem of death. Where death was but a prelude to eternal life, hell and heaven could be themes of serious discourse, and domination on earth had a reduced importance. But with the decline in religious belief went a decline in the power of belief in eternal life. In its place arose the stark prospect that death meant the total annihilation of the self. (Hamlet, as Max Horkheimer points out, "is the embodiment of the idea of individuality for the very reason that he fears the finality of death, the terror of the abyss.")

Many of these fears were staved off by work. Although religion declined, the significance of work was that it could still mobilize emotional energies into creative challenges. (For Tolstoy, as later for the Zionists in the Israeli *kibbutzim,* work was a religion; A. D. Gordon, the theoretician of the cooperative communities, preached redemption through physical labor.) One could eliminate death from consciousness by minimizing it through work. As *homo faber,* man could seek to master nature and to discipline himself.

Work, said Freud, was the chief means of binding an individual to reality. What will happen, then, when not only the worker but work itself is displaced by the machine?

FRIEDRICH GEORG JUENGER

The mechanical sterility of modern sports

The influence of technology upon man is apparent not only in man's work; we see it also in his favorite amusements, and in his favorite sports. Sports presuppose and are, in fact, impossible without the technically organized city. The technical terms of our modern sports are largely of English origin. This is owing to the British head start in industrialization, particularly in the first half of the nineteenth century. Engineers and technicians from all over the world then traveled to England to round out their technical education. Later, when America had become the technically leading nation, sports too became Americanized. Sports receive little support from technically backward countries, and none at all from the vast regions which so far have not been industrialized.

Sports, then, may be defined as a reaction to the conditions under which man lives in the large cities. This reaction is dependent upon the increasing mechanization of motion. "Savages" do not practice sports. They exercise their physical faculties; they play, dance, and sing, but there is nothing sportslike in these activities, even if they are performed with virtuosity. Our best sportsmen significantly hail from the industrial districts where mechanization is at its highest, particularly from the cities. Farmers, foresters, professional hunters, and fishermen, those whose movements are free of mechanical compulsion, rarely practice sports. The headway that sports are making in the rural districts is in fact a yardstick of advancing mechanization, particularly the mechanization of farming.

For the operation of that machinery changes the muscular development and with it the operator's movements. In older generations, lifelong hard manual labor had produced that heaviness and hardness of body, that clumsiness typical of the peasant. Now these features are disappearing. He becomes nimble and more agile since the machine relieves him from direct contact with the soil. The driver of a tractor or a combine has a body different from that of the ploughman or the mower.

It is not easy to draw a sharp line between play and sports, because there is hardly a game that cannot be practiced as a sport. The Olympic Games of the Greeks, obviously, were not sports but festivals of a religious character, combined with contests. They cannot be called sports simply because of the absence of the industrial scene, which is the background of what we moderns term sports. What we call Olympic games in memory of antiquity are highly technical sports to which flock the specialists from all countries. There is a difference between the man for whom hunting or swimming, fishing or rowing are natural pursuits, parts of his life, and the man who practices hunting, swimming, fishing, or rowing as a sport. The latter obviously is a technician who has developed to perfection the mechanical side of his activity. The equipment of the modern sportsman alone indicates this. To get an impression of the growing mechanization, we need only look at the tools used in sports, all those elaborate fishing rods and reels, all those scientific golf balls and clubs, the stop watches, time clocks, measuring devices, starting machines, and so on. In the exact timings of motions and split-second recordings of modern sports we find again that organization and control of the consumption of time that characterize technology.

And is not the sportsman's lingo a language of typically mechanical hardness?

Finally, let us consider the organization of the sports business itself: the athletic teams, their training, their scores, their lists of members, and their records. Plainly the popularity of modern sports is connected with the advance of mechanization, and the sports themselves are practiced more and more mechanically. This is evident not only in automobile races, air races, or speedboat races, where engines are used; we see the same thing in such sports as boxing, wrestling, swimming, running, jumping, throwing, weight-lifting. Even in these the individual turns himself into a machine, a fighting or record-breaking machine, whose every motion is controlled and checked by machinery until it becomes mechanical. Consequently sportsmen today are becoming professionals, who make a profitable business of their special talents.

Doubtless sports are an activity which, with increasing mechanization, is becoming more and more indispensable to man. We find, too, that the discipline to which sports subject the human body results in extraordinary performances. However, there is a peculiar sterility in the sports business of today which can be traced to the mechanization of sports activities and to their mushrooming into huge technical organizations. Long observation makes this ever more evident. They lack completely all spontaneous movement, all free improvisation.

A man who starts to jump and run for the sheer joy of jumping and running and who stops when the mood has left him is entirely different from the man who enters an athletic event in which, under guidance of technical rules and with the use of time clocks and measuring apparatus, he jumps and runs in an attempt to break a record. The high pleasure that swimming and diving give us is due to the touch of water, its crystal freshness, its coolness, purity, transparency, and gentle yielding. This delight, obviously, is of no significance in contests where professional swimmers perform. For the purpose of such contests is to find out which swimmer has the most perfect technique and consequently reaches the goal faster than the rest. Training for record-breaking is essentially an intensification of will power aimed at complete mastery over the body which has to obey mechanically. Such an effort may be quite useful and effective. But the more the training for, and the breaking of, records become ends in themselves, the more sterile they grow.

The physique of the modern athlete betrays the one-sided training to which it is subjected. His body is trained, but it is anything but beautiful. The body-building, as effected by specialized sports, does not achieve beauty, because it lacks proportion, something a body devoted to special training no more can have than a mind narrowed down to highly specialized interests. When the sports-trained body is considered beautiful, it is due not merely to the absence of a trained eye, to insufficient study of the nude. No, an appraisal of this sort also expresses the fact that the human body is judged by mechanical criteria such as muscular dimensions and, in particular, by the specialized training it shows. These criteria, however, lack appreciation for the quiet, effortless fullness of beauty; they do not consider relaxed easiness or charm and grace. These viewpoints are deficient in spirituality as well as in sensuality. Unbalance and exaggeration of physique as bred by modern sports are most striking with women. Both their bodies and their faces acquire hardened, sterile traits. Modern sports are incompatible with any kind of artistic life and activity; they are essentially unartistic and unspiritual by nature.

A comparison suggests itself between the sportsman and the ascetic, who is also a professional, though in quite a different sense. The training of the sportsman has an ascetic trait, and through all sports we find a certain puritanism, a strict hygiene of physical habits, which controls sleep, nutrition, and sex life from the viewpoint of efficiency. Sportsmen are not a group of people who exuberantly express their abundance of vital energy, but a tribe of strict professionals who rigidly economize their every ounce of strength, lest they waste a single motion of their money-making, fame-making physique.

GARY SHAW

Meat on the hoof

After our first week with Hewlett [the "brain coach" at the University of Texas] I knew our education, like football, was to be spelled D-I-S-C-I-P-L-I-N-E, and that I needed to start psyching myself to be ever ready.

As an aid to this mechanical preparation, our lives were strictly regimented. Hewlett had arranged our fall classes in the morning and early afternoon. We went from one to another, from desk to desk, until two P.M. Then we prepared for our football workout. For me, it was sometimes hard to tell the difference between my classes and workouts. In both I quickly finished one part, then moved on to the next. The object was to get through them and accomplish my mission, their defeat. And after succeeding, I would move on to another course—another contest.

We were usually at the field house by two-thirty for taping. By three-thirty we were on the field. Workouts lasted until about five-thirty. By the time we showered and got back to the dorm it was time for supper at six. My first semester the freshmen were to be at a required study hall at seven. Study hall was over at ten. Back to the dorm and to bed. Every activity was oriented toward getting us disciplined and well oiled. Success and winning meant denial, doing what was not easy—not liked. . . .

When we joined the varsity, this regimentation and its seriousness was increased. In fact, very few things were important enough to interfere with [Coach] Royal's tight organization. For example, the day President Kennedy was shot in Dallas, the varsity was on the practice field preparing for Texas A & M at their regularly scheduled time—two hours after Kennedy's death. Royal told us that this is what President Kennedy would have wanted us to do. . . .

In the time requiring our physical presence we had at least a thirty- to forty-hour work week. Interestingly enough, the university will not let anyone who is working over thirty hours take a full course load (anything over nine hours), yet all of us were taking a bare minimum of ten hours and most of us twelve to fifteen hours. . . .

Obviously, for Hewlett, the only important factor was winning the grades. And he could tell us how to get there—in fact, he always spoke of how well he knew the ins and outs of the university. . . .

An example of this "educational expertise" was his handling of the university faculty. He encouraged their full support by allowing selected "inside" glimpses of Royal's program. . . .

One student-athlete to come out of this academic climate was our freshman coach, Pat Culpepper. Culpepper had been All-American both on the field and scholastically. . . .

His initial speech about education came at the end of our first week. "Men, you are at the university for two reasons—and only two reasons—to play football and to get an education. To do these two things you must sacrifice all else, because that's what it will take. And men, I realize that there will be many temptations to take your minds off these objectives, but to be a winner, you must deny yourself. It is a Spartan existence; but for this Spartan life you will be held in special esteem, the campus will look up to you, and you will be part of the Texas football tradition."

We were special. And I did feel pride in the realization of how tough I'd have to be, that the others couldn't go through what I would. . . .

I was determined to be completely dedicated to both football and school. If I wasn't on the field or in class, I was studying. And any time I strayed from these duties I felt immediately guilty. In fact, there was only about thirty minutes during the day when I felt free from my discipline. This was the half-hour interval between leaving my last class and going to the field house. This was the most valued time of my freshman year. In this brief thirty minutes I had one place to which I always escaped, one place where I felt completely free but secure. It seems rather ludicrous now, but my best moments as a freshman Longhorn were spent at the same time every day, in the same toilet stall, and on the same john. And I am thoroughly convinced that being able to lock that stall, and then sit and read a magazine in total privacy for thirty minutes each day, enabled me to survive that first year.

My Culpepper-like dedication to disciplined study lasted until the middle of my second semester and then suddenly collapsed. From this point until I graduated I usually concerned myself with finding the shortest routes to the end results. And like most of my teammates, I began going to any lengths to avoid studying. . . .

So far as we were concerned, our education was just another external measure. And so most of us, including myself, became interested in finding the easy courses rather than the stimulating ones. . . .

Unfortunately, any number of other means to our ends, including cheating, came to be widely used and pretty much accepted, or at best ignored. . . .

Coach Royal, of course, would have said he was against our cheating, but whether he was or not, it was basically not in conflict with his exclusive emphasis on end results. . . .

The American male who ceaselessly pushes himself to the top, while trying to score as the office stud on the side, is going in the same direction I was. This same inner belief of "what makes a man" is also what creates millions of fanatical fans in America who, under the right circumstances, would have been on the field with us. We have surrendered our identities to some stereotyped stallion gone mad. And the more this horse seems to be disappearing from our culture, the more fervidly we cling to the saddle. The new institutional representative and spokesman for this horse has become American sports, especially football. So what I was caught up in was the extreme of what most of us American men are caught up in, and I couldn't seem to disentangle myself. Football was not just an activity for me, it had become my way of dealing with life—"playing the game." I played to win at everything, which meant I could never let down my defense for a moment for fear an opponent would score against me; and as a result, like most American men I was basically without real human contact, alone and scared. The more

threatened I felt as I began to wander away from my ego pump, football, the more I felt I had to score somewhere else.

Maybe this is the biggest reason why many never leave football, although while in its grips they are never really secure as men. Though they have to constantly prove themselves on the field, at least there they know the rules well, and they're good enough to win frequently. Whereas to leave this world would only mean that they would have to score somewhere else in a more uncertain, less controlled environment. And football will continue to have appeal to those not in it for this same reason. They envy football players because their rules for being a man are clear—in football you know when you've won or lost, unlike many of their work-life encounters. But they fail to see that a clear-cut victory leads only to another challenge in a perpetual rat race, even more restricting than the one they're in. As long as there is an attempt to hold on to this simple view of life as a series of challenges and victories with a few winners and many losers, then we will be trapped in an anxious and basically frustrating existence. . . .

Sadly, most football players seem just as driven all their life; there are never enough victories. . . . After football they must win at getting the most money, selling the most insurance—drive, drive, and in the background some high school alma mater plays on. Like cotton candy there is never enough until finally, if you're lucky, your system throws up from a total lack of nutrition. But this cotton rot is the eternal prize held in front of the donkey. And supporting this donkey's powerful reluctance to quit his running is the inability to admit that his achieved tastes of victory were not worth the price—not worth the unpleasant experiences that were required to get there. "Everybody wants to win—some just can't pay the price." What if we all simply decide it ain't worth it? . . .

The guilt and anxiety of quitting football were growing into a firm resentment, a clear hate of what I'd seen the past four years. It was a resentment that touched some inner base. I wanted to act.

Chachie [a fullback] and I started talking to

each other several times a week. On each occasion we discussed football and what it had demanded of us. Our thoughts crystallized rapidly and we took turns attacking the abuses and hypocrisy of college football. I became incensed as I recalled some of the personal scenes I'd witnessed on a football field, the total disregard by the coaches of us as people, the complete sham of portraying us as student-athletes to the public, and the psychological misery we'd gone through and seen our friends go through. What could we do? We decided we couldn't let it go any further.

One November night in 1966 at two in the morning, Chachie woke me with an excited rap on my window.

"I've got it, I've got it!" he said. . . .

"We're going to do an exposé! We're going to tell all! We're going to have a news conference and let everyone know about shit drills and everything else that goes on!" . . .

I knew the extent of the problem was far deeper than exposing the abuses of college football. . . .

It's not just that football is so popular and that attacking it would endanger the enjoyment these people have on Saturday afternoons. And it runs much deeper than the fact that football is a big business, and big businessmen happen to like one another's company. No, I think it runs right to the core of the American psyche. . . . Only a few get to be winners, and you make it by competing and by defeating others. Life is a big football game. It's why politicians like Nixon praise football so much. It's why Nixon loves to be thought of as the quarterback, and why he constantly reminds us of his losing in 1960, and then "fighting back" to defeat Humphrey in 1968—thus proving his worth as a winner. To attack football is to attack the major exhibit of the masculine view of the world. And on a gut level, the winners in this survival-of-the-fittest code sense the connection. Thus to condemn the method of college football would be to condemn their simplistic world view and focus light on the shallow, deprived existence that depends on glory, fame, and power. It would be much more strongly resisted than an attack on the church or most other American institutions

(if not all) because the football code is much more their lifeblood, and their lifeblood in its purest, most elemental form. It is a lifeblood that they accurately sense is already being eroded by youth and the new culture. . . . Football is the strongest remaining unquestioned remnant of an old culture, and the struggle to change its current form is no less than the conflict between an old culture and a new culture.

Philip Slater says in *The Pursuit of Loneliness* that if change does not affect the motivational roots of a society then it is not real change. The development of a cooperative society where individual worth and strength is not based on defeating others cannot be accomplished by using the old culture's rules. To concentrate on competing against and defeating those in power is to replace one winner with another. Instead we must use our energies to discover our real wants and then move toward fulfilling them.

LANCE RENTZEL

When all the laughter died in sorrow

It was obvious by Wednesday that my teammates [on the Dallas Cowboys] had heard the rumors [of my being questioned for indecent exposure]. No one came out and said anything, but I could sense they were looking at me strangely. I didn't know whether to say anything or not. . . .

Then I got a call telling me that the *Oklahoma City Times*—from the town where my family was prominent, and where I grew up—had plastered the whole story all over the front page, and there was a good chance that it might be picked up by the wire services and released across the entire country.

That night I knew what I had to do. There was a team meeting at the Hilton Hotel, where we stayed before our home games. About fifty of us were crowded into the meeting room. Some were standing because there weren't enough chairs for us all. Landry walked in and opened the meeting. He told the team that I had something I wanted to say. . . .

Because of the confined space, everyone seemed almost on top of me, and all I could feel was a sudden burst of shame. In a sense, I had never really been one of them. Mostly I lived a different way of life from theirs. Different kinds of friends, different backgrounds. I dressed differently, wore my hair longer, acted less conservatively than most. When I was single, I avoided the parties of the married crowd and went my own way, because I felt a little out of place. After I married Joey,* I still stayed away because a couple of the other wives had not been friendly to her. Now I was going to ask them to bear with me, and I wondered if they would accept such a plea.

"I suppose you've all heard a lot of stories about me in the last few days, and I feel you should hear from me what's going on. Well, the stories are pretty much true, and I want you to understand the truth about it, so that you'll know how to handle it. . . . I guess everybody makes mistakes in his life. Well, I've made some bad ones. I'm in serious trouble and I don't know what's going to happen."

I got that much out without too much difficulty; then I began to choke badly. . . .

"I want to apologize to you. If I've embarrassed you as teammates, I'm really sorry. I hope that you'll want me to stay on the team, and that you'll support me and consider me a friend—because that's what I want to be. That's what I want above all."

I sat down and there was not a sound for a second or two, then a few loud swallows, including my own. . . .

I started to cry, I couldn't help it, I fought it, holding my hand in front of my mouth. I looked up and saw that I wasn't the only one in tears. I wanted to run from the room, I began wishing [Coach] Landry would turn out the damn lights and start the film so I could

_____

*Ed. note: Joey Heatherton, an actress and entertainer.

hide in the darkness, and it seemed like forever before they did.

Then, in the dark, Landry tried to bring everyone's attention back to the game, to watch the Green Bay kicking teams on film, but you could feel how impossible that was, I'd ruined that for the moment at least. Then this incredible thing happened: a hand grabbed my shoulder, a huge hand, and it held on, firmly, supportively, and then, from the other side, a tap on the arm, then again. The room was dark and the coach was talking, but there was a shuffling and a sound of scraping chairs, as one after another they moved to make contact with me. They wanted to remain anonymous and did not wish to be open about it, but they wanted to convey the unspoken message: "We're with you." I wondered how I could have doubted them. I knew one thing: I'd never forget that moment.

The meeting ended and the team went to dinner. The guys at my table talked normally, as they always did the night before a game. At times I forgot the trouble I was in and talked as if nothing had happened. Dan Reeves came up and whispered, "Everyone makes a mistake, but few people have the courage to stand up and admit it the way you did. We're all on your side." During the rest of the meal, other players and coaches approached me; each came alone and said something in his own way to let me know he was not judging me. They understood what I was going through and they felt for me. And now, for the first time, these men who hardly ever weaken or display their feelings were saying things they ordinarily wouldn't. It was interesting noticing who spoke to me and who didn't, although I realized that the ones who remained silent were not necessarily against me. Everyone reacts differently in a moment like this. . . .

When I got to Carl Oates's office [on Monday], Bob Strauss was there to give me the bad news: charges had been filed that morning, the publicity was already out, clattering off press wires throughout the country, and I was a doomed man. . . .

The news that evening was overwhelming. Every newspaper in America played it up, and it was on television coast to coast. Several sportscasters in New York said I no longer belonged in the world of sports. . . .

It was only the beginning. Whatever happened from here on in, this flurry of international publicity (carried by the wire services all the way to Japan, Australia, and Vietnam) was just the start of my problems. I knew wherever I went, or whatever I did, I was a marked man from this day on.

My phone never stopped ringing. I got calls from everywhere, all of them offering support, but the one I appreciated the most was from Craig Morton. "We'll see you at 9:30 in the morning," he said, "in time for practice." For the team had voted unanimously to ask me to continue playing. I was completely surprised by this. Once again, I realized how much these guys meant to me. They were willing to share my guilt in order to help me out. I knew how much I wanted to play, how much I *needed* to play, especially now when all the world was caving in on me, when my mind was going to be burdened with too many pressures, when my life threatened to become rootless and ridden with shame. If I could play ball, if I could be part of this team, if I could spend at least part of my day driving my body and my concentration toward this new Cowboy surge to the championship, everything else would be that much more tolerable. There was no legal or NFL rule to prevent me from playing. The team wanted me back, and I needed to go back. When Bob Hayes stopped in to chat—he had tried to call but couldn't get through—I told him, yes, I'd be there in the morning. . . .

At 11:30 Tom Landry called. He was very sympathetic but full of doubts about the consequences if I continued to play. He asked me to think about it from all points of view. How would the public react to my remaining with the team? Would the criticism of me increase, and if so, would that affect my performance? Would criticism be directed toward the team, and would it affect their playing?

I thought about it a minute and realized that he was making some valid points. I had to stay away until the case was legally resolved, or I would cause a great deal of abuse to be focused on the team, as well as myself. And this would certainly hamper the Cowboys' comeback.

There was no getting around it. I couldn't play.

The next morning I went out to the Cowboy training quarters, about six or seven miles northeast of town, through a pleasant area that's just beginning to be developed. The building itself was temporary, walled by corrugated metal but very pleasant inside, with thick carpets, a pleasant lounge, and inside the locker rooms huge individual compartments. . . . It had been a second home for me in the way an office can be for a man who loves his work.

So now I was leaving this home for what, at the moment, read as a two-week vacation. I maintained the belief that I would be back, so I talked to them again, I told them that I was going on the move list, the best solution for the time being, and I thanked them all for their support: it meant a lot to me.

After hearing what I had to say, they asked me to leave the meeting. They wanted to discuss it among themselves, hoping that maybe they could figure out some way in which I could play. So I went back to the locker room and sat by my compartment, all alone. The room was totally silent, and it crossed my mind that this was the first time I'd ever been in it without dozens of others, that its silence was ominous, suggestive of my changing status. I sat there, hands clasped in front of me, and I looked up at the rows of locker stalls, reading the names above them and suddenly feeling like a hero-worshiping fan who had somehow managed to sneak inside. Morton, Hayes, Lilly, Garrison . . . I was so locked into being a part of them. Green, Hill, Reeves, Renfro, Rentzel. Yes, Rentzel. This was me, this was what I did. I played on this team and these were my friends. I sweated with them, worked with them, won with them, suffered with them. I would be nothing without being a part of this team. Football had been the opening door to everything that was worthwhile in my life (even Joey, I could not help thinking). And now all I could do was wonder if I'd ever be back.

My head was swimming with these things when Cornell Green beckoned me to come back to the meeting room. Lee Roy Jordon delivered the team message: yes, they all wanted me to play, they wanted very much for me to play, especially since they were winning ball games again and there was a chance that they could come through for the division title. But then, they understood the problem, that it was a bad situation for everyone; if I felt it was best that I go on the move list, they accepted it as an unfortunate reality. They appreciated my feelings and my concern for them. They wanted me to know that anything they could do for me, they would do it at the asking.

I was very touched. Lee Roy told it very well.

"You all will never know how much your support means to me," I said. "I promise you one thing, and remember this: no matter how bad things get, I won't ever quit. Ever. It may take a while, but I'll be back. So long."

And that was it. I walked out, unaware that I would never return.

JOSEF PIEPER

Leisure, the basis of culture

In order to gain a clear notion of leisure we must begin by setting aside the prejudice—our prejudice—that comes from overvaluing the sphere of work. In his well-known study of capitalism Max Weber quotes the saying, that "one does not work to live; one lives to work," which nowadays no one has much difficulty in understanding: it expresses the current opinion. We even find some difficulty in grasping that it reverses the order of things and stands them on their head.

But what ought we to say to the opposite view, to the view that "we work in order to have leisure"? We should not hesitate to say that here indeed "the world of topsy-turvydom," the

world that had been stood on its head, has been clearly expressed. To those who live in a world of nothing but work, in what we might call the world of "total work," it presumably sounds immoral, as though directed at the very foundations of human society.

That maxim is not, however, an illustration invented for the sake of clarifying this thesis: it is a quotation from Aristotle; and the fact that it expresses the view of a cool-headed workaday realist (as he is supposed to have been) gives it all the more weight. Literally, the Greek says "we are unleisurely in order to have leisure." . . .

This is perhaps the point at which to anticipate the objection: "What does Aristotle honestly matter to us? We may admire the world of antiquity, but why should we feel under any obligation to it?"

Among other things, it might be pointed out in reply that the Christian and Western conception of the contemplative life is closely linked to the Aristotelian notion of leisure. It is also to be observed that this is the source of the distinction between the *artes liberales* and the *artes serviles,* the liberal arts and servile work. . . .

Leisure, it must be clearly understood, is a mental and spiritual attitude—it is not simply the result of external factors, it is not the inevitable result of spare time, a holiday, a week-end or a vacation. It is, in the first place, an attitude of mind, a condition of the soul, and as such utterly contrary to the ideal of "worker" in each and every one of the three aspects . . . : work as activity, as toil, as a social function.

Compared with the exclusive ideal of work as activity, leisure implies (in the first place) an attitude of non-activity, of inward calm, of silence; it means not being "busy," but letting things happen. . . .

Leisure is a receptive attitude of mind, a contemplative attitude, and it is not only the occasion but also the capacity for steeping oneself in the whole of creation. . . .

Leisure is not the attitude of mind of those who actively intervene, but of those who are open to everything; not of those who grab and grab hold, but of those who leave the reins loose and who are free and easy themselves—almost like a man falling asleep, for one can only fall asleep by "letting oneself go." . . . When we really let our minds rest contemplatively on a rose in bud, on a child at play, on a divine mystery, we are rested and quickened as though by a dreamless sleep. . . .

Compared with the exclusive ideal of work as toil, leisure appears (*secondly*) in its character as an attitude of contemplative "celebration," a word that, properly understood, goes to the very heart of what we mean by leisure. Leisure is possible only on the premise that man consents to his own true nature and abides in concord with the meaning of the universe (whereas idleness . . . is the refusal of such consent). Leisure draws its vitality from affirmation. It is not the same as non-activity, nor is it identical with tranquillity; it is not even the same as inward tranquillity. Rather, it is like the tranquil silence of lovers, which draws its strength from concord. . . . And we may read in the first chapter of Genesis that God "ended his work which he had made" and "behold, it was very good." In leisure man, too, celebrates the end of his work by allowing his inner eye to dwell for a while upon the reality of the Creation. He looks and he affirms: it is good. . . .

And *thirdly,* leisure stands opposed to the exclusive ideal of work *qua* social function. A break in one's work, whether of an hour, a day or a week, is still part of the world of work. It is a link in the chain of utilitarian functions. The pause is made for the sake of work and in order to work, and a man is not only refreshed *from* work but *for* work. Leisure is an altogether different matter; it is no longer on the same plane; it runs at right angles to work. . . . And therefore leisure does not exist for the sake of work—however much strength it may give a man to work; the point of leisure is not to be a restorative, a pick-me-up, whether mental or physical; and though it gives new strength, mentally and physically, and spiritually too, that is not the point.

Leisure, like contemplation, is of a higher order than the *vita activa* (although the active life is the proper human life in a more special sense). . . .

The point and the justification of leisure are not that the functionary should function faultlessly and without a breakdown, but that the functionary should continue to be a man—and that means that he should not be wholly absorbed in the clear-cut milieu of his strictly limited function; the point is also that he should retain the faculty of grasping the world as a whole and realizing his full potentialities as an entity meant to reach Wholeness.

Because Wholeness is what man strives for, the power to achieve leisure is one of the fundamental powers of the human soul. Like the gift for contemplative absorption in the things that are and like the capacity of the spirit to soar in festive celebration, the power to know leisure is the power to overstep the boundaries of the workaday world and reach out to superhuman, life-giving existential forces which refresh and renew us before we turn back to our daily work. Only in genuine leisure does a "gate to freedom" open. Through that gate man may escape from the "restricted area" of that "latent anxiety" which a keen observer has perceived to be the mark of the world of work, where "work and unemployment are the two inescapable poles of existence."

"Then it's agreed—one million for research in recycling and two million to publicize it."

14

THE
MORALITY
OF
BUSINESS

In capitalist countries, there are businessmen; in communist ones, there are only workers and officials. This chapter on the morals of business and businessmen, therefore, refers only to capitalist societies.

The most devastating attack leveled against business morality has come from Karl Marx. The immorality that Marx inveighs against is not immorality in business, for example, corruption, theft, or the like, but the immorality *of* business. The whole enterprise, at its root and in its logic, is rotten. By its very success, Marx argues, business has substituted money values for every kind of tie between men and every kind of human activity. The bourgeoisie "has resolved personal worth into exchange value. . . . The bourgeoisie has stripped of its halo every occupation hitherto honored and looked up to with reverent awe. It has converted the physician, the lawyer, the priest, the poet, the man of science, into its paid wage laborers." In the rest of the selection, Marx shows how capitalism has been exploitative and expansionist, creating "a world after its own image."

The solid bourgeois, whom Marx pilloried, was the champion of the free market—the classic liberal, who, today in America, is often referred to as a conservative. The defense of the free market is based on both the economic freedom and the political liberty that a free economy secures. Moreover, capitalism is supported for its influence on individual morality because it allegedly creates an atmosphere in which individual choice and responsibility are at their greatest. Milton Friedman presents the case for the free market, contending that "underlying most arguments against the free market is a lack of belief in freedom itself."

In the next article, however, Nicholas Eberstadt points out that throughout most of Western history, businessmen were not free to pursue their private ends. From ancient Greek times until the Industrial Revolution, political and social controls were designed to assure that business operated in the public interest. The Industrial Revolution, however, brought the giant corporation, with its attitude of "the public be damned." Eberstadt sees today's movement toward corporate responsibility as an attempt to restore the old Western tradition.

Wayne Leys then argues that by the 1960s there had already been a marked rise in the standards of business ethics. He claims that deception, for example, was far more rampant in the nineteenth century: "'Complete sewing machines' were being offered for a dime and the expectant mail-order purchaser received a needle." Today, a promoter "makes his plans, keeping in mind certain rights of customers, competitors, investors, employees and neighbors. He must avoid cutthroat competition, but not be guilty of collusion. . . . He must provide job security, but not in a way that can be called feather-bedding." These limits—the latest being minority hiring quotas and environmental standards—are set by the government to make business socially responsible.

But these controls have failed to prevent widespread abuses, claims consumer advocate Ralph Nader in the next selection. According to Nader, "In the ideology of American business, free competition and corporate 'responsibility' are supposed to protect the consumer; in practice, both have long been ignored." The result has been "an assault on the health and safety of the public" from "dangerous industrial products, by-products, and foods."

However, labor-union official Gus Tyler insists in the following article, there are limits on what can be expected from "corporate responsibility." Arguing that the nation should not "shirk its collective responsibility by unloading onto the corporations that which the corporations cannot do," Tyler points

out that corporate funds ultimately come from "all kinds of plain people of limited means who count on proper (profitable) investment of their funds, just to have the income now or later to make ends meet. Hence, the prime business of a corporation is the business of making money for its investors." Corporations cannot, therefore, be primarily concerned with helping society at large.

One way in which some corporations have sought to remain profitable is by expansion overseas. Many analysts warn that these largest corporations, whose operations span several countries, pose a threat today. These multinational firms may wield great power through their subsidiaries and remain beyond the reach of any nation's sovereignty. Robert Heilbroner discounts these fears, claiming that "all the multinational companies are, in fact, national companies that have extended their operations abroad." He ridicules the notion that foreign operations or foreign control bodes danger to national governments: "What difference does it make to our national sovereignty if Valium or chocolate bars are made by a Swiss rather than a U.S. firm?" Admitting that these giant complexes can have pernicious effects on developing countries, Heilbroner maintains that this has long been true of foreign investment and is not a new departure.

In sharp opposition to Heilbroner's article is a report by William Carley on the recent international bribery scandal. There, it becomes apparent that the corporate bribery offenses will not be fully prosecuted because such cases would require an international investigation that is beyond the power of any nation's sovereignty. Thus, for the present, corporate officers appear to be immune from legal control.

Karl Marx and **Friedrich Engels.** See above, p. 127.

Milton Friedman, born in 1912, is Paul Snowden Russell Professor of Economics at the University of Chicago. A contributing editor of *Newsweek,* he is also the author of several books on the economy, including *A Program for Monetary Stability* and *A Theoretical Framework for Monetary Analysis. Capitalism and Freedom,* excerpted here, was published in 1962.

Nicholas N. Eberstadt, born in 1956, is a student at Harvard University. He has worked on a project on corporate responsibility for the Rockefeller Foundation. "What History Tells Us About Corporate Responsibility" appeared in *Business and Society Review* in 1973.

Wayne A. R. Leys, born in 1905, taught philosophy at the University of Chicago until 1963. He was a member and director of various projects devoted to cultural exchange, including the National Conference of Christians and Jews, and was lecturer to several universities and governmental agencies. He wrote *Ethics and Social Policy* (1941) and (with C. M. Perry) *Philosophy and the Public Interest* (1959). "Ethics in American Business and Government," excerpted here, first appeared in *The Annals of the American Academy of Political and Social Science* in 1968.

Ralph Nader. See above, p. 103. "The Great American Gyp" was first published in *The New York Review of Books,* November 1968.

Gus Tyler is assistant president of the International Ladies Garment Workers Union and director of the union's political and educational departments. He was on the planning committee for the nation's bicentennial program, American Issues Forum and has participated in many government conferences. A syndicated columnist for United Features, he is also the author of *Organized Crime in America* and *The Economics of Scarcity.* "On the Limits of Corporate Responsibility," reprinted here, first appeared in *Dissent* in 1974.

Robert L. Heilbroner, born in 1919, is Norman Thomas Professor at the New School for Social Research, where he has been a member of the faculty since 1963. Among his major works are *The Worldly Philosophers, The Making of Economic Society, Between Capitalism and Socialism,* and *An Inquiry into the Human Prospect.* "None of Your Business" was first published in *The New York Review of Books* in March 1975.

William M. Carley is a columnist for the *Wall Street Journal* in which the article reprinted here first appeared in July 1976.

KARL MARX and FRIEDRICH ENGELS

Manifesto of the communist party

The bourgeoisie, historically, has played a most revolutionary part.

The bourgeoisie, wherever it has got the upper hand, has put an end to all feudal, patriarchal, idyllic relations. It has pitilessly torn asunder the motley feudal ties that bound man to his "natural superiors," and has left remaining no other nexus between man and man than naked self-interest, than callous "cash payment." It has drowned the most heavenly ecstasies of religious fervor, of chivalrous enthusiasm, of Philistine sentimentalism in the icy water of egotistical calculation. It has resolved personal worth into exchange value and, in place of the numberless indefeasible chartered freedoms, has set up that single, unconscionable freedom—free trade. In one word, for exploitation, veiled by religious and political illusions, it has substituted naked, shameless, direct, brutal exploitation.

The bourgeoisie has stripped of its halo every occupation hitherto honored and looked up to with reverent awe. It has converted the physician, the lawyer, the priest, the poet, the man of science into its paid wage laborers.

The bourgeoisie has torn away from the family its sentimental veil, and has reduced the family relation to a mere money relation. . . .

The bourgeoisie cannot exist without constantly revolutionizing the instruments of production, and thereby the relations of production, and with them the whole relations of society. Conservation of the old modes of production in unaltered form was, on the contrary, the first condition of existence for all earlier industrial classes. Constant revolutionizing of production, uninterrupted disturbance of all social conditions, everlasting uncertainty and agitation distinguish the bourgeois epoch from all earlier ones. All fixed, fast-frozen relations, with their train of ancient and venerable prejudices and opinions, are swept away, all new-formed ones become antiquated before they can ossify. All that is solid melts into air, all that is holy is profaned, and man is at last compelled to face with sober senses his real conditions of life and his relations with his kind.

The need of a constantly expanding market for its products chases the bourgeoisie over the whole surface of the globe. It must nestle everywhere, settle everywhere, establish connections everywhere.

The bourgeoisie has through its exploitation of the world market given a cosmopolitan character to production and consumption in every country. To the great chagrin of reactionists, it has drawn from under the feet of industry the national ground on which it stood. All old-established national industries have been destroyed or are daily being destroyed. They are dislodged by new industries, whose introduction becomes a life and death question for all civilized nations, by industries that no longer work up indigenous raw material, but raw material drawn from the remotest zones: industries whose products are consumed not only at home, but in every quarter of the globe. In place of the old wants, satisfied by the productions of the country, we find new wants, requiring for their satisfaction the products of distant lands and climes. In place of the old local and national seclusion and self-sufficiency we have intercourse in every direction, universal interdependence of nations. . . .

The bourgeoisie, by the rapid improvement of all instruments of production, by the immensely facilitated means of communication, draws all, even the most barbarian, nations into civilization. The cheap prices of its commodities are the heavy artillery with which it batters down all Chinese walls, with which it forces the barbarians' intensely obstinate hatred of foreigners to capitulate. It compels all nations, on pain of extinction, to adopt the bourgeois mode of production; it compels them to introduce what it calls civilization into their midst, i.e., to become bourgeois themselves. In one word, it creates a world after its own image.

MILTON FRIEDMAN

Capitalism and freedom

Fundamentally, there are only two ways of co-ordinating the economic activities of millions. One is central direction involving the use of coercion—the technique of the army and of the modern totalitarian state. The other is voluntary co-operation of individuals—the technique of the market place.

The possibility of co-ordination through voluntary co-operation rests on the elementary—yet frequently denied—proposition that both parties to an economic transaction benefit from it, *provided the transaction is bi-laterally voluntary and informed.*

Exchange can therefore bring about co-ordination without coercion. A working model of a society organized through voluntary exchange is a *free private enterprise exchange economy*—what we have been calling competitive capitalism. . . .

Despite the important role of enterprises and of money in our actual economy, and despite the numerous and complex problems they raise, the central characteristic of the market technique of achieving co-ordination is fully displayed in the simple exchange economy that contains neither enterprises nor money. As in that simple model, so in the complex enterprise and money-exchange economy, co-operation is strictly individual and voluntary *provided*: (*a*) that enterprises are private, so that the ultimate contracting parties are individuals and (*b*) that individuals are effectively free to enter or not to enter into any particular exchange, so that every transaction is strictly voluntary.

It is far easier to state these provisos in general terms than to spell them out in detail, or to specify precisely the institutional arrangements most conducive to their maintenance. . . . The basic requisite is the maintenance of law and order to prevent physical coercion of one individual by another and to enforce contracts voluntarily entered into, thus giving substance to "private." Aside from this, perhaps the most

difficult problems arise from monopoly—which inhibits effective freedom by denying individuals alternatives to the particular exchange—and from "neighborhood effects"—effects on third parties for which it is not feasible to charge or recompense them. . . .

So long as effective freedom of exchange is maintained, the central feature of the market organization of economic activity is that it prevents one person from interfering with another in respect of most of his activities. The consumer is protected from coercion by the seller because of the presence of other sellers with whom he can deal. The seller is protected from coercion by the consumer because of other consumers to whom he can sell. The employee is protected from coercion by the employer because of other employers for whom he can work, and so on. And the market does this impersonally and without centralized authority.

Indeed, a major source of objection to a free economy is precisely that it does this task so well. It gives people what they want instead of what a particular group thinks they ought to want. Underlying most arguments against the free market is a lack of belief in freedom itself.

The existence of a free market does not of course eliminate the need for government. On the contrary, government is essential both as a forum for determining the "rules of the game" and as an umpire to interpret and enforce the rules decided on. What the market does is to reduce greatly the range of issues that must be decided through political means, and thereby to minimize the extent to which government need participate directly in the game. The characteristic feature of action through political channels is that it tends to require or enforce substantial conformity. The great advantage of the market, on the other hand, is that it permits wide diversity. It is, in political terms, a system of proportional representation. Each man can vote, as it were, for the color of tie he wants and get it; he does not have to see what color the majority wants and then, if he is in the minority, submit.

It is this feature of the market that we refer to when we say that the market provides economic freedom. But this characteristic also has implications that go far beyond the narrowly economic. Political freedom means the absence of coercion of a man by his fellow men. The fundamental threat to freedom is power to coerce, be it in the hands of a monarch, a dictator, an oligarchy, or a momentary majority. The preservation of freedom requires the elimination of such concentration of power to the fullest possible extent and the dispersal and distribution of whatever power cannot be eliminated—a system of checks and balances. By removing the organization of economic activity from the control of political authority, the market eliminates this source of coercive power. It enables economic strength to be a check to political power rather than a reinforcement. . . .

One feature of a free society is surely the freedom of individuals to advocate and propagandize openly for a radical change in the structure of the society—so long as the advocacy is restricted to persuasion and does not include force or other forms of coercion. It is a mark of the political freedom of a capitalist society that men can openly advocate and work for socialism. Equally, political freedom in a socialist society would require that men be free to advocate the introduction of capitalism. How could the freedom to advocate capitalism be preserved and protected in a socialist society?

In order for men to advocate anything, they must in the first place be able to earn a living. This already raises a problem in a socialist society, since all jobs are under the direct control of political authorities. It would take an act of self-denial whose difficulty is underlined by experience in the United States after World War II with the problem of "security" among Federal employees, for a socialist government to permit its employees to advocate policies directly contrary to official doctrine.

But let us suppose this act of self-denial to be achieved. For advocacy of capitalism to mean anything, the proponents must be able to finance their cause—to hold public meetings, publish pamphlets, buy radio time, issue newspapers and magazines, and so on. How could they raise the funds? . . .

In a capitalist society, it is only necessary to

convince a few wealthy people to get funds to launch any idea, however strange, and there are many such persons, many independent foci of support. And, indeed, it is not even necessary to persuade people or financial institutions with available funds of the soundness of the ideas to be propagated. It is only necessary to persuade them that the propagation can be financially successful; that the newspaper or magazine or book or other venture will be profitable. . . .

In this way, the market breaks the vicious circle and makes it possible ultimately to finance such ventures by small amounts from many people without first persuading them. There are no such possibilities in the socialist society; there is only the all-powerful state. . . .

But we are not yet through. In a free market society, it is enough to have the funds. The suppliers of paper are as willing to sell it to the *Daily Worker* as to the *Wall Street Journal*. In a socialist society, it would not be enough to have the funds. The hypothetical supporter of capitalism would have to persuade a government factory making paper to sell to him, the government printing press to print his pamphlets, a government post office to distribute them among the people, a government agency to rent him a hall in which to talk, and so on.

Perhaps there is some way in which one could overcome these difficulties and preserve freedom in a socialist society. One cannot say it is utterly impossible. What is clear, however, is that there are very real difficulties in establishing institutions that will effectively preserve the possibility of dissent. . . . By contrast, it is clear how a free market capitalist society fosters freedom.

NICHOLAS N. EBERSTADT

What history tells us about corporate responsibility

The full significance of the corporate responsibility movement cannot be seen without reviewing history. Only then can we understand that "the free enterprise system as we know it" is the exception, not the rule, of Western political economy. . . .

A brief review of history will demonstrate that an industrial revolution less than two hundred years old has allowed business to circumvent checks on power—and requirements of responsibility—as old as our civilization. Were corporate leaders to review the past, they would see that today's corporate responsibility movement is neither the preaching of self-appointed saviours nor the plotting of economic nihilists; it is a historical swing to recreate the social contract of power with responsibility, and as such may well become the most important and welcomed reform of our time. . . .

Classical Greece

The businessman's rung on the Greek social ladder was only slightly higher than the slave's. Economic activity was divided into household management, which was encouraged, and moneymaking, which was disapproved of. Character development was important in the Greek system of values, and business was thought to promote base emotions. . . .

Community spirit marked Greek life. The community, or polis, cultivated such devotion among its citizens that the Athenian aristocracy appointed a special governor when they became aware that their economic system was impoverishing "middle class" citizens; the aristocracy abided by his decisions to cancel all outstanding debt, limit homestead size, and embargo food exportation until domestic poverty was conquered. Business was expected to be of social service to the community. Ostracism was not an unthinkable punishment for immoral business practices, and corporal punishment was frequently the penalty for fraud. . . . Respect for nature seems to have influenced industry's environmental practices. It appears that standards of conservation and ecological balance were enforced upon the mining and lumbering interests. There was no doubt in the Greek citizen's mind that business existed to serve the public. According to one scholar, Dr. Raymond Bauer, . . . "The Greeks were particularly offended by the suggestion that material gains from business were to be used merely as the owner wished, without regard for the interests of the community."

The medieval period, 1000–1500 A.D.

The Catholic Church distrusted both the businessman and the business system. It branded the profit motive anti-Christian and adopted a policy toward business expressed by the motto, *Homo mercator vit aut numquam Deo placere potest*—the merchant seldom, or never, pleases God. Orations against the evils of business were as vehement as they were frequent. . . . By virtue of its international structure and its monopoly on education, the Church dicta saturated medieval culture so entirely that businessmen doubted their own moral worth. Frequently, merchants urged their children to pursue less "dangerous work," and sometimes they made compliance a condition of inheritance. . . .

In the Dark Ages, the Church had questioned the validity of property and commerce. Later, it maintained that if business *had* to exist, it should be used in the public interest. . . . The good businessman would be honest in motive and actions, sell at a "just price" to provide a "living wage," and use his profits in a socially responsible manner. Business could not be abolished, but it could be controlled. . . .

The businessman's obligations, however, extended beyond honesty. He was expected to care for his guildmembers and for the well-being of his community. Most guilds supported their sick members and provided for their dead members' dependents; some even established unemployment funds. Many guilds voluntarily sponsored municipal improvements. "Helping to educate the poor, encouraging local artists, building hospitals and orphanages . . . all came to be common practice," wrote Dr. Clarence Walton. In addition, wealthy individuals spent vast amounts on the poor. Jakob Fugger actually established a foundation to provide low-cost housing in his hometown (his subsequent plan to supply the poor with free grain in perpetuity was frustrated by the town council).

During the Middle Ages the percursor of the

corporation appeared, lacking both the immortality and legal personality it later enjoyed. In many "corporations," God was a major partner, and at the end of each year His profits were distributed among the poor. When a "corporation" liquidated, God was usually the first-Principal to be reimbursed. Social responsibility produced economic results: despite the poverty of the times, the common man in England and elsewhere enjoyed a standard of living in 1500 not to be attained again for more than three centuries.

The medieval concept of social responsibility was defective in one way: its view of the community was narrow, and it condoned the exploitation of "outsiders." This practice became a tradition in the mercantile period, and exploiting outsiders, it was discovered in the industrial period, was not demonstrably different from exploiting one's neighbors, so long as one was familiar with neither.

The mercantile period, 1500–1800

As the Church atrophied, Catholic dogma gave way to Calvinist doctrine, which glorified the thrifty and industrious businessman. As the famed historian R. H. Tawney has said, Calvinism assured merchants and industrialists that "the forces of the universe" were on their side, "taught them to feel they were a chosen people, made them conscious of their great destiny in the Providential plan and resolute to realize it." The emerging nation-states which jockeyed for the position of international power the papacy had left vacant, realized their national strength depended on their commercial and industrial production. The solid policy of mercantilism rested, in Professor Walton's words, upon "a conviction that the government actively encourage industrial development and farm prosperity." . . . The businessman gained respectability and dignity in England: on the continent prominent business leaders joined the nobility, and the business class was granted influence in national affairs.

The social obligations of business increased with the businessman's status. Nowhere was this clearer than in the country which had most enthusiastically promoted business, England. According to England's "harmony of interests" theory, business was to act in the national interest because the state supported it. . . .

Businesses which provided outstanding public service were given special privileges. These businesses, like the Virginia Company and the East India Company, were called corporations, and were granted limited liability and legal personality forever. Some corporations earned their charters by pursuing national interests abroad, others by attempting to alleviate domestic social problems. A number of companies were established solely to employ the poor in impoverished communities and underdeveloped industries. "A complete absence of graft leaves no room for suspecting their [the corporation members'] honesty. . . . [this was mercantilism] in its most ambitious form . . . representing the nearest approach to national planning ever made in England."

Just as business met national social needs, the businessman met local needs. "The failure of a London merchant to settle some conspicuous charitable trust or gift was generally regarded as little short of shocking. . . ." Those businessmen who did not contribute to charity were frequently fined the amount judged to be an adequate gift. . . .

An implicit tenet of mercantilism was the exploitation of foreigners. Although more than three million blacks were enslaved and shipped to the New World, not even the most moral were aroused. The practice of selective piracy was actually applauded by the nations with the strongest fleets. The acceptance of the principle of exploitation gradually soured Calvinist and mercantile principles. As Professor Tawney observed, "To urge that the Christian life must be lived in a zealous discharge of private duties—how necessary! Yet how readily perverted to the suggestion that there are no vital social obligations beyond them! To suggest that the individual is responsible [for his own moral welfare], that no man can save his brother, how true the indispensable! Yet how easy to slip from that truth into the suggestion that society is without responsibility, that no man can help his brother!"

The industrial period, 1800–1930

The industrial revolution which swept through America in the nineteenth century carried with it new attitudes toward business and the businessman. By the late 1800s, the industrialist had replaced the landholder in the aristocracy of wealth, and the businessman had come to represent absolute virtue. Social Darwinists explained his success in terms of natural selection: "It is because they are selected that wealth . . . aggregate under their hands. . . . All who are competent [in the role of millionaire] will be employed in it." Religious leaders hold the entrepreneur's wealth to be a sign of his moral excellence: "In the long run, it is only to the man of morality that wealth comes. . . . Godliness is in league with riches." . . .

Social Darwinists and laissez-faire economists . . . rejected the proposition that business was responsible for the state's social welfare. Herbert Spencer, a leading Social Darwinist, argued that society's only obligation to the lazy, sick, and intemperate was to prevent them from procreating, so that the human species might become stronger. To prevent business from acting as an arbiter of social justice, in his opinion, was unpardonable. Social Darwinists and laissez-faire economists agreed that the role of government should be to encourage the growth of unregulated business. Legislatures, courts, and Congress quickly adapted themselves to the individualist philosophy. By the end of the Civil War, charters were obtainable under any business pretext, and were all but impossible to revoke. Tariffs were raised to prevent foreign competition; corporate and personal income taxes were repealed; and the corporation, by law a citizen, enjoyed full constitutional privileges.

The giant corporation came to dominate the economy. By the late nineteenth century the two hundred largest manufacturing concerns added more to the GNP than the next hundred thousand largest. Some corporations virtually had the power of governments, and "this enormous concentrated economic power gravitated into the hands of a few, raising up a corporate ruling class with almost unlimited authority."

Unfortunately, the character of the great corporate leaders made the hope of corporation-promoted social welfare unrealizable. Many captains of industry held their fellow citizens and their government in contempt. Although scholars do not agree on whether William Vanderbilt said, "The public be damned!" they have ascertained that, upon being confronted with the possibility of having acted illegally, his father exploded, "Law? What do I care about the law? Ain't I got the power?" John D. Rockefeller, Sr., an advocate of active competition, forced railroads to pay him for shipping competing oil, bribed attorneys general to suppress anti-trust investigations, and it is alleged, even dynamited competing refineries in his attempt to monopolize the oil industry. Jay Gould, a prominent financier, drove at least one of his partners to suicide, and was wanted for arrest in several states.

While corporate profits and the cost of living soared, wages actually declined. The average worker was paid so poorly that the Bureau of Labor Statistics concluded it was impossible for many workers to provide for their families. Industrial accidents occurred with appalling frequency, and in even as inoffensive an industry as cigar manufacturing, almost three-fourths of all employees fell ill within six months of starting work. Housing was so squalid that rats sometimes ate children alive. In congressional testimony it was estimated that the most conscientious and thrifty miner could not save more than four dollars a year if he bought merchandise from the company store.

The monopolies, pools, and trusts which the captains of industry cultivated often successfully defied the laws of market pricing. . . . Market control was often an incentive to lower product quality. This was particularly true in the food industry: milk was commonly preserved with formaldehyde; meat was sometimes sold rotting or filled with vermin.

The stockholder, who legally controlled the corporation, was constantly cheated by "stock watering" (a trick from which Vanderbilt once made $23 million); counterfeit shares; and calculated news releases, many of them false.

Attempts to reform the corporation were, for the most part, unsuccessful. The Populists, a loose combination of farmworkers and wage laborers, effected minor reform but lacked leadership, insight, and organization, and consequently remained isolated in the Midwest. The Progressives, comprised of the Populists, small businessmen, and many middle-class professionals, forced large corporations into compliance with standards of common honesty—and actually dissolved the Standard Oil trust—but were ineffective in improving the quality of the laborer's life or restoring free competition to the market system. World War I silenced the reformers, and the postwar boom restored faith in the business system. President Coolidge exemplified the attitude toward industry: "The business of America is business. . . . The man who builds a factory, builds a temple."

Indeed, business might never have turned back toward responsibility and accountability if the culmination of corporate irresponsibility had not been the collapse of the economic system. . . . By 1932, one of every four workers was unemployed, and the GNP had declined by half. Americans were offered the choice between rugged individualism and business autonomy or economic security. The generation raised on the gospel of wealth gladly forfeited the former.

The corporate period, 1930–present

Although the National Association of Manufacturers might explain the workings of the economy in terms of the small businessman and the little factory, the American market system today is controlled by a handful of corporations. In 1928, at the zenith of their pre-Depression power, the two hundred largest corporations owned 30 percent of the nation's manufacturing assets. Today they own slightly under 60 percent. The ten largest alone employ nearly 5 percent of the labor force. In many instances, foreign policy has been directly shaped to accommodate the policy of the large corporation, the energy crisis being the most recent example. The large corporation, however, influences more than politics and economics; it determines quality of life, even for those not employed by it.

Since the Depression, the corporation increasingly has been regarded as an institution which, like the government, has social obligations to fulfill. Through minimum wage and collective bargaining regulations, required disclosure of corporate information, and the establishment of agencies to promote nondestructive competition, the government restated business's responsibilities toward workers, shareholders, and other businesses. Business's social obligations were further reaffirmed by a new generation of corporate managers, many of them college-educated and heavily influenced by liberal arts humanism.

Still, this trend was not continued in full before the Thirties. The war dominated business and industry in the following decade and, during the Cold War, corporations assumed that business could fulfill its social obligations simply by standing as an anti-Communist institution. Consequently, while America's social problems became ever more apparent, corporate commitment stagnated. Ralph Nader brought the issue of corporate responsibility into the news in 1965 with what was branded a radical philosophy. He argued that business, like government, exists to serve. Consequently, he reasoned, the large corporation, which in many ways acts as a subnational government, must be held accountable for its action or inaction. The public has accepted this philosophy enthusiastically.

Nader's philosophy is not new. He is merely synthesizing over twenty centuries of Western tradition with our present environment, which is something of a postindustrial one. . . . Business seldom has enjoyed so much power with so little responsibility. The extent to which responsibility and accountability are accepted by or imposed upon corporate capitalism will be the measure of our adjustment to industrial and postindustrial life.

WAYNE A. R. LEYS

Ethics in American business and government: The confused issues

It is not difficult to paint a flattering portrait of the executives who run our corporations and public agencies. All that we have to do is to bring out the family album and look at the flinty visages of the executives of a century ago. Although there are notable exceptions, today's executives generally have higher moral standards, more awareness of duties, more concern for values.

The awareness of duties

During the second half of the nineteenth century, morality appeared to many observers to be losing its importance. The disappearance of moral scruples can be gauged by looking into P. T. Barnum's (1884) book, *How I Made Millions (or the Secret of Success)*. It is the story of high-pressure selling of everything from Jenny Lind to circuses. Barnum's first success was in exhibiting, during 1835, the old Negro nurse of George Washington, Joice Heth, alleged to have been 161 years old. Barnum recorded one deception after another, sometimes at his competitors' expense, often at the customer's expense, not infrequently even at his own expense. Even when he told how he himself had been cheated, Barnum reported the gamesmanship with glee. This was the period when "complete sewing machines" were being offered for a dime, and the expectant mail-order purchaser received a needle.

By contrast, today's promoter is conscious of a multiple of "Thou-shalt-nots." He makes his plans, keeping in mind certain rights of customers, competitors, investors, employees, and neighbors. He walks many a tightrope. He must avoid cutthroat competition, but he must not be guilty of collusion. He feels the pressure to be concerned with the welfare of his associates, but he must not invade their privacy. He must provide job security, but not in a way that can be called feather-bedding. He must avoid overcharging, but he must remember that his plant and his product face numerous inspections that protect various rights and keep certain costs rigid. . . .

No doubt, the decision-maker of 1968 thinks about many more rules and is conscious of the rights of many more parties than the decision-maker of 1868. In the intervening time, just about every segment of the population has raised Cain with some set of businessmen or some group of public officials. They campaigned for hostile public regulation and policing. The rights to which they laid claim were not always recognized; but, after noisy legislative hearings had been held, there was usually a new regulation, either in the statutes or in a code of ethics.

Concern for values

Executives now do more thinking about values as well as duties. Never before has there been so much information about the goods and services that are being produced. . . .

It is now orthodox to assert that management ought to be responsible, and responsibility requires information about what the enterprise is doing for everyone affected by the enterprise. This concern extends, under prodding, to such by-products as stream and air pollution, traffic congestion and, even, to unpleasant international relations. No longer is the complaint clerk some old grouch, preferably deaf. High-level Ombudsmen are being given power to deal with a wide range of dissatisfactions. In-service seminars are designed to remove occupational blindspots and broaden the value consciousness of specialists.

All this is by way of recognizing that not all values are represented by a corporation's current profit-and-loss statement or by a public agency's dollar-budget. Community good will, the health of employees, good taste, and the advancement of the arts are now matters of concern, and not only because they may affect next year's profit-and-loss statement or next year's appropriation.

RALPH NADER

The great American gyp

The consumer movement [has relentlessly documented] that consumers are being manipulated, defrauded, and injured not just by marginal businesses or fly-by-night hucksters, but by the U.S. blue-chip business firms whose practices are unchecked by the older regulatory agencies. Since the consumer movement can cite statistics showing that these practices have reduced real income and raised the rates of mortality and disease, it is not difficult to understand the growing corporate concern. . . .

What has taken place during the last few years may be seen as an escalating series of disclosures. The charges made by independent Congressmen and people like myself almost always turn out to be understatements of the actual conditions in various industries when those industries are subsequently exposed in Congressional hearings and investigations. As these charges get attention, demands for new legislative action increase. This, at least, has been the case with the exposure of defects in vehicles, industrial and vehicle pollution, gas pipelines, overpriced or dangerous drugs, unfair credit, harmful pesticides, cigarettes, land frauds, electric power reliability, household improvement rackets, exploitation in slums, auto warranties, radiation, high-priced auto insurance, and boating hazards. How many people realized, for example, that faulty heating devices injure 125,000 Americans a year or that poorly designed stoves, power mowers, and washing machines cause substantial injury to 300,000 people annually? Or that, as Rep. Benjamin Rosenthal recently revealed, the food rejected by Federal agencies as contaminated or rotting is often re-routed for sale in the market? These abuses are now starting to be discussed in the press and in Congress.

One result of the detailed Congressional hearings has been a broader definition of legitimate consumer rights and interests. It is becoming clear that consumers must not only be protected from the dangers of voluntary use of a product,

such as flammable material, but also from *involuntary* consumption of industrial by-products such as air and water pollutants, excessive pesticide and nitrate residues in foods, and antibiotics in meat. A more concrete idea of a just economy is thus beginning to emerge, while, at the same time, the assortment of groups that comprise the "consumer's movement" is moving in directions that seem to me quite different from the ones that similar groups have followed in the past. Their demands are ethical rather than ideological. Their principles and proposals are being derived from solid documentation of common abuses whose origins are being traced directly to the policies of powerful corporations.

This inquiry is extending beyond the question of legal control of corporations into the failure of business, labor, and voluntary organizations to check one another's abuses through competition and other private pressures. It is becoming apparent that the reform of consumer abuses and the reform of corporate power itself are different sides of the same coin and that new approaches to the enforcement of the rights of consumers are necessary. . . .

In the ideology of American business, free competition, and corporate "responsibility" are supposed to protect the consumer; in practice both have long been ignored. Price-fixing, either by conspiracy or by mutually understood cues, is rampant throughout the economy. This is partly revealed by the growing number of government and private antitrust actions. . . .

Even greater dangers arise when the failure of large industry to compete prevents the development of new products that might save or improve the lives of consumers. . . .

Ideally, one of the most powerful forces for consumer justice would be the exercise of corporate responsibility or private "countervailing" and monitoring forces within the corporate world. Unfortunately for believers in a pluralist economic system, recent decades have shown that the economics of accommodation repeatedly overwhelms the economics of checks and balances. . . .

The current assault on the health and safety of the public from so many dangerous industrial products, by-products, and foods has resulted in violence that dwarfs the issue of crime in the streets. (During the last three years, about 260 people have died in riots in American cities; but every two days, 300 people are killed, and 20,000 injured, while driving on the highways.)

What the consumer movement is beginning to say—and must say much more strongly if it is to grow—is that business crime and corporate intransigence are the really urgent menace to law and order in America.

GUS TYLER

On the limits of "corporate responsibility"

The current interest in "corporate responsibility" arises from a mounting concern over tensions in our society and from a recognition of the decisive role corporations play in our lives. In the next decade, there will undoubtedly be considerable movement by corporations into the social area—out of social pressures and enlightened self-interest. These acts of "corporate conscience" will be viewed by many as the answer to our most pressing social problems.

The object of this article is neither to deny the positive aspects of corporate initiative in the social area nor to discourage the development of corporate responsibility. Rather, this article seeks to explore *limits* of the corporate role—so that the nation will not shirk its collective responsibility by unloading onto the corporation that which the corporations cannot do.

The 1973 statement of the Committee on Economic Development (CED) on "Social Responsibilities of Business Corporations" recognizes the necessary limits of a company's commitment to the societal interest. "Corporations are necessarily limited," the paper points out, "by various internal constraints on what and how much they can do to improve society." In this connection, two major restraints are noted: (1) "No company of any size can willingly incur costs that would jeopardize its competitive position and threaten its survival." (2) Management

must concern itself with realizing a level of profitability that its stockholders and the financial market consider to be reasonable under the circumstances.

These two constraints—both of which are compulsions bearing down on even the most socially minded executive—are of sufficient weight to slow down almost any major corporation impulse to social do-goodery. The first constraint—to stay competitive—means that a corporation cannot take on any sizable added costs that would cause it to lose out to its rival in the marketplace. Social goodwill, therefore, can operate only in that thin area of cost advantage a corporation is willing to surrender to its competitors without losing its competitive edge. The second constraint is even more compelling, for even if a corporation can *survive* against competition but appears to be offering a less than expected return on investment, that corporation will lose the confidence (support) of shareholders and the financial market. Indeed, the most immediate threat will come from a more short-run, narrow-interest, socially unconcerned operator (or operators) who will move in on the depressed company for a killing by buying up the stock, by rallying the shareholders, and by hitting the target at a moment of its disfavor in financial circles. . . .

What then is a business corporation—by its very nature? It is a profit-making enterprise. The men who organize it do so to realize profit; the people who buy stocks expect returns on investment; the financiers calculate their rates and their risks against anticipated earnings and values; the managers and executives are under duress to justify the expectations of owners, investors, lenders.

Because business corporations are what they are, must be, and should be, they really have only one constituency: the shareholders. To talk of employees, consumers, and the public-at-large as constituents is unnecessarily confusing—and even dangerously illusionary. A constituent is someone who has a voice in choosing a representative who will reflect the interests of his constituents. In that sense, the shareholder is a constituent: he elects the corporate executives who are expected to champion the interests of the shareholder—i.e., to make money. The employees, the consumers, the ecologically concerned public-at-large are not constituents: they have no voice in choosing the corporate executives. The employees, if they are unionized, are constituents of another organization, electing their own leaders to represent them. Sometimes these two constituencies—management and labor—have common interests, such as increasing the market for the product or protecting the market against foreign competition. At other times, these constituencies—management and labor—clash over how to divide the corporate income, or how to set work rules, etc. In the same manner, the consumers compose a separate constituency, although rarely do they find the kind of organized expression typified by a corporation or a union. The financial community—the banks and other lenders—have a special relationship with corporations, whereby the financier may often opt to be a constituent. In those cases where the financing institution has one or more of its men sitting on the corporate board, it is clearly a constituent—sometimes, *the* constituent.

This does not mean that the corporation, with its imperatives dictated by its nature as directed by its constituents, can disregard the other constituencies in society. As one "little republic" (to use Blackstone's appellation for a corporation) living alongside other "little republics," the corporation must work out a *modus vivendi et operandi* with its neighbors. Many of the conflicts arising between corporations and other constituencies are inherent in the corporate being. For instance, the ancient tug-of-war between management and labor is inherent in the contest over "who gets what." The friction between producer and consumer is inherent in the desire of both parties to get as much as possible for what has been put out. The more recent collision between manufacturers and the public over pollution is inherent in the corporation's need to produce as cheaply as possible and to avoid such outlays as are not necessary to the conduct of its own business.

In the last half-century, the business corporation has adjusted policies to accommodate the other constituencies. Unions have been recog-
308

nized with attendant changes in wage and fringe benefit policies; consumer power has been recognized with attendant changes in product; environmentalist protest has been recognized with attendant changes in productive methods; ethnic militancy has been recognized with attendant changes in hiring and promotion policies; hard-core unemployment has been recognized with attendant changes in manpower training. While labor, consumer, environmentalist, racial minority, or jobless may complain that the corporations have not gone far or fast enough, the fact remains that they have moved—and they have moved contrary to the compulsions of their impersonal corporate beings. . . .

It might seem easy to instill a regnant sense of social responsibility in the corporate world. The number of people in charge of that world is relatively small. One account estimates that 100 industrial firms own about half the assets in all manufacture. The number at the pinnacles of finance should be smaller. By a process of careful enlistment, it should be possible to compose a congenial congregation of about 200 who are the real power. If they could be persuaded as to the right course for America by a faculty composed of Ralph Nader, Ken Galbraith, Charles Reich, and Billy Sunday, the job would be done.

But, alas, it is not that simple. Our problem does not stem from either the stupidity or the malevolence of our top 200. (They are likely to be better informed and better intentioned than most.) It is not the man but his stars that are to blame—those stars that compose the constellation in whose orbit he inexorably moves.

The movers of money are, in a sense, caught in the orbit of the masses they handle. . . . Today, ownership has become more *impersonal*:

Most U.S. corporate wealth is *controlled*—not by individuals, or families, but by an alliance of management and financial institutions. . . . What is new, a contribution of the post-war years, and particularly the last decade, is the shift from individual to institutional corporate ownership. This is the era of the financial institution, not the personal investor.[1]

[1]Richard J. Barber, *The American Corporation* (New York: E. P. Dutton, 1970), p. 20.

This impersonality robs the corporation of personality. The corporation becomes what it has long been legally named in some countries: a *société anonyme,* a being without a name. The corporation is now twice removed from being a true *persona*: first, it was set up to be recognized under the law as a *persona ficta*; and now the persons who hid beyond the *persona ficta* have been replaced by *persona ficta* called "institutions."

What are these institutions? They are mutual funds, pension funds, insurance companies, trust funds, and—above all—banks that move their own funds and manage personal and common trusts and pension funds.

Although banks play a central role in almost all of these, they are not the only money managers. But whoever the money managers are, they have one thing in common: a responsibility to serve their constituencies. In these cases, the constituents are the people (or funds) entrusted to the managers of the money. The first responsibility of the manager is to the millions of little people who buy into mutual funds, who depend in their old age on pension funds, who place their trust in the financial wisdom of a bank. Indeed, if a fund or bank manager were so spiritually inclined, he might well think of himself as the righteous servant of the people championing their cause *against* the great corporation by demanding a maximum return on the invested monies. No doubt, some money managers see themselves in this hallowed light—as makers and monitors of a people's capitalism.

This quick vivisection of the body corporate uncovers no locus for a social conscience. The corporation, like the banks, gets its funds increasingly from institutions. These institutions (banks) get their funds from other institutions, like pension funds. These pension (etc.) funds really belong in the ethical and, ultimately, legal sense to all kinds of plain people of limited means who count on proper (profitable) investment of their funds, just to have the income now or later to make ends meet. Hence, the prime business of a corporation is the business of making money for its investors—and for its managers, who must carry this risky responsibility.

In pursuit of this prime purpose, corporations do many noxious things; they plan obsolescence, pollute the environment, fool consumers, underpay labor, evade taxes, and turn out products and services that are useless or harmful. In most cases, the corporate board is not aware of the evil; in other cases, the evil is accepted as the lesser evil—as compared with closing a plant or getting wiped out by merger or bankruptcy.

ROBERT L. HEILBRONER

None of your business

The term "multinational corporation" has become familiar only recently. Writing in these pages just five years ago, I felt obliged to explain that the multinationals were not merely giant corporations that did a world-wide export business, but giants whose manufacturing or servicing facilities were located around the globe, so that Pepsi-Cola, to take an example, could be bought in Mexico or the Philippines (or another 100-odd countries) not because the drink was turned out in America and then shipped abroad, but because it was produced and bottled in the country where it was consumed. . . .

Can one . . . make some sense of the multinational presence? With much trepidation, I shall try.

We must begin by recognizing that the fundamental process behind the rise of the multinational corporation is growth, the urge for expansion that is the daemon of capitalism itself. Why is growth so central, so insatiable? In part the answer must be sought in the "animal spirits," as Keynes called them, of capitalist entrepreneurs whose self-esteem and self-valuation are deeply intertwined with the sheer size of the wealth they own or control.

But growth is also a defensive reaction. Companies seek to grow in order to preserve their place in the sun, to prevent competitors from crowding them out. Hence the struggle for market shares has always been a central aspect of the capitalist system, lending color to the robber baron age, taking on a more restrained but no less intense form in the age of the modern "socially responsible" firm. . . .

309

Only recently . . . have we begun to describe the sequence of events that drives a firm to make the decisive leap across national boundaries, with all the headaches and problems that such a venture entails—foreign governments to deal with, foreign languages to speak, foreign currencies to worry about. . . . Any number of stimuli may finally tempt an expanding company to make the leap. It may have begun to penetrate a foreign market with exports, and then may decide to locate a production facility abroad in order to avoid a tariff that impedes its exports. It may locate a manufacturing branch abroad to forestall—or to match—a similar step by one of its rivals. It may seek the advantages of manufacturing abroad because wages are cheaper. . . .

This phenomenon of expansion, with its aggressive and defensive roots, emphasizes an extremely important aspect of what we call "multinationalization," which is that all the multinational companies are in fact *national* companies that have extended their operations abroad. They are not, as their spokesmen sometimes claim, companies that have lost their nationality. Two giant companies—Shell and Unilever—have in fact mixed nationalities on their boards of directors, and IBM never wearies of boasting that Jacques Maisonrouge, president of the IBM World Trade Corporation, is French. But I can see little evidence that IBM is not an "American" company, notwithstanding; and no evidence that any other of the giant multinationals cannot be unambiguously identified as having a distinct nationality. . . .

Thus I think we must view the world of very large, expansive national enterprises, extending their operations abroad, as a change in degree, not kind, from the world of very large expansive enterprises still contained within national borders. . . .

Here it is useful to review the basic characteristics of monopoly capitalism. An economy dominated by the kinds of expansive organizations I have described sooner or later encounters extreme difficulties of economic coordination. We do not know if a world of atomistic enterprises would run as smoothly as the theory of pure competition suggests, and we never shall know. We do know that an economy dominated

by giant firms encounters serious problems in dovetailing its private operations so as to provide substantially full employment, maintain a stable level of prices, and produce the full array of goods and services needed by the population. In every capitalist nation this has led to what is euphemistically called a "mixed" economy—an economy in which the world of business is restrained, guided, subsidized, protected, buttressed by a growing array of public instruments and agencies. Governments, for all their ideological skirmishes with business, have always been the silent partners of business; indeed, as Adam Smith was explicit in declaring, private property would not exist a minute without government.

In what way does the multinational change this basic picture? I must confess that I do not think it changes it at all. I am aware, of course, of the much discussed erosion of "sovereignty" caused by the ability of the multinationals to locate their plants in this country or that one, or to transfer their profits from one nation to another by means of arbitrary pricing. But is this significantly different from the failure of nation–states to exercise control over companies *within* their national boundaries? What effectiveness does the United States have, for example, in directing the location of the investment of General Motors inside the United States, or for that matter in affecting the design of its products, its employment policies, etc.? What difference does it make to our national sovereignty if Valium or chocolate bars are made by a Swiss rather than a U.S. firm?

Of course, there are some differences, mainly having to do with the flows of funds across our national borders. But in the absence of the flows generated by the multinationals—the export of capital out of the U.S., the import of profits back—there would be the flows of funds generated by normal exports and imports, equally capable of working international monetary mischief, equally difficult to control.

The situation is somewhat different with regard to the underdeveloped countries. Foreign corporations play a powerful and sometimes pernicious role in determining the pace and pattern of the economic advance of these nations. They often support technologies and social

310

structures that are inimical to the rounded development of the backward areas—for example in shoring up corrupt and privileged classes and in encouraging some countries to concentrate agricultural production on exports rather than on badly needed food for local consumption. The technology they introduce is as often as not deforming rather than transforming for these countries . . . ; the profits they earn are often extremely high.

But is this a *new* condition of affairs? . . . It was, after all, under the drive of foreign capital that such countries as Brazil and Honduras and Rhodesia first became adjuncts of the modern industrial system, each producing a single commodity for the world market. If there is any remarkable change to be noted, it seems to be the long overdue assertion of political independence on the part of these one-time economic colonies, and their attempts to impose much stricter forms of supervision over the foreign bodies embedded so firmly and dangerously in their midst. Indeed, where is the process of the subordination of private international economic power to local political control more evident than in the places where the multinationals are most visible—the oil-producing regions of the world?

In suggesting that the role of the multinationals may be exaggerated, I do not wave away the charge that these companies exercise vast influence, both overtly and covertly. I only maintain that this is an old rather than a new state of affairs.

What remains, then, of the multinational phenomenon? Certainly some new and very important problems have been introduced. The problem of the trade unions, facing companies that can offset the growth of labor strength in one nation by transferring production to another nation, is one. The ability to juggle profits by arbitrary pricing is another. The prospect of a dangerous coalition of world-wide national corporate power with world-wide national political power is a third: witness the case of Chile, and the covert operations we hear about in other Latin American countries.

Yet with regard to the proposition that the multinationals represent a wholly new phase of capitalism I have become increasingly doubtful.

Throughout the capitalist world the trend toward bigness and unwieldiness is evident, and the difficulties of managing national economies are front page news. This is driving all industrialized nations, whatever their ideologies, toward a system of centralized planning: socialism, a cynic might say, has become the next stage of capitalism. But I cannot view the international scope of economic power as constituting a special feature of this "socialism."

Suppose that every multinational corporation, whatever its national base, suddenly had its foreign affiliates lopped off and awarded as prizes to the management of domestic enterprise—that, for example, GM lost its plants in Germany to Volkswagen, or that Olivetti-owned factories in the U.S. were transferred to Pitney-Bowes. In some of the underdeveloped countries such a shift would be regarded as a windfall—and it would indeed be one for those nations where the benefits of ownership could be widely distributed and not simply taken over by small groups which are already too rich and powerful. (Where are such countries?) But would the problems of capitalism as a social order radically change? Would the management of unemployment, inflation, pollution, energy, workers' alienation, corruption, or any other of the evils of our time be greatly lessened or worsened? That capitalism will have to make far-reaching adjustments to keep the lid on things I do not for a moment doubt; but that capitalism has entered a new stage, in which corporations will fundamentally change the intrinsic problems of the system by extending the international reach of their operations, is an assertion that I do not believe has yet been convincingly demonstrated.

WILLIAM M. CARLEY

Despite early gains, anti-payoff campaign is beginning to sputter

Like a number of other companies involved in the foreign-bribery scandals of the past few years, Northrop Corp. settled a Securities and Exchange Commission suit last year [1975] by agreeing not to pay any more bribes.

But this year the aircraft maker disclosed that some of its men were still at it. Northrop said a communications subsidiary based in Rome, Page-Europa S.p.A., had made $861,000 in payoffs to get business in Italy, Greece, Portugal, Somalia and Turkey from 1969 to 1975. About $129,000 of the payments were made after the consent decree was signed.

It may not be exactly bribery-as-usual these days (Northrop did report the case and did ultimately fire the Page-Europa officials involved, it should be noted), but the year-long anti-bribery drive led by the SEC and the Senate Subcommittee on Multinationals is clearly having a limited impact.

Other signposts:

—Except for a few spectacular resignations of top executives at companies like Gulf Oil Corp. and Lockheed Aircraft Corp., very few executives involved in briberies have been fired, demoted or even transferred. To the contrary, many businessmen still defend bribe-paying abroad as necessary to meet the competition from other countries.

—The Internal Revenue Service, responding to an anguished outcry from major accounting firms, has backed off on a new policy to ask outside auditors certain questions about corporate payoffs whenever the IRS checks a company's books.

—Efforts to draft legislation against bribery are ensnarled in intramural squabbling, with the result that Congress seems unlikely to enact any anti-bribery bill this year except for an arms-sales measure already passed.

Most analysts acknowledge that bribery disclosures by the SEC and the Senate subcommittee, as well as corporate investigations triggered by those disclosures, have brought some solid steps toward a cleanup. Some argue that the government has done enough and that business, at least for now, should be left to reform itself. . . .

But others doubt that there will be any lasting change in the practice of payoffs unless the government continues its crackdown. "I fear that many companies will keep on paying bribes if they can get away with it, because the potential rewards are so great and the risks are minimal," Sen. William Proxmire says. Though over 100 companies have admitted improper payments, "nobody has gone to jail," he says. "Only three corporations have fired their chief executive officers. At most, there has been unfortunate publicity."

"It's completely illusory to think anything will change," says Jerry Levinson, chief counsel of the multinational subcommittee. "I think that once the publicity has faded, many of these guys will go back to the same old philosophy of 'sell, sell, sell any way you can.'"

Whatever happens in the future, present government efforts have run into considerable antipathy. At a Conference Board seminar on illegal payments last month in New York, for example, representatives of the SEC, the Senate subcommittee and the IRS were peppered by hostile questions from an audience of 400 businessmen, auditors and attorneys. "Why is the IRS conducting this inquisition?" Meade Emory, assistant to the commissioner of the IRS, was asked. (He denied any inquisition.)

A chairman of the Conference Board meeting, Charles Bowen, chairman of Booz, Allen & Hamilton consultants, was asked in an interview what he thought of the government's anti-bribery drive. "A bunch of pip-squeak moralists running around trying to apply U.S. puritanical standards to other countries," he replied. Would he fire a worker for paying bribes abroad? Mr. Bowen was asked. "Hell, no! Why fire him for something he was paid to do?"

Even some companies now wanting to clean house face difficulties because so many company people have been involved, one Senate investigator says. . . .

Companies are also clinging to foreign consultants even though they have served as conduits for bribes. . . .

A problem has also surfaced with U.S. companies' overseas managers, most of whom are foreign nationals who may have spent their careers in countries where payoffs have been a way of life. One SEC official says, "Companies are telling us that when the corporate president flies over and announces to the overseas people that all of a sudden they have to stop paying off, they just don't believe him." . . .

Many companies are still subject to arm-twisting to make payoffs abroad. "If you have technology that a small country needs and can't duplicate, like IBM or Kodak, you can get by without paying off," a government investigator says. "But what will you do tomorrow if you have a $20 million offshore oil-drilling rig blocked in the harbor and a government official who is demanding a bribe?"

At home or abroad, the corporate drive for profits can put heavy pressure on employees to get results by whatever means, and some companies are still paying off. Besides the Northrop case, Allied Chemical Corp. disclosed last month that it made a domestic payoff earlier this year. . . .

While Allied and Northrop reported their affairs to the SEC, indications are that some other companies aren't bothering. One SEC enforcement official says, "I've had a number of lawyers tell me certain of their clients are ignoring legal advice to disclose; they're going to keep mum, keep on paying off and take their chances."

Attempts by government agencies to catch corporate bribe payers are generating stiff opposition. The IRS is trying to crack down because some companies have been paying bribes and then deducting them as a normal business expense, thus cutting their tax bill. The IRS decided to put 11 questions on bribery, slush funds and overseas bank accounts to corporate managers when reviewing a company's tax return, hoping to get honest answers. As a check, the agency decided to put the same questions to the outside accountants who audit the company's books.

Accountants were infuriated, charging that the IRS move would disrupt their confidential relationships with clients. . . .

The result was a compromise under which the accountants are to sign a letter stating that, to the best of their knowledge, belief and recollection, management's answers to the 11 questions are accurate. IRS officials think this will still serve as an effective check on management. Others worry it will allow some accountants to continue the practice which, according to one critic, amounts to, "I didn't look, and I didn't find anything." . . .

Congress now has passed an arms-sales law compelling disclosure of consultant fees to the State Department and in some cases to law-enforcement agencies and Congress. (The law covers government-to-government sales as well as company-to-government transactions.)

Business representatives don't like the new law. "We'll be policed so we're nice and clean" while foreign firms can bribe at will, says Marshall Garrett, director of international service for the Aerospace Industries Association. When competing with foreign firms, "we'll have to keep our gloves on, while they can fight with bare knuckles."

Where arms aren't involved, a variety of measures are proposed. Disclosure measures provide for reports to foreign government purchasers, to the U.S. government and in some cases to the public. Some bills would give competitors the right to sue bribe-paying rivals on ground they had engaged in an unfair trade practice. Other measures would simply outlaw bribes.

The bill just cleared by Mr. Proxmire's Senate Banking Committee would make it a crime for U.S. companies to bribe foreign officials. But Commerce Secretary Elliot Richardson, chairman of an administration task force on slush funds, doubts it's enforceable. "Successful prosecution of offenses would typically depend upon witnesses and information beyond the reach of U.S. judicial process," he says. "Other nations, rather than assisting in such prosecutions, might resist cooperation because of considerations of national preference or sovereignty." The Commerce Secretary says a treaty would be the best solution, but he concedes that step is a long way off.

15

RACISM

Racism has many faces, some inflamed and vengeful, some cool and apparently indifferent. Still others may conceal themselves behind effective disguises. The simplest consequence of these faces is—as E. Franklin Frazier notes—that whites and blacks do not know each other very well. The purpose behind the selections in this chapter is to depict the varied looks of racism, to understand their human costs, and to assess, however briefly, possible ways of overcoming racism in American society.

In the opening selection, Kenneth B. Clark views racism as part of the general moral crisis of today. Racism is one example of the divergence between America's professed ideals and its realities. "The crisis of inconsistencies in American life—the American dilemma—is primarily a crisis of moral ambivalence."

Next comes E. Franklin Frazier, who discusses the nature of race prejudice, the essence of which is to deny a person his individuality and to conceive of him only as a member of a stereotyped racial group. As a result of such prejudice, Frazier points out, whites and blacks in America "do not know each other as human beings." In a moving statement, Ralph Ellison indicates that a person who is viewed as a stereotype rather than as a total human being becomes an "invisible man," incapable of being seen by those blinded with prejudice.

Leonard Bloom then analyzes some of the moral and social costs of racism and discusses how integration can affect prejudice. Bloom cites evidence from studies of integrated housing complexes to claim that, contrary to the familiar saying, familiarity breeds tolerance. The implication is that racism can be reduced by policy decisions aimed at integration.

Jesse Jackson, however, writes that blacks must assume complete responsibility for their lives and cannot permit themselves the luxury of self-pity. He calls for a show of moral strength among blacks to overcome the despair and poverty of the ghetto. He also offers suggestions as to how this new responsibility may be embodied in specific courses of action.

By itself, different skin color is not a sufficient explanation for the existence of racism. Differences in color have no meaning until men confer significance upon them. The roots of racism lie not in the skin, but in the mind. The violence of lynchings, the humiliation of tauntings, and the face of hatred are all prepared for in emotion-laden thought. Robert Coles recounts how these roots take hold. He reports how children first learn of the existence of racism and how they are taught to participate in it.

There are signs, however, that racial attitudes are changing. In the final selection in this chapter, Martin Kilson assesses some of these changes and urges the continuance of innovative public policy to bring about integration and the realization of the American dream for all.

Kenneth B. Clark, born in 1914, has taught psychology at the City College of New York since 1942. His 1950 report on the psychological effects of school segregation was prominently cited by the Supreme Court in its 1954 decision in *Brown* v. *Board of Education,* ruling "separate but equal" schools unconstitutional. He is the author of *Prejudice and Your Child, Dark Ghetto,* and *Pathos of Power.* "The American Dilemma" was first published in the *New York Times* in February 1975.

E. Franklin Frazier was born in 1894 and educated at Howard University and the University of Chicago. He was professor of sociology at Howard until his death in 1962. He was chairman of a committee of experts on race for UNESCO and president of the International Society for the Scientific Study of Race Relations. His books include *The Negro in the United States* (revised edition, 1957), excerpted here, and *Black Bourgeoisie.*

Ralph Waldo Ellison, author of essays and stories on blacks and American culture, was born in 1914. He has been writer-in-residence at Rutgers University and a visiting fellow at Yale and is currently Albert Schweitzer Professor in the Humanities at New York University. In 1969 he was awarded the Presidential Medal of Freedom. *Invisible Man,* excerpted here, won the National Book Award for 1953 and was named by a Book Week poll in 1965 as the "most distinguished single work" published in the previous twenty years.

Leonard Bloom, born in 1911, has taught sociology in several American universities and since 1971 has been on the faculty of the Institute for Advanced Studies at the Australian National University in Canberra. He has written extensively on the subject of race relations, and among his works are *The Managed Casualty* (with John Kitsuse), *A Blanket a Year* (with F. L. Jones), and *The Social Psychology of Race Relations* (1971), excerpted in this volume.

Jesse L. Jackson, clergyman and civic leader, was born in 1941 in North Carolina and, after advanced study at the Chicago Theological Seminary, was ordained to the ministry of the Baptist church. A close associate of Martin Luther King, he was founder (with others) of Operation Breadbasket, a joint project of the Southern Christian Leadership Conference, and founder and executive director of Operation PUSH (People United to Save Humanity). "Give the People a Vision," which appeared originally in the *New York Times Magazine* in April 1976, was written with the assistance of Bryant Rollins of the *New York Times.*

Robert Coles, born in 1929, is now research psychiatrist at Harvard University Health Services. Author of many books, his *Children of Crisis* in three volumes took no less than eight distinguished literary awards, including the Pulitzer Prize for Volumes 2 and 3. He is on the editorial board of *The American Scholar.* "It's the Same, but It's Different" was written for a conference of the American Academy of Arts and Sciences in 1965 and was published in *The Negro American* (1967), edited by Talcott Parsons and Kenneth Clark.

Martin Kilson is a professor of government at Harvard. His publications include *Political Change in a West African State* and *Political Dilemmas of Black Mayors.* "Whither Integration?" first appeared in *The American Scholar* in the fall of 1976.

KENNETH B. CLARK

The American dilemma

In assessing the social, political and human strength and potential of America, one can concentrate on such large issues as America's role in Southeast Asia and such other international problems as its fluctuating relations with its economic and ideological allies and adversaries; the persistent and manifold and overtly cruel forms of racism; the more subtle manifestations of inter-ethnic conflicts and the rejection of the poor, the aged and the infirm in a nation that prides itself on its affluence; and the fact that a highly developed technological society that has pioneered in space exploration continues to tolerate large-scale decay of the residential portions of its inner cities, deterioration of public education and accelerated pollution and wastage of its natural and human resources.

What is the basic systemic problem—the fundamental problem of perspective, value and character—that seems to be inherent in the chronic crises plaguing American society? Obviously the answer to this question is not to be found in deprivation and poverty of resources.

The paradoxical problem of American society is that it has been too successful; it is affluent and efficient even as it has legitimized and accepted pervasive dishonesties as the price of apparent success. When dishonesty appears to work, it is difficult to argue persuasively for honesty.

So far, America has been able to have its democratic ideals and pursue the cruelties of racism. Today the majority of Americans will vote yes in favor of desegregation of the public schools—but a greater majority will vote against busing of students to obtain desegregated schools. Many Americans under the banner of democratic egalitarianism will argue and insist upon their right to keep less desirable, "less equal," Americans out of their communities and schools.

These and related inconsistencies could be explained as examples of the nonrationality of the human species. . . . [But] I do not believe that this is a logical or rational problem. The crisis of inconsistencies in American life—the American dilemma—is primarily a crisis of moral ambivalence. It is an honesty-dishonesty dilemma that pervades all dimensions of our social, economic, political, educational and, indeed, our religious institutions.

This systemic dilemma within American society is complicated and probably made all the more virulent because it is inextricably entangled with status striving, success symbols, moral and ethical pretensions and the anxieties and fear of personal and family failures.

The conflicts in the American character structure and social system—conflicts intensified by the frequently fulfilled promises of upward mobility—must be resolved if the individuals are to continue to pursue the goals of status and success.

Reality, efficiency and morality are defined as if they were synonymous: That is real and moral which leads to success. If this is found to be too abstract an approach even for a pragmatic morality, then outright moral cynicism and hypocrisy are available as alternative approaches to personal success and effectiveness.

These devices for the resolution of the pervasive moral conflicts of our society can place tremendous stresses and strains upon some sensitive human beings. These individuals—probably a minority—are required continuously to measure their desire to function in terms of ethical and moral principles against their desire to avoid personal failure and ineffectiveness.

In a pragmatic, efficiency-dominated society, it is difficult for an ethically sensitive person to be taken seriously in the making of "tough-minded," "hard-headed" decisions. Promotions don't come easily to them. They are not likely to survive the severe "realistic" screening process that selects candidates for office.

American democracy, with its divergent and competing racial, ethnic and class groups cannot afford to elect to high office individuals who genuinely place ideals and ethical values above personal advantages and "realistic" moral compromises.

Indeed, the concern with honesty and human

values becomes the sign that an individual is not practical enough to be entrusted with the responsibilities of making realistic political and economic decisions.

The virulence of this ethical and moral sickness is indicated by the fact that the symptoms, flagrant or subtle, are accepted by sophisticated realists—the controllers, policy-makers and decision-makers of our society—as normative, competitive, and necessary for efficiency, affluence and effectiveness.

In short, they are interpreted as signs of health.

Those who insist that they are signs of a severe social disease can be dismissed as starry-eyed moralists, sentimentalists and understandably without influence or power. As a matter of fact, the few serious moral critics of our society do not have constituents. Intellectually and temperamentally they cannot appeal to the masses. Neither can they expect support from radicals of the right or the left because they tend to be as much concerned with methods as they are with ends; they cannot accept moral ends through immoral means.

The moral schizophrenia pervasive in the American society appears to be no more curable by words than is personal schizophrenia curable by psychotherapeutic preachments. Political, religious, civil-rights panaceas have been tried and found palliative at best and cruelly disillusioning at worst.

The essential for hope is to be found in that critical minority of human beings who insist upon being unrealistic, who for some still unknown set of reasons continue to argue that human beings are somehow capable of the possibility of empathy, compassion and sensitivity even as cruelty and hostility and insensitivity and rationalized dishonesty now dominate.

Fortunately for the future of a civilized society there exist these human beings who, while they are not nominated for high office and if nominated are not elected, nonetheless remain concerned about moral and ethical values and justice in the affairs of men.

They also seem to have the courage to risk the repeated expressions of their concern and thereby serve as a gnawing and irritating conscience to those who have attained success.

In the final analysis only these individuals provide the hope for that ultimate type of realism that is defined by the capacity of a society to survive rather than to be destroyed eventually on the altar of human barbarity.

E. FRANKLIN FRAZIER

The Negro in the United States

Before analyzing the nature of race prejudice, it is necessary to consider first the nature of prejudice in general. As indicated in the etymology of the word, prejudice is a pre-judgment in the sense that it is a judgment concerning objects and persons not based upon knowledge or experience. The most elemental manifestation of prejudice in this broad meaning of the word is to be found in the personal likes and dislikes and preferences and antipathies which everyone exhibits in regard to food, clothes, and art as well as persons. Although these so-called personal idiosyncrasies, tastes, or prejudices are often deep-seated and appear to be organic reactions, they have been conditioned by the experiences of the individual in his group life. The experiences which are responsible for personal taste and idiosyncrasies are often forgotten. In fact, prejudices may not result from personal experiences with objects or persons. Very often prejudices or dislikes of objects and persons are reactions acquired from other persons or they are attitudes taken over from the culture of the group.

Race prejudice . . . is a special form of prejudice directed toward some racial group. Like prejudices and dislikes in general, race prejudice consists of certain preconceived attitudes which are not based upon scientific knowledge or facts concerning a racial group. The very term racial prejudice, it should be noted, suggests an important element in the phenomenon which we are analyzing. Race prejudice is directed not

319

against an individual with certain observable characteristics but against the individual as a member of the category "race." The categoric picture which a prejudiced person carries in his head affects even his perception of an individual identified with a race that is the object of his prejudice. It is probably true that to most white people all Negroes look alike, just as to Negroes who have prejudices against Chinese all Chinese look alike. When a person has prejudice against a racial group, a person identified with the racial group fails to emerge as an individual. With true insight into the nature of prejudice, Sinclair Lewis has the enraged neighbors, who have discovered that Neil Kingsblood has some remote Negro ancestor, declare that they are going to drive out the black, thick-lipped brute.

Since race prejudice is "an attitude with an emotional bias," the reasons which a person offers for his prejudice are "rationalizations" rather than "reasonable grounds" for his attitude. In providing reasons for his attitude he is attempting to make it appear logical or justifiable. For example, whites often justify their prejudice against Negroes on the grounds that the latter are lazy, lacking in intelligence, or immoral. When they undertake to justify their prejudice against Japanese, they give other "reasons" since they do not attribute these qualities to Japanese. The relation of rationalizations to race prejudice may be observed in many ways, such as in the changing reasons which have been advanced against the education of the Negro. The first reason advanced for not educating the Negro was that he was not capable of being educated. After numerous Negroes acquired an education, it was argued that education unfitted the Negro for labor and made a criminal of him. The latest rationalization which is heard among some whites is that education makes the Negro unhappy.

The prejudice which one has against a member of a racial group may lead one in a conflict situation to desire to exterminate the object of one's prejudice. But, as in other human relations, a *modus vivendi* is generally established in regard to the racial group which is the object of prejudice. This involves primarily the question of status. During the period of slavery when the inferior status of the Negro was fixed, race prejudice tended to be absent. Whatever racial prejudice was manifested toward the Negro was directed against the free Negro. In a society based upon slavery, there was no place for a free Negro. The reference here to "place" is not to "place" in the spatial sense, but to place in the social sense or *status*. Those who are prejudiced against a racial group are generally eager to keep the members of the racial group in a subordinate social status. This explains why the Negro maid with her cap and apron may enter a hotel from which a Negro college professor or scientist is excluded. . . .

One of the truly remarkable phases of race relations in the United States is the fact that whites and Negroes do not know each other as human beings. Most of the sentimental talk of southern whites to the effect that they know Negroes simply reveals the barriers which have been erected between the races since Emancipation. Southern whites know the stereotype of the Negro which provides a certain moral justification for the white's behavior and attitudes toward Negroes. Nor has the northern white known the Negro since he has only reacted to a different stereotype. White Americans do not know Negroes for the simple reason that race prejudice and discrimination have prevented normal human intercourse between the two races.

RALPH ELLISON

Invisible man

I am an invisible man. No, I am not a spook like those who haunted Edgar Allan Poe; nor am I one of your Hollywood-movie ectoplasms. I am a man of substance, of flesh and bone, fiber and liquids—and I might even be said to possess a mind. I am invisible, understand, simply because people refuse to see me. Like the bodiless heads you see sometimes in circus sideshows, it is as though I have been surrounded by mirrors of hard, distorting glass. When they approach me they see only my surroundings, themselves, or figments of their imagination—indeed, everything and anything except me.

Nor is my invisibility exactly a matter of a bio-chemical accident to my epidermis. That invisibility to which I refer occurs because of a peculiar disposition of the eyes of those with whom I come in contact. A matter of the construction of their *inner* eyes, those eyes with which they look through their physical eyes upon reality. I am not complaining, nor am I protesting either. It is sometimes advantageous to be unseen, although it is most often rather wearing on the nerves. Then too, you're constantly being bumped against by those of poor vision. Or again, you often doubt if you really exist. You wonder whether you aren't simply a phantom in other people's minds. Say, a figure in a nightmare which the sleeper tries with all his strength to destroy. It's when you feel like this that, out of resentment, you begin to bump people back. And, let me confess, you feel that way most of the time. You ache with the need to convince yourself that you do exist in the real world, that you're a part of all the sound and anguish, and you strike out with your fists, you curse and you swear to make them recognize you. And, alas, it's seldom successful. . . .

Most of the time (although I do not choose as I once did to deny the violence of my days by ignoring it) I am not . . . overtly violent. I remember that I am invisible and walk softly so as not to awaken the sleeping ones. Sometimes it is best not to awaken them; there are few things in the world as dangerous as sleepwalkers. I learned in time though that it is possible to carry on a fight against them without their realizing it.

LEONARD BLOOM

The social psychology of race relations

There is no direct connection between race and culture. Nations and states, language and culture, are the products of history and cannot be understood apart from a study of their internal development and external relations. Moreover, the fantastic social and technological developments of the last five hundred years have occurred within far too short a time for any genetic changes to have taken place, and are spreading throughout the world far too rapidly for genetic factors to have any influence.

Possibly the most striking example of rapid cultural change is the modern history of Japan, which has developed from feudalism to modern industrialism in barely a century. The development of Africa since about the late 1940s or early 1950s illustrates the same point. For example, Zambia became an independent state on 24 October 1964, and within a few months a university was founded, education was greatly extended and the Development Plan inaugurated a rapid urbanization–industrialization. The culture of pre-independence was well on the way to far-reaching modernization. Did the inhabitants of Zambia one day in 1964 become suddenly fitted genetically to share the achievements of the technology of the Western world, when they were not so fitted before? The only change was in the social and political status and organization of Zambia. . . .

Costs and distortions of racialism

The true costs of discrimination and prejudice are both moral and psychological, and are in terms of unquantifiable, often concealed, but nevertheless real values, damaging both to the quality of society and its members.

One example suffices. During the three years 1965–7 in the U.S.A., rioting and racialism cost the deaths of 130 citizens and the injury of over 3,600. Nearly 29,000 arrests were made, and the estimated damage to property and the economic loss was about $714 millions. This period included major riots at Watts, Newark and Detroit. After the murder of Martin Luther King in April 1968, rioting and looting broke out across the U.S.A. from Washington, D.C. to Oakland, California; from Denver to Tallahassee; and in Washington, D.C. alone more than 20 people were killed.

The intangible, concealed costs were the civic disruption and insecurity, the hardening of misunderstanding between whites and non-whites and the cutting short of social and political dialogue. The encouraging of a tough frontier philosophy of attempting to suppress social distress with violence is matched by a counter-philosophy that only violence will bring about social improvements. When the expression of social distress is effectively suppressed, the processes of estrangement and rebellious despair may be hastened.

The calculable costs of law enforcement are considerable, growing and purely destructive. In Los Angeles, for example, the police have experimented with a giant troop-carrier of 20 tons carrying hoses, a smoke-screen producer, tear-gas launchers, and a 0.30 calibre machine-gun. The Detroit police have claimed eight armoured troop-carriers, and Cleveland, Ohio, is deciding on helicopters. Money spent on armaments cannot be also spent upon improving the quality of life.

Economic costs and losses, although assessable, are arbitrary and meaningless in moral terms. The damage done to the fragile bonds of society is enduring, pervasive and possibly irreversible. An indirect economic cost is the wastage—psychological and social—of talents and skills that are atrophying, unexplored and unemployed, and are summarized in the statistics that the teenage unemployment rate for Negro youth is nearly 26%, and of Negro unemployment in the one hundred largest cities is nearly 7%—far higher figures than for the white population.*

---

*Ed. note: The national unemployment rate in 1969 was 3.3 percent for whites and 6.3 for nonwhites. Comparable figures for 1970 were 5.4 percent and 9.2 percent.

Pettigrew (1964) has shown that if the acquisition of skills of non-whites in the U.S.A. continues at the 1950–60 rates, clerical workers would get proportional representation in 1992, skilled workers in 2005, professionals by 2017, sales workers in 2114, business managers and proprietors in 2730. This implies that even the brightest and most ambitious non-white child cannot realistically look forward to professional or vocational equality with a white child. The non-white child has to overcome a powerful social inertia if he is to rise above the depressive effects of low status and negligible opportunities. It is harder, and more discouraging, for a non-white child to strive for excellence because the rewards are far away and almost unreachable, and the models almost non-existent. The inaccessibility and irrelevance of rewards leads to a lack of interest in education, which in turn reinforces the lack of incentives to rise above a low status.

The explanation of Pettigrew's observation is outlined in the U.S. Civil Rights Commission Report, 1967: segregated education facilities are "inherently unequal." In the deep South only 3.2% of all Negro children in Mississippi, 3.5% in Louisiana, and 6% in South Carolina (for example) attended schools with white children. Indeed, the vast majority of Negroes who entered first grade in 1955 completed their high school in 1967 without ever having attended a class with a white student. Not only was this another obstacle to *psychological* integration, but there is a large body of evidence that suggests that school systems are improved when they are desegregated, because of the efforts that then have to be made to improve the total school system rather than its white segment. More generally, Negro college attendance was proportionally about 50% that of whites. In Washington, D.C., for example, until the school board was restrained in mid-1967, the education of white pupils cost $100 more per head than did that of Negro pupils. At school the Negro drop-outs rate is 60% higher than that of whites, and by the twelfth grade the average reading-level of Negro pupils is about three years behind that of white.

The education of the "disadvantaged" is in content, style and values inadequate for remedying the child's overall disabilities, let alone educating him to take his place as an equal in an integrated society.

The "disadvantaged" child becomes the disadvantaged adult whose economic and social contribution to his society is less than society can afford and his personality can tolerate.

In general, the environmental press of the American colour-caste system tends to develop conceptions of self in Negro children and youth which result in defeated behaviour, as far as academic and political development are concerned. (Kvaraceus, 1965.)

Further, the disadvantaged child lives amidst a clash of cultures and values: those of the low status group to which he belongs, and those of the middle classes which dominate the larger society. . . .

The changing of situational determinants

Underlying all attempts to change prejudice and discrimination by the manipulation of groups and group attitudes and values, is the fostering of contact between members of hostile or antipathetic groups. Contact is no guarantee of understanding; but lack of contact is a partial inducement to misunderstanding and fantasy. Even conflict can, in some circumstances, be useful and creative in initiating a change towards a more stable and satisfying society. Where conflict is natural and functional, for example, where one group is striving to improve its status and reduce its insecurity, this can (1) alter the social structure and make possible the beginnings of social change; (2) extend social communication between sections of a society that were insulated from each other, as a dialogue between American whites and non-whites is opening in the U.S.A., although it is still shrill and ugly . . . ; (3) enhance social solidarity among the lower-status groups, as is happening among American Negroes . . . ; (4) facilitate personal identity, in that it offers a means for protest, assertion and the possibility of success, however limited.

It is the nature and quality of contact, not its frequency, that determines its effect upon the individual's attitudes and behaviour. It is paradoxical that there is probably more casual interracial contact in South Africa than in most multi-racial states, yet it would be a feat of irresponsibility to argue that race attitudes and behaviour in South Africa are benign. Contact does not necessarily diminish prejudice, nor does it inevitably increase understanding and sympathy. Contact will *tend* to change attitudes when it generates—or increases—the expectation that change is probable; otherwise contact can be superficial, casual, tense or hostile and is more likely to increase than decrease prejudice.

Simpson and Yinger (1965) have summarized the main effects of contact:

(i) Equal status contact . . . is likely to reduce prejudice; (ii) Stereotype-breaking contacts that show minority groups in roles not usually associated with them reduce prejudice; (iii) Contacts that bring people of minority and majority groups together in functionally important activities reduce prejudice.

A striking example of equal-status contact was experienced by many soldiers of the U.S.A. towards the end of World War II when platoons of Negroes were attached in terms of complete equality to white companies. This policy followed an executive order of President Roosevelt, which declared:

I do hereby reaffirm the policy of the U.S. that there shall be no discrimination in the employment of workers in defense industries or government, because of race, creed, color or national origin.

An army needed to be raised, industry was needed to supply it, and the state could not afford to lose the services of any person. The problems of race relations in the army were similar to those in the rest of American society, and the responses of both Negro and white soldiers reveal, in rarely-reported detail, the successes and failures of this "experiment in race relations." Officers and sergeants in twenty-four companies that had Negro platoons were interviewed on their attitudes towards racial separation in the army, and an overwhelming majority of the white soldiers, from the North or from the

South, approved of Negro soldiers being segregated in separate units, the most frequent reason given being "the fear of friction." Yet, in answer to the question, "Some army divisions have companies which include Negro platoons and white platoons. How would you feel about it if your outfit was set up like that?" the proportion of white enlisted men who would "dislike it very much" was only 7% in a company with a Negro platoon, increasing to 62% in units with no coloured platoons in white companies. After some time a sample of platoon sergeants in 24 companies that had Negro platoons were asked, "Has your feeling changed since having served in the same unit with coloured soldiers?" More than three-quarters replied "Yes, have become more favourable." None replied that their feelings had become less favourable or more unfavourable. In answer to the questions, "How well did the coloured soldiers in this company perform in combat?" more than 80% replied, "Very well," and only 1% gave the mildly unfavourable answer, "Not so well." A platoon sergeant from South Carolina expressed the changing attitudes:

When I heard about it, I said I'd be damned if I'd wear the same shoulder patch they did. After that first day when we saw how they fought, I changed my mind. They're just like any of the other boys to us.

The authors of the study *The American Soldier* (Stouffer *et al.,* 1965) observed that although the integration of whites and coloured soldiers was imperfect, it could not be expected that it would be because the army was not insulated from the conflicts and strains of civilian life. Nevertheless, even men who initially objected to integrated units accepted them and in many cases their attitudes improved. Indeed it seems no exaggeration to write of "the revolution in attitudes that took place among these men as a result of enforced contacts."

Of course, this study does not answer the question whether enforced contacts would ameliorate attitudes in other situations. The peculiarity of this situation was that the demands and dangers of total war made it impossible to permit choice to those with hostile attitudes and the only practical and expedient policy was to insist that all soldiers were treated as having equal status regardless of their race. The authors discuss the recommendations of an official board that investigated the major points of racial friction encountered in the army, and while neither denying nor minimizing the difficulties, tensions and misunderstandings that a policy of integration entails, agree with the board that a policy of integration is the only policy possible within the context of the American democratic tradition. Further, the alternative policy of allowing separation and discrimination to continue is more likely to encourage racialism and prejudice than to avoid friction points.

Few studies of behaviour change in situations of equal-status contact include a wide range of everyday activities, but housing is one area of life that permits "real life" study. Deutsch and Collins (1951) investigated two housing schemes in the neighbouring cities of New York and Newark. The projects in Newark housed both Negro and white families in segregated units. In New York, Negro and white families were assigned to apartment buildings without regard to their race. The housing schemes were for poor families, all were in mainly Negro neighbourhoods, "considerably deteriorated and characterized by much delinquency," with similar proportions of white and Negro families.

Interviews with the housewives suggested that prejudice was sharply reduced in the integrated projects, and this finding was supported by an examination of the numbers of tenants who moved away and their reasons, the housewives' interracial experiences before they moved into the apartments, and a comparison of the housewives who knew about the pattern of occupancy before they applied for an apartment with those who did not know. The authors consider that their investigations

discredit a notion that has characterized much of social-science thinking in the field of race relations . . . that "state-ways cannot change folkways" . . . Official policy, executed without equivocation, can result in large changes in behavior despite initial resistance to that policy.

The principal changes arose less from deliberate policy to create better race relations than from the emergence of many situations in which equal-status contact was inevitable and "physical and functional proximity" inescapable. In the integrated projects more than 95% of the women interviewed indicated that they were likely to get to know coloured people, compared with 30% and 21% of the housewives in the segregated bi-racial schemes. This striking difference is accounted for by the places the housewives described as most likely meeting-places: the actual buildings in which they lived, outside on benches and the laundry in or near the buildings. In the segregated projects it was less easy for those informal meeting-places to become equally available to both races. Similar differences appeared in neighbourly activities such as helping with another woman's shopping, visiting, going to the movies together, sewing clubs. In the integrated projects many of the white women were neighbourly in this way, but in the segregated projects, very few. Interviews with the Negro housewives and their children confirmed these different patterns of contact: "in effect, living in the integrated projects produces a *behavioral* change with respect to race relations for many of the white people." The different housing schemes developed group norms or standards about racial issues. In the integrated projects white housewives *expected* approval and support if they were friendly with a Negro resident, and by contrast, in the segregated projects the housewife expected to be socially ostracized by the other white women if she happened to be friendly with a Negro. But the most striking evidence of the development of norms was the friendship patterns of the children. The children in segregated projects went to unsegregated elementary schools and had the opportunity to mix with members of the other race. Yet no such child, whatever his choice of friends in the school, would have a child of another race as a friend in activities within the project. On the other hand, children in the integrated projects played together in the project as freely as in school, and visited one another's homes.

Finally, the effects upon interracial attitudes in the projects differed. Through their experiences in the integrated projects, white housewives tended to shift their attitudes towards Negroes in a more favourable direction, and few of the tenants in the segregated projects did so. The housewives in the integrated projects were far less prejudiced than those in the segregated projects, and among the housewives in the integrated projects "their experiences in the project with Negro people have become partially *generalized,* so that they now have more favorable attitudes toward Negroes as a group," even outside the project.

Interviews illustrate the changing attitudes. One woman said:

I thought I was moving into the heart of Africa. . . . I had always heard things about how they were. . . . they were dirty, drink a lot . . . were like savages. Living with them my ideas have changed altogether. They're just people . . . they're not any different.

The authors claim their findings are consistent with the growing evidence that equal-status contacts can change prejudiced attitudes and discriminatory behaviour, provided that (1) the behaviour of the "objects of prejudice" does not conform with the beliefs of the prejudiced; (2) the amount and closeness of the contact is sufficiently realistic and compelling to resist the tendency to become distorted to fit the old stereotypes; (3) the contact is in such conditions that the prejudiced person cannot interpret the behaviour of the object of prejudice as due to the situation rather than to his personal qualities. If the friendly Negro store-clerk is primarily behaving as a store-clerk *should* behave, then his friendliness is unlikely to have any effect upon the attitudes of a prejudiced person; (4) the prejudiced person is exposed to social influences which strongly and clearly conflict with his retaining his prejudiced behaviour.

JESSE L. JACKSON

Give the people a vision

It is time, I believe, to reexamine the causes of the social and economic plight in which black Americans—and particularly the poor blacks of the Northern cities—still find themselves, despite the legal advances of the 60's. Since so many past analyses of this problem have failed to bring about satisfactory improvement, I think it is time to suggest some new approaches, based largely on new values. It is my view that such a fresh start offers the best hope not only of lifting up the black people but of saving America's cities.

I also believe that it is fruitful to think of these problems within a larger context—the relationship between the United States and the third world. For the white racist attitudes that are part of the problem at home have also been an often unconscious element in the policy failures of the white political leadership vis-à-vis the emerging nations, most recently in Africa. And the natural pride of American blacks in the achievement of black leaders abroad is a factor in their own struggle.

As a starting point, let us take a noteworthy statistic: There are now 130 black mayors in the United States. We blacks have populated the cities; we must now learn to run them. The need is urgent. The ethical collapse, the heroin epidemic, the large numbers of our people who are out of work and on welfare, and the disruptive violence in our schools all indicate that the cities may be destroying us.

The thrust of my argument is that black Americans must begin to accept a larger share of responsibility for their lives. For too many years we have been crying that racism and oppression have kept us down. That is true, and racism and oppression have to be fought on every front. But to fight any battle takes soldiers who are strong, healthy, spirited, committed, well-trained and confident. This is particularly true when the enemy is as tough and elusive as American racism. I don't believe that we will produce strong soldiers by moaning about what the enemy has done to us.

It is time, I think, for us to stand up, admit to our failures and weaknesses and begin to strengthen ourselves. Here are some of the things I am talking about:

There is a definite welfare mentality in many black communities that derives perhaps from slavery but that must now be overcome.

We have become politically apathetic. Only 7 million out of 14 million eligible black voters are registered to vote. Yet politics is one key to self-development. In terms of votes, we have more potential strength than labor or any other single bloc. We have a responsibility to use it to the full.

We too often condemn blacks who succeed and excel, calling them Toms and the like, when the ideal ought to be for all of us to succeed and excel.

We are allowing a minuscule minority of criminals in our midst to create disorder, ruin our schools and sap the energy we need to rebuild our neighborhoods and our cities.

Many leaders who are black, and many white liberals, will object to my discussing these things in public. But the decadence in black communities—killings, destruction of our own businesses, violence in the schools—is already in the headlines; the only question is what we should do about it. Others will object that to demand that we must meet the challenge of self-government is to put too much pressure on the victims of ancient wrongs. Yet in spite of these objections, in spite of yesterday's agony, liberation struggles are built on sweat and pain rather than tears and complaints.

In facing up to the new reality of black concentration in the Northern cities, the flight of whites to the suburbs, and the decay of the inner cities—particularly their black communities—in many parts of the country, many black and white leaders demand Federal aid as the only solution. More Federal aid is certainly needed, but money alone, or in combination with minor reforms, will not significantly change the welfare system, reduce crime, build enough new houses, improve education, restore stable families or eliminate drug abuse. A multitude of Federal antipoverty and urban-renewal programs should have proved that by now. But if more Federal money will not solve the problem, what will? . . .

We black Americans can rebuild our communities with moral authority. We need a blueprint, such as an urban Marshall Plan, but at its base there must be moral authority and sound ethical conduct.

This is not unrealistic. It was the moral authority of the civil-rights movement, not the Federal marshals—who stood back initially and let whites have their way with the demonstrators—that changed the face of the South. It was a disciplined struggle—and such a struggle can be waged again, to good purpose, in the cities of the North.

We need to tell our young people in those cities: "All right, we'll get all the state and Federal money that we can; but first and foremost, we need to put your hands and your bodies and your minds to work building our communities." What we must do for our young people is challenge them to put hope in their brains rather than dope in their veins. What difference does it make if the doors swing wide open if our young people are too dizzy to walk through them?

I often wonder what would happen if Coleman Young, the Mayor of Detroit, who has inherited a city of much moral and economic decay, were to go into one of Detroit's stadiums and had 50,000 or 60,000 people in there—just as Jomo Kenyatta has done, and Castro, and President Samora Machel of Mozambique—and delivered a resounding State of Detroit message.

"All right, people," he could say, "Detroit needs 200 doctors in the next 10 to 15 years, and here is what we will do to make certain that it happens. And we will need 200 lawyers and 400 electricians and 250 nurses, and here is what we will do to make sure it happens. I cannot pass a law about these things, but I am appealing to you parents and you children to cooperate. Parents, you must keep your children at home every night from 7 to 9 to study, and get them into bed by 10. Every morning the city will provide

physical-training directors in city parks. We will close off one block in every neighborhood for half an hour every morning for exercise—we want you out there getting your bodies healthy for this struggle for independence."

I have been visiting major cities across the country, preparing for a crusade next fall that will stimulate people along these lines. Everywhere I go, from Washington to Los Angeles, I meet young people in schools that the politicians have given up on. I frequently find myself addressing 3,000 or 4,000 young people in a rundown assembly hall. Each time I suggest a program of self-development, they respond with overwhelming enthusiasm. . . .

Our program is simple. We want to get black men from the neighborhoods to replace the police in patrolling the school corridors and the street corners where the dope pushers operate. We want all parents to reserve the evening hours of 7 to 9 for their children's homework. We want student leaders and athletes to help identify and solve discipline problems before they get out of control. We want the black-oriented media to find ways to publicly reward achievers. We want the black disc jockeys, who reach more black kids than the school principals, to inform and inspire as well as entertain.

A crucial element in our program is the black church. The church is the most stable influence in the black communities. It is the only place where all segments of the community come together, once a week. An estimated 11 to 13 million men, women and children are members of black churches. Historically, the black church has been involved in or behind every black movement of any significance. I have been involved with high schools in Washington, Chicago and Los Angeles that are working with churches, and if there is anything the experience has shown me, it is that black ministers still carry moral authority with our people, except for a hard-core few, and most people want moral authority.

America is in the midst of a crisis, both in regard to its cities and in regard to its position in the world. Black Americans, inheritors of the role of the restless and disenfranchised minorities of the past who helped make America strong, have a historic opportunity to show that the cities can be saved. We can do so by stimulating change in the schools and the communities we control.

Also by virtue of our special empathy for the colored peoples of the third world, and particularly Africa, black Americans can contribute to the foreign-policy debate by exposing the racism at the root of some of our Government's worst domestic and foreign blunders. It would be tragic if our nation lost its potential for true greatness by letting racist legacies deflect it from its proper course.

Vital though this second task may be, it must, for the moment, take second place. The first and immediate task for American blacks is to rise up from the decadence in which we too often find ourselves in the cities, and to do so by the force of our will, our intellect, our energy and our faith in ourselves. It is a historic opportunity we cannot afford to miss.

ROBERT COLES

It's the same, but it's different

My clinical impression—slowly consolidated over these past years of working with Negro children—is that most of the "usual" problems and struggles of growing up find an additional dimension in the racial context. In a very real sense being Negro serves to organize and render coherent many of the experiences, warnings, punishments, and prohibitions that Negro children face. The feelings of inferiority or worthlessness they acquire, the longing to be white they harbor and conceal, the anger at what they find to be their relatively confined and money-less condition, these do not fully account for the range of emotions in many Negro children as they come to terms with the "meaning" of their skin color. Sally's grandmother said more concisely what I am struggling to say: "They can

scream at our Sally, but she knows why, and she's not surprised. She knows that even when they stop screaming, she'll have whispers, and after them the stares. It'll be with her for life. . . . We tell our children that, so by the time they have children, they'll know how to prepare them. . . . It takes a lot of preparing before you can let a child loose in a white world. If you're black in Louisiana it's like cloudy weather; you just don't see the sun much."

The "preparation" for such a climate of living begins in the first year of life. At birth the shade of the child's skin may be very important to his parents—so important that it determines in large measure how he is accepted, particularly in the many Negro marriages which bring together a range of genes which, when combined, offer the possibility of almost *any* color. What is often said about color-consciousness in Negroes (their legendary pursuit of skin bleaches and hair-straightening lotions) must be seen in its relentless effect upon the life of the mind, upon babies, and upon child-rearing. A Negro sociologist—involved in, rather than studying, the sit-in movement—insisted to me that "when a Negro child is shown to his mother and father, the first thing they look at is his color, and then they check for fingers and toes." I thought such a remark extreme indeed, until two years later when I made a point of asking many parents I knew what they thought of it—and found them unashamedly in agreement.

As infants become children, they begin to form some idea of how they look, and how their appearance compares with that of others. They watch television, accompany their mothers to the local market or stores downtown. They play on the street and ride in cars which move through cities or small towns. They hear talk, at the table or in Sunday school, or from other children while playing. In the time they enter school, at five or six, to "begin" to learn, they have already learned some lessons of self-respect (or its absence) quite well.

I have been continually astonished to discover just how intricately children come to examine the social system, the political and economic facts of life in our society. I had always imagined myself rather sensible and untouched by those romantic nineteenth-century notions of childhood "innocence." As a child psychiatrist I had even committed myself to a professional life based on the faith that young children see and feel what is happening in their family life—and if properly heard will tell much of it to the doctor, whether in words, in games, or with crayons. Yet I had never quite realized that children so quickly learn to estimate who can vote, or who has the money to frequent this kind of restaurant or that kind of theater or what groups of people contribute to our police force—and why. Children, after all, have other matters on their minds—and so do many adults.

I do not think Negro children are, by definition, budding sociologists or political scientists, but I have been struck by how specifically aware they become of those forces in our society which, reciprocally, are specifically sensitive to *them*. They remark upon the scarcity of colored faces on television, and I have heard them cheer the sight of a Negro on that screen. In the South they ask their parents why few if any policemen or bus drivers are colored. In the ghettos of the North they soon enough come to regard the Negro policeman or bus driver as specially privileged—as indeed he is, with his steady pay, with his uniform that calls for respect and signifies authority—and perhaps as an enemy in the inevitable clash with "whitey."

"The first thing a colored mother has to do when her kids get old enough to leave the house and play in the street is teach them about the white man and what he expects. I've done it with seven kids, and I've got two more to go; and then I hope I'll be through." She was talking about her earnest desire to "be done with" bringing children into the world, but she had slipped into a recital of how Negro mothers must be loyal to the segregationist customs of Southern towns. Still, she preferred them to the North; and so did her son, a youth I had watched defy sheriffs (and his mother's early admonitions) in Alabama and Mississippi for several years. "In the North," her son added, "I'd have learned the same thing, only it's worse, because there a mother can't just lay it on the line. It

takes time for the boy to get the full pitch, and realize it's really the same show, just a little dressed-up, and until he makes that discovery, he's liable to be confused. The thing we're not down here is confused." . . .

For that matter, it is not simply that Negro children learn the bounds of their fate, the limits of the kinds of work allowed to them, the extent of their future disfranchisement, the confines of their social freedom, the edge of the residential elbowroom permitted them, the margin of free play, whim, or sport available to them now or within their grasp when they are grown. They learn how to make use of such knowledge, and in so doing gain quite gradually and informally an abiding, often tough sense of what is about them in the world, and what must be in them to survive. . . .

When I lived in Mississippi I had a home in a small town. For a long time I was not interested in the civil rights issue: there was none in the state at that time. The people I knew were intelligent and kindly—all of them white, middle-class people who were born in the state, brought up from their first days by Negro "mammies." . . . After I became interested in how young Negroes lived and got along with whites, I went with a doctor and his wife one day to the colored section of our town. They had always ignored laundromats, would not think of buying a washing machine; Louisa had been washing and ironing their sheets and shirts for years. Louisa and her mother had taken care of the doctor's wife when she was a child: "She fed me as a baby. I was the first baby she cared for; she learned from her mother how to do it—I don't remember much of it; I just remember Louisa smiling and helping me choose a dress to wear for a party at school, and maybe a game or two she played with us." Later that day this very sensitive woman told me of an experience she *did* remember, and quite clearly: "I think I was seven or eight, and I went with my mother to a five-and-dime store. It was one of those old ones; I can still see the counters, and the fans going. They hung in rows from the ceilings. . . . Anyway, we were walking down the aisle, and I bumped right into a nigra woman. I said, 'Excuse me, ma'am,' and right in front of her my mother told me never to use 'ma'am' with the colored. It was O.K. to say 'excuse me,' because that showed I was a well-mannered girl; but 'ma'am' was different. . . . I had trouble making sense of that, and I asked my mother her reasons for being so against using 'ma'am' with the nigra. She tried to tell me that it was the way we did things in the world, but it never made sense to me. . . . I think what *did* make sense to me was that I had to obey my mother's wish. Then you grow older, and you stop trying to make sense of things like that. You just know that there are things you can do, and things you can't, and that's it. My brother once tried to get my parents to explain to him why he had to wear a tie one place, and not another. It was the same thing. My daddy just said, 'Jimmie, that's the way it is, and that's the way we have to do it.'"

MARTIN KILSON

Whither integration?

According to most indicators, between World War II and the 1970s white attitudes toward blacks changed markedly for the better. True, the change was uneven, often precarious, and usually forthcoming only grudgingly. Yet there has been change. For example, by 1970 only 30 percent of whites, nationwide, opposed the principle of school integration, and only 40 percent of whites in the South opposed it. Most whites also favored the principle of integration in public accommodations, housing, jobs, et cetera. The problem, however, is getting whites to translate agreement on *integration in principle* into *integration in fact*. This is difficult indeed, for most whites refuse to admit that the historical treatment of blacks in terms of racial caste has significantly constrained their access to equality in American life. A Harris poll taken in December 1972 showed that only 40 percent of whites agreed that Negroes were discriminated against in regard to "getting full equality," 38

percent in regard to "the way treated as human beings," 40 percent in regard to "getting skilled labor jobs," 29 percent in regard to "getting quality education in public schools," 40 percent in regard to "getting white-collar jobs," 22 percent in regard to "wages paid," and 51 percent in regard to "getting decent housing"—the last being the only issue on which a majority of white Americans considered blacks distinctly disadvantaged because of race. . . .

Clearly, then, there remains a profound discrepancy between, on the one hand, the postwar open-mindedness of a majority of whites toward the principle of integrating blacks into American life and, on the other hand, the transformation of this favorable outlook on racial matters into concrete changes in housing, schools, and jobs. This discrepancy plays havoc with all efforts of federal public policy to sustain racial change in these basic spheres of American life. Moreover, the precarious position of public policy in racial matters sine 1968 is reinforced by a widespread alienation of voters toward government, with only 15 percent of the population currently believing that the federal government "does the best job." . . .

Yet, on the more sanguine side, Negroes over the past two decades made serious political advances along with real economic and educational gains. Increases in the number of registered voters, actual voting, candidacies, and elected officials among Negroes have been nothing less than astonishing. . . .

Integration, in the wider sense in which I have been discussing it here, is measurable by more than indicators of social change. Cultural phenomena weigh heavily as well. Many of the important cultural tendencies that are pertinent for racial integration had their origins in the counterculture and new styles of life that developed in the 1960s. New cultural patterns and images related to racial matters—particularly in the spheres of cross-ethnic marriage, popular culture, and the mass media—are now available to young Americans, enabling fundamental change in the character of American society.

The growth of cross-ethnic marriages, including interracial marriages, has been extraordinary. . . . Among Negroes between 1960 and 1970 there were 64,789 black-white marriages—a 26 percent increase over the previous decade. Moreover, in the decade 1950–60 there were for the first time slightly more white male–black female marriages—25,913 of them, a margin of 417 over black male–white female marriages. Although marriages of this character declined in 1960–70, doubtless owing to the rise of virulent black militancy and the polarization of racial feeling that it brought in its wake, such marriages, and interracial marriages in general, are expected to increase markedly in the current decade. Experts agree that white male–black female marriages are an important index of fundamental change in the historical pattern of racial-caste labeling in America, and hence of the ultra-stigmatization under which Negroes have lived.

Less easy to generalize about, but more pervasive, has been the increased presence of the Negro in popular culture, and in a new and different perspective. Rock music, for example, is the first successful mode of mass music—played and listened to by millions of white kids of all classes and ethnic groups and in all regions of the country—to contain a distinctly Negro cultural motif, albeit of lower-class Negro origin. . . . No other generation of white popular musical artists, however much their music was earlier shaped by Negro forms, has shown the same degree of deference to Negroness. This new and unprecedented cultural diffusion between blacks and whites at least supports racial-caste dissolution; for if more whites—the young in particular—consider the Negro and his ethnicity an increasingly valid source of their own style, they might also begin to consider the Negro a legitimate member of American society.

In the media—television, textbooks, magazines, the press, movies—the old degrading image of the Negro as a superstitious, maniacially smiling, lazy coon that for so long dominated the view of the Negro in popular culture is just about dead. Television in particular has helped to effect this change. Millions of white families now see on their TV screens richly variegated portrayals of blacks in American life. . . . It would of course be foolish to infer from this turnabout in the popular projection of the Negro that a radical change has occurred in the character of American race relations; yet it would be equally foolish to conclude that it is of no consequence whatever, save in the marketing of products in a capitalist economy. Indeed it is precisely because capitalism has endorsed this dramatic change in the popular image of blacks that I would expect its impact to be significant. Few things in American civilization succeed as thoroughly as capitalist-linked success, and however much one may bemoan this feature of our culture, it is a powerful institutionalizing force.

Over a generation ago, Gunnar Myrdal argued that the resolution of the "American Dilemma"—the nonfreedom of racial caste in a society whose primary premise was freedom itself—would occur when the American creed of equal opportunity for all individuals was extended to blacks and whites alike. Thus far the resolution of that dilemma, while well under way, has remained only partial. And it will continue to be so, Myrdal believes, until whites face up to the moral cowardice that lies at the heart of it.

Certainly the split personality, aided and abetted by moral confusion, that the average white displays in the process of extending the American creed is a continuing obstacle to racial integration. For example, in the area of sports—where Negroes now have a preponderant role after their fitful entry in the late 1940s and early 1950s—one finds much moral ambivalence in racial matters. Consider the city of Boston, where Irish youth cheer on the Celtics' Jojo White or Charlie Scott at the Boston Garden, or Jim Rice of the Red Sox at Fenway Park, but the next day shout "dirty nigger" at black children being bused into formerly white schools. Fortunately, most Negro leaders today are quite capable of open-mindedness toward this kind of ambivalence in the racial perceptions of the average white, who might be willing to change in one sphere of cultural and social life but in other spheres remains constrained by past habits and current anxieties.

Another and less sympathetic response by

Negro leaders is warranted, however, in regard to the neoconservative white intellectuals and publicists whose current arguments regarding racial integration amount to adding insult to injury. These neoconservatives would have us believe that the American creed would have shed its white-only status quite of its own accord—without the pressure of the civil rights movement, the general cultural shifts of the 1960s, and the public policy initiatives of the Kennedy and Johnson administrations. The latter in particular come in for the loudest criticism from the neoconservatives. They condemn any role for government in racial integration beyond that of night watchman. Such transgression, they claim, can only produce bureaucratic excesses and profound distortions of the traditional American values of individual achievement—values that white ethnic groups like Jews, Irish, Slavs, and Italians presumably have assimilated. Nathan Glazer's book *Affirmative Discrimination* propounds this thesis; it is sharply critical of affirmative action in hiring policies for blacks, women, and Spanish-speaking citizens.

This neoconservative attack on racial integration—and it is, in the final analysis, nothing less—is riddled through with unexamined assumptions. For one thing, the white ethnics' experience with upward mobility did not entail any special deference to individualism, insofar as individualism led them to reject assistance from government. . . .

It is equally curious that the neoconservatives, despite their claim to realism, have paid little attention to what underlies the fears of white ethnics in regard to federal support of racial integration: the economics of scarcity under which the United States has been living since the end of the Vietnam War. In particular, much of the bad feeling that has of late accompanied the affirmative action program is not racial or sexual but economic. . . . Which brings us back again to the need for innovative public policy—a policy that will give all who have been held down a chance for a leg up without knocking down those who have already attained significant upward mobility.

Finally, it has to be understood that integration is not a matter of interest exclusively to Negroes. The best of our leaders, black and white, have always understood it in a wider context—as a necessity for the nation at large. "I have a dream," announced Martin Luther King, Jr., before he was brought down, and that dream, as he elaborated upon it, was not for Negroes alone but for every American. It was a dream of a society without hunger and without meanness, a society in which everyone could live his life to the best of his God-given limitations. That dream has seemed to fade in recent years. . . . It remains the best dream we have, and the truest American vision.

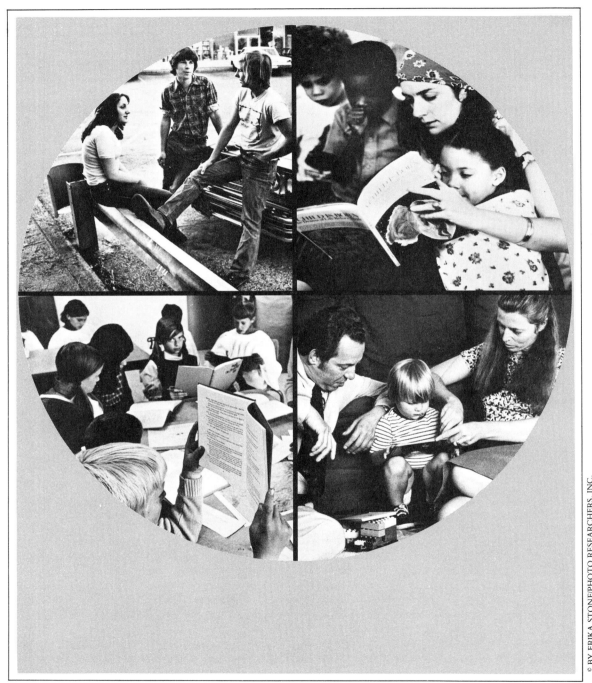

Agents of Moral Education. *Who is responsible for moral education today—the family, the school, the church or the peer group.*

A distinctive feature of moral thought today is its realization that it confronts problems and situations for which moral responses have not been developed. This condition decisively affects moral education. Consider, for instance, its effects on the time-honored way of moral education—teaching by example—where a teacher or an elder would be regarded as a model and would be imitated by the young. This kind of moral education presupposed a teacher who embodied a stable and unified morality. This presupposition has been shaken precisely because few moralities are today self-confident in their understanding of the world in which we live. This lack of confidence may be seen in their constant changes and experiments. As a result, people seem to be in the position of students seeking to understand how to act morally but who lack teachers who can impart this knowledge. The selections in this chapter address the question of how moral behavior can be taught in this time of moral uncertainty and put forward various suggestions to bring about some compelling moral renewal.

Most of these excerpts consider the role of the schools and teachers in moral education. (The role of the family in moral education has already been considered in Chapter 3.) In the university, the primary way a professor can serve "moral forces," argues Max Weber, is by helping his students bring about a greater "self-clarification" and a "sense of respon-sibility." Weber says that this may be done by leading students to recognize those facts that are "inconvenient" for the particular moral positions they may hold.

For Emile Durkheim, the primary school, not the university, is the central institution for moral education. Only the primary school can instill those impersonal rules of discipline that Durkheim believes compose the core of morality. He considers the task of the teacher to be twofold: to enforce the rules scrupulously and to convey to the students that the rules exist impersonally and do not rely on his personal authority. Then, in explicit opposition to Durkheim, comes Jean

16

MORAL
EDUCATION

Piaget, who argues that schools should aim to develop the character trait of "autonomy" in students, rather than discipline, and the spirit of "cooperation" rather than that of obedience.

Drawing upon classic philosophic accounts and modern psychological insights, Martin Buber describes the powers and limits of a teacher to reach his pupils and those personal qualities and manner of instruction of a teacher that are necessary for the moral development of students. For Buber, all "education worthy of the name is essentially education of character."

In the next selection, John Dewey argues that all morality is social, and "moral judgment and moral responsibility are the work wrought in us by the social environment," that is, by the way others react to our acts. Trying to instill moral principles in a child is futile, Dewey argues, if the child soon learns that society does not, in fact, condemn violation of such principles. Dewey urges us to use science so that we can better observe, and thus understand and shape, human interrelationships.

In the final article, Amitai Etzioni notes the current concern with teaching morality and reviews some of the methods now being used in the schools. But, following the argument presented by Dewey, Etzioni points out that formal attempts to teach morality are being undermined by the societal ethos of competition and success, evidenced in the "hidden curriculum" of the schools. He concludes that "before the schools can effectively provide moral education, the surrounding society must work to reform itself so that its members are less concerned with success and material achievements, and more concerned about the quality of life and individual conduct."

NOTES ABOUT THE AUTHORS

Max Weber. See above, p. 277.

Emile Durkheim was a French sociologist, born in 1858. His books *The Elementary Forms of Religious Life* and *Suicide* are standard reference works in the field. He died in 1917.

Jean Piaget is a Swiss psychologist, born in 1896. He has taught at Swiss universities and is at present director of the International Center of Genetic Epistemology at Geneva, which he founded. He has written extensively in the field of children's education, proposing that children pass through three stages of mental development, culminating in the ability to deal with abstractions. *The Moral Judgment of the Child,* excerpted here, was published in 1965.

Martin Buber, Israeli theologian, was born in 1878 in Vienna. A scholar of Hassidic Judaism, he taught social philosophy at Hebrew University, Jerusalem. His best-known works are *Good and Evil* (1953) and *I and Thou* (1958). "The Education of Character" is from *Man and Man* (1965). Buber died in 1965.

John Dewey, philosopher and educator, was born in 1859. He was a leader of the philosophical movement known as "pragmatism." Opposed to traditional education that stressed rote learning, he emphasized the need to consider the student's physical, moral, and intellectual development. His books include *Democracy and Education, Reconstruction in Philosophy,* and *Human Nature and Conduct,* excerpted here and first published in 1922. Dewey died in 1952.

Amitai Etzioni, born in 1929, has taught at Columbia since 1958. He is currently director of the Center for Policy Research. His many books include *Active Society, A Comparative Analysis of Complex Organizations,* and *Genetic Fix.* "Do as I Say, not as I Do" appeared originally in the *New York Times Magazine* in September 1976.

Science and politics

Fellow students! You come to our lectures and demand from us the qualities of leadership, and you fail to realize in advance that of a hundred professors at least ninety-nine do not and must not claim to be football masters in the vital problems of life, or even to be "leaders" in matters of conduct. . . .

Finally, you will put the question: "If this is so, what then does science actually and positively contribute to practical and personal 'life'?" . . .

[Science can help you] to gain *clarity*. Of course, it is presupposed that we ourselves possess clarity. As far as this is the case, we can make clear to you the following:

In practice, you can take this or that position when concerned with a problem of value—for simplicity's sake, please think of social phenomena as examples. *If* you take such and such a stand, then, according to scientific experience, you have to use such and such a *means* in order to carry out your conviction practically. Now, these means are perhaps such that you believe you must reject them. Then you simply must choose between the end and the inevitable means. Does the end "justify" the means? Or does it not? The teacher can confront you with the necessity of this choice. He cannot do more, so long as he wishes to remain a teacher and not to become a demagogue. He can, of course, also tell you that if you want such and such an end, then you must take into the bargain the subsidiary consequences which according to all experience will occur. Again we find ourselves in the same situation as before. These are still problems that can also emerge for the technician, who in numerous instances has to make decisions according to the principle of the lesser evil or of the relatively best. Only to him one thing, the main thing, is usually given, namely, the end. But as soon as truly "ultimate" problems are at stake for us this is not the case. With

this, at long last, we come to the final service that science as such can render to the aim of clarity, and at the same time we come to the limits of science.

Besides we can and we should state: In terms of its meaning, such and such a practical stand can be derived with inner consistency, and hence integrity, from this or that ultimate *weltanschauliche** position. Perhaps it can only be derived from one such fundamental position, or maybe from several, but it cannot be derived from these or those other positions. Figuratively speaking, you serve this god and you offend the other god when you decide to adhere to this position. And if you remain faithful to yourself, you will necessarily come to certain final conclusions that subjectively make sense. This much, in principle at least, can be accomplished. Philosophy, as a special discipline, and the essentially philosophical discussions of principles in the other sciences attempt to achieve this. Thus, if we are competent in our pursuit (which must be presupposed here) we can force the individual, or at least we can help him, to give himself an *account of the ultimate meaning of his own conduct*. This appears to me as not so trifling a thing to do, even for one's own personal life. Again, I am tempted to say of a teacher who succeeds in this: he stands in the service of "moral" forces; he fulfils the duty of bringing about self-clarification and a sense of responsibility. And I believe he will be the more able to accomplish this, the more conscientiously he avoids the desire personally to impose upon or suggest to his audience his own stand.

Moral education

Morality is not . . . simply a system of customary conduct. It is a system of commandments. We were saying, first of all, that irregular be-

---

**Ed. note:* World view.

havior is morally incomplete. So it is with the anarchist. (I use the word in its etymological sense, referring to the man so constituted as not to feel the reality of moral imperatives, the man who is affected by a kind of color-blindness, by virtue of which all moral and intellectual forces seem to him of the same order.) Here we confront another aspect of morality: at the root of the moral life there is, besides the preference for regularity, the notion of moral authority. Furthermore, these two aspects of morality are closely linked, their unity deriving from a more complex idea that embraces both of them. This is the concept of discipline. Discipline in effect regularizes conduct. It implies repetitive behavior under determinate conditions. But discipline does not emerge without authority—a regulating authority. Therefore, to summarize . . . we can say that the fundamental element of morality is the spirit of discipline.

However, let us be clear about the meaning of this proposition. Ordinarily, discipline appears useful only because it entails behavior that has useful outcomes. Discipline is only a means of specifying and imposing the required behavior, so it derives its *raison d'être* from the behavior. But if the preceding analysis is correct we must say that discipline derives its *raison d'être* from itself; it is good that man is disciplined, independent of the acts to which he thus finds himself constrained. . . .

Since morality is a discipline, since it commands us, it is evident that the behavior required of us is not according to the bent of our individual natures. If morality merely bids us follow our individual natures, it need not speak to us in an imperative tone. Authority is necessary only to halt, to contain rebellious forces, not to encourage existing forces to develop in their own way. It has been said that the function of morality is to prevent the individual from encroaching on forbidden territory; in a sense, nothing is more accurate. Morality is a comprehensive system of prohibitions. That is to say, its objective is to limit the range within which individual behavior should and must normally occur.

We now see what end is served by this necessary limitation. The totality of moral regulations really forms about each person an imaginary

338

wall, at the foot of which a multitude of human passions simply die without being able to go further. For the same reason—that they are contained—it becomes possible to satisfy them. But if at any point this barrier weakens, human forces—until now restrained—pour tumultuously through the open breach; once loosed, they find no limits where they can or must stop. Unfortunately, they can only devote themselves to the pursuit of an end that always eludes them. For example, should the rules of conjugal morality lose their authority, should husband-wife obligations be less respected, should passions and appetites ruled by this sector of morality unleash themselves, being even exacerbated by this same release, then, powerless to fulfill themselves because they have been emancipated from all limitations, such passions would entail a disillusionment which translates itself graphically into statistics of suicide. Again, should that morality governing economic life be shaken, and were the ambitions for gain to become excited and inflamed, knowing no bounds, then one would observe a rise in the annual quota of suicides. One could multiply such examples. Furthermore, it is because morality has the function of limiting and containing that too much wealth so easily becomes a source of immorality. Through the power wealth confers on us, it actually diminishes the power of things to oppose us. Consequently, it lends an increment of strength to our desires, which makes it harder to hold them in check. Under such conditions, moral equilibrium is unstable: it requires but a slight blow to disrupt it.

Thus, we glimpse the nature and source of this malady of infiniteness which we suffer in our day. For man to imagine that he has before him boundless, free, and open space, he must no longer see this moral barrier, which under normal conditions would cut off his view. He must no longer feel these moral forces that restrain him and limit his horizon. But if he no longer feels them, it is because they no longer carry their normal measure of authority, because they are weakened, because they are no longer what they ought to be. The notion of the infinite, then, appears only at those times when moral discipline has lost its ascendancy over man's will. It is the sign of the attrition that emerges during periods when the moral system, prevailing for several centuries, is shaken, failing to respond to new conditions of human life, and without any new system yet contrived to replace that which has disappeared. . . .

So we come to this important conclusion. Moral discipline not only buttresses the moral life, properly speaking; its influence extends further. In effect, it follows . . . that it performs an important function in forming character and personality in general. In fact, the most essential element of character is this capacity for restraint or—as they say—of inhibition, which allows us to contain our passions, our desires, our habits, and subject them to law.

The individual human being is someone who can leave his imprint upon everything he does, a mark appropriate to himself, constant through time and by means of which he recognizes himself as distinct from all others. But insofar as our inclinations, instincts, and desires lack any counterbalance, insofar as our conduct hangs on the relative intensity of uncontrolled dispositions, these dispositions are gusts of wind, erratic stop-start affairs characteristic of children and primitives, which as they endlessly split the will against itself, dissipate it on the winds of caprice and preclude its gaining the unity and continuity that are the essential preconditions of personality. It is precisely in this development of self-mastery that we build up moral discipline. It teaches us not to act in response to those transient whims, bringing our behavior willy-nilly to the level of its natural inclinations. It teaches us that conduct involves effort; that it is moral action only when we restrict some inclination, suppress some appetite, moderate some tendency. At the same time, just as any rule about anything that is relatively fixed or invariable stands above all individual caprice, and as moral rules are still more invariable than all the others, to learn to act morally is also to learn conduct that is orderly, conduct that follows enduring principles and transcends the fortuitous impulse and suggestion. Thus, will is generally formed in the school of duty. . . .

To act morally, it is not enough—above all, it is no longer enough—to respect discipline and to be committed to a group. Beyond this, and whether out of deference to a rule or devotion to a collective ideal, we must have knowledge, as clear and complete an awareness as possible of the reasons for our conduct. This consciousness confers on our behavior the autonomy that the public conscience from now on requires of every genuinely and completely moral being. Hence, we can say that [another] element of morality is the understanding of it. Morality no longer consists merely in behaving, even intentionally behaving, in certain required ways. Beyond this, the rule prescribing such behavior must be freely desired, that is to say, freely accepted; and this willing acceptance is nothing less than an enlightened assent.

Here it is, perhaps, that the moral conscience of contemporary peoples is confronted with the greatest change: intelligence has become and is becoming increasingly an element of morality. Morality, which originally was completely a function of the act, the content of the behavior that constituted the act, now depends more and more upon knowledge. For a long time now we have imputed social value only to an act that was intentional, that is to say when the actor pictured ahead of time what the act involved and what bearing it had on the rule. But now, beyond this first level of awareness, we require another, which goes deeper into the nature of things—the symbolic explanation of the rule itself, its causes and reasons for being. This explains the place we accord the teaching of morality in our schools. For to teach morality is neither to preach nor to indoctrinate; it is to explain. If we refuse the child all explanation of this sort, if we do not try to help him understand the reasons for the rules he should abide by, we would be condemning him to an incomplete and inferior morality. Such teaching, far from harming the public morality—as has sometimes been alleged—is henceforth its necessary condition. . . .

In reality . . . the nature and function of school discipline is . . . not a simple device for securing superficial peace in the classroom—a device allowing the work to roll on tranquilly. It is the morality of the classroom, just as the discipline of the social body is morality properly

339

speaking. Each social group, each type of society, has and could not fail to have its own morality, which expresses its own make-up.

Now, the class is a small society. It is therefore both natural and necessary that it have its own morality corresponding to its size, the character of its elements, and its function. Discipline is this morality. The obligations we shall presently enumerate are the student's duties, just as the civic or professional obligations imposed by state or corporation are the duties of the adult. On the other hand, the schoolroom society is much closer to the society of adults than it is to that of the family. For aside from the fact that it is larger, the individuals—teachers and students—who make it up are not brought together by personal feelings or preferences but for altogether general and abstract reasons, that is to say, because of the social function to be performed by the teacher, and the immature mental condition of the students. For all these reasons, the rule of the classroom cannot bend or give with the same flexibility as that of the family in all kinds and combinations of circumstances. It cannot accommodate itself to given temperaments. There is already something colder and more impersonal about the obligations imposed by the school: they are now concerned with reason and less with feelings; they require more effort and greater application. And although—as we have previously said—we must guard against overdoing it, it is nevertheless indispensable in order that school discipline be everything that it should be and fulfill its function completely. For only on this condition will it be able to serve as intermediary between the affective morality of the family and the more rigorous morality of civil life. It is by respecting the school rules that the child learns to respect rules in general, that he develops the habit of self-control and restraint simply because he should control and restrain himself. It is a first initiation into the austerity of duty. Serious life has now begun.

This, then, is the true function of discipline. It is not a simple procedure aimed at making the child work, stimulating his desire for instruction, or husbanding the energies of the teacher.

It is essentially an instrument—difficult to duplicate—of moral education. . . .

Since it is through the teacher that the rule is revealed to the child, everything depends upon him. A rule can scarcely have any authority other than that with which the teacher invests it—that is to say, the idea of which he suggests to the children. The question comes to this: what conditions must the teacher fulfill in order to radiate authority?

Of course, certain personal qualities are necessary. Notably, the teacher should be decisive, have some will power. Since the imperative character of the rule derives from the fact that it silences all doubts and hesitations, the rule cannot appear obligatory to the child if applied indecisively—if those charged with teaching it to him do not seem always certain of what it should be. However, these are really secondary considerations. What is above all important is that the teacher really feel in himself the authority he must communicate and for which he must convey some feeling. It constitutes a force that he can manifest only if he possesses it effectively.

Now, what is the source of the teacher's authority? Does it derive from a physical power with which he is armed, from his right of punishment and reward? The fear of punishment is something altogether different from respect for authority. It has a moral character and moral value only if the penalty is regarded as just by those subjected to it, which implies that the authority which punishes is itself recognized as legitimate. However, this is what is in question. It is not from the outside, from the fear he inspires, that the teacher should gain his authority; it is from himself. This cannot come to him except from his innermost being. He must believe, not perhaps in himself or in the superior quality of his intelligence or will, but in his task and the greatness of that task. It is the priest's lofty conception of his mission that gives him the authority that so readily colors his language and bearing. For he speaks in the name of a God, who he feels in himself and to whom he feels himself much closer than the laymen in the crowds he addresses. So, the lay teacher can and should have something of this same feeling. He also is an instrument of a great moral reality which surpasses him and with which he communicates more directly than does the child, since it is through his intermediation that the child communicates with it. Just as the priest is the interpreter of God, he is the interpreter of the great moral ideas of his time and country. Whatever is linked with these ideas, whatever the significance and authority attributed to them, necessarily spreads to him and everything coming from him since he expresses these things and embodies them in the eyes of children. . . .

However, the dominant part played by the teacher in generating this feeling—the personal role that he plays—entails a danger that we must guard against. Indeed, there is reason to fear lest the child develop the habit of associating the notion of rule itself too narrowly with the person of the teacher—lest he view the regulations of the school too concretely as the expression of the teacher's will. So it is that people throughout time have needed to view laws of conduct as instituted by a divine personality. Such a conception runs contrary to the end we want to achieve. The rule is no longer a rule if it is not impersonal and if it is not represented as such in our minds. The teacher must therefore be committed to presenting it, not as his own personal doing, but as a moral power superior to him, and of which he is the instrument not the author. He must make the students understand that it imposes itself on him as it does on them; that he cannot remove or modify it; that he is constrained to apply it; and that it dominates him and obliges him as it obliges them. On this condition alone will he be able to evoke a sentiment that, in a democratic society like ours, is or ought to be at the very foundation of the public conscience: this is the respect for legality, the respect for impersonal law deriving its ascendancy from impersonality itself. From the moment when the law is no longer embodied in a specific person who represents it in a palpable manner, the mind must necessarily seize upon some general and abstract conception of law and respect it as such. Indeed, is it not true that the only thing that survives or can survive in a society where the prestige of class and dynasties is no longer recognized is the impersonal authority of law? For it cannot weaken without all of collective discipline giving way. Unfortunately, we cannot hide the fact that such an idea runs counter to customs deeply rooted for centuries, and that a whole education is necessary to imbue men's minds with it. The school would fail in one of its principal obligations if it disregarded this task.

JEAN PIAGET

The moral judgment of the child

The analysis of the child's moral judgments has led us perforce to the discussion of the great problem of the relations of social life to the rational consciousness. The conclusion we came to was that the morality prescribed for the individual by society is not homogeneous because society itself is not just one thing. Society is the sum of social relations, and among these relations we can distinguish two extreme types: relations of constraint, whose characteristic is to impose upon the individual from outside a system of rules with obligatory content, and relations of cooperation whose characteristic is to create within people's minds the consciousness of ideal norms at the back of all rules. Arising from the ties of authority and unilateral respect, the relations of constraint therefore characterize most of the features of society as it exists, and in particular the relations of the child to its adult surrounding. Defined by equality and mutual respect, the relations of cooperation, on the contrary, constitute an equilibrial limit rather than a static system. Constraint, the source of duty and heteronomy, cannot, therefore, be reduced to the good and to autonomous rationality, which are the fruits of reciprocity, although the actual evolution of the relations of constraint tends to bring these nearer to cooperation. . . .

This . . . brings us to a second point: the parallelism existing between moral and intellectual development. Everyone is aware of the kinship between logical and ethical norms. Logic is the morality of thought just as morality is the logic of action. Nearly all contemporary theories agree in recognizing the existence of this parallelism—from the *a priori* view which regards pure reason as the arbiter both of theoretical reflection and daily practice, to the sociological theories of knowledge and of ethical values. It is therefore in no way surprising that the analysis of child thought should bring to the fore certain particular aspects of this general phenomenon.

One may say, to begin with, that in a certain sense neither logical nor moral norms are innate in the individual mind. We can find, no doubt, even before language, all the elements of rationality and morality. Thus sensori-motor intelligence gives rise to operations of assimilation and construction, in which it is hard to see the functional equivalent of the logic of classes and of relations. Similarly the child's behaviour towards persons shows signs from the first of those sympathetic tendencies and affective reactions in which one can easily see the raw material of all subsequent moral behaviour. But an intelligent act can only be called logical and a good-hearted impulse moral from the moment that certain norms impress a given structure and rules of equilibrium upon this material. Logic is not co-extensive with intelligence, but consists of the sum-total of rules of control which intelligence makes use of for its own direction. Morality plays a similar part with regard to the affective life. Now there is nothing that allows us to affirm the existence of such norms in the pre-social behaviour occurring before the appearance of language. The control characteristic of sensori-motor intelligence is of external origin: it is things themselves that constrain the organism to select which steps it will take; the initial intellectual activity does actively seek for truth. Similarly, it is persons external to him who canalize the child's elementary feelings; those feelings do not tend to regulate themselves from within. . . .

In the first place it should be noticed that the individual is not capable of achieving this conscious realization by himself, and consequently does not straight away succeed in establishing norms properly so-called. It is in this sense that reason in its double aspect, both logical and

moral, is a collective product. This does not mean that society has conjured up rationality out of the void, nor that there does not exist a spirit of humanity that is superior to society because dwelling both within the individual and the social group. It means that social life is necessary if the individual is to become conscious of the functioning of his own mind and thus to transform into norms properly so called the simple functional equilibria immanent to all mental and even all vital activity.

For the individual, left to himself, remains egocentric. By which we mean simply this— Just as at first the mind, before it can dissociate what belongs to objective laws from what is bound up with the sum of subjective conditions, confuses itself with the universe, so does the individual begin by understanding and feeling everything through the medium of himself before distinguishing what belongs to things and other people from what is the result of his own particular intellectual and affective perspective. At this stage, therefore, the individual cannot be conscious of his own thought, since consciousness of self implies a perpetual comparison of the self with other people. Thus from the logical point of view egocentrism would seem to involve a sort of alogicality, such that sometimes affectivity gains the ascendant over objectivity, and sometimes the relations arising from personal activity prove stronger than the relations that are independent of the self. And from the moral point of view, egocentricism involves a sort of anomy such that tenderness and disinterestedness can go hand in hand with a naïve selfishness, and yet the child not feel spontaneously himself to be better in one case than the other. Just as the ideas which enter his mind appear from the first in the form of beliefs and not of hypotheses requiring verification, so do the feelings that arise in the child's consciousness appear to him from the first as having value and not as having to be submitted to some ulterior evaluation. It is only through contact with the judgments and evaluations of others that this intellectual and affective anomy will gradually yield to the pressure of collective logical and moral laws.

In the second place, the relations of constraint

and unilateral respect which are spontaneously established between child and adult contribute to the formation of a first type of logical and moral control. But this control is insufficient to eliminate childish egocentrism. From the intellectual point of view this respect of the child for the adult gives rise to an "annunciatory" conception of truth: the mind stops affirming what it likes to affirm and falls in with the opinion of those around it. This gives birth to a distinction which is equivalent to that of truth and falsehood: some affirmations are recognized as valid while others are not. But it goes without saying that although this distinction marks an important advance as compared to the anomy of egocentric thought, it is none the less irrational in principle. For if we are to speak of truth as rational, it is not sufficient that the contents of one's statements should conform with reality: reason must have taken active steps to obtain these contents and reason must be in a position to control the agreement or disagreement of these statements with reality. Now, in the case under discussion, reason is still very far removed from this autonomy: truth means whatever conforms with the spoken word of the adult. Whether the child has himself discovered the propositions which he asks the adult to sanction with his authority, or whether he merely repeats what the adult has said, in both cases there is intellectual constraint put upon an inferior by a superior, and therefore heteronomy. Thus, far from checking childish egocentrism at its source, such a submission tends on the contrary partly to consolidate the mental habits characteristic of egocentrism. Just as, if left to himself, the child believes every idea that enters his head instead of regarding it as a hypothesis to be verified, so the child who is submissive to the word of his parents believes without question everything he is told, instead of perceiving the element of uncertainty and search in adult thought. The self's good pleasure is simply replaced by the good pleasure of a supreme authority. There is progress here, no doubt, since such a transference accustoms the mind to look for a common truth, but this progress is big with danger if the supreme authority be not in its turn criticized in the name of reason. Now, criticism is

born of discussion, and discussion is only possible among equals: cooperation alone will therefore accomplish what intellectual constraint failed to bring about. And indeed we constantly have occasion throughout our schools to notice the combined effects of this constraint and of intellectual egocentrism. What is "verbalism," for example, if not the joint result of oral authority and the syncretism peculiar to the egocentric language of the child? In short, in order to really socialize the child, cooperation is necessary, for it alone will succeed in delivering him from the mystical power of the world of the adult. . . .

Cooperation alone leads to autonomy. With regard to logic, cooperation is at first a source of criticism; thanks to the mutual control which it introduces, it suppresses both the spontaneous conviction that characterizes egocentrism and the blind faith in adult authority. Thus, discussion gives rise to reflection and objective verification. But through this very fact cooperation becomes the source of constructive values. It leads to the recognition of the principles of formal logic in so far as these normative laws are necessary to common search for truth. It leads, above all, to a conscious realization of the logic of relations, since reciprocity on the intellectual plane necessarily involves the elaboration of those laws of perspective which we find in the operations distinctive of systems of relations.

In the same way, with regard to moral realities, cooperation is at first the source of criticism and individualism. For by comparing his own private motives with the rules adopted by each and sundry, the individual is led to judge objectively the acts and commands of other people, including adults. Whence the decline of unilateral respect and the primacy of personal judgment. But in consequence of this, cooperation suppresses both egocentrism and moral realism, and thus achieves an interiorization of rules. A new morality follows upon that of pure duty. Heteronomy steps aside to make way for a consciousness of good, of which the autonomy results from the acceptance of the norms of reciprocity. Obedience withdraws in favour of the idea of justice and of mutual service, now the source of all the obligations which till then had

343

been imposed as incomprehensible commands. In a word, cooperation on the moral plane brings about transformations exactly parallel to those of which we have just been recalling the existence in the intellectual domain.

Is there any need, by way of conclusion, to point to the educational consequences of such observations? If education claims to be the direct application of what we know about Child Psychology, it would not be necessary. It is obvious that our results are as unfavourable to the method of authority as to purely individualistic methods. It is, as we said in connection with Durkheim, absurd and even immoral to wish to impose upon the child a fully worked-out system of discipline when the social life of children amongst themselves is sufficiently developed to give rise to a discipline infinitely nearer to that inner submission which is the mark of adult morality. It is idle, again, to try and transform the child's mind from outside, when his own taste for active research and his desire for cooperation suffice to ensure a normal intellectual development. The adult must therefore be a collaborator and not a master, from this double point of view, moral and rational. But conversely, it would be unwise to rely upon biological "nature" alone to ensure the dual progress of conscience and intelligence, when we realize to what extent all moral as all logical norms are the result of cooperation. Let us therefore try to create in the school a place where individual experimentation and reflection carried out in common come to each other's aid and balance one another.

MARTIN BUBER

The education of character

Education worthy of the name is essentially education of character. For the genuine educator does not merely consider individual functions of his pupil, as one intending to teach him only to know or be capable of certain definite things; but his concern is always the person as a whole, both in the actuality in which he lives before you now and in his possibilities, what he can become. But in this way, as a whole in reality and potentiality, a man can be conceived either as personality, that is, as a unique spiritual-physical form with all the forces dormant in it, or as character, that is, as the link between what this individual is and the sequence of his actions and attitudes. Between these two modes of conceiving the pupil in his wholeness there is a fundamental difference. Personality is something which in its growth remains essentially outside the influence of the educator; but to assist in the moulding of character is his greatest task. Personality is a completion, only character is a task. One may cultivate and enhance personality, but in education one can and one must aim at character.

However—as I would like to point out straightaway—it is advisable not to overestimate what the educator can even at best do to develop character. In this more than in any other branch of the science of teaching it is important to realize, at the very beginning of the discussion, the fundamental limits to conscious influence, even before asking what character is and how it is to be brought about.

If I have to teach algebra I can expect to succeed in giving my pupils an idea of quadratic equations with two unknown quantities. Even the slowest-witted child will understand it so well that he will amuse himself by solving equations at night when he cannot fall asleep. And even one with the most sluggish memory will not forget, in his old age, how to play with x and y. But if I am concerned with the education of character, everything becomes problematic. I try to explain to my pupils that envy is despicable, and at once I feel the secret resistance of those who are poorer than their comrades. I try to explain that it is wicked to bully the weak, and at once I see a suppressed smile on the lips of the strong. I try to explain that lying destroys life, and something frightful happens: the worst habitual liar of the class produces a brilliant essay on the destructive power of lying. I have made the fatal mistake of *giving instruction* in ethics, and what I said is accepted as current coin of knowledge; nothing of it is transformed into character-building substance.

But the difficulty lies still deeper. In all teaching of a subject I can announce my intention of teaching as openly as I please, and this does not interfere with the results. After all, pupils do want, for the most part, to learn something, even if not over-much, so that a tacit agreement becomes possible. But as soon as my pupils notice that I want to educate their characters I am resisted precisely by those who show most signs of genuine independent character: they will not let themselves be educated, or rather, they do not like the idea that somebody wants to educate them. And those, too, who are seriously labouring over the question of good and evil, rebel when one dictates to them, as though it were some long established truth, what is good and what is bad; and they rebel just because they have experienced over and over again how hard it is to find the right way. Does it follow that one should keep silent about one's intention of educating character, and act by ruse and subterfuge? No; I have just said that the difficulty lies deeper. It is not enough to see that education of character is not introduced into a lesson in class; neither may one conceal it in cleverly arranged intervals. Education cannot tolerate such politic action. Even if the pupil does not notice the hidden motive it will have its negative effect on the actions of the teacher himself by depriving him of the directness which is his strength. Only in his whole being, in all his spontaneity can the educator truly affect the whole being of his pupil. For educating characters you do not need a moral genius, but you do need a man who is wholly alive and able to communicate himself directly to his fellow beings. His aliveness streams out to them and affects them most strongly and purely when he has no thought of affecting them.

The Greek word character means *impression*. The special link between man's being and his appearance, the special connexion between the unity of what he is and the sequence of his actions and attitudes is impressed on his still plastic substance. Who does the impressing? Everything does: nature and the social context, the house and the street, language and custom, the world of history and the world of daily news in the form of rumour, of broadcast and newspaper, music and technical science, play and dream—everything together. Many of these factors exert their influence by stimulating agreement, imitation, desire, effort; others by arousing questions, doubts, dislike, resistance. Character is formed by the interpenetration of all those multifarious, opposing influences. And yet, among this infinity of form-giving forces the educator is only one element among innumerable others, but distinct from them all by his *will* to take part in the stamping of character and by his *consciousness* that he represents in the eyes of the growing person a certain *selection* of what is, the selection of what is "right," of what *should* be. It is in this will and this consciousness that his vocation as an educator finds its fundamental expression. From this the genuine educator gains two things: first, humility, the feeling of being only one element amidst the fullness of life, only one single existence in the midst of all the tremendous inrush of reality on the pupil; but secondly, self-awareness, the feeling of being therein the only existence that *wants* to affect the whole person, and thus the feeling of responsibility for the selection of reality which he represents to the pupil. And a third thing emerges from all this, the recognition that in this realm of the education of character, of wholeness, there is only *one* access to the pupil: his *confidence*. For the adolescent who is frightened and disappointed by an unreliable world, confidence means the liberating insight that there is human truth, the truth of human existence. When the pupil's confidence has been won, his resistance against being educated gives way to a singular happening: he accepts the educator as a person. He feels he may trust this man, that this man is not making a business out of him, but is taking part in his life, accepting him before desiring to influence him. And so he learns to *ask*. . . .

If this is the teacher's standpoint towards his pupil, taking part in his life and conscious of responsibility, then everything that passes between them can, without any deliberate or politic intention, open a way to the education of character: lessons and games, a conversation about quarrels in the class, or about the problems of a world-war. Only, the teacher must not forget the limits of education; even when he enjoys confidence he cannot always expect agreement. Confidence implies a break-through from reserve, the bursting of the bonds which imprison an unquiet heart. But it does not imply unconditional agreement. The teacher must never forget that conflicts too, if only they are decided in a healthy atmosphere, have an educational value. A conflict with a pupil is the supreme test for the educator. He must use his own insight wholeheartedly; he must not blunt the piercing impact of his knowledge, but he must at the same time have in readiness the healing ointment for the heart pierced by it. Not for a moment may he conduct a dialectical maneuver instead of the real battle for truth. But if he is the victor he has to help the vanquished to endure defeat; and if he cannot conquer the self-willed soul that faces him (for victories over souls are not so easily won), then he has to find the word of love which alone can help to overcome so difficult a situation. . . .

The great character can be conceived neither as a system of maxims nor as a system of habits. It is peculiar to him to act from the whole of his substance. That is, it is peculiar to him to react in accordance with the uniqueness of every situation which challenges him as an active person. . . . In spite of all similarities every living situation has, like a newborn child, a new face, that has never been before and will never come again. It demands of you a reaction which cannot be prepared beforehand. It demands nothing of what is past. It demands presence, responsibility; it demands you. I call a great character one who by his actions and attitudes satisfies the claim of situations out of deep readiness to respond with his whole life, and in such a way that the sum of his actions and attitudes expresses at the same time the unity of his being in its willingness to accept responsibility. As his being is unity, the unity of accepted responsibility, his active life, too, coheres into unity. One might perhaps say that for him there rises a unity out of the situations he has responded to in responsibility, the indefinable unity of a moral destiny.

346

All this does not mean that the great character is beyond the acceptance of norms. No responsible person remains a stranger to norms. But the command inherent in a genuine norm never becomes a maxim and the fulfilment of it never a habit. Any command that a great character takes to himself in the course of his development does not act in him as part of his consciousness or as material for building up his exercises, but remains latent in a basic layer of his substance until it reveals itself to him in a concrete way. What it has to tell him is revealed whenever a situation arises which demands of him a solution of which till then he had perhaps no idea. Even the most universal norm will at times be recognized only in a very special situation. . . .

It may be asked whether the educator should really start "from above," whether, in fixing his goal, the hope of finding a great character, who is bound to be the exception, should be his starting-point; for in his methods of educating character he will always have to take into consideration the others, the many. To this I reply that the educator would not have the right to do so if a method inapplicable to these others were to result. In fact, however, his very insight into the structure of a great character helps him to find the way by which alone (as I have indicated) he can begin to influence also the victims of the collective Moloch,* pointing out to them the sphere in which they themselves suffer—namely, their relation to their own selves. From this sphere he must elicit the values which he can make credible and desirable to his pupils. That is what insight into the structure of a great character helps him to do.

JOHN DEWEY

Morality is social

Our intelligence is bound up, so far as its materials are concerned, with the community life of

---

Ed. note: A Semitic god to whom children were sacrificed.

which we are a part. We know what it communicates to us, and know according to the habits it forms in us. Science is an affair of civilization not of individual intellect.

So with conscience. When a child acts, those about him re-act. They shower encouragement upon him, visit him with approval, or they bestow frowns and rebuke. What others do to us when we act is as natural a consequence of our action as what the fire does to us when we plunge our hands in it. The social environment may be as artificial as you please. But its action in response to ours is natural not artificial. In language and imagination we rehearse the responses of others just as we dramatically enact other consequences. We foreknow how others will act, and the foreknowledge is the beginning of judgment passed on action. We know *with* them; there is conscience. An assembly is formed within our breast which discusses and appraises proposed and performed acts. The community without becomes a forum and tribunal within, a judgment-seat of charges, assessments and exculpations. Our thoughts of our own actions are saturated with the ideas that others entertain about them, ideas which have been expressed not only in explicit instruction but still more effectively in reaction to our acts.

Liability is the beginning of responsibility. We are held accountable by others for the consequences of our acts. They visit their like and dislike of these consequences upon us. In vain do we claim that these are not ours; that they are products of ignorance not design, or are incidents in the execution of a most laudable scheme. Their authorship is imputed to us. We are disapproved, and disapproval is not an inner state of mind but a most definite act. Others say to us by their deeds we do not care a fig whether you did this deliberately or not. We intend that you *shall* deliberate before you do it again, and that if possible your deliberation shall prevent a repetition of this act we object to. The reference in blame and every unfavorable judgment is prospective, not retrospective. Theories about responsibility may become confused, but in practice no one is stupid enough to try to change the past. Approbation and disapprobation are ways of influencing the formation of habits and

aims; that is, of influencing future acts. The individual is *held* accountable for what he *has* done in order that he may be responsive in what he is *going* to do. Gradually persons learn by dramatic imitation to hold themselves accountable, and liability becomes a voluntary deliberate acknowledgment that deeds are our own, that their consequences come from us.

These two facts, that moral judgment and moral responsibility are the work wrought in us by the social environment, signify that all morality is social; not because we *ought* to take into account the effect of our acts upon the welfare of others, but because of facts. Others *do* take account of what we do, and they respond accordingly to our acts. Their responses actually *do* affect the meaning of what we do. The significance thus contributed is as inevitable as is the effect of interaction with the physical environment. In fact as civilization advances the physical environment gets itself more and more humanized, for the meaning of physical energies and events becomes involved with the part they play in human activities. Our conduct *is* socially conditioned whether we perceive the fact or not.

The effect of custom on habit, and of habit upon thought is enough to prove this statement. When we begin to forecast consequences, the consequences that most stand out are those which will proceed from other people. The resistance and the cooperation of others is the central fact in the furtherance or failure of our schemes. Connections with our fellows furnish both the opportunities for action and the instrumentalities by which we take advantage of opportunity. All of the actions of an individual bear the stamp of his community as assuredly as does the language he speaks. Difficulty in reading the stamp is due to variety of impressions in consequence of membership in many groups. This social saturation is, I repeat, a matter of fact, not of what should be, not of what is desirable or undesirable. It does not guarantee the rightness or goodness of an act; there is no excuse for thinking of evil action as individualistic and right action as social. Deliberate unscrupulous pursuit of self-interest is as much conditioned upon social opportunities, training and assistance as is the course of action prompted by a beaming benevolence. The difference lies in the quality and degree of the perception of ties and interdependencies; in the use to which they are put. Consider the form commonly assumed today by self-seeking; namely command of money and economic power. Money is a social institution; property is a legal custom; economic opportunities are dependent upon the state of society; the objects aimed at, the rewards sought for, are what they are because of social admiration, prestige, competition and power. If money-making is morally obnoxious it is because of the way these social facts are handled, not because a money-making man has withdrawn from society into an isolated selfhood or turned his back upon society. His "individualism" is not found in his original nature but in his habits acquired under social influences. It is found in his concrete aims, and these are reflexes of social conditions. Well-grounded moral objection to a mode of conduct rests upon the kind of social connections that figure, not upon lack of social aim. A man may attempt to utilize social relationships for his own advantage in an inequitable way; he may intentionally or unconsciously try to make them feed one of his own appetites. Then he is denounced as egoistic. But both his course of action and the disapproval he is subject to are facts *within* society. They are social phenomena. He pursues his unjust advantage as a social asset.

Explicit recognition of this fact is a prerequisite of improvement in moral education and of an intelligent understanding of the chief ideas or "categories" of morals. Morals is as much a matter of interaction of a person with his social environment as walking is an interaction of legs with a physical environment. The character of walking depends upon the strength and competency of legs. But it also depends upon whether a man is walking in a bog or on a paved street, upon whether there is a safeguarded path set aside or whether he has to walk amid dangerous vehicles. If the standard of morals is low it is because the education given by the interaction of the individual with his social environment is defective. Of what avail is it to preach unassuming simplicity and contentment of life when communal admiration goes to the man who "succeeds"—who makes himself conspicuous

and envied because of command of money and other forms of power? If a child gets on by peevishness or intrigue, then others are his accomplices who assist in the habits which are built up. The notion that an abstract ready-made conscience exists in individuals and that it is only necessary to make an occasional appeal to it and to indulge in occasional crude rebukes and punishments, is associated with the causes of lack of definitive and orderly moral advance. For it is associated with lack of attention to social forces.

There is a peculiar inconsistency in the current idea that morals *ought* to be social. The introduction of the moral "ought" into the idea contains an implicit assertion that morals depend upon something apart from social relations. Morals *are* social. The question of ought, should be, is a question of better and worse *in* social affairs. . . .

At present we not only have no assured means of forming character except crude devices of blame, praise, exhortation and punishment, but the very meaning of the general notions of moral inquiry is matter of doubt and dispute. The reason is that these notions are discussed in isolation from the concrete facts of the interactions of human beings with one another—an abstraction as fatal as was the old discussion of phlogiston, gravity and vital force apart from concrete correlations of changing events with one another. Take for example such a basic conception as that of Right involving the nature of authority in conduct. There is no need here to rehearse the multitude of contending views which give evidence that discussion of this matter is still in the realm of opinion. We content ourselves with pointing out that this notion is the last resort of the anti-empirical school in morals and that it proves the effect of neglect of social conditions.

In effect its adherents argue as follows: "Let us concede that concrete ideas about right and wrong and particular notions of what is obligatory have grown up within experience. But we cannot admit this about the idea of Right, of Obligation itself. Why does moral authority exist at all? Why is the claim of the Right recognized in conscience even by those who violate it in deed? Our opponents say that such and such a course is wise, expedient, better. But *why* act for the wise, or good, or better? Why not follow our own immediate devices if we are so inclined? There is only one answer: We have a moral nature, a conscience, call it what you will. And this nature responds directly in acknowledgment of the supreme authority of the Right over all claims of inclination and habit. We may not act in accordance with this acknowledgment, but we still know that the authority of the moral law, although not its power, is unquestionable. Men may differ indefinitely according to what their experience has been as to just *what* is Right, what its contents are. But they all spontaneously agree in recognizing the supremacy of the claims of whatever is thought of as Right. Otherwise there would be no such thing as morality, but merely calculations of how to satisfy desire.

Grant the foregoing argument, and all the apparatus of abstract moralism follows in its wake. A remote goal of perfection, ideals that are contrary in a wholesale way to what is actual, a free will of arbitrary choice; all of these conceptions band themselves together with that of a non-empirical authority of Right and a non-empirical conscience which acknowledges it. They constitute its ceremonial or formal train.

Why, indeed, acknowledge the authority of Right? That many persons do not acknowledge it in fact, in action, and that all persons ignore it at times, is assumed by the argument. Just what is the significance of an alleged recognition of a supremacy which is continually denied in fact? How much would be lost if it were dropped out, and we were left face to face with actual facts? If a man lived alone in the world there might be some sense in the question "Why be moral?" were it not for one thing: No such question would then arise. As it is, we live in a world where other persons live too. Our acts affect them. They perceive these effects, and react upon us in consequence. Because they are living beings they make demands upon us for certain things from us. They approve and condemn—not in abstract theory but in what they do to us. The answer to the question "Why not put your hand in the fire?" is the answer of fact.

If you do your hand will be burnt. The answer to the question why acknowledge the right is of the same sort. For Right is only an abstract name for the multitude of concrete demands in action which others impress upon us, and of which we are obliged, if we would live, to take some account. Its authority is the exigency of their demands, the efficacy of their insistencies. There may be good ground for the contention that in theory the idea of the right is subordinate to that of the good, being a statement of the course proper to attain good. But in fact it signifies the totality of social pressures exercised upon us to induce us to think and desire in certain ways. Hence the right can in fact become the road to the good only as the elements that compose this unremitting pressure are enlightened, only as social relationships become themselves reasonable.

It will be retorted that all pressure is a non-moral affair partaking of force, not of right; that right must be ideal. Thus we are invited to enter again the circle in which the ideal has no force and social actualities no ideal quality. We refuse the invitation because social pressure is involved in our own lives, as much so as the air we breathe and the ground we walk upon. If we had desires, judgments, plans, in short a mind, apart from social connections, then the latter would be external and their action might be regarded as that of a non-moral force. But we live mentally as physically only *in* and *because* of our environment. Social pressure is but a name for the interactions which are always going on and in which we participate, living so far as we partake and dying so far as we do not. The pressure is not ideal but empirical, yet empirical here means only actual. It calls attention to the fact that considerations of right are claims originating not outside of life, but within it. They are "ideal" in precisely the degree in which we intelligently recognize and act upon them, just as colors and canvas become ideal when used in ways that give an added meaning to life.

Accordingly failure to recognize the authority of right means defect in effective apprehension of the realities of human association, not an arbitrary exercise of free will. This deficiency

349

and perversion in apprehension indicates a defect in education—that is to say, in the operation of actual conditions, in the consequences upon desire and thought of existing interactions and interdependencies. It is false that every person has a consciousness of the supreme authority of right and then misconceives it or ignores it in action. One has such a sense of the claims of social relationships as those relationships enforce in one's desires and observations. The belief in a separate, ideal or transcendental, practically ineffectual Right is a reflex of the inadequacy with which existing institutions perform their educative office—their office in generating observation of social continuities. It is an endeavor to "rationalize" this defect. Like all rationalizations, it operates to divert attention from the real state of affairs. Thus it helps maintain the conditions which created it, standing in the way of effort to make our institutions more humane and equitable. A theoretical acknowledgment of the supreme authority of Right, of moral law, gets twisted into an effectual substitute for acts which would better the customs which now produce vague, dull, halting and evasive observation of actual social ties. We are not caught in a circle; we traverse a spiral in which social customs generate some consciousness of interdependencies, and this consciousness is embodied in acts which in improving the environment generate new perceptions of social ties, and so on forever. The relationships, the interactions are forever there as fact, but they acquire meaning only in the desires, judgments and purposes they awaken.

We recur to our fundamental propositions. Morals is connected with actualities of existence, not with ideals, ends and obligations independent of concrete actualities. The facts upon which it depends are those which arise out of active connections of human beings with one another, the consequences of their mutually intertwined activities in the life of desire, belief, judgment, satisfaction and dissatisfaction. In this sense conduct and hence morals are social: they are not just things which *ought* to be social and which fail to come up to the scratch. But there are enormous differences of better and worse in the quality of what is social. Ideal morals begin with the perception of these differences. Human interaction and ties are there, are operative in any case. But they can be regulated, employed in an orderly way for good only as we know how to observe them. And they cannot be observed aright, they cannot be understood and utilized, when the mind is left to itself to work without the aid of science. For the natural unaided mind means precisely the habits of belief, thought and desire which have been accidentally generated and confirmed by social institutions or customs. But with all their admixture of accident and reasonableness we have at last reached a point where social conditions create a mind capable of scientific outlook and inquiry. To foster and develop this spirit is the social obligation of the present because it is its urgent need.

AMITAI ETZIONI

Do as I say, not as I do

The hottest new item in post-Watergate curriculums is "moral education," an attempt by educators to instill moral values in youngsters by using newly designed teaching methods. With many believing that people in the United States do not live as moral and honest lives as they used to, according to Gallup, moral education is now favored by four out of every five Americans.

But moral education means rather different things to different people—from teaching respect for the law as embodied in police officers and other authority figures, to instilling "good manners," to developing the capacity to form one's own standards and judgments. Though the goals of moral education are at best contradictory, a significant number of the nation's public schools are nonetheless forging ahead. . . .

In the search for an appropriate way to get moral values across, a variety of approaches are being tried.

350

In 1970, Jane Elliott, a teacher at Community Elementary school in Riceville, Iowa, wanted to teach her third-grade students the injustice of discrimination, but sensing that just talking about the arbitrariness and unfairness of race prejudice would be too academic to have much impact, her inspiration was to appeal directly to the children's capacity for emotional experience and empathetic insight by declaring a day of discrimination against the blue-eyed. . . .

After reversing the roles for a day, Mrs. Elliott had every child write about how it felt to be discriminated against. Though to many adults her procedure may sound heavy-handed, as far as her students were concerned the experience "took." . . .

In the context of the current moral-education drive, what Jane Elliott did in 1970 is of particular interest because despite the successful results she was reported to have achieved, few schools have followed her lead.

One Monday morning, the students in a Pittsburgh junior high school started their civics class not with a rehash of government branches, the meaning of "checks and balances," or that pragmatic addition of recent years, how to fill out Form 1040A, but with a brief "moral dilemma": "Sharon and Jill were best friends. One day they went shopping together. Jill tried on a sweater and then, to Sharon's surprise, walked out of the store with the sweater under her coat. A moment later, the store's security officer stopped Sharon and demanded that she tell him the name of the girl who had walked out. He told the storeowner that he had seen the two girls together, and that he was sure that the one who left had been shoplifting. The storeowner told Sharon that she could really get in trouble if she didn't give her friend's name."

"Should Sharon tell?" the teacher asked. . . .

What educators who favor this moral-dilemma approach stress is that, first of all, it elicits a discussion in which the teacher tolerates free expression of student viewpoints and, second, such give-and-take improves student awareness of moral issues, and leads to higher levels of moral reasoning.

According to Harvard's Lawrence Kohlberg,

most often cited by moral-dilemma advocates, children move from an amoral stage toward concern for the needs and feelings of others. It is useless, he argues, to try to get children at the most primitive stage of moral development—in the early years where they only do what is right to avoid punishment or to gain approval—to suddenly understand principles or modes of reasoning at the highest level. But it is possible, through proper classroom dialectics, to help children move toward a point where they wish to be ethical because they themselves think it's right.

By far the most prevalent method of classroom ethics teaching today is paper-and-pencil assignments. The main champion of this approach is Prof. Sidney B. Simon of the University of Massachusetts. . . . More than 1,000 schools [are] using his "values-clarification kits." . . . An example of the technique is as follows:

Exercise one: "Write down 20 things you love to do." Pause. "Now that you have all made your lists, state *the five* things you love to do *best of all.* Check the things you love to do alone; X the things you love to do with other people; . . . things that cost less than $3 to do." . . .

The whole idea of values clarification is *not* to instill or introduce any particular values, new or old, but to help students discover those they already have. Having to decide which 15 items to leave out, which five to include, leads the youngsters to an understanding of how values work, the choices inevitably involved. . . .

Values-clarification exercises differ from most other work-book assignments in one way: Any and all answers are considered "right" as long as one can give a reason for them. . . .

Some claim that it is precisely its amorality that makes the values-clarification package so popular in the public schools—it protects them from having to choose *whose* values to teach.

Whatever method of teaching morals is employed—there is not yet enough data available to support the superiority of any one technique—there are other ways schools communicate moral values.

It has long been understood that children

learn from their parents by emulation—as is acknowledged in the well-known saw: "Do as I say, not as I do!" The same notion is equally applicable to the ethics taught in school: The way teachers, administrators, coaches and other school officials interact with the children teaches ethical values by example. Mrs. Elsa Wasserman, a counselor to the Cambridge, Mass., public schools, explains: "The governance structure of many schools teaches students that in school they have no significant control over their lives; that they must conform to arbitrary rules or be punished; and that they should go along with what the majority thinks and does even when they disagree." This is the "hidden curriculum."

Talking to students, one finds that the core of the hidden curriculum revolves around grades, athletics and student behavior. The attitudes and actions students observe on the part of school officials with regard to these are not often ones which convey the importance of standing up for ethical principles. . . .

In marked contrast to the idealism of a few years back that sought to replace grades with more meaningful evaluations, many of today's students believe their life's fate hangs on getting into the "right" college—which in turn depends on getting high grades. Thus, for quite a few students the notion that cheating on exams or term papers is a serious ethical issue is about as quaint as the medieval scholastic debate over how many angels can stand on the head of a pin.

Among the students with whom I have spoken, attitudes seem to be less cynical toward sports than toward grades. . . . Football seems to be the focus of the most intense pressures to win—and, therefore, the greatest temptations to win at any price. . . .

The hidden-curriculum emphasis on high grades and winning in sports suggests that grades and sports are still considered important tools for instilling the American "success ethic" and that stimulating the drive for success is still a major mission of the American school. The success drive has ethics-undermining side-effects, however, if built into its creed is the attitude conveyed by the late football coach Vince Lombardi's oft-quoted motto: "Winning is not the most important thing, it's the *only* thing." Unbounded competition is incompatible with ethical codes because it puts self (or one's team) above the rules of the game.

Of all the approaches to moral education, the one which focuses on reform of the hidden curriculum is likely to be both the most relevant and the most difficult to accomplish, because teachers and students are less aware of its moral implications than they are of the formal curriculum, and because its roots lie in the community. . . .

Most of America is probably far from ready for . . . a radically egalitarian approach in the public schools. But most schools may be ready for limited reforms to bring the hidden curriculum more in line with what is taught in ethics classes—awarding grades on the basis of merit rather than on conformity to the teacher's views or docility in the face of authority, emphasizing respect for the rules in sports rather than just playing to win.

The objection may be raised that schools structured to produce more ethical youth would fail in their major mission of adequately preparing their students for later life, in which "success" often entails bending, if not violating, the rules. One could counter this criticism by maintaining that it is the schools' job to educate their students morally—over and above the prevalent societal standards. At the very least, then, the students will have some principles to compromise later on; and though their standards may become eroded, nonetheless they will not become as unethical as they would have had they started out with no scruples at all. True, most schools cannot proceed very far in promoting values not shared by the community at large. Before the schools can effectively provide moral education, the surrounding society must work to reform itself so that its members are less concerned with success and material achievements, and more concerned about quality of life and individual conduct.